INDIAN ADMINISTRATION

TEXT AND PROBLEMS

INDIAN ADMINISTRATION

For the Aspirants of Civil Services–Central and State, Honours and Postgraduate Students of Different Indian Universities

Dr. VISHNOO BHAGWAN
M.A., Ph.D., H.E.S.(I)
Joint Director, Higher Education, Haryana (Retd.)

Dr. VIDYA BHUSHAN
M.A., Ph.D., H.E.S.(I)
Joint Director, Higher Education, Haryana (Retd.)

S. CHAND & COMPANY PVT. LTD.
(AN ISO 9001: 2008 COMPANY)
RAM NAGAR, NEW DELHI-110055

S. CHAND
PUBLISHING
empowering minds

S. CHAND & COMPANY PVT. LTD.

(An ISO 9001 : 2008 Company)

Head Office: 7361, RAM NAGAR, NEW DELHI - 110 055
Phone: 23672080-81-82, 9899107446, 9911310888 Fax: 91-11-23677446
www.schandpublishing.com; e-mail: helpdesk@schandpublishing.com

Branches

Ahmedabad : Ph: 27541965, 27542369, ahmedabad@schandpublishing.com
Bengaluru : Ph: 22268048, 22354008, bangalore@schandpublishing.com
Bhopal : Ph: 4274723, 4209587, bhopal@schandpublishing.com
Chandigarh : Ph: 2725443, 2725446, chandigarh@schandpublishing.com
Chennai : Ph. 28410027, 28410058, chennai@schandpublishing.com
Coimbatore : Ph: 2323620, 4217136, coimbatore@schandpublishing.com (Marketing Office)
Cuttack : Ph: 2332580; 2332581, cuttack@schandpublishing.com
Dehradun : Ph: 2711101, 2710861, dehradun@schandpublishing.com
Guwahati : Ph: 2738811, 2735640, guwahati@schandpublishing.com
Hyderabad : Ph: 27550194, 27550195, hyderabad@schandpublishing.com
Jaipur : Ph: 2219175, 2219176, jaipur@schandpublishing.com
Jalandhar : Ph: 2401630, 5000630, jalandhar@schandpublishing.com
Kochi : Ph: 2378740, 2378207-08, cochin@schandpublishing.com
Kolkata : Ph: 22367459, 22373914, kolkata@schandpublishing.com
Lucknow : Ph: 4026791, 4065646 lucknow@schandpublishing.com
Mumbai : Ph: 22690881, 22610885, mumbai@schandpublishing.com
Nagpur : Ph: 6451311, 2720523, 2777666, nagpur@schandpublishing.com
Patna : Ph: 2300489, 2302100, patna@schandpublishing.com
Pune : Ph: 64017298, pune@schandpublishing.com
Raipur : Ph: 2443142, raipur@schandpublishing.com (Marketing Office)
Ranchi : Ph: 2361178, ranchi@schandpublishing.com
Siliguri : Ph: 2520750, siliguri@schandpublishing.com (Marketing Office)
Visakhapatnam : Ph: 2782609 visakhapatnam@schandpublishing.com (Marketing Office)

First Edition 1994
Subsequent Editions and Reprints 1996, 2000, 2005, 2011
Reprint 2016

ISBN : 978-81-219-0402-5 **Code :** 1017A 163

This book is for Sale in India & other SAARC Countries only.

PRINTED IN INDIA

By Nirja Publishers & Printers Pvt. Ltd., 54/3/2, Jindal Paddy Compound, Kashipur Road, Rudrapur-263153, Uttarakhand and published by S. Chand & Company Pvt. Ltd., 7361, Ram Nagar, New Delhi -110 055.

PREFACE TO THE FIFTH EDITION

We feel immense pleasure in placing meticulously revised and thoroughly updated version of our well received and widely acclaimed humble venture - Indian Administration.

We assure our esteemed readers that the subject matter of handy volume in their hand is fairly exhaustive so as to meet the requirement of the aspirants of administrative services and the young scholars who will like to opt for Public Administration as one of their disciplines for embarking upon a meritorious administrative career. The chapters pertaining to top functionaries whose political acumen and administrative calibre get ample opportunities to be tested in coalitional politics necessitating judiciousness practical sagacity, marked adaptability and above all unimpeachable integrity have been paid special attention.

A few new topics viz Women Empowerment sizable reservation for the OBC and keenness to accommodate minorities in the public services ; well conceived Electoral Reforms leading to examplary conduct of elections of XVth Lok Sabha and that of State Assemblies in the largest democracy of the world; Aggravation of Law and Order problem resulting in the inception of New Protective Agencies at the Central and State levels and a fair assessment of their working as regards redressal of genuine grievances of the masses ; the appraisal of the role of the President at the Centre and the Governors in the States on account of Hung Parliament and State Assemblies and Fractured mandate ushering in era of coalition governments ; the significance and likely misuse of Article 356 ; the passage of 73rd and 74th amending acts resulting in the strengthening of grass root democracy in the urban and rural areas — all these political events and their consequences have been dispassionately debated and analytically appraised.

We have made the budding citizens conscious of the political constraints and administrative bottlenecks which are gradually eating into the very vitals of our Democracy. We have tried to emphasise the re-orientation of our Administrative structure and strengthening of the foundations of our political edifice which is facing fast erosion due to rampant corruption, red tapism and at times officiousness and circumlocation. We aim at attaining the presitive glory of prestigious Indian Administration in the hoary past as it used to be the envy of even the alien invaders and ambitious rulers.

We are confident that this all–comprehensive, thoroughly revised and updated Edition will earn a word of praise.

We gratefully acknowledge the special pains undertaken by our dynamic publishers — Messers S. Chand for the expeditious publication of this well designed volume.

Authors

PREFACE TO THE FIRST EDITION

Indian Administration has been written primarily to serve the requirements of the young students appearing for the civil services examinations. It may not be deemed presumptuous on our part to claim that none of the existing books on the subject covers the entire syllabus of the said examination or furnish up-to-date information. Hence we have made a modest attempt to place a handy volume at the disposal of the aspirants of top administrative services just to enable them to acquire a basic understanding of the various facts on Indian administration. Besides, this latest book on the subject would amply cater to the needs of the students of Public Administration of various universities and also serve the general readers who would like to acquaint themselves with the administrative system of the country since Kautilya's times.

The topics which have been highlighted in the volume are Evolution of Indian Administration, Environmental Setting, Political Executive at the Union level, Structure of Central Administration, Centre-State relations, Public Services, Machinery for Planning, Public Undertakings, Control of Public Expenditure, State Administration, District and Local Administration, Welfare Administration and Issue Areas in Indian Administration.

A sincere effort has been made to portray analytically hard facts and naked realities dispassionately in easy language and lucid style. The authors are equipped with rich experience of teaching post-graduate classes for over three decades and have held top administrative posts in the hierarchy of Haryana Education Department. They have seen from close range the working of administrative machinery, the serfdom of bureaucracy to political masters and appalling apathy of the administration to public woes and worries. The authors feel that in the context of Indian ethos the administrative structure of the country is structurally sound but operationally perfunctory and faltering. More structural changes will be of no avail without the dedicated will on the part of the political rulers and the administrators alike to operate the fast decaying system conscientiously and honestly.

We are confident, the present volume will meet the requirements of promising scholars and competitors for the coveted administrative jobs in the country. We will welcome all constructive comments and concrete suggestions and incorporate them in the next edition.

We are indebted to our dynamic Publishers M/s. S. Chand and Company Ltd. for taking special pains in bringing out this voluminous edition expeditiously.

AUTHORS

CONTENTS

EVOLUTION OF INDIAN ADMINISTRATION

"No study has so potent an influence in forming a nation's mind and a nation's character as a critical and careful study of its past history. And it is by such study alone that an unreasoning and superstitious worship of the past is replaced by a legitimate and manly administration".

— R.C. Dutt

CONTENTS :

(A) ANCIENT ADMINISTRATION

Public Administration in India is a relic of the past. It has a deep historical perspective and a perpetual tradition of evolution. Arthashastra of Kautilya (Chanakya) is a manual of Public Administration and a rich heritage of India till date.

Arthashastra embodies values, norms and beliefs pertaining to public administration in ancient India. It is, in fact, a treatise on politics, public administration, ethics, economics, international politics and finance. Kautilya was of the view that, "The state must be based on sound economic foundations so as to enable men to realize the aims of life to lessen as much as possible the struggle for existence at home, to lessen the dependence of the community on the outside world, to be in a position to help other sections of humanity in distress and thereby to ensure an existence conducive to the happiness of men in this life and pave the way to a brighter one beyond".[1]

A peep in the hoary past also reveals that different forms of Governments existed in the primitive past but Monarchy eventually supplanted them all. With the passage of time, it was firmly entrenched on the soil of India and in fact it became the linchpin of the social arch. An appraisal of Mahabharata times also clearly reflects that elected Kings were strongly favoured and it used to be emphasised that there could be no sacrifice without a king. During the *Vedic* era, the Kings were not only elected by the people but they were *ousted* by them as well. The choice of the king was made by the *'rajkritas'* or *'rajkartarah' i.e.*, kingmakers. In due course, the election system was replaced by hereditary kingship. As such, the eldest male heir was to ascend the throne after the death of the king. If hereditary succession was found unsuitable for the august office or suffered disqualification on account of certain special default, another member of the royal family was installed on the throne. The establishment of hereditary kingship gave rise to the theory of divine origin of the institution of kingship. Thus, the king was sanctified with a divine halo. However, only a righteous king was regarded as divine. The monarch was allowed to remain as the head of the state if he promoted the welfare of his subjects[2]

[1] *N.C. Bandopadhyaya : Kautilya Vol. 1, (1927 ed) P. 67*
[2] *Ibid., p. 51*

The Vedic monarch ruled with the assistance of popular Vedic bodies, the *'Samiti'* and *'Sabha'*. The word *'Samiti'* denotes *meeting together* in an assembly. The king was required to attend the *'Samiti'*. The *Sabha* in literal terms meant a body of citizens sitting together. Those who were entitled to seat therein were thus invested with lustre. The Sabha acted as the national judicature. The Vedas clearly indicate that in the earliest times the national life and activities were expressed through popular assemblies and institutions.

King in Mahabharata times

The king was not above law. He had to be governed by the rules enumerated in the *'Sastras'*. He was expected to follow the advice of higher officials and in the event of crisism, he was guided by the learned Brahmans. Mahabharata refers to the duties of the king as – (i) to please the people; (ii) to protect them; (iii) to seek their welfare; (iv) to punish wrongdoers; (v) to practise the virtues of promptitude, energy, truthfulness, self restraint, humility, righteousness, fortitude and compassion; (vi) to see that his subjects observed their respective duties.

Functions of the King

A king combined in himself the main functions — executive, judicial, and military. The following were his functions : (i) the king hired and fired directly or indirectly the officials connected with the affairs of the state. The latter obeyed his commands and were accountable to him for their assigned functions; (ii) the administration of justice was done in the King's name and at times he presided over the Royal Court of Justice; (iii) he executed the judgement of the Courts and exercised his prerogative of mercy in suitable cases; (iv) though he was not vested with the legislative powers yet he could issue royal edicts, pertaining to administrative business, which had the force of law; (v) he was the supreme commander of the military forces of the country and many a time he led the army personally on the battlefield. Keeping in view the above functions, Kautilya calls the "king as the centre of authority".

Checks on the King's authority : The ancient Hindu political thinkers refer to two types of checks on the authority of Kings *viz.* (a) preventive and (b) retributive. The former prevented a king from degenerating into a tyrant. They were internal as well as external which were further subdivided into religious and political checks. During studentship, the prince lived the life of a *Brahmachari i.e.*, observed complete celibacy and underwent a rigorous life, studying different types of subjects. Kautilya emphasizes that the king should have control over the senses and forego lust, shed anger, greed, vanity, haughtiness and gaiety. The latter checks suggest imposition of fines, deposition and tyrannicide for wrongs committed by them[1]. The subjects could migrate to another country better governed, thus causing loss of revenue to the king. They could throw him out and enthrone his relation found more suitable. Mahabharata, in fact, suggested the most drastic remedy 'right to tyrannicide' if there was no other alternative.

Republics in the past : Besides Monarchies, Republics also existed. The Hindu Republics constitute an illustration of communal self-governing habits of the post Vedic age. The Greek observers have showered praises on the laws and the administration of laws in the Republican states of India. Justice reigned supreme. Discipline was the order of the day. Valorous deeds were instilled in the individuals and the commitment of such deeds was a matter of honour and ambition. However, a systematic philosophy of Republicanism could not find its roots in ancient India because by the time political theorising emerged, republicanism was on its decline.

A full chapter which has been devoted to ***'ganas'*** in ***'Santi Parva'***, refers to the constitution

[1] *P. Sharma : Public Administration in India, 1978 ed. p.3.*

of 'ganas'. Gana Mukhiya was the leader of the *'Gana'*. The assembly comprised of the qualified citizens who could neither know nor discuss the secret policy of the state. It remained the privilege of the 'Gana Mukhiya'. A Governing Council, responsible for determination of policy and its execution also existed.

Buddhist literature also reveals the working of a Republic. The following factors were said to have catered to the success of the Republics — (i) full and frequent public assemblies; (ii) meeting and carrying out undertakings in secret; (iii) not enacting anything not already established; (iv) acting according to the ancient institution of *vajjians* as established in former days; (v) honouring and supporting the *vajjian* elders and following their advice[1]. Some prominent features of Republicanism were : excessive formality and ritualism of the Government; strict control over individuals and families through executive edicts and also legislation : adoption of distinctive symbols and devices; superiority of Kshatriyas over the Brahmins in social set-up. However, Majumdar states "*Empire builders like Chandragupta Maurya and Samudra Gupta impartially destroyed all the states irrespective of their form of government*"[2].

Chandragupta Maurya's Time

Chandragupta played a pioneering role in bringing under his direct supremacy the entire country from Afghanistan to the Bay of Bengal and from the Himalayas to beyond the Vindhya mountains. To exercise effective control over the imperial system, Kautilya — the Prime Minister of Chandragupta, framed a complex administrative machinery. The central executive controlled the Home province but the distant provinces were ruled by the Governor appointed by the Centre. From a purely administrative point of view, the provinces were divided into districts and sub-districts and fairly competent officers were used to be put in charge of them. Chanakya refers about them as '*Gopas*' and '*Sthanikas*'. The Inspection staff of the Central Government visited these provinces and submitted periodic reports about their functioning to the Central Government. Parts of Empire were governed by local *'rajas'* who were allowed varying degrees of autonomy and who owed nominal allegiance to the suzerain authority. Some of them paid the annual tribute and could be called to assist the suzerain at the time of foreign invasion. However, these *'rajas'* enjoyed internal autonomy. The less important of them were subjected to suspension of the Imperial Government. The standard of efficiency varied from state to state. There have been good Kings assisted by capable ministers but there have been incompetent kings assisted by incapable administrators who could hardly maintain peace and order and brought untold misery and sufferings to the people. A historian is of the view that "on the whole the administration was considered to be efficient".

Ghoshal refers to the following branches of political organisation during the Maurya Empire — (a) security and progress of the state; (b) public security and welfare; (c) state control over popular recreations; (d) state planned foundations of towns and construction of architectural monuments; (e) status of religious sects and Ashoka's relation with the Buddhist *Viharas* and, (f) status of the autonomous people and of foreign subjects[3].

It may not be out of place to point out that during the post-Vedic to pre-Mauryan periods, the Kings levied taxes on the subjects in lieu of protection they offered to the people. However, there is no mention about this fact during Gupta and post Gupta periods.

Brahmans in this era were the custodians of the law books and interpreted the texts of the king. They imposed checks on the Kings' authority. Some feudatories held titles like '*Maharathis*' and lords *'Mahabhojas'* who wielded greater authority because of matrimonial relations and family

[1] *A.K. Majumdar : Concise History of Ancient India vol. II (1980 ed) pp.137-38.*

[2] *Ibid p.143*

[3] *U.N. Ghoshal : A History of Indian Public Life Vol. II (1966 ed) – p. 183.*

ties and exercised some control on the royal power. Besides, the royal power used to be restrained by the ministers as well. Invaribly, the king did not act against the wishes of the Council of Ministers.

Administrative Structure

During the period (500-750), the king was the most prominent element in the administration, in fact he was the focal point of administration. However, he exercised his authority through *'mantrins'*, *'amatyas'* and *'sachivas'*. The *'mantrins'* were the confidants of the king and his principal advisers. They were considered custodians of public interest. Kautilya in 'Arthashastra' portrays the *'Amatyas'* as the regular cadre of service from which higher officials *viz.* chief priests, ministers, and treasurers, were recruited. The *'Amatyas'* were assigned the duties of fortification, collection of the royal dues, punishment of the criminals, agricultural operations and territorial welfare. The *'Sachivas'* — officials of a particular cadre — were more of executors of King's order, rather than his counsellors.

The others who constituted the King's *entourage*, included *'Parishadas'* or assembly men; the *'arthkarins'* — the executive officers, five in number in the cabinet to deal with state business and *'Dharmikas'* — the judges or the interpreters of laws. Besides, there were *'Tirthas'* — eighteen other officers of the state; *'Mantri'* — the Chief *Councillor* — to advise the king in secret; *'Purohita'* — the chief priest to render advice on matters pertaining to succession; *'Yuvaraja'* — the Crown Prince who preceded the 'Senapati'; *'Chamupati'* the commander-in-chief of the army; *'Dvarapata' 'Chamberlain* and *'Antaravesika'* — the supervisor of the *'Harem'* exercising control over the forces working inside the palace area; *Dravya Samchayakrit* — the chief steward dealing with financial administration; *'Kritya Krityeshu Charthan Viniyoja'* — the chief executive officer, to determine the execution of public business; *Pradeshta* — the chief judge for administering justice; *'Nagar adhyaksha* — the superintendent of justice; *Sabhadhyaksha* — the president of the Assembly; *Dandapala* — the chief criminal judge; *Durga Pala* — the warden of the forts; *'Rashtrantapalaka'* — the warden of the marches and *Atavipalaka* — in charge of forests[1].

In Maurya and Gupta Empires, the State was divided into Divisions and the Divisions into districts. The Provinces were governed by the Governors, known as Tatapadha — *'pargrahita'*. They invariably hailed from the royal family and were appointed by the king. The District officers were appointed by the provincial Governor. They possessed both the administrative and judicial powers. The District Administrator as the nominee of the State safeguarded the royal interests as well as those enumerated in the grants for the religious and charitable purposes.

The *Grama* (village) constituted the smallest unit of the administration. The head man — the elder of the village was the linchpin of the village administration. The village administration was run by a Panchayat (village council). The panchayat was equipped with both the executive and judicial powers. The village officers maintained law and order and acted as custodians of life and property of the villagers.

The city headed by the *nagarka purapala* (Governor) formed a separate administrative unit. The city had its own *'adhishtanadhikarana'* (city council) which was divided into committees. The latter were the functional bodies and the council in the co-operative society, looked after general local affairs *viz.* finance, sanitation, water supply etc. The village and city autonomy comprised the seminal principles of ancient administration in India. Frank Moraes rightly stated that before the Mughal or British eras, the stress was on self governing institutions and a cooperative life[2].

A critical survey of the political set-up in India between 500 and 750 AD reveals that it was not a unitary system. It was a sort of federal feudalism though some of the historians do not accept this contention. The traits of modern federalism — *viz* a written constitution, clear demarcation of spheres of power, co-ordination of federal and state authorities, were conspicuous by their

[1]*B.N. Puri : History of Indian Administration, vol. 1, pp. 19-20*

[2]*Frank Moraes : Jawaharlal Nehru, A Biography, 1956 ed., p. 407*

absence. Hence, it has been termed as a tributary system.

Kautilya's view of Monarchy and its limitations

Kautilya refers to Magadha Imperialism as a centralised system. "Justice had become royal, even law tended to be royal[1]". King was the symbol of state[2]. The king was the standard of sovereignty to rally loyalty and hold the realm together. However, the king, in the words of Kautilya, has no personal likes; it is the like of the subjects that shall be followed by him[3]. The king's utility was great. He saw to the transfer of ministers and ministry and was the co-ordinating spirit in the Government. On account of his high sense of sacrifice, old traditions and envious position, the king stood far higher than the ministers and ruled them. If people found the actual Governors bad, the king remained the centre of hope and reform and avoided disruption[4]. Thus the ministers came and went but the king remained intact. Even a powerless king epitomised the state. Hence the king is not to be despised. The Kings' office is that of Indra and Yama, visible inflictor of punishment and bestower of reward. On those who despise him, even divine punishment descends[5].

However, Kautilya — the greatest votary of monarchy — stated that matters of state should be discussed by the Council of Ministers and whatever the majority decides the king should carry out. In his words "when there is an extraordinary matter, the *Mantrins* and the Mantri-Parishad should be called together and informed. In the meeting whatever the majority decided to be done should be done by the king[6]". It is evident that the king is not even given the power of veto. Emphasising the importance of the Parishads, Kautilya remarks that Indira was called "thousand eyed", although he had two eyes because he had thousand wise members in his Mantri Parishad or Council of State, who are regarded as his eyes."[7] Kautilya in a way limits the authority of the king by stressing the importance of the Parishad (modern Council of Ministers).

Besides, the hermits and the recluse thinkers (living in forests) who were repositories of past experience in social and political matters, and comprised of a set of clean and impartial thinking, could understand the complexities of administration and advise the king without reserve and fear. These hermits though leading a retired life were not absolutely out of touch with the community and the world of politics. As such, they could apprise the king of the correct view of a difficulty in administration[8]. Theirs' was quite an effective, restraining and sobering influence on the king. Kautilya emphasises in Artha-sastra that a bad government offends ascetics and recluses[9].

Thus a significant constitutional progress is discernible in ancient Hindu polity which could neither be equalled nor surpassed by any polity of antiquity. Kautilya's Arthashastra is a manual on administrative acumen. Dr. K.P. Jayaswal remarks "constitutional or social advancement is not a monopoly of any particular race. I am not a believer in the cheap wisdom which preaches that political greatness is inherent in some people.... *There is no such thing as blue-blood in political and constitutional evolution. Political and constitutional progress is a creation of circumstances and human forces. And even if such blue-blood be a reality, it is certainly present in the veins of the Hindu"[10]*

(B) MEDIEVAL ADMINISTRATION (750 - 1200 AD)

During this period, the king was the fountain of authority. The executive, the judicial and

[1]*Artha-Shastra p. 150*
[2]*Ibid Ch 6, 95 (p. 254)*
[3]*Ibid Chap 19, 16 (p. 39)*
[4]*Ibid Chap 1, 127 (p. 320)*
[5]*Ibid Chap 15, 11 p. 29*
[6]*K.P. Jayaswal : op. cit. p. 225*
[7]*Ibid Bk. I, Ch. 15 : 11 (p. 29)*
[8]*Ibid Bk. II, 2; p. 49*
[9]*Ibid Bk-I, Ch. 4; (p. 9)*
[10]*K.P. Jayaswal : op. cit. (5th ed., 1978) p. 353*

the military powers were vested with him. As the head of the State, he was responsible for the protection of the people and acted as the custodian of their welfare. He administered law impartially and was required to see that the lower courts rendered justice properly. He maintained law and order in the State, by eliminating the irreconcilable forces and then expanded his territory. Besides, he promoted '*dharma*', '*artha*' and '*kama*' in order to accelerate progress of society in religious, socio-economic and aesthetic fields. During this era, trade, agriculture and industry flourished. Hence the country's resources were augmented and it possessed fabulous wealth in gold, silver and pearls. In spite of progress in politics, poetics, philosophy and chemistry and prosperity due to addition of economic sources, India remained a divided house. Political unity remained a mirage and feuds amongst rulers of the states were frequent.

Administration was run by the ministers who were respected and honoured particularly if they were competent. The *Pradhana* — P.M. was the most important of the ministers, the *Sachiva* — the war minister was second in the hierarchical ladder. The other important ministers were the foreign minister, the *Pradvivaka* — the head of the judicial department, the revenue minister and the treasurer. The ministers were not only the servants of the king but also the trustees of the people. They protected the interests of the people by exhorting the King not to deviate from the right path.

The provincial Governors appointed by the king maintained law and order, and collected revenues. Village was the lowest administrative unit kept under the control of headman who played paternal role to the inmates of the village by taking care of their economic prosperity and abiding happiness.

During the early Rajput regime, the '*Pratihara*' administration was headed by the ruler who was hereditary and was required to heed the advice of his court and particularly his experienced ministers and counsellors comprising it. A powerful feudal class, a prominent segment of the Royal Court was a potent check on the king and was graded next to the ruler in status and authority. The Royal court was divided into two sections — Mahasthana and Abhyantarasthaana — the inner court. The latter was composed of the closest confidants of the ruler — the rajini, the yuvaraja, the ministers and the senapati. The Mahasthana, consisted of mantrins, senanayaks, mahapratiharas, mahasamantas, dharmastheyas, 'learned brahmins', poets, physicians, scholars well versed in sastras, jesters and courtiers. This assembly discussed non-secret matters of common interest.

The ministry termed as 'mantrimandala' was an important component of *mahasthana*. The ministers were removable by the king and ran the administration. Sandhivigrahika — a minister for peace and war, Aksapatalika — the Chief Accounts officer, 'Lihandagarika' in charge of the royal treasury and ornaments; Mahadandanayakar', Senapati, Niyuktaka — a departmental head — were the main ministers.

The extensive tracts of the Pratihara Empire were held by feudatories bound to their own lords by terms of service. The rest of the empire was grouped under the heads — Bhuati Mandala, Visaya, Pathaka, Charturasitika and Dvadasaka. Bhuati was the biggest division. The civil affairs were managed by a non-official body known as 'Varikas'. The village administration was run by a village Panchayat and Grampati or Gramkuta — the headman.

The Rajput administration in a way was a blend of militarism, feudalism and a divine monarchy. The rulers were more keen for the acquisition of military glory rather than promotion of public welfare. The rulers evoked respect but not attention or gratitude. Invariably, civil and military appointments were given to the Brahmans and the kshatriyas. Hence, the rest of the people did not evince any interest in the political affairs. The Rajput Kings did not interfere in the local administration. As such, the local population developed in itself initiative and self reliance.

The Rajputs did not present a united front. They could not contain the invasions from the North West. Some of them foolishly welcomed an attack by the Muslim rulers if it was planned against some rival of theirs. Hence within a few years, the greater chunk of our territory went into the hands of the Muslims.

Islamic society and Government were organised on the basis of divine injunctions incorporated in the Holy Quran. According to the Quran, the real master and sovereign of the Universe is Allah and the Muslims are expected to obey him. Hence as per Islamic conception, the state is only a tool to serve the head in the attainment of its objects or the ideal of *millet* of Islam as revealed through the medium of Prophet Mohammad. *Thus the nature of the Islamic state became communal. It conceived of only the Muslims — the faithfuls — as its citizens. Hence, all the political ideas and functions of the state came to be centred around the person of the Monarch*[1].

Delhi Sultanate

There were two categories of sultans — (i) Ala-ud-din and Mohammad-bin Tughlaq who tried to incorporate innovations which were hated by orthodox Muslims and (ii) Firoz Tuglaq and Sikundar Lodi who were staunch believers of Islamic tenets and principles, and hence believed in ruling the States strictly in accordance with the Islamic laws. They adapted themselves to Islamic injunctions, theology and law, and did not treat religion separate from politics and administration. The Sultanate may therefore be portrayed as a junior member of the Islamic Commonwealth of Nations.

The Sultan in this era was the Chief Executive and the keystone of the administrative arch. He acted as the highest court of appeal and his subordinates presented all petitions to him. Next to the Sultan was the *Wazir* who was the chief adviser of the former and officiated in his absence. The Wazir was assisted by the *Naib-Wazir*, the Accountant General (*Mushrif-i-Mamalik*), the Auditor General (*Mustauf-i-Mamalik*), *hazirs* (Superintendents) *waqufis* (inspectors) and several other officials. *Aziz-i-Mamalik* was the head of the military department. As such, he was concerned with the building up of the army and supply of war material. He was assisted by *Naib-aziz-i-Mamalik*. Qazi-ul-Quzat headed the judiciary. The records of the departments were maintained by the *Dabir-i-khas*. *Barid-i-Mamalik* was in charge of department of Information and Intelligence. Agricultural administration was looked after by '*Amir Kohi*'.

The Royal Household was looked after by *wakil-i-dar* assisted by *Naib-wakil-i-dar*. *Amir-i-Hajili* known as '*Barabak*' as well was the chief of the protocol. He was assisted by a *naib-barabak*. Other important officials included the '*Khasin*' — the royal treasurer, '*Sarjaudar*' — the royal bodyguard, '*Sharabdar*' — in charge of royal drinks; *chasnigir* — the taster of the royal food; *Muthdar* — the keeper of the royal seal and *Shabna-i-fil* and *Akhurbek* in charge of the elephants and horses separately.

The empire was divided into a number of provinces. Each province was governed by a *Wali* — Governor or *hazim* or *naib sultan* who was appointed by the Emperor. He was assisted by a *Naib-quzuil-quzat* — a high qazi in the capital and naib *mustakharj*— a revenue officer who was required to realise arrears from the *amils* and supervise the collection of the provincial revenues. The kingdom used to be divided into '*Sarkars*', corresponding to big divisions. The '*Sarkars*' were administered by the Governors though the revenue administration of a *Sarkar*' was kept under a '*DIWAN*' APPOINTED BY THE 'SULTAN'. The '*Diwan*' was not subservient to the Governor. He was assisted by a *Mushrif*— an accountant and *mustaufi* — an auditor. *Bakshi* — the paymaster of the army; *Qazi* - the judge, *kotwal* etc. were also important officials in the 'Sarkar'.

Next to the division was 'Pargana' or Shiqq which looked after the executive and land revenue. The '*Shiqqadar*' headed a small army and possessed a 'jagir' for his maintenance. At the Pargana level there were other officials *viz., Amil*, the Collector of revenue to deal with the central and provincial revenue '*Diwan*', *fotahadar* — the local treasurer, *daroga* — the superintendent of accounts; *amin* — the surveyor; *kanungo, munsif, thaneder, patwari*, etc. The 'diwan' in the Sarkar was the executive head of the 'Pargana'.

[1]*U.N. Day : The Mughal Government quoted in P. Sharan's Public Administration in India (1978 ed.) p. 8*

An appraisal of the sultan's regime reveals that the division of Empire into subhas, sarkars and parganas, had taken proper shape. District and Revenue administration had clearly emerged. Proper records, ensuring security to the tenants and adequate returns to the state were brought into existence. Espionage and the postal system confined to the royal mail had developed substantially. A standing Army maintained by the centre defended the territorial integrity of the country. The contribution of the '*walis*' and '*vaasals*' in men and resources was regularly available. It has been observed that the later phase of the Delhi Sultanate was more or less an experiment in administering the vast territory inhabited by communal and feudal elements which always constituted a standing threat to the central authority.

During the Sultanate, prior to the Divine Right theory, projecting a monarch as a shadow of God, encountered opposition at the hands of orthodox Muslim thinkers, though it was a transient phase and the theory gathered momentum in the ensuing Mughal era.

(C) THE MUGHAL ADMINISTRATION

(Babar to Aurangzeb i.e. 1526 to 1707)

Babar's historic victory in the battle of Panipat in 1526 enabled him to establish Mughal rule in India. However, he did not live for long and breathed his last in December, 1530. Humayun—his eldest son, ascended the throne of Agra on December 30, 1530. Fulfilling the desire of his father, he gave Sambhal to Askari, Alwar to Hindal and the provinces of Kabul, Kandhahar, Punjab Hissar and Feroza to Kamran. Thus he was required to feel contented with the newly conquered empire. He faced many trials and tribulations. He succeeded in recovering his kingdom after persistent efforts but unfortunately he met with an accident and was succeeded in 1556 by Akbar the Great — the monarch known for magnanimity and secularist approach. Akbar was succeeded by Jahangir known for Adal-i-Jhangiri — a just and fair king of Mughal period. Jahangir was succeeded by Shahjahan — designated by the Historians as the architect king. Aurangzeb — the successor to Shahjahan, ascended the throne through intrigues and manipulation. He tarnished the image of his forefathers by sowing the seeds of dissension and betraying communal tinge in his approach to the Hindu community. He died on March 3, 1707. Mughal empire met its decline during and after his reign. The last of the Mughals—Bahadur Shah who played an active role in the mutiny of 1857, died as prisoner in exile in Rangoon.

An overall appraisal of the Mughal administration reveals that it was more of a military rule and a sort of centralised despotism. The sovereign was both head of the state and that of the faith. For the Muslims, particularly the other section, the Monarch was the 'shadow of God'. This idea reached high watermark in the times of Akbar and Humayun. The Mughal emperor headed the administration. He had no Cabinet as such but his secretaries functioned as ministers. He was the fountain of all authority, omnipotent and omnicompetent, and was under no bounds or restraints. Whether or not the ministers and *wazirs* be consulted was his sweet will. The Mughal rule was hierarchical in structure. As such, the monarch was the pillar around which the whole administrative machinery revolved. The emperor was the embodiment of justice. He not only rendered proper justice but made provisions through which justice could be administered. A famous historian remarks, "Though the Mughals came to India as conquerors and foreigners, they set up traditions and conventions which were calculated to endear them to the Indian subjects. The emperor's appearance at the Jharokha for popular '*Didar-a-Roz*' offered, the opportunity to the people to approach them with their petitions, their personal attention to minute details of administration and their regular inspection tours and pageants throughout the empire, even apart from their generally enlightened and benevolent policy in all matters, served to impart to their autocratic rule the appearance of government by consent. This noble gesture was largely the creation of Akbar's statesmanship. It was sustained during the next two reigns of Jahangir and Shahjahan, but was progressively undermined by the reactionary policy of Aurangzeb. Nevertheless, the main framework of the administrative organisation though in a considerably attenuated form endured till the English East India Company stepped into the shoes of the Mughal Emperors".[1]

An appraisal of individual contribution of Mughal emperors in the field of administration will enable us to conclude that the Mughals, with the exception of Akbar-the Great, did not make significant contribution in this domain.

Babur (1525 to 1530)

Babur was no administrative genius. He was only a plain warrior with statesman-like instincts. He founded the Mughal empire in India in 1526. He followed the administrative plan already in existence. He entrusted the dominions to his officers with a clear understanding that each was responsible for efficient administration of the districts under his control. However, he did not let Amirs gain what the Crown lost as it happened in the past. In the words of Rushbrooke Williams, "....During the reign of Babur this does not become apparent partly because he was invested with the prestige of a conquerer and partly because the time was too short for the consequences of his policy to make themsclves felt. Even before he died, however, the symptoms of radical unsoundness with administration are not far to seek. The old haphazard financial system entirely failed to provide means for the upkeep of the professional soldiers.....who were paid directly from the royal revenue. *Babur suddenly found himself with an empty treasury".*[2]

Humayun (1530 to 40), (1540 - 53 Exile) and (1555 - 56)

Rushbrooke Williams remarks, "....But in the time of Humayun there is a repetition of the old story of financial breakdown accompanied by revolution, intrigues and the dethronement of dynasty".[3] When Humayun arrived in Delhi, he dedicatedly devoted himself to general superintendence of the affairs of the kingdom and personally watched the progress of his armies which he had deputed to reduce provinces. He discussed various defects in the system of government and set himself to devising means of improving it. He split the Empire administratively into several great divisions each of them to have a local capital and a Board of administration for directing local affairs. To each of these divisions was assigned a considerable military force under an able General in order to render it independent of assistance from the others. The Emperor was to accord unity to the whole by paying them a visit with an army of 1200 horses under his own immediate command and readily available to him to move in any direction. Erskine remarks, "for this plan, however, he never had time. Had he even possessed, sufficient steadiness, he might not have carried it into execution".[4]

Second, he divided all the affairs of the Government into four departments viz., *Atashi, Hawai, Abi* and *Khaki*. For the conduct of business of these departments, he appointed four ministers. *Atashi* department functioned under 'Khwaja Amid-ul-Mulk. It was concerned with the artillery, the making of arms, weapons of war, various sorts of engines and other such things, which necessitated the use of fire. The *Hawai* department was entrusted to Khwaja Lutfulla. It was concerned with the ward robe, kitchen, stable, and some other important affairs. *Abi* department functioned under the superintendence of Khwaja Hasan. The department comprised of a Sherbat Khana, Suji Khana, the digging of canals and the works related to water and rivers. *Khaki* department was kept under the management of Khwaja Jalal-ud-din Mirza Beg. Agriculture, erection of buildings, resumption of khalisa lands and some household affairs constituted this department.

---

[1]*Sri Ram Sharma : Mughal Government and Administration p. 260.*
[2]*Rushbrooke Williams : An Empire Builder, pp. 161-62.*
[3]*ibid*
[4]*Erskine : Babur and Humayun II, pp. 526-27*

The wise king also divided the days of the week and fixed one day to each of the classes. Saturdays and Thursdays were for pious men. Visits from literary and religious men were allowed on this day. Sundays and Tuesdays were fixed for staff officers. As such, the entire Government business and the duties connected with the management of the country were discharged on these days.

Akbar the Great (1556 - 1605)

Moreland calls the Administration of Akbar as 'severely practical'. Akbar's administration reveals that it was a centralised monarchy acting through bureaucratic machinery. All the strings of administration were gathered together ultimately in the Emperor's own hands. His administrative system favoured the direct relation between the state and the individual peasant, the assessment and collection of revenue being controlled from the centre and the officers having to account in details for all receipts.[1] For the sake of administrative convenience, the following departments were created — Military, Revenue, Justice and Religion. Prof. J.N. Sarkar has described the Mughal administration as under :

Central Government

The chief departments of the Mughal administration were : (*i*) The Exchequer and Revenue under High Diwan. (*ii*) The Imperial Household under Khan-i-Saman. (*iii*) The Military, Pay and Accounts office under the Imperial Bakshi. (*iv*) Canon law both civil and criminal under the Chief Qazi. (*v*) Religious Endowments and charity under Chief Sadar. (*vi*) Censorship of public morals under Muhtasib. (*vii*) The Artillery under Mir Atish or Darogha-i-topkhana; (*viii*) Intelligence and Posts under the Darogha of Dak-Khana (The (*vi*) and (*vii*) were less in importance but ranked almost like departments).

The numerous Karkhanas (factories and stores) each under a *darogha* or superintendent were not categorised as Departments. Most of them functioned under Khan-i-Saman.

Officers Under the King

The following were the officers functioning under the king.

The Bakshi or Paymaster

The salaries of the military commanders calculated in terms of contingents under them, were passed by the paymaster of the Army. At a later stage, this officer was called 'Mir' or first Bakshi. He had three officers under him-Bakshis second, third and fourth.

The Khan-i-Saman or High Steward

This officer was the head of the Imperial household. In the words of Mannuci, "He had charge of the whole expenditure of the royal household in reference to both great and small things".[2] The personal staff of the king was under his control. He supervised the Emperor's daily expenditure. Often wazir's were chosen from among the 'Khan-i-Samans'.

The Qazi-ul-quzat or Chief Judge

The qazi of the imperial camp made all appointments of local qazis in various parts of the Empire.

The Sadar-us-Sadur [Chief Sadar]

The officer was the chief civil judge and supervisor of the endowments of land made by the

[1] *Moreland : India at the death of Akbar, pp. 33-4.*

[2] *J.N. Sarkar : Mughal Administration, p. 26n*

emperors or princes for the support of pious men, scholars, and monks. He had to see that such grants were expended for the right purpose and he had also to scrutinize applications for fresh grants. He was the Emperor's almoner and spent the vast sums which the Emperor set apart for charity in the month of *Ramzan* and other holy occasions.

Muhtasib or Censor of Public Morals

He had also to see that Muslims led lives according to the prophet's commands and did not indulge in forbidden things. The sale of intoxicating drink was to be prohibited in the cities and the prostitutes were not to be allowed residence therein as it was opposed to the sacred law. Instructions to him ran :

"Give good counsel and warning to those who violate the Quoranic precepts. Quoranic precepts do not show harshness. First send advice to the leaders of these people and if they do not listen to you then report the case to the Governor".[1]

The Chancellor (Wazir)

The Chancellor of the Empire - the Prime Minister termed as Wazir or Vakil, exercised dictatorial authority like the Peshwas in India or the Mayors of the Palace in medieval France. Next to the king was the Wazir, the Prime Minister. He was Diwan as well. He received all revenue papers and returns and despatches from the provinces and the field armies. He represented the king on ceremonial occasions. He wrote letters 'by order' in his own person though under the emperor's directions. With the exception of payment to the field army and the workmen of the state factories, all other payments were made through the department only. Some of the eminent Wazirs were well versed in Persian prose as well and acted as secretaries in drafting royal letters to foreign rulers on behalf of their monarchs. Often he led short expeditions as his proximity to the king was indispensable. *"Thus in its origin, the Wazir's post was a civil one and his assumption of the supreme military direction was abnormal and a mark of Imperial decadence".*[2]

The provincial administration was a prototype of the central administration. Provincial and district administrations were based on the 'suba' and 'sarkars', as units with their heads called 'subedars' and 'faujdars' assisted by the 'diwans' and 'amalguzars' respectively. On the last days of Mughal rule, the Sarkar was replaced by a larger administrative unit termed as 'Chakla'. Below the 'Sarkar' was the 'Pargana' headed by the Shiqqdar'. Decentralisation was considered indispensable for a huge empire of the Mughals. However, the latter did not disturb the local set up under Muqaddams and 'Chandbaris'. The border areas were administered by 'Faujdars' while that of the port areas by 'Mustsaddi'. Kotwal was the head of the police at the metropolis whereas the Qazis and Sadars headed the judicial administration. Assessment and collection of revenue were controlled by the Centre and the officers had to account in details for all receipts. Revenue administration and military organisation comprised the main pillars for holding up the structure of the state.

Administration at Lower Level

Administration at the lower level was carried out by the officers in charge of the administrative unit at that level. However, sanction of the imperial and provincial Governments in such cases was a foregone conclusion. The vigilant and competent lower administrative machinery was considered, to a great extent, responsible for the security of empire and its peaceful and efficient administration. Mansabdars were the chief officers of the localities. The 'mansab' was a commission held by the officers of the Emperor. It was a hierarchical system consisting of the 'mansabdars' ranging from those commanding 20 horsemen to those commanding 5000. In

[1] *Ibid, pp. 30-31*
[2] *J.N. Sarkar : op. cit. (1952 ed), pp. 22-23*

between, innumerable grades existed the officers who rose from grade to grade according to merit and also patronage. Besides, the system was the fusion between the civil and military functions. Keeping in view the vastness of the Indian administrative system JN Sarkar remarks, "*The mughal system at one time spread over practically all the civilised and organised parts of India. Nor is it dead in our own times. Traces of it still survive - But the new has been built upon the old, our present has its roots in our past*".[1] For Muslims, the mughal rule undertook socialistic functions, but for non-Muslims, it followed the policy of least interference. It discharged only the police functions and collected revenues. JN Sarkar remarks that the socialistic activity in the broadest sense of the modern state was left to the community, the society or the caste brotherhood. The aim of the Government is thus extremely limited, materialistic, and almost sordid".[2]

Jahangir (1605-27)

Dr. Beni Prasad remarks, "*The political side of Jahangir's history is interesting enough but its virtue lies in cultural development*".[3] He was more a patron of art and literature and a lover of nature. His attitude to religion was not so rational as that of his father but he was not an electic or a Christian at heart".[4] In fact he was a liberal muslim whose religious belief and practices were generally based on a tolerant understanding of the principles of other faiths. He was a fairly successful ruler and administrator. In the words of Dr. Srivastava, "He had the capacity of appreciating the need and circumstances of the age and the good sense to continue the administrative system and policy devised by Akbar".[5] He was, however, not a statesman who could initiate administrative reforms and legislate for the good of the generation yet to be born. Neither he possessed idealism nor genius of his father. Hence the administrative machinery left by his father remained untouched. The Vakil or Vakil-i-Mulaq remained the highest dignitary next to the Emperor and so was the case of other ministers. **The difference between his administration and that of his father lay in the fact that the latter being the just judge of human character appointed right men to right offices whereas Jahangir, many a time, fitted square pegs in the round holes, swayed by extraneous considerations.**

Shahjahan (1628-58)

Shahjahan was a capable administrator and a statesman. He systematised the administration particularly, 'the mansabdari system'. He effected a cut in the salaries of '*mansabdars*' and empowered them to maintain in their services the exact number of troops required for their several ranks. In the 20th year of his reign he issued a circular that a *mansabdar* who held a *jagir* in India must maintain one-third of the troops indicated by his rank. One who held *jagir* outside India, was required to maintain one-fourth of the troops per his rank.

He maintained his ancestral tradition of personally administering justice. Offenders were few. Those discovered, were tried on the spot, according to law, and with concurrence of the law officers. Appeals could be made to the Governor or Diwan or the Qazi of the Suba if any individual was dissatisfied with the decision made on the spot. Further appeals could be made to a Chief Diwan or Chief Qazi if dissatisfaction still prevailed. Cases pertaining to blood and religion could become subjects of reference to His Majesty[6].

Moreland is appreciative of Shahjahan's financial administration. He described the reign of Shahjahan as 'a period of agrarian tranquillity"[7]. This prosperity is said to be due to his "careful

[1] *Ibid op. cit., p. 3*
[2] *Ibid pp. 4-5*
[3] *Beni Prasad : History of Jahangir, pp. 430-36.*
[4] *R.C. Majumdar and others : An Advanced History of India, p. 467*
[5] *Ashirbedilal Srivastava : The Mughal Empire (1979 ed.), pp. 288-89.*
[6] *Rai Bhari Mal's Eulogy in Lubh-ul-Tawarikh-in-Hind : E and D Vol. VII: pp. 172–73.*
[7] ***Moreland** : op. cit., p. 131.*

administration" which raised the income of the state beyond all precedents.[1] The vast wealth was concentrated in the hands of the Emperor and the nobility and spent in war and luxury was not extorted from the indigent peasantry as is generally alleged. He provided '*Caravan serais*' with proper equipments to render travelling within the empire as safe as possible. These *serais* were fortified places with bastions and strong gates mostly built of stone or bricks. They were not meant for soldiers. They had separate abodes for men and women. However, the historians feel that he was not as tolerant to Hindus as his father or grandfather. The acts of persecution and religious bigotry he indulged in, reveal that "*there was already a setback in the tide of liberalism so well begun by Akbar*".[2] Besides, corruption creeped in his administration. His fondness for money impelled him to enhance the burden of the people and caused untold sufferings to them. "His love of presents accorded sanction to a pernicious custom of gilded bribery. The offering of 'nazars' and presents became common not only at the royal court and camp but also in the households of imperial nobles and officers and became responsible for a great deal of corruption in administration".[3] His extortion of money from the unwilling masses and classes and his sensual tastes set a poor standard of public and private morality. During his reign were sown the seeds of reaction which became eventually the main causes of the downfall of his dynasty and the **fall of his empire.**

Aurangzeb (1658-1707)

In the words of Sarkar, ".....under him the Mughal Empire reached its greatest extent and the largest single state ever known in India from the dawn of history to the rise of the British power was formed". His reign has been portrayed as "the turn of the tide" by some historians. His administration was in fact a highly centralised despotism. All authority was concentrated in the hands of the Emperor who, like Louis XIV, of France, was said to be his own Prime Minister. He looked personally into the petty details of administration. He read the petitions personally and wrote orders personally or dictated them. His ministers and officers were strictly under his control and dared not share with him the initiation or formulation of policy. He was conscious of the royal prerogative and was strict in the enforcement of his orders. He emphasised, "If a single rule is disregarded, all the regulations will be destroyed". The over-centralisation of his administration and his parochial outlook reduced the ministers to the position of glorified clerks. They were neither left with any initiative nor showed fearlessness in assuming responsibility. Hence, all this resulted in the degeneration of administration. He being the believer of the Islamic theory of the State, followed the 'Shariat' in everything political, administrative or economic. He tried to convert India into an Islamic state. Thus the theory of 'religious tolerance' followed by his forefather Akbar stood exploded.

Though the framework of the administration remained the same as under his forefathers and father, a seachange occurred in the manner and the spirit in which the institutions functioned. As in the time of Akbar, every province was headed by a Governor and had a Diwan, and other officers who were hired and fired by the Emperor. His provincial administration suffered a setback as he was out of Northern India for 25 years and was continuously at war in Deccan'. The local chiefs and zamindars disregarded law and order and the central authority was gradually facing erosion on account of unending wars and the policy of religious intolerance rigidly adhered to by the fanatic king.

He believed in the Islamic theory of taxes and remitted non-Islamic taxes and imposed the Pilgrims tax and Jaziya on Hindus, just to get compensated for the loss in the revenue caused by

[1] *Ibid p. 126*
[2] *Sri Ram Sharma : op. cit., p. 268*
[3] *Ashirbadilal Srivastava : op. cit., p. 326*

the abolition of illegal taxes and *abwalas*. The mode of collection and assessment of revenues as introduced by Akbar was abandoned and it was substituted by a 'farming system' which allowed the contractors in place of officials to realise the revenue from the cultivators. This led to deterioration of the lot of the subjects. The Mughal army, during his reign, increased considerably as he was indulging in wars throughout his life. The expenditure on the army during his reign was double to that of Shahjahan's rule. Discipline in the army was on the other hand comparatively on the wane and morale of the troops, was at the lowest ebb.

He restored Islam to its original position as the religion of the state and made a sustained effort to convert India into a Muslim country. He had faith in the Islamic theory of Kingship. As such, the Islamic theory of sovereignty in its unalloyed form became the guiding principle of the Emperor.

An analytical appraisal of the Mughal era reflects that the Mughal Emperors were equipped with onerous authority and possessed enormous powers. They headed the State as well as the Government. They held the office of the Commander-in-Chief of the Army and acted as the defender of Islam and the spiritual head of the Muslim community. Hence they levied *Zakat* on the latter and expended it on building mosques, subsidizing theologians and helping out Muslim paupers. They were invariably assisted by four to six ministers who could not initiate policy but render them advice which was not binding. Therefore, the Council of Ministers of the Mughal era cannot be considered analogous to the modern cabinet. The Mughal Emperor was a thorough autocrat. However, from Akbar to Shah Jahan, the Mughal Emperors can be categorised as benevolent despots. Aurangzeb was, however, a fanatic despot who was mainly responsible for the downfall of the Mughal Empire. The descendants of Aurangzeb could hardly make any contribution worth the name.

(D) THE BRITISH ADMINISTRATION

The unrivalled position of the Portuguese in monopolising trade with the East was an eyesore for some of the maritime powers, England, in particular. Hence some prominent London merchants held a meeting in Founders Hall with the Lord Mayor in the chair on September 22, 1599 and decided to petition the Queen to incorporate them into a Company for trading with the Indies. On December 31, 1599 they succeeded in procuring a Royal Charter. Thus, the East India Company under the name 'The Governor and Company of merchants trading into East Indies' came into existence. In the initial stages, the Company had a commercial purpose but later it became imperialistic. After the demise of Aurangzeb in 1707 the Mughal empire faced disintegration and the Central administration was totally eclipsed. It led to the rise of innumerable petty rulers fighting among themselves. The Company made the most of the golden opportunity and entered the political arena. Soon it managed to have a hold over several parts of the country. The Battle of Plassey in 1757 paved the way for the territorial aggrandisement of the Company. Mir Jafar who was installed Nawab of Bengal after this historic battle recognised the English sovereignty in Calcutta. He granted lands sufficient to enable the Company to maintain a military force. He accepted the residence of a servant of the Company at his Durbar. He even granted 24 Paraganas to the Company on his elevation as the Nawab.

The territorial acquisitions of the East India Company were on the increase thereafter. Eventually, it produced a startling effect in England. The Britishers in general, clamoured for an immediate parliamentary intervention. Expensive wars launched and ruthlessly fought to satisfy the lust of a few avaricious individuals, the colossal fortune amassed by the Company servants who posed themselves as petty oriental *Nawabs,* the shabby behaviour of the agents of the Company towards the Indian masses, induced the British Parliamentarians to put restraints on the powers of the company. No less than five Acts were passed regarding the Indian affairs. The Company was asked to deposit pounds 400,000 as a tribute to the country's exchequer for retaining the territorial acquisitions and revenue. Thus, within two years of the acquisition of Diwani, the British

Government commenced interference openly in the affairs of the Company and secured a share in the spoils.

The calculations of the British Government that the Company had amassed an inexhaustible mine of riches were not wholly true. It had a debt of more than six million pounds to pay off as it had undertaken to pay huge tributes and pensions to the Mughal Emperor and Nizam in India, and the British Government at home. Besides, it had to maintain huge military establishments. Its warring ventures also had exhausted its sources. A visit of famine in Bengal from 1769-72 dealt a severe blow to its already deteriorating economic position. Hence it was left with no alternative except asking the Government for a loan of one million pounds. This exposed the economic destitution of the Company and led the British Government to pass a series of Acts for effecting administrative and political improvements in the Company's rule over India. We discuss below some of the important acts which eventually resulted in the 'takeover' of Indian affairs by the British Queen Victoria in 1858. However, for the Indians, the transfer of power from the company to the British Monarch was hardly fruitful. In fact it was an exercise from the 'frying pan to fire'.

Regulating Act (1773)

It is an important landmark in the growth of the Indian administration under the British rulers. Before 1773, there was no central authority in the country. The East India Company's dominions in India were extending to Bombay, Bengal and Madras, each of these Presidencies was governed by the Governor-in-Council responsible to the Court of Directors in England. The hallmark of the organisation of Government during 1773-1861 was the gradual concentration of authority at the Centre. This was intended to ensure a close control over the Presidencies of Bombay and Madras in time of peace as well as during war.

The Act of 1773 aimed at the unification of India e.g.,

(*i*) It appointed a Governor General and four councillors for the Presidency of Fort William in Bengal.

(*ii*) The Governor General and his councillors were vested with the whole civil and military government of the said Presidency.

(*iii*) The Governor General and Council were empowered to superintend and control the government and management of the Presidencies of Bombay and Madras. They could not commence hostilities or conclude treaties with native powers without obtaining the previous sanction of the Governor General and the Council.

(*iv*) The subordinate Presidencies were required to obey the orders of the Supreme Government and the offending Governors-in-Council could be suspended by the Governor General-in-Council.

(*v*) The Governor General-in-Council were empowered to make rules and regulations, and issue ordinances for the good order and civil management of the Company's settlement at Fort William and other factories and places subordinate to it.

The Directors of the Company were required to submit to the Treasury the entire correspondence regarding the revenues and to place before one of the Secretaries of State those parts of it which dealt with the Civil and Military administration of the Company in India. Besides, all governments in India were to pay due obedience to the orders of the Directors and were to keep them informed of all matters concerning the interests of the Company.

The Act was subjected to severe criticism. In the words of Bouten Rouse *"The object of the Act was good but the system that it established was imperfect"*. G.N. Singh opines *"The main cause of imperfections was the novel nature of problem with which the Parliament had to deal"*[1]. The Act no doubt did a good thing by empowering the Governor General-in-Council to exercise control over two Presidencies but it made a mistake of making exceptions to the rule. On the plea

[1]*G.N. Singh : Landmarks in Indian Constitutional and National Development, p.18-19*

of 'emergency' they could flout the authority of Governor General-in-Council. Both Bombay and Madras Governments launched wars with Marathas and Hyder Ali respectively, without reference to the Governor General-in-Council.

Besides, the control of the Parliament over the Company affairs remained inadequate and ineffective. Though the copies of all civil and military despatches received from the Governor General-in-Council by the Directors were to be placed before the Ministry within a fortnight, yet it did not establish any effective machinery to scrutinize those reports and urge the Government for necessary action. Roberts has very well portrayed the flaws of the Act which had aimed at improvement in the Company's administration. In his words, "It had neither given the state a definite control over the Company nor the Directors a definite control over their servants, nor the 'Governor Generals' a definite control over Madras and Bombay."[1] Despite these defects, the Regulating Act was a great landmark as it was the first of its series subjecting to some extent the control of the Indian affairs in the hands of the Parliament. In the words of Lyall, "The Act gave a definite and recognizable form to the vague and arbitrary powers of sovereignty that had developed upon the Company."[2] It was by the Act of 1773 that for the first time, the British nation as a nation assumed the actual responsibility of the government of the territories won by the servants of the trading corporation. There was a gradual growth of feeling that the Britishers through their Parliament rather than through a trading concern should be responsible for British rule in India. Prof. Keith thus remarked '*The Act altered the constitution of the company at Home; changed the structure of the Company in India; subjected in some degree the whole of territories to some supreme control in India and provided in a very efficient manner for the supervision of the Company by the ministry.*"

The Act of 1781 and Pitts India Act 1784

The Amending Act 1781 removed some of defects of the Regulating Act. It strengthened the position of the Governor General-in-Council vis-a-vis the Supreme Court. It also recognised and legalised the legislative powers of the Governor General-in-Council over Bengal, Bihar and Orissa.

The next Act which is considered of some significance is the Pitts India Act 1784.

The Act introduced changes mainly in the Company's administration at Home. Some of its clauses effected modifications in the contribution of the Supreme Government and Presidencies in India.

(*a*) The Act established a Board of six Commissioners for the affairs of India, known as the Board of Control. It was vested with the power of appointing any of Company's servants. Further, it was empowered to superintend, direct and control all Acts, operations and concessions relating to civil and military government or revenue of the British territorial possessions in East India.

(*b*) The Court of Directors were to be bound by all orders of the Board touching the civil and military government and the revenues of India.

(*c*) The Act reduced the number of members from four to three in Governor-General's Executive Council.

(*d*) The appointment of the Governor General was made by the Directors with the approval of the Crown. However, such approval was not needed whenever the Governors and the members of the Executive Council were appointed.

(*e*) The Board of Control was empowered to send secret orders and directions regarding secret matters such as declaring of war, making of peace or negotiating with any of the native Princes or States in India, to the Secret Committee of the Court of Directors.

(*f*) The Governor General and the Council were empowered to superintend, direct and control the several presidencies and governments in matters concerning war or peace or application of

[1] *Robert: 'Cambridge History of India' Vol. V, p. 119.*
[2] *Lyall : British Dominion, p. 131*

revenues or fees during war or transactions with the country powers. Thus the control of the Governor General over other Presidencies was strengthened. It was no longer qualified by the provisions that the subordinate governments could in cases of urgent necessity act on their own and without obtaining leave from Bengal.

The constitutional importance of the Act lies in the fact that it formed the basis of the Indian Constitution till 1858.

In the words of Principal Sri Ram Sharma "The Pitt's India Act altered the foundations of the direction of Indian affairs in England. The Court of Proprietors lost its political power. The Directors now played second fiddle to the British Government who possessed almost unlimited powers of issuing orders which the Directors were bound to obey."[1]

The system of dual control made the Company's administration dilatory and cumbersome. In the words of Lord Palmerstone "The functions of government and the responsibility have been divided between the Board of Control, the Court of Directors, and the Governor General in India. The opinion of the Directors used to be given due weight by the Board as they were equipped with administrative experience concerning Company's affairs in India. Since the mass of business had to pass through their hands, they could wield considerable influence. In the words of Tucker, Chairman of the Court of Directors... "the administration of India is now vested in the national government. This is very much the case no doubt but.... we are still left in a position to exert some moral influence with effect." The Court of Directors made all appointments from petty clerk to the Governor General. The Board of Control had the power to Recall but it was very frequently resorted to. The dual system (Court of Directors Vs. Board of Control) enhanced influence but without entrusting responsibility. The Board of Control as an annexe to the Ministry enabled the British Government to exercise its influence on the Indian administration though it had not to bear any responsibility regarding the conduct of the company's affairs. Besides the Board of Control with the connivance of the Governor General followed a course, not likable by the Directors. The Directors also did not lag behind in intrigues and retaliatory measures. All this caused further deterioration in the Company's affairs.

Act of 1786

In 1786, another act was passed to amend the Act of 1783. It empowered the Governor General to override the Council and act on his own responsibility whenever he deemed fit. An Act passed in 1793 enhanced powers of the Governor General and the Governors by enabling them to override the majority of the Council concerned. It clearly stated that all orders etc. should be made by the Governor General (or the Governors as the case may be) in-Council. The procedure remained in force till the introduction of responsible Government in the country.

During the period 1800-1833, the secretariat was expanded to cope with the voluminous work. Several departments viz. the Persian Department, the Ecclesiastical Department, the Clothing Board and the Board of customs, salt and opium were established, abolished or merged with one another. In 1829 the name of the Board of Revenue at Calcutta was changed to the Sadar Board of Revenue and another such Board was created at Allahabad in 1833.

The Charter Act of 1833

The Act of 1833 was portrayed by Lord Morely as the, *"most important measure of the Indian Government between Mr. Pitt's Acts of 1784 and Queen Victoria's assumption of the powers of Government in 1858."* No doubt, the Act introduced some changes of far reaching importance both in the Company's Government in India and its administration at Home. Some of its important provisions are as follows:

(*i*) The Company was deprived of its commercial privileges and its monopoly of trade with

[1]*Sri Ram Sharma : A Constitutional History of India, p. 29*

China and for tea. It was asked to wind-up its business with all convenient speed.

(*ii*) The Governor General of Bengal was made the Governor General of India. The Act vested the superintendence, direction and control of the whole civil and military government in the Governor General-in-Council in India.

(*iii*) The Governor General's Council was enlarged for legislative work by the addition of a Law member. His duties were confined to the making of laws and regulations and he was not allowed to attend or vote at the meetings of the council except at meetings for making laws and regulations. Though the law member could not participate in the Executive business of the council, yet the Governor General-in-Council were advised to avail of the presence without his vote, as intimate knowledge of the business transacted in the council could be of use to him in the discharge of his legislative functions.

(*iv*) The power of making laws in India was concentrated in the hands of the Governor General-in-Council. Formerly, there were different bodies of the statute laws in force in India. The Hindu and Mohammedan laws, and usages were most obscure and uncertain due to a variety of texts and conflicting interpretations.

The Act clearly laid down that the jurisdiction of the Governor General-in-Council extended to all persons and all courts, all places and all things.

The Charter Act of 1833 is considered the most significant measure enacted by the British Parliament during the 19th century. In the words of Morley, it is, "*the most extensive measure of the Indian Government between Mr. Pitt's Act of 1784 and Queen Victoria's assumption of the powers of Government in 1858.*" Dr. Ishwari Prasad remarks, "The Charter Act of 1833 was also significant in so far as it made certain important provisions regarding the government of India and marked the beginning of Indian legislature." **The Act undoubtedly removed some of the glaring defects in the system of administration. It effected uniformity in general administration by concentrating the executive and financial administration in the hands of the Governor General.** It established the supremacy of the Crown and Parliament in the management of the Indian affairs by clipping the wings of the Directors. It introduced uniformity in the laws of the Government by establishing the legislative supremacy of the Central Government and undoing the diversities in the laws of different Presidencies.

Act of 1853

The Charter Act of 1853 is also a measure of constitutional importance as it did not renew the Company's charter for any definite period. It reflected that, Company's end was getting written on the wall and was fast approaching. The Act reduced the number of Directors from 24 to 18. Out of eighteen, six were to be appointed by the Crown. It dealt a severe blow to the Court of Directors. The Governor General's Council was re-constituted and the Commander-in-Chief was given an extra-ordinary membership in the Council. The Act also specified that six additional members were to be associated with the Executive Council only for legislative purposes. Among those six members, one was to be an official representative from each of the provinces while the Chief Justice and a judge of the Supreme Court were the other members. Thus now there were twelve members of the legislative council. All laws were subject to the consent of the Governor General. All legislative functions were vested in the Council. Obviously, the legislative and executive functions of the Governor General's Council were separated for the first time, and legislation was treated as a special function of Government.

The Directors were deprived of patronage. The covenanted civil service was thrown open to competition to all natural born subjects of Her Majesty under the rules to be framed by the Board of Control.

The Act authorised the appointment of a body of Commissioners to examine and consider the recommendations of the Indian Law Commission which had ceased to exist by that time. In fact, it was the outcome of their labour that the Indian Penal Code and Civil and Criminal Procedure

Codes were at last enacted into law.

Though the Act reduced the authority of the Directors considerably, yet the Dual system of Government still persisted. However, non-renewal of the Company's Charter for a specific number of years and reduction of the powers of the Directors was in fact quite revealing. At no distant future, the Company was to be asked to wind up. In fact, the Indian Mutiny accelerated the process.

Government of India Act 1858

The 1857 Revolt, generally termed as Mutiny by disgruntled and dispossessed Nawabs and Rajas against the Britishers by the British or pro-British historians but construed as the first battle of independence by the Indian patriots and historians, drove the last nail into the coffin of Company's rotten rule. "Inevitably, the blame for the 'debacle' fell on the Company and its rule was doomed".[1]

The 1858 Act, which was passed on August 2, 1858 transferred the Government of India from the Company to the Crown. India was henceforth to be governed by and in the name of Her Majesty. Some of the main provisions of the Act were :

(*i*) The Act abolished the Court of Directors and the Board of Control, and vested their powers with one of Her Majesty's principal secretaries of state – a minister of the British Cabinet.

(*ii*) The latter was empowered to superintend, direct and control all acts, operations and concerns, related to the Government and Indian revenues.

(*iii*) The Secretary of State was to be assisted by a Council of India consisting of 15 members, 8 of whom were to be appointed by the Crown and the remaining 7 were to be elected by the existing Court of Directors. The Act also laid down that more than half, at least nine members – must have served or resided in India for at least 10 years and must not have left India more than 10 years before their appointment.

(*iv*) The Secretary of State had a separate office known as the India Office which enabled him to discharge his functions smoothly. His salary and expenses of his establishment were paid out of the revenues of India.

(*v*) The Governor General and the Governors of the Presidencies were to be appointed by the Crown and the members of their Council by the Secretary of State in Council. Lieutenant Governors were to be appointed by the Governor General, subject to the approval of Her Majesty.

(*vi*) Appointments to the covenanted Civil Service were to be made through open competition, under rules to be made by the Secretary of State–in–Council with the assistance of the Civil Service Commissions.

(*vii*) It was also laid down that except for preventing or repelling actual invasion or under other urgent necessity, the Indian revenues should not be consumed to defray the expenses of military operations carried on beyond the external frontiers of India without the consent of both the Houses of Parliament.

(*viii*) The Act also laid down that whenever an order directing the commencement of hostilities was communicated to India, it must be presented to both the Houses of Parliament within three months of its issue, and if Parliament was not in session, within one month after the next meeting of the Parliament.

(*ix*) The treaties entered into by the Company were to be binding on the Crown. All contracts, covenants, liabilities and engagements entered into by the Company were to be binding on the Crown.

The significance of the Act lies in the fact that it dealt a *coup–de- race* to the system of double government at Home. The establishment of India Council in 1858 was another measure of great importance. Its predecessor - the Court of Directors - exhibited colossal ignorance about the

[1]*A.B. Keith : op. cit., p. 20*

Indian affairs as it had never been to India. The members of the Council on the other hand were fully aware of the petty details about the Indian affairs as they were supposed to be equipped with ten years residential or service qualifications in India before their appointment. The Council could, therefore, put a curtain upon the power of the Secretary of State. However, it was more a consultative body without any attribute of a modern Cabinet. They generally saw eye to eye with the Secretary of State in all matters. Hence, the Council proved to be an appendage having outgrown its utility.

The Act, though constitutionally speaking significant, did not grant any political right to the Indians. Nor did it allow them any share in the administration of their own country. Hence, the Royal proclamation announcing this transfer of power, couched in dignified language and breathing spirit of British magnanimity and justice, could not fulfil the aspirations of the Indians. They considered this change as a change from the frying pan to the fire. In the words of Dr. Prasad, "*The Act of 1858 was the culmination of the process begun by Pitt in 1784 and merely dressed the seat of power and responsibility with the outward semblance of authority*".[1] No attempt had been made to associate Indians with the Indian affairs. Loyalists, like Sir Syed Ahmed Khan emphasised that the recent 'outbreak' would have been avoided if the natives had been admitted in the Legislative Council. In his words, "It is highly conducive to the welfare and prosperity of Government......indeed it is essential to its stability.....that the people should have a voice in its Councils.....the voice of the people alone can check the error in the bud and warn us of dangers before they burst upon and destroy us........".[2] Besides, this defective system of lawmaking, the debatable role of the Indian Legislative council and the absence of change in the Indian administrative system, the unhappiness of the Provincial Governments over the meagre share they were assigned in the legislation, concerning their territories, led to the passage of Indian Councils Act, 1861.

During this phase, the hallmark of the Company's exploitative designs was to make the most of economic gains and territorial annexations with the sole motive of securing their trade and retaining its monopoly. Hence the officials of the Company did not effect fundamental changes in the sphere of administration. Only minimal administrative changes were made to control the revenue collection more effectively. Tara Chand, a renowned historian rightly remarks, "*......Imperialistic Britain treated dependent India as a satellite whose main function was to sweat and labour for the master to subserve its economy and to enhance the glory and prestige of the empire*".[3]

The Act of 1861

The main provisions of the Act affecting the administration were as follows :

(*i*) It enlarged the Executive Council of the Governor General by providing for an additional Law member. Thus the strength of the Council was raised to five.

(*ii*) Governor General was empowered to make rules and regulations for the transaction of business in the Council. It led to the rise of portfolio system.

(*iii*) The Secretary of State retained the power of appointing Commander-in-Chief as an extraordinary member of the Council. It led to the emergence of Portfolio system.

(*iv*) The Council of the Governor General was enlarged by the addition of not less than six nor more than twelve additional members provided that not less than one-half of the additional members so nominated shall be non-official members.

(*v*) The powers of the Legislative Council were extremely limited to legislation. Previous sanction of the Governor General was made essential for introducing in his Council any measure affecting the army, the foreign and political relations, the public debt, posts and telegraphs, religions and religious rites of any class of people in India.

---

[1] *Dr. Ishwari Prasad : History of Modern India, p. 230.*
[2] *As quoted by C.L. Anand in Government of India, p. 84.*
[3] *Tara Chand : History of the Freedom Movement in India, Vol. II, p. 474.*

(*vi*) Every Bill passed by the Governor General-in-Council required his assent to become an Act. Every Act passed by the Legislature in India was subject to disallowance by Her Majesty acting through the Secretary of the State-in-Council.

(*vii*) The Governor General was authorised to exercise a veto as well and, issue ordinances in emergency. He could alter or reverse any law passed by the Provincial Government.

(*viii*) The Act restored legislative powers to the Presidency Governments of Bombay and Madras. As such, their executive councils were expanded for the purpose.

(*ix*) The Provincial Legislative Councils were empowered to make laws and regulations, not affecting provisions of any act of parliament for the peace and good government of the Presidency. However, they were debarred from making laws on any of the following subjects : (*a*) measures affecting army; (*b*) the foreign and political relations; (*c*) the public debt; (*d*) coinage and currency; (*e*) the religion or religious rites and urges of any class of people (*f*) customs and other taxes.

(*x*) Every Bill passed by the Provincial Council required not only the assent of the Governor but also the Governor General and was subject to disallowance by Her Majesty the Queen acting through the Secretary of State.

(*xi*) In the expanded councils not less than 4 and not more than 8 members were added, out of whom not less than half were to be non-officials and invariably Indians. The Governor General was empowered to create similar bodies for North Western-Province and Punjab.

Thus the Act of 1861, a first milestone on the road leading to responsible government by the Indians, sought to make a beginning in the direction of seeking association of the Indian people with the work of legislation though under the strict control of the Governors in the Provinces and of the Governor General at the Centre. However, there is no denying the fact that this act tried to render the Executive Government too strong to be handicapped by an expansion of the legislature and restored the legislative powers of the local governments without affecting central control.[1]

The Indian Councils Acts 1892

The Indian Councils Act 1892 was the first result of the Indian National Congress which came into existence in 1885. It took up the question of reform of the legislature which had proved to be inadequate and disappointing to the people. The enlightened classes of the country clamoured for the expansion of the Councils and also enhancement of their functions. It was realized that the Legislative Councils could not have discussion on financial matters except when a proposal for new tax was taken up. The Government also did not have the opportunity to explain its policy or reply to hostile criticism or seek information or express their wants. The Indian National Congress in its first session passed a resolution'....the Congress considers the reform and expansion of the Supreme and existing Local Legislative Councils by the admission of a considerable proportion of elected members....essential and holds that all budgets should be referred to these Councils for consideration, their members being moreover empowered to interpellate the executive in regard to all branches of administration". In the next session, the Congress demanded the increase of members of the Legislative Councils and also election of at least half of them. They also suggested that the elected members of the Legislative Councils of the Governor General should be elected by the elected members of the Provincial Legislative Councils who should be elected by the members of the Municipal Councils, District Boards, Chambers of Commerce and Universities. The attitude of the Government was sympathetic in the initial stages though later on, it was the reverse. However, the Viceroy (Lord Dufferin) was convinced of desirability of further associating Indians with the government of the country. He was conscious of the fact that their presence at the Councils' meetings and according assent to the measures would popularise the Government. He remarked in 1886, ".....if they.....had a native party behind them, the Government

[1]B.B. Misra : *The Administration History of India (1834-1947), General Administration (1970 ed.), p. 32*

of India would cease to stand up as it does now as an isolated rock in the middle of a tempestuous sea, around whose base the breakers dash themselves simultaneously from all the four quarters of the heaven". The 1892 Act was the result of such feelings of a Viceroy embodied in the despatch sent to the Government in England. C.L. Anand remarks, "Lord Dufferins' despatch is an important constitutional document not only for the reforms ultimately embodied in the Act of 1892 but also for the fact that it laid down the principle of decentralisation, increasing association of Indians and maintenance in the English hands of the supreme control and authority which after years were repeatedly held to be the guiding principles of constitutional changes in India".

Main Provisions of the Act

(*i*) The number of additional members in the supreme council was increased to not less than ten and not more than sixteen and, in the case of Bombay and Madras councils to not less than eight and not more than twenty. The maximum additional members for Bengal and N.W. Provinces and Oudh to twenty and fifteen respectively.

(*ii*) It was also laid down that 2/5th of the members were to be non officials among the additional members.

(*iii*) The Governor General-in-Council was empowered with the approval of the Secretary of State-in-Council to make regulations for the nomination of additional numbers and prescribe the manner in which such regulations should be carried into effect.

(*iv*) The Governor General-in-Council was authorised to make rules, subject to the sanction of the Secretary of State-in-Council for the discussion of annual financial statements and the string of questions.

(*v*) The Governors-in-Council and the Lt. Governors were also empowered to frame similar rules with the sanction of the Governor General-in-Council.

(*vi*) The local legislatures were empowered with the previous sanction of the Governor General to repeal or amend the acts of the Central Government.

(*vii*) The Act authorised the Council to discuss the annual financial statements (though not to vote the budget item by item).

(*viii*) The members of the Council were empowered to ask the questions on matters of public interest. However, six days's notice for asking such questions was made obligatory. The President of the Council could disallow a question without assigning reason.

(*ix*) The Act cautiously introduced an elective element in the Councils. The word election was carefully avoided. It did not provide for direct election. However, the mode of indirect election produced result which turned the balance of power against the landed aristocracy and placed legal practitioners in a dominant position.

The achievements of the Act were of quite a great significance. The Act laid down the foundations of a representative government. The opinions of the Indians who were only one-third of the Council were accorded proper attention and listened to with deference. "The election principle though denied was indirectly introduced. Gladstone himself remarked, "......while the language of the Bill cannot be said to embody the elective principle it is intended to pave the way for the adoption of that principle". The Act enabled the non-officials to have free and full discussions on the financial policy of the Government. The Government also got an opportunity to remove misapprehensions and meet their criticism. Another significant advance lay in empowering the council to put interpellations on matters of public interest. Frazer has well summed up the gains of the Act in the words. "*It was an attempt at compromise between the official view of the Councils-pocket legislatures and the educated Indian view of them as embryo parliaments. While no efforts were made to enlarge the boundaries of the educated class to provide them with any training in responsible Government or to lay the foundations of a future electorate to control them, the Act deliberately attempted to deal with the effective idea*".[1] No doubt the Act did not mark the

[1]*Frazers : Indian under Curzon and after, p.4.*

beginning of Parliamentary Government in India yet it is decidedly an important milestone on the road leading to the establishment of Parliamentary Government at a later stage. The seed sown in 1892, at a much later date, sprouted and grew into a big tree despite the perpetual attempts of the white bureaucrats to sterilize and kill it.

The Indian Councils Act 1909

As already referred, the moderate leadership in the Congress was to a great extent instrumental in the enactment of the Indian Councils Act of 1892. However, no sooner than before, the Congress became an eye sore for the imperialists. Hence, they sought to sharpen the application of their theory of divide and rule to sow the seeds of dissensions between the two major communities — Hindus and Muslims. George Francis Hamilton's (Secretary of State for India) letter to Lord Curzon (Viceroy) on September 2, 1897 is revealing, "I think the real danger to our rule in India not now but say 50 years hence is the gradual adoption and extension of western ideas of agitation and organisation and if we could break the educated Hindu party into two sections holding widely different views, we should by such a division strengthen our position against the subtle and continuous attack which the spread of education must make upon our system of government".[1] Thus the shrewd British rulers befriended Sir Aga Khan and Lord Minto, the then Viceroy and made him the mouthpiece of the Muslims for sinister demand for separate electorates. Lord Morley — the liberal secretary of state, made Minto conscious of the nefarious scheme fraught with grave dangers to the Indians' unity and a retardation of the growth of national spirit. However, he did not assert. The emergence of the Muslim League on December 30, 1906 and its vehement support of the demand of the communal electorates resulted in the acceptance of the concept of 'separate electorates' in the Act of 1909. **Hence, Lord Minto has been called the 'father of communal electorates'.**

Main Provisions of the Act

(*a*) The Imperial and Provincial Legislative Councils were expanded. For the Imperial Legislative Council, the maximum number of additional members was raised from 16 to 60; the number of such members for the Councils of Bombay, Madras and Bengal, was raised from 20 to 50, for U.P. from 15 to 50 and for all others it was fixed at 30.

(*b*) Each Council was to consist of three types of members — nominated officials, nominated non officials, and elected members. The Secretary of State was particular to retain a substantial official majority in the Imperial Legislative Council which consisted of 37 officials and 32 non officials. Of the 37 officials, 28 were nominated by the Governor General, and the rest were ex-officio, *viz.*, 6 ordinary members of his council and 2 extra ordinary members, *i.e.*, the Commander-in-Chief and the Head of the Province where the Council happened to meet and also the Governor General. Of the 32 non officials, 5 were to be nominated by the Governor General and the rest were to be elected. In the case of 27 elected seats in the Imperial Legislative Council, 6 were allotted to the landholders, 5 to the non-Muhammadans and one to the Muhammadan landholders and one each to the Bengal and Bombay Chambers of Commerce. The remaining 13 were to be filled up by the non-official members of the nine Provincial Councils

(*c*) In the case of the Provincial Legislative Councils, the Secretary of State did not think it desirable to maintain even a bare official majority as he did not expect any danger in conceding a non official majority in the local councils. Evidently, the non officials could not have forged a united front because they did not represent a homogeneous electorate. For instance, Madras Legislative Council consisted of 26 non officials and 21 officials. Out of 21 officials, the Governor and three members of his council and the Advocate General were the *ex-officio*. The remaining 16 were nominees of the Governor. Of the 26 non officials 5 were nominated and 21 were elected. The Government thus clearly enjoyed a majority in the Council. Out of 21 elected members, 2

[1]*Tara Chand : The History of the Indian Freedom Movement, Vol. II, p. 56.*

each were elected by Muhammadans and Zamindars, 3 by the landholders other than the Zamindars, 1 each by the Corporation of Madras, University of Madras, the Madras Chamber of Commerce, the Madras Traders Association and the Planting Community and the rest of the 9 members by the Municipal Councils, District and Taluka Boards.

(*d*) The functions of the Legislative Councils were enlarged. The members were empowered to ask questions and supplementary questions and move resolutions on matters of general public interest. The resolutions could be moved and votes taken on the votable portions of the budget.

(*e*) Some changes took place in the composition of the Executive Council as well. The Secretary of State for India-in-Council were empowered to raise the membership of the Executive Councils of Bombay and Madras Presidencies from 2 to 4 of whom at least half must have worked for at least 12 years in the service of the Crown in India. The Governor General-in-Council were empowered to establish an Executive Council in Bengal of not more than 4 members with the approval of the Secretary of State for India.

(*f*) A declaration of intention to secure the appointment of an Indian to the Governor General's Council and those of the Governors was incorporated in the Act. Lord Sinha was appointed the first Law Member on the Governor General's Executive Council.

However, the reforms embodied in 1909 fell short of the expectations of the agitated Indians. The Reforms in the words of Dr. Zacharias had given to the people, 'the shadow rather than substance'. In fact, the reforms established a sort of "Constitutional autocracy". The intentions of the authors of the Act have been well portrayed in the Report on the Constitutional Reforms of 1918 in the words, "*They hoped to blend the principle of autocracy derived from Mughal Emperors and the Hindu Kings with the principle of constitutionalism derived from the British Crown and Parliament to create a Constitutional autocracy.......*"

The Act set natives against the natives. It sowed the seeds of dissensions between the two major communities on account of introduction of separate electorates. According to P. Woodruff "*the introduction of separate constituencies was a deep laid plot aimed at dividing the communities and providing an excuse for extending British rule for ever........it was a Machiavellian politics*".[1] Franchise was restricted and there was lack of direct contact between the members and their constituencies. Hence the legislatures, both at the Centre and the Provinces, could not claim themselves as the true representatives of the nation. Further, the Act created glaring inequalities between the voters of the different communities.

The existence of a strong official block in the Imperial Council reduced the importance of the elected members to a farce. In the Provincial Councils, a non official majority could not be of any practical use to the Indians. The nominated non officials always danced to the tune of the Government. Hence the elected non officials were reduced to a minority. The limited powers of the Councils also undermined their utility. Lord Morley's remarks elucidate these facts, "The provision of non-official majority in the Provincial Councils would not matter much, for the power of these Councils even were very limited and the Heads of the Government had the power to veto the measures". Thus the Provincial Councils were relegated to the position of mere registering bodies. They merely registered the decrees of the Executive.

The Act gave undue importance to the vested interests who were puppets in the hands of the British Government and were opposed to the national interests.

The Act exhibited over centralisation of administration. The control of the Centre over provincial Councils was not relaxed. The Central Government administered not less than 1/3 of the entire revenues of the state. Even in the domain of legislation and administration, the Central Government exercised excessive control over the Provinces. All the bills passed by the Provincial Government needed the assent of the Governor General. In

[1]*Phillip Woodruff : The Men Who Ruled India, p. 209.*

all initial matters of administration, the Indian Government issued instructions to the Provincial Governments. Hence *the councils were dubbed as 'cynical and calculated sham' and reforms introduced by the Act as mere 'moonshine'*.

Whatever the flaws, the Act in the words of Ramsay Macdonald, was *"a compromise between bureaucracy and democracy inevitably a shortlived necessary experiment"*. Lord Morley described these reforms as, "the opening of a very important chapter in this history of relations of Great Britain and India" and "the turning over of a fresh leaf in the history of British responsibility to India".

The Act of 1919

The Act of 1909 failed to satisfy the Indian's aspirations as it involved no transfer of power. Even a moderate Congressman like Gokhale who wanted to give these reforms a trial was utterly disillusioned. The policy of association of Indians with the Indian affairs still remained a mockery. Only two Indians were appointed to the Indian Council of the Secretary of State and one Indian each to the executive councils of the Governor General and the Governors. Even the British writers pointed out the inadequacy of these reforms, particularly when the English Government was involved in the Great War. In the words of Professor C.H. Philips, *"Lacking a clearly distinguishable and steadily British policy towards the growth of politics in India, Morley and Minto were driven to devising not so much a coherent plan as a series of expedients to meet the particular and admittedly difficult situations"*.[1]

Montagu Declaration

Thus came the famous Montagu Declaration of 1917 that pledged of progressive realization of self government in India. The Declarations are as follows : "The policy of His Majesty's Government with which the Government of India are in complete accord is that of increasing associations of Indians in every branch of the administration and the gradual development of self-governing institutions with a view to the progressive realization of responsible government in India as an integral part of the British Empire. They have decided that substantial steps in the direction should be taken as soon as possible.........."

Montford Report

Montagu visited India to appraise the situation personally. Consequently, a report, the result of collaboration and mutual consultation of the Secretary of State, Montagu and the Viceroy (Lord Chelmsford) was published in July, 1918. It stated, *"The provinces are the domain in which the earliest steps towards the progressive realisation of responsible government should be taken. Some measure of responsibility as soon as conditions permit......."*. This report became the base of the Government of India Act 1919 which furnished a slightly refined version of the policy of apparent association.

Main Provisions of Act of 1919

(*i*) The Government of India Act 1919 introduced the Bicameral system comprising of Council of State and the Legislative Assembly in the Central Legislature. The total strength of the Council of State was not more than 60 out of which 33 members were elected and 27 nominated. The Legislative Assembly consisted of 145 members out of which 104 were elected and the remaining were nominated. The Central legislature was empowered to consider, pass or reject legislation and the annual budget of the 'Government of India'. The authors of the Act retained autocracy at the Centre though they exhibited keenness to make it responsive to public opinion. Hence the

[1]*Philips : India, p. 107*

changes introduced in the Executive (Government) at the Centre were not significant.

(*ii*) The maximum limit imposed on the membership of the Governor General's Executive Council was removed.

(*iii*) A pleader of the Indian High Court was also made eligible for appointment as the Law member.

(*iv*) Of the six members of the Governor General's Council other than a Commander-in-Chief, three were required to be Indians. This was done to implement the policy of increasing the association of Indians to every branch of administration. However, Indian members were allocated portfolios of minor significance.

(*v*) The Executive Council was to be responsible to the Secretary of State (S.o.S.) and not to the Central Legislature. The Government was still responsible to the Parliament through the S.o.S.

(*vi*) The Governor General-in-Council was further vested with the power of certifying bills, restoring cuts and promulgating ordinances.

Theoretically the Executive authority was vested with the Governor General-in-Council, yet in reality the Governor General asserted his supremacy over the Council. This was not a part of the whole but constituted the whole. He enjoyed commanded position and exercised a dominating influence.

(*vii*) The Act demarcated the Central and Provincial subjects. The Central List had the most important subjects such as defence, foreign affairs, railways, customs and tariff, currency and coinage etc. The Provincial List included comparatively less significant subjects *viz.*, local self government, public health, public works, irrigation and agriculture, forests etc. The provincial subjects were again divided into two parts – 'reserved' and 'transferred'.

(*viii*) The reserved subjects being important, were placed under the charge of councillors who, along with the Governor, were made responsible to the Secretary of State and the central legislature. These subjects included finance, justice, revenue, irrigation, famine relief etc. The 'administration' of 'transferred' subjects *viz.*, local self government, medical administration, education, public health, agriculture, forests etc., was vested with the ministers responsible to the Provincial Legislative Council. This division of subjects into 'Transferred' and 'Reserved' at the Provincial level and entrusting them to the two different authorities was termed as Dyarchy.

This dyarchical arrangement was the first advance towards the progressive realization of responsible government in the provinces, without of course, handing over all provincial departments to popular ministers. "For it was feared that while their administrative experience was limited, their responsibility to legislatures might cause instability, even a complete breakdown".[1]

(*ix*) The Central and Provincial Legislatures were empowered to legislate on their respective list of subjects. A good deal of autonomy to the provinces was conceded in the administration of their related subjects. Under the Act, some heads of revenue, were also provided for the provinces. The provinces could borrow money and raise taxes. The devolution rules undoubtedly gave some independence to the provinces in their working spheres, yet the overpowering influence of the Government of India over the provinces was not minimized.

(*x*) The control of the Secretary of State for India over the Central and Provincial administration was reduced. The salary of the Secretary of State was henceforth, to be paid out of the British revenues.

(*xi*) The Constitution of the India Council underwent a great modification. It was not to consist of not less than 8 and not more than 12 members, half of whom at least must have served or resided in India for not less than ten years at the time of their appointment. The Secretary of State was given wide discretion to direct the manner in which the business of the Secretary of State-in-Council or the India Council was to be transacted.

[1]*B.B. Misra : op. cit., p. 71.*

An Appraisal

The Act of 1919 gave a rude shock to the Indians who were clamouring for "self-government" embodying the right of "self-determination". The Act was universally denounced. Mrs. Annie Beasent described the scheme as "ungenerous for England to offer and unworthy for India to accept". In fact, a few concessions extended to the Indians were hedged with so many restrictions and limitations that its purpose of introducing partial responsible government and associating Indians with the Indian affairs stood defeated. The following lacunae of the Act establish its futility.

(i) Dyarchy a dismal failure : Dyarchy which was supposed to be a bridge between the British Bureaucracy and the Indian people proved to be a bridge, weak and unstable. It was utterly a failure as the division of subjects was haphazard and illogical. In the words of K.V. Reddy, a Minister of Madras, "I was a minister for Development without the forests. I was the minister for Agriculture minus Irrigation......Efficacy and efficiency of a minister of Agriculture without having anything to do with irrigation, agricultural loans but improvement loans and famine relief is better imagined than described'. Moreover a Governor did not act as a Constitutional head. There was a lack of harmony between the services and the ministers. Besides, Finance Department was a Reserved department. As such, the Transferred Departments had to bank upon this 'Reserved Department' for execution of their programmes and projects. The principle of collective responsibility could also not be followed by the ministers as they constituted a house divided against itself. The Governors also exercised undue control over the services. Hence they danced to the tune of the Governors rather than followed the dictates of the ministry. Thus Dyarchy could not be worked in the way it had been intended by the authors. The ministers behaved as yesmen of the Government. They could not remain in power without the support of the official block. Thus the very purpose of Dyarchy stood defeated.

(ii) Central Executive lacked representative character :Central Executive was a yesmen body of the Governor General. It was hardly a representative body. Since these members were removable only by the Secretary of State, they did not feel any responsibility to the Central Legislature. Moreover, the Indian members preferred to be henchmen of the Governor General and assist him in gathering requisite information about the Indian affairs.

(iii) Limited authority of Central Legislature : The Central Legislature had very limited authority. It could neither control the executive, nor formulate legislation. It did not control the purse either. Nearly sixty per cent of the Budget was non votable. As regards the remaining forty per cent, the Governor General was empowered to restore any demand for grant refused or reduced by the Central Legislature. The Governor General could also authorise any expenditure in emergency of which he was the sole judge. Previous sanction of the Governor General was required to introduce certain bills. He could veto a bill passed by the Central Legislature and by his special power of certification pass any bill and sign it as a permanent law. The second chamber was created to checkmate the Assembly and constitute impregnable citadel of reaction.

(iv) Narrow Franchise and Assembly unrepresentative : The Franchise too was restricted. High Property qualifications and holding of titles etc., made the upper House custodian of the vested interests. The qualification of the Assembly members was also high. Weightage to the minorities was continued. The Assembly was thus undemocratic in character. Hence the introduction of partial responsible government at the Centre was an illusion as yet.

Whatever its flaws, the Act was a landmark in the constitutional development of India. It was a first milestone on the highway leading to self government at no distant future.

It marked the end of benevolent despotism and the dawn of a new era of responsible government. In the words of Coupland, "*.....Now Indians were to govern, so to speak on their* *own. They were to take charge of great departments of provincial administration not as official nominees but as the leaders of the elected majorities in their legislatures and responsible to them".*[1] The introduction of dyarchy effected a radical change in the conception of provincial government. The association of the Indians with legislation and administration developed in them a sense of responsibility which could at a later stage, prove immensely useful to them in running self-government. The pace of Indianisation in services also increased with the presence of Indian ministers as heads of various departments. The Indian ministers could effect much needed reforms and eradicate evils which the Britishers were reluctant to touch, fearing allegations of interference in the customs and belief's of the natives. In the words of Principal Sri Ram, "....Several creditable pieces of social legislation were undertaken which the foreign rulers of the country had avoided in their reluctance to interfere with established customs and beliefs The departments were renamed, reshaped and merged".[2] **In August 1921 Deptt. of Education was renamed as Deptt. of Education and Health. In 1923 PWD was merged with Deptt. of Industries. In April 1924, Board of Revenue was reconstructed and entrusted customs, excise etc., as well.**

The work of the central legislature was also in no way less commendable. It could exercise considerable influence on the executive and afford to be critical of the attitude of the Government.

Hence, it can be concluded that, despite many shortcomings, *the Act was an Act of great administrative and constitutional importance.*

The Government of India Act 1935

The Act of 1919 did not come up to the expectations of the Indian people. The dyarchical experiment which was made in the Indian provinces from 1921 to 1937 proved to be a dismal failure. Hence, to placate the Indian leaders, the Government sent its statutory commission (known as Simon Commission) in 1928 to India to submit its report on the implementation part of the new constitutional reform based on the Montford scheme. The commission was boycotted. Hence to appease the public opinion, Lord Irwin, the Viceroy, proclaimed that the goal of British policy was 'Dominion Status'. The Round Table Conferences of 1930, 1931 and 1932 held in London, could not resolve the tangle as the British leaders were not prepared to extend political concessions which would strike at the roots of the British empire. Besides, the cursed policy of 'counterpoise of natives against natives' became more effective at this stage that had its manifestations in the 14-point programme of Jinnah and in the representation of Indian India (Princes), in the Round Table Conferences. On the basis of conclusions in Round Table Conferences and a few modifications in it, a White Paper was issued by the British Government in March, 1933. A joint select committee appointed in April 1933, discussed the details in the White Paper and submitted its report on November 22, 1934 which was still more reactionary. The suggestions of the committee were thoroughly discussed and a bill was drafted and introduced in the House of Commons on February 5, 1935. It was passed by the House of Commons on June 4, 1935 and the House of Lords in July, 1935. The bill ultimately became the 1935 Act with the assent of the King on August 2, 1935.

Main Provisions of the Act

The Act effected important under mentioned changes in the administrative structure.

(i) Establishment of Federal Form of Government : It provided for the establishment of the Federal form of Government which was to consist of eleven Governors Provinces, six Chief Commissioners Provinces and of such Indian States as would agree to form the Federation. Obviously, it was obligatory for the British provinces to join the Federation, yet it was purely

[1]R. *Coupland: A Restatement p. 113*
[2]*Sri Ram Sharma: op. cit., pp 194-95*

voluntary action on the part of each state. The Federation was to consist of Federal Executive and Federal Legislature. The Federal Legislature was to be Bicameral. The Federation could not come into existence as the Princes opposed it tooth and nail, fearing a curb on their autonomy. The British Government felt the pulse of the Nation and postponed the introduction of Federation. The Government continued its working under the provisions of 1919 Act with modifications.

(ii) Indian Council replaced by Advisers : The structure of the Home Government also underwent a change. The India Council was dissolved. Its place was taken by a set of advisers to the Secretary of State for India whose number was fixed between three to six. The Secretary of State had the right to consult these advisers individually or collectively. Their advice was not, however, binding on him.

(iii) Introduction of Dyarchy at the Centre and Provincial Autonomy in Provinces : The Act provided for the introduction of Dyarchy at the Centre, though Dyarchy in the provinces was abolished and Provincial autonomy was introduced. The Governors were given special responsibilities to act in their individual judgement and assume all powers in the case of a breakdown of constitutional machinery. Thus it was easy for them to override the ministers.

Provincial autonomy as explained by the Authors of the Act meant establishment of responsible governments in the provinces and relaxation of central control over them. Both these proclaimed concessions were denied in actual reality. In the presence of communal electorates and special responsibilities of the Governors, the ministers could neither forge a united front nor effectively exercise their powers. The Governor General also on the plea of special responsibilities could interfere in the affairs of the provinces. Thus the autonomy in actual sense meant *autonomy of the Governors who were more autonomous than the ministers.* In the words of Rajendra Prasad (ex-President of India), "*It would be mere camouflage and a fraud to declare that such and such subjects had been transferred when the responsibilities with regard to them was reserved with the British. The wide powers vested in the Governor, Governor General and also in the Crown and the Parliament negatived the very essence of the Provincial autonomy - the great prize awarded to the Indians*".

(iv) Provision of Safeguards : The safeguards constituted the most controversial feature of the Act. Normally, the safeguards are a bulwark against undesirable tendencies which the constitutional pandits want to avoid. The safeguards provided in the Act were incompatible with the democratic norms and were deliberately provided to perpetuate British rule in India by vesting with the Governor General and Governors such drastic powers as could be arbitrarily used. The Governor General and Governors were vested with special responsibilities related to— (*a*) prevention of grave menace to the peace and security of India or a province; (*b*) the protection of legitimate interests of the minorities; (*c*) safeguarding of the rights of services; (*d*) protecting the rights of the Indian states and the dignity of the Indian rulers; (*e*) the prevention of discrimination against the British goods. On the ground of these special responsibilities, the Governor General or the Governors could interfere in the affairs of the ministers. In all these matters of special responsibilities, the Governor General and Governors possessed individual judgement which meant that they were required to consult the ministers but they might or might not act on their advice.

Besides, in the proposed Federation Defence, External Affairs, Ecclesiastical Affairs, and administration of Tribal Affairs were to be Reserved Departments. The Governor General had to deal with them in his own discretion. They were to be completely outside the purview of popular ministers. While acting in his own discretion or exercising individual judgement, the Governor General had to act according to the instructions of the Secretary of State. The Governors had to follow the instructions of both the Secretary of State and the Governor General.

These safeguards were meant to curb the national forces and appease the reactionary forces of India. They were, according to Rajendra Prasad, designed to protect the interest of "*birds of passage who came from thousand of miles, made hay while the sun shone and then disappeared in the evening of their days to enjoy the fruits in their native land again or to keep the Indian communities warring with one another".* Maulana Azad also commented, "*The Government of India Act, 1935" provided for provincial autonomy but there was a fly in the ointment.* Special powers were reserved to the Governors to declare a state of emergency and once a Governor did so, he could suspend the constitution and assume all powers to himself. Democracy in the provinces could therefore function only so long as the Governors permitted it. The position was even worse so far as the Central Government was concerned...."[1]

(v) *Establishment of a Federal Court.* The Act provided for the establishment of a Federal Court which came into existence on October 1, 1937. It consisted of a chief justice and six other judges who were to be appointed by the British monarch. The Federal Court was vested with both original and appellate jurisdiction. Besides, it was entrusted advisory jurisdiction as well. The Governor General could seek its advice on any point of law though the Act was not clear as to whether or not this advice was to be binding on the Governor General. The Federal Court was to be a Court of Record as well. Its proceedings and judgements were to be officially recorded and cited as an authority before subordinate courts.

Federal Court not a Supreme Court : The Federal Court was not a Supreme Court as is necessitated in a federal structure. Its decisions were not to be final. Appeals from its decisions could be carried to the judicial committee of Privy Council without its permission, in certain cases *viz.*, (*a*) cases involving an interpretation of the constitution or any order-in-council; (*b*) those involving an interpretation of an agreement made for the administration of federal laws within the territories of a state; (*c*) those relating to the extent of legislative and executive authority vested in the Federation by virtue of an Instrument of Accession executed by a state. Apart from the above cases, appeals could be carried to the Privy Council with the permission of the Federal Court or His Majesty-in-Council.

Though the federation did not come into existence, the Federal Court performed those functions which an impartial judicial tribunal is expected to perform in a federal polity. It decided the disputes between Centre and the Provinces and did not allow them from crossing their legal boundaries. The Court acted as a palladium of people's civil liberties. For instance during World War II, thousands of Indians were detained under Section 26 of the Defence of India Rules where a regular case was instituted against the said section of the Defence rule, Chief Justice Gwyer declared the section *ultra vires*. The inaugural address of its Chief Justice reflects the functions it was expected to perform. He remarked. *"The Federal Court will become like similar courts in other countries at once, the crucible in which the flux of current political thought is tested and refined, and the anvil on which the more stable and permanent elements of it are hammered into shape to take their place in that armoury of ideas with which each generation seeks to solve its own problems*....It would be its endeavour to look at the Constitution not with the cold eyes of an anatomist but as a living and 'breathing organism which contains within itself as all life must, the seeds of future growth and development......".

(vi) *Office of High Commissioner retained :* The office of High Commissioner for India in the U.K., which was created under section 29 of the 1919 Act, for the performance of commercial and agency function which were formerly discharged by the Secretary of State for India. The Act of 1935 retained this office and did not suggest any substantial change in the position, status or functions of the High Commissioner. However, he was now to be appointed by the Governor General and not Governor General-in-Council if, of course, a Federation came into existence. Since the Federation did not materialise, his appointment did not undergo a change.

(vii) *Separate Electorates further extended :* Separate electorates were not only retained but were further extended to Anglo-Indians, Indian Christians and Europeans as well. They were keen to extend it to Harijans as well but Mahatma Gandhi's fast unto death prevented them from doing so.

(viii) *Franchise qualifications relaxed :* The Act lowered the property and literacy qualifications for franchise with the result that 35 million people were entitled to vote.

[1]*Azad A.K. : India Wins Freedom, p. 12*

(ix) Burma and Aden accorded new status : The Act separated Burma from India. Aden was also transferred from the administrative control of the Indian Government to the colonial office. Thus Burma appeared on the map of India as a separate country and Aden became a Crown Colony. Burma was henceforth to be deemed a part of the Governor's province known as "Central Province and Berar".

(x) Federal machinery as contemplated : Though the Federation remained a mirage, yet federal machinery contemplated in the Act may be briefly referred. The Federal Executive was to consist of (*a*) Governor General and Crown's Representative; (*b*) the Councillors; (*c*) Ministers. The Governor- General was to be a cornerstone of the Federal edifice. He was vested with a lot of discretionary authority in executive, legislative, and financial matters. Besides he was allowed to exercise individual judgement on 'special responsibilities' of the Governor General. He could seek advice of the ministers on these matters enumerated as 'special responsibilities' though that advice was not binding on him.

The Federal legislature was to be a Bicameral legislature composed of a Council of State comprising not more than 260 members, 156 from British Provinces and 104 from the Indian states, and a Federal Assembly consisting of 375 members of which 250 were to be allotted to the British Provinces and 125 to the Indian states. The representatives of the British provinces in the Assembly were to be indirectly elected by the respective provincial legislatures by the system of 'proportional representation'. The indirect election of the lower House was unprecedented and was said to be an experiment in election, eventually it was to be made direct. The representatives of the Indian states were to be nominated by the respective rulers. Surprisingly 150 representatives of provinces in the Council of State were to be directly elected and 6 were to be nominated by the Governor General.

The Federal legislature was equipped with legislative and financial powers. It was to control the executive as well. It was not vested with the power of amending the constitution or amending or repealing Acts of British parliament applicable to India. The legislative and financial powers were also hedged with many restrictions. The Governor General was vested with Veto power and also authority to reserve the bills for the consideration of His Majesty, the King. He could have issued ordinances and pass Governor General's Acts. Likewise over 80% of the Budget was to be non votable. Regarding the rest of 20% of the expenditure which was votable, the Governor General was empowered to restore a grant refused or reduced by the Assembly on the plea of special responsibility. No proposal of taxation or borrowing could come before the House except on the Governor General's recommendation. Thus initiation and the last word in the matters concerning finance was also to rest with the Governor General. Palande remarked, *"The absence of financial power imparted an air of unreality to the responsible government and tended to reduce it to a mockery"*.[1]

Reaction of Leaders to the Act and its evaluation : The Act of 1935 entailed scathing criticism at the hands of all political parties of India. M.A. Jinnah, condemned it as, "thoroughly rotten, fundamentally bad and totally unacceptable". Jawaharlal Nehru denounced it as a machine with strong brakes and no engine". Pt. Madan Mohan Malviya condemned it as "democratic from without". Rajagopalachari called the new Constitution as "Worse than Dyarchy". Churchill on the other hand called it "an undue exaltation of the principle of self government".[2] Churchill's fear was unjustified as the autonomy offered to the provinces was more of autonomy of the Governors rather than the ministers. The Ministries were established in 1937 in the provinces, though the Congress run ministries tendered resignation in 1939, and non Congress ministries being puppets of the British Government persisted till the attainment of independence. However, a critical appraisal of the working of provincial autonomy in the Congress and non Congress

[1]*M.R. Palande : Introduction to the Indian Constitution, p. 84*

[2]*Parliamentary Debates, House of Commons, Vol. 297 (1935), Cols. 1650-55*

ministries reveals that in the former it worked satisfactorily whereas in the latter, it was more of a mockery. The 'special responsibilities' and the vast discretionary powers vested with the Governors were on full play in non-Congress provinces. The Instrument of Instructions was flagrantly flouted by the Governor. They frequently intervened and vetoed the measures passed by the Provincial legislatures. On the other hand, solidarity in the Congress ranks and marked ability of the Congress High Command deterred them from playing similar mischiefs in the Congress dominated provinces.

However, after resignation of the Congress ministries in 1939, autocratic rule of the Governors was installed in. Thus the dream of self government once again became an illusion. Secondly, autonomy would have meant relaxation of central control over the provinces. The appointment of the Governors by the King rather than Governor General was thought to be a substantial step in this direction. It was expected that the Governor General would not interfere in the provincial affairs. But, in actual fact, the central control over the provinces was in no way relaxed. The special responsibilities (of the Governor General) could enable him to man the affairs in the provinces as he deemed fit. The directives of the Governor General to the Governors of U.P. and Orissa over the release of political prisoners bear ample testimony to this fact.

Even in the provincial legislation, the Governor General could be assertive, as certain bills needed his prior permission before introduction and certain bills after passage required his final assent. He could reserve the bills for the consideration of His Majesty or return them for the reconsideration of the provincial legislatures. The Act had clearly specified that while withholding his assent to the bills, issuing ordinances in his discretion, enacting Governor's Acts restoring grants and exercising special responsibilities, a Governor was to act under the direction and control of the Governor General.

Such sweeping powers of the Governor General could easily place the whole of the financial, administrative and legislative machinery of the province at his disposal. Principal Sri Ram Sharma rightly remarked, "*Provincial autonomy had already been throttled by its authorities before its corpse was presented to the eleven provinces on April 1, 1937* ". Thus, it can be concluded that there existed a world of difference between the real significance of the word 'autonomy' and the so-called autonomy bestowed upon the Indians by the benign masters. However, it was certainly another milestone on the highway leading to the goal of complete independence in 1947.

Since the Federal mechanism of Government could not be established, the Government of India continued functioning under the provisions of the Act of 1919 with minor modifications till the passage of the Independence Act 1947.

World War and After

During the War, the British Government made many attempts to end the stalemate. In August 1940, Viceroy Lord Linlithgow offered to enlarge the size of the Executive Council so as to include in it more Indians and also suggested that the Constitution would be devised in consultation with all shades of opinions after the War. *The August 1940 offer* failed. It was followed by *Cripps Mission in 1942.* It emphasised that after war India would have Dominion status and a new Constitution would be framed by the Constituent Assembly subject to its ratification by the British Parliament. A treaty between the British Government and Indian Constituent Assembly would be signed to provide for the complete transfer of power. The Government undertook to accept the Constitution subject to the conditions - (*a*) the right of any province to retain its present constitutional position, provision being made for its subsequent accession if it so decides; (*b*) the signing of a Treaty which shall be negotiated between Government and the Constitution making body to cover up all matters arising out of transfer of the responsibilities to the Indians and to protect the rights of social and religious minorities. It was an attempt at separation.

Nehru commented, "*any proposal to cut up India into parts was a painful one to contemplate....to think of partitioning India at this stage went against the whole current of modern historical and economic development. It seemed to be fantastic in the extreme*".[1] *Gandhi described these proposals as a 'postdated cheque'*.

Next came the ***Wavell plan of 1945***. A conference of the Indian leaders with the Viceroy was held at Simla to consider this Plan but nothing could materialize on account of vast differences between the Congress and the League leaders.

The Cabinet Mission Plan of 1946 is the next important attempt to solve the *impasse*. It rejected the demand for the country's partition as raised by the Muslim League. It suggested a three tier system - a Union Centre; an intermediary authority representative of the Groups of contiguous provinces and the Indian provinces. It also chalked out a scheme for the formation of the Constituent Assembly consisting of the representatives of the provinces and of the native states. It also suggested the formation of an Interim Government consisting of the leaders of the major political parties.

The Cabinet Mission plan had a controversial but on the whole a sympathetic reception in India and after the due deliberations, clarifications and negotiations, was accepted by the Congress and the Muslim League. Both these major parties agreed at the long term proposals. But they failed to agree at short-term proposals. The views of the top Congress leaders bear an ample testimony to the fact that the Plan was not a denial of reality. Gandhiji remarked, "It is the best document the British Government could have produced in the circumstances". In the words of Maulana Azad, "*The acceptance of the Cabinet Mission Plan by both the Congress and Muslim League was a glorious event in the history of the freedom movement in India. It meant that the difficult question of Indian freedom had been settled by negotiation and agreement, and not by methods of violence and conflict*".[2]

After prolonged discussions, the Congress joined the Interim Government in September, and the Muslim League followed it, about a month or so after. However, the Government could not run smoothly due to the obstructive role of the Muslim League members who had entered the Government to wreck it rather than work it. The British Government decided to convert the policy of 'Divide and Rule' to 'Divide and Quit'. Hence, on February 20, 1947 Prime Minister Attlee made a historic declaration that the British would leave the country by June, 1948. In his words (before Parliament), "*....The present state of uncertainty is fraught with a danger and cannot be indefinitely prolonged. His Majesty's Government wish to make it clear that it is their definite intention to take the necessary steps to effect the transfer of power into responsible Indian hands by a date not later than June,1948* ".

Mountbatten Plan

The gordian knot was cut when the Congress leaders accepted *Lord Mountbatten's Plan of June* 3, 1947 which suggested the partition of the country. Lord Mountbatten remarked, "The whole plan may not be perfect but like all plans its success will depend on the spirit of goodwill with which it is carried out. I have always felt that once it was decided in what way to transfer power, the transfer should take place at the earliest possible moment but the dilemma was that if we waited until a constitutional set up for All-India was agreed, we should have to wait a long time particularly if partition was decided on. Whereas, if we handed over power before the Constituent Assembly had finished their work, we should leave the country without a Constitution. The solution to this dilemma is that His Majesty's Government should transfer power over to one or two Governments of British India, each having Dominion status as soon as the necessary arrangements

[1]*Jawaharlal Nehru: Discovery of India, p.465*

[2]*Azad : op. cit., p. 151*

can be made.......". The Plan was accepted both by the Congress and Muslim League. Lord Mountbatten proceeded to implement it without any delay.

Act of 1947

On July 4, 1947 the Independence Bill was introduced in the House of Commons and was passed by both the Houses of Parliament within two weeks. The Act provided for the end of the British rule in India on August 15, 1947 and the establishment of the Dominions of India and Pakistan, which were allowed to secede from the British Commonwealth. In the words of Prime Minister Attlee, *"The Act did not lay down a new Constitution for India providing for every detail. It was far more in the nature of an enabling bill, a bill to enable the representatives of India and Pakistan to draft their own Constitutions"*.

Main Provisions of the Act

(*i*) It provided for the establishment of two Dominions - India and Pakistan on August 15, 1947.

(*ii*) The territories of the Dominions were demarcated. The division of the Punjab and Bengal was to be effected according to the Boundary Commission award.

(*iii*) The Act abolished the office of the Secretary of State for India and his Advisers and provided a Governor General for each Dominion. However, one Governor General may serve in a dual capacity.

(*iv*) Each Dominion was to have a sovereign legislature which was to be vested with full powers of making laws for the dominion concerned. The Constituent Assemblies of the two Dominions were to serve as their representative legislatures.

(*v*) The Governors of the provinces were to be nominated by the Dominion Cabinets. They were to follow the advice given by their ministers under all circumstances.

(*vi*) The appointments to civil services and reservation of posts by the Secretary of State were to be discontinued. The Act made a provision for the maintenance of the then existing conditions of service as well as pensionary rights as regards those services which had to continue service under the Government of either of the new Dominion or of any province.

(*vii*) The paramountcy of the British Crown over the Indian native States lapsed, and also its connection with the Tribal Areas ended on August 15, 1947. Thus, the States were declared free to accede to India or Pakistan or remain independent. All treaties and agreements between the British Crown and the States and all the obligations of His Majesty's Government towards the rulers of states ended with the lapse of paramountcy.

(*viii*) It was also provided that the relations of the British Government with the new Dominions were to be conducted through the Commonwealth Relations Office.

(*ix*) The title of "Emperor of India" was dropped from the royal style and titles of the King of England.

An Appraisal

The Indian Independence Act was the swansong of the British rule over India. It opened a new era. It was indeed the noblest and the greatest law ever enacted by the British Parliament. It was described to be a gracious and dignified farewell. Lord Samuel described it "*an event unique in history - a treaty of peace without war*". Jawaharlal remarked before the Constituent Assembly on August 15, 1947, **"Long years ago, we made a tryst with destiny and now the time comes when we shall redeem our pledge not wholly or in full measure but very substantially. At the stroke of midnight hour when the world sleeps, India will awake to life and freedom".**

The Act however left one blot on the British escutcheon for all times to come. It left a sad trail of memory behind - a vivisected India and its aftermath. In fact, the partition of India not only frustrated the long cherished dream of a united India but left an indelible imprint of bloodbath and perpetual animosity on both sides of the frontiers of India and Pakistan.

Besides, the independence of the Rulers of States (Indian India) was a calculated and a nefarious move which could have posed a great problem for the Indians. If these states had not acceded to India and decided to remain independent, India would have been turned into a hydraheaded monstrosity. It would have remained a divided House and its hardwon independence would have been jeopardized by any clever and unscrupulous invader as in the past. In fact, it was a vicious parting kick to a country which had groaned under the heels of the British Imperialists for over three centuries. The Mountbatten Plan (June 1947) marked the triumph of the British colonial policy of Divide and Rule now converted into the policy of Divide and Quit. Many diehard conservative politicians like Churchill fondled a hope that Indian Independence would soon appear to be a mirage and the Britishers would once again be requested to rule over India torn with strife and animosities, and ravaged with civil war and anarchy. However, it proved to be a wishful thinking.

The Independence Act resulted in the establishment of two Dominions - India and Pakistan. In its resolution of December 13, 1946 the Constituent Assembly proclaimed its firm resolve to soon convert the Indian Dominion into an Independent Sovereign Republic and framed a new Constitution which was enforced on January 26, 1950. It is, however, crystal clear that all these measures of constitutional reforms were designed by the Imperialists to safeguard the interests of the British empire. The policy of 'association of Indians with Indian affairs' and 'progressive realization' of self governing institutions was a big hoax justifying a great deal the political axiom, *"Imperialism and popular government have nothing in common. They differ in spirit, in policy, in method"*.[1]

Some Conviction

The British administrative system in India had some set convictions and beliefs *viz.*, (*a*) The British Government believed in the oriental display of pomp and show it had inherited as a legacy of the Grand Mughal Empire. It revelled in this splendour till its end. (*b*) It set its face firmly against interference in the religious and social customs and traditions of Indians. (*c*) Contrary to the proclamation of Queen Victoria, before the passage of the 1858 Act the superior public services of the country were treated as a preserve of the Englishman. "Then the British rule was considered to be compatible only with the British holding key positions in administration".[2] (*d*) The executive work necessitated co-operation of the Police and at times of the Army, which may not be possible if senior executive position is held by an Indian. (*e*) **The Britishers attached the highest value to the officer's experience of District Administration. However, British bureaucracy in India remained subdued to the Parliament and the Political Executive.**

Internal Administration (1858 - 1947)

Before we come to the close of this chapter, it is essential to portray the all powerful bureaucracy during the British era. After the winding up of the company the administrative machinery was reorganised in consonance with the administrative principles and political ideals of the British. In fact, the Indian administration became more efficient and fairly up to date, due to the unitary control of the British Parliament. The Indian officials were responsible only to the Secretary of the State. As such, they had not to satisfy any other authority. It was rather difficult

---

[1]*Hobson : Imperialism, p. 150*

[2]*S.R. Maheshwari : op. cit., pp. 6-10*

for the Secretary of the State to control the administration from a far distance. Hence he always stood by the actions of the officials. It led to the rise of an omnipotent bureaucracy of India which was headed by the superior Indian civil service. Blunt is of the view that these services became *"the practical owners of India, irremovable, irresponsible and amenable to no authority but that of their fellow members"*. The ability and integrity of the civil services was an acknowledged fact but they suffered from superiority complexes. As such, a big void between the representatives of the rulers and the ruled was yawning too wide to be abridged. The sympathy and mutual understanding which constitute the bedrock of good administration were conspicuous by their absence.

The isolationist policy of the British Civil services was due to the horrible happenings during the Mutiny (1857), otherwise during the earlier period they were comparatively more friendly to the Indians. Besides the discovery of steam navigation, the construction of the Suez canal and the appearance of telegraph and overland route brought them in closer touch with their home country. More and more Britishers got settled in the towns. Hence there was hardly the necessity of social contacts with the Indians. Office and club life kept them busy in their narrow shells. According to Dr. Majumdar, *"he remained to all intents and purposes a foreigner and knew little of their feelings, sentiments and aspirations"*.[1] Blunt also observed, "the Anglo Indian official of the Company days loved India in a way, no Queen's official dreams of doing now, and loving it, he served it better".

The Indians were, by and large, of the view that the state of affairs could improve only if Indians were inducted in the services. The Act of 1793 had laid down that none but covenanted servants of the company could hold any office with a salary of more than (pound) 800 a year. Evidently the Indians could fill any high post if they were regular officials who had entered into covenant with the East India Company and after 1858 with the Secretary of State. Thus the Charter Act of 1833 legalising the appointment of Indians to the highest offices of the state was a mockery.

The system of open competition which was introduced in 1853 was re-affirmed in 1858. The competition was thrown open to all natural born subjects of Her Majesty whether Indians or Europeans. The maximum age limit was kept at 23 years to be reduced to 22 years in 1859. In 1866 the maximum age was further reduced to 21 years. Finally the selected candidates were to be kept on probation in England for one year but now this period was enhanced to two years. It was very cumbersome for the Indians to pass this examination particularly when the medium of examination was English. Besides, journeying to England was expensive. The British Government eventually realised the inadequacy of the Indian element in the superior civil service. In 1870, the appointment of Indians to the higher offices without examination was authorised by an act but it was actually implemented in 1879. In 1879, the rules adopted ordained "that a proportion not exceeding one-sixth of the total number of covenanted Civil servants appointed in any year by the Secretary of State should be natives selected in India by the local governments subject to the approval of the Governor General-in-Council". These officers termed "Statutory Civil servants" were recruited from "youngmen of good family and social position possessed of fair abilities and education". Indians, however, preferred open competitive examination and denounced the system of nomination. In order to enable Indians equitable chances, they recommended holding of examinations simultaneously in India and England. In 1877, a deliberate attempt was made to keep out Indians by further lowering the age of Civil services to 19. It led to agitation by the Congress and a demand for simultaneous examinations and employment of more Indians.

In 1866, a Public Service Commission appointed by Lord Dufferin to investigate the problem, rejected the demand of simultaneous examinations for covenanted service and advised the abolition of the Statutory Civil Service. Instead, it was proposed by them that posts hitherto reserved for covenanted service should be thrown open to a local service and be called "Provincial

[1]*Dr. R.C. Majumdar : op. cit. p. 848.*

Civil Service'. The latter was to be separately recruited in every province either by promotion from lower ranks or by direct recruitment. The terms covenanted and uncovenanted were substituted by Imperial and Provincial and below the latter a subordinate Civil Service too was created. These recommendations were accepted. The covenanted Civil Service was hitherto to be known "Civil Service of India" and the Provincial Service was to be named after the particular province. A list was prepared of posts reserved for the Civil Service of India, but open to the new Provincial Service and the Local Governments were authorised to appoint an Indian to any such 'listed post'. In other branches of administration, *viz.*, Education, Police, Public Works and Medical Departments, there were similar Divisions into imperial, 'provincial' and subordinate services. The first was exclusively meant for the Englishmen and the latter two for the Indians.

The above system remained in vogue till the end of the British rule. It effected an improvement but the Indians were still unhappy as they aspired for the higher services as well. In 1893, the House of Commons again passed a resolution, favouring simultaneous examinations in England and India for the I.C.S. The resolution was conveyed to the Government of India for opinion. Lord Lansdown's Government consulted the Provincial Governments, exhibited opposition to the principle contained in the Resolution. Hence, the proposal was set at naught.

During the initial years of the 20th century, Indians agitated for a greater share in the Public services. A Royal commission on Public services was appointed in September, 1912 under the chairmanship of Lord Islington. G.K. Gokhale, a moderate Congressman, was one of its members. The Report of this Committee was deferred till 1917 on account of the Great War. Its recommendations were :

(*i*) the recruitment of Indians to the I.C.S. through the London Examination;

(*ii*) 25 per cent of the posts in the superior civil service to be filled from among Indians, partly by direct recruitment and partly by promotion from the lower services;

(*iii*) holding of an examination in India for the recruitment of civilians. Thus the Indian's demand was conceded in a changed form.

Thereafter the Montagu - Chelmford Report adopted a still more sympathetic and liberal attitude than the Islington Commission on the question of Indianisation of the I.C.S. Their recommendations were :

(*i*) 33 per cent of superior posts to be recruited in India and this percentage to go up by 1.5 per cent annually; (*ii*) all social distinctions in the matter of appointments were to be abolished;

(*iii*) In all public services for which there is recruitment in England open to Europeans and Indians alike, there must be a system of appointment in India. For four years, the principles laid down in the Report were followed but the members of superior service felt perturbed over growing Indianisation of the services. The Secretary of State-in-Council introduced a scheme under which all Indian officers, selected for appointment before January 1, 1920 and not permanently employed under the Government of India, were permitted retirement before the completion of tenure on a pension proportionate to their length of service.

Lee Commission's (1923-24) Report

In order to remove other irritants, a Royal Commission was set up with Lord Lee as its Chairman in June, 1923. The Lee Commission submitted its report in 1924. Its main recommendations, most of which were accepted by the Government were as under :

(*i*) The All India Officers of the I.C.S., the Indian Police Service, Indian Forest Service and the Irrigation branch of the service of Engineers may continue to be appointed and controlled by the Secretary of State-in-Council while services in the 'Transferred' departments be controlled by the Provincial Governments except the Indian Medical Service, for which each province was to appoint in its Civil Medical department a certain number of officers lent by the Medical department of the Army in India.

(*ii*) Twenty per cent of the officers to be recruited by promotion from Provincial Civil Service and of the remaining eight per cent, half should be British and half Indians; (*iii*) Immediate establishment of a Public Service Commission which was to be composed of five wholetime members.

The Act of 1935 defined the rights and status of the civil and military officers in the provinces and the proposed Federation guaranteed their existing privileges regarding pay, promotion, leave and pension. It provided for the establishment of a Federal Public Service Commission and Provincial Public Service Commissions. Two or more Provinces might agree that one Commission shall serve a group or that all the Provinces shall use one Commission. The functions of the Commissions were to be purely of an advisory nature. They had to make recommendations to the ministers which might or might not, at least in some cases, be accepted.

New Constitutional Frame Work

Thus, it is clear that the foundations of bureaucratic machinery which had to play a vital role in the running of the administration of Independent India had been firmly laid, prior to the attainment of Independence. The three-fold classification of the civil services as existed during the British rule was perpetuated under the new constitutional framework. Thus, we were to have three classes of Public services – All India services, Central services and the State services. The All India services are common to the Union and State Governments and they consist of the officers who are not exclusively for either of the Governments. The Central services deal with the administration of the Union subjects. They work under Union government. The State Services administer State subjects.

Article 312 of the Indian Constitution empowers the Rajya sabha to pass a special resolution by special majority that it is necessary and expedient in the national interest to create some new central services. It enables the Parliament to make law for such a purpose. The Indian Forest service, the Indian Engineering Service and Indian Economic Service were added through such an arrangement. In very recent past the Central Government has been contemplating of contributing of all India Judicial Services as well. Moreover fundamental changes have been made regarding recruitment and working conditions of the civil services functioning at the Central or State level. Through Sixth Pay Commission radical changes in the pay scales and working conditions of the employees have been made. It has led to the boosting of the morale of the employees and improve their performance. However corruption among the services has become almost cancerous. It is strange that lucrative incentives and handsome salaries have not been able to make them feel contented and play the role of public servants in the real sense

***

CONSTITUTIONAL FRAMEWORK

> *"This cannot be done by the wisest of lawyers sitting together in conclave; it cannot be done by small committees trying to balance interests and calling that constitution making; it can never be done under the shadow of an external authority. It can only be done effectively when the political and psychological conditions are present and the urge and sanctions come from the masses."*
>
> **— *Jawaharlal Nehru***

CONTENTS : (A) Framework of Indian Constitution

(B) Indian Federation

(C) Parliamentary Democracy

(D) Planning

(E) Socialism

(F) Human Rights

(A) FRAMEWORK OF INDIAN CONSTITUTION

As said in the preceding chapter, India was freed from the foreigners' yoke on August 15, 1947 and embarked upon a new era – era of hopes and aspirations , peace and prosperity, planning with plenty, unity in diversity. Hence a new framework of the Constitution, embodying the ideals and long cherished aspirations of the teeming millions was envisaged. In the words of Jawaharlal Nehru the stupendous task of the architects of freedom was "to free India through a new Constitution" to feed the starving people and to clothe the naked masses and to give every Indian the fullest opportunity to develop himself according to his needs".[1] On August 14, 1947, in his midnight speech before the Constituent Assembly, Nehru portrayed nationalist sentiments in the words, *"Long ago we made a tryst with destiny and now the time comes when we shall redeem our pledge not wholly or in full measure but very substantially.......".* Hence, the Fathers of the Constitution framed a Constitution which could be instrumental in bringing about 'social revolution', usher in 'national renaissance' and safeguard the country against fissiparious tendencies which in the past kept India as a house divided against itself.

On August 29, 1947 the Constituent Assembly set up a Drafting Committee of seven eminent members under the chairmanship of Dr. B.R. Ambedkar. B.N. Rao, a constitutional expert assisted the Committee as an advisor. Pt. Nehru, a visionary, Sardar Patel, the iron man of India and a pragmatist, were the main sources of constant guidance and inspiration. In fact, Nehru, Patel, Rajendra Prasad and Maulana Azad constituted an 'ogligarchy within the Assembly'. Their personal popularity, marked ability and practical sagacity, made a member of the Assembly remark, *"the government rested in the hands of those who were utterly incapable of doing any wrong to the people".*[2]

The Drafting Committee submitted the Draft to the President of the Constituent Assembly after 141 days's strenuous work on February 21, 1948. Eight months' period was allowed for its hairsplitting

[1] *Constituent Assembly Debates, Volume II, p. 316*

[2] *Brajeshwar Prasad : CAD, 18 p. 760-61*

all over the country. The total number of amendments tabled was approximately 7,635, out of which 2,473 amendments were actually moved. After elaborate discussions, the Draft was finalised on November 26, 1949. It took the Assembly 2 years 11 months and 20 days to frame the Constitution.

The 12th session of the Assembly held on January 24, 1950 elected Rajendra Prasad as the first President of the Indian Union. The members of the Assembly–legal and political luminaries–affixed their signatures on the official copies of the Indian Constitution which came into force on January 26, 1950. Most of the articles and clauses were supported by a thumping majority, almost unanimously. Austin thus remarks, "Had the Constitution come from the Constituent Assembly sanctioned by a meagre majority opposed by many it would have been attacked as unworthy of general support and unrepresentative of India's best interests".[1]

The Constitution enshrines Indian's cherished goals — the dawn of an era of liberty, equality and justice. It was drafted with the welfare of the then "four hundred million Indians in mind". On account of its democratic ideals it was hailed by the top democracies of the world as 'a glorious chapter in the history of man's march on the highway of progress and prosperity'.[2] We give a sketchy portrayal of its framework though in the following chapters, a detailed account has been given.The basic aims and objectives of the Indian polity are embodied in the objective resolutions ratified by the Constituent Assembly on January 22, 1947 and are found in the Preamble to the Constitution of 1950.

Preamble

The preamble is not an integral part of the Constitution and as such does not have any legal force behind it. Still, it is no less significant. It contains lofty ideals which the architects of the Constitution have laid before the future Governments of India. It indicates the source, the sanction, the pattern, the objects, and the contents of the Constitution. The Preamble runs as follows : "*We, the people of India having solemnly resolved to constitute India into a Sovereign Democratic Republic and secure to all its citizens justice, social, economic and political; liberty of thought, expression, belief, faith and worship; equality of status and of opportunity and to promote among them all fraternity assuring the dignity of the individual and the unity and integrity of the Nation...... In our Constituent Assembly, this 26th day of November 1949 do hereby adopt, enact and give to ourselves this Constitution.*" The Swaran Singh Committee recommended amendment in the Preamble. As such, words 'secular' and 'socialistic' were added after 'sovereign democratic' according to the 42nd amendment of the Constitution passed by the Parliament in November, 1976 and, assented to by the President of India on December 11, 1976.

Evidently the Preamble embodies the sovereignty of the people like the Preambles of Constitutions of the U.S.A., Australia, France and Italy.

It embodies the noblest ideals of justice, liberty, equality and fraternity. It also reflects that right from the very beginning, the Fathers of the Constitution stood for sovereign, democratic Republic. The addition of words 'secular' and 'socialist' before 'sovereign democratic' and 'integrity' before unity reveals the intentions of succeeding leadership. The Constitution is thus apt to protect the religious minorities and provide just rights for minorities, depressed and other backward classes and tribal areas so that they enjoy parity as the recipients of social, economic and political justice. Besides all are to be provided freedoms of thought, expression, belief, faith and worship, etc. The Constitution is to strive 'to guarantee to the people justice based on social, economic and political equality, equality of opportunity and equality before law'.

These laudable objectives as enshrined in the Preamble remained as a beacon light for the framers of the Constitution and also the future leadership, who were to be responsible for shaping the destiny of the nation. India became a sovereign democratic Republic on January 26, 1950 and incorporated

[1]*Austin, G : The Indian Constitution coverstone of a Nation, p. 25*

[2]*Dr. Vishnu Bhagwan : Indian Constitution — an Appraisal, 1999 ed., p. 13.*

an impressive chapter of Fundamental Rights and also Directive Principles which were to be fundamental in the governance of the country, in pursuance of the ideals embodied in the Preamble. However, we did not sever our relations with British Commonwealth of Nations. We embraced its membership on the condition that it will hitherto be designated as 'Commonwealth of Nations'. We accepted King as the symbol of Commonwealth unity. Obviously, such an arrangement for future 'give and take' with U.K. and other members of Commonwealth did not impair our sovereignty.

Fundamental Rights

One of the most conspicuous features of the Indian Bill of Rights is that it is the most elaborate in the world. The voluminous size of the chapter is due to the enumeration of seven rights in the minutest details alongwith a set of limitations imposed upon them. **However, now there are six Fundamental Rights as the 44th amendment Act 1978 deleted the right to property from chapter III.** As such, it ceased to be a Fundamental Right. The Fundamental Rights which still form Part III of our Constitution are as follows : Right to equality; right to freedom; right against exploitation; right to freedom of religion; cultural and educational rights; right to constitutional remedies. A brief explanation of these rights will apprise the reader of the contents of these **Fundamental Rights.**

Right to Equality (*Articles 14 to 18*)

Article 14 guarantees equality before the law to all persons and not the citizens alone. No law can discriminate unfairly between one group of citizens and another in relation to the same matter or between the citizens and foreigners.

V.N. Shukla referring to equality before law opines. "The rule is that all should be treated alike and not that unlike should be treated like".[1]

Article 15 lays emphasis on prohibition of discrimination on the basis of sex, religion, race, caste, place of birth, etc., in respect of access to shops, public restaurants, hotels and places of public entertainment, and the use of wells, tanks, bathing ghats, roads and places of public resort, maintained wholly or partly by state funds or dedicated to the use of general public. However, the Government is authorised to make special provisions for women and children, the advancement of any socially and educationally backward classes and the scheduled castes and scheduled tribes.

Article 16 guarantees equality of opportunity in matters of employment to any of the offices of the Union or the states. Further, no citizen is to be discriminated against on the grounds of religion, race, caste, sex, descent, place of birth or residence. In this case also, some exceptions have been provided. Parliament may confine employment under state and local authority to residents. A state may also provide for the reservation of appointments or posts for backward classes which are not adequately represented in the services under the state. The offices concerned with religious institutions may be reserved for the adherents of a particular religion

Article 17 abolishes untouchability and forbids its practice in any form. The enforcement of any disability arising out of untouchability is to be treated as a punishable offence.

Article 18 abolishes all titles and the State is prohibited from conferring titles on any person except the titles of military or academic distinction.

Dr. Jenning was, however, of the view that the abolition of untouchability and titles are egalitarian and constituted in fact the fulfilment of longstanding commitments of the Congress to the Indian masses. He goes to the extent of emphasising that Articles 17 and 18 do not comprise Rights. Article 17 removes a social disability and Article 18 imposes restrictions on public officers which could have been imposed by administrative regulations. He remarked, *"It seems to be no*

[1]*Shukla V.N. : The Constitution of India (1972 ed.) p. 27*

breach of this right to equality if Shri John Brown became Dr. John Brown or General John Brown or Pandit John Brown or Mr. John Brown or Rotarian John Brown or even Sir John Brown, M.B.E. or if he rolls round in a gold plated car or loads his wife with jewellery and silk sarees but if like the present lecturer, he becomes an impecunious 'Knight', the right to equality is broken"[1]

Right to Freedom (*Articles 19 to 22*)

Article 19 is the palladium of traditional individual freedoms. It assures freedom of speech and expression; freedom to assemble peacefully and without arms; freedom to form associations or unions; freedom to move freely throughout the territory of India; freedom to reside and settle in any part of the territory of the country and, freedom to practise any profession or to carry on any occupation, trade or business. However, the Constitution imposes specific limitations on their exercise and enjoyment. Four reservations viz., laws relating to libel, slander and defamation; contempt of court; decency or morality and security of the state, restrict freedom of speech. The Constitution Amendment Act 1951 added three more reservations *viz.*, friendly relations with foreign states; public order and incitement to an offence. The Constitution (Sixteenth Amendment) Act, 1963 added "Sovereignty and integrity of India as one of the grounds for imposing restrictions on freedom of speech and expression, assembly and forming of associations or unions. The right to move freely is also subject to such restrictions as are imposed by any existing law or such as the State may impose in the public interest or to safeguard the interests of any Scheduled Tribes. Likewise in emergencies such as war, a citizen may be legally prohibited from entering or leaving the affected area in the interest of public health. The Government may also extern any person from any part of the country for a particular period in the interest of the maintenance of law and order or detain a person in the public interest.

The Right to reside is hedged with restrictions in the interest of the general public or for the protection of the interests of Scheduled Tribes. The Right to practise any trade or profession is subjected to the right of the State to prescribe professional or technical qualifications. The Constitution (First) Amendment Act 1951 empowered the State to reserve to itself the right to carry on any trade, business, industry or service, either directly or through State controlled corporations to the complete or partial exclusion of private citizens. It will not be out of place to point out that the reasonableness of any law permitting nationalization of any trade or business cannot be a subject of judicial review.[2]

Articles 20 to 22 confer personal liberty. Article 20 requires that no person shall be convicted of an offence except for violation of a law in force at the time of the Commission of the Act. Besides, no person is to be prosecuted and punished for the same offence more than once; no person accused of an offence is to be compelled to stand witness against itself. Likewise no person is to be detained without being informed of the grounds for his arrest. Article 22 permits an arrested person to consult and be defended by a lawyer of his own choice. Besides, he is to be produced before the magistrate and is not to be kept in custody beyond a period of 24 hours without orders from a magistrate. Preventive Detention which was initially for three months cannot be made for more than two months (after the passage of 44th Amendment), without the intercession of an Advisory Board constituted for the same. Detention is permissible if the Advisory Board justifies it. M.V. Pylee justifies the provision of Preventive Detention as such, *"Until and unless every party or group accepts constitutional means to achieve its objectives and practices the special provisions such as the preventive detention law may still be needed in India"*.[3] Acharya Kripalani describes it as a "lawless law". Bakshi Tek Chand dubbed it "as a charter of oppression and denial of liberty. A staunch communist like A.K. Gopalan opined that Preventive Detention Act is "designed to crush the political rivals of the Congress".

[1]*Sir Ivor Jenning : Some characteristics of the Indian Constitution, pp. 36-7.*
[2]*Saghir Ahmed V. State of U.P., A.I.R. 1954, S.C. 224 : Ramchandra Palai V. State of Orissa, A.I.R. 1956, S.C. 298.*
[3]*Pylee M.V. : Constitutional Government in India, 1965, pp. 263-64.*

Even Dr. Ambedkar had admitted that no part of the draft Constitution invited such a vehement criticism at the hands of the critics as the Articles dealing with 'personal liberty'. It was apprehended that (*i*) detenus will be unduly tortured or subjected to inhuman treatment during the detention, (*ii*) the Government may constitute packed Board to toe their line of action and ditto their point of view, (*iii*) provision for the maintenance of families during the detention of detenus will not exist, (*iv*) the period of 3 months (later reduced to 2) to allow police to prepare their case for detention needed to be cut down to a fortnight or maximum one month.

However, preventive detention in general was considered as a check on disruptionists and the crying need of the hour. In the words of K.M. Munshi, "where the rule of law prevails, preventive detention is the only remedy to meet the dangers of subversion from infiltration or coercive mass demonstration". Prof. Gladhill rightly remarks, *"Preventive detention is an administrative necessity in India and likely to cause less human misery than might result from likely alternative measures to deal with persons who cannot be successfully prosecuted for their activities though they are menace to public security and order"*. Austin describes it as a psychological deterrent and hopes that it would not bring about downfall of liberty.

Right against Exploitation (*Articles 23, 24*)

Article 23 prohibits traffic in human beings and *'Begar'* and other similar forms of forced labour. Any contravention is punishable as an offence under the law. Traffic in human beings includes traffic in women and children for immoral purposes. However, the State is empowered to impose compulsory service for public purposes. In doing so, the State shall not make any discrimination on grounds of religion, race, caste or class, or any of them.

Article 24 prohibits the children below the age of 14 years from employment in any factory or mine or in any other hazardous labour.

It is, however, distressing that in actual practice traffic in human beings particularly in women for immoral purposes, still persists in disguised form. Moreover children are apt to be exploited so long as Poor Houses or Work Houses as in the U.K. are not provided. After all children–hailing from poor and pauper families also have to survive somehow. Shri. M. R. Singhal – the present Social Welfare Labour and Employment Minister in Sheila Dixit's Ministry formed after third consecutive victory in Delhi Assembly elections made a critical remark regarding Child Labour Act which gives a package of 20 thousands only to such poor families for not sending children for child labour jobs. He said, "this is not just enough". He suggested a job to the family concerned. Besides schools, hostels, for board and lodging be constructed as free facilities.

The Maharashtra Assembly passed bill for the welfare and amelioration of the plight of the domestic help on December 28, 2008[1]. The Maharashtra labour Minister described it a laudable step in keeping with the State's image. Just to throw them out of jobs is not enough. They have to be provided crumbes to eat and proper accommodation in schools and provision of mid-day meals. If a member of such families who is adult is provided a job, it will be indeed appreciable. Presently, the families of such children who are working as domestic help to earn their livelihood and in some cases helping parents to make both ends meet, are feeling frustrated.

Right to Freedom of Religion (*Articles 25 to 28*)

These rights include both the personal and social aspects of religion and are equally enjoyed by all persons living in India, citizens and aliens. Article 25 guarantees to all persons freedom of conscience and authorises them to profess, practice and propagate, any religion subject to the 'prescribed limitations of public order, morality and health'. However, the article empowers the state to regulate or restrict any economic, financial, political or other secular activity associated with

[1] *Hindustan times : December 29, 2008 p.1.*

religious practice to provide for social welfare and reform, or to throw open the Hindu religious institutions of public character to all classes and sections of Hindus. It, however, clearly states that wearing and carrying of *Kirpans* shall be deemed to be included in the profession of the Sikh religion. It reflects that Article 25 is an 'article of faith in the Constitution' as it recognises the principle that the real test of a true democracy is the earmarking of identity to insignificant minority.

Article 26 allows freedom to manage religious affairs. Hence every religious denomination possesses the right to :

(*i*) establish and maintain institutions for religious and charitable purposes;
(*ii*) manage its own affairs in matters of religion;
(*iii*) own and acquire movable and immovable property
(*iv*) to administer such property in accordance with law.

Article 27 restricts the imparting of religious instructions in an educational institution wholly maintained out of State funds. However, this is not to apply to an educational institution established under any endowment or trust requiring imparting of religious instructions in such an institution. Moreover, no person can be compelled to participate in religious instructions or religious worship in an educational institution recognized or financially aided by the State. In case of a minor, consent of the guardian will have to be sought for attending such instructions or worship.

The provisions relating to religious freedom clearly reflect that ours' is a secular state in letter and spirit. Keeping in view these provisions of the Constitution, Nehru remarked, *"We call our state a secular state.... What exactly does it mean ? It does not obviously mean a state where religion as such is discouraged. It means freedom of religion and conscience including freedom for those who have no religion. It means free play for all religions subject only to their not interfering with each other or with the basic conceptions of our state...."*.[1] Though the state observes complete neutrality in religious matters, it is not debarred from adopting measures of social reforms and imposing checks on the abuse of religious freedom, endangering public order, health or morality.

Cultural and Educational Right (*Articles 29 to 30*)

Besides individual rights and freedoms, the Constitution recognises and guarantees certain non political rights of the religious, cultural, and linguistic minorities, groups, or sections of the people.

Article 29 guarantees to every minority right to preserve its language, script and culture. No citizen is to be denied admission in the State or State aided educational institutions on the grounds only of religion, race, caste, or language.

Article 30 deals with the right of minorities to establish and administer educational institutions of their choice. A newly inserted clause 39(1A) states that in making any law providing for the compulsory acquisition of any property of an educational institution established and administered by a minority, the State is to ensure that the amount so fixed is such as would not restrict or abrogate the right so guaranteed. Since Article 31 had been deleted, this clause was inserted by the 44th Constitution Amending Act (1978) to enable a minority to establish and administer a similar institution at another location.

Section (2) of Article 30 prohibits the State from extending aid to those educational institutions that discriminate on the basis of either religion or language.

Thus the State is not allowed to dictate to the minority the nature of educational institutions it shall have. It is for the minority to decide the pattern of educational institution it should have, so as to enable it to conserve its culture. Moreover, the State is to adopt an impartial attitude while granting financial assistance to these institutions run by the minorities.

[1]*Jawaharlal Nehru's monthly circular to the State Congress Committee. India News August 14, 1954.*

Right to Constitutional Remedies (*Articles 32 to 35*)

The citizens have been authorised to move the Supreme Court and the High Courts by appropriate proceedings for the enforcement of the Fundamental Rights. The Supreme Court and the High Courts can issue directions or orders or writs in the nature of '*habeas corpus, mandamus, prohibition, quo warranto, and certiorari*' under Article 32. Article 33 provides that Parliament may by law determine as to what extent any of the rights conferred by chapter III (Fundamental Rights) shall in their application to armed forces, or the forces charged with the maintenance of public order, or persons employed in any bureau or other organisations established by the state for purposes of intelli- gence or counter intelligence, or persons employed in telecommunication systems set up for the purpose of any force, bureau or organisation of the members of Armed Forces be restricted or abro-gated so as to ensure proper discharge of their duties and the maintenance of discipline amongst them.

Article 32 provides for indemnity to public servants and others for any action taken by them for maintenance on restoration of order in any area where martial law was in force.

Article 35 empowers Parliament to make laws with respect to any matter under clause 3 of Article 16. Clause (b) of this article provides that in case of Acts already in existence which provide punishment for breach of fundamental rights, unless and until Parliament makes another provision such laws would continue in operation.

The importance of this right was very well portrayed by Dr. Ambedkar in the words, **"It is the very soul of the Constitution and the very heart of it"**.[1] P. B. Gajendragadkar, former Chief Justice of India, described this right as a very distinguishing feature of the Indian Constitution and a cornerstone of the democratic edifice raised by the Constitution.[2]

Conclusion

Thus the chapter of Fundamental Rights is instrumental in preserving individual liberties and establishing the democratic way of life based on the cardinal principles of equality and justice. Austin is of the view..... "the Fundamental Rights have both created a new equality and had been absent in traditional Indian (largely Hindu) society and have helped to preserve individual liberty".[3] K.M. Pannikar also holds that "*Fundamental Rights in India have been the source and inspiration of the Reform legislation as under their aegis the Indian Parliament has been active in the matter of 'social legislation' whether it be called by a Hindu Code Bill or by another name*".[4] However, the critics allege that the Rights are not sacrosanct as they can be infringed in the name of reasonable restrictions to further national interests.

The critics also refer to the ambiguity of words used in the chapter of Rights. 'Public purpose', 'traffic in human beings', 'hazardous employment', 'amount and minorities' - all these words smack of vagueness. It has been resulting in confrontation between the Parliament and the Judiciary. Hence amendments have followed in quick succession.

Suspension of these rights during emergency has also entailed scathing criticism. Similar powers were vested with the President of Germany according to article 48 of the 1926 Constitution and it eventually resulted in the rise of Hitler's dictatorship. Another notable leader, H.V. Kamath pointed out in the Constituent Assembly, "I fear that by this single chapter we are seeking to lay the foundation of a totalitarian state....where the rights and liberties of the millions of innocent men and women will be in continuous jeopardy".[5] The passage of 42nd and 44th amendments has clarified the position. The President is apt to act on the advice of the council of ministers on all matters eventually. Thus, the President remains a mere constitutional 'head'.

[1] *Constituent Assembly Debates, Volume VII, No. 23, p. 953.*

[2] *Gajendragadkar P.B. : The 'Constitution of India' – the Philosophy and basic postulates, pp. 60-62*

[3] *Austin, G : The Indian Constitution - Cornerstone of a Nation, p. 114*

[4] *Pannikar, K.M : Hindu Society, p. 57.*

[5] *C.A. Debates, Vol. IX, p. 559*

The critics also refer to the omission of economic rights which constitute the fabric of democracy and denounced the 'Right to Private Property'. The abolition of the latter by the 44th amendment and its being reduced to a statutory right and inclusion of the right to work as a duty has, however, taken the sting out of this criticism on this ground.

Though these comments are not without much of weight, yet it will not be an exaggeration to say that Fundamental Rights constitute the cornerstone of our national liberty which we endearingly cherished and attained after trials and tribulations. Even the restrictions on the Rights have been described as judicious by legal luminaries like Justice Shelat who said, ".....these fundamental rights must yield to reasonable restrictions the imposition of which may become necessary to satisfy the changing necessities and situations which might arise from time to time".[1] Hence the rights were not intended to be sacrosanct. The framers of the Constitution wanted them to be dynamic realities and not obstacles in the way of progress and prosperity of our infant democracy. They exist for the fulfilment of a new social and economic order as envisaged in the Directive Principles of State policy (Part IV of the Constitution). Hence Austin remarks, "....in no other constitution, expression of positive or negative rights has provided so much impetus towards changing and rebuilding society for the common good".[2]

Directive Principles of State Policy (*Articles 36 to 51*)

The Directive Principles of State Policy which have been incorporated in Articles 36 to 51 in Chapter IV of the Constitution have been borrowed from the Constitution of Ireland. At home the immediate source of this Chapter is the Instrument of Instructions under the Government of India Act 1935. They form a very comprehensive political, social and economic programme of a modern welfare state. They set forth 'the humanitarian socialist precepts that were and are the aims of the Indian Revolution. However, they neither form the complete blueprint nor do they constitute a cut and dried and rigid programme. They reflect the aspirations of the founding fathers who expected every government to strive to establish economic democracy in a politically emancipated country.

These principles have not been arranged logically. Hence it is difficult to classify them. However, we may group them as : Socialistic, Gandhian, Liberal Intellectualistic and General : The General group may include all those principles which are not covered by the above classification.

Socialistic. The socialistic principles aiming at the establishment of a welfare state in India are widely spread over the articles. Article 39 enjoins upon the State to direct its policy towards

(*i*) securing adequate means of livelihood for both men and women on equal basis;

(*ii*) distributing the control and ownership of the material resources of the community so as to subserve the common good;

(*iii*) operation of the economic system in a manner that it does not result in the concentration of wealth and means of production to the common detriment;

(*iv*) enforcing equal pay for equal work for both men and women;

(*v*) avoidance of abuse of health and strength of workers, men, women and children, and also avoiding compulsion of undertaking vocations unsuitable to their age;

(*vi*) protection of childhood and youth against exploitation and moral and material abandonment;

Article 41 seeks to ensure the right to work, to education and to public assistance in cases of unemployment, old age, sickness and disablement and other cases of undeserved want.

Article 42 makes a provision for securing just and humane conditions of work and for maternity relief.

Article 43 secures for all workers, agricultural, industrial or otherwise, work, a living wage,

---

[1]*Rajendra Prasad Endowment Lectures : The Spirit of the Constitution, p. 31*

[2]*Austin G : op. cit., p. 115*

conditions of work, ensuring a decent standard of life and full enjoyment of leisure and social and cultural opportunities. The 42nd amendment (43A article) secures the participation of workers in the management of undertakings or organisations engaged in any Industry. Article 46 exhorts the state to promote with special care the educational and economic interest of the weaker sections of the people and in particular of the scheduled castes and the scheduled tribes and to protect them from social injustice and all forms of exploitation. Article 44 aims at uniform civil code.

Article 47 urges the State to raise the level of nutrition and the standard of living of its people and the improvement of the public health.

The Amendment Act of 1976 added a few more Directive Principles which further the cause of socialism. Free legal aid to the poor, security for the citizens, equal justice and promoting of workers' participation in the management, fall in this category (Article 39 A).

The objectives referred to above. embody the main tenets of a socialistic pattern of society. Hence Jennings remarks, *"The ghosts of Sidney and Beatric Webb stalk through the text of Part IV of the Constitution"*.

Gandhian Principles. Gandhian ideology finds a prominent place in some of these objectives stated as under :

(*i*) the state shall organise village panchayats and endow them with such powers as may enable them to function as units of self government;

(*ii*) the state shall promote with special care the educational and economic interests of Harijans, Scheduled Tribes and weaker sections of the community;

(*iii*) the state shall strive to promote cottage industries on an individual or co-operative basis. in the rural areas.

(*iv*) the state shall take steps for preserving the breeds of milch cattle including cows and calves and for prohibiting their slaughter;

(*v*) the state shall endeavour to effect prohibition of consumption except for medicinal purposes of intoxicating drugs and drinks which are harmful to health.

Liberal Intellectualistic

(*i*) The State is to endeavour to secure for the citizens a uniform civil code throughout the territory of India. (*ii*) The State is to endeavour to provide within a period of 10 years from the commencement of the Constitution for free and compulsory education for children below and up to the age of 14 years. The long pending bill, right to education, assuring free and compulsory education for children between 6 and 14 years got the union cabinet's nod on October 30, 2008.

On December 15, 2008, right of children to free and compulsory education 'bill' was introduced in Rajya Sabha. The highlights of the bill are:-

(*a*) It seeks to promote free and compulsory education to children between 6 to 14 years.

(*b*) Every school will have to earmark atleast 25% seats in class I for free and compulsory education.

(*c*) It seeks to do away with the practice of school taking capitation fees before admission and subjecting the child or parents to any screening procedure.

(*d*) It seeks ban on tuition fees

(*e*) It ensures that the child is not subjected to physical punishment or mental harassment. The violation would be liable to disciplinary action.[1] After the passage of the child literacy will go of considerably.

(*f*) The state shall strive to organise agricultural and animal husbandry on modern and scientific lines.

[1] *Times of India : December 16, 2008 parliamentry Diary.*

(*g*) The state shall take steps to separate the judiciary from the Executive.

(*h*) The state shall endeavour to promote international peace and security, maintain just and honourable relations between nations, foster respect' for international law and treaty obligation, encourage, settelement of international disputes by arbitration (Article 51).

(*i*) Another directive principle which catered to the protection and improvement of the environment and safeguarding forests and wild life of the country was added in chapter IV.

General

Articles 36 and 37 are merely concerned with the definition and application of the Directive Principles. Article 36 provides that in this part unless the context otherwise provides, the state has the same meaning.

Article 37 provides that these principles shall not be enforceable by any court of law and are nevertheless fundamental in the governance of the country. It shall be the duty of the state to apply these principles in making laws. Article 49 makes it obligatory for the State to protect every monument or place or object of artistic or historic interest which Parliament considers of national importance.

Evaluation

The Directive Principles have been vehemently criticised by the critics. The communists describe these "Directives as decoratives". T.T. Krishnamachari portrays these Directive principles as, *"a veritable dustbin of sentiments....."*. Sir B.N. Rau regards them as *"mere moral precepts for the state authorities"*[1]. K.T. Shah describes them as a "Cheque payable by the bank concerned at its convenience". K.C. Wheare calls them *"manifesto of aims and aspirations"*. All this and more was said about them as they were not made justiciable. They were described as vague and also illogically arranged. They were declared unnatural by some critics in a sovereign state like India. Why does a sovereign nation look to directions or instructions ? What is the guarantee that future generations or governments would pay any heed to them? Some critics challenge their soundness. Does not prohibition cause monumental loss to the State Exchequer ? Is morality enforceable ? Prohibition where introduced was rejected with impunity. Andhra Pradesh and Haryana are the recent examples where prohibition was introduced but abolished when it proved to be a big drain on state exchequer and smuggling of liquor and illicit distillation became the order of the day. The critics like Dr. Jennings describe them "as brake on the wheels of national progress". Jennings opines, "*....the ideals embodied in this chapter may not simply become outmoded and antiquated in the next century. They might act as citadels of reaction as well and thus clog national progress*".

Dr. Jennings goes to the extent of saying that **"Directive Principles are nothing but collection of political principles derived from English political experience of the 19th century. They are deemed to be unsuited for India in the middle of 20th century"**. The critics also apprehend that a uniform civil code throughout the country was envisaged to tyrannize the minorities. The laws passed by the majorities might be an imposition on minorities whose culture, customs, and rites, differ from that of the majority community. Keeping in view all these points of criticism, a critic describes them as 'ingenious blend of pious wishes, noble aspirations, moral precepts, and economic maxims, which ultimately degenerate into sublime nonsense'.

These comments are rather exaggerations. These principles are not meaningless as they have been portrayed by some critics. In this age of democracy, vigilant public opinion is the real force behind the these idealistic principles. No Government can afford to ignore these Directives. The Act of 1976 made them justiciable. A.K. Gokhale, the then law minister, thus remarked, "The Bill is aimed at spelling out expressly the high ideals of socialism, secularism, and the integrity of nation

---

[1] *Noorani, A.G. : Reviewing Fundamental Rights – an article in Indian Express, New Delhi, Sept. 4, 1980.*

to make directive principles more comprehensible and give them primacy over those fundamental rights around which the vested interests had built their bulwark to thwart socio-economic reforms".[1]

Their constitutional sanctity is also unchallengeable. Their violation has been deemed as contrary to the Constitution and as violation of a constitutional principle legally enforceable. In Gopalan Vs. State of Madras, C.J. Kania opined that, directive principles do not, "*represent a temporary will of the majority but the deliberate wisdom of the nation expressed through the Constituent Assembly.....By declaring them to be fundamental in the governance of the country, the Constitution has invested them with a certain sanctity*".

Besides, they are an insurance against extremes. These principles are apt to induce the conservatives to introduce reforms necessitated by the exigencies of the time and also exercise restraint on the radicals if they intend effecting sweeping reforms. In the words of Dr. Ambedkar, "*They have left enough room for people of different ways of thinking with regard to reaching of the ideal of economic democracy*".[2]

It is also asserted that these Directives have proved to be fundamental principles of a new social and economic order. The abolition of Zamindari System, the nationalisation of the Banks, the abolition of privy purses, the curtailment of right to private property through 24th and 25th amendments and ultimately removal of private property right from the Chapter of Fundamental Rights, clearly reflect that they have been given precedence over Fundamental Rights. Their practical utility lay in the fact that they have been instrumental in the removal of ambiguities of the constitution. In Gopalan Vs. State of Madras, C.J. Kania rightly remarked "Most of the Fundamental Rights are subject to reasonable restrictions which may be imposed for public purposes or in public interest. The courts can be and have been guided by the Directive Principles in determining whether the actual restrictions placed by law in the exercise of Fundamental Rights are reasonable or are in public interest, or whether they subserve a public purpose."[3] M.C. Setalwad. former Attorney General of India, also pointed out, "...Those fundamental axioms of state policy though of no legal effect have served as a useful beacon light to Courts.....Restrictions imposed by law on the freedom of citizens may well be reasonable if they are imposed in furtherance of the Directive Principles"

These Directives have been of advantage to the Planning Commission as well. The latter has realized that economic pattern to be attained through National Planning has been clearly laid down in the Directive Principles of State Policy. Hence the Planning Commission is apt to follow these principles while formulating these plans. Keeping in view all these facts, one can agree with Ayyer (Alladi Krishnaswamy), "*No ministry responsible to the people can afford light-heartedly to ignore the provisions in Part IV of the Constitution*". They have served as signal posts to the Legislature and the Executive and beacon lights to the Courts.

For instance, the Supreme Court in its historic judgement on May 10, 1995 in a Bigamy case exhorted Govt of India to give effect to Article 44 on Uniform Civil Code and directed it to inform the Apex Court of the progress made in this direction by August 9, 1996. It proves that the bar in article 37 on the enforcing of these principles has not deterred the judiciary from giving effect to a Directive Principle indirectly by interpretation.

An appraisal and a detailed analysis of efforts made by the Governments—Central, State and Local, in implementing these principles over the period of years and their glorious achievements in this respect establishes their practical utility. The abolition of zamindari, jagirdari and ryotwari systems resulting in the amelioration of the lot of tillers and catering to the growth of socialism, the network of Panchayati Raj institutions, the establishment of All India Khadi and Village Industries Board, All India Handicrafts Board, All India Handloom Board etc. to encourage cottage

[1]*Socialist India : October 30, 1976, p.15*
[2]*Constituent Assembly Debates, Volume VI, pp. 494-95*
[3]*1950, S.C.R. 88.*

Industries, the separation of judiciary from the executive in many states, consistent efforts to protect historic buildings and monuments, Indian Government's perpetual effort to develop friendly relations with the neighbours and also the Russian, the British, the Arabs, the Africans and in the most recent past with the Americans. Beside, the introduction of free and compulsory primary education for children below the age of 14 years in many states and eventually the passage of right to education (December 15, 2008) in the Rajya Sabha with hope to get it passed by the Lok Sabha and eventually the President are some of the glaring examples to prove that these principles have not been pious wishes or mere noble aspirations. However with the substitution of liberalism and free market economy socialism envisaged through directive principles stands eclipsed.

Fundamental Duties

The 42nd amendment Act added IVA part to chapter IV and introduced article 51A enumerating the duties. This was done on the pattern of the Soviet Constitution. The Following are the duties incorporated.

(*i*) To abide by the constitution and respect its ideals which inspired our national struggle for freedom.

(*ii*) To cherish and follow the noble ideals which inspired our national struggle for freedom.

(*iii*) To uphold and protect the sovereignty, unity and integrity of India.

(*iv*) To defend the country and render the national service when called upon to do so.

(*v*) To promote harmony and the spirit of common brotherhood amongst all the people of India, transcending religious, linguistic, regional and sectional diversities to renounce practices derogatory to the dignity of women.

(*vi*) To value and preserve the rich heritage of our composite culture.

(*vii*) To protect and improve the natural environment including forests, lakes, rivers, and wild life and to have compassion for living creatures.

(*viii*) To develop scientific temper, humanism, and spirit of enquiry and reform.

(*ix*) To safeguard public property and to abjure violence.

(*x*) To strive towards excellence in all spheres of individual and collective entity so that the nation constantly rises to higher levels of endeavour and achievement.

Evaluation

The articles on duties are quite impressive yet they have entailed a scathing criticism. In fact this addition in the constitution is a mixed bag of expectations and exhortations. Some of these duties are enforceable otherwise too. Their mention is just superfluous. Any Indian is expected to abide by the constitution or respect the National Flag. The critics also emphasise that duties incorporated are not exhaustive. For example, honest payment of taxes is conspicuous by its absence.

Second, they are ambiguous and beyond the comprehension of a layman. Terms as scientific temper, humanism, composite culture, the spirit of enquiry and collective entity, are beyond the comprehension of an average Indian.

Third, some of the duties display mere sentiments and do not concur with the realities. The cherishing of noble ideals which goaded us to the freedom struggle has wider ramifications. In the words of a lawyer, "*The duties may be spelt out in a more concrete form. One is left guessing, the noble ideals - 'Duties' - should be such and so worded as to catch the imagination of the common man*".[1]

---

[1]*Chawla D.D. : The Concept of Fundamental Duties - 'Socialist India', October 23, 1976, pp. 44-45.*

Fourth, they appear to be an appendage to Part IV of the Constitution. As such, they are mere moral precepts and not justiciable. They could have been part and parcel of the Fundamental Rights chapter and made enforceable.

However, it is wrong to assume that they are mere pious declarations. The 42nd amendment established primacy of the Directive Principles over the Fundamental Rights, and deprived the Courts of the power of striking down any clause of the Amending Act.

There is some justification in the above criticism. However to assume that they are mere pious declarations is farther from truth. If the 42nd amendment could establish primacy of Directive Principles over Fundamental Rights and deprive the Courts of striking down any clause of an Amending Act, it can hopefully be conceived that the Fundamental Duties will not be violated as they also constitute part IV of the Constitution. Dholakia aptly remarks, *"Parliament is empowered to impose appropriate penalty or punishment for any noncompliance with or refusal to observe any of these Fundamental Duties".*[1]

Moreover the uniqueness of Fundamental Duties lies in the fact that they have tried to dispel superstition and eradicate fanaticism, regional chauvinism and linguistic antagonism, by incorporating duties like developing scientific temper, humanism and the spirit of enquiry and reform. Besides renunciation of practices derogatory to the dignity of women and preservation of the rich heritage of India's composite culture, are the noble ideals to uplift our fast deteriorating society. Hence the Fundamental Duties may not be treated as a mere assertion of sentimentalism.

The Union Executive[2]

Ours is a parliamentary democracy. As such the President, the nominal head, the Prime Minister heading a Council of Ministers as the real head, constitute the Union Executive. In the words of Dr. Ambedkar "at the head of Indian Union there is a functionary called the President of the Union. The title of this functionary reminds one of the President of the United States. But beyond identity of names there is nothing in common between the form of government prevalent in America and the form of government envisaged under the Indian Constitution.....under the Indian Constitution the President occupies the same place as the British Monarch under the English Constitution. He is the head of the State but not of the government. He represents the nation but does not rule the nation. He is the symbol of the nation. His place in the administration is that of a ceremonial device or a seal by which the nation's decisions are made known"[3].

Article 53 vests the executive power of the Union including the supreme command of the Defence forces in the President. Quite contrarily, provisions in Articles 74, 75 and 78 are indicative of real powers having been vested with the Council of Ministers. Article 72 also explains his powers of granting pardon and commuting, suspending and remitting, sentences in certain cases. Article 155 vests with him power of appointing Governors whereas Articles 124(2), 217, 316 and 324, empower him to appoint judges of the Supreme Court and High Courts and Chairman of Public Service Commission. Articles 148, 324 and 280 authorise him to appoint Comptroller and Auditor General, Chief Election Commissioner and Finance Commission. Articles 339, 340 and 344, empower him to appoint commissions on backward classes and also on official languages. Articles 350 to 360, equip him with emergency powers. Article 123 vests him with power of promulgating ordinances.

These powers seem to be enormous, and, apparently, make his authority onerous but prior to the passage of the 42nd amendment, he had to exercise his powers on the advice of the Council of Ministers and only conventionally (India being a parliamentary democracy), that advice was binding

[1]*Dholakia, H.C. : Forty Second minus Forty Fourth : Some plus points in journal of Constitutional and Parliamentary Studies Vol. XIII, Nov. 4, 1979, p. 401.*

[2] *See details in chapter III.*

[3]*Constituent Assembly Debates, Vol. VII, pp. 33-34.*

on him. It had raised doubts and apprehensions due to controversial statement of first President Rajendra Prasad in a Law Institute. However, the President could ask the Council of Ministers to reconsider their advice. The 42nd Amendment Act 1976 and the 44th Amendment Act (1978) set at rest all possible speculations and made the advice of the Council of Ministers binding upon the President. (According to 44th Amendment, the President may require the Council of Ministers to reconsider such advice. However the President shall act in accordance with the advice tendered after such reconsideration.)

Thus a convention has been embodied in an act and the possibilities of President rejecting the advice in case he belonged to the party opposite to that of the Prime Minister have been set at naught for all times to come.

The method and matters pertaining to election of the President as well as Vice President have been discussed under articles 54, 55, 58, 61 and 71, and also amendment Act of 1974 regulating the Presidential and Vice Presidential elections.[1]

A.P.J. Abdul Kalam – a nuclear scientist, a Missile man, held the august office from July 25, 2002 as the 12th President for one term i.e. 5 years. Thereafter Mrs. Pratibha Patil was elected as the President of India.

Vice President

The Constitution provides for the Vice President (Article 63) and the office is modelled to some extent, on a similar institution in the U.S.A. Like his counterpart in U.S.A. he is the *ex-officio* Chairman of the Upper House (Rajya Sabha), and presides over its meetings. When the President is unable to discharge his functions because of absence, illness or any other reason, the Vice-President acts as President and discharges the former's functions till the President resumes his duties. If the President resigns, dies or is removed from office, the Vice President on such occasions will act as President until a new elected President assumes his office. While discharging those functions he is entitled to all such emoluments and allowances as are enjoyable by the President.

Dr. Ansari is the present incumbent of this office. He succeeded Bhairon Singh Shekhawat (now late).

Council of Ministers

Articles 74, 75 and 78, refer about the Council of Ministers. However, details regarding functions and powers of the Council of Ministers have not been provided in the Constitution.

Article 74 provides that there is to be a Council of Ministers with the Prime Ministers as the Head to aid and advice the President in the exercise of his functions. The 42nd amendment Act 1976 has made this advice binding on the President. Article 75 explains the process of forming of the Council of Ministers. According to this Article, the Prime Minister is to be appointed by the President and the ministers are appointed on the advice of the Prime Minister. The ministers are to hold office during the pleasure of the President. However, in actual practice, the President is apt to call the leader of the majority party to act as the Prime Minister and constitute his Council of Ministers. It will interest the reader to know that on 15th August 1947, there were 18 ministries in the central cabinet whereas presently (on May 28, 2009), it consisted of 33 Cabinet Ministers, 7 Ministers of States (Independent charge) and 30 ministers of state. In toto the P.M will be assisted by 79 members of Council of Ministers.[2]

A minister is to cease to be a minister if he does not become a member of either House of Parliament within a period of six consecutive months if already he does not figure as M.P. in either of the two Houses of the Parliament. The ministers are collectively responsible to the House of

[1]*Hindustan Times May 29, 2009*

[2]*See the detail of Prime Minister in Chapter III.*

People (Lok Sabha). Collective responsibility to Parliament and holding office during the pleasure of President are self contradictory. However, in parliamentary democracy, it is the former which matters and makes or mars the ministry and not the latter.

The Constitution enjoins upon the Prime Minister (*i*) to communicate to the President all decisions taken in the Council of Ministers pertaining to the administrative affairs of the Union and proposals for legislation; (*ii*) to furnish such information as the President calls for and, (*iii*) to submit for the consideration of the Council of Ministers if it is so required by the President, any matter on which a decision has been taken by an individual minister but which has not yet been considered by the Council collectively.

Prime Minister (P. M)

In a Parliamentary Democracy. Prime Minister is the real head of the government. President as already explained is a mere constitutional ruler, a figure head, a rubber stamp. Prime minister vis-a-vis 'his Council of Minister is described as a '*moon among the lesser stars*'. a '*Sun around whom the ministers revolve like planets*'. Since he enjoys position of ascendance over other ministers, he is not to be portrayed as '*primus inter pares*' i.e. first among equals' like chairman of federal council in Switzerland. Briefly speaking, the powers of the Prime Minister are as under:-

(i) He forms the government. The constitution is candid on this point. The President appoints the ministers, on the advice of the P.M. After the passage of 42nd amendment Act 1976, the advice is *binding* on the President. However, in coalitional era as during NDA's rule under A.B Vajpayee as P.M. and latter followed by UPA's rule under Dr. Man Mohan Singh, the hands of the P.M. were fettered. He can not annoy the coalition partners and even he might not have liked to be in M.P's were made the ministers.

After the 15th Lok Sabha elections, The position of UPA of impressed substaintly and Dr. Manmohan Singh had freer hand to choose his team comparatively.

(ii) He allocates portfolios to the Ministers. The coalitional compulsions compel the P.M. to earmark portfolios to the coalition *parties* according to their choice. The example of Mamta Banerjee who pressed for Railway department eventually agreed to have Railways. Though in the preceding this time Mamta Banerjee asked for Railways and suceeded in her mission.

(iii) He can shuffle his pack as he pleases. Dr. Manmohan Singh shuffled his pack on October 25, 2006 and inducted young blood. After Terrorists attack on Bombay, the Home Minister–Shiv Raj Patil was replaced by the Finance Minister. Shiv Raj Patil resigned on moral grounds, a face sarving device in politics as per entries views. Recently Shashi Tharoor Minister of State External Attairs was made to quit.

(iv) He is chairman of the Cabinet. He presides over its meetings. In case of differences of opinion he can be assertive provided that he has the solid backing of the majority in the Lok Sabha and backing of the party High command.

(v) He is the coordinator of the governmental business. Coordination is brought about through committies of the cabinet. However, general supervision of the departments is to be done by him.

(vi) He is the leader of the Lok Sabha. He makes policy announcements. All baffling issues are addressed to him. He assists the speaker in maintaining order and discipline in the House.

(vii) He is the link between the President and the Council of Ministers. He is to furnish any information, the president seeks about a particular department. The President through Prime Minister can ask the entire Council of Minister to take up a matter on which an individual minister had taken a decision.

(viii) He is the spokesman of governmental policy on all matters of domestic and foreign policy. His is a decisive role in this respect. P.M., A.B. Vajpayee made historic declaration of triple nuclear explosions of Pokhran on May 11, 1998. Recently, 'India, USA Nuclear Deal' for Civil purposes made by Dr. Manmohan Singh put the very future of his government at stake as he sought vote of confidence from the Lok Sabha. Withdrawl of support by lay the Left could have led to big political crises had SSP of M. S. Yadav not come to P.M.'s rescue.

(ix) P.M. is the leader of the Nation. It is said when P.M. speaks the Nation has spoken. The words of K. R. Srinivasan about Pt. Nehru (as P.M.) are significant in this respect. " When he enters an Assembly, be it a select committee or a mass rally the effect is invariably the same. All eyes converge towards him, all hands clap in eager affectionate welcome as of a preordained tone. The men are a little out of breath. The women are almost overwhelmed" Likewise Mrs. Indira Gandhi symbolized the Nation which considered her a gleam of hope in the hour of distress. Rajiv Gandhi- a dynamic young P.M took the nation to the path of modernization and Liberalization. A. B. Vajpayee and Dr. Manmohan Singh have streered the Nation in coalitional era with great dedication and strong calibre.

(x) He makes major appointments viz. governors, ambassadors, members of UPSC etc. though in the name of the President. He can effect removals of ineffective and incapable functionaries. An appraisal of the functions and powers enumerated above reveal that the P.M. is the linchpin of the cabinet, a leader of the nation, spokesman of his party's ideology and thinking on the floor of the House and an envoy of the Nation when abroad to attend conferences or various meets. The word of first PM of India J.L.Nehru vis-a-vis C.D. Deshmukh after a tiff are revealing "I am also something after all, I am the Prime Minister of India and the Prime Minister is the Prime Minister...., the PM the is the linchpin of the Governmen."

Attorney General of India

The Attorney General, formerly known as Advocate General is the highest law officer of the Government of India. He is appointed by the President of India and holds office during the pleasure of the latter. The Constitution states that he must possess the same qualifications that are necessary for a judge of the Supreme Court. In other words, he must be a citizen of India. He must have served as a judge of some High Court for at least 5 years or as an advocate in some High Court for not less than 10 years or that he must be a distinguished jurist. He can quit his office by tendering resignation to the President as was done by G. Ramaswamy on Nov. 10, 1992 on health grounds.[1] He is removable by the President as well. He is allowed to enjoy all the privileges and immunities permissible to a member of Parliament. When he is called in the House, he occupies a seat on the Government benches.

His Functions and Powers : He is the adviser of the Government of India in such matters of legal and constitutional importance as are referred to him by the Government. He also discharges such other duties of a legal character as are assigned to him by the President from time to time.

(2) He appears on behalf of the Government in all cases including suits and appeals, before the Supreme Court or any High Court in which the Government is a party. He may be asked to appear before the court on behalf of the Parliament or its presiding officer. For example, former A.G., G. Ramaswamy represented Union Govt., in a petition against the abolition of Privy purses of rulers before the Supreme Court, and supported the 26th amendment strongly.[2]

(3) He is required to appear and represent the point of view of Government of India in matters of references made by the President to the Supreme Court for seeking its advisory opinion.

(4) He has been authorised the right of audience in all courts of India and Commissions of Enquiry. G. Ramaswamy appeared before the Verma Commission of Enquiry probing the assassination of former Prime Minister Rajiv Gandhi.[3] However, he cannot hold briefs for any party except the Government of India or some State Government or some other establishment as maintained by the Union or State Governments.

---

1. *Hindustan Times dated November 11, 1992.*
2. *Ibid, Nov. 7, 1992.*
3. *Hindustan Times dated Nov. 11, 1992.*

(5) While appearing before the Supreme Court, he has precedence over all other advocates. The Supreme Court can issue notice of any proceedings to the Attorney General and the latter also can seek an audience in any Court.

(6) He may be invited by the Speaker to speak in the House in order to give his opinion on matters of legal and constitutional importance. The members of the House may seek clarifications from him in the House but cannot cross-examine him.

(7) The Speaker may also obtain the opinion of the Attorney General on matters of legal and constitutional importance though that opinion is not binding upon the speaker.

(8) He has to advise on the competence of the Parliament to pass laws without impinging the guaranteed Fundamental Rights and without transgressing the legislative field demarcated for the States under the Federal system.

The above functions and powers of the A.G. reveal that he is the principal officer of law whose main function is to render advice to the Government of India in legal and constitutional matters and to play the role of its representative in a Court of law as was done by former A.G. in Privy purse case.[1] Unlike that of his counterpart in the U.K., he is neither the member of Council of Ministers nor accountable to the Parliament. In Pt. Nehru's times a proposal was mooted to merge this post with that of law minister but due to vehement opposition, it was shelved.

Parliament

The Central legislature comprising the President and two Houses - the Council of State (Rajya Sabha) and the House of People (Lok Sabha) constitute the Parliament. In a way, the Constitution envisages a bicameral legislature. The President is not an integral part of Parliament yet his participation in the legislative process is ensured because constitutionally he has been made a part of the Indian Parliament. Being the chief executive authority, his executive power is co-extensive with the legislative power which makes it necessary that he should become an integral part of the legislature.[2]

The Rajya Sabha (Council of State)

Article 80 states that the Council of States (Rajya Sabha) consists of (*a*) 12 members having special knowledge or practical experience in literature, science, art and social service to be nominated by the President and (*b*) representatives of the States and the Union Territories not exceeding 238. At present the Rajya Sabha is composed of 233 elected and 12 nominated members. As such, its strength is 245. It is a continuous House and is not subject to dissolution. Its tenure is 6 years, one-third of its members retiring after every two years. Election to the House is indirect. The representatives from each state are elected by the elected members of the legislative assembly of the state according to the system of proportional representation by means of a single transferable vote system. The representatives of each Union Territory are chosen in such a manner as may be prescribed by a law made by Parliament.

Article 84 states that a person to be elected to the Council of States must be a citizen of India, must have attained 30 years of age and must possess such other qualifications as may be prescribed under some law made by the Parliament. The House is not subject to dissolution. As such, each member enjoys tenure of six years.

The Vice President is the *ex-officio* Chairman of the House. The Council of States elects a Deputy Chairman from among its own members and he presides during the absence of the Chairman or when the latter acts as the President of India. The Chairman is removable from the office by a

[1]*Petition against 26th amendment filed in 1972, Report in Hindustan Times, November 7, 1992.*

[2]*C.A.D. VIII, p. 1198.*

resolution of the House provided at least 14 days notice has been given by a majority of all the then members of the Council of State and agreed by the House of the People (Lok Sabha). The Deputy Chairman is also removable in the like manner except that the resolution of his removal does not require the consent of the lower House. Their salaries are determined by Parliament and are chargeable on the Consolidated Fund of India.

Functions and Powers of Rajya Sabha

Briefly speaking, the Rajya Sabha plays only a secondary role in legislation, control over purse or the executive. Following are its functions :

(*a*) It is equipped with coordinate legislative powers with the Lok Sabha except with regard to money bills. It cannot reject the non-money bills. It can suggest amendments and delay them maximum for 6 months.

(*b*) In financial matters, its position is still weaker. Money Bills cannot be initiated in the Rajya Sabha. It can delay the money Bills maximum for 14 days. It may suggest amendments in the money Bills which may or may not be accepted by the Lok Sabha. Whether a Bill is a money Bill or not, is to be decided by the Speaker of the Lok Sabha.

(*c*) The Council of Ministers is responsible to the Lok Sabha. However, the members of the Rajya Sabha can criticise the acts of omission and commission of the Government and bring it to disrepute. Through questions and supplementary questions, they can seek information. They can move adjournment motions to discuss vital affairs concerning the State. They can move resolutions and impress upon the Government to follow a particular policy. They cannot oust the Government by passing a vote of no-confidence.

(*d*) It participates in the amendment of the Constitution. A majority of total and 2/3 of its members present and voting is required to pass an amending bill. In case of a deadlock between the two Houses over an amending Bill, a joint session of both the Houses can resolve the issue. Since the number of members in the lower House is double to that of the upper House, the point of view of the lower House generally prevails.

(*e*) Besides, the Rajya Sabha participates in the election of the President and the Vice-President.

(*f*) It possesses coordinate powers with the Lok Sabha in matters of impeachment of the President.

(*g*) Its approval is essential for the continuance of proclamation of emergency beyond two months.

(*h*) A judge of the Supreme Court or High Court is removable for misbehaviour or incapacity on an address passed by both the Houses of Parliament. However, majority of total and 2/3 of the members present and voting is needed for the purpose. Evidently it explains the role of the Rajya Sabha.

(*i*) The Vice President of India is elected by both the Houses - the Rajya Sabha and the Lok Sabha - and is removable by resolution of Rajya Sabha agreed upon by the Lok Sabha.

(*j*) The Rajya Sabha may, by a resolution passed by majority of total and 2/3 of its members, present and voting affirm that a particular subject enumerated in the State List is of national importance. Then the Parliament takes it over and can legislate on it. However such a resolution remains in force maximum for a period of one year.

(*k*) On its advice, Government of India can constitute All India Services whose members, appointed by the Union Government, would actually serve the State Government.

On the analysis of the functions and powers stated above, one may conclude that Rajya Sabha plays only a second fiddle to the Lok Sabha. It is only a revisory Chamber and serves as a drag on Lok Sabha's coach. In the words of Gopalaswamy Ayyengar, it was created "to hold dignified debates on important issues and to delay legislation which might be the outcome of the passions of the moment". Its sobering, dignifying and ennobling influence on the legislation of the country cannot be underestimated. It has played the role of 'House of Elders' fairly effectively. It could tone down radical measures like the Hindu Code Bill and defeat the 24th Constitution amending Bill (1970), and be instrumental in getting discussions on the 43rd amending Bill (1977) postponed. On March 8, 1999 the Central cabinet recommended revocation of Presidents' rule in Bihar as the BJP and its allies did not have the requisite majority in the Rajya Sabha and wanted to avoid humiliating defeat in the Upper House. This speaks of practical utility of the Rajya Sabha. In a way, it can checkmate the misuse of Article 356 if it is dominated by the opposition party and the party in power in the Lok Sabha indulges in highhandedness.

However, unlike the Senate in U.S.A., it does not serve the purpose of a second chamber in the Federal State. It does not act as the custodian of the rights of the Indian states which have not been accorded equal representation as in the case of the U.S.A. Senate. B.D. Jatti, a (former Chairman of Rajya Sabha) prophesied :

"In view of the present political setup in the country a situation may arise when the governments in a number of states may be run by political parties other than the party at the centre and this will have its impact on the Rajya Sabha. Then the Rajya Sabha will have an important role to play in handling the problem of federal government".[1] The example of revocation of President's Rule in Bihar quoted above explains the possibility of its assertive role.

The Lok Sabha (House of People)

It is the representative Chamber of the Indian Legislature. Articles 81 and 82 provide that Lok Sabha will consist of not more than 525 members directly elected by the voters in the States and not more than 20 members representing the Union Territories. If the Anglo Indian Community is not adequately represented, the President can nominate not more than 2 representatives of this community in the Lok Sabha. Each state is allotted seats in the Lok Sabha in such a manner that the ratio between that number and the population of the state is (so far as practically feasible) the same for all states. Thus States are divided into territorial constituencies in such a way that the ratio between the population of each constituency and the number of seats allotted to each state is, so far as practicable, the same throughout the state.

In General Election 2004 held in April-May there were 423 Lok Sabha constituencies for general candidates; 79 constituencies reserved for scheduled caste candidates; 41 reserved for Scheduled Tribe candidates. Thus the total seats for the Lok Sabha were 543 (elected). 67, 14, 87, 930 were the electorates in general elections Rs. 13000 millions was the expenditure incurred on the election.[2]

The 14th Lok Sabha consisted of 543 elected members out of which 44 women candidates were elected. The elections were completed completed on May 17, 2004. Two were nominated by the President to represent the Anglo-Indian Community. An amendment in the constitution in 2001 laid down that the strength of the Lok Sabha till 2025 will remain the same.

The 15th Lok Sabha Elections were held in May, 2009 in five phases. The UPA comprising Congress; Trinamool Congress; DMK; NCP; National Conference. JMM; Muslim League; V C K and Kerala Congress could win 261 seats. The NDA led by BJP comprised of BJP; JD (U); Shiv Sena; AD; AGP; RLD and TRS could win 159 seats only.

The left parties could win 24 and others 99. The Congress in its independent capacity emerged as the largest party and improved its tally by capturing 206 seats. The BJP was the next though it could win only 116 seats.[3]

[1]*The Tribune dated January 26, 1975.*
[2]*India Today 2008.*
[3]*Time of India, May 19. 2009*

Article 84 lays down that only those persons can contest election to the Lok Sabha who are citizens of India; are 25 years old or more and possess such other qualifications as are specified by the Parliament. Article 102 provides certain disqualifications which debar a person from contesting elections viz., holding an office of profit in the Government; of unsound mind; insolvent, noncitizen; otherwise disqualified by Parliament. The 52nd Amendment Act 1985 debars a person from membership of House if he defects or is expelled by the Party concerned or if an independent member forms a party after the expiration of 6 months from the date on which he took the seat in House.

However, this term during the emergency can be extended by the Parliament maximum for one year at a time and cannot be extended for more than 6 months after the emergency has ceased to exist.

Article 105 grants the members powers, privileges and immunities. It assures the members freedom of speech in Parliament and grants immunities from proceedings in the Court in respect of anything said or votes given by them in Parliament or any of its committees. They are granted similar immunities in respect of the publication by or under the authority of either House or Parliament, of any report, paper or proceedings.

The Lok Sabha is presided over by the Speaker who is elected by the House from among its own members. When the House is dissolved the speaker is not to vacate the office until immediately before the first meeting of the House. The Speaker draws such salaries and allowances as are determined by the Parliament. The same are chargeable on the Consolidated Fund of India. The Speaker is a non party man in the House though he does not get sentence of exile from politics like the British speaker. He remains a partyman outside the House. Hence the Indian speaker does not hold office for life. The maxim 'once a speaker always a speaker' applies to the British speaker and not his counterpart in India who does not cease to be a party men outside the house. In fact the objectivity and detachment exhibited by the British speaker has enabled him to become a symbol of the dignity and independence of the House as well as the guardian of the rights and privileges of the members in the true sense. However, Patil belonged to Congress (I) – the largest party. The main Opposition Party – BJP – expressed itself in favour of his candidature. Likewise, Sh. M.L. Joshi was the unanimous choice of the 13th Lok Sabha after the tragic death of Speaker Balyogi in air crash and Som Nath Chattergee of the CPM was the unanimous choice of the 14th Lok Sabha in 2002. The trend is very commendable and is in keeping with the dignity of the House. On june 3, 2009 Meira Kumar-a Dalit and daughter of Congress stalwart–Babu Jagjiwan Ram was unanimously elected as the first woman speaker of the Lok Sabha. The trend is very commendable and is in keeping with the dignity of the House.

Powers of the Speaker

The speaker is equipped with all those powers which a Presiding officer of a House is supposed to have. Briefly speaking, his powers are as follows :

(*i*) To preside over the House; (*ii*) to determine the order of the business; (*iii*) to decide the admissibility of questions and disallow questions not conforming to rules; (*iv*) to allocate time for discussion; (*v*) to accord consent to a motion of adjournment; (*vi*) to appoint a Chairman of Selection Committee; (*vii*) to put a motion to vote; (*viii*) to maintain discipline and decorum in the House; (*ix*) to recognise the members; (*x*) to decide points of order. (*xi*) to expel a member from the House; (*xii*) to act as guardian of the privileges of the members of the House; (*xiii*) to shield the House against the encroachments of the Government; (*xiv*) to act as the *ex-officio* Chairman of some of the committees of the House such as Rules Committee; (*xv*) to certify whether a Bill is a money Bill or not; (*xvi*) to adjourn the House if there is no quorum; (*xvii*) to control the secretariat of the House; (*xviii*) to refuse to accept the resignation of a member of the House in case he finds its submission under duress.[1] M.N. Kaul ex-secretary Lok Sabha well summed up the position and powers of the Speaker, "*Such is the important position which the speaker holds and although normally he just presides, watches and controls the debates in any crisis, his powers which have a political significance, come into being. The two powers which we think of every day importance are very vital : one is the power to admit notices of questions, amendments, actions etc.....and the other is to enforce strictly the rules of procedure which are a guarantee for the minority......All these seem normal things but it is in a crisis that the power of the speaker and his influence on the Parliament is really gathered up*".[2] S. N. Chatterjee played very dignified and balanced role during vote of confidence for UPA government over Indo-USA Nuclear issue for civil purposes. He maintained dignity of the chair by refusing to follow the dictate of his party at the risk of his age old links with the party.

Powers of Lok Sabha (Functions)

The word 'function' is a large word and comprises both powers and duties.[3] Lok Sabha is the real legislature. Its powers can be summarised as legislative, financial, electoral, executive, and miscellaneous.

Legislative

It is authorised to make laws on 99 subjects in the Union List, 52 subjects in the concurrent list; and 61 subjects in the State list and, also residual matters, not covered by the three lists. It can also make laws on the state subjects if the Rajya Sabha considers them of national interest.[4] Legislatures of two or three states can also pass a resolution that the Parliament should make a law on a specific matter in the State List. During emergencies also, Parliament can make laws for the entire country or any particular state where the central rule is imposed under article 356.

Financial

The Lok Sabha passes the budget. Rajya Sabha can delay a money Bill only for 14 days. Money Bills can be initiated only in the Lok Sabha. Lok Sabha has the exclusive privilege of authorising expenditure. The demands for grants are submitted to the Lok Sabha.

Electoral

Article 54 vests electoral functions with the Parliament. Both the Houses participate in the election of the President and the Vice President. Since the strength of the Lok Sabha is double to that of the Rajya Sabha, the importance of the Lok Sabha in these elections is self evident.

Executive

According to Article 75(3) the Council of Ministers is collectively responsible to the Lok Sabha. A vote of no confidence in the Lok Sabha, against the Council of Ministers leads to its resignation. The Houses can reject the Bills introduced by the Government. The Ministers in charge of various departments can be interrogated and censured by the members of the House. Through questions, supplementary questions, and adjournment motions on questions of vital importances, the Government can be taken to task on the floor of the House.

Miscellaneous

(*i*) It participates in the impeachment of the President. (*ii*) It can move for the removal of

---

[1] *33rd Amendment Act 1973.*

[2] *The Hindustan Times Weekly, February 7, 1954.*

[3] *CAD Volume IX, p. 1122.*

[4] *Referedin powers of Rajya Sabha.*

judges of Supreme Court and High Courts through a process of Impeachment (*iii*) It participates in the amendment of the Constitution. (*iv*) Proclamation of emergency is subject to approval by the Lok Sabha (along with Rajya Sabha). (*v*) The House serves as a mirror of public opinion and a sort of public forum. (*vi*) It can take preventive actions against the members and the outsiders who impair dignity of the House and indulge in breach of privileges of the House. In 1978, Mrs. Indira Gandhi was expelled from the House for breach of privileges. The resolution of expulsion was rescinded on May 7, 1981. Keeping in view these functions of Lok Sabha, Dr. M.P. Sharma remarks, "If the Parliament is the supreme organ of the State, the Lok Sabha is the supreme organ of its Parliament. In fact for all practical purposes it is the parliament".[1]

Though Parliament of India exercises vast control over legislation, holds purse strings, an oust the council of ministers, possesses electoral and other miscellaneous powers, 'yet it is not considered a sovereign legislature as is the case with the British Parliament. The laws passed by the Indian Parliament can be declared null and void by the Apex Court if the judges find them violating the constitution. That is not the case with the British Parliament. Judiciary cannot put such curbs on its sovereign authority.

Legislative Procedure

As the Constitution lays down only broad outlines of legislative procedure, each House of Parliament has framed its own rules of procedure in details. Article 107 provides that, subject to the provisions in Articles 109 and 117, dealing with money Bills and other financial Bills, a Bill may be introduced in either House of Parliament. Article 109 lays down that a money Bill should not be introduced in the Rajya Sabha and after having passed a money Bill the Lok Sabha will transmit it to the Rajya Sabha for its recommendations. The latter shall within 14 days from the date of receipt of the Bill return the same with its recommendations to the Lok Sabha. The Lok Sabha may either accept or reject all or any of the recommendations made by the Rajya Sabha. If the Rajya Sabha fails to return the Bill within 14 days, it will be deemed to have been passed by both the Houses at the expiry of 14 days and the Bill is then sent to the President for his formal assent which is a foregone conclusion.

A Bill other than a money Bill is also to be passed by both the Houses of Parliament. If a Bill which has been passed by one House, say the lower, and transmitted to the other House is rejected or the amendments suggested are disagreed with or more than six months have elapsed from the date of the receipt of the Bill by the other House (say Rajya Sabha), without passing it, the President may summon a joint session of both the Houses to resolve the deadlock between both the Houses. This procedure is, however, not applicable to a money Bill. While reckoning the period of 6 months, no account is to be taken of the period for which the House remains prorogued or adjourned for more than 4 consecutive days. If at the joint sitting, the Bill is passed by a majority of the total members present and voting, it will be deemed to have been passed by both the Houses. In joint sittings, the Lok Sabha is apt to have upperhand because of its double strength. When a Bill is passed by both the Houses it is placed before the President who may accord his consent or return it. If it is not money Bill the President can send it to the Houses for reconsideration. The Bill so returned will be reconsidered by the Houses and if it is passed again by the Houses with or without the amendments and presented to the President for his assent, the President shall not withhold his assent.[2]

It may also be pointed out that the procedure in the case of Private Members Bill is the same as the Government Bills except for some special features, viz., notice for leave to introduce the Bill must be accompanied by a statement of objects and reasons; the recommendation and sanction of the President for the consideration or introduction of the Bill memoranda, the financial repercussions

[1] *Dr. M.P. sharma: op. cit. p 166.*
[2] *Article. III*

of the Bill. A notice may be disallowed if it is incomplete in any respect or the Bill is otherwise defective. The Speaker can disallow notice of a Bill if he feels that it is not proper to include it in the list of Business. There is a Committee on Private Members Bill which consists of not more than 15 members nominated by the Speaker. The Chairman also is appointed by the Speaker from among its members.

A legislative bill is required to be read three times in each House before it can be deemed to have been passed by the Parliament. An ordinary bill may be introduced by a minister or a private member. In the former case, it is termed as Government Bill and in the latter case, it is categorised as a Private Members Bill. A Government Bill and a Private Members Bill has to undergo an identical procedure. The three Readings of a Bill actually involve four stages. The first Reading means 'Motion to introduce the Bill and on its adoption, the Bill is deemed to have been introduced. The second Reading has two stages. In the first stage, discussions on principles of the Bill and its provisions take place. At the second stage, clause by clause, discussion and consideration of the Bill as reported by a Select or Joint Committee takes place. The third Reading is a formal affair. It refers to discussion on the motion that the Bill be passed.

The Bill is then referred to the other House for its concurrence. If the receiving House passes the Bill in the same form in which it came from the House of its origin, it is presented to the President for his assent. The President may give his assent, withhold it or send the Bill back for reconsideration. In the latter case, if the Bill is again passed by the two Houses with or without amendments, it is again presented to the President for his assent which can no longer be withheld and the Bill becomes a law.

If the Bill passed by one House is amended by the other, the Bill is sent back to the House where it originated. In case of persistence of disagreement, the President calls a joint session and the vote is taken. Joint session is convened when a Bill is rejected by the other House or if more than six months elapse from the date of the receipt of the Bill by the other House without the Bill being passed by it.

THE UNION JUDICIARY

The Constitution of India provides for the Supreme Court at the apex of the judicial hierarchy. The Constitution does not fix up the number of judges. Hence in the beginning it consisted of a Chief Justice and 7 other judges raised to 10 in 1956 to 13 in 1960, to 17 in 1977 and to 25 in May 9, 1986. Thus at present it consists of a Chief Justice and 25 other judges. They are to be appointed by the President. They hold office until they attain the age of 65 years. Article 124(3) states that a person shall not be qualified for appointment as a judge unless he is a citizen of India and has been a judge of High Court or two or more of such courts in succession for at least 10 years, or in the opinion of the President is a distinguished jurist. According to Articles 127 (1) and 128 of the Constitution; a judge of a High Court can be appointed as *ad hoc* judge of the Supreme Court. Likewise, retired judges of the Supreme Court and High Courts can act as judges of the Supreme Court.

Their independence has been assured by Article 124(4). A judge, according to it, is not removable from office except by an order of the President passed, after an address by each House of the Parliament duly supported by a majority of the total membership of the House and by a majority of not less than 2/3 of the members present and voting, is presented to the President. Such a removal can be asked for, on grounds of proved misbehaviour or incapacity.

Jurisdiction

Briefly speaking, the Supreme Court has original, appellate and advisory jurisdiction.

The original jurisdiction of the Court covers any dispute between the Centre and any state or states on one side and one or more states on the other or between two or more states.

Article 32 empowers it to issue directions or orders or writs including writs in the nature of *habeas corpus, mandamus, prohibition, quo warranto and certiorari* to enforce the Fundamental Rights. K. Suba Rao, former Chief Justice once remarked, "*It had already salvaged some freedom and I hope and trust that it will salvage more in the near future*".[1] The Supreme Court has served as palladium of Fundamental Rights and custodian of Indian Constitution.

Appellate

The appellate jurisdiction can be divided into four categories of cases, viz. Civil, Criminal, Constitutional and Special.

In civil matters, prior to the 30th Constitution amending Act 1972, appeal could lie to the Supreme Court if the High Court certified that any of the three conditions were satisfied - (*i*) the amount or value of the subject matter of dispute is not less than Rs. 20,000. The 30th amendment Act 1972 which imposed a limit on cash or value of property regarding which appeal was to be carried to the Supreme Court, has since been removed;

(*ii*) the judgement, decree or final order involving directly or indirectly some claim or question respecting the property of the value of Rs. 20,000 **(No limit is there since 1972)**.

(*iii*) the case is fit for appeal to the Supreme Court irrespective of value.

As regards criminal cases there are two modes of appeals, viz.,

(*i*) If the High Court has reversed an order of acquittal of an accused and sentenced him to death.

(*ii*) If the High Court has withdrawn for trial before itself any case from any court subordinate to its authority and has in such a trial convicted the accused person and sentenced him to death. Secondly, an appeal lies to the Supreme Court from a decision of High Court in criminal proceedings if the High Court certifies that the case is a fit one for appeal to the Supreme Court.

According to Article 132(1) an appeal shall lie to the Supreme Court from any judgment, decree or final order of a High Court, whether in a Civil, Criminal or other proceedings, if the High Court certifies that the case involves a substantial question of law as to the interpretation of the Constitution. If the High Court refuses to give such a certificate, the Supreme Court can grant special leave to appeal if the Court is satisfied that the case involves a substantial question of law as to the interpretation of the Constitution.

Special Appeals

Article 136 states, "Notwithstanding anything in this chapter, the Supreme Court may in its discretion grant special leave to appeal from any judgment, decree, sentence or order in any tribunal in the territory of India. The only exception to this all embracing judicial review is the decisions of Courts constituted under any law relating to Armed Forces. In the words of D.D. Basu, "*It vests in the Supreme Court a plenary jurisdiction in the matter of entertaining and hearing appeals by granting special leave against any kind of judgment or order made by any Court or Tribunal (except a Military Tribunal) in any proceedings and the exercise of this power is left entirely to the discretion of the Supreme Court, unfettered by any restriction and this power cannot be curtailed by any legislation short of amending the article itself*".[2]

Advisory Jurisdiction

According to Article 143(1) the President is empowered to refer to the Supreme Court any question of law or act of public importance. There is no constitutional compulsion for the Court to give its advice. In 1978 for example, Chief Justice Chandrachud on the Special Courts Bill opined that it was not binding on the Supreme Court to give its opinion if, "we come to the conclusion that we cannot answer". The advice of the Supreme Court is, however, not binding on the President. Referring to the importance of this jurisdiction, Pylee remarks, "Advisory opinions are a help to preventing litigation or reducing it to a considerable extent".[3] In the recent past, under Article 143(1)

[1] *K. Subha Rao delivering setalvad lecture at Bombay 'University'*
[2] *Basu D.D. : An introduction to the Constitution of India p. 232.*
[3] *Pylee : M.V. : Constitutional Government of India p. 439*

the President made a reference to the Supreme Court for an opinion on the question whether any Hindu temple existed prior to the construction of Ram Janam Bhoomi and Babri Masjid. In the recent past, former President K.R. Narayanan sought clarification on consultation process as laid down in a 1993 judgment for appointment and transfer of judges following an *impasse* over the recommendations by a former Chief Justice (M.M. Punchi)[1].

To quote a few more examples of recent past – on October 24, 1994 the supreme court returned to the President the reference made to it whether Ram temple actually existed at the place where Babrimasjid was built. Such a presidential reference was considered by the apex court as unnecessary and superfluous. Again on July 22, 2004 on the Sutlej Yamuna link canal construction matter, the Central Government through president sought Supreme Courts' opinion whether or not – (1) The Punjab Termination of Agreement Act 2004 was constitutionally valid and whether or not it affects the agreement on sharing of the waters of the Ravi, Bease and Sutlej among Punjab, Haryana, Rajasthan and Himachal Pradesh. The opinions of the court in the above cases amply prove the beneficient result of the advisory jurisdiction M.V. Pylee holds "... *Advisory opinions are a help to prevent litigation or reduce it to a considerable extent.*"

A Court of Record

Article 129 makes the Supreme Court a Court of Record as well. The records of such a court are retained for perpetual value and testimony. Its power to punish for contempt follows from it. In the words of Dr. Ambedkar, *"the Court of Record is a Court the records of which are admitted to be of evidentiary value and they are not to be questioned when they are produced before any Court. As a matter of fact, the power to punish for contempt necessarily follows from that position".*[2]

Custodian of the Constitution

The Constitution of India is more akin to the American Constitution in this respect. The Supreme Court enjoys unique position in this respect. It is competent to exercise the power of reviewing legislative enactments. Thus it makes the court a powerful instrument of Judicial Review. In the words of Justice B.K. Mukherjee..... "In India, it is the Constitution that is supreme and Parliament as well as state legislature must not only act within the limits of their respective spheres as demarcated in the three lists....Part III of the Constitution guarantees to the citizens certain Fundamental Rights which the legislative authority can on no account transgress. A state law to be valid must in all cases be in conformity with the constitutional requirements and it is for the judiciary to decide whether any enactment is unconstitutional or not". Exercising its power of judicial review, the Supreme Court struck down Bank Nationalization legislation and privy purses abolition order passed by the President and upheld 25th amendment Act establishing precedence of Directive Principles pertaining to Socialism over the Fundamental Rights. Though the scope of judicial review in India is not as wide as in the U.S.A., yet it is more than enough to consider the Supreme Court as a powerful agency to control the activities of both the legislature and the executive. Chief Justice Kania rightly prophesied, "*....Within the limits prescribed, we are quite sure that the Supreme Court will be able to make a substantial contribution towards the formation of India into a great country retaining its own civilization, traditions and customs......*"

Comptroller and Auditor General

Article 148 refers to the appointment and conditions of service of the Comptroller and Auditor General who is to act as financial watchdog of the Parliament over the expenditure of public money.

---

[1]*Hindustan Times: October 29, 1998*

[2]*C.A.D. Volume VII, p. 352.*

He is appointed by the President for a period of 6 years. The Constitution is silent about his qualifications. In fact such a person is recommended to him by the Cabinet. He may quit his office any time by tendering resignation to the President or he may be removed by the President in case a special address is passed by each House of Parliament by special majority (absolute majority of the whole House and 2/3 of members present and voting) on the grounds of proved misbehaviour or incapacity. His salary and other conditions of service are determined by Parliament and are not variable to his disadvantage after the appointment. The administrative expenses of the office of the Auditor General including salaries, allowances and pensions payable to persons serving in his office are chargeable on the consolidated fund of India.

His functions

The following are the functions of the Comptroller and Auditor General:

(*i*) To perform such duties and exercise such powers in relation to the Accounts of the Union and the State Government as defined in an act of Parliament or in the absence of any such legislation as entrusted to him by the Government of India Audit and Accounts Order of 1936. Surprisingly, the Parliament has so far passed no such legislation.

(*ii*) To examine the accounts of the Union Government and submit a report to the President and in case of State Governments to submit such a report to the Governor.

(*iii*) To assist the Public Accounts Committee (PAC) by detecting the points of question in accounts and leaving it to the former to pursue the matter as it deems fit.

(*iv*) To submit his report to the Public Accounts Committee regarding the factual verification of matters if a case is so referred to him by the ministry concerned and to attend the meeting of PAC when it sits to finalize its report.

(*v*) To assist the Committee on Public undertakings in pursuing such matters as have been raised in the audit reports.

(*vi*) To furnish any information sought for, to either House of Parliament through Public Accounts Committee.

(*vii*) To exercise administrative control over the offices of the Auditors working in State capitals and in pursuance thereof to prescribe the form and the manner in which these accounts are to be prepared and maintained.

An analysis of these powers reveals that he has hardly anything to perform by virtue of being the Comptroller of India. He does not possess power to control the receipts and issue of public funds and his jurisdiction commences after the incurring of the expenditure. However, as Auditor General he is the custodian of public revenues. Dr. Pattabhi Sitaramayya describes him, **"supreme arbiter of India's Finances"**.

Chief Election Commissioner

The Constitution provides for an independent agency termed as Election Commission which is vested with the power of superintendence, direction and control of preparation of electoral rolls required for the conduct of all elections to the Parliament, the State legislatures, and the elections to the offices of the President and the Vice President. Its chairman is designated as the Chief Election Commissioner who is appointed by the President subject to the provisions of law made by the Parliament. He holds office during the pleasure of the President. He can tender his resignation to the President. He is removable by the President in case a special address charging him with proved misbehaviour or incapacity is passed by each House of Parliament with absolute majority as well as with 2/3 majority of the members present and voting. His emoluments and conditions of service are not variable to his disadvantage during the term of his service. His functions are as follows :

(*i*) To get the electoral rolls for the election to the Parliament and all state legislatures including local bodies prepared and revised subject to the provisions of the Constitution.

(*ii*) To exercise superintendence, direction and control over all matters pertaining to the elections of the President, Vice President, Parliament and State Legislatures.

(*iii*) To advise the President and Governors regarding the incurring of disqualifications by a member of the Union and State legislatures subsequent to his elections.

(*iv*) To appoint election officers for enquiring into the doubts and disputes arising out of or connected with the election arrangements.

(*v*) To advise the President to appoint regional election commissioners.

(*vi*) To requisition from the President such staff as he may deem essential for the conduct of elections.

(*vii*) To settle disputes regarding allotment of symbols to the parties at the time of elections.

(*viii*) To reserve the right to prepare or restore for Central broadcasts and telecasts allocating particular days and time to particular parties.

(*ix*) To order for rectification of a clerical mistake made by the Delimitation Commission with the prior approval of this authority.

(*x*) To visit the disturbed areas and make appeals through the mass communication media to pacify the people asking for the rectification of electoral records or procedures.

(*xi*) To waive the conditions of not holding an election until the electoral rolls are revised and order re-poll in exceptional situations.

(*xii*) To exempt a person from the disqualifications imposed by a judicial decision.

(*xiii*) The most important function of the CEC is to see that the elections are conducted in fair and peaceful manner.

(*xiv*) To see to the rigid following of ceiling on the election expenses. Even the revision of this ceiling can be sought from the government through him.

(*xv*) To see to the avoidance of impersonation cases, the introduction of identity cards to the voters was the idea emanating from the mind of TN. Seshan.

(*xvi*) President of India is to seek the advice of the CEC and EC if the question of disqualification of a member of Parliament crops up Invariably, the advice is accepted. At the state level the Governor has to seek such advice.

The functions mentioned above reflect that the CEC and his team play a vital role in the conduct of General Election. J.M. Lyngdoh a former CEC was awarded Ramon Magsaysay Award in 2003 for 'convincing validation of free and fair elections as the foundation and best hope of secular democracy in India. This prestigious award is the Asian version of Noble Prize of the year. Mr. Naveen Chawla is the CEC at present.

Thus we can conclude that the Chief Election Commissioner holds an independent office charged with the onerous task of holding free and fair elections in the country. In the early stages, some members of the Assembly had expressed apprehensions regarding exercise of political influence on his appointment. It is however, a matter of satisfaction that men of unquestionable integrity and highest judicial probity have been appointed to this office and as such, "various apprehensions regarding political influences creeping in the appointment of the Chief Election Commissioner have also been belied in practice".[1] During his tenure as Chief Election Commissioner (CEC), T.N. Seshan, created history as very effective CEC. He succeeded in introducing drastic reforms in the electoral

[1] *R.P. Bhalla: Elections in India, p.9.*

practices during the General Elections and ushering in era of congeniality before, during and after General Elections. J.M. Lyngdoh followed the footsteps of his predecessor to a great extent. Peaceful conduct of elections in J & K and Gujrat during his tunure speak volumes about his calibre as CEC.

Presently also the Election Commission has done wonders in holding elections fair and peaceful in J & K in December 2008. Despite the terrorists threat of boycott of election the turn out in election was over 60 per cent which has opened the eyes of the disruptionists. The general Lok Sabha election held in May 2009 have also been conducted peacefully.

Special Officer for Scheduled Castes and Scheduled Tribes

Article 138 provides for a Special Officer for Scheduled Castes and Scheduled Tribes. He is appointed by the President to investigate all matters concerning safeguards provided for these communities under the Constitution in the fields of their representation in the legislatures and services. He is designated as the Commissioner for Scheduled Castes. He is assisted by ten assistant commissioners each in charge of a region. The Commissioner submits annual report to the President which is laid before both the Houses of the Parliament. The Report throws light on the all-round augumentation of the tempo of work pertaining to the Welfare of the Scheduled Castes, Scheduled Tribes and Backward classes, in the social, educational, economic, and political spheres. Originally the reservation was made for 10 years though the period had been extended four times. Special funds for their allround development have been earmarked. The Commissioner also looks into matters relating to the registering of progress under various schemes.

Commission for Backward Classes

Article 340 empowers the President to appoint a Commission consisting of such persons as he deems fit to investigate the conditions of socially and educationally backward classes of India and the problems they are confronted with. Thereafter, it makes recommendations regarding the steps to be taken by the Union or the State Government for mitigating their grievances and ameliorating their lot. It also recommends the grants for the purpose to be sanctioned both by the Union and the State Governments. It lays down the conditions subject to which such grants are to be made. The Commission shall investigate into those matters as are referred to it and present to the President its report. The report along with a memorandum explaining the action taken thereon is to be laid before both the Houses of Parliament by the President.

Tribes Advisory Council

A Tribes Advisory Council is to be setup in each state, having Scheduled Areas and in those states which have Scheduled Tribes but not Scheduled Areas. Such a Council is to consist of not more than 20 members of whom about 3/4 are to be representatives of the Scheduled Tribes in the Legislative Assembly of the State concerned. If the number of representatives of the Scheduled Tribes in the Legislative Assembly has been less than the number of seats in the Tribes Advisory Council to be filled by such representatives, the remaining seats should be filled up from amongst the other members of those Tribes in the State. The Advisory Council advises on such matters pertaining to the welfare and advancement of the Scheduled Tribes as are referred to it by the Governor of the State. The Governor is authorised to make rules, prescribe the number of members, mode of appointing members and the Chairman as well as the officers and servants of the Council, the conduct of its meetings and procedure and like matters.

STATE GOVERNMENT IN BRIEF

State Executive

The Governor is the formal head of the State and the real executive powers are exercised by the Chief Minister and the Council of Ministers. Article 163 provides a Council of Ministers to aid and advise the Governor in discharging the functions. According to Article 164, the Chief Minister is to be appointed by the Governor and the other ministers are appointed by him on the advice of the Chief Minister. The Governor is apt to call the leader of the majority party to form the Government. Since our's is a parliamentary government, the Council of Ministers as per Article 164(2) are collectively responsible to the lower House i.e. the Legislative Assembly of the State. Thus the lower House and not the Governor can oust the Council of Ministers. In the coalitional era, i.e. after 1967 the Governors have been playing very effective, though at times demoralizing, role in the State politics. They have been making full use of discretionary powers in ousting a particular coalition Government on the directions of their political mentors — the Central Government. The position and powers of the Chief Minister are analogous to the Prime Minister at the Centre.[1]

State Legislature

The Constitution provides for legislature for every State in the Union. The legislature of each State is to consist of the Governor and the House or Houses of the State concerned. In some of the states, the legislature is bicameral, i.e. have two Houses viz., Legislative Assembly and Legislative Council. Article 169 provides for the abolition and creation of second chambers. The State Legislative Assembly can pass a resolution by a 2/3rd majority of the votes of the members present and voting and by a majority of its total membership asking Parliament to enact a law for the abolition and creation of a Legislative Council. It is not to be deemed as an amendment of the Constitution.

The strength of the Legislative Council is not to exceed 1/4th of the members of the Assembly. It is not to be less than 40 in any case. Broadly speaking 5/6th of the members of the Council are to be indirectly elected and 1/6th are to be nominated by the Governor. Its composition is as follows :

(*i*) 1/3rd are to be elected by the members of Legislative Assembly (Vidhan Sabha) from amongst persons who are not its members.

(*ii*) 1/3rd are to be elected by the local bodies of the State.

(*iii*) 1/12th are to be elected by the graduates of 3 years standing.

(*iv*) 1/12th are to be elected by the teachers of 3 years standing in secondary school and above.

(*v*) The remainder i.e. 1/16th are to be nominated by the Governor from among persons having knowledge and/or practical experience in respect of such matters such as Literature, Science, Art, Cooperative Movement and Social Service.

As regards their qualifications, a member of the Legislative Council (Vidhan Parishad) must be a citizen of India; must not be less than 30 years of age, must possess such other qualifications as may be prescribed by the State Legislature. The Council is not subject to dissolution but 1/3rd of its members retire after every two years. Its tenure is 6 years like that of the Rajya Sabha. The Council is presided over by the Chairman elected by its members.

There were only ten legislative councils to begin with. Gradually Punjab, West Bengal, Andhra Pradesh, Tamil Nadu (formerly Madras) abolished Councils. Madhya Pradesh abolished it but decided to re-establish it. The Punjab Government has been again contemplating to revive it. The growing disillusionment with the Legislative Councils resulting into their abolition reflects that the Councils

[1]*See details in chapter V.*

are either not popular or their utility has been minimal. In fact, they are considered *'Rolls Royce institutions in a bullock cart country'*. They have been portrayed as ornamental superfluities by the critics. They do not serve useful purposes even as revisory chambers. Neither they control the purse nor they can put a curb on the autocratic tendencies of the Executives. Hence, they have been acting more or less as ditto chambers, as they can detain a non money Bill maximum for a period of four months. As such, time is not far off when the remaining states may also abolish them and save a big drain on the state exchequer.

Legislative Assembly

The Vidhan Sabha of each State consists of not more than 500 and not less than 60 members according to its population. They are elected directly on the basis of adult suffrage. Article 332 provides for reservation of seats in the Assembly for the Scheduled Castes and Tribes on population basis. Article 333 empowers the Governor to nominate to the assembly Anglo Indians, in case the community is not adequately represented.

The term of the Assembly is 5 years. The Amendment Act of 1976 (42nd) extended the tenure to six years which was again reduced to five years by the 44th amendment Act. During the proclamation of emergency, the life of the Assembly can be prolonged for one year at a time but in no case beyond six months after the proclamation ceases to operate. The qualifications and disqualification for an MLA are the same as in the case of Lok Sabha. Each Assembly has a speaker elected by its members immediately after elections. The position and powers of the speaker are analogous to its counterpart at the Centre.

The Legislative Assembly is virtually the state legislature even where the Legislative Council exists. The latter can delay a money Bill for 14 days and non money Bills maximum for four months. It is the Assembly which controls the executive and also the purse. It participates in the election of the President of India and also amendment of the Constitution.

On account of numerous limitations, the state legislatures are not sovereign entities. They work as vassal legislatures under the over lordship of the Parliament of India. Certain Bills cannot be moved in the state legislature without the previous sanction of the President. Certain Bills are invalid unless they receive the President's assent after having been reserved for President's consideration. During emergency, Parliament can make laws regarding subjects included in the State List. Regarding concurrent subjects, the will of the Parliament prevails. Rajya Sabha by a resolution can declare a particular state subject as of national interest. In such case, the parliament will make laws on the state subject though for a period of one year. The financial autonomy of the state is also limited. Unlike Government of India, it cannot borrow outside the territory of India without the consent of the Union Government.

State Judiciary

The High Court stands at the apex of the State judicial organisation. The Constitution establishes a High Court in each of the constituent states. The parliament is empowered to establish a common High Court for two or more states. Each High Court consists of a Chief Justice and such other judges as the President may from time to time determine. The President appoints the Chief Justice of a High Court after consultation with the Chief Justice of India and the Governor of the State concerned. While appointing a judge, the president consults even the Chief Justice of the High Court concerned. A person may not be qualified for appointment as a judge of the High Court unless he is a citizen of India and has held a judicial office for at least 10 years or has served as an advocate for at least 10 years in one or more High Courts. The Act of 1976 (42nd amendment) further added to the qualifications. A distinguished jurist; one who has been a member of Administrative Tribunal, and one who has held a government post requiring special knowledge of law can also be appointed as judges. A judge is to hold office till the age of 62 years. The Union Law Minister is toying with the idea of raising it to 65 years. He is removable by process of impeachment – the way a judge of the Supreme Court is removed. Their salaries and allowances are not variable to their disadvantage after their appointment and are chargeable on the Consolidated Fund of India.

The Constitution does not provide for the original jurisdiction of the High Courts. The present jurisdiction of the High Courts is governed by the letters, patents and Central and Provincial Acts. Civil and Criminal jurisdiction of the High Court is mainly governed by the civil and criminal procedure codes. The High Courts of three Presidency towns of Calcutta, Bombay and Madras possess an original jurisdiction – both in civil and criminal cases arising within the Presidency towns. The rest of the High Courts possess original jurisdiction in matters of admiralty, probate, matrimonial and contempt of court cases only. The appellate jurisdiction of the High Court extends to both civil and criminal cases. Its power of superintendence extends to all courts and tribunals throughout the territory. Article 226 vests all High Courts with the power of issuing prerogative writs and orders, directions and writs for the enforcement of Fundamental Rights. It can take over cases from subordinate courts regarding the interpretation of the Constitution. Article 229 empowers the Chief Justice to appoint its other officers and servants. It is a Court of Record as well. As such it is equipped with all the powers of such a court. It will not be out of place to point out that 42nd amendment 1976 had deprived the High Court of the power of deciding the constitutional validity of a central law. However, this power was restored to it by the 44th amendment Act passed in 1978. Further, the parliament has extended the jurisdictional competence of the High Courts by enlarging the original jurisdiction in matters of revenue or its collection and also empowering it to issue writs not only for the protection of Fundamental Rights but also for other purposes. They can now settle disputes relating to election of members to the Union and State Legislatures.

(B) INDIAN FEDERATION

The Republic of India is a 'Union of States'. The word Federation is conspicuous by its absence. Perhaps the word 'union' was intended to connote a higher degree of integration. In the words of Dr. B.R. Ambedkar,..... "the committee has used the term Union instead of Federation but the Committee has preferred to follow the language of the preamble to the British North America Act 1867 and considered that there are advantages in describing India as a Union although its constitution may be federal in structure. In fact, the framers of our constitution were governed by the experiences of American and Australian constitutions. The good points of these Federations were owned and the lacunae avoided".

Besides, the Fathers of the Indian Constitution were fully conscious of their grim past. India had always been a plaything in the hands of alien invaders because of internal bickerings, mutual antagonism and perpetual animosities among its rulers and ever prevalent fissiparous tendencies. Absence of a strong centre had been the cause of jeopardization of India's independence by the Muslim invaders and later British rulers. Hence, the framers of the Constitution did not like history to repeat itself. They were keen to give autonomy to the units to the extent practically feasible, but not at the cost of a strong centre which alone could hold the union strong. The existence of a strong centre is hardly inconsistent with the theory and practice of Federalism. We had to evolve our own pattern of Centre-State relations in the light of India's historical background and its political and social conditions. Besides India's hoary past, the aftermath of independence was also not roseate. Partition had brought in its wake untold misery and sufferings on account of communal riots. The drama of barbarism and carnage was enacted on the soils of India and Pakistan. The seeds of communalism had been firmly sown. Feuds and fights in the name of religion or language could be envisaged in future as well. Besides, the Independence Act had conferred option on the Indian states to join either India or Pakistan or remain independent. It was a vicious parting kick by the Britishers to keep Indian house divided against itself. The states could choose to remain independent and not integrate with India. Hyderabad, Junagarh and Kashmir posed a problem. Thus, our newly independent country was faced with grave problem of possible disintegration. In these stirring circumstances, the Union Government could not, in fact have kept the Centre weak. The Draft Constitution took note of these tendencies. It did not like to leave it to the Supreme Court to strengthen the Centre by a process of judicial interpretation. In the words of Ashok Chandra, *"The divergence between the provisions of the Indian Constitution and the other Federal Constitutions have their origin in many complexes, including those arising out of partition and the inclination of the Indian mind to break away from tradition."*[1] Dr. Ivor Jennings opined, "India has a Federation with a strong centralising tendency"[2] Dr. Munshi, a distinguished jurist, described our Constitution, "a quasi-federal union invested with several important features of a unitary government".[3] D.D. Basu a critic of the Indian Constitution remarks, "The Constitution of India is neither purely federal nor unitary but is a combination of both. It is a union or composite of novel type". Really Indian Federation is a federation with unitary bias. We may call it a 'Quasi-Federal'. We analyse below the federal features and centralising tendencies inherent in the Indian Constitution.

Federal features

Indian Federation is a stable union of former princely states and British Indian provinces which have lost neither their entity nor claim for more autonomy. Its federal features are : A dual polity; rigidity and supremacy of Constitution; provision of an independent judiciary for settling disputes between the Centre and the States. A brief explanation of these elements of Indian Federation is as follows :

(a) A Dual Polity

Under a federal system, the Centre and States possess autonomous powers within their respective spheres of functioning. The powers are as such distributed under the Constitution There are three distinct lists - Union, State and Concurrent as per Article 246 of the Constitution. The Union List presently contains 99 items (though formerly 97) and the Union Government alone is competent to make laws on them. The State list comprises 66 items though the number was reduced to 61 following the 7th and 42nd amendments. The state legislature can make laws on these subjects. In the concurrent list 52 subjects (though formerly 47) are included. Both the Parliament and the State legislatures are empowered to make laws on them. However, in case of a conflict between the Parliament and the State legislature over a concurrent subject, the will of the Parliament prevails. Thus a dual polity exists in clear cut terms.

(b) Rigidity and Supremacy of the Constitution

The Constitution is both written and rigid. Most of its clauses and articles are not easily amendable. Absolute majority of total and 2/3rd of the members present and voting is required to effect amendments. Some of the specified and comparatively more important matters require majority of half of the state legislatures as well besides the above quoted majorities of the Parliament. This reflects excessive rigidity of our Constitution. However, it is contended by the critics that its rigidity cannot be matched with that of the American Constitution. Ninety three[4] amendments have taken place in the Indian constitution which reflects it, is not too rigid.

The supremacy of Constitution is the hallmark of the Indian Federation. The provisions of the Constitution are binding on both the governments. Neither the Union, nor the State government can contravene them. Neither of the governments can alter the distribution of powers as earmarked in the Constitution. This can be done only through an amendment procedure which is quite cumbersome.

---

[1] *Ashok Chandra : Federation in India p.37*

[2] *Ivor Jennings: Some Characteristics of the Indian Constitution (1953) P. I*

[3] *K.M. Munshi : The President under the New Constitution, (1967), p. 1.*

[4] *India 2008 : Govt of India, Publication Division p. 38-52*

(c) Independence of Judiciary

Another pre-requisite of a federation - independence of judiciary – is also ingrained in our Constitution. The Supreme Court is an independent and impartial body on whom the states can count for an impartial interpretation of the Constitution and vindication of their position. "To this extent our constitution is more federal than that of Switzerland or Russia".[1]

A.B. Keith adds two more tests of federalism : (*i*) the right of units to frame their own Constitutions (*ii*) their right to define the privileges of their legislators. India does not fulfil the first additional test though it does meet the second. However, it is not known whether a state legislature could define its privileges in contravention of a law of the Parliament.

Dr. V.K. Rao emphasises that a federation should opt for double citizenship. In his words, "By far a greater test is whether the states as units have their own citizens apart from mere residents on whom state laws exclusively operate".[2] The Indian Federation lacks this characteristic. Article 14 accords equal protection of laws to all persons. Article 19 permits freedom of movement, acquisition of property, and practising of any profession throughout the territory of India. Article 301 assures freedom of trade, commerce, and intercourse throughout the territory of India. In this respect the units have a far lesser degree of status than the units of American Federation.

It is, however, not an exaggeration to conclude that Indian Federation possesses most of the pre-requisites of a Federation viz., written, rigid, and supreme Constitution, proper distribution of powers between the Centre and the states, and impartial judicial Tribunal. Dr. B.R. Ambedkar aptly remarked about our Constitution, **"It establishes a dual polity with the union at the centre and the states at the periphery, each endowed with sovereign powers to be exercised in the field assigned to them respectively by the Constitution-....Both the Union and the States are created by the Constitution; both derive their respective authority from the Constitution. The one is not subordinate to the other in its own field; the authority of one is coordinate with that of the other".**[3] However as stated earlier, our federation has strong "Centralizing tendency" which prompts the critics to say that our Federation is a federation with unitary bias - a fact which is irrefutable. Now, we explain below unitary bias which is clearly reflected in the constitution.

Unitary Bias

The unitarianism is reflected through the following facts :

(*i*) *Division of Powers :* In the threefold division of powers, the most important subjects have been included in the Union List which is comprehensive. Even on the concurrent subjects, comprising 52 subjects, the Parliament possesses an overriding authority over the state legislatures. On the subjects in the State list, Parliament can legislate for a year if the Rajya Sabha passes a resolution supported by a majority of the total and not less than 2/3rd of the members present and voting that the matter is of national importance or interest (Article 249). Article 253 also empowers the Parliament to make laws implementing any treaty, agreement or covenant with another country or 'any' decision made at any international conference, association or other 'body'. Besides, the Constitution vests the residuary subjects with the Union unlike the U.S.A where such subjects are assigned to the States.

There has also been a tendency to encroach upon the State list. The 42nd amendment transferred education, forests, population control and family planning and a few more subjects to the concurrent list. Evidently this gives an upperhand to the Union Parliament in more subjects than initially provided in the Constitution.

---

[1] *V.K. Rao : Parliamentary Democracy in India, p. 280.*

[3] *Ibid p.280*

[3] *C.A.D. Vol. VIII, p. 927*

Besides, the Union Government possesses the right of issuing general instructions and directions in certain cases, and requisitioning of Union Law in the States. The states are also required to manage their affairs in a way as would not obstruct or prejudice the exercise of the executive power of the Union. Hence Srinivasan holds "*despite formal division of power the over-riding control of the Centre over the units testifies to the fact that the very nature of this distribution of power is noticeably centripetal*".[1]

Emergency Powers of the President

During the proclamation of emergency due to war, civil war or imminence thereof, the Union Government can give directions to the State Government as to how they should exercise their powers. Even the Parliament may acquire authority to make laws regarding the State subjects. Under article 356, the President on the report of the Governor or on his own enquiry can take over the administration of the State till the situation ceases to be abnormal.[2] In such an eventuality, the President assumes himself or allocates to any of the executive, functions of the State Government concerned and can entrust functions of the State legislature to the Parliament. Articles 360(3) empowers the Union Government to give directions to any state and ask it to observe such canons of financial propriety as may be specified in the directions to meet the financial difficulties and in order to restore the financial stability or credit of India. The President can issue directives for the reduction of salaries and allowances of public servants both working in the Union and the States. All money Bills passed by the State legislature during the financial emergency are subject to the control of the Government of India. The Governor heading the state administration, is a nominee of the President and holds office during the latter's pleasure. Invariably, he acts according to the dictates of the Centre. Their role, after 1967 in the coalitional non Congress governments is 'self-revealing'.[3] The Union Government through the Governor, reduced the autonomy of the states where non Congress governments were formed, to a mere farce. U.P. during the Governorship of Mr. Romesh Bhandari is a concrete example of the Central interference through the Governor in the state politics. Hence the appointment of head of the State by the President contravenes the principles of genuine federation.[4]

Appointments of Comptroller and Auditor General and Election Commission by Centre

In order to effect uniformity in financial administration, the President is empowered to appoint the 'Comptroller and Auditor General who supervises the financial meticulousness of both the Union and the States. The critics describe it as the control of the Central Government over the units through a Central functionary. Likewise, the Chief Election Commissioner and other members of the Election Commission are appointed by the President, though they direct, supervise and control, elections both of the Parliament and the State legislatures. This also vividly reflects Centralization.

Common all India Services

In a Federal state, centrally administered services negate the concept of distribution of powers. In India such services are appointed by the Union Government on the recommendation of the UPSC whose members are appointed by the President of India. The All India services operate both at the Centre and in the States and run the administration of the entire country. It reveals that the administrative machinery even at the state level is controlled by the civil services appointed by U.P.S.C.—a Central Government body which has a paramount fidelity to the Union Government. It is held that such services were created in fact to combat purely parochial tendencies and effect national integration. However, this is clearly a centralising tendency.

---

[1] *N. Srinivasan : Democratic Government in India, p. 203.*

[2] *See details in the chapter pertaining to centre and state relations.*

[3] *See details in the chapter in State Executive.*

[4] *See details in the chapter pertaining to centre and state relations.*

Unified Judiciary

Unlike that of the U.S.A., India opted for a single judiciary. The High Courts of the States are deemed as branches of the Supreme Court which is equipped with supervisory authority.

The High Courts are constituted and organised by the Union authorities. The American States on the other hand, have their own High Courts but branches of the Supreme Court in the form of District and Circuit Courts also separately exist in each state. In other words, there is double judiciary in the U.S.A. unlike that of India where single judiciary has been provided. This is certainly a centralising trend.

Financial Dependence

The sources of revenue exclusively earmarked for the states have not proved adequate to meet their requirements. Hence they have to bank upon the Centre for financial assistance in the form of a share of proceeds of some of the Union taxes and Grants-in-aid. Though the Constitution fixes the taxes fully assigned or shared with the states yet the proportion of the latter's share in many cases is determinable by the President. Such financial dependence on the Centre is apt to bring, in its wake, dependence in policy and administration as well. Besides, the Finance Commission whose members are appointed by the President is responsible for distributing net proceeds of the joint sources of revenue and allocating among the states of their respective shares. It also lays down the principles governing Grants-in-aid. This tightens the noose round the States' necks further.

Centralised Constitution Amending Power

The Indian states unlike Canadian Provinces or American states do not possess independent power of constitutional amendment. Even a decision to create or abolish the Legislative Council requires an Act of Parliament. Moreover except for a few specific matters where satisfaction of at least one half of the state legislatures is needed, the Constitution can be amended by the Parliament. The states do not come in picture. This detracts a great deal from the autonomy of the State.

Absence of Inviolability of the Units

The territories of the Units forming the Indian Federation are not inviolable. Article 3 of the Constitution empowers the Parliament to (*i*) form a new state by separation of territory from any state or by uniting two or more states or parts of states or by uniting any territory to a part of any state; (*ii*) increase the area of any state; (*iii*) diminish the area of any state; (*iv*) alter the boundaries of any state and (*v*) alter the name of any state. However, the President is required to ascertain the views of the States concerned though it is not obligatory to accept that advice. This is not the case in the U.S.A. In fact the redrawing of the map of India has been done through a simple majority in the Parliament. A few states like Jharkhand, Uttaranchal (Uttarakhand), Chattisgarh have come into existence through this process of simple majority. This reveals the predominance of the Centre.

Centres' approval on certain State Bills

Article 31(3) lays down that certain Bills will not be valid unless they are reserved for the consideration of the President and are assented to by him. For example, laws passed by the State legislature for the acquisition of property, laws in respect of current matters, repugnant to earlier laws of Parliament, laws providing for the imposition of taxes on the sale or purchase of commodities declared by the Parliament to be essential for the life of the community and derogating the powers of the High Courts must be reserved for President's assent. Certain Bills require the previous sanction of the President before they are introduced in the state legislature viz., Bills seeking to impose restrictions in the public interest on the freedom of trade, commerce, or intercourse within or without that state. The Central supremacy over legislation is thus established.

Uniformity of Civil and Criminal Code

The Constitution provides for uniformity in fundamental laws - Civil and Criminal. To avoid diversities of laws, the Civil and Criminal Courts have been placed in the Concurrent List. Thus in case of conflict, the will of the Parliament prevails. It indicates that the Indian federation maintains unity in all basic matters. Dr. B.R. Ambedkar defended such a provision saying, "up to a certain point diversity does not matter. It may be welcomed as being an attempt to accommodate the powers of government to local needs and requirements. But this diversity when it goes beyond a certain point is capable of producing chaos and has produced chaos in many federal states".

Settlement of Inter-State disputes

The Union Government has been empowered to effect coordination among the States and settle their mutual disputes. An inter-State Council may be set up by the President to settle disputes among the states and investigate and discuss matters of common interest and make recommendations for coordination of policy and action thereon. Disputes regarding the distribution or use of waters of inter-state rivers maybe regulated by a law of the parliament. Cavery River water dispute between the three southern states and Yamuna water dispute between Delhi and Haryana are the glaring examples of Centre's intervention.

Welfare of Scheduled Tribes and Backward Classes

The Welfare of the Scheduled Tribes and Backward Classes has been entrusted to the President who can appoint a Commission to investigate their plight. In the light of the recommendations of the Commission, the President may issue directions to the State Governments for the amelioration of their lot. Mandal Commission Report on the Backward Classes vitiated the political and academic atmosphere. It appeared that the State Governments were reduced to mere units of local administration in the Unitary System of Government. In the words of V.K. Rao, **"The Centre plans, the Centre decides, the Centre directs, and the States are unable to do anything positive except waiting at the door of the Planning Commission for doles".**[1]

Dominance of one Party

The Congress has been at the helm of affairs except for brief spells of time. This smoothened the functioning of our federal system. Many issues of political and legal significance could be solved through the mechanism of a Party itself. The Congress High Command had been keeping a tight grip on the organisation, the distribution of party tickets for elections, making and unmaking of state ministries, election, selection and removal of Chief Ministers, imposition of emergency under article 356. The Centre State conflicts were thus reduced to a minimum. The opposition parties denounce the role of Congress for dilution of the principles of the federal system. The communist parties have been clamouring for more autonomy of the states and loosening of the Centre's noose. With the passage of time, gradual, the rise and the dominance of regional parties may also become the main cause of the Union-State-confrontation. For instance, they have been dictating terms to BJP when it was in power at the Centre, on account of the latter's dependence on their support. The AIADMK has been a great irritant for the Centre during NDA government's rule. Likewise in the previous UPA government and also the present, small a regional allies are the irritants at times.

Unequal Representation to Units in Upper House

Unlike federations in the U.S.A., Australia and Switzerland Indian Federation does not make provision for equal representation to the States irrespective of their size and population. Such an equal 'representation is accorded to safeguard the interests of the units composing federation'. The critics attribute it to unitarian spirit of the Constitution.

---

[1] *V. K. Rao : Planning and Problem of Administration- an article in journal of Political science vol XIV NO 4, p.167*

Administration of Union Territories

The Union Territories are still administered by the President through an Administrator appointed by him. The constitutional setup of these Union Territories vary as their circumstances differ widely. The Parliament has been authorised to make appropriate arrangements by law for each case. In Andaman and Nicobar islands and Lacadive, Minicoy and Amindivi Islands, the President is authorised to make regulations having the force of law. Even a law passed by Parliament for these territories is amendable and repealable by a regulation of the President. According to M.P. Sharma, "*....the states of these territories in relation to the Union is like that of the subdivision of a Unitary state to its Central Government*".[1]

Planning Commission

In the words of B.B. Jena, "the Planning Commission which functions like super cabinet has proved to be a bandmaster which calls the tune of the economic policy of the country". The Planning Commission, it is held by the critics, has reduced the Indian states to mere beggars at its doors.

Maintenance of law and order

The paramount control of the Centre over the states is also discernible from the use of coercive machinery to protect and maintain the establishments of Government of India located in states of India. In opposition governed states, such coercive authority has often been over manifested. The Central Reserve Police Force was despatched to Kerala to quell the employee's agitation in September, 1968. The CRPF fired at the mob in the Steel Plant at Durgapur on March 24, 1969 resulting in heated exchanges between the West Bengal Home minister (a Communist) and the Union Home Minister. Three weeks later CRPF was again in action in Cossipure Gun and Shelling factory. The 42nd amendment (1976) Act empowered the Centre to deploy armed forces to deal with a grave situation of law and order in any state. It further strengthened the position of Centre. In the most recent past terrorist attack in Bombay could be controlled by the centre through Commandoes, CRPF and Defence Forces as state of Maharashtra failed miserably to save the rich heritage from the onslaught of the terrorists from Pakistan.

Single Constitution

A single constitution has been provided wherefrom the Centre as well as the State Governments derive their powers. Thus the States have no constitution of their own, Jammu and Kashmir being an exception. It is unlike American and Swiss Constitutions.

Conclusion

The above quoted facts establish it beyond any doubt that the process of unification and centralization has been taken to extreme limits. There is a dire necessity of a working balance between the requirements of national unity and autonomy of states. Dr. B.R. Ambedkar's contention, "Our Constitution would be both unitary as well as federal according to the requirements of time and circumstances", should be made true in letter and spirit. The autonomy of the states should not be in jeopardy on the pretext of Constitutional breakdown.

Surprisingly the Sarkaria Commission appointed by Mrs. Indira Gandhi in March 1983 in its report released on January 30, 1988 outrightly rejected the demand for curtailing the powers of the Centre and maintained that a strong Centre was imperative to preserve national unity and integrity of the country. However, its suggestions to activate Inter-State Council and Zonal Councils, and retention of National Development Council, the appointment of non-political individual as the Governor on the

[1] *Dr. M.P. Sharma : The Government of Indian Republic, p. 91*

advice of the Chief Minister, the invoking of article 356 very sparingly, enlarging financial resources of the states, extensive consultation with the states before the Centre legislates on the subject included in the concurrent list, can go a long way to dispel suspicion from the minds of the critics regarding excessive centralisation of the Indian Federation. The Inter-State Council has since been set up. Its first meeting was held on September 24, 1991 and some concrete suggestions regarding legislative relations between the Centre and the states were made. For example, extensive consultation with the states before legislating on a subject in the concurrent list was suggested by the Inter-State Council to the Centre. P.V. Narasimha Rao's (ex-Prime Minister of India) emphasis on the need to foster the cooperative spirit in the working of the Federal system at the Governor's Conference held on December 27-28, 1991 was a laudable step reflecting the intentions of the then Congress Government. Professor Rasheeduddin Khan rightly said, *"There is a historic warning focus in India to put our house in order before accumulated problems erode and dismantle our unique federal policy"*.[1] The BJP Government appeared to be conscious of possible erosion of federal polity during its tenure before the dissolution of 12th Lok Sabha. Hence it has been avoiding invocation of Article 356. In case of Bihar, however, it made an effort to destabilise the RJD Government led by Rabri Devi (wife of L.P. Yadav, ex-CM) twice. In the first attempt, it failed due to K.R. Narayan, President of India's advice for reconsideration and secondly the opposition's majority in Rajya Sabha proved deterrent and it revoked the President's rule after 24 days on March 8, 1999. It is a welcome development. The overawing hegemony of the Centre over the States is on the wane. The regional parties and their leaders at state level have been lending and at times marring stability to the national parties, both BJP and now the Congress as well because neither of them held sway at the Centre on account of lack of the requisite majority and has at to fall back upon these parties to minister the absolute majority.

(C) PARLIAMENTARY DEMOCRACY

India had been groaning under the heels of the foreign rulers for years. The Indians as such had faced the turbulent times at the hands of the tyrants. They had striven hard for the attainment of democratic institutions particularly since the establishment of Indian National Congress in 1885. The Britishers have been playing a double game since their pitching tents on the Indian soil. The East India Company made the Indian rulers fight against each other whereas the British Crown after take over of the reins of Government from the East Indian Company soon after Mutiny (1857) in 1858 placated the 'moderates' and crushed the 'violent revolutionaries' and tortured the 'extremists'. They did not feel satisfied with an attempt of dividing the nationalist ranks. Even the seeds of communalism were sown by introducing the Separate Electorates. Eventually the wedge was caused, too wide to be a bridged between Hindus, Muslims, Sikhs and Indian Christians. The moth-eaten representative institutions were being established though they were devoid of real powers and authority. The Act of 1919 introduced partial responsibility through a novel experiment of Dyarchy. The Act of 1935 went ahead by abolishing Dyarchy - otherwise a dismal failure - after 16 years of experiment and introducing provincial autonomy in the provinces. However, this autonomy though seemingly a democratic experiment on the lines of parliamentary system of government was hedged with many restrictions. It was nullified on account of overriding powers of the Governors in the Provinces and the Governor General at the Centre who was over all responsible for the maintenance of law and order in the country. Franchise was restricted to propertied classes and educated few. The Joint electorates clamoured for by the Nationalists congress had not been conceded. Federal mechanism of government as envisaged by 1935 Act could not be introduced due to the opposition of princely states and lack of good will on the part the Britishers.

Thus at the time of deliverance from the foreign yoke, it was thought essential that the virus of communalism should no longer be allowed to inject our body politic. Hence separate electorates were abolished and joint electorates were introduced. Rêstrictions on franchise were done away with

[1] *Rasheeduddin Khan : Federal India : A design for change.*

to bring vested interests at par with the common man. Universal Adult Franchise was adopted. The framers of the Constitution were keen to gain from the parliamentary institutions tried by the Britishers during our freedom struggle. Hence, they retained the British model of parliamentary democracy before them, though as already said, on account of peculiar circumstances, we were confronted with, the federal mechanism of government (unlike that of U.K.) was conceived as well. The Reserved powers or host of discretionary powers of the Governors as the Heads of the States as provided by Act of 1935 were dispensed with. Like the British monarch, the President of India was to be only a nominal head. The Prime Minister was to be the real head running the Government of the country. At the state level, a Governor was to be a constitutional ruler and the real powers were to be exercised by the Chief Minister. Thus, the first requisite of Parliamentary Government in India, i.e. two heads, real and nominal, stood fulfilled. However, prior to the passage of the 42nd amendment Act, the President acted on the advice of the Council of Ministers only conventionally. After the enactment of the Amandment Act the advice of Council of Ministers has become binding on governor. Hence the possibility of controversy between President and Prime Minister, particularly if they are drawn from different political parties, are set at naught.

The controversy between the President and the Prime Minister was raked up when President Rajendra Prasad' in speech in Law Institute remarked that research should be made on the powers of the President. It provoked Prime Minister Jawaharlal to emphasise, "…..our *Constitution makes the President constitutionally rather like the King or Queen of England. If this was not so, you can see the whole question of responsibility of the Cabinet and of the parliament would suffer*". In fact the expression 'aid and advice' as used in article 74(1) remained a mere constitutional euphemism to keep up the dignity of the august office of the President. As already said, the advice was even then more or less binding on the President. However, the 42nd amendment Act set at rest the speculations and possibilities of their mutual discords for all times to come by making the advice of the Council of Ministers binding on the President.

Leadership of the Prime Minister

Leadership of the Prime Minister is an acknowledged fact in a parliamentary democracy. Prime Minister is the architect of the Council of Ministers. He can shuffle his pack as he pleases. However, it is expected that he would consult his senior colleagues before constituting the cabinet. Nehru very rarely consulted them. N.V. Gadgill, a senior colleague was kept out of the cabinet and nobody was consulted. Nehru's statement in the parliament on July 30, 1956 over his controversy with C.D. Deshmukh reveals the onerous authority of the Prime Minister vis-a-vis a minister. He said, **"I am also something after all. I am the Prime Minister of India and a Prime Minister is the Prime Minister.....in the Constitution the Prime Minister is the linchpin of the Government....."** Morarji Desai had to quit Nehru's cabinet as he tried to be near equal to Nehru K. Hanumanthaiah compared Nehru with a '*Banyan tree*' which gives shade but under which nothing grows'. These remarks though a bit exaggerated reveal the working of the office of Prime Minister as envisaged under the constitution. Lal Bahadur Shastri, during the short span of his tenure, set the precedence of collective leadership. He invariably took colleagues in confidence for each and every matter of national significance. Mrs. Indira Gandhi also took senior colleagues in confidence so long as she did not command overwhelming majority in the Lok Sabha and she was politically a novice. When she won the convincing majority and became the irrefutable leader of Congress (I), she shuffled her pack as she pleased.[1] Rajiv Gandhi during his tenure as the PM gradually emerged as an assertive leader. A former President Giani Zail Singh once remarked, *"Rajiv Gandhi gave me lot of respect in public but started humiliating me and was even disrespectful"*.[2] Rajiv Gandhi is said to have been considering the President's impeachment for flouting conventions and the latter was thinking of former's dismissal on the basis of corruption and negligence.[3] As per Gianji's version, Rajiv Gandhi

[1] *See details in chapter on Central Executive*
[2] *Hindustan Times dated November 5, 1992*
[3] *Ibid "Rajiv wanted to impeach me" Zail Singh, p.1*

stopped the recording of his address which was to be telecast to the nation on his retirement. Hence he had to speak extempore. In Giani Zail Singh's words, *"It was purely a dispute between a Prime Minister and a President and I wanted to prove it to the world that the chair of the President was higher than that of the Prime Minister".*[1]

This reflects that Rajiv Gandhi too was an assertive leader vis-a-via the President of India. He made the President Giani Zail Singh realize that dismissal of a popularly elected Prime Minister was not a child's play. Hence President could not take drastic action, he was wishfully contemplating. V.P. Singh could not be an effective leader as he was heading a precarious majority of discordant elements. The BJP supported him from outside without entering the Government. Likewise, Prime Minister Chandra Shekhar was on the mercy of Congress supporting him from outside. Hence, he too, could not prove assertive and be that effective. P.V. Narasimha Rao headed the largest party in Parliament and could eventually turn it into absolute majority with the support of AIADMK and Muslim League. Hence he believed in keeping consensus and the team of ministers and the adherents of his way of thinking appeased. This enabled him to lend stability to his government for 5 years. He took the President into confidence, kept him informed on all important policy decisions. Thus we can conclude that in general the Prime Minister vis-a-vis ministers, as said by Jennings, is like *"the sun round whom the ministers revolve like planets"*. **Much, however, depends upon the personality of the incumbent of the office, the majority that he enjoys in the Lok Sabha and his political and administrative acumen. The Prime Ministers heading coalition governments** — Deve Gowda, I.K. Gujral (of United Front) and even A.B. Vajpayee cannot be kept in the category of assertive PMs as their coalition partners and those who lent them support too often asked for pound of flesh and 'withdrawal of support threat' hanged like a *Sword of Damocles* on their heads as they enjoyed only a precarious majority. Even Dr. Manmohan Singh had to face such a music at the hands of some coalition partners. The support of Left from outside was a constant irritant and eventually on Indo-Us governments nuclear Deal for civil purposes, decided to withdraw the support and put the governments survival in jeopardy.

Membership of Parliament

The Council of Ministers are invariably drawn from the Parliament. If a particular minister is not a member of parliament, he is required to seek its membership within six months. Lal Bahadur Shastri inducted Mrs. Indira Gandhi in the cabinet when she was not a member of Parliament. Subsequently, a seat in the Rajya Sabha was vacated for her and she was duly elected to it within a specified period. In Indira's own cabinet Ch. Bansi Lal was inducted as Defence Minister of India though he got elected to Rajya Sabha later within 6 months. In the alternative, a seat of the Lok Sabha can be got vacated and the minister concerned can be asked to contest by-election. This happened in case of Narasimha Rao. However, this is done only if the party High Command is sure of victory of the contesting candidate in a particular constituency. 'A minister must be a member of parliament' and then act as the saviour of the public interest, is a democratic practice which has been rigidly adhered to.

Collective Responsibility

The Council of Ministers is collectively responsible to the parliament. "All for one and one for all" principle applies in a parliamentary democracy. For a collective national policy formulated by the entire Council of Ministers, the entire Council will tender resignation and not a particular minister who is directly concerned with the policy.

If, however, any minister differs, he has to tender resignation or accept the majority point of view. The critics allege that the humiliating military defeats of the Indian military forces at the hands of the Chinese should have normally resulted in the resignation of the entire Nehru Cabinet but

[1]*Ibid.*

V.K. Krishna Menon - the Defence Minister alone was made the scapegoat and made to resign. In fact the policy of appeasement of India to China and apparent display of cordiality by Chinese leaders was only an artifice to hoodwink Indian leaders and stab them in the back so as to humiliate them in the eyes of the Indian masses. Evidently, the Central Government headed by Pt. Jawaharlal Nehru was responsible for falling prey to the political suaveness of Chinese leaders, but Krishna Menon was made to own the responsibility for not arming Northern borders effectively and hence the nerve-wrecking military debacle was to be faced by the Indian forces and face humiliation. The rest of the ministers remained silent spectators to his political misfortune. In the words of Krishna Menon, "*So the collective responsibility in the sense that a decision once made is everybody's is very largely a myth—certainly in the Indian cabinet. Even today one Cabinet member speaks almost like a Swatantra Party man, another member speaks more with the emphasis of Gandhi's philosophy, a third one speaks perhaps as a Socialist and so on....*"[1] During NDA rule, this generally happened. In Dr. Manmohan Singh's tenure as head of the UPA there has been some restraint in this trend.

Individual Responsibility

Each minister is individually responsible to the parliament for the department he holds. He has to resign if majority in the Lok Sabha goes against him regarding a policy formulated by him. This does not amount to vote of no confidence against the entire Council of Ministers. Lal Bahadur Shastri as Railway Minister in J.L. Nehru's Cabinet set a fine precedent when he resigned on account of two railway accidents in quick succession in the southern railways. Likewise, Dr. Karan Singh, Minister of Civil Aviation and Tourism in Indira Gandhi's cabinet resigned when Avro Crash occurred on March 15, 1973 at Secunderabad. However. His resignation was not accepted though he was praised both by the Government and the opposition for his sense of responsibility and love for democratic traditions. Another laudable precedent was set by Madhavrao Scindia. Madhavrao Scindia - Minister of state for Railways in Rajiv Gandhi's Council of Ministers owned moral responsibility when the Bangalore - Trivandrum Express went off the rails over Ashtamudi Lake in Kerala on July 8, 1988 and resigned. His resignation was not accepted by the Prime Minister. He again tendered resignation owning moral responsibility for T.U. 154 Passenger aircraft crash on runway of Delhi Airport on January 9, 1993, as he happened to be Civil Aviation and Tourism Minister. His resignation was accepted. The critics pointed accusing fingers on a former finance minister Dr. Manmohan Singh, who presided over the whole network of the financial system and despite the securities scam which shattered public confidence in the financial system and did incalculable harm to the small investor, did not bear the cross. This was denounced as a great setback to the principle of individual responsibility In the words of S.N. Misra, "....Such is the seachange in the political culture that this key word - responsibility - of parliamentary democracy is as good as banished from the political lexicon of the ruling class. The new creed appears to be that majority equals moral authority". Likewise at a later stage, C.K. Jaffer Sharief - the Railway minister did not tender resignation particularly when the Delhi High Court had given adverse verdict against him in the bogies purchase case involving Rs. 170 crores. No doubt he had appealed to the Supreme Court against the decision and won the case, but grace lay in his resignation there and then. The Prime Minister could have restrained acceptance till the decision of the highest tribunal. Likewise, Sharad Pawar, ex-Defence Minister did not set a good precedent by not resigning in the wake of Bombay High Court ruling regarding allotment of land to a cooperative society of some IAS officers in Bombay during his Chief Ministership. The High Court indicted Sharad Pawar for non application of mind in a case involving demolition of a school building and benefitting officials at the cost of the weaker sections of society.

---

[1]*Michael Brecher : Succession in India (1968 ed) p. 247.*

These instances of Dr. Manmohan Singh, Sharief and Sharad Pawar prompted S.N. Misra to remark, "the tenets of the new faith represented by Dr. Singh, Sharief and Sharad, are bound to spread disastrously". This is the most depressing aspect of the political scenario during U.F. coalition ministries headed by Deve Gowda and I.K. Gujral and also later BJP Government, led by A.B. Vajpayee. In not too distant a past (November 26, 2008) terrorists attack on Bombay and mass killing of the people and destruction of property considered prestigious and almost legacy of the nation reflected weakness of the Home Ministry. This attack had been preceded by terrorists' attack in Delhi a few months earlier. Hence it was considered unpreparedness of the nation and the Government to face such possible onslaught despite warnings by the concerned intelligence agencies. Hence the Maharashtra CM had to resign and the accusing fingers compelled the Home Minister Shiv Raj Patil to resign on the so called moral grounds. Actually the Home Minister's wild denunciation due to the repeated terrorists attack's compelled him to resign which was portrayed as nothing short of an expulsion from the council of ministers or a graceful dismissal.

In fact, such type of negligence on the part of ministers should induce the ministers to tender resignations of their own and set precedents of individual responsibility which is facing a gradual decline, infact a sort of erosion from our soil. The days of L. B. Shastri or Dr. Karan Singh owning individual responsibility for an accident seemed things of the past. It is a matter of great relief that Civil Aviation Minister P. Patil offered resignation to the Prime Minister on May 22, 2010 after Manglore Air Crash on 22nd May killing 158 passengers"[1] The P.M. refused to accept the resignation.

Sound Opposition

Though India followed a British pattern of parliamentary democracy, yet healthy and sound opposition, the very soul of parliamentary democracy is as yet a far cry. A plethora of political parties embracing conflicting ideologies and professing different faiths have emerged with the passage of time. The ruling party has been no exception. Congress (O), Congress (I), Congress (S) and recently Trinamul Congress under Mamata Banerjee (W. Bengal) establish the fact. Janata Dal was later split in clearcut two Dals - Janata Dal (Ajit) and Janata Dal (V.P. Singh). Later, a splinter group of Janata Dal under Laloo Yadav called as RJD came into existence. Communist Party of India (CPI), Communist Party Marxist (CPM), Communist Party of India- Marxist-Leninist (CPI-ML) reflect divisions in Communist ranks. Jan Sangh and BJP constitute splinter groups of Hindu fundamentalists. Akali Dal has four such factions. In not too distant a past Gurcharan Singh Tohra came out of Prakash Singh Badal's Akali Dal and stood by Jathadar Ranjit Singh, who was removed by P.S. Badal's Akali Dal and formed his separate Akali Dal. Referring to such splinter groups and factions sprouting like mushroom in Indian political scenario, DMK has another potential rival in AIADMK. Nehru rightly remarked "They hold together I suppose because of the stress of circumstances and sometimes there are marriages of convenience, sometimes followed by rapid divorces". What Jawaharlal said decades ago was referred by Dr. Karan Singh a scholar politician in the recent past "*....the successful working of a parliamentary democracy requires the existence of a single party or cohesive grouping capable of providing a credible alternative to the ruling party*"[2]. Till date the opposition has remained divided into factions and splinter groups. Hence it failed to raise a united voice. The stalling, of proceedings of the House and hurling at each other microphones of and caring a fig for the speakers shouts to stop it and seeking the help of Marshall to throw out certain members reflect that healthy opposition is as yet a far cry.

Homogeneity of People

Indians do not constitute a homogeneous population. Their outlooks differ and their ideas vary. They profess different faiths and embrace different ideologies. Hence the bond of the political party is torn asunder to help out a co-religionist or co-casteist. The crossing of floors is also frequent

---

[1]*Hindustan Times May 23, 2010. p. 1.*

[2]*Dr. Karan Singh : Great statesmanship needed — an article in the Tribune dated April 2, 1989.*

and has resulted in unprincipled politics. A government based on shifting loyalties and leaders depending on floating, indecisive and vacillating electorates is apt to prove weak, ineffective and ever faltering. The emergence of hung parliaments in the Xth, XIth, XIIth XIIIth and XIVth the General elections reflected the mood of the electorates. It appears they were not prepared to give clear mandate. Instead they had given fractured mandates in five successive elections. This resulted in coalitional politics at the Centre and the Central Government falling back on the fragile crutches - the regional parties and the communal or the communist outfits. Thus, era of political instability ushered in since the fall of one party dominance and the frustration of the dream of a stable government supported by absolute majority. Thus it was concluded that the emergence of the biparty system alone would help in checkmating a marked heterogeneity of the Indian voters and result in the healthy growth of parliamentary democracy by returning one party with absolute majority and the other automatically forming the healthy and viable opposition. The XV the Lok Sabha elections held in May, 2009 have revived hopes for the national parties to emerge stronger if they believe in disciplined politics. The Congress has gained grounds and the UPA is more confident the regional parties and the dictatorial left parties have been rebuffed this angures well for our democracy.

Political homogeneity

Political homogeneity - an important characteristic of parliamentary democracy - has been accorded due recognition in the Indian politics at the Centre. Since the inception of our Constitution, Congress has been the dominant party except for a few brief spells for the opposition parties and then congress emerging as the largest party as is case at present. Hence the ministers comprising the Cabinet constituted homogeneous team. Nehruji in his first Cabinet had drawn ministers from non-partymen and also non-Congress and even anti-Congress leaders. The experiment proved a failure. Hence one by one, such ministers came out of his Cabinet. Thereafter the Congress party invariably did not venture on drawing talent from outside the party. Mrs. Indira Gandhi inducted eminent men from public life in her Cabinet only if they happened to be her loyalists. The Janata Cabinet of Morarji Desai contrastingly was drawn from four parties which had merged together and CFD headed by Jagjiwan Ram, just to oust the Congress. Hence the cabinet could not last for long. The ministers on account of discordant views pulled in the opposite direction. It was reestablished when Janata Dal under V.P. Singh formed the Government with the support of BJP and communist parties. How could conflicting views be reconciled? The hopes of smooth sailing proved to be a wishful thinking. The United Front ministries after XIth General Elections also could not last longer as they had formed a coalition and got support from the Congress from outside. The Congress pulled the rug both the times. The U.F. Government could survive the first shock by agreeing to drop the Prime Minister Deve Gowda but I.K. Gujral, the next P.M., could not save the sinking ship when the Congress President again proclaimed withdrawal of support. The BJP Government headed by A.B Vajpayee has also been facing constant pinpricks at the hands of coalition partners viz. AIADMK, Trinamool Congress, Akali Dal and Haryana Lok Dal. The UPA headed by Dr. Manmohan Singh after XIVth Lok Sabha polls tells the same tale. The Congress won the fractured mandate in 2004 elections and had to seek support from like minded secular parties. The Left lent its support from outside. However for the implementation of economic reforms in view of liberalization and modernization, it faced pinpricks, at the hands of the Left in particular. Eventually on Indo-US Nuclear deal for civil purposes, the Left withdrew support and UPA government decided to seek confidence Vote. The SSP headed by M.S. yadav proclaimed its support to Dr. Manmohan Singh. The Government emerged victorious and an important deal with USA, was struck but the governments' future was at stake because of an ally which was anti USA and pro communist. In fact, the coalition governments do not constitute homogeneous teams. Their views differ. Their ideologies conflict. They are persistent to have a pound of flesh whenever opportunity crops up by sounding a threat of gunning down the Government. Thus, whenever they so desire, they blow their own trumpets and take credit of salvaging the Government if the government dances to their tune. They do not hesitate to bring down the government if it does not play their tune. Thus, invariably they succeed in grinding their own axe. This has given a set back to Indian parliamentary democracy and at times pushes it perpetually on tenterhooks.

The XVth Lok Sabha elections results have changed the political secenario a bit. Still we are far away from the 'absolute majority' party government which alone can lend stability to parliamentary system of government.

Administrative responsibility to Parliament

Administration comes under close scrutiny of parliament at the time of discussions on the budget. Each ministry, department and office, is on trials and toes. It can hope to get money sanctioned only if its activities during the year are minutely examined and approved after discussions. About two months of parliamentary sittings are devoted to these discussions. Still they are neither adequate nor detailed. Questions pertaining to policy economy, complaints, grievances, adequacy or inadequacy of the projects, schemes and outlays are raised and the minister concerned is to give satisfactory explanation. However, the parliamentarians generally remain dissatisfied with these explanations. Hence the Parliament has devised the method of scrutinizing the matters through the special committees, viz., the committee on Estimates, Public Accounts Committee and Committee on Public undertakings.[1] Besides these committees, the administration is answerable to other scrutiny committees as well., viz. the Committees on Government Assurances, Committee on Subordinate Legislation and Committee on Petitions.

Such a control on administration is indispensable as the administrative bureaucracy responsible for running the administration of a department is generally afflicted by bureaucratic maladies. Red tapism, circumlocution, officiousness and corruption, generate a crisis of confidence. Hence, if parliament does not control ruling bureaucrats in the name of ministerial control, it does little to justify its very existence. In a socialist state aiming at the welfare of the masses, the parliament is supposed to act as watchdog of public funds. Parliament in fact represents the popular sovereignty. Its direct as well as indirect control over administration is a logical conclusion to which the demands of socialism and the goals of welfare administration have much meaning and substance.[2]

Parliament exercises control over the administration through motions of no confidence, questions, short notice questions, half an hour discussion, call attention motions, adjournment motions, zero hour discussions, Budget discussions, after President's speech in the parliament on the day of the opening session. Referring to the importance of discussions on the Finance Bill, G.V. Mavlankar, the first speaker of Lok Sabha, said on March 24, 1950. *It is an acknowledged principle that any subject can be discussed on the Finance Bill and any grievance ventilated, the principle being that the citizen should not be called upon to pay unless he is given through parliament the fullest possible latitude of representing his views and conveying his grievances"*. This, in fact, is an effective way to air genuine and pressing grievances, pinpoint related administrative issues and observe and discuss the sidelights.

Lack of Decorum in the Legislatures

During the last few years, the Central and State legislatures have lost credibility of being mirror of public opinion and truly representative bodies. In the recent past, there was unprecedented uproar

[1]*See deatils in the Chapter – Control on Public Enterprises*
[2]*B. Mehta : Dynamics of State Administration (1975 ed) p. 107.*

uproar on 'Action Taken Report', on security scam in the parliament. Likewise on many other issues, viz. Indo-USA Nuclear Civil Deal 'vote for cash', terrorists attack on Jamiah Milia area of New Delhi, 26 Nov., 2008 in Bombay. The parliament witnessed rowdyism of the worst type and no fruitful discussion could take place. The recurrent unruly scenes in state assemblies of U.P., Haryana and Tamil Nadu speak volumes about the lack of proper decorum in the elected bodies representing the masses. The role of speakers in the state assemblies has been invariably partial and hardly in consonance with the dignity of the chair of a speaker. This impairs the dignity of the legislature and eclipses our parliamentary democracy.

Conclusion

An appraisal of the functioning of Indian parliamentary democracy reveals that it lacks certain essential prerequisites. Healthy conventions for the proper blossoming of Parliamentary democracy have not as yet developed. Even the top governmental institutions at the state level have been in disrepute. Money power has played havoc at the time of general elections and there have been scandles of 'cash for question's in the parliament and also allegation in the very recent confidence vote, of cash for votes said to have been given to parliamentarian in a vote of confidence. In fact it was more of a theoritical gesture than a reality horse trading, opportunism and defections have been the order of the day. Corruption has been rampant in the three branches of the government, judiciary being no exception and, unbridled nepotism on caste and clan basis, has vitiated the administrative machinery. However, it is hoped that with the dawn of enlightenment, development of national outlook, emergence of healthy opposition on the pattern of Great Britain and gradual evolution of healthy parliamentary conventions, parliamentary democracy is apt to attain success. A switchover to Presidential type of government as suggested by dismal prophets is hardly acceptable as a panacea of the ills of our democracy. There is no denying the fact that our parliamentary democracy, despite lack of pre-requisites of a parliamentary systems of government, has been able to steer the ship of the state safely through tempestuous times viz. during wars with the neighbours, terrorists attack on the parliament, selected and prestigious places in Delhi, Jaipur, Assam, Jammu and Kashmir and on Nov 26, 2008 in Bombay. However, the emergence of sound party system, on the lines of U.K. can go a long way in adding to the strength and stability of the parliamentary system of government. The critics may call it a wishful thinking, but it is hoped against hopes that disillusionment with coalitional era due to the frequent emergence of hung parliaments may eventually lead to the complete disillusionment with the regional, nonsecular and pro enemy parties and eventual emergence of two party system as is the case in UK. Such a development may lead to the inception of an ideal parliamentary system in the largest democracy of the world.

(D) PLANNING

Planning is a relic of the past. In 1938, the Indian National Congress set up the National Planning Commission under the Chairmanship of Pt. Jawaharlal Nehru. Eight prominent economists of Bombay prepared the Bombay Plan in 1943. Simultaneously M.N. Roy prepared People's Plan. After the attainment of independence the Planning Commission (see details about Planning Commission in Chapter VII) was established in 1950 under the chairmanship of Jawaharlal Nehru. Thus an era of economic planning ushered in 1950 when the first five-year plan commenced in 1951.

Salient Features of Planning

(a) An advisory Body

The Planning Commission has been set up to act as an advisory body and lay down guidelines of the plans. Thus, "Planning in India is not imperative or authoritarian but is based on inducement and permission".[1]

[1] *Dr. Rajesh Chadha : "Indian economy" – as contributed in General Studies Manual 1992 P.F. 11 (edited by Dr. Tara Chand).*

(*b*) *Limited Centralisation*

All decisions and choices are made in a decentralised manner with the exception of certain critical decisions having a strong bearing on the nation as a whole.

(*c*) *Democratic Socialism.*

India's economic planning strives to blend the virtues of the socialist and capitalist economic systems. The Indian economy, in fact, is a mixed economy and both private and public sectors have been given importance in their respective spheres. However, till recent past, the public sector was given more importance in the economic development of India. Since the dawn of era of liberalization and modernization, private sector has become predominant.

(*d*) *Development oriented.*

Emphasis has been laid on the establishment of a strong infrastructure of basic and heavy industries.

Objectives of Planning

The long term objectives of planning in India have been almost identical in all the Five year plans. The objectives are interconnected with one another.

(*a*) *Economic Growth*

All plans aimed at raising the level of national and per capita income.

(*b*) *Self Reliance*

Self Reliance has been construed as a vital requirement for economic growth. Hence reduction in the dependence on foreign aid and concessional foreign capital has been envisaged as the donors can exercise political influence on the decision making process of the recipient country.

(*c*) *Employment Generation.*

Provision of jobs to the unemployed and more work to the underemployed has been the aim of planning.

(*d*) *Promotion of Social Justice.*

For promoting social justice, planning keeps two sub objectives in view – (*i*) Eradication of poverty, (*ii*) Narrowing down of inequalities of income and wealth.

Achievements of Planning

Its major achievements are as follows :

(*i*) Building up of a strong infrastructure in the areas of energy, irrigation, transport, education and public health.
(*ii*) Development in science and technology.
(*iii*) Rapid industrialization in consumer and capital goods industries.
(*iv*) Diversification of exports and import substitution.

Failures

Though its achievements seem to be quite impressive, yet its failures cannot be overlooked. They are as follows :

(*i*) Slow rate of growth of national income and per capita income.
(*ii*) Large unemployment in actual practice
(*iii*) Social Justice remained mostly in jeopardy as planning could neither provide a national minimum level of living nor reduce inequalities of income and wealth.

Synopsis of Individual Plans

The First 5 Year Plan (1951-56)

It accorded the highest priority to agriculture at the cost of heavy industries in particular. Evidently low priority was given to the industries in general. The main aims of the Plan were : (*i*) To achieve self sufficiency in food grains production, (*ii*) To rehabilitate the Indian economy shattered by the Second World War and the partition of the country. (*iii*) To check inflation, (*iv*) To build economic overheads and (*v*) To provide social justice.

The First Plan was instrumental for the spread of Community Development Projects throughout the country with the sole objective of raising the level of living of the people through improved agricultural efficiency. The Plan was indeed quite successful in the domains of Agriculture, Irrigation and Community Development. The national income also exceeded the targetted rate.

The Second Plan (1956-61)

The success of the First Plan boosted the launching of the second plan. The philosophy behind this plan was to give a 'big push' to the economy in order to enable it to 'take off' in the context of economic development. This Plan laid emphasis on Industrialisation–basic and heavy industries, in particular. It also aimed at augmenting of national income, adding to employment opportunities and curtailing inequalities of wealth and income.

The Plan was confronted with numerous problems, viz., the Suez crisis; failure of the monsoons, cropping up of inflationary trends and the depletion of foreign exchange reserves and a severe set back to rice production. Despite this, the Plan met with some success and national income and per capita income were enhanced by 3.9 and 1.9 per cent respectively.

The Third Plan (1961-66)

The first two plans geared up the Indian economy. The Third Plan aimed at making India self reliant and to have self generating economy. The Plan aimed at achieving more than five per cent growth rate in national income and self-sufficiency in food grains production. It also stood for expansion of basic industries like steel, chemicals, fuel and power etc., creation of substantial employment opportunities, provision of greater equality of opportunities and reduction of economic disparities.

The Third Plan proved to be a failure. Agricultural and Industrial production could not achieve the target. It was mainly due to the Chinese aggression (1962) and the Indo-Pakistan conflict (1965). Evidently production priorities became defence oriented. Monsoons were also poor in all the plan years except in 1964-65. The utter failure of the Plan induced the Government to declare a Plan Holiday for the remaining three years, i.e., 1966-69.

The Fourth Plan (1969-74)

The Plan Holiday period (1966-69) witnessed three annual plans. In 1966-67 economy was further shattered due to drought. Hence agriculture got a further set back. Industrial development also was eclipsed. In the next two years, a process of recovery was discernible. Price levels showed a decline on account of improvement in foodgrains production. The foreign exchange position registered an improvement. "By 1969, the economy had absorbed the shocks, it had received during the Third Plan". Hence the Fourth Plan was launched with great aspirations in April, 1969.

The principal objectives of the Fourth Plan were :- Progressive achievement of self reliance; growth with justice; balanced regional development. Some emphasis was laid on social justice and equality, creation of employment and provision of a national minimum to the people.

An appraisal

The 4th plan was a tame affair. The first two years did indicate encouraging results but the last three years were rather disappointing. On account of infrastructural, raw materials and industrial relations bottlenecks, underutilization of the existing capacity was discernible. The Indo-Pak Conflict (1971) and the emergence of Bangladesh refugees problem further worsened the situation.

The Fifth Plan (1974-79)

The twin principal objectives of the Fifth Plan were 'eradication of poverty' and 'achievement of self reliance'. In order to fulfil these objectives, the fifth plan aimed at 5.5 per cent growth rate in gross domestic product; employment generation; a national programme for minimum needs, viz., elementary education, drinking water, medical care in rural areas, nutrition, home sites for landless labour, rural roads, rural electrification, and slum improvement; social welfare; emphasis on agriculture, key and basic industries and consumption of goods production; adequate public procurement and distribution system; restraint on non-essential consumption and reduction in economic, social and regional inequalities.

An appraisal

The Non-Congress Government comprising opposition alliances terminated the plan in 1978. However, the performance in food grains and cotton cloth was quite satisfactory. In the case of sugarcane, coal, petroleum, fertilizers, mild steel and the electricity, the performance was below the targets. In the case of raw cotton, paper and paperboards, cement and mill cloth performance was rather dismal. The national income went up at the rate of 6.2 per cent though the target was 5.5 per cent. This can be rated as good performance.

The Sixth Plan (1980-85)

Non Congress Government formulated the plan for the period 1978-83 and termed it as the "Rolling Plan". The Congress Government which came in power after two years of Janata misrule abandoned the concept and a new sixth plan was launched for the period 1980-85.

Objectives

The basic objective of the Sixth Plan was the removal of poverty. The formulation of this plan kept in view a perspective of 15 years ahead (1980-95). Hence the plan aimed at achieving economic and technological self reliance; reduction of poverty and eradication of unemployment; development of indigenous energy sources; improvement of the quality of life of the poorest through the Minimum Needs Programme; curtailment of inequalities of income and wealth through better redistribution, and population control. The plan involved all sections of people in the process of development.

An appraisal

An appraisal of the plan reveals that the economy grew at the rate of 5.4 percent per annum though the target of growth in national income was 5.2 percent. Likewise development of agriculture, and services went beyond the target - 3.8 to 4.3 percent in agriculture and 5.5 to 6.6 percent in services. In manufacturing and mining sectors, performance has been rather poor, i.e. 6.6. to 3.7 per cent. This performance offset the good performance of agriculture and service sector. The sixth plan expected a saving rate of 24.5 percent in 1984-85 but it came down to 23.3 per cent. Though the progress in the output of commercial energy was evident - the country remained confronted with power shortages. Hence it adversely affected many basic industries. However, it is heartening to note that many employment generating rural development programmes were initiated during the Sixth Plan.

The Seventh Plan (1985-90)

The Seventh Plan was initiated on April 1, 1985. The plan was designed with a long term perspective for the period 1985 to 2000. The long term development strategy accorded the highest priority to creation of more opportunities for productive employment. Further efforts were put in to slacken the rate of population growth and raise the nutritional level of the people. Energy planning also was an important ingredient of long term planning.

Main Objectives

It laid emphasis on the policies and programmes which could increase the growth of foodgrains production, enhance employment opportunities and raise productivity. The growth rate of gross domestic product was aimed at five per cent during this Plan.

Strategy

The development strategy during this plan aimed at generation of productive employment. Hence it aimed at launching of a direct attack on the grave problems of poverty, unemployment and regional imbalances. Further it was thought indispensable to effect substantial economy in the use of resources. These improvements could be effected through the augmentation of human resources, greater selectivity in the development and use of domestic technological capabilities, widespread introduction of new technologies in agriculture factories and offices, greater emphasis on capacity utilization and better project implementation and following up of policies that would cause reduction of costs of production in the industrial sector in particular.

Sectoral Allocation

In the VIIth plan, the Plan outlay was Rs. 1,80,000 crores at 1984-85 prices. It was inclusive of current development outlay of Rs. 25,782 crores and gross investment of Rs. 1,54,218 crores. Gross investment in the private sector was to be Rs. 1,68,148 crores. It meant a total investment of Rs. 3,22,366 crores of which 94 per cent was to be financed from domestic resources. Thus the actual public sector outlay amounted to be Rs. 2,22,169 crores.

An appraisal

It is heartening to note that many of the targets laid down for the Seventh Plan were exceeded. This can be attributed to the good performance of economy in 1989-90. For instance, as against plan target of 5 per cent, the average annual rate of GDP (Gross Domestic Product) touched 5.6 per cent. In agriculture, the average annual growth rate went up to 4.1 per cent though the target was 4 percent. Such an achievement was creditable particularly when during the first 3 years of plan, the monsoons were much below the mark. Increase in per capita income was recorded at 17% (i.e. 3.4% per annum). Jawahar Rojgar Yojna (JRP) was launched to provide additional employment. Due emphasis was laid upon the development of smallscale and cottage industries. Several significant decisions were taken in order to achieve competitiveness of international standard in the economy. The industrial production increased at an average rate of 8.5 per cent only, 2 percent below the Plan target of 8.7 percent. Mining and quarrying and electricity generation exhibited a growth of a 5.7 and 9.4 percent respectively. It fell short of the plan targets of 13 and 12 percent respectively. This was, however, compensated partially by increase in the manufacturing output to the extent of 8.8 per cent per annum as against 8 percent of target. In spite of the fact that the output and growth targets of the VIIth plan had gone up, an imbalance in the pattern of financing the plan with the contribution of resources from Public sector savings, falling short of target, was discernible. According to Dr. Rajesh Chadha, "The determination in the savings performance of the public sector which has put the planning process under considerable strain is an important factor underlying the persistent fiscal imbalances". In fact, a big gap between the income and the expenditure of the Government was responsible for huge fiscal deficits. Imbalances between aggregate demand and domestic output which occurred on account of excessive deficit financing resulted in inflationary pressures and expectations. Besides, the fiscal deficits of the Government spilled over into current account deficits or the balance of payments had to be financed either by running down of foreign exchange reserves or through fresh external borrowing, each entailing its own attendant problems.

The Eighth Plan (1992-97)

Abnormal circumstances overtook the country in 1991, though the performance of the Indian economy in recent years had substantially improved and attained the targets to a substantial extent. There has, however, been accentuation of unrest and discontentment on account of appalling poverty rampant unemployment, illiteracy, ill health and rapid decline in living conditions of the poor and economically backward sections.

The Congress Government postponed the VIIIth Plan to 1992. The Plan envisaged decentralisation of the planning process, involving reorientation of the focus, and priorities of Planning and also its process and mechanism. The process was expected to be enriched and made more effective by taking the masses along, both in planning and its implementation through democratic decentralisation and a closer linkage of the Planning Commission with the State Planning organisations.

Objectives

The main objective of the Plan was to ensure that the needs of the masses were fulfilled and the quality of their life improved. Hence Planning was expected to promote rapid overall development and diversification of the economy and strengthen the infrastructural base. The state required to generate adequate employment and secure a basic standard of living to everyone, the poor in particular through planning. Besides, the plan catered to the needs of ecologically sustainable development. "*Without doubt the eighth plan is a milestone in the great task of nation building*".[1] The plan had to keep in view the need for (*a*) continued reliance on domestic resources for financial investments; (*b*) increased technical capabilities for the development of science and technology and (*c*) modernization and competitive efficiency so that Indian economy can keep pace with and take advantage of global developments.

Though the VIIIth plan estimate was almost double the VIIth Plan, the actual enhancement in the public sector outlay was kept only 52 percent over the revised public sector outlay of the Seventh Schedule.

As regards the resource mobilisation, the Planning Commission emphasised the necessity for utmost financial discipline both at the Centre and in the states to reduce fiscal deficit, curtailment of unproductive expenditure, efficient management of public sector units and rationalisation of various developmental schemes.

It was emphasised that the process of planning and implementation needs modification so as to involve people in development processes through the democratic institutions of the local governments and voluntary organisations.

Highlights of 8th Plan (1992-97)

In the recent past, our BOP (Balance of payment) position was close to disaster. Inflation was on its climax despite a sound and broad based industrial growth. We were confronted with a disgusting and bleak scenario. Hence such a desperate economic situation necessitated courageous steps to put the nation back on the pathway of prompt and sustainable development. Thus, the then finance Minister - an eminent economist - introduced radical reforms. "Liberalisation was the hallmark

[1] *Yojna : August 15, 1992 Issue, p. 3*

of the Economic Reforms Programme which was amply reflected in the new trade and industrial policy. *Measures such as tightening of monetary policy to counter inflationary pressures and cut in government expenditure were mainly intended to reverse the trend of rising fiscal deficits thereby effecting much needed fiscal discipline. Policy regarding foreign investment was restructured to make it more attractive. In a nutshell, all these measures sought to achieve our objective, i.e. to make the Indian economy strong, viable and compatible with the global economic environment*".[1] At this crucial juncture, 8th five year plan was envisaged. It assumed a special significance as a vehicle of development and, as an instrument to meet mounting fiscal and budgetary deficits; critical situations in the balance of payments; a high rate of inflation. Its highlights are as under:

(*a*) The 8th Plan provided a new orientation to planning consistent with the new thrusts in economic policy and ensured that the public sector investment rested on a sound source base and the current account deficit was limited to a level sustainable by normal capital flows.

(*b*) During the Plan, steps were taken to curb the fundamental weakness in India's balance of payments situation, so that India's economy might not be disrupted.

(*c*) A reasonable degree of price stability was envisaged for the smooth functioning of the economic system, for protection of the interests of the poor and preventing deterioration in the mobilisation of resources.

(*d*) Deficit financing in the terms of the Central Government borrowings from the Reserve Bank was to be kept at a level consistent with a reasonable degree of price stability.

(*e*) The Public sector investment as envisaged in the 8th plan necessitated that the dissavings of the Government must come down sharply. Improved fiscal management leading to the generation of more savings by Government, underlined the financial pattern of public sector in the 8th plan. Hence, the existing trend of increasing dissavings of the Government was reversed.

(*f*) Four fold focus of approach to the Plan was as follows :

(*i*) Clear privatisation of sectors/projects for investment in order to facilitate operationalisation and implementation of the policy initiatives in the fiscal trade and industrial sectors and human development.

(*ii*) Making available the resources for the priority sectors and ensuring their effective utilization and completion of projects on schedules, avoiding cost and time overturns.

(*iii*) Creation of a social security net through employment generation, improved health care, and provision of extensive education facilities throughout the country.

(*iv*) Setting up of appropriate organisations and delivery systems to ensure that the benefits of investment in the social sectors reached the beneficiaries.[2]

(*g*) Keeping in view the above approach the following *objectives* were given priority :

(*i*) Generation of adequate employment so as to eradicate unemployment by the end of the 20th Century;

(*ii*) checkmating of population growth through mass cooperation and effective scheme of incentives and disincentives,

(*iii*) eradication of illiteracy by universalisation of elementary education among people between 15 and 35 years of age;

(*iv*) provision of safe drinking water and primary health care facilities, immunisation, accessibility for all villagers and elimination of scavenging;

[1] *Yojna : Eight Five Year Plan Vol. 36 August 15, 1992 p. 3*

[2] *Yojna : Eight Five Year Plan Volume 36 August 15, 1992 p. 81*

(*v*) growth and diversification of agriculture to attain self-sufficiency in food and surpluses for export;

(*vi*) strengthening the infrastructure (energy, transport, communication, irrigation) in order to lend support to the growth process;[1]

(*h*) The above mentioned objectives were to be kept in mind to cater to the following needs :

(*i*) perpetual reliance on domestic resources for financing investment;

(*ii*) augmentation of the technical capabilities for the development of science and technology;

(*iii*) modernization and competitive efficiency in order to enable the Indian economy to keep pace with global development.

Plan financing

Financial investment was originally to be of Rs. 7,98,000 crores and outlay of Rs. 8,71,000 crores. It necessitated massive domestic effort as net outflow from abroad was to be kept at moderate level, i.e. 1.6 per cent of GDP. Public sector investment was to be 45.3 percent of aggregate compared to 47.8 percent as initially conceived. Public sector investments at the rate of 10 percent of GDP was to come from borrowings out of savings of households to the extent of 70.4 per cent, 9.71 percent from the rest of the world and the balance from its own savings.

Keeping in view the highlights of Planning described above and comparing them with our experience of Planning for the last forty five years or so, it can be concluded that if the latter dampened people's initiatives and their sense of responsibility towards building the nation, the former played a major role in strengthening the physical infrastructure in order to support the growth process on a sustainable basis.

IXth Plan (April 1, 1997 - March, 2002)

The IXth plan was supposed to commence on April 1, 1997. A paper on IXth Plan was prepared by Madhu Dandavate, Dy. Chairman, Planning Commission during the U.F. Government. He tendered resignation and the BJP Government appointed Jaswant Singh as Dy. Chairman, Planning Commission. When the latter was elevated to the office of Minister, External Affairs, K.C. Pant, formerly, Chairman, Finance Commission was appointed, Deputy Chairman of the Planning Commission. He assumed office on February 6, 1999.

The Ninth Plan could not commence on April 1, 1997 due to frequent changes in the Government. However, the Annual plans were undertaken by the Government. Unfortunately even annual plan of 1998 could not be prepared due to fall of the U.F. Government.

According to Approach Paper, total investment proposed was Rs. 22,05,000 crores. Out of it, Rs. 8,75,000 crores was to be expended in the public sector and Rs. 13,30,000 crore in private sector. The plan aimed at achieving 7% growth rate per annum. The fall of the BJP Government in May 1999 was a temporary set back to the planning process.

Objectives

The main objectives of the Planning were :

(1) Priority to agriculture and rural development : With a view to generating employment and eradicating poverty, the Plan accorded priority to agriculture and rural development.

(2) Stability in prices : The Plan aimed at maintaining price stability in order to accelerate the growth rate of the economy.

[1]*Ibid, p. 82.*

(3) Nutritional security : It aimed at ensuring food and nutritional security for all weaker sections of the society, in particular.

(4) Minimum basic services : It stood for providing minimum basic services viz. safe drinking water, primary health care facility, primary education for all during the specified period and housing facility.

(5) Reduction in population growth : It aimed at reducing the growth rate of population.

(6) Environmental protection : It stood for ensuring environmental protection in the development process, eliciting cooperation of the people.

(7) To effect socio-economic change : It aimed at empowering women and socially weaker sections and minorities as agents of socio-economic change.

(8) Impetus to people's co-operation : It stood for developing Panchayati Raj Institutions, co-operatives and voluntary organisations in order to enable them to contribute to the economic development of the country.

(9) Self-Reliance : It aimed at attaining the goal of self-reliance.

To sum up, it can be concluded that the Ninth Plan stood for achieving the goal of 'growth with equity'.

Sectoral Programmes : Certain laudable programmes were framed for different sectors during the IXth Plan. They were as under :

1. Agricultural Development : The growth rate of agriculture was enhanced from 3.5% in the 8th plan to 4.5% in the 9th plan. Rs. 36,658 crore was to be spent on the development of agriculture and allied activities by adopting following measures :

(i) Different techniques were adopted for agricultural development suiting climactic and geographical conditions of different regions.

(ii) Production of manure and high yielding variety of seeds was increased.

(iii) Credit was made available to agricultural sector on a large scale at low rates of interest.

(iv) More importance be accorded to crop Insurance to protect small and marginal farmers.

(v) Research in agricultural sector be conducted and education be imparted to agriculturists regarding scientific methods of cultivation.

(vi) Production in activities allied to agriculture viz. animal husbandry, horticulture to be accorded more importance.

(vii) Special efforts to be made to promote the export of agricultural products.

(viii) Cooperative movement to be made more efficient as was based on professionalism.

2. Rural Development : In order to alleviate poverty and increase employment opportunities, the following rural development programmes will be vigorously pursued :

(i) Self employment plans to be coordinated with different regional plans and Area Development Programmes under Panchayati Raj.

(ii) Rural youth to be imparted job-oriented training for self-employment.

(iii) Rural artisans to be provided modern tools and technologies to augment their productivity and income,

(iv) Seven primary services (for the rural area's development), viz. drinking water, primary education, primary health services, houses for homeless, nutrition etc. to be accorded priority. In toto, Rs. 74,942 crores will be expended on Rural Development.

3. Irrigation : The Irrigation projects under progress to be completed and those already existing to be fully utilized.

(i) Minor irrigation projects to be further expanded

(ii) Water resources to be economically developed. Rs. 57,735 crore is to be expended on Irrigation and Flood control.

4. Industrial Development : Industrial growth rate was fixed at 9.3%. Hence greater emphasis was laid on the development in the infrastructure.

(i) Number of industries without licence was increased. The number of industries which require licences will be brought down.

(*ii*) Percentage of foreign capital in certain industries was increased from 74% to 100%.

(*iii*) 51% investment was made in many industries in public sector. Their management will be made more efficient.

(*iv*) National Renewal Fund was used to compensate Labourers rendered unemployed or who sought voluntary retirement.

Tenth Plan's (2002-2007)

The Xth Plan was conceived against a back drop of great expectations arising from applandable performance viz GDP growth reaveling 4.5% decelaration of population growth below 2% for the first line in the lest 4 deceds increase of litirary from 5.2% in 1991 to 6% in 2001 emergence of softwar and, It as new source of strength loorting confidence almost India potential to compatitive with world democracy. In fact, the 10th plan offered an opportunity to luclid upon the gain of the fast and address the weaknesses that had cropped up. The country a Reform Plan irrated of a new resource plan.

On October 29, 2002 the 10th five-year plan targeting **8 per cent growth** annually during 2002-07 was approved by the Union Cabinet. Its main points are highlighted are as follows :

1. An outlay of Rs 15,92,300 crore including gross budgetary support of Rs. 706000 crore has been earmarked.

2. The Central Plan will have an outlay of Rs. 9,21,291 crore and the outlay for the states and the Union Territories was Rs. 6,71,009 crore.

3. Planning Commission proposed Rs. 78,000 crore as the contribution of disinvestment proceeds towards Rs. 9,21,291 crore central plan outlay over the next five years. Evidently, disinvestment proceeds were to finance 11% of the Central budgetary support to the Plan.

4. The Plan document carried forward key reforms particularly in the domain of agriculture to generate 50 million jobs in the next five years. Besides it raised FDI[1] flow to 7.5 billion dollars annually.

5. The Plan focussed on the improvement of quality of life of people as well. It referred to reduction in poverty ratio from 26% to 21% by 2007.

6. The Plan made a provision for potable drinking water in all villages; cleansing of major polluted rivers; growth in gainful employment, increase in literacy rate from 65% to 75%; universalisation of elementary education by 2003.[2]

7. The growth target was kept at 8%.

Speaking on the targets of plan reform the Planning Commission the P.M remakred. This should be plan for the poor. this should be a plan fudals-Adecasis and Back and clears and this should be a plan for all those regions that have eagged behind development". [3] It frcussed ono the remoral of regional and gender unilalanes which shaken the social falrid of our connture.

Mid Term appraisal of the 10th plan

The mid term apparisal of the 10th plan was accorded approval by the National Development Council in June 2005. A comprehensive assessment of the performance of the economy as a whole and its performance in undivided sectors keeping in view the plan target was made and duly presented

[1] *Ibid, p. 82.*

[2] *Completition world : January 2003 Issue P.157*

[3] *Dr. Rudra Dutt:* 10th plan: Approach etc in competitive world

to the NDC. Its highlights were ; (i) The economy was statisfactory in many areas. (ii) The average GDP for inotival 3 years are 6.5% through anticipation was 3% though largest was 8%.

XIth Plan 2007-2012

11th plan. The Indian economy on the eve of the 11th plan (2007-12) was on sounder footing than it was a few years ago. The economy at the time of ushering in of the 11th plan exhibited 7.8 per cent GDP serving rate at 34.8 percent of GDP and the Investment rate at 35.9 percent of GDP. Foreign direct Investment inflows, exports, foreign exchange reserves were on the ascendence and in general the fiscal position was perpetually improving. Evidently 11th plan could not have expected a better economic environment.

The approach paper to the 11th 5 yearly plan document "Towards faster and more inclusive growth" was approved by the National Development Council. The 11th Plan was later approved by the Planning Commission.

Priority Areas of the 11th 5 year Plan

Agriculture, Irrigation and water resources education health, infrastructure and employment along with programmes for upliftment of SCs/STs, OBC, minorities, women and children. In the initial years government realized that the economic growth though accelerated failed to be all inducive. Benefit of growth could hardly reach the farmers landless labourers and persons working in unorganised sector. The 11th plan recognises the necessity of promotion of social typed. Justice and the need of growth process that can help aleviation, of poverty, generation of employment and ensuring of essential services viz health and education for all sections of society.

Total proposed public investment in the 11th plan Rs. 3644718 crores. The GDP growth target towards the end of Plan was conceived as 10 percent though the average growth rate of 9 percent-envisaged. However the 11th plan did not consider GDP as the end in itself. In was considered as a means to achieve higher standard of living. Recession has however given set back to GDP which infact is a global phenomenon still we are far better off than most of the global powrs.

Global recession and all round melt down has given a great set back to our fast growing economy and so long as recession continues achievements of targets is likely to be affected in India as well. GDP growth has come to stand still. It's likely to remain 7 per cent and even less. Our targets were as follows:

I. Income and Poverty : (i) To accelerate growth rate of GDP from 8% to 10% and then maintain it at 10% in the next 5 year plan in order to double the income by 2016-17. (ii) To enhance agricultural growth rate to 4 per cent. (iii) To create 58 million new employment opportunities (iv) To curtail educated unemployment rate to below 5% (v) To increase wage rate of unskilled workers by 20% (vi) To reduce poverty by 10% points *i.e.* from existing 20 percent to 10 percent.

II Education: (i) To curtail drop out rate of children from elementary school from 52.2 % in 2003-04 to 20% by 2011-12 (ii) To develop minimum standards of education in elementary schools and ensure quality of education (iii) to increase literacy rate for persons of 7 years of age or more to 85 percent (iv) To reduce gender gap in literacy from 21% to 10% (v) To increase the percentage of each child going to higher education from the current 10% to 15% by the end of the 11th plan.

III Health: (i) To reduce infant mortality rate to 28 and maternal mortality rate to 1 per 1000 births.

(ii) to reduce fertility rate to 2-1 (iii) to make provision for clean drinking water for all by 2009 (iv) To curtail mal-nutrition among children of age group 0-3 to half of its level. (v) To reduce anaemia among women and girls by 50% by the end of the 11th plan.

IV Women and Children: (i) To raise the sex ratio for age group 0-6 to 935 by 2011-12 end to 950 by 2016-17.

(ii) To ensure that at least 33% of the direct and indirect beneficiaries of all government schemes are women and girl children.

(iii)To see that all children enjoy a safe childhood without any compulsion to work.

V Infrastructure: (i) To provide electricity to all villages and BPL households by 2009 and 24 hours supply by the end of plan.

(ii) To ensure all weather road links to all habitations with-population of 1000 and above, by 2009.

(iii) To link every village with telephone by November, 2009 and to provide broad band connectivity to all villages.

(iv) To provide homesheds to all by 2012.

VI Environment: (i) To increase forest and tree cover by 5%

(ii) To attain WHO standards of air quality in all major cities by 20.1.12.

(iii) To treat all urban waste water by 2011-12 and to clean river water (iv) To increase energy efficiency by 20% by 2016-17.

It may be stated that the resource allocation makes it clear that the plan is committed towards achievement of faster and more inclusive growth.

(C) Basic assumptions of the plan: The faster and inclusive growth as has been projected in the 11th five year plan will require investment of 35.1% of GDP. The share of private and public sectors is as follows: Public sector.............11.2% of GDP

Private sector ....23.9% of GDP

It clearly reflects that the current plan is more dependent on, private investment. As such, private sector's it may be stated that the resource allocation makes it clear that the Plan is committed towards achievement of faster and more inclusive growth in the development investment. As such private sectors role in the development process of economy is more prominent.

(D) Strategy of the 11th five yearly plan: The main ingredients of strategy of the 11th plan are as follows:

1. Quick growth: In a rapid growing economy alone the income of the masses can be enhanced and amelioration of their lot is possible.

2. Inclusive growth: The growth should be universal. Hence government should adopt policies that ensure broad based growth benefitting all parts of the country', rural areas in particular.

3. Priority Area: The growth rate should be doubled in priority area viz agriculture, health education, employment and labour.

4. Focus on private sector: The private sector comprising small scale enterprises farming and the corporate sector has to play vital role in the attainment of objectives of faster and more inclusive growth. Since this sector accounts for 70% of the total investment in the economy our policies must cater to the creation of environment in which enterpreneurship can flourish.

It is thus quite evident that the public sector is mainly dependent on the development of infrastructre, agriculture education and health and the private sector has to render assistance to the public sector and play significant role in developing industrial and service sectors.

The Challenges Presently, the main challenges before the economy are sustaining the growth momentum and achieving the GDP of 9 percent. reduction of inflation and to keep it at single digit level; agricultural growth; expandrig industry fast by 10.5% per year, effective fiscal management and augmentation of agricultural growth to accelerate general growth in the country. The global recession has adversely affected the economy all the world over, India being no exception. It is another big challenge– to keep pace with global recession and come out of it. Its heartening to note that economic growth in the first quarter 2009-10 India economic growth has uses to 6.1%. As per an Editorial. The push given by way of debt barriers and higher procurement prices fairmer and social development schemes enabled million in rural areas to turn from modest income earners to mers. The gavent an economy a boost..." Parnate Mukherjee remarked" The queen shoots an un finally taking not. In the next two to three years our economy will require growth rate of a percent the pre down tween period "

(E) SOCIALISM (in India)

Prof. C.M. Joad rightly remarked "Socialism is like a hat which has lost its shape, as everybody wears it". After the attainment of independence in 1947, Pandit Jawaharlal Nehru came at the helm of affairs as the Prime Minister of the country. Though born in an aristocratic family, Nehru was considerably influenced by concepts of Socialism as practised in USSR and Gandhism at a later stage. Hence he got enamoured of a socialistic pattern of society right from the very beginning. He became plan minded, on account of the Russian influence. As early as 1937, he headed the Planning Committee appointed by the Indian National Congress but the then Congress could not have much say as the Central Government run by alien masters held its sway. The Central Government as already stated, was run by the Governor General and his Council.

With the inception of independent era, Planning Commission was set up in March, 1950 with Jawaharlal Nehru as its Chairman. Jawaharlal Nehru and his socialistic brand in the Congress pleaded for incorporation of socialistic directives in the IVth Chapter of the Constitution. The Directives which aimed at securing a social order for the welfare of the people ensuring: were to serve as the beaon light for the future governments. They were as under.

(*i*) Adequate means of livelihood, for all citizens.

(*ii*) Ownership and control of material resources of the community and their distribution for common good.

(*iii*) Non concentration of wealth and means of production to common detriment.

(*iv*) Equal pay for equal work for men and women.

(*v*) Saving the health and strength of workers from abuse forced by economic necessities.

(*vi*) Protection of child and adult labour.

(*vii*) Opportunities to children to develop in a healthy manner and in conditions of freedom and dignity and protection of childhood and youth against exploitation and moral and material abandonment.

(*viii*) Public assistance in the event of old age, unemployment, sickness and physical disablement.

(*ix*) Provision for just and humane conditions of work and maternity relief.

(*x*) Living wage and decent standards of life and employment of leisure.

(*xi*) Workers' participation in the management of industrial establishments.

(*xii*) Minimisation of inequalities in income and elimination of inequalities in status, facilities and opportunities.

(*xiii*) Provision for legal aid, ensuring non-denial of justice for economic or other reasons.

The Gandhian principle of promotion of cottage industries is also one of the directives which aims at ameliorating the lot of poor classes by enabling them employment opportunities and providing them cheap Khadi cloth. Organisation of village panchayats to function as units of self-government was another laudable Gandhian principle incorporated in the chapter. This was to help vast section of villagers to gain self confidence and manage their own affairs and solve their primary problems. According to a scholar, both these principles aim at *Sarvodaya*—pure Socialism.[1]

The Directive Principles stated above refer to the ideals of socio-economic character. These are the directives which the Legislature and the Executive are expected to keep in view while framing laws or issuing orders. They aim at establishing a socialistic state based on the welfare of the people.

[1] *S.N. Aggarwal : Socialism and Sarvodaya : Hindustan Times, January 1, 1995.*

According to K.V. Rao, "the philosophy underlying these provisions is 'Fabian Socialism' without the socialism, for only the nationalisation of the means of production, distribution, and exchange is missing'.[1] In fact the principles enumerated above laid down the framework of a democratic socialistic order as envisaged by Gandhi and conceived by Nehru. Dr. Ambedkar, the architect of the Indian Constitution rightly opined, **"If these Directive Principles of State Policy are not socialistic in their direction and their content, I fail to understand what more socialism can there be"**.[2]

The inclusion of 'Right to Private Property' as Fundamental Right in Chapter III of the Indian Constitution made a mockery of the Indian brand of socialism. There have been numerous legal conflicts regarding the implementation of Directive Principles pertaining to socialism and the right to Property as Fundamental Right. Which was to be given precedence - a fundamental right or non- justiciable Directive Principle - was a moot question. The Supreme Court has been giving contradictory judgments at different times and in different climes. Recently, the Supreme Court took a firm stand that the Directive Principles could not override the Fundamental Rights and must conform to and run subsidiary to the latter. In the *State of Madras* Vs. *Champa Karan Dorairajan*, the Supreme Court (1951) had upheld the decision of the High Court of Madras and ruled that the chapter on Fundamental Rights was sacrosanct and not liable to be abridged by any legislative or executive enactment or order. In another case of State of Madras Vs. C.R. Srinivasan, the Supreme Court held that the Directive Principles being nonjusticiable could not override Fundamental Rights. It led the ruling party to enact the first Amendment in 1951. "It provided that nothing shall prevent the state from making any special provision for the advancement of a socially and educationally backward class of citizens or for the Scheduled castes and the Scheduled Tribes". In *State of Bihar* Vs. *Kameshwar Singh* and *'Bijoy Cotton Mills Ltd.* Vs. *the State of Ajmer'*, the Supreme Court gave precedence to Directive Principles. In the former case, the validity of Zamindari Abolition Act was challenged on the plea that it violated the Right to Property. Justice M.C. Mahajan upholding the validity of the Zamindari Abolition Act opined that the abolition was intended to do away with the concentration of large tracts of lands in the hands of a few individuals and benefit a large number of tenants obviously for public purpose. In the famous *Gokalnath case* (1967), the Supreme Court rejected the Government's plea that if parliament was not given the power to amend the Constitution, it would be difficult to implement the Directive Principles and there will be a revolution in the country. The Chief Justice remarked, "*The Fundamental Rights and the Directive Principles of the State Policy enshrined in the Constitution formed an integrated scheme and were elastic enough to respond to the changing needs of the society*".[3] This opinion clarified that both the Directive Principles and the Fundamental Rights are on equal footing and the earlier theory of subordination of Directive Principles to Fundamental Rights stood exploded. Secondly the Fundamental Rights are not to be treated as static. They must respond to the changing needs of society reflecting the aspirations of the people. The Judges portrayed Directive Principles as the conscience of the constitution and the reservoir of the people's aspirations. Thus the doctrine of 'integrated scheme' and 'elasticity' of Fundamental Rights establish that the Fundamental Rights must be interpreted in the light of the Directive Principles so that the state might implement its socio-economic obligations as imposed on it by Part IV of the Constitution and also the Preamble of the Constitution particularly after the passage of the 42nd amendment Act (1976).[4] In the words of a scholar, to interpret the Fundamentals in the light of Directive Principles is "*definitely to give new meaning, new content and new dimension to the former so that not only the latter could be implemented fully and effectively but the former could find themselves in tune with the changed conditions and the new social order brought about by implementation of the directive principles*".[5] The 24th and 25th

[1] *K.V. Rao : Parliamentary Democracy of India, Ed. II, p. 353*

[2] *CAD Vol VIII p. 40*

[3] *Golak Nath v. State of Punjab (1967), SA.C.J. 436.*

[4] *Words 'socialist' and 'secular' were added in the Preamble by the 42nd Amendment Act, 1976.*

[5] *R.P. Krishna Shethy : Fundamental Rights and Socio-economic justice in the Indian Constitution, p. 103.*

amendment Acts (1971) aimed at removing the hindrances to the implementation of Directive Principles contained in Article 37, (as posed by provisions in Part III, relating to Fundamental Rights).

In the famous *Kesavananda Bharti case*, the Supreme Court upheld Article 31(C) and recognised the competence of the legislature for enacting laws to give effect to the Directive Principles as contained in clause (b) and (c) of Article 39. It also opined that though article 368 empowers the Parliament to amend the Constitution, the said power could not be exercised so as to alter the basic structure of the Constitution. The 42nd Amendment Act nullified the effect of the above case and provided that no law giving effect to the policy of the state towards securing for all any of the Directive Principles shall be deemed to be void on the ground that it is inconsistent with or abridges the rights conferred by Articles 14, 19 or 31.[1] Article 368 was also amended, debarring the Courts from questioning the validity of amendments which conferred upon the Parliament unlimited powers to amend any provision of the Constitution.

The controversy continued. In *Minerva Mills case,* the validity of 42nd amendment was questioned. On May 9, 1980 section 55 and section 4 of the Act were declared void by the Supreme Court. Section 4 amended article 31C which had exempted from challenge any law which enforced any of the Directive Principles on the ground that it violated Articles 14 and 19. The Minerva Mills case re-established the supremacy of the Fundamental Rights and every law or amendment made in furtherance of the Directive Principles was subjected to the scrutiny of the courts which had to determine as to whether or not it was violative of Fundamental Rights, particularly of Articles 14 and 19.

It is evident from the above controversy that these Directive Principles were intended to be fundamental in the governance of the country. They aimed at the establishment of socialistic order. The abolition of Zamindari system and Privy purses of the former rulers, bank nationalization, ceiling on the rural and urban land and the gradual transfer of surplus land to the weaker sections of people have been substantial steps towards the establishment of social and economic justice in the country. The eventual abolition of right to property as a fundamental right was another milestone in this direction. Promotion of cottage industries, establishment of Panchayati Raj and right to work as a directive are steps in this direction as well.

Right to equality and right against exploitation are the laudable fundamental rights which help in ushering in an era of equality, justice and social security - the ingredients of socialism. However, the right to equality is not supposed to prevent the state from making any special provisions for women and children. The Constitution Amendment Act (1951) also provided that Article 15 or clause 29 will not prevent the state from making any special provision for the advancement of any socially and educationally backward classes of citizens or for scheduled castes and scheduled tribes. Likewise posts may be kept reserved for Backward Classes. The right to equality thus protects all categories of the citizens against all types of discriminations. It bans all kinds of untouchability-specified or unspecified. The right to equality does not mean levelling down of the people. Instead, it fosters social revolution, by creating egalitarian society, free from the trammels of economic disabilities and social inequalities.

Right against exploitation puts an end to '*Begar*' and traffic in human beings for immoral purposes. Thus, bonded or forced labour has been constitutionally prohibited. The children below the age of 14 years are not to be allowed to work in hazardous factories or mines steps are being taken to educate such children and give economic assistance to their families after the passage of right to education in 2009. In case of Delhi Child Labour Act had laid down a package of Rs 20,000 for each such family but the present minister of social welfare in Sheila Dixit's cabinet has requested the government to revise this package and employ one member of the family of each such child who is deprived of an opportunity to serve in hazardous factory. After all children were being put

[1] *The 44th Amendment Act, 1978 deleted from Fundamental Rights chapter the Right to Private Property.*

to torture by poor parents out of compulsion. Maharashtra also is thinking of doing something substantial for domestic helps. These steps do help in the establishment of a socialistic pattern of society as they aim at ending all types of exploitation—the legacies of Imperialists.

The 42nd Amendment (1976) substitutes the Preamble 'Sovereign Democratic Republic' by a Sovereign, Democratic, Socialistic, and Secular Republic.' Liberty of thought, expression, belief, faith and worship' as provided by Right to Freedom of Religion' necessitated a clear mention of the word 'secular' in our Preamble to highlight the basic tenet of our policy. The addition of the word 'socialist' in the Preamble reveals the aspirations of the then leadership of the country to save the future governments from deviating from the socialistic pattern of society. Perhaps they might not have liked socialism to be deduced at will from the Directive Principles or the Fundamental Rights referred to above. Hence they incorporated socialism in the Preamble itself so that posterity might remain conscious of the fundamental objectives to be kept in mind before framing the governmental sketch and designing progressive laws of the land.

However, our socialism is of a unique type. We have catered to a mixed economy system since the times of first Prime Minister Jawaharlal Nehru – the votary of socialism and planning. His strong leanings to the erstwhile Soviet Union and the latter's perpetual support to India in matters, economic political and diplomatic detracted him from a capitalistic economic structure – the type existing in the U.S.A. How-ever, exigencies of time demanded the existence of a private sector along with the public sector. Healthy competition between the two sectors was thought indispensable to improve our completely shattered economy and take no chances by a complete switch over to socialism. Socialism of the type prevalent in ertwhile USSR, China and other communist countries toeing the line of Karl Marx, Lenin, Stalin and Mao, believed in a ruthless dictatorship to wipe out capitalist structure of society which was considered highly discriminatory, thoroughly acquisitive, and totally exploitative. Democracy in such socialistic regime was only a mockery though they made tall claims for the same. Dr. Finer, writing about the so-called Russian thorough going democracy remarked, "Russian leaders wrested authority from the Czars and usurped it and gave to the people crumbs baked on guns and revolvers." Evidently, Russian socialistic democracy worked within the iron-framework of the Communist Party. Hence it was hardly democratic. The Party which ruled USSR presented a monolithic structure. The trappings of mass democracy and mass participation could not mask the entrenched position of the dictatorial elite which dominated both the Party and the Government. In the words of Fainsod, "*the political realities of Soviet life speak the unmistakable language of one party dictatorship in which ultimate power is deposited in a narrow ruling group*."

The collapse of the Soviet Union and explosion of myth of its sound economy revealed hollowness of this brand of socialism. India after the fall of Soviet Union and installation of Congress Government under Narasimha Rao started paying only lip homage to Socialism. The UF Governments under Deve Gowda and I.K. Gujral and after XII Lok Sabha polls, the BJP under A.B. Vajpayee toed the line laid down by Narasimha Rao. Adoption of new economic measures in the recent past reflect our strong leanings to an American pattern of economy. More and more emphasis is being laid on privatization and curb on deficit financing to rejuvenate our economy's so as to enable us to get maximum assistance from the International Monetary Fund and the World Bank. The latest measures include encouraging foreign investors to collaborate with the Indians and set up enterprises in India for improving economy. Thus we are now taking to liberalisation and modernisation. Hence our GDP has gone up. Even during the global recession indias' economy's comparatively sound. We hope to augment GDP to 8 percent in the near future. Inflation also came down through inflation in edibles sky high.

These steps towards liberalization have entailed scathing criticism at the hands of the Leftists, the C.P.I. and C.P.I(M) in particular. They call it a complete 'sell out' to world Bank and I.M.F. and an open invitation to Americans' hegemony. They have expressed apprehensions of being duped by foreign capitalists at no distant future and India once again losing hard-won economic independence at the hands of the foreign capitalists who eventually may rule our economy. However, this is going rather too far though a setback to the concept of socialism cannot be denied, during the previous regimes of Congress under Narsimha Rao, of U.F. under Deve Gowda and I.K. Gujral and also in the BJP regime, under A.B. Vajpayee and the present congress government at the centre. This may not be too heavy a price for effecting sound economy and ushering in an era of abiding prosperity. No doubt, Socialism under the current philosophy of Liberalisation is fast becoming a relic of the past. We are fast drifting to USA both economically and diplomatically. Indo-USA Nuclear Deal for civil purpose aims at improving our economy and making India as a global power. Evidently, we have chosen a different path to safeguard the economic interests of our country. We hope to eradicate poverty by keeping pace with the technological revolution in the western world. If the poor is protected and our country becomes richer by following the concepts of free market economy and economic liberalization, we wont be considered losers. Socialism may however be in jeopardy as it had its trial for a few decades in our country and poor became poorer and then, rich richer. Hence a switch over to liberalization and modernization was the crying need of the hour.

E. Human Rights: The autocratic dictators like Hitler in Nazi Germany, Mussolini in Italy. Franco in Spain King–the Emperor in Japan and Stalin in Soviet Union trampled the rights of the people down their heels. They gagged the press, crushed freedom of speech and thoughts and abrogated all the civic freedoms without which a human being is reduced to a mere dumb driven cattle. The mass persecutions of gews in Germany, the extermination of the capitalist classes (the hourgeous) in Soviet land, the slogans of war and expansion in Italy proclaiming 'war is to man and maternity to women the tall claims of Germans Nordia race is the superior most race in the world, resulting eventually in ghastly tragedy – the world—world war II which shook the saver politicans of the world to the last fiber. Hence, there was spontaneous awakening all the world over and a craze to usher in era of peace and tranquility. President Roosevelt of USA proclaimed in 1941 the dire necessity of four feeedoms viz freedom of speech, freedom of worship, freedom from want and freedom from fears. It was construed as a step towards laying foundation of durable peace and human dignity.

UN Charter and Human Rights (1945): With the end of hostilities in 1945 and the incepton of the United Nations Organisation, a new era of the post world war dawned. The UN charter proclaimed, the objectives of the UN as the promotion of social progress and opting for better standard of life in larger freedom. It clearly affirmed faith in fundamental human rights in the dignity and worth of human beings:

A Universal Declaration December 10, 1948: The universal declaration of Human Rights was proclaimed on December 10, 1948. The member states of the UN were called upon to adopt and implement all these rights in their respective countries. Since then all the world over, December 10 is celebrated as the Human Rights Day. We state below a synopsis of the Human Rights as incorporated in the Declaration of 1948.

The Declaration of Human Rights comprises a Preamble and 30 articles. These rights may be grouped as follows.

A Civil Rights (i) All human beings are born free and are equal in dignity and rights. All are equal before law.

(ii) Everyone has the right to life, liberty and security of person. Nobody is to be held in slavery. As such, the slave trade is to be prohibited in all forms (iii) No one is to be subjected to torture or inhuman treatment or punishment. No one is to be subjected to arbitrary arrest, detention or exile (iv) Everyone has the right to freedom of thought, conscience and religion. Everyone has the right of opinion and expression.

(v) Everyone has the right to freedom of peaceful assembly and association. However, no one is to be compelled to belong to any association.

(B) Political Rights: (Articles 14, 15 and 21) (i) Everyone has the right to participate in the government of the country directly or indirectly through properly elected representatives (ii) Everyone has the right of equal access to public services in his country (iii) The will of the people is the basis of the authority of the Government. This will is to be expressed through periodic elections by secret ballot. (iv) None is to be deprived of his nationality nor anybody is to be denied the right to change his nationality. (v) Anybody can seek and enjoy in other countries asylum from prosecution.

(C) Economic Rights: (i) Everyone has the right to own property. None is to be deprived of property arbitrarily. (ii) Everyone has the right to social security which enables a person having no source of income to be supported by the government (iii) Everyone has the right to work and also protection against unemployment. Everyone has the right to equal pay for equal look. (iv) Everyone possesses the right to standard of living adequate for the health and well-being of himself and his family. It comprises proper food, clothing, housing, medical care and necessary social services.

(D) Social Rights: (i) Men and Women of full age have the right to marry. Marriage shall take place with full consent of the intending spouses (ii) The family – a natural and fundamental unit of society– is entitled to full protection by society and the state.

(iii) Motherhood and childhood are entitled to special care and assistance (iv) Everyone posseses the right to education. Education may be free at least in the elementary and fundamental stage (v) Education is to promote understanding tolerance, friendship among all nations and social groups. It furthers the activities of the United Nations for the maintenance of peace.

(E) Cultural Rights: (i) Everyone possess the right to freely participate in the cultural life of the community. Everyone as such can enjoy the arts and share in scientific advancements and zeap its benefits. (ii) Everyone has the right to the protection of the moral and material interests resulting from scientific literary or artistic production of which be is the author.

Significance of the Human Rights Declaration: The Declaration commands significance of the highest order. It is not only addressed to all nations but to all people in the world. It has acquired the character of world law. The Declaration is of vast significance on the following grounds.

(a) Universality of Rights: The Declaration of Human Rights has attained marked universality. Not a single dissenting voice was expressed against it. Article 2 laid down, "Everyone is entitled to all the rights and freedoms set forth in the Declaration without distinction of any kind. The declaration is applicable to all territories and countries and not self governing countries alone.

(b) Violation of human Rights– an international concern : The saga of Nazi Germany and Fascists strangulation of civic freedoms was too fresh in the memories of the terribly agonised humanity and as such hardly ineffacrable from minds. Hence the UN laid down promotion of human rights as the principal purpose of its very inception. A gross violation of Human Rights was considered a potential threat to internal peace and was to be construed as a matter of international concern. Under the UN charter, the Security Council is determinant of the existence of any peril to peace. It decides as to what action is necessitated to maintain international peace.

(c) Its impact on constitutions; The declaration of Human Rights embodies major contentsof the American Bill of Rights and that of Charter of Rights of Great Britain. The Declaration as such had great impact-on several constitutions of India, Indonesia, Pakistan, Togo, Haiti, Bangladesh are

Significance of Human Right In India: The significance of the Human Rights for India lies in the facts as under:

A craving since Colonial Era: India has been a votary of Human Rights since its subjugation by the British. The Indians have been subjected to inhuman treatment at the hands of the British imperialists the day they landed on our soil as the traders in the guise of East India Company. After Mutiny of 1857 which was in fact first battle of India's independence Queen victoria took over government of India and abolished Court of Directors and Board of control of East India Company and Victoria became the Queen Empress of India. For Indians it was it change from 'frying pan to fire'. Perpetuation untold sufferings and denial of civic liberties during the tyrannical British rule. The Indians realized, the value of political emancipation which alone could be followed by civic freedoms. Hence

India which had suffered the pangs of servitude and subjugation to the alien rulers, contributed substantially to draft a universal declaration of Human Rights. India was a signatory to six Human Rights Couvenants.

India strongly espoused the cause of Human Rights as it stood for both the human values, democratic norms and international cooperation. India zealously participated in the discussions on the Human Rights in the sessions of UN commission on the Human rights. India's role in the 54th sessions of the Commission on Human Rights held in Geneva was laudable. The craving for Human Rights induced the fathers of the Indian constitution to specify in the PREAMBLE of the Indian constitution– the constitution will secure to its citizens justice-social economic and political; liberty of the thought, expression belief, faith and worship; equality of status and opportunity and fraternity assuring the dignity of the individual and unity of the nation. These ideals laid down in the preamble were accorded realistic shape by incorporating Fundamental Rights and Directive Principles in chapters of the Indian Constitution.

Provisions of the Indian Constitution: The seven fundamental rights, later reduced to 'six' by the 44th amendment which abolished right to property are : (i) Right to equality (ii) Right to freedom (iii) right against exploitation; (iv) right to freedom of religion (v) cultural and educational rights (vi) right to constitutional remedies

Right to Property being very controversial was taken out of the list of Fundamental Rights by the 44th amendment and was reduced to status of legal right only. The details of these rights are given in the following pages to apprise the readers of our Fundamental Rights in detail.

The Directive principles also secure social and economic freedoms. They require the state to provide work to everybody give equal pay for equal work for men and women and impart elementary education for children below the age of 14 years. The Right to education passed by the parliament in the recent past in 2009 implements the directive principle regarding elementary education more firmly.

Human Rights Commission (at National level 1992-93) : We established two prominent commissions-National commission for women in 1992 and Human Rights commission in 1993. The N.C for women established on January 21, 1992 made an appraisal of the legal and constitutional safeguards of women and recommended remedial measures and advised the Government on welfare activities pertaining to women in the country. In the recent past women in the rural local bodies have been provided 1/3 of the total seats as per 73rd amedment in the constitution. Like wise in the urban local bodies according to get 74th Amendment Act women get 1/3 of the total seats. The efforts are being made to get them 33% reservation in the state legislator assemblies and also the parliament. In the recent past Rajya Sabha succeeded in passing the Bill for according them 33% of reservation in the Parliament. The Bill could not be presented in the Lok Sabha due to opposition of even government's allies. On the International Women Day function in 2001, the HRD minister expressed hopes that a law was soon to be enacted to tackle the widespread problem of domestic violence against women.[1] Chief Justice Dr. A.S. Anand also held that though the constitution accorded an equal status to the two sexes this had not been reflected adequately in reality."[2] Later the prohibition of women from domestic violence Act 2005 was enacted. The prohibition of child marriage Act 2006 (notified in 2007) was also passed.

Human Rights Commission 1993: The HRC performs the following duties: (1) It enquires into complaints of violation of Human Rights (2) It pays a visit to any jail to find out the living conditions of the prisoners (3) It reviews acts of terrorism that impede the enjoyment of human rights (4) It promotes research in the domain of human rights and makes people conscious of human

1. *Hindustan Times: March 9, 2001 p.11*
2. *Ibid*

rights (5) It incourages the effect of the governmental organisation in furthering the cause of human rights.

How it functions: It is equipped with powers of civil court. It can summon witenesses evidences and affidavits, forward the case with record of facts to a magistrate. To quote an instance, on April 9, 2000 the HRC directed the kerala government to make payment of Rs. 50,000 as interim compensation to the family of a prisoner who received fatal injuries white discharging perilous kitchen duties in Kottarakara Jail. Likewise the commission played a conspicious role in the campaign against terrorist and disruptive activities act in the recent case.

Non Governmental Organisation:(NGOS) A close link between government and NGOs is indispensable, if human rights are to be effectively protected. Such organisations have sprouted in USA, Africa, Europe. Latin America and many Asiatic countries India also over 2000. NGOs have been actively attracting public attention to human rights abuse. These organizations have unearthed extreme cases servitude in the form of bounded labourers and carpet boy and have highlighted the molestation of women undertrials and also single working women.

We may conclude that frantic effort, are afoot both by the Government and the NGOs to secure human rights. The NHC and Slate HRCs are quite active in their respective role at their levels. But despite their efforts, in caste ridden society and not devoid of gender bias, the under priviliged are subjected to atrocities. The fair sex also is being treated unfairly. It is possible with the gradual empowerment of women lessoning of gender bias more of human approach to the under privileged people and the frantic efforts of the NGOs and the governmental agencies human rights may be enjoyed by one and all without any discrimination and become a proud privilege of every democratic citizen and envy of underprivileged and bounded classes in the various works and corners of the world.

Attempts for impetus to Universal Declration of Human Right (UDHR): The under mentioned conventions which were religiously followed after the UDHR have given impetus to the attempts for the safeguard of Human Rights. (1) Convention on the Prevention and punishment of the Crime of Genocide 1948. (2) Convention on the Political Rights of Women 1952. (3) Covenant on Economic Social and Cultural Rights 1966. (4) Covenant on Civil and Political Rights 1966. (5) Optional protocol to the International Covenant on Civil and Political Rights 1966. (6) Convention on the Non applicability of statutory limitations to war crimes and crimes against humanity - 1968. (7) Convention on the suppression and Punishment of the Crime of Apartheid - 1973.

These covenants/conventions have been instrumental in providing a legal sanctity to the DHRD. As such these Rights are binding upon every nation. Besides the above a few more conventions have cropped up for the protection of the rights of children women workers migrant workers bounded labour forced labour the prostitutes 'apartheid etc.' The UDHR (1948) and the conventions adopted thereafter have considerably influenced the Unity of Nations. As such they have eventually incoporated these rights in their respective constitutions and have championed the cause of Human Rights. In 1981, even the UN General Assembly was invoked by some member states to consider the inception of International Human Order, which should aim at provoking the states to declare that the grants and progress of society and the stability of governments of states are inextricably and inseparately linked with the growth, progress and stability of human beings and as such all development programmes should be designed and executed at the level of the people — the main instruments and principal beneficiaries of the evolutionary process.

It is heartening that today the human Rights and Freedoms constitute the bedrock of the 21st Century global democracies. Hence, the tempo should be perpetually maintained by ending inequalities among sovereign nation states and assuming Freedoms to all the people of the world irrespective of discriminations on the basis of race, sex, language, religion, culture, nationality, place of residence and citizenship.

***

CENTRAL POLITICAL EXECUTIVE

Political Executive at the Union level

"The President is the head of the State but not of the Executive."

—*Dr. B.R. Ambedkar*

CONTENTS : (A) The President of India
(B) Vice President
(C) Prime Minister
(D) Council of Ministers (COM)
(E) Cabinet Committees

The President, the Prime Minister, and the Council of Ministers constitute the Union executive. India has opted for a parliamentary form of government. Hence President is a constitutional ruler, a nominal head of the state and the Prime Minister and his COM the *real executive.* The Constitution vested executive powers with the President and laid down that he is to be advised and aided by the Council of Ministers in the exercise of these powers. Hence it remained only conventional till the passage of 42nd (1976) and 44th (1978) amendments Acts when it was enjoined on the President not to flout the advice of the Ministers. These amendments made the advice of the Council of Ministers binding on the President. However, the advice which was made binding on the President according to 42nd amendment Act enabled the latter by the 44th amendment Act to get the Bill reconsidered by the Council of Ministers. After such a reconsideration, however, the advice of the Council of Ministers cannot be flouted. Thus the position of the President vis-a-vis Prime Minister who heads the Council of Ministers is crystal clear. The former is the titular head of the State whereas the latter is the real head of the Government.

(A) THE PRESIDENT OF INDIA

His Election

According to Article 54, the President is to be elected by an Electoral College consisting of (a) the elected members of both the Houses of the Parliament; (b) the elected members of the Legislative Assemblies of the States. The election of President shall be held in accordance with proportional representation by means of a single transferable vote and the voting at such election is to be through secret ballot.[1] The Constitution provides uniformity in the scale of representation of the different states. Besides, parity between the states as a whole and the Union is aimed at. For securing such a parity between the Union and the states and uniformity among the states, the undermentioned formula is adopted. Every elected member of the Legislative Assembly shall have as many votes as there are multiples of one thousand in the quotient obtained by dividing the population of the states by the total number of elected members of the Assembly. In brief, the number of votes which each M.L.A of a state has

[1] *Article 55.*

$$= \frac{\textit{Population of the State}}{\textit{Total number of elected member of the State Legislative Assembly.}}$$

If by this division, the remainder is 500 or more it will be counted as one.

The number of votes which each M.P. gets

$$= \frac{\textit{Total votes of elected M.L.A's}}{\textit{Total number of elected M.P's}}$$

Fraction exceeding one half will be counted as one. It is thus obvious that the framers of the Constitution avoided direct election so that the President may not claim a superior position which is not in consonance with the principles of parliamentary government.

Thirteen Presidential Elections have taken place so far.

Pratibha Patil a nominee of the UPA was elected as the President of India. The former Vice President B. S. Shekhavat candidate of NDA lost election against her.

Qualifications

A candidate for this august office is to be equipped with the following qualifications: (a) He should be a citizen of India. (b) He should have completed 35 years of age. (c) He should possess qualifications prescribed for a member of the Lok Sabha. (d) He should not hold any office of profit under the Government of India or the Government of any State or under any local or other authority.

Tenure and Removal

He is elected for a period of 5 years.[1] He is re-eligible. It's however hoped that he would not contest for the third time. He is removable from office by a process of impeachment for the violation of the Constitution.[2] The impeachment charge is to be initiated by either House of Parliament. The charges are contained in a resolution, signed at least by 1/4 th of the total members of the House. The resolution is to be passed by a majority of not less than 2/3rd majority. The President ceases to hold office from the day such a resolution is passed.

Salary

The President was drawing Rs 50, 000 salary on December 30, 2008, President Pratibha Patil gave assent to the Law passed by the Parliament. The Presidents' salary has been hiked presently, it is 1.50 lakhs p.m. This salary has been given with retrospective effect *i.e.* january 1, 2006. Evidently he President Abdul Kalam will also be entitled to arrears[3].

Powers of the President

The President of India as a head of the State is vested with wide powers, *viz*, executive, military, diplomatic, legislative, financial, judicial and emergency.

(*i*) Executive Powers

The Supreme executive power of the Union is vested in the President who can exercise it directly or through subordinates. However as already said, after the passage of 42nd Act re-enforced by the 44th Amendment Act, the advice of the Council of Ministers has become binding on him. Following are his executive powers : (a) the entire administration of Government of India is conducted in his name. (b) He is to make rules of business for the Government of India and allocate work to the ministers.[4] (c) He is to be kept informed by the Prime Minister of all decisions of the

[1] *Article 65(i)*

[2] *Article 61*

[3] *Hindustan Times January 4, 2009*

[4] *Article 77(3)*

Cabinet and supplied with such other information, as he might call for. (d) He is to submit a decision of any individual minister for the consideration of the Council of Ministers.[1] (e) He possesses the power of appointing the Prime Minister and on his advice the ministers, the judges of the Supreme Court and the High Courts, the Governor of the States, the Attorney General, the Comptroller and Auditor General, the chairman and members of the Public Service Commission, the members of Finance, Election and the Official Language's Commission.

A former President K.R. Narayanan's recommendations to the Supreme Court that scheduled caste and scheduled tribe candidates be considered for appointment as Judges has revived discussion on his role. Till this recommendation he had steered clear of political controversies but by proposing affirmative advice in judicial appointments, he stepped into the cesspool of politics. The issue of reservation is controversial. Hence the President who was held in high esteem due to his early actions regarding President's rule in U.P. and Bihar should not have dragged his name and office into political contours. His written proposal to the Supreme Court was an act of avoidable indiscretion.[2] (f) He is empowered to appoint a commission to investigate into the conditions of all backward classes. (g) He possesses the power of directing, controlling and coordinating the State Government from time to time. (i) He can appoint Inter-State Council to advise him upon coordination of policy and settlement of disputes between the states. (j) The administration of Union territories is directly under him.

(ii) Diplomatic

(a) He accredits and receives Ambassadors and other diplomatic representatives (b) All treaties and international agreements are negotiated and concluded in the name of President but subsequently they are ratified by the Parliament.

(iii) Military

He is the Supreme Commander of the Defence Forces of the country though the exercise of these powers is regulated by law. In fact, in the event of war, acting on the advice of his Council of Ministers, he can employ forces to repel invasion, pending a formal declaration of war by the Parliament. He can declare a national emergency in anticipation of parliamentary decisions and get the emergency proclamation subsequently ratified by the parliament under Articles 352 and 353.

(iv) Legislative

The parliament is composed of President and the two Houses of Parliament. Though he is not a member of parliament yet he possesses vast legislative powers : (a) He summons and prorogues the Parliament and dissolves the Lok Sabha. Article 85(i) compels the President to summon parliament within six months of the previous session. In case of a deadlock between the two Houses on a non-money Bill, he can convene joint session of both the Houses.[3] (b) He can dissolve the Lok Sabha on the advice of the Council of ministers. President Sanjeeva Reddy dissolved the Lok Sabha on August 22, 1979[4] on the advice of Prime Minister Charan Singh who had lost majority It sparked off controversy. After the Xth General elections A.B. Vajpayee, whose party captured the largest number of seats in the Lok Sabha, formed the government, but before facing the vote of confidence as stipulated by the President, he requested him to dissolve the house. The President accepted the advice after ascertaining that none else was in a position to form the Government.

To quote an example after the XI General Elections again there was hung parliament and people had given fractured mandate. As such, UF (United Front) with outside support of left

[1] *Article 78*

[2] *Sunil Sondhi : President's Role – an article in the Hindustan Times, January 28, 1999.*

[3] *Article 79*

[4] *Hindustan Times, August 23, 1979.*

parties and the Congress formed the Government. When Congress President decided to withdraw support second time, I.K. Gujral, the second U.F. Government P.M., advised the President for the dissolution of the Lok Sabha. The President accepted the advice after consultation with Attorney General and the country faced the XII General Elections. (c) He may address either House of Parliament or both Houses assembled together and seek attendance of the members for that purpose. This is analogous to the Speech from the Throne in England. (d) He may communicate messages to either Houses of Parliament. However, this power is not as effective as is the case in the U.S.A. (e) A Bill passed by the Parliament is to be presented to the President for his assent. He may give his assent or withhold it in the case of a non-money Bill, return it to the House for reconsideration. However, if the Bill is again passed by the House with or without amendment, he must accord his consent. In case of Bills passed by the State legislature but reserved by the Governor for his consideration, he may give his assent or withhold it. (f) No Bill for the formation of a new State and the alteration of areas, boundaries or names of the existing states can be introduced in either House of Parliament except on the recommendation of the President. (g) For the introduction of certain types of Bills in the State legislature, his prior sanction is essential. (h) He nominates 12 members of the Rajya Sabha from among persons having special knowledge, or a practical experience in the fields of of literature, science, art and social services.[1] He is empowered to nominate two Anglo-Indians to the Lok Sabha if no Anglo-Indian is elected to the House. He can also nominate one member from NEFA. (*i*) He can promulgate ordinances when parliament is not in session and circumstances so necessitate it. For instance on January 7, 1993 the President promulgated the ordinance for the acquisition of 69.703 acres of land in and around Ram Janambhoomi-Babri Masjid complex at Ayodhya.[2] The ordinance resulted in transfer of the right, title and interest in relation to this area to the Central Government with immediate effect. The Government was required to pay compensation to the owners of land and property. It is strange that no maximum time limit has been prescribed for the duration of an ordinance. However, it ceases to operate six weeks after the reassembly of the Parliament. Issue of two ordinances requested by the Council of Ministers was turned down by President Dr. S.D. Sharma on March, 14, 1996 as Lok Sabha Elections were at hands and Government had failed to enact legislation on two matters embodying these ordinances. It was denounced as a partisan attitude of the President. However, it reflects that President could give assent in the matter. According to Ayyanagar in a symposium on 'Law and Democracy in India', "Ordinance making power of President is a negation of Parliamentary Democracy".[3] C.L. Anand, a legal luminary also commented. "It is a serious limitation on the democratic principle of government for which there is no parallel in other democratic constitutions such as, those of Great Britain, the U.S.A and the British Dominions......the President is the sole judge of the necessity for issuing the ordinance. There is no restriction as regards the subject matter of ordinance."[4] (j) He appoints the acting Chairman of the Raja Sabha, in case the office falls vacant during the period the Vice-President is to officiate as the President of India or when the office of the Deputy Chairman is also vacant and none of the six members of the panel of chairmen is available.

(*v*) Financial Powers

The Constitution provides that the President shall cause to be laid before the parliament a statement of the estimated receipts and expenditure of the Government of India for the year (b) No demand for grants is to be made except on the recommendations of the President. (c) The Contingency

---

[1]*Article 80 (3)*

[2]*The Hindustan Times dated January 8, 1993, p. 1*

[3]*The Tribune dated February 9, 1959*

[4]*C.L. Anand : The Constitution of India p. 210*

Fund is at his disposal. He may make advance out of it to meet unforeseen expenditure, pending its authorisation by the Parliament.[1] (e) He is to determine the State's shares of the proceeds of income tax and the yearly grants-in-aid to certain states in lieu of their share of the jute export duty. (f) He is to constitute a Finance Commission after every five years. (g) No money Bill can be introduced in the Parliament except on President's recommendation.

(*vi*) Judicial Powers

The President can grant pardons, reprieves, or remissions of punishments. He can suspend, remit, or commute the sentence of any person convicted of any offence in all cases where the punishment or sentence is by Court Martial and in other cases where sentence is one of death or where offences committed against a law relating to a matter to which the executive power of the Union extends. The power of pardon is also to be exercised on the advice of the Council of Ministers.

(*vii*) Emergency Powers

The Constitution provides for three kinds of emergencies (a) Emergency due to war or external aggression or internal disturbance or threat there of (Article 352), (b) Emergency resulting from the failure of constitutional machinery in the states (Article 356), (c) Financial Emergency (Article 360). A brief account of these article pertaining to emergencies will enlighten the reader of their effects and consequences.

(A) Article 352

The President may proclaim emergency if he is satisfied that there exists a grave menace threatening the security of India or part thereof or there is a likelihood of such a threat (Article 352). In other words, such a proclamation may be made before the actual occurrence of war or external aggression or internal disturbance and may be revoked by subsequent proclamation. This has to be laid before both the Houses of Parliament and shall cease to operate at the expiry of two months unless it has been approved by both the Houses. If the proclamation is made when the Lok Sabha stands dissolved or is dissolved during the period of two months and the Rajya Sabha accords its approval, then the proclamation is to be approved by the newly elected Lok Sabha within thirty days of its first sitting, otherwise it will cease to operate. The 42nd Amendment of the Constitution (1976) empowers the President to make proclamation in respect of whole of India or of such part of its territory as may be specified in the proclamation. The 44th amendment (1978) safeguards the country against abuse of this power. It provides that the President shall not issue a proclamation unless the decision of the Union Cabinet to this effect is communicated to him in writing.[2]

Consequences

(a) The parliament is vested with unlimited powers to make for the whole or any part of India with regards to any of the matters enumerated in the State list. Laws so passed shall cease to have effect six months after the expiry of proclamation of emergency. (b) The parliament may extend its own life for one year at a time. However, such an extension in its term is not to last beyond six months after the expiry of the proclamation. (c) The Union Government can give direction to the states in the exercise of its powers (d) The President may modify any of the provisions related to the distribution of revenue between the Union and the States for securing adequate means for the Union to meet the emergency. Such orders must be placed before each House of Parliament. (e) The Fundamental Rights pertaining to the seven freedoms and the restrictions imposed by Article (19) on the executive and the legislature are suspended. He is authorized to suspend the right to constitutional remedies as well.

[1]*Article 267 (1)*
[2]*Article 352 (1)*

Such a state of emergency was thrice at work, on October 26, 1962 during the Chinese invasion on N.E.F.A. and Ladakh, in December 1971 when Pakistan attacked India, and on June 26, 1975, in the name of grave danger to internal security. Rumours of imposition of Emergency were again afloat due to incursion of intruders in Kargil, with the support of Pakistan Army. The 44th amendment 1978 proposes several safeguards to prevent abuse and misuse of provisions concerning internal and external emergency. The proclamation can be issued only when security of India or any part of its territory is threatened by armed rebellion. Secondly, emergency is to be declared on the written advice of the cabinet. Thirdly, the declaration of the president without the approval of Parliament can remain in force for one month. Fourthly, such a proclamation is revokable by a subsequent proclamation. Fifthly, the approval by the parliament will require absolute majority in both the Houses and 2/3rd majority of the members present and voting.

(B) Article 356

Emergency due to failure of constitutional machinery in a state or internal disturbance can be declared either on the report of the Governor or on President's own initiative when the Government of the State cannot be carried on, according to the provisions of the Constitution (Article 356). Each such proclamation is to be laid before the parliament and is to cease to operate at the expiry of two months unless it is approved by the Parliament before the end of two months. Such a proclamation is also issued for six months. The duration can be extended for six months at a time. The 42nd Amendment Act 1976 extended period of emergency from six months to one year at a time but it was undone by the 44th amendment Act in 1978. The maximum period for the operation of such a proclamation remained three years even after the passage of the 44th amendment.[1] This type of emergency was used for the first time in the Punjab on June 20, 1951. On February 9, 1999 President's rule was imposed in Goa[2] and approved by the Lok Sabha on February 24, 1999[3] and for a brief stint of 24 days in Bihar on February 12, 1999[4]. It was revoked in Bihar on March 8, 1999[5] as requisite majority in Rajya Sabha for its approval was not available with the ruling coalition. President's Rule was imposed in U.P. on march 8, 2002 and the newly constituted assembly was kept in suspended animation for two weeks after a fractured mandate in the assembly elections. However, the present government at the centre has used this article sparingly. Both the NDA and now the UPA government did not make the misuse of this article. Hence clamours against it have eventually died down.

Consequences

(*i*) The President can assume to himself all or any of the functions of the concerned State and the powers of the Governor or any other authority in the State except the State legislature. (*ii*) The powers of the State legislatures should be exercised by or under Parliament's authorisation. (*iii*) The President may assume to himself any of the powers of the State Government except the powers vested in a High Court. (*iv*) He may make such provisions which he thinks necessary or desirable for achievement of the object of the proclamation. (*v*) He can authorise any expenditure from the Consolidated Fund of the State when the Lok Sabha is not in session. Such a proclamation was first issued on June 20, 1951 in the Punjab when after the fall of Gopi Chand Bhargav Ministry, no ministry could be formed and the President decided to take over. Thereafter this proclamation has been invoked on numerous occasions in almost all the states of India. Its use has been very frequent

[1] *59th amendment March 30, 1988 replaced armed rebellion by internal disturbance*

[2] *Ibid, February 10, 1999.*

[3] *Ibid, February 25, 1999.*

[4] *Ibid, February 13, 1999.*

[5] *Ibid, March 9, 1999.*

after 1967 when the opposition parties came to power in the states and the Congress ruled at the Centre. The installation of Non- Congress Governments twice at the Centre for a brief spell of time also led to issuing of a proclamation of such a type of emergency in Congress ruled states. In a way, this emergency provision has been often abused and democracy has been held to ridicule. Janata Government on April 30, 1977 was responsible for invoking this proclamation in nine Congress ruled states of Punjab. Haryana, Himachal Pradesh, Uttar Pradesh, Bihar, Rajasthan, Madhya Pradesh, Orrisa and West Bengal. On February 18, 1980, the non-Congress Governments in nine states faced dissolution of their Assemblies and dismissal of Ministries at the instance of the ruling Congress (I) at the Centre through the invocation of Article 356.[1]

All this reflects that President's rule which was designed to preserve political unity against the threat of dysfunctional diversities ultimately proved to be an instrument for establishing central predominance. Dr. B.R. Ambedkar's fears have come out to be true. He had said "*I do not altogether deny that there is a possibility of these Articles being abused or employed for political purposes*".[2] The dismissal of B.J.P's Government on December 15, 1992 and dissolution of State Assemblies in H.P., M.P. and Rajasthan, described as 'commanded performance of Governors', proved this fact[3] in those years. On account of wide denunciation of Article 356 there have been discussions and debates on its scrapping altogether or curtailing its use to substantial extent so that it may not become an instrument of high handedness in the state politics. As already said the NDA and now UPA made its usc and that too when no other alternative seemed to be insight. On July 7, 2008 the CM Gulam Nabi Azad got conscious of losing confidence in the Assembly after the withdrawal of PDP's support. Hence he resigned. In order to avoid any horse trading governor's rule was installed by the centre and by December, 2008 elections had taken place and popular government– a coalition of National Conference and Congress was set up.[3]

(C) Article 360

A proclamation of Financial emergency can be issued if the President is satisfied that the situation has arisen whereby the financial stability or credit of the country or any of its parts is threatened (Article 360). Such a proclamation also will cease to operate at the end of 2 months unless before the end of such a period, it has been approved by both the Houses of Parliament. The proclamation is approved by the Rajya Sabha if the Lok Sabha stands dissolved. However, within 30 days of its next sitting, the approval of the Lok Sabha must be sought.

Consequences

During the operation of such a proclamation, the Union Government may give such financial directions to the state authorities as it deems fit (b) salaries of Union officers as well as that of the States including that of judges may be reduced. (c) All money Bills after they are passed by the legislature of a state must be reserved for President's assent. The President may adopt any measure for the restoration of the country's financial stability.

The language of Article 360 is, however, ambiguous. It is not clear whether such an emergency will apply to the entire country or to some of its part or parts.

It is apprehended by the critics that instead of dealing with a situation of emergency, it might

[1] *On December, 1992 by invoking Article 356, President's rule was imposed in U.P. on the recommendation of Council of Ministers and State Assembly got dissolved as the U.P. Government failed to protect the Ram Janmabhoomi Babri Masjid structure from extensive damage despite its pledge to the Supreme Court, the Central Government, and National Integration Council.*

[2] *Constituent Assembly Debates Vol IX, p. 177*

[3] *Hindustan Times, December 16, 1991.*

result in the emergence of a situation of greater emergency. Finance deserves very careful and calculated handling. An unfounded step in this direction may usher in an era of economic instability and financial insecurity resulting in confusion and chaos. In the words of V.K. Rao *"Far from restoring confidence the declaration itself might lower our credit, create a panic and thus itself might bring about a financial instability. What is required in a grave economic crisis is expert analysis, cool thinking and a workable plan but not a panicky declaration"*[1]. However, so far no such emergency has been invoked. During the current global recession and economic instability in all the world over our economy has shown till now the signs of stability. Inflation had fast gone down though it has again gone up. Presently GDP is fairly sound comparatively. Many concrete steps have bean taken by the government and Reserve Bank of India to maintain our economy in sound position and save it from recession.

The 6th pay commission has given big hike in salaries of the employees and also the pensioners. The Government has hiked the salaries of the political executive and more recently judges of Apex and High Courts as well. This indicates that our economic condition is sound enough to avoid financial emergency.

Position of the President

A critical appraisal of the powers of the Indian President reveals that his powers are enormous and apparently his authority onerous. However, in a parliamentary form of government, the head of the state is required to be a mere figurehead — a sort of constitutional ruler. India being a parliamentary democracy, conventionally the President acted on the advice of the Council of Ministers for whatever he did. However the first President of India — Dr. Rajendara Prasad, did not feel satisfied with the actual exercise of powers and on his being ignored by the Prime Minister. Hence his outburst in a law Institute, "research may be made on the powers of the President", sparked off great controversy and provoked Prime Minister Nehru to remark, "Our Constitution makes the President constitutionally rather like the King or Queen of England. If this were not so you can see the whole question of responsibility of the Cabinet and the Parliament would suffer......"[2] Alexandrowiz also holds, *"the examination of constitutional practice in the post independence years shows beyond doubt that........ the President is by convention reduced to a mere figurehead while the ministry is the real executive"*[3] In fact, the President was not intended to be either a dictator or an autocrat. Dr. Radha Krishnan — a philosopher President, had been unhesitatingly airing his views when India was facing reverses at the hands of Chinese. On January 25, 1963 he emphasised, "Our credibility and negligence are responsible of our reverses" in NEFA. In a broadcast on January 25, 1964 he cautioned the nation against complacency towards corruption and remarked, "It would be well to recognize that the tolerance of our society for weak, inefficient and unclean administration is not unlimited." Despite occasional criticism of the Government, Dr. Radha Krishnan pulled on quite smoothly with Nehru, Shastri and Mrs. Indira Gandhi. The relationship of President Neelam Sanjiva Raddy and Prime Minister Morarji Desai were not cordial. There was practically no rapport between the two. Hence generally there had been no formal consultation with the President by the Prime Minister. He once remarked *"I am not a President to play the second fiddle. This they know at Delhi"*[4]. However, consultations between Mrs. Gandhi and Reddy were frequent and regular. Likewise Gyani Zail Singh and Mrs. Indira Gandhi had no problem with each other except vast differences on 'Operation Blue Star' in the Punjab. About this operation, President was absolutely kept in dark. He is said to have learnt about it on the radio.[5] Gyani Zail Singh was generally by

[1] *V.K. Rao : Parliamentary Democracy of India, p. 295.*

[2] *Hindustan Times dated July 8, 1957.*

[3] *C.H. Alexandrowiz : Constitutional Development in India (1957) p. 143.*

[4] *The Statesman, New Delhi October 10, 1977.*

[5] *The Times of India, New Delhi April 21, 1997.*

passed by Rajiv Gandhi during his tenure of Prime Ministership. Regular consultation between the two was very occasional. In first two years of his prime ministership Rajiv Gandhi called Gyaniji only twice. Even the opposition did not hesitate to highlight such cold shouldering to the President on the floor of the House though the Prime Minister refuted it and informed the House that he and his ministers have been regularly informing the President on important developments of public interest. The same was repudiated by the President *"I am constrained to say that certain well established conventions have not been allowed. I have not been briefed on matters relating to accords finalised in respect of Assam, Punjab and Mizoram"*. In his letter dated March 9, 1987 to the Prime Minister, Gyaniji said *"The delicate relationship has to be nurtured by mutual trust, concern for conventions and emphatic and free exchange of views"*[1]

Gyaniji had confessed in an interview with the author of the book 'Rajiv Gandhi, Many Facets' that he was considering the dismissal of Rajiv Gandhi in 1987, on grounds of 'corruption and negligence' but restrained from taking the action keeping in view the larger national interests. The President claims that he did not take this step because the Prime Minister apologized for his lapses and also because his successor might turn out to be a weak person which could have resulted in the transition of power from a democratically elected Government to the armed forces"[2]. Gyaniji also pointed out that the Prime Minister was "actively considering my impeachment"[3]. He further points out, *"It was purely a dispute between a Prime Minister and a President and I wanted to prove it to the world that the chair of the President was higher than the Prime Minister*[4]*."* In case Gyaniji had really dismissed the Prime Minister commanding 2/3rd majority it would have amounted to a *coup* against a 'duly elected Prime Minister' and in fact against parliamentary democracy itself. One cannot speculate repercussions of any abnormal act. However, it would have certainly degenerated into a ruthless military dictatorship or in case of failure of such an action the impeachment of too arrogant a President who, in a fit of emotions, lost balance of mind. However, Gyaniji was too shrewd a politician. He had remarked earlier, "Just because Rajiv Gandhi has humiliated me in so many ways does not mean that I can dismiss him or sanction prosecution proceedings. I must act with dignity and propriety."[5] In fact, a youthful Prime Minister unaware of constitutional proprieties and political complexities, surrounded by sycophants and some short-sighted politicians departed from well-accepted conventions. He flouted Article 78 of the Constitution and did not communicate with the President.

President Venkataraman who assumed office on July 25, 1987 followed the illustrious tradition set by eminent Presidents like Rajendra Prasad, Dr. Radhakrishnan and Dr. Zakir Hussain. He had always been of the view that the President should not stay beyond the powers enshrined in the Constitution. He should not consider himself as a second seat of authority." He can guide, advise and warn the necessary action by protecting it. Otherwise his role is limited."[6] He could work smoothly with all the four P.M's[7] objectively and effectively. President K. R. Naryanan asserted a couple of times and was partrayed as Hero President. Abdul Kalam also enjoyed reputation of a very gracious president having very smooth relations with the P.M. The present President-Pratibha Patil is too gentle and easily agreeable to the governments' way of thinking.

A brief survey of functioning of some of the incumbents of this august office clearly reveals that prior to the passage of the 42nd and 44th amendments, the President could afford to be assertive. The acceptance of advice of the Council of Ministers was conventional though the Founding Fathers wanted this convention to be rigidly followed. However, an advice is an advice and convention is

[1]*Extract from letter of President to Prime Minister dated March 9, 1987 as reported in Indian Express.*
[2]*Hindustan Times, November 5, 1992*
[3]*Ibid*
[4]*Ibid*
[5]*In an interview with Pritish Nandy, editor of Illustrated Weekly, Bombay, July 19-25, 1987 issue.*
[6]*Hindustan Times Sunday Magazine, July 5, 1987.*
[7]*Rajiv Gandhi, V.P. Singh, Chandra Shekhar and P.V. Narasimha Rao.*

not justiciable. Hence the advice was made binding by 42nd amendment. However, the 44th amendment made it binding after reconsideration of it by the Council of Ministers. Evidently, the above quoted controversies as in the case of Gyaniji vs Rajiv Gandhi — may not be ruled out if the two functionaries are not considerate to each other or if both suffer from complexes, one of being democratically elected leader of the majority party and the other the first citizen of the country.

The President can, however, exercise discretionary powers when no party commands majority in the Lok Sabha. When Moraji Desai tendered resignation, no political party commanded clear-cut majority in the Lok Sabha. The leader of the largest party–Y.B. Chavan refused to form the Government. The president bypassed the claim of Babu Jagjiwan Ram, the leader of the Janata Party and invited Ch. Charan Singh, the leader of the Lok Dal to form the Government. In abnormal circumstances when the Government is weak, unstable and insecure, due to factional feuds, and political degeneration, unable to checkmate social and economic chaos and safeguard freedom and security of the country, the President as saviour of the constitution, can play a role, more than that of an ornamental head. In normal circumstances or if the country is led by a dynamic prime minister he is to act as a 'dignified emollient' in the Indian constitutional mechanism. "He is not expected to embarrass the Government but to strengthen its hands in dealing with them"[1]. President's influence is apt to be more effective if after getting elected to this august office, he effaces from mind all his political affiliations, avoids meddlesome obstructiveness, acts with a complete constitutional rectitude and impartiality and plays the role of a guide, a philosopher and a friend to the ministers, leaving the role of their master to the Prime Minister.

President Naryanan gave a jolt to I.K. Gujral, a former P.M. heading U.F. Government by asking him to reconsider their recommendation regarding imposition of President's rule in U.P. Thus BJP Government in U.P. got a new lease of life.

In case of Governor of Bihar recommending President's rule in Bihar in the recent past, K.R. Narayanan (Ex-President) advised the Central Cabinet to reconsider the decision of their endorsing the views of the Governor. It led to withdrawal of recommendation. Evidently an Ex-President played his role effectively. He was portrayed as a 'man of action', 'a hero in the present political situation'. In a coalitional political era, President alone can guide the ship of state and bring the nation out of morass of political instability and stalemate which has at times shaken the very foundation of our parliamentary democracy since the dawn of era of coalition governments.

(B) VICE PRESIDENT

Article 63 provides for a Vice President as well. The Vice President as already said is elected by both the Houses of Parliament at a joint session by secret ballot in accordance with the principle of proportional representation by means of a single transferable vote system. Evidently, his method of election is different from that of the President and also his counterpart in the U.S.A. The election is conducted by the Election Commission subject to constitutional requirements.

The candidate for the office of Vice President must be (a) a citizen of India; (b) must not be less than 35 years of age; (c) must be qualified for election to Rajya Sabha; (d) must not hold any office of profit under any Government within the territory of India' (e) must not be a member of either House of the Parliament or any House of the State legislatures. If he is already a member, he is required to tender, resignation before he assumes the office of the Vice President.

The Vice Presidents salary has been hiked three fold with retrospective effect i.e. January 1, 2006. This has been done in view of pay hike for the employees as per 6th Pay Commission Report. The political executive could not be expected to get less salary than the cabinet secretary. Previously Vice President was getting Rs 40,000 as salary. On December 30, 2008 the president gave assent to

[1]*The Times of India dated August 19, 1974 – V.V. Giri's Press Interview.*

the law passed by the parliament hiking the salaries of President and Vice President threefold. In other words, Vice-President's salary as such is *Rs. One Lakh and twenty thousands per month*. He gets other perks and allowances as well.

He holds office for a period of 5 years. He may however, resign his office before the expiry of the end of his annual tenure. The letter of resignation is to be addressed to the President . He is re-eligible to the same office. He is removable from his office by a resolution of the Rajya Sabha passed by a majority of all the then members of Rajya Sabha and agreed to by the Lok Sabha. According to Article 67(b) he is to be served 14 days notice before a resolution of removal is served on him.

Presently Dr Hamid Mohammad Ansari is the Vice President of the country. He stepped in the shoes of B.S. Shekhawat who contested for presidents' office but lost.

Functions

His office in fact is that of 'His superfluous Highness". He is not equipped with much of authority. Twofold functions have been entrusted to him. He is the *ex-officio* Chairman of the Rajya Sabha. In this capacity, he exercises powers of a presiding officer including right to exercise a casting vote in case of a tie. He is not a member of Rajya Sabha. Hence he has not been given a right to vote in the House.

The Vice President assumes the office of the President if the latter falls vacant temporarily because of the President's resignation, ailment, removal or death. The election of the President must take place within six months of the occurrence of the vacancy. During the period, the President fails to perform his function as a president, the Vice President acts as the President and exercises all his functions. It is evident that Vice President can act as the President maximum for a period of six months unlike that of the American Vice President who remains President of the U.S.A. for the remaining period of his tenure if Presidency falls vacant.

The Vice President of the U.S.A. is supposed to possess the same qualifications as that of the President. His method of election is the same as that of the American President. The Indian Vice President presents a contrasting picture. He is not elected by the same Electoral College which elects the President. His qualifications differ from that of the President. The process of removal of the two Vice Presidents also differs. The Vice President of the U.S.A. unlike the President of USA is not removable from the office by a process of impeachment. The Indian Vice President can be ousted from the office if the Rajya Sabha passes a resolution to this effect and the same is agreed upon by the Lok Sabha. The process of impeachment has been provided only for the Presidentship of the Indian Republic.

The Office of American Vice Presidency has been subjected to contemptuous remarks viz "unique in its lack of functions", "His superfluous Highness"; "the most insignificant that ever the invention of men contrived"; "a man in a catalytic fit conscious of all that goes on but has no part in it" — These epithets portray the position of the Vice President of the U.S.A. In fact the position of India's Vice President is still worse. Hence these epithets much more portray the position of the Indian Vice President as well. However, this office has been a stepping stone to the Presidency in some cases. B. S. Shekhawat aspired for the Presidency but suffered defeat as Pratibha Patil the present incumbent won the majority of the Electoral College.

(C) PRIME MINISTER

The Prime Minister of India like his counterpart in the U.K. is the 'keystone of the Cabinet arch', nay, 'the constitutional arch' as well. He enjoys a pivotal position. The Constitution expressly provides for the office of the Prime Minister. He is the formal head of the Council of Ministers enjoying primacy over the rest of the Ministers. According to the Constitution, the Prime Minister is to be appointed by the President. The Constitution is, however, silent as to how the President is to choose the Prime Minister. It does not also state whether he should necessarily belong to the Lok Sabha or may be a member of either House of Parliament. According to the letter of the law, the Prime Minister may be appointed without being a member of either House of Parliament (as was the case of P.V. Narasimha Rao and later Rajiv Gandhi after Indira Gandhi association). However in such cases, he must seek election to either House of the parliament within a period of six months. It, in fact, impairs the principle of ministerial responsibility.

Conventionally, the President is apt to summon the leader of the majority party to form the ministry. In case of a multiple party system if none is in a position to muster absolute majority and a coalition government is to be formed the President can exercise some discretion and summon the leader of any party, who in his opinion, can constitute a ministry. During the first three General Elections, the President was not confronted with any problem as Jawaharlal Nehru was always emerging victorious as the leader of the Congress Party enjoying majority support in the House. After his sudden death, problem was posed. Congress President K. Kamaraj adopted the consensus method and Lal Bahadur Shastri was assigned Prime Ministership on this basis. The same problem cropped up when Shastriji died of heart failure in January, 1966. This time election between the main contenders — Morarji Desai and Mrs. Indira Gandhi could not be averted. The members of the Parliament elected Mrs. Indira Gandhi as their leader. After the fourth General Election in 1967, contest between Morarji Desai and Indira Gandhi was avoided as the former withdrew willingly and agreed to play the second fiddle by accepting deputy prime ministership. However this was a moonshine. Soon there was a parting of the ways, leading to split in the Congress and mid-term poll, giving a massive verdict in Mrs. Gandhi's favour. Thus the President had not to face problem in choosing or summoning the leader to form the Government. After 1977 elections, Janata Party with its allies – CFD and CPI(M) won a comfortable majority. Hence the allies through consensus formula chose Morarji Desai as the leader. Evidently the President could easily call him to form the Government and act as the Prime Minister. Obviously even in case of an alliance forming the Government, the President could not exercise any discretion. However after the fall of Morarji Desai, due to split in the party, the President did use discretion by calling Chaudhary Charan Singh, Lok Dal leader to form the Government, ignoring the claim of Babu Jagjivan Ram of the former CFD and later leader of Janata Party.

The possibility of arising of ticklish situations was averted in 1980 when Mrs. Indira Gandhi of the Congress was triumphant in the General Elections and Sanjiva Reddi — a stalwart of Janata Party was the President. Keeping in view her 2/3rd majority in the Lok Sabha, the President unreluctantly called her to form the Government.

After Mrs. Gandhi's death, Gyani Zail Singh's role in choosing Rajiv Gandhi as the next Prime Minister particularly when he was politically a novice, is worth appreciation. In Gyaniji's words, on his calling Rajiv Gandhi to act as the Prime Minister "Rajiv's sweetness and simplicity appealed to me. He seemed a man capable of leading the nation and appealing to the masses. He was gentle, softspoken, decent."[1] In Janata Dal's regime after Rajiv's defeat, President Venkataraman's role has been very balanced. During his Presidential tenure, four Prime Ministers viz Rajiv Gandhi, V.P. Singh, Chandra Shekhar, P.V. Narasimha Rao have been installed on the Prime Ministerial saddle, without display of partisanship or misuse of discretionary authority by the President. In the case of janata Dal Prime Minister V.P. Singh holding the rein of the Government, and after his fall Janata Dal (S) leader Chandra Shekhar forming the Government, the President had to exercise a lot of judiciousness, as both of them had to assume office under extraordinary circumstances. In the case of the former, the major coalition partner – BJP – had to extend support from outside the Government i.e. on the floor of the parliament only whereas in the case of the latter a splinter group of Janata Dal was to get support of the largest party – the Congress (I) which had refused to join the Council of Ministers. However, in both the cases, the coalition partners had named the leader. The President

1. *The Illustrated Weekly of India, Bombay, July 19-25, 1987, pp. 12-13.*

was not expected to exercise discretion while making a choice though utmost caution was very much required. Hence, the President's objective approach to the formation of Governments, though of non-Congress parties, is praiseworthy.

After XIth General Elections, hung Parliament was returned. The BJP was the largest party. A.B. Vajpayee, leader of the Party was invited to form the Government by the then President and he was asked to prove his majority within stipulated period. Since he could not muster the majority, he tendered resignation after about 13 days. Thereafter the United Front which was extending support to Congress (I) from outside was invited to form the Government. Deve Gowda (a dark horse) a former C.M. Karnataka was the choice candidate. Since the Congress President could not pull on well with him Congress withdrew support and agreed to support U.F. provided that it replaced the leader. Deve Gowda bowed out and I.K. Gujral emerged out as the leader. In both cases leader had been chosen by the Front and President could not assert. After XIIth General Elections, BJP again emerged as the largest party and established its majority on the floor of the House with the support of allies. Hence A.B. Vajpayee was called to act as P.M. Presently, Dr. Manmohan Singh heads the U.P.A. Government, with Congress as the largest party in the Alliance for about 4 years Left parties extended support to him from outside without forming Government. But on Indo-USA Nuclear Deal for civil puposes" the Left parties withdraw the support and SSP headed by M.S. Yadav extended hands of friendship and enabled Dr. Singh to win the vote of confidence and save his sinking ship. Again after the, 2009 general election, the UPA won the majority and formed the government with Dr. Manmohan Singh as the leader. It is the second tenure of Dr. Singh, the P.M. of India.

His Functions

The functions of the Prime Minister are enormous and authority onerous. He has been rightly compared with his counterpart in U.K. and termed as the 'keystone of the cabinet arch,' a 'moon among the lesser stars' or the 'sun' around whom the ministers revolve like planets'. His functions are as follows:

(A) To form the Government

The President appoints the Council of Ministers on the advice of the Prime Minister. His advice is binding. The President cannot impose a minister on the Prime Minister. The latter chooses his team. Pt. Nehru chose nonparty leaders who were men of calibre, in his earlier cabinets but the experiment had been rather a failure. One by one, such non Congress ministers resigned. Commenting on these cabinets V.K. Krishna Menon remarked, "Perhaps it will be wrong to call them composite cabinets but they certainly contained persons who were not Congress party members or even if they were, very new entrants...These cabinets may therefore be regarded as more formal."[1] Though the P.M. is not fettered with any constitutional restriction on his choice, yet his hands are tied to a considerable extent by geographical considerations, due representation to various communities and party necessities, calibre of the minister, his experience as parliamentarian or administrator, his personal likes and dislikes, sincerity and loyalty, to the chair.

A strong Prime Minister may not be led by the party High Command or extraneous considerations. Regarding the exclusive powers of the Prime Minister in Cabinet formation, Lal Bahadur Shastri remarked *"I have not consulted a single person in so far as the formation of my Cabinet was concerned. Even additions and alterations were my own. In the matter of appointment of Ministers of my Government, I have been secretive. I want to keep this to myself in future also if and when the occasion arises...It is but natural that I should take the whole responsibility for this on my shoulders."*[2] Mrs. Gandhi also constituted her cabinet without consulting the Congress President or her Deputy Prime

---

[1]*Michael Brecher : Succession in India (1966) p. 97*

[2]*D.R. Mankekar : Lal Bahadur : A Biography*

Minister. Later she held both the offices — Congress President as well as that of P.M. "She consulted but did not show the full cabinet list to her Deputy Prime Minister. She paid a courtesy call on Kamaraj and showed him the list...but more changes were made in the next two hours when the swearing in ceremony took place. It was a blunt display of being unfettered"[1]. However it will not be out of place to point out that Prime Minister in case of a coalition Government does not have much of a say in the formation of ministry as the coalition partners through a mutual agreement decide the nominees to the Council of Ministers. P.V. Narasimha Rao after Xth General Elections reconstituted his Council of Ministers on January 18, 1993. It was composed of 15 Cabinet, 13 ministers of State with Independent charge, 27 ministers of State and 3 deputy ministers."[2]

However in coalitional era after XIth, XIIth XIIIth, XIV and XV General Elections, the PMs heading the coalitional teams had to appease coalition partners for their survival. Deve Gowda, I.K. Gujral — PMs of UF after XIth General Elections, and A.B. Vajpayee after XII and XIII and Dr. Manmohan Singh after XIV and XVth General Election could not be master of their will. The ministers were chosen by the coalition leaders according to the choice of the high command of the coalition partner. At times P.M. heading a coalition on having a precarious majority at his back had to act according to the dictates of powerful allies in order to lend stability to his government and remain in power. After XV the Lok Sabha Election, Congress under Dr. Manmohan Singh's leadership be cowed down by coalition partners as was the case earlier as; the Congress has improved its majority and BJP and Left had suffered set back.

Shuffling his Pack

He not only appoints ministers but is instrumental in their dismissal or removal as well. Hence it is said 'He can shuffle his pack as he pleases.' If the difference of opinion between him and any minister arises, it is the latter who has to resign. The Constitution enjoins upon the President to dismiss a minister 'though it is always done on the advice of the Prime Minister'. Dr. B.R. Ambedkar remarked "No person shall be retained as a member of the cabinet if the prime Minister says that he shall be dismissed."[3] In fact, dismissal is too harsh a step. Hence an undesirable minister is generally dropped out while reconstituting the Cabinet. An ambitious minister acting as a pinprick may be elevated to Governorship of a state or ambassadorship of a small country. Mrs. Indira Gandhi reshuffled her Council of Ministers six times between 1971 and 1974. She followed the practice in 1980 and 1983 as well Rajiv Gandhi during his first 2½ years of tenure shuffled and reshuffled his Council of Ministers nine times. He did not hesitate in dropping his close ally and a cousin Arun Nehru, and G.S. Dhillon at a later stage. V.P. Singh dropped Ch. Devi Lal, his mentor. In the recent past Dr. Manmohan asked Shiv Raj Patil to tender resignation when there was lot of pressure from his party to make him quit as Home Minister due to repeated terrorists attacks in Delhi and later the worst being on Bombay (Mumbai) on November 26, 2008. However, he owned the responsibility and tendered registration on moral grounds. During first tenure of Dr. Manmohan Singh and the second tenure as well some incompetent or defaulting ministers were dropped and new dynamic MPs were inducted. According to Dr. B.R. Ambedkar holding of "such an authority is in consonance with the principle of collective responsibility." He remarked *"The prime minister is really the keystone of the arch of the cabinet and unless and until we create that office and endow that office with statutory authority to nominate and dismiss ministers, there can be no collective responsibility."*[4] On January 18, 1993 and Feb. 10, 1995 P.M. drastically revamped his cabinet and thoroughly shuffled junior level portfolios.[5] On June 10, 1995 three ex-C.M.s were inducted in the cabinet.[6] However, in coalitional

[1] *M. Becher : Succession in India (1967) Asian Survey, July 1967, pp. 434-45.*

[2] *Hindustan Times dated January 19, 1993 and January 20, 1993.*

[3] *Constituents Assembly Debates Vol VII, p. 1159.*

[4] *Ibid*

[5] *Hindustan Times; January 19, 1993*

[6] *Ibid June 11, 1995*

era after preceding four General Elections, reshuffling of his pack according to P.M.'s choice has been a tough affair. In fact, some of the ministers taken from certain parties dance to the tune of their political mentors rather than the P.M. It is the political leader of a coalition ally who matters for survival of a minister in the COM e.g., in the regime of A.B. Vajpayee, Jaya Lalita — AIADMK Supremo — mattered for the ministers taken from her party. Likewise George Fernandes (Defence Minister) leader of Samta Party commanded more allegiance and elicited more obedience from the ministers drawn from his party. A coalition partner may quit of his/her own choice. Mamta Banerjee of Trinamool Party is another example. She rejoined the Vajpayee Government and preferred to remain a minister without portfolio (Dec. 2003) until she got a portfolio of her choice. Many such examples can be quoted. As already referred Shashi Tharoor - Minister of External Affairs is existed in the current tenure of the present P.M.

Allocation of Portfolios

It is his prerogative to allocate portfolios and divest the erring ministers of important portfolios. However, important party leaders must get prominent portfolios otherwise they feel humiliated and can create problems for the leader. Morarji Desai resigned when Mrs. Gandhi relieved him of Finance. Morarji Desai during his tenure of 27 months as P.M. effected minimal changes. Rajiv Gandhi changed portfolios very often. Later P.V. Narasimha Rao also had been often toying with the idea of changing portfolios and dropping some erring ministers with whom he had not been satisfied. On January 18, 1993 he thoroughly shuffled junior level portfolios though left heavy weights untouched. For example Shankaranand was shifted from Petroleum to Health and Family welfare, Rajesh Pilot from Communications to Home.[1] On February 10, 1995 re-allocation of portfolios was done e.g. Pranab Mukherjee and Madhavrao Sindhia were assigned External Affairs and Human Resource & department whereas Buta Singh and Ajit Singh Civil Supplies and Food respectively.[2] Such reallocation of portfolios is not frequently done in coalitional era. To quote another example, Mamta Banerjee leader Trinamool Congress was toying with the idea of joining A.B. Vajpayee's Council of Ministers, if Railway portfolio was earmarked for her party. However, It was opposed tooth and nail by Samta Party whose leader Nitish Kumar happened to hold independent charge of Railways and George Fernandes took it as a challenge to his party. Hence the matter was dropped as both were reluctant to change their respective stand. On February 3, 1999 over-burdened P.M. entrusted some of his ministries and Departments to five of his ministerial colleagues by way of additional charges.[3] Recently after November 26, 2008 terrorists attack on Bombay Home Department was entrusted to P. Chidambaram Ex Finance Minister and Shiv Raj Patil had to quit on moral grounds. Likewise Parnab Mukherjee was assigned Finance. Mamta Banerjee after XV Lok Sabha election joined hands with Congress leading UPA and succeeded in having portfolio of her choice for herself and some of her colleagues. In coalition such assertiveness is expected of the coalition partners.

A Chairman of the Cabinet

As a chairman of the cabinet, he presides over the meetings of the cabinet and determines as to what business is to be transacted in these meetings. In the case of varied opinions of the cabinet, he can assert and can get his decision accepted by the cabinet. He controls the agenda of the cabinet meetings and may reject or accept proposals for cabinet discussions. However, in the case of coalition Government, he has to include all those items in the agenda which the individual ministers consider worthy of discussions. There lies the strength and stability of the coalition Government. He is required to appease all the coalition partners in order to lend stability to his Government.

---

[1] *Ibid*
[2] *Ibid Feb. 11, 1995.*
[3] *Ibid February 4, 1999, p. 1*

As a Coordinator

He is the chief coordinator of the Government business. He is required to coordinate the activities of various heads of the ministries. This coordination is effected by the cabinet committee as well. However, general supervision of the Government departments is still done by him. He is to be consulted by the departmental heads on vital departmental issues and innovative measures. Hence he is known as linchpin of the cabinet.

As a Leader of the Lok Sabha

The Prime Minister is the leader of the Lok Sabha. In this capacity, he makes all important announcements. All questions on critical and baffling issues are addressed to him. He initiates and leads the debates of a general nature. He comes to the rescue of his colleagues on the floor of the House. He assists the speaker in maintaining order and discipline in the House. He has to keep liaison with the leader of the opposition and other opposition parties in order to *abridge the areas of disagreement. In the words of Kaul "The P.M. exercises direct influence on the course of business. The whole policy of the Government and measures dealing with the course of its business is concentrated in his person."*[1] He possesses the power of dissolving the House as well. On December 7, 1970 the President dissolved the House on the advice of the P.M. In January, 1977 Mrs. Gandhi again asked the President to dissolve the House. In August, 1979 Charan Singh advised the President to dissolve the House and order new Elections. Likewise when A.B. Vajpayee, the leader of the largest political party after XIth General Elections after 13 days of Prime Ministership found that he had failed to win the support of the Lok Sabha, he did not face Vote of Confidence on the floor of the House. Instead he tendered resignation to the President. I.K. Gujral (U.F.) recommended dissolution of the Lok Sabha when he lost support of the Congress and as such majority in the Lok Sabha. It led to the XII General Elections. The advice tendered by the P.M. was widely criticised. In fact this advice which is apt to be accepted by the President stands like Sword of Damocles on the heads of recalcitrant members of the House. The role of the P.M as a Leader of the House is to be balanced, rational and dignified. A recent example of first tenure of Dr Manmohan Singh as P.M. reveals how he faced stiff opposition at the hands of the opposition and how Left parties (supporters from outside) eventually withdrew their support. Dr. Manmohan Singh decided to seek confidence of the Lok Sabha on the famous Indo-US Nuclear Deal, which he thought essential for India's economy. He won the confidence as SSP led by Mulayam Singh of their own, decided to support him considering the deal of great significance for boosting India's economy. 'Risking the Governments' survival for the sake of Nations' eventual welfare is expected of the Leader of the House. Eventually he won a prestigious victory in the House.

A Channel between the President and the Cabinet

The P.M. serves as a channel of communication between the President and the Council of Ministers. He furnishes to the President the latest and requisite information relating to legislative and administrative affairs. He conveys messages of the President to his colleagues. No minister is authorised to see or communicate with the President without the permission of the P.M. Gyani Zail Singh complained that Rajiv Gandhi did not take the President in his confidence for many matters that transpired between him and the Cabinet. A.B. Vajpayee — the P.M. after the XIIIth Lok Sabha elections kept the President Abdul Kalam informed almost on all important political and international developments by his frequent and regular visits to the latter. The same is being done by Dr. Manmohan Singh. His visits to the former and present president -Pratibha Patil have been after brief intervels and as frequent as desired by the president. That makes the functioning smooth and cordial and convinces the Nation that the two leaders are functioning smoothly in their interest.

---

[1]*Shekder Kaul : Practice and Procedure of Parliament p. 102.*

Vast Patronage

He enjoys vast patronage regarding major appointments though they are made in the name of the President. He may consult his colleagues if he so desires while making such appointments. The appointments of the chiefs of the Army, Navy and Air force, Chief Justice and judges of the Supreme Court and the High Courts, Comptroller and Auditor General of India, Election Commissioner, Attorney General, Ambassadors, High Commissioners, Chairman and members of UPSC, Governors and Lt. Governors fall in this category. However recommendations made by the Prime Minister heading a caretaker Government may not be accepted by the President. For instance, Sanjiva Reddy did not induct two new judges recommended by Morarji Desai heading a caretaker Government. In a coalitional era, as we have at present, pound of flesh may he demanded by the coalitional partners conscious of razor thin majority of the largest party. Hence the P. M. is expected to dole out some of these ornamental and lucrative posts for the coalition partners as well.

Spokesman of the Government

He is the spokesman of the Government on all matters of domestic and foreign policy. His role in shaping policies is decisive. He is the representative of the country in the International and Commonwealth conferences. Jawahar Lal Nehru, Indira Gandhi, Rajiv Gandhi, A. B. Vajpayce and now Dr Manmohan Singh have left indelible imprint on such conferences and meets. For instance their contribution in NAM (Non aligned Meet) has been commendable. Rajiv Gandhi's role in the establishment and stabilisation of SAARC has been highly eulogised even by the foreigners. Tashkent declaration was made on the initiative of Lal Bahadur Shastri. Mrs. Indira Gandhi was instrumental in taking decisions on complex and complicated matters like Indo-Soviet Treaty and creation of Bangladesh. Likewise, Indo-Sri Lanka accord was Rajiv Gandhi's brain wave. The credit for victory in two wars with Pakistan in 1965 and 1971 goes to P.M. Lal Bahadur Shastri and Mrs. Indira Gandhi respectively though they were not manning personally the defence of the country. In the recent past, A.B. Vajpayee took the initiative of travelling by bus to Pakistan (W. Punjab) with a view to bring about peace and harmony between the two neighbours and open the vistas of trade. His visit to Pakistan resulted in famous 'Lahore Declaration' signed on February 21, 1999. P.M. Vajpayee said "we wont permit wars" 'was a clear indicator of our craving for peace and smooth relations with the neighbours. The credit for Indo-US Nuclear Deal for Civil purposes goes to a great extent to the P.M. Dr. Manmohan Singh. His occasional warm meetings with George Bush President of USA and other pivotal leaders of USA and the world reflect his statesmanship and sound knowledge of the utility of such a Nuclear Deal for the economic amelioration of our countrymen by no longer remaining isolated in nuclear world.

The Prime Minister is also expected to keep a grip on the economic affairs of the country. The popularity of the Government is likely to decline if people remain economically destitute and prosperity eludes the nation. Hence the Prime Minister is the Chairman of the Planning Commission and the National Development Council. The 21 points economic programme of Mrs. Gandhi to eradicate poverty and the industrial liberalisation and other social reforms to gear up the stagnant economy by the P.V. Narasimha Rao's Government and now Dr Manmohan Singh's are glaring instances to prove prominent role of the Prime Minister in the economic affairs. His strenous efforts for clinching Nuclear Deal with USA is a glaring example of best spokesmanship of our P.M. The Prime Minister however works in close relation with the Finance Minister and the chairman of the planning commission.

As Chief Advisor of the President

The Prime Minister is the Chief advisor of the President. In emergencies, in particular, the President is apt to consult him. However, the Prime Minister Mrs. Indira Gandhi declared internal

[1]*Hindustan Times February 22, 1999 p. 1 : 'Indo-Pak Bus Diplomacy'*

Emergency in June, 1975 without consulting the President. She did not seek his advice on 'Operation Blue Star' in the Punjab. He is said to have learnt of it from the news bulletin. Rajiv Gandhi did not consult the President on various accords. It resulted in unpleasantness between the two top functionaries and there were wild speculations of President's impeachment by the Parliament and Rajiv Gandhi's dismissal by the President. This fact was later openly confessed by the former President Gyani Zail Singh in an interview with an author of the Book – 'Rajiv Gandhi, many facets'.[1] Evidently smooth sailing of our parliamentary government demands that the Prime Minister should always advise the President on the matters of vital importance before precipitating action. Such an advice, as already said, is apt to be binding as per 42nd and 44th amendments in the Constitution, but the President will like to have the consolation of being kept informed and asked to make the formal announcements from the President's House.

Leader of the Nation

The Prime Minister is not only the leader of the party or head of the Government but also the leader of the Nation. He steers the ship of the state through turbulent times. The first three General Elections have been fought by the Congress in the name of Nehru. 'Vote for the Congress and strengthen the hands of Nehru' has been the slogan of the Party to hypnotize the masses. Likewise Mrs. Indira Gandhi symbolized the Nation. Some over enthusiastic advisers did not hesitate proclaiming, *"India is Indira and Indira is India."* The Congress in her times won a massive mandate of the people. Likewise Rajiv Gandhi epitomized the aspirations of the masses when he won with thumping majority. He carved for himself a niche in Indian history and in fact Indian's mind. 'Indira wave', 'Rajiv wave' brightened the future of the Congress party and established it beyond any doubt that Charismatic personalities do matter in sweeping the electorates off their feet and also confronting the onslaughts of the unscrupulous invaders on the territorial integrity of the country. In the XIIth, XIIIth and XIV General Elections, the BJP fought elections projecting A.B. Vajpayee as the future P.M. The other parties could not specifically project any leader. The electorates though gave a fractured mandate, yet returned BJP with the largest majority, in the XII and XIII General Elections. However, over confidence of the BJP leaders inducing them to prepone the XIV General Elections by a few months led to their debacle and Congress emerged as the largest party. Mrs. Sonia Gandhi did not project her name. It was being rumoured that she will head the government if Congress is elected as majority party. The Nation gave a fractured mandate but she managed to get the maximum seats. The credit goes to her that despite persuasion of the party men, she declined to accept the office of Prime Minister and proposed Dr. Manmohan Singh for the prestigious assignment. That added to her prestige further. She was the chair-person of UPA and considered the mentor of the victory of UPA led by congress. In the XVth Lok sabha she trounced opposition, BJP in particular and further established superiority of the Congress. She again reposed faith in Dr. Manmohan Singh and decided to be the leader of the Nation from the wings.

As leader of the Party

The Prime Minister has emerged as the leader of the Party. In fact, the Congress Presidents have been toeing the line of the Prime Ministers like Jawaharlal Nehru and Mrs. Indira Gandhi prior to the split of the Congress. Both these leader remained on the helm of the affers. Indira was portrayed as 'India' and personified the congress. Pt. Nehru dominated the party till he lived. Nobody could defy him. If anybody had the courage to do so, he was ousted. A congress leader said "Nehru is like a "Banayan tree which gives big shade but under which nothing grows". Since the inception of Congress (I), Mrs. Indira Gandhi epitomised the hopes and aspirations of her party. She was the political mentor of many upcoming politicians. Rajiv Gandhi too was both the Congress President and the Prime Minister. His writ ran through the Congress circles. Later on, Kamlapati Tripathi, the

[1]*Hindustan Times dated November 12, 1992.*

working president of the Congress placed his resignation in the hands of Rajiv Gandhi to revamp the party structure. P.V. Narasimha Rao happened to be both the President and the Prime Minister and ran both the offices of the country as he deemed fit. He was acknowledged as the leader by the loyalists of the Congress. Congress President of Karnataka was made to quit finally on the instance of the Congress President on November 11, 1992. The communication of Janardhan Poojary, General Secretary of the Congress to Bangarappa, makes the fact crystal clear. "The Congress had sent a team of observers to Karnataka. On the basis of the report submitted by the observers the Congress President has decided that you should step down as the Chief Minister of Karnataka immediately. You are therefore asked to submit your resignation to the Governor forthwith." If the two offices are combined, the P.M. becomes all powerful, as it is evident from the language of the communication quoted above. Deve Gowda, I.K. Gujral — both P.M.s under U.F. Government at the Centre after XIth General Elections, though belonged to Janata Dal, but were not the Party Presidents. Hence they did not have the advantage of combining in themselves the two offices and make their writ run in the Party as well. During the A.B. Vajpayee (BJP) as the P.M. the office of the President of BJP and L K Advani held by Naido. Both have been pulling on very smoothly. Presently P.M. Dr. Manmohan Singh and Mrs. Sonia Gandhi Congress president are pulling on very smoothly. Hence PM.'s authority is on the ascendance and his position getting stronger than that of any other leader of the Party.

An analytical appraisal of the powers of the Prime Minister reveals that he is in the real sense a keystone of the constitutional arch. He dominates the cabinet, shields his faltering colleagues on the floor of the House, serves as a chief link between the President and the Cabinet, acts as a spokesman of the Governmental policy, enjoys vast patronage as the appointing authority, acts as the leader of the party and above all personifies the Nation. Pt. Nehru's assertion in the Lok Sabha on July 30, 1956 refuting the charges of C.D. Deshmukh (ex-Finance Minister) reflects pivotal position of the P.M. vis-a-vis ministers. *"I am also something after all. I am the Prime Minister of India and the Prime Minister is the Prime Minister. He can lay down the policy of government...and that.. in the constitution the Prime Minister is the linchpin of Government.."*

Though the Prime Minister enjoys a predominant position, still he, as per norms and conventions of parliamentary democracy, must act as captain of the team and not play the over awing boss. If he does so, the ministers can revolt and put him in an embarrassing position. Mrs. Indira Gandhi suffered a severe setback when she failed to contain a senior minister B. Jagjivan Ram whose untimely exit proved suicidal to her political career. Rajiv Gandhi's failure to pull on smoothly with V.P. Singh and Arun Nehru changed the phase of history. V.P. Singh eventually became the Prime Minister and Rajiv Gandhi was reduced to a mere leader of the opposition. One wrong move on the chessboard of politics can doom a Prime Minister. Dr. Jennings rightly remarks, *"The office of the Prime Minister is necessarily what the holder chooses to make it and what other ministers allow to make it."* A Prime Minister like Pt. Nehru and Mrs. Indira Gandhi dominated the Indian scene like huge colossus. Nehru's pre-eminence is compared with Churchill at Westminster during the Second World War and of Mrs. Indira Gandhi with Joan of Arc. Referring to the pre-eminence of Pt. Nehru, Dr. Radha Krishnan remarked *"Many of his cabinet colleagues and party high ups receive the shock of their lives when Nehru asks them to explain obscure reports published in the papers with the relevant cuttings pasted faithfully on the note paper"*. Mrs. Gandhi had acquired "complete control over administrative machinery by bringing all intelligence service directly under her charge and building up her own secretariat". The cabinet colleagues and the party leaders were virtually afraid of this oft designated *"soft dove with sharp claws"*. She had developed the reputation of never forgetting and more ominously she never forgives".

In fact, the leaders of the party look to the prime minister as the source of power and bank upon him/her for their electoral triumphs and future prospects. Hence a prime minister enjoying comfortable majority; equipped with administrative acumen, strong mental calibre and above all an understanding heart, serves as a beacon light for his colleagues, a ray of hope for the party leaders, and a saviour for the nation in peril. He epitomizes the hopes and aspirations of the teeming millions. He serves as their moral rudder and political gyroscope in tempestuous times. However, he is acknowledged as a leader both of the party and the cabinet only if he has sterling qualities of head and heart, excels his contemporaries in administrative calibre, practical sagacity and political acumen and has a comfortable majority of his party men at his back. Jones referring to Indian counterpart in Great Britain observes *"the office of the P.M. has great potentialities but the use made of them depends on many variables — the personality, temperament and, ability of the Prime Minister, what he wants to achieve and the methods he uses.* It depends on his colleagues, their personalities, temperaments and abilities what they want to do and their methods. Prime Minister who can carry his colleagues with him can be in a very powerful position but he is only as strong as they let him be"[1].

PMs Secretariat

Prime Minister's Secretariat Now Termed as Prime Minister's Office

The inception of P.M's secretariat took place in August 1947 i.e., after the attainment of Independence. It was brought into existence to serve the purpose of a centre of information and a channel of communication between the Union council of ministers and the Prime Minister. However, it was not concerned with the formulation of decisions. Lal Bahadur Shastri as P.M. leaned too heavily on the Secretariat owing to his ill health in 1964. It reassumed the role of a regular department working under a Secretary. The Secretariat was no longer an information bureau. It became a top decision influencing body. Mrs. Indira Gandhi during her tenure as P.M. reorganised the Secretariat so as to function as a reservoir of knowledge and a potent agency of liaison between the Union ministries and the State Governments while tackling the problems of national importance. The RAW (Research and Analysis Wing) was activized to keep the P.M. apprised with matters and men in the country. During the initial years of her tenure the RAW's role in politics within the Union and State Government was prominent.

It's Role

P.M.'s Secretariat (now PMO) played a momentous role as under :

(*i*) It brought about coordination among the Ministers, the P.M. and the Civil Services. (*ii*) It has been instrumental in keeping powers concentrated at the top level. For example in Mrs. Indira Gandhi's tenure as P.M. the trio—P.N. Haksar, L.K. Jha and Yashpal Kapur—excercised predominant influence and wielded considerable authority. It was no less than that of a Union Minister of the Cabinet rank. In 1974, the P.M's Secretariat issued a circular to all the Union Ministers on October 8, 1974 exhorting them to communicate to the P.M.'s secretariat copies of the statements required to be made on the floor of the Parliament and also the notes on supplementary questions on such statements.

The role of the P.Ms secretariat had been on fire at the hands of parliamentarians. During the tenure of Morarji Desai as P.M., Janata Party made a fervent appeal for a thorough probe into the activities of the RAW of the Secretariat. Hence about 600 officer working in the RAW were transferred to their parent states. Thus P.Ms secretariat was divested of powers and shorn of its name.

The Prime Minister's office now consisted of the Principal Secretary, the Private Secretary and a few personnel assistants. The rest of the staff was transferred. Morarji Desai attributed unpopularity of the earlier Congress Governments to the centralisation of decision making apparatus under the P.M. He emphasised that the system had resulted in the concentration of power in the hands of Mrs. Indira Gandhi and a coterie of officials in the P.M's secretariat and cabinet secretariat thus throwing democratic process of decision making to the winds. However, this was his way of thinking which could last till his continuance as P.M.

[1]*G. W. Jones: 'The Prime Minister's Powers" in Anthony King (ed) : The British Prime Minister p. 190.*

Present Position and Functions of PMO

Presently the PMO's office, located in the South Block is headed by the Principal Secretary to the PM. Later the Principal Secretary of A.B. Vajpayee (P.M.) happened to be the National Security Advisor to the PM. as well. The PMO included the anti-corruption unit and the public wing dealing with grievances.

Its comparatively more significant functions are as follows :

(*i*) It provides secretarial assistance to the P.M.

(*ii*) It submits those files to the P.M. of which he holds the direct charge for orders. If the ministry functions under some other cabinet minister or minister of state holding Independent charge of the ministry, more matters are dealt with by the cabinet minister or the minister incharge. Only important policy issues which the minister feels should be placed before the P.M. for orders may be sent to the PMO. The P.M. has been traditionally holding the charge of the Departments of Space, Atomic Energy and Ministry of Personnel, Public Grievances and Pensions. However there is no rigidity about it.

(*iii*) As the P.M. is the chairman of the Planning Commission, relevant files are forwarded to the PMO for his comments and clearance.

(*iv*) The PMO directly operates PM's National Relief Fund and the National Defence Fund.

(*v*) Special packages announced by the PM for the states are monitored in the PMO and periodical reports are submitted to the PM.

(*vi*) Besides the above, the following matters necessitating the PM's personal attention are mooted in the PMO :

(*a*) Important Defence related matters.

(*b*) Important policy matters.

(*c*) Decorations—Civilian and Defence requiring Presidential approval.

(*d*) Proposals for effecting appointments of Indian heads of Missions abroad and requests for grant of agreement for foreign heads of missions posted to India.

(*e*) Important decisions relating to the Cabinet Secretariat.

(*f*) Appointments of members of State Administrative Tribunals, the Central Administrative Tribunals, UPSC, Election Commission, Appointment of members of Statutory/Constitutional Committees, Commissions attached to the various ministries.

(*g*) All the vital matters pertaining to the administration of the civil services and administrative reforms.

(*h*) The judicial appointments requiring Presidential approval.

(D) COUNCIL OF MINISTERS

Article 74 of the Constitution provides that there shall be a Council of Ministers with the Prime Minister as the head to aid and advise the President in the exercise of his functions. Article 75 on the other hand lays down that the President shall appoint the Prime Minister and the other ministers shall be appointed by the President on the advice of the Prime Minister.

The President appoints as Prime Minister a person who heads the majority party or parties(in case of coalition) in the Lok Sabha. The Prime Minister may also belong to the Rajya Sabha. For example, Mrs. Indira Gandhi was a member of Rajya Sabha when she was tipped for the office of the Prime Minister in 1966. The Council of Ministers consists of the Prime Minister, Cabinet ministers, State ministers, the deputy ministers, and parliamentary secretaries. The Constitution does not fix the size of the Council of Ministers. The Prime Minister decides its size, according to the exigencies of the time and the requirements of the situation. However, the Prime Minister is required to consider the claims and views of the prominent members of the parliamentary group of his party in both the Houses. The states are to be adequately represented. The minorities are not to be ignored. The Scheduled Castes and the backward classes are to be given due recognition. Men of calibre and those equipped with rich parliamentary experience are to be accorded preference. On account of all these considerations, the size of the Council is apt to be unwieldy. It has been varying from 50 to 60. Nehru's Council of Ministers has been often unwieldy though in 1962 he talked of austerity measures and cut in the Council of Ministers. Lal Bahadur Shastri's ministry consisted of 51 members out of which sixteen were cabinet ministers. Mrs. Indira Gandhi kept the number of ministers around sixty and the cabinet ministers varied from 15 to 18. Morarji Desai as the P.M. kept the total below 40 though during the initial four months, he had only 19 cabinet ministers. In December, 1984 Rajiv Gandhi's Council of Ministers consisted of 40 ministers out of which 14 were of the cabinet rank. In October, 1986 its number was raised to 58, out of which 17 were Cabinet ministers. On October 22, 1987 the Council of Ministers consisted of 17 cabinet ministers, 8 ministers of state with independent charge, 29 ministers of state and 3 deputy ministers i.e. 57 in all. On February 15, 1988 the number of Ministers was 60 out of which 16 were the cabinet ministers. Again on June 25, 1988 the Council of Ministers was reshuffled. It consisted of 20 cabinet ministers, 37 ministers of state and 7 deputy ministers[1]. On June 21 1991, P.V. Narasimha Rao constituted a Council of Ministers consisting of 58 ministers of which 16 were cabinet ministers.[2] On January 18 1993 Rao's Council of Ministers (CoM) consisted of 15 Cabinet, 13 ministers of state (independent charge), 27 ministers of state and 3 deputy ministers. On June 1, 1996, 21 membered CoM headed by UF Governments' P.M. (of Janata Dal) was constituted. On June 28, 1996 it was expanded — 5 cabinet ministers and 9 ministers of state were added. On July 5, 1996 further expansion took place — cabinet ministers 19, Minister of state (Independent charge) 9, and Ministers of state 11. I.K. Gujral's CoM constituted on May 1, 1997 consisted of 19 cabinet ministers and 21 ministers of state. Only one new cabinet minister Jaipal Reddy was added, rest of the ministers of Deve Gowda (CoM) were retained. A.B. Vajpayee's CoM on 13th October 1999 after 13th Lok Sabha elections was composed of 25 Cabinet ministers and 44 ministers of state.

The Council of ministers of Dr. Manmohan Singh (UPA Govt.) consisted of 34 Cabinet Ministers including P.M. (Later Shibu Soren was removed on conviction by a court seven Ministers of state (Independent charge) and 439 ministers of state after 2004 General election. The new council of minister after 15th Lok Sabha elections on May 22, 2009, extended on May 28 consisted of 33 cabinet ministers 7 Ministers of States (independent charge) and 39 ministers of states. Thus, P.M Dr. Manmohan Singh's COM was composed of 79 Ministers, to begin with.

The Council of Ministers holds office during the pleasure of the President.[4] The President can dismiss a minister if he loses the confidence of the Lok Sabha and the Prime Minister. The Prime Minister, as already said, is the creator, the preserver and the destroyer of the Council of Ministers. If a member of the Council of Ministers is not a member of parliament he will cease to be a minister, if at the expiration of 6 months, he's not elected to either House of the Parliament. The salaries and allowances of the ministers are determinable from time to time by Parliament.

The Prime Minister, as already said, acts as the channel of communication between the President and the Council of Ministers. As such, he communicates to the President all decisions of the Council of Ministers, relating to the administration of the affairs of the Union and proposals for legislation as the President may call for and if the President so requires submit for the consideration of the Council of Ministers any matter on which a decision has been taken by a minister but which has not been considered by the Council of Ministers (Article 78).

[1]*Hindustan Times:June 26, 1988.*

[2]*June 22, 1981*

[3]*Hindustan Times: May 29, 2009*

[4]*Article 72 (2)*

The Cabinet

The ministers of cabinet rank constitute the Cabinet. The cabinet is considered is the 'keystone of the constitutional arch', though the constitution is silent about it. A cabinet minister heads the executive department and plays vital role in the formulation of the national policies and their implementation. The ministers of state also assist the Cabinet ministers unless they hold independent charge of a department. The deputy ministers also assist the ministers in day to day work. Generally, younger politicians are appointed as deputy ministers so that they may acquire administrative experience essential for the conduct of the business of the Government.

The size of the cabinet has, however, been varying from 15 to 20 in the past. The size of the cabinet is kept small to facilitate concentrated discussions and frequent decisions. Dr. Manmohan Singh's cabinet after the 15th Lok Sabha election consisted of 33 cabinet ministers which evidently is unwieldy. The advantages of a small cabinet are as follows :

(*i*) Less burden on the public exchequer. (*ii*) Coordination problem is eased (*iii*) Team spirit is fostered (*iv*) It is conducive to the healthy growth of public life and political parties (*v*) Healthy development of democracy is made possible and undue public criticism of government policies is considerably curtailed. The cabinet meets once a week, only the ministers of cabinet rank attend the meetings.

Functions of Cabinet

In the words of Pylee "*The cabinet is the formulator of national policies, the higher appointing authority, the arbitrator of inter-departmental disputes and the supreme organ of coordination in the Government.*" The following are some of the important functions of the Cabinet :

(a) Policy determining Functions

Cabinet is a deliberative and policy formulating organ. It decides all national and international problems confronting the country. It meets regularly once a week for this purpose and formulates decisions on all vital issues and other matters emerging from various ministries. The cabinet accepts the by panals report on the Pay hike of the Government employees. On engaged 14, 2008 the union cabinet accepted the recommendation of the 6th Pay Commission duly modified by the committee of secretaries. The package marks a zero of 21% over what the Pay panal had recommended. The salary hikes are wef 1.1.2006. It benefits 50 lakh central government employees the states also here accepted the pay hikes.

(b) Legislative

Cabinet is the main link between Executive wing of the Government and the Legislature. It is the hyphen that joins, the buckle that fastens the Executive and the Legislative departments together. In fact, the cabinet directs Parliament for action and gets approval of its policy from the majority in the parliament. Important legislation is always initiated by the cabinet or by non-cabinet ministers with the permission of the cabinet. It has been correctly said that the cabinet legislates with the advice and the consent of the Parliament. Besides, the cabinet fixes up time for summoning and prorogation of parliament. Likewise the dissolution of the parliament, prior to the completion of its tenure which amounts to curtailing the tenure of the elected representatives of all parties. Hence such a vital issue is decided by the cabinet.

(c) Control over Finance

The Cabinet controls the purse in actual practice. The Finance Minister keeps his colleagues in the picture, enquires about their demands but decision is purely his own. The Tax proposals on which depends popularity of the party in power are shown to the Prime Minister by the Finance Minister. The proposals are revealed to the Cabinet on the day the Budget speech is to be delivered.

The Cabinet can suggest modifications to the Budget proposals after their presentation to the Parliament. C. Rajagopalachari vehemently criticised the Budget proposals of 1963-64 which was in fact a reflection on the Budget procedure itself. In his words "The way in which Budgets are made and got ready for presentation, leaves no room for the whole or material section of the Cabinet to examine and advise upon it or even go through it. In order to safeguard secrecy, all consultation is avoided. The Budget is hatched by the officials working under the nominal guidance of the Finance Minister.... If both the Prime Minister and the Finance Minister happen to be persons blissfully ignorant of the business of the Budget making when all the economy of the country comes under the direct or indirect influence of the budget, the consequences are.....disastrous".

Supreme Control of the Executive

The executive authority is vested with the President and the offices subordinate to him. The cabinet ministers are the real functionaries. The policy determined by the Cabinet and approved by the Parliament is to be implemented by the individual ministers, according to the directions of the Cabinet. No deviation is permissible to any individual minister as otherwise it amounts to the impairment of party discipline. The cabinet thus functions as the supreme national executive. It supervises, superintends and directs the work of the civil services spread over the Indian territory.

As a Coordinator

The Cabinet is the main coordinating agency. It is required to effect coordination among all ministers and departments of Government. Generally the departmental matters are settled at the level of concerned ministers. However, if they fail to sort out their mutual differences, the P.M. acts as the coordinator and arbitrator. Finally the matter if otherwise irreconcilable, is placed before the Cabinet whose decision is to be accepted by the concerned ministers. The minister who even now differs will have to tender resignation.

Vast Patronage

All major appointments of key positions are taken up in the Cabinet before they are made public. This means seeking the approval of the Cabinet. In real practice, this is said to be a mere formality. However the formal control of the cabinet over the appointments cannot be denied.

Delegated Legislative Authority

In a welfare state, enormity of legislation and also its complexity induces the parliament to delegate legislative authority to the Executive. The Parliament passes the bill in the skeleton form and the details are to be filled up by the executive, obviously by the Cabinet who with the active assistance of bureaucrats and the experts in the respective fields frames the detailed legislation in the form of executive orders. This type of authority is delegated also to meet exigencies of times or when the Parliament is not in session. All such orders at a later stage are approved by the parliament. As such they have statutory authority.

Control over Foreign Policy

The Cabinet formulates the foreign policy of the Union and determines Indian relations with the foreign countries. The Foreign Affairs minister formulates the policy in consultation with the Prime Minister. Jawaharlal Nehru held the portfolio personally. P.V. Narasimha Rao, the former P.M. also held the portfolio of External Affairs, though he was being actively assisted by the minister of state for External Affairs. Later on, a full fledged cabinet minister was appointed as External Affairs Minister. A.B. Vajpayee P.M. also held the charge for some time. Later, Jaswant Singh was assigned the portfolio of External Affairs Ministry. In Dr. Manmohan Singh's cool formerly held Parnab Mukherjee holds the charge of external affairs ministry. Since reshuffling was in Mukherjee ceased to be incharge of External Affairs. Presently, S.M. Krishna heads the department.

Miscellaneous

Cases pertaining to proclamation of Emergency under Articles 352-360, those relating to cessation or commencement of a 'State of War', proposals for the creation of new public corporations or companies; proposals relating to the appointment of Public Committees of enquiry and consideration of the reports of these committees; proposal to vary or reverse a decision previously taken by the Cabinet; proposal to withdraw a prosecution instituted by the Government are some of the other important matters which are referred to the Cabinet.

These functions of the Cabinet are quite exacting. Its control over legislation, finance, executive and its coordinative authority make it a supreme executive. Its real importance is very much linked with the type of person at the helm of affairs as the P.M. In fact the Cabinet stands partially eclipsed by the Cabinet committees. Dr. B.R. Ambedkar remarked *"The Cabinet has become a merely recording and registering office of the decisions already arrived at by committees. They work behind an iron curtain."*[1] However it still remains the keystone of constitutional arch.

(E) CABINET COMMITTEE

The Committee system at this level is analogous to that of Great Britain. The Prime Minister constitutes these committees to facilitate quick despatch of business and ensure expert examination of the issues at hand. The Cabinet committees ordinarily are authorised to make final decisions though they are to be communicated to the Cabinet which may review them.

The Cabinet, as already said, meets once a week. As such, it has neither the time nor the ability to tackle all the ticklish administrative problems. Hence two types of committees have emerged out –permanent and *ad-hoc*. An *ad-hoc* committee is setup to tackle a particular problem. It goes out of existence after reporting on the matter entrusted to it. It is generally comprised of ministers concerned with it. For example, in July, 1987 a special Cabinet committee was setup under Rajiv Gandhi to tackle the drought faced by the country. Likewise in October 1991, a Cabinet Committee under the chairmanship of the P.M. was constituted to monitor prices.

The Janata Government dismantled superfluous administrative set up. Hence in 1977 there were six Cabinet committees, viz., Political Affairs Committee; Committee on Economic Affairs; Parliamentary Affairs Committee; Appointment Committee; Committee on Accommodation and Informal Group of Ministers on Price Situations. The number and the names of the Cabinet committees do not remain unchanged. However, some of the committees – Political Affairs; Economic Affairs; Parliamentary Affairs and Appointments have existed under both Congress and Non-Congress Governments. The following Cabinet Committees are the important ones.

(a) Political Affairs Committee

It functions under the chairmanship of the P.M. Its other members are Home, Defence, External Affairs and Finance Ministers. It deals with all important matters pertaining to both internal developments and foreign relations.

(b) Economic Affairs Committee

It also is chaired by the P.M. while the Finance minister, the Rural Development minister and the Industry minister, are its other members. It directs and coordinates governmental activities in the economic field and regulates the working of national economy.

(c) Committee on Parliamentary Affairs

The Home minister is the chairman of this committee. The Information and Broadcasting

[1]*Dr. B.R. Ambedkar's statement at the time of resignation from the Cabinet on October 11, 1951.*

Minister, the minister for Labour, the Law minister and the Minister for Parliamentary Affairs are its other members. The committee looks after the day to day progress of the Government business in the parliament, just to secure the smooth passage of legislation. Further, it determines the Government's attitude to non-official Bills and resolutions coming up before the Parliament.

(d) Appointment Committee

It functions under the chairmanship of the Prime Minister. The Home minister and the minister concerned are its other members. Its functions revolve round some key appointments. First it takes decisions regarding secretariat appointments, of the ranks of deputy secretary and above, Chairmen, managing directors, and general managers of State owned Public Corporations, companies and enterprises and Governors of Reserve Bank. Besides, it is required to take decisions regarding all other appointments which are made by the Government or which necessitate the approval of Government of India and which are salaried appointments.

It also takes decisions on all cases of disagreements between the Department concerned and the Union Public Service Commission in regard to any appointment.

Certain recently appointed important comittees also may be mentioned.

1. Committee on the welfare of schedule castes and scheduled tribes: Members from both the Houses are drawn in this committee. It serves and considers all matters concerning the welfare of the scheduled castes and scheduled tribes which fall within the purview of the Union Government. It keeps a watch whether constitutional safeguard for these classes have been duly implemented.

2. General Purposes committee: It advises speaker/chairman on matters concerning affairs of the House which do not fall within the purview of any other committee.

3. Joint committee on offices of profit: It examines the composition and character of committee and other bodies appointed by the Central and State governments and Union Territories' Administration and recommends as to which officers ought to or ought not to disqualify a person from being chosen as a member of either House of Parliament.

4. The Library Committee: It consists of members drawn from both the Houses. It considers matters concerning the Library of Parliament.

5. Committee of Empowerment of women (29th April 1997): Its members are drawn from both the Houses of the Parliament. It secures status, dignity and equality for women in all fields.

6. Ethics committee (March 1997): On March 4, 1997 the Ethics committee of Rajya Sabha was constituted.[1]

Composition: The Prime Minister constitutes the above mentioned committees. Their membership varies from 3 to 8.

Functions: They are entrusted two functions viz. (a) coordinating the various ministers, and (b) decentralising the policies.

They can also be employed to keep critical problems under continuous review. Further by inclusion of non Cabinet ministers in their deliberations the committee system extends Cabinet's coordinating activity to wider governmental affairs.

At times the Political Affairs Committee serves as Super Cabinet.

(e) Ad hoc Committees

Besides these sub committees, *ad hoc* committees are also set up, for example to deal with

[1]*India 2008 : 31-2*

the problems of prices, review the performance of the Public Undertakings, Export promotion and Import substitution, denudation of forests and trees and increase in agricultural prices in view of the increased power rates.

How the Committees are involved?

A subject necessitating cabinet decision may either come directly to the appropriate committee or may be referred to it by the cabinet itself for indepth scrutiny before the latter arrives at some decision. Though the Cabinet is the highest policy making body in the Government, some of these Cabinet committees have emerged out as real centres of authority and the Cabinet has been simply dittoing their decisions.

There are two types of such committees – (a) Committees which are constituted from time to time, to enquire into and report on specific subjects (b) Select or Joint committees which are appointed to consider and report on a particular bill. These committees are distinguishable from other ad hoc committees in as much as they are concerned with bills and the procedure to be followed by them as laid down in the rules of procedure and directions by the speaker/chairman.[1]

An Appraisal

An appraisal of the actual functioning of these committees reveals that by and large, they have not proved very effective. In the words of Chanda 'the purpose of forming the Cabinet committees for securing coordination and for reaching quick decisions might also be largely defeated since these committees now include the bulk of the cabinet ministers".[2] The opinion of the Administrative Reform Commission (1966-70) also is not very encouraging. They reported "Some of the committees have not met regularly. Several important subjects are not covered by these committees. Further, they can take up a matter only if it is referred to them by the Minister concerned or by the Cabinet".[3] The ARC suggested that these deficiencies may be eradicated from their working. Second, they should cover between them all important areas of Government activity. Third, each cabinet committee should meet regularly so that sustained attention is given to complex problems. Fourth, the progress of implementation of important policies and programmes may be kept under constant review.[4]

Cabinet Secretariat—A Brief History (Its Origin)

Before the passage of the Councils Act of 1861, the Governmental business used to be conducted by the Governor General-in-Council. The Council functioned as a joint consultative board. With the enormity and the complexity of governmental business, the work of the various departments was dispersed among the members of the Council. Only more important cases were tackled by the Governor General and the Council collectively.

During the Viceroyalty of Lord Canning and the passage of the Council Act 1861, the portfolio system was introduced and inception of the Executive Council took place. The Secretariat of the Executive Council of Viceroy was led by his private secretary who did not attend the Council's meetings. Later Lord Willington permitted his Private secretary to be by his side at these meetings. The practice was perpetuated. In November, 1935 the Private secretary was accorded the additional designation of Secretary to the Executive Council. With the inception of interim government in September, 1946 the Executive Council Secretariat was designated as Cabinet Secretariat.

---

[1] *India 2008 Govt of India Publication p.31-2*

[2] *Ashok Chandra : Indian Administration, (1958) p. 95*

[3] *The ARC Report on the machinery of the Govt. and its procedures of work (1968) p. 11.*

[4] *Ibid.*

Its functions, underwent a change after the attainment of Independence in August 1947. It was no longer concerned with circulating of papers to Ministers and Ministeries. It became a coordinating agency for effecting coordination among the ministries. An Economic committee of the Cabinet established with its secretariat at Ministry of Finance in 1949 was transferred to the Cabinet secretariat in 1950 and was named 'Economic Wing' and eventually was made a part of the Secretariat in 1955. In 1954, the Organisation and Methods Division was set up under the Cabinet secretariat which was later transferred to Ministry of Home Affairs in 1964.

In 1957, the "Defence Committee of the Cabinet" was set up under Cabinet Secretariat. In 1991 this wing was transferred to the Defence Ministry. In 1961 department of statistics was created under the Cabinet secretariat though in February 1973 it was transferred to Ministry of Planning. In 1962 Department of Special Economic Coordination was established under Cabinet secretariat and later transferred to Ministry of Economic Defence Coordination. The department does not exist at present.

The Bureau of Public Enterprises was brought under the control of Cabinet secretariat only for a few months—January to June, 1966. Later it was transferred to department of Economic Affairs under Ministry of Finance and again in 1985 it was entrusted to the Department of Public Enterprises under ministry of Industry.

In June, 1970, three departments viz., Department of Electronics; Department of Scientific and Industrial Research and Department of Personnel were set up under the Cabinet secretariat. In July, 1970, Directorate General of Revenue Intelligence-cum Directorate of Enforcement was set up under Cabinet secretariat. Later this Directorate was transferred to the Department of Personnel in August 1970. In 1971 the Department of Electronics became an independent department. Likewise Department of Personnel and Administrative Reforms was transferred to the Ministry of Home Affairs. Presently the latter is an ingredient of Ministry of Personnel, Public Grievances and Pension.

In July, 1981, Department of Ocean Development was created under the Cabinet secretariat. It became independent department in February, 1982. In March, 1988 Directorate of Public Grievances was created in the Cabinet secretariat.

The Cabinet secretariat functions under the direct charge of the PM though its Administrative Head is the Cabinet Secretary who is also the ex-officies chairman of the civil service Board as well. It provides secretarial assistance to the Cabinet and the Cabinet committees and serves as the custodian of the documents of the Cabinet meetings. N.R. Pillai was the first Cabinet Secretary who served in this capacity from February 6, 1950 to May 13, 1953. Kamal Pande has been serving in this capacity since November 1, 2002. He has since retired in the recent past.

Its functions

As per government of India (alocation of business Rules 1961) cabinet secretorial finds a place is the first schedule to the Rules, the subjects alloted to it are as under. In the initial stages the Cabinet secretariat was entrusted the following functions : (*i*) Submission of cases to the Cabinet and its committees. (*ii*) Preparation of the records of the decisions arrived at and also of the follow up actions while executing these decisions. (*iii*) Exhorting the Committee of the secretaries which meet periodically to consider and advise on the problems necessitating interministerial consultation and coordination (*iv*) Formulating the rules of business and allocating the business of the Union Government to the various ministries and the departments as per directions of the Prime Minister and with the formal approval of the President. (*v*) Procuring and circulation to the President, the Vice President the Council of Ministers and other distinguished functionaries the notes and periodical summaries on important developments in each ministry. (*vi*) In recent amendment the CBI like RAW (Research and Analysis Wing) has become part of Cabinet secretariat.

Since 1980, its functions have enhanced resulting in sharp criticism about the style of its functioning and the supervisory role it gradually established over the working of the whole government. Even Prime Minister Rajiv Gandhi was compelled to take stock of the things and see as to how best the secretariat could improve its role without unduly interveaning in the performance of the ministries and departments. The Cabinet secretariat with reformed role still exists. Monitoring, coordination and promotion of new policy initiatives are still its important functions. Its growing importance is revealed from the fact that even the latest amendment (January 30, 2003) in the Government's allocation of business rules the CBI was detached from the Ministry of Personnel and was instead made a part of Cabinet Secretariat headed by the Cabinet Secretary. The latter is required to report directly to the Prime Minister.

According to Govt. of India publication. "The cabinet secretariat is seen as a useful mechanism by the departments for promoting inter-ministerial coordination since the cabinet secretary is also the head of the civil service. The Secretaries felt it necessary to keep the Cabinet Secretary informed of development informations from times to time. The transaction of Business Rules also required them to keep the cabinet secretary informed specially if there are departures from these rules."

Composition of Cabinet Secretariat

Since the times of Rajiv Gandhi, the Cabinet secretariat has been expanded to the size of a full fledged Ministry. It comprises a secretary—the ex-officio Chairman of CSB[1], four additional secretaries, four joint secretaries, a special secretary, three directors and several deputy secretaries. Besides, the Information Advisor and the Security Advisor in the PMs secretariat are also its members. They too are of the rank of secretaries. Such high class composition has made its role very significant and has entailed comments on the style of its functioning. The post of Cabinet Secretary has become more of a political appointment.

Conclusion

The Cabinet secretariat is still considered as a useful mechanism by the various departments for promoting inter-ministerial coordination. The Cabinet Secretary serves as a focal point. He is kept informed of developments by the secretaries particularly when there is a necessity of departure from the business rules.

1. *Hindustan Times January 31, 2003, p. "Advani gets Roses—Amendment—Business Rule.*

STRUCTURE OF ADMINISTRATION

> *"Routine business is always more urgent and calls for less intellectual effort than sitting down to think seriously about something that may happen next year, sometime never". It is only by the creation of a separate policy department, a general staff freed from administration as a whole that it is possible to secure fore-thought and effective planning"*
>
> ***— L.S. Amery : Thoughts on Constitution (1953)***

CONTENTS: (A) The Secretariat
(B) The Office
(C) Secretariat — Then and Now
(D) A.R.C.'s Recommendations
(E) Field Organisations
(F) Boards and Commissions
(G) Ministers

The Constitution of India does not make any provision for the machinery of administering public affairs. Article 77(1) specifies that all executive business of the Government of India shall be expressed to be taken in the name of the President. Article 77 (3) lays down that the President shall make rules for the more convenient transaction of the business of the Government of India and for the allocation among Ministers of the said business.

The Central Secretariat has three services- (i) Central secretariat service (CSS) (ii) Central Sercretariat stenographer service (CSSSS) (iii) The Central Secretariat clerical service (CSCS). The grades of selection Grade and Grade I of CSS and the senior principal Private Secretary and Principal Private secretary (CSSS) are centeralised. The section officers grads D, C, A and B (merge) of CSS and LDS and UDS are decentralised.

(A) THE SECRETARIAT

Although the Constitution is silent about the word Secretariat, Article 77(3) indicates the way for the allocation of business rules among the departments and ministries. The ministries and departments enumerated in the 'allocation of Business rules' are collectively known as the Secretariat — the nerve centre of Government. The number of such ministers and departments varies from time to time depending on the volume and variety of work priorities, valuational orientation, political expediency ...A "ministry may comprise one or more allied Departments or may not have any separate Departments as such"[1] The ministry is headed by a minister who is assisted by career bureaucrats—the Secretary, Additional Secretaries, Joint Secretaries, Directors, Deputy Secretaries and Under Secretaries, the Section Officers. There are Assistants, Upper and Lower Division Clerks, Typists to run the machinery as per the dictates of the superior officers.

---

[1]*S.R. Maheshwari, Public Administration in India Paper in II P.A. Twelfth Advanced Professional Programme in Public Administration 1986-87 p. 9.*

The Indian Secretarial system is based on two distinct principles of administrative philosophy—(i) Separation of policy making function from that of its execution (ii) A cadre of officers operating on the tenure system controlling a permanent staff. In the words of L.S. Amery, "It is only by the creation of a separate policy Department General staff freed from administration as a whole, that it is possible to secure thoughtful and effective planning"[1]. It is known as split system.

Advantages of Split System

The Following advantages are cited of the prevalent split system.

(*i*) Freedom from operational involvements enables the formulation of policy to plan in terms of the overall national requirements and objectives. (*ii*) The Secretary being an impartial adviser to the Minister examines objectively the proposals emanating from the executive agencies keeping in view the broader point of view of the Government as a whole. The secretary is not only a secretary to the minister but the Government as a whole. (*iii*) The separation results in keeping the secretariat of smaller size. (iv) Over centralisation is avoided as the executive agencies alone are concerned only with the implementation of policies in the area earmarked for them.

Functions of the Secretariat

Following arc the functions of the Secretariat related to the Ministries and the Departments :

(*i*) To assist the ministers in the process of policy making.

(*ii*) To assist in the framing of legislation, rules and regulations.

(*iii*) To formulate sectoral planning and programmes.

(*iv*) To accord and to secure administrative and financial approval to operational programmes and plans and their subsequent modifications.

(*v*) To exercise supervision and control over the executive departments or semi autonomous field agencies, regarding the execution of policies and programmes as well as their evaluation.

(vi) To interpret policies framed by the policy makers.

(*vii*) To coordinate and assist other branches of Government and maintain contact with State Administration.

(*viii*) To initiate measures to develop greater personnel and organisational competence both in the Ministry and Department and its executive agencies.

(*ix*) To help the minister in the discharge of his parliamentary responsibilities.

(*x*) To help frame the Budget and control the expenditure to be incurred on the activities of thc Ministry and Department

(*xi*) To evaluate work done by the executive agencies.

(*xii*) To guide and direct the executive agencies in the performance of their tasks[2]

Role of the Secretariat

As an office the Secretariat is to serve as an organisation to assist the Government in the fulfilment of its responsibilities.

As a concept, its role assumes greater significance due to the following reasons: (*i*) It assists the ministers in the formulation of Governmental policies embodying the manifesto displayed by the party of the minister at the time of election. Besides, it has to provide adequate data, relevant information and also quote precedents to enable the minister to finalize policies on the problems, not conceived in the manifesto. (*ii*) It renders assistance to the minister in the legislative work as

[1]*P. Sharma : Public Administration in India, p. 107*

[2]*S.R. Maheswari : op cit. 1989 ed : reprint 1992, p. 30*

well. The legislative leadership in fact, devolves upon the Government on account of enormity and complexity of legislation. The secretariat formulates the draft of legislation to be initiated on the floor of the House. It collects all relevant information for the minister to enable him to reply to supplementary questions in the Parliament. (*iii*) It enables the Government to examine the emerging problems in the light of past practices and precedents. Such an examination helps in ensuring objectivity and continuity. Hence S.R. Maheswari calls it "institutionalized memory"[1] (*iv*) It serves as a clearing house, preliminary to governmental discretion, as it conducts an elaborate scrutinising of a problem by taking a comprehensive view of it and in consultation with and approval of Ministry of Law and Ministry of Finance. (*v*) It plays the role of a channel of communication between the states or with the Planning and Finance Commissions. (*vi*) It also ensures that field office executes with efficiency and economy, the policies and decisions of the Government.

An appraisal of the above functions of the secretariat makes us conclude that it is a pivotal institution in the administrative system of our country and is the nerve-centre of the Government. *According to Administrative Reforms Commission, "The secretariat system of work has lent balance, consistency and continuity to the administration and serves as a nucleus for the total machinery of a ministry. It has facilitated inter-ministry coordination and accountability to parliament at the ministerial level. As an institutionalised system, it is indispensable for the proper functioning of Government*".[2]

The prestigious position of the secretariat is discernible also from the fact that the personnel of the secretariat are paid higher salaries than those working in the field agencies and the field. They get special pay as well for serving in the secretariat.

Tenure system

The superior positions in the secretariat are managed by officers who hail from the states and also from certain central services for a specified period. After serving for a specified period, they revert to their respective states or services. This arrangement is termed as the Tenure System. It is a relic of the past. Since 1905, the system is in vogue. Lord Curzon was the originator of the system. The various committees and commissions appointed in the Britisher's time viz., Secretariat Procedure Committees (`1919), the Simon Commission (1930), the Maxwell Committee (1937) lent support to this practice. Following are the arguments for and against the system.

Arguments for the system

First, the rotational system exercises a wholesome and steadying influence on the function of the Federal system of government. Such a role is significant on account of lack of cordial relations between the Centre and the States particularly when different political parties come in power at the Centre and in the states.

Second, it is advisable that the Secretariat be manned by experienced persons of the district. It is vital that the officers are exchanged between line and staff work.

Third, a longer tenure at the Secretariat is apt to disrupt living contact with administration at field level. In order to get acquainted with the practical bearings of policies of the Secretariat upon the lives and interests of the people, it is essential to opt for Tenure system.

Fourth, Tenure system benefits the states as well. They are in a position to requisition the services of officers, possessing rich experience and having familiarity with the national approach to the administration and problems.

Fifth, very lengthy tenure enables an officer to enjoy stability at one place. However very short tenure creates uncertainty. Hence, if tenure is neither too long nor too short, it suits the employees.

---

[1] *Ibid*

[2] *Report of the ARC study Team on the Machinery of Govt. of India and Procedure Growth 1967 : p. 30*

Sixth, the Secretariat service is coveted as it confers upon officers a number of special advantages. Hence an unbroken stay in the Secretariat would create two classes of bureaucrats — the 'haves' and the 'have nots'. Such a dichotomy shakes, the morale of the latter.

Seventh, since most officers are entitled to a spell of stay at the Secretariat, it accords equal opportunities for all.

Eighth, the Secretariat can easily get rid of incompetent persons as the tenure post automatically brings to an end one's stay at the Secretariat.

Ninth, it secures and consolidates administrative unity of the country.

Tenth, it secures the independence of the civil service as it serves as a check against too long subservience to the higher levels of functionaries — both official and political.

Arguments against Tenure system

The Tenure system has entailed comments as under :

First, the system does not ensure specialisation in this age of specialisation. work in the ministries, it is contended, is becoming of specialised nature.

Second, district experience is not said to be indispensable in many areas of activities which are being performed by the Central Government at present.

Third, it gives impetus to 'office dominated administration' as it strengthens the office at the cost of the officer. A new officer is too much dependent on the office.

Conclusion

In fact, the Tenure system had not been adopted even in the British era in some of the prominent departments viz. Foreign and Political, Indian Audit and Accounts, Posts and Telegraphs, Customs and Income Tax Departments. The Central Secretariat service has thrown a challenge to the Tenure system officially prevalent in some of the departments. A sizable number of posts of Under and Deputy Secretaries are being manned by this service. Even Joint Secretaries are not immune from this impact. The specialists who preponderate in the secretariat service are not subject to rotation to areas far away from the secretariat. The Tenure system was further eclipsed and considerably modified due to the creation of a Finance Commerce Pool in 1958 and the Central Administrative Pool in 1957. The Finance Commerce Pool helped in meeting the specialised needs of the economic department, whereas the Central Administrative Pool which is composed of officers drawn from the I.A.S., Allied and State services, was an attempt to overcome the uncertainty both in the matter of supply and quality of officers. There are a good number of officers in the secretariat who have never been reverted to their original places of posting. Thus it has been observed, ".......everywhere it operates, it appears to be followed more in the breach than in observance".[1]

Otherwise too, technically speaking, the Indian Government cannot claim to own a permanent Civil Service except the central secretariat service. Hence, the middle and the higher management positions have always been filled by getting officers from State Government and certain Central Services deputed. (External Affairs, Railways, Post and Telegraph ministries have been the exceptions in this respect). Such officers are equipped with first hand and fresh experience of working in the field. Hence the decisions emanating from the Union Government are not devoid of reality and are to a great extent meaningful to the people. Besides, the experience of working in the Secretariat enables the Civil servants to be fully abreast of the objectives underlying the policies and programmes which they have to execute ultimately. Thus the implementation of a policy is in consonance with the objectives of a given programme eventually leading to its success. Dr. Maheswari

[1]*Shriram Maheshwari op cit p. 36.*

has rightly said, ".......*each level of government comes to gain direct insight into the others' constraints and concerns and this itself facilitates reaching a healthy equilibrium in a federal system*".[1] Hence this principle of staff has been firmly entrenched on our soil, though with slight modifications conceived from time to time.

It has been rightly suggested that the tenure system must remain rhythmic. The civil servants must revert to their parent departments on completion of their tenure of deputation so that vacancies are filled up by fresh blood attuned with the latest problems in the field. It is however unfortunate that the reverse flow of officers is treated as "punishment posting" and the civil servants returning to the parent departments are not whole heartedly welcomed.

Hence the early deputationists show reluctance to go back to their original cadre and make frantic efforts through their political mentors to stick to the Headquarters or to get absorbed in Government run organisation in Delhi for the transient period. In the meanwhile, they are ready for second deputation. Hence, in actual practice, a group of officers, having an inordinate liking for central assignments, has emerged both in the ministries and the agencies manning the economic affairs. They ultimately aim at a coveted place in an International organisation like the World Bank or its subsidiaries. Such imbalances and distortions are disgusting and highly alarming. Hence they must be checkmated. A rhythmic operation of Tenure system must be ensured.

Theoretically, the Tenure system for different grades is as follows : Under Secretary .....3 years, Deputy Secretary....4 years, Joint Secretary....5 years, Secretary.......5 years.

Structure

No uniform terminology can be conceived to portray the Central Secretariat which comprises a complex organisation of various ministries and departments. A ministry may have more than one Department. The large ministries viz. Defence, External Affairs, Home, Finance, Human Resource Department, have more than one department. A Department may be defined as an organisational unit for discharging specific functions under the administrative control of a Secretary —potent component of the Secretariat. A minister is incharge of a ministry. He is the political head assisted by a Minister of state and a Deputy minister if his ministry is large. The Secretary is incharge of the department. A ministry having more than one department under it, will obviously have more than one Secretary; one of these secretaries invariably will be holding a superior position to that of the rest. For example ministry of Defence which comprises three departments, has three Secretaries — The Defence Secretary; Secretary of the Defence Production Department and Secretary of the Defence Supply Department. Though all the three Secretaries are in the same pay scale, yet the Defence Secretary is ranked as the highest of the three. Besides attending to his normal work, he coordinates the work of the other two Secretaries.

Functions of a Secretary

The Secretary performs three fold functions.

(*i*) He acts as Chief Adviser to the Minister as regards policy and administrative affairs (*ii*) He is responsible for conducting of administration under his control, efficiently and economically. (*iii*) He is required to represent his ministry before Public Accounts Committee.

In the words of N. Gopalaswami Ayyangar, "a secretary should not be immersed in files and burdened with routine. It is essential that he should have time to grasp the overall picture, size up the problems facing Government in the field allotted to his charge and think and plan ahead. All these are the proper functions and must be efficiently performed. Failure to make adequate provision in this respect cannot be compensated by mere increase in the establishment under his control".[2]

[1]*Maheshwari op cit p. 36.*

[2]*Report of the Reorganisation of the Machinery of Government, 1949, New Delhi Govt. Publication 1957, Para 14.*

The ARC has also described his role as "coordinator policy guide, reviewer and evaluator". He is fully authorised to give general or specific instructions for certain cases or type of cases which are submitted to him directly. Besides, he is to keep himself fully informed of the work of Ministries/ Departments by asking for weekly summaries of the cases dealt with at the lower levels.

Deputy Secretary's Functions

The Secretary is assisted by special and additional secretaries, Joint Secretaries and Deputy Secretaries. A Deputy Secretary acts on behalf of the Secretary and is in charge of a Secretariat Division holding responsibility for disposing off work assigned to him. He is to move through the Joint Secretary. He submits papers relating to important cases to him. The Under Secretaries assist the Joint and Deputy Secretaries for the disposal of Government business and is in charge of a branch in the ministry. As such, he exercises control over the branch personnel for dispatch of government business and maintenance of discipline.

Under Secretary's Functions

The role of the Under Secretary has been well portrayed by Maxwell Committee in the words, "The Under Secretary should ordinarily intimate action on all inward communications but he should not hesitate even at that stage to bring a receipt immediately to the notice of the Deputy Secretary for any instructions which the latter might wish to give. The Under Secretary should dispose of minor cases on his own volition. Comparatively more important files he should submit to the Deputy Secretary in such a form that in the ordinary course, the Deputy Secretary should be enabled to deal with the case promptly : Under Secretaries should also attempt to reduce as far as possible the number of files to be formally submitted to the Deputy Secretary by taking the latters' verbal orders in appropriate cases. One of the great losses in recent years in the working of the Secretariat Departments is the practical disappearance due to various causes of the summary and draft of the efficient Under Secretary".

It may also be pointed out that the functionaries at these different levels discharge their functions in the best interests of the Government of India as a whole. The Secretary as such is the Secretary to the Government of India and not the ministry concerned alone.

This should be true normally at the lower level as well. In reality, however, there is a tendency of thinking in terms of departmentalization. As such, the Secretary and officers below him think in terms of their respective departments, division or a branch respectively. All this is detrimental to the organisational harmony and happiness and hardly in consonance with the attainment of organisational goals.

(B) THE OFFICE

Below this galaxy of top bureaucrats, there exists a permanent but less qualified office. The office is coterminous with the sections. The section invariably functions under one Under Secretary. Each section functions under a Section Officer who is required to supervise the work of dealing hands generally 3 to 7, usually 5. Four of them are the Assistants and fifth a U.D.C. Besides, there is ancillary staff at both levels, personal assistants, stenographers and peons for officers and employees for record duties and office services in the section. The office serves as the foundation sustaining the superstructure. It serves as the 'organisational memory' as it embodies in itself the specialised knowledge and precedents. This function has its relevance and due importance in view of the prevalent Tenure system.

Two Under Secretaries work under a Deputy Secretary who is in charge of a division whereas the former mans the branches. Two Deputy Secretaries work under a Joint Secretary who constitutes the effective decision making level, working directly under the Secretary and the Minister.

Functions of the Office

The office performs two types of functions to be performed automatically in any case communicated to the office without specific directions and functions to be performed on the directions of an officer.

Automatic Functions

The automatic functions are as under : (*i*) To see that all papers referred in correspondence or notes are properly arranged, linked and paged, as well as have correct marginal references (*ii*) To verify facts and see that they are correct. (*iii*) To point out laws and rules. (*iv*) To provide other relevant facts and figures as are available in the department. (*v*) To put up precedents or papers embodying previous decisions and policy and to point out the relevant portions of the papers being put up. (*vi*) To invite attention to the statutory or customary procedure required for the disposal of a case. (*vii*) In a routine case or cases having established precedents to put up a draft for approval. (*viii*) To suggest a cause of action wherever possible at the proper time.

Functions under Direction

In this category the following functions can be enumerated : (*i*) To examine the case thoroughly and see that all matters necessitating decisions are put up. (*ii*) To tabulate and summarise information if necessary. (*iii*) To formulate drafts according to the orders.

Layout of office

As already said, the layout of the office is as follows :

Under Secretary

↓

Section Officers (C I and II)

↓

Assistants

↓

Clerks (Division I and II)

Besides there is one daftri and one peon attached to each officer.

Functions of Section Officer

The superintendent is the in-charge of a section and is termed as the Section Officer. He functions as a supervisor over the staff working under him. He is thus termed as the firstline supervisor in the Secretariat hierarchy and handles the minor complicated cases himself. Besides his other important duties are : (*i*) Distribution of work among the staff of his section. (*ii*) To render help and furnish advice to them. (*iii*) To effect coordination of work (*iv*) To see to efficient disposal of work. (*v*) To use proper methods for the processing of cases. (*vi*) Timely submission of periodic reports (*vii*) Proper maintenance of section records. (*viii*) To ensure strict compliance of instructions regarding top secret documents. (*ix*) To maintain order and discipline in the section.

Duties of an Assistant

The following are the duties of an Assistant : (*i*) To examine and put up notes on cases and their submission to the Section Officer after proper paging, referencing and maintenance of diary and other related records. (*ii*) He is also authorised for direct submission of cases to the Branch officer concerned.

Duties of Clerk

The lower division clerk performs routine functions such as collection of previous papers, maintenance of files and registers, indexing, recording and despatch of mail and typing of drafts prepared etc. The upper division clerk also performs similar set of functions. Besides, he gives his noting on simple cases and assists in their disposal.

Method of Recruitment

The lower division clerk is recruited directly through a competitive examination which is being organised by the Staff Service Commission since 1976. The direct recruitment of Upper Division Clerks was abandoned as these posts are now filled by promoting Lower Division Clerks. The posts of Assistants are filled partly by direct open recruitment through a competitive examination and partly by promotion of upper division clerks. The Section Officers posts are filled partly by direct recruitment through a competitive examination and partly through promotion of Assistants. A blend of direct and indirect recruitment, two distinct age groups, reflecting two sub-cultures are represented at these levels in the Secretariat.

The office system suffers from certain lacunae viz. excessive noting and file shifting, resulting in delay and inefficiency. These pitfalls of the system have been pointed out by every committee and every special officer who has ever dealt with the subject and also by every officer who has been in the Secretariat. Still these defects remain firmly embedded in the system as they are inherent in it. It is increasingly being realised that if consistency and continuity of Government policy are thought to be essential and if the element of continuity is to be the contribution of the office, the need of the 'office first', cannot be minimised. The office is apt to acquaint the newly joined officers about the work just to justify its ever expanding existence. Otherwise too, a new officer has to rely on the 'office' for guidance and full information about 'ins and outs' of the department/Division. Traditionally a man's career may be made or marred by the length of his notes on those collections of papers.

Besides, according to a rule, the 'officer' is apt to suggest that other departments must be consulted. This leads to postponement or avoidance of decisions as file is marked to the other department.

It may not be out of place to point out that with the ever-increasing number of departments, the device of sending the file to all interested or concerned departments, results in intolerable and undue delay and adds to the complication of the process.

(C) SECRETARIAT — THEN AND NOW

In 1946 there were 20 Departments. though some of them created during War were purely of temporary nature. On August 15, 1947, there were 18 ministries in all — a new designation for departments. Since then the number has been on the ascendance partly due to the increase in the work load and partly due to political expediency just to accommodate political aspirants for ministerial berths.

The nomenclature of the ministries also undergoes change as per requirements of the times and the wishes and aspirations of the party in power. The number of Ministeries in U.P.A Government has been about 49.

Since attainment of independence and the ushering in an era of planning in particular, in the fifties, the functions of the Government have become manifold. Hence the Government of India is no longer functioning in the North and South Blocks only. A plethora of Bhawans have come into existence. The allocation of Business Rules in the recent past makes Central Government responsible for over 2,000 items of work despite our federal structure and the states being made directly responsible for developmental and regulatory activities.

In A.B. Vajpayee's Government, Welfare Ministry was renamed as "Ministry of Social Justice and Empowerment". The decision to rename the ministry was guided by a stronger commitment to the value of equality and social and economic liberation. A.B. Vajpayee on the eve of Dr. Ambedkar Jayanti said, "In an unequal society where the scheduled castes, scheduled tribes and backward classes are still suffering from historical disabilities, what they want is social justice and empowerment and not mere welfare". Likewise, in Manmohan Singh Government new Ministeries have been created in the name of 'Aam Admi' welfare.

Characteristics of the Secretariat System

(*i*) The Secretariat has been rapidly expanding, (*ii*) Activities of House keeping nature are being manned by one third of the Secretariat (*iii*) It has taken up significant amount of original work as well as work of an infructous nature. (*iv*) A plural headed structure is emerging in the administration as the ministers are usually assisted by more than one Secretary. As such, the principles of 'one Secretary for one ministry' is on the wane. (*v*) The office of a Joint Secretary is provided as a regular feature. (*vi*) Principles of unity of command and unity of control are gradually becoming relics of the past as the norm of an employee reporting to only one person is fast receding to the background e.g. in Ministry of Defence, the Deputy Secretary reports to a number of Joint Secretaries. (*vii*) The Secretariat suffers from a high degree of departmentalism and has developed secretariat thinking.

The following table gives an idea of the growing number of Secratariat Services Staff

CENTRAL SECRETARIAT SERVICES

Structure of Administration[1]

Service	CSS Grade	CSSS No. of Posts	CSCS Grade	No. of Posts	Grade	No. of Posts
1.	Sr. Selection Grade (Group 'A' Gazetted)	110	——	——	——	——
2.	Selection Grade (Group 'A' Gazetted)	330	Sr. PPS Group 'A' Gazetted	68	——	——
3.	Grade- I (Group 'A' Gazetted)	1405	PPS Group 'A' Gazetted	182	——	——
4.	Section officer (Group 'B' Gazetted)	3000	PS (A and B) (group 'B' Gazetted)	1598		
5.	Assistant (Group 'B' Gazetted)	4905	Grade C/PA (Group 'B' Non-Gazatted)	2793	——	
6.	——	——	Grade 'D' Grade 'C' Non-Gazetted	1958	UDC/LDC Group 'C' Non-Gazetted	9115
Total		9750		6599	——	9115

[1] *Research Reference and Training Division, 9750 Publication Division Ministry of Information and Broadcasting Government of India: India 2008 A Reference annual p.39.*

An appraisal of the Secretariat

The Secretariat as a concept is indispensable but its functioning has entailed criticism at the hands of the critics. The following are the main points of criticism.

(*i*) Cases at the secretariat level are unduly delayed due to — (*a*) excessive dependence of higher officials on their subordinates; (*b*) absence of adequacy in service training; (*c*) frequent transfers; (*d*) undue interference of top officials; (*e*) over delayed decision making, (*f*) personnel devoid of feeling of responsibility; (*g*) decision implementation at snails speed, (*h*) over centralisation; (*i*) delayed action on the documents received and prolonged correspondence; (*j*) increasing number of levels; (*k*) lack of decision making powers at different levels; (*l*) awaiting unwanted consultations with the higher officers on petty matters; (*m*) completion of similar papers selected to common causes at one place.

Such an exasperating delay breeds corruption.

(*ii*) Secretariat is blamed for empire building and is engaged in the transaction of business which is either out of its purview or of an infructuous nature.

(*iii*) The Secretariat — a policy-making body encroaches upon the domain of the executive agencies. It impairs administrative efficiency as the Secretariat is prevented from concentrating on policy making and weakens the executive agencies on account of encroachment on their domain.

(*iv*) The Secretariat has been turned into an overgrown institution. Too many personnel in the Secretariat are engaged in the unnecessary work.

The additional staff asked for in fact remains underworked. They remain more occupied in ventilating their grievances which sap their morale.

(*v*) The personnel in the Secretariat suffer from superiority complex. At times, they are arrogant and display vanity. They hardly assist or encourage the executive. The Secretariat has, in fact, become an inhibiting factor. The secretariat could act more efficiently if it could project effectively, the experience gathered in the field by its officers. This emphasises the necessity of Tenure system as discussed in the preceding pages.

(*vi*) The Secretariat is said to have monopolised the most efficient staff. As a result, the executive agencies are suffering from some kind of "anaemia in terms of both power and qualified manpower".

The criticism referred to above is quite valid. The Secretariat must be purged of weakness and impurities that seem to have creeped in it. Efforts should be made to root out these shortcomings. Things may show an improvement if the following points are kept in view :

(*a*) Noting on the part of lower level should be minimised and the references may be earmarked to the appropriate authority forthwith or to an authority not exceeding two levels below the authority involved in the decision making.

(*b*) The senior level officer should direct and lay down the manner to be followed for disposal of the cases and should get the cases reviewed regularly.

(*c*) Sufficient powers should be delegated to the appropriate level to curtail undue delay and cumbersome procedure.

(*d*) The Secretariat should only deal with policy making functions. The non policy formulation functions should be left over to the executive agencies.

(*e*) Its functioning should be specifically laid down so that dominance of the 'office' could be avoided.

(*f*) There must be systematic transfer of officers between the Secretariat and the field agencies so that realities are kept in view during the course of functioning.

(*g*) No special allowances be paid to the officers when deputed to the Secretariat after a period of one year. In the initial year they are to be compensated for the dislocation caused due to shifting. The Secretariat will cease to be alluring and the officers won't pull the political strings to prolong their stay at the Secretariat level.

(D)ARC'S RECOMMENDATIONS

Reference to ARC's recommendations in this context will not be out of place. These recommendations were mostly made to checkmate procedural delays and curtail cumbersome procedures:

(A) Non secretariat organisations engaged mainly in planning, implementation and review of single development programmes or several allied programmes covering sizable activities of the Ministry and having a direct bearing on policy making must be integrated with the secretariat of the concerned ministry. Such amalgamation has its special significance regarding activities of scientific and technical character and those necessitating a high degree of functional specialisation. (*ii*) The heads of non secretariat organisations which are integrated with the Secretariat should work as the principal advisers to the Government in their respective areas and should command a status appropriate to the nature of their duties and responsibilities. They may retain their present designations. A formal *ex-officio* status may not be conferred upon them. (*iii*) In all other cases the existing distinction between policy-making and executive organisations may be continued. Such distinction is vital for protecting the operational autonomy of the regulatory executive agencies and such developmental executive organisation, as are mostly engaged in promotional activities, privatization of a service or production and supply of a commodity. (*iv*) Executive functions which are being performed by an administrative ministry or Department having no close bearing on policy making should be transferred to an appropriate secretariat Agency or to a new executive organisation created for the purpose, depending on the volume of work. (*v*) Policy personnel in Departments and Ministries dealing with scientific and technical matters or with functions of a highly specialised character should include persons having specialised experience or expertise.

(B) (*i*) In non staff ministries a setup of three staff officers should be provided : (*a*) an office of Planning and Policy; (*b*) a Chief Personnel office; (*c*) A Finance office. An administrative Department with a heavy charge or with functions which have no close affinity with the work of other Departments may have a separate planning and policy office. (*ii*) The office of planning and policy should include the planning cell recommended in the ARC record of machinery for planning. The office should be continuously engaged in formulating long term policies carrying out policy studies and evolving well-articulated policy statements. It should also deal with the parliamentarian's work of the Department/Ministry. (*iii*) The chief personnel officer in a Ministry should formulate and co-ordinate overall personnel policies, initiate measures for promoting personnel development and service rules of cadres administered by the Ministry. It may look after office, management 'O and M' and general administration (*iv*) Each of the staff offices should be manned by staff having specialised knowledge and experience. The head of each 'staff office' should be invariably of the rank of a Joint Secretary though he may be of the rank of Additional or Deputy Secretary depending on the quantum of work. (*v*) Besides three staff officers each ministry should have a Public Relation Office as well. (*vi*) The head of the substantive work wings may deal directly with the chiefs of the three staff offices as also with the Secretary and minister on matters of technical or operational policy. Proposals pertaining to long term policy should be processed through the Planning and Policy Office.

(C) (*i*) Distribution of work between the wings of a Ministry/Administrative Department and within the Divisions of a Secretariat wing should be based on considerations of rationality, manageability of charge and unity of command. (*ii*) Each secretariat wing should have its separate identity and the budget should appear as a distinct unit in the budget of the ministry. Its head should enjoy adequate administrative and financial powers. (*iii*) The head of the wing should be primarily responsible for good administration, within the wing, effective supervisions and control of staff and maintenance of high standards of disciplined conduct. (*iv*) The head of the wing should have considerable voice in the formulation of the wing budget, creation of posts subject to budget provisions, spending of budgeted funds and appointments of personnel to the wing and their transfer therefrom. He should, therefore, possess the necessary powers for effective day to day personnel management in the wing, e.g., powers to sponsor staff for training, to grant honorarium, to impose minor penalties and to fill short leave vacancies.

(D) (*i*) (*a*) Only Two levels of consideration below the minister viz. Under secretary/Deputy Secretary and Joint secretary/Additional secretary/Secretary Work should be assigned to each of the two levels on the lines of desk officers system. Each level should be empowered to execute substantial amount of work on its own and should be given the necessary staff assistance. (*b*) The staffing pattern within a wing may be flexible to facilitate the employment of officers of various grades. (*c*) The duties and requirements of various jobs in the secretariat at each of the two levels may be clearly defined in detail on the basis of scientific analysis of work content.

(*ii*) For smooth and effective working of the proposed 'desk officer' system the following measures will be essential viz. (*a*) introduction of a functional system of the file index; (*b*) maintenance of guard files or card indices which will contain all important precedents, (*c*) adequate provision for 'leave reserve'; (*d*) adequate stenographic and clerical help.

(*iii*) (*a*) In each ministry or major administrative Department, a Policy Advisory Committee to consider all important issues of long-term policy and to inject thinking inputs from different areas of specialisation into problem solving, be setup. The committee, should be headed by the secretary of the ministry and should include the heads of the three staff offices and heads of important substantive work wings. The head of governing bodies of important research and training institutions and boards and corporations outside the Government may be co-opted as members of the Policy Advisory Committee for such items of work as are of interest to them. (*b*) Self contained papers or memoranda setting out problems, their various alternate solutions, merits and demerits of each alternative etc. should be prepared for consideration by the committee and the decision arrived at, should be duly recorded in minutes.[1]

(E) FIELD ORGANISATIONS

In the words of L.D. White, "Field institution is a self–contained unit performing a designated function or activity of which there may be only one or a small number". W.F. Willougby thus explains the system of field organisation "The bulk of the work is performed at scattered stations or ports and the office at the seat of government consists merely of the headquarters for the exercise of the function of general direction and control over the field stations".

Importance

The importance of the field organisation can be discerned from the following facts :

(*a*) The number of field personnel is many a time more than that of the officials functioning at the centre as there is only one employee out of every 160 who works at the Headquarters (at the Centre) while the rest of them work in the field. (*b*) A welfare state like that of India necessitates a sizable field service to meet the needs of the citizens. (*c*) There is fast expansion of regulatory activities of the Government (*d*) The technical advancement particularly in Transport and Communication has caused expansion of field organisation. (*e*) It is the crying need of the day to establish field organisation for making provision of the requisite services to the countrymen at the doorstep level. (*f*) Under any situation the existence of field organisation is imperative. A country, for example, has to maintain diplomatic missions abroad.

---

[1] *As quoted in Public Administration in India by Dr. Hoshiar Singh, Dr. Mohindar Singh Ed. 1987, reprint 1990 pp. 157-161.*

Patterns of Field Organisation

Professor Willoughby, a pioneer in the field of public administration, has demarcated between the unitary and multiple type of field organisations. In a unitary system, the field units of an organisation remain under the supervision and control of the regional head. The regional head is responsible to the central headquarters for the functioning of his field units. He holds complete charge of the field services and the staff working in these units is responsible to him. A single line of command runs from the central office to the regional head of the field units and those heading field units receive it from their immediate boss at the regional level. In the unitary pattern, the directives issued to the field units are communicated through the regional head to a field unit. Under the multiple type of field organisation, there is a direct communication between the central office and the field unit. The middle officer does not intervene in the supervision and control of the field agencies. The field units do have their regional supervisory authoritieis but there is no singular authority to control the units working in the field.

In the case of India, the business of the Government is transacted at the Capital though numerous administrative sub-centres exist throughout the country to serve the needs of the attached areas as the Centre is not in a position to govern and administer the whole country at its own level. In India such field organisations are termed as subordinate offices.

Unitary System

The layout under a unitary system may be explained diagrammatically by quoting an instance of Post Office Department :

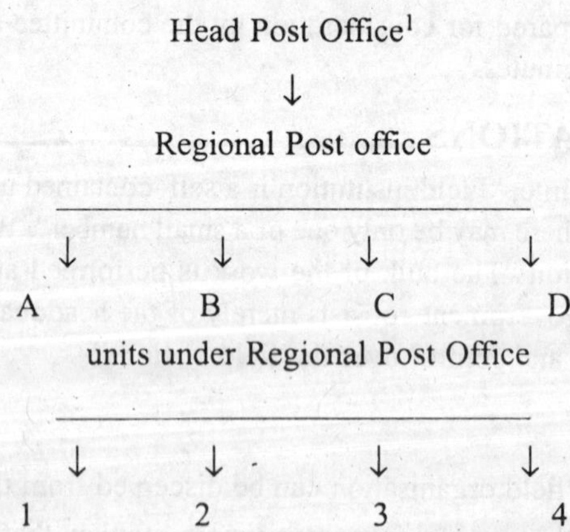

The diagram quoted above reflects that the units of a regional post office have been kept under the control of the Regional head who in his turn is responsible to the head office for the working of the regional office and its units.

Multiple system

The diagram given below refers to the working of the field units under Multiple system :

[1] *Ibid*

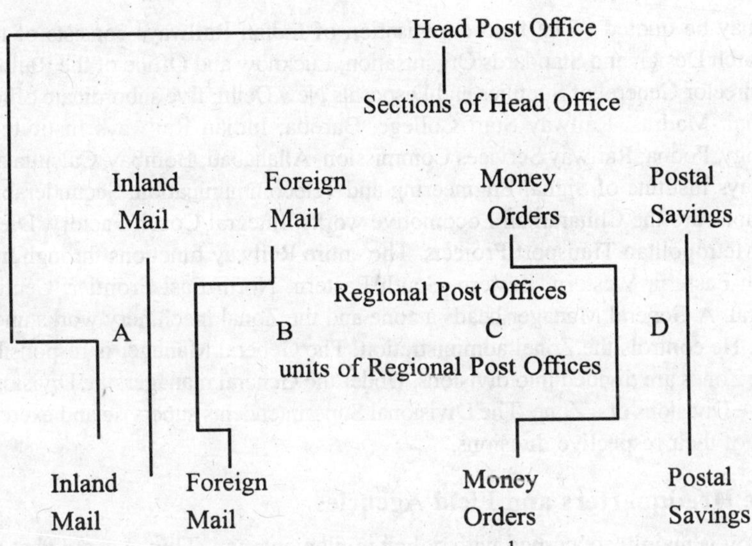

1

The diagram given above clearly indicates the direct relationship of sections of the Head Post Office viz. Inland Mail, Foreign Mail, Money Orders and Postal Orders and Postal Savings with its respective units in the Regional Post Office. There is no Department that has followed or adopted the complete unitary or multiple system. For the smooth working of the Department, a blend of the two systems is generally found in operation.

For example, the Ministry of Labour has four attached offices : (*i*) The Director General of Employment and Training is assisted by two directors who are assisted by deputy and assistant directors technical as well as non-technical staff. (*ii*) The Chief Labour Commissioner is assisted by a joint Labour Commissioner, three deputy Chief Labour Commissioners, three Labour Enforcement officers at the Headquarter and thirteen Regional Commissioners. The Field organisation also consists of one deputy Chief Labour Commissioner and 159 Labour Enforcement Officers. (*iii*) The Director General of Factory Advice Service and Labour Institute is at Bombay and three Regional Labour Institutes at Calcutta, Kanpur and Madras. (*iv*) The Directorate of Labour Bureau headed by a director assisted by two offices of the Bureau each at Chandigarh and Simla

There exist 21 subordinate offices and 6 autonomous organisations. More prominent subordinate offices are as follows : Director General of Mines Safety, Dhanbad; Offices of the Welfare Commissioners at Bangalore, Jabalpur, Bhubaneswar, Karma, Bhilwara, Kalichedu, Panji, Allahabad and the office of the Deputy Welfare Commissioner at Barbil, Central Government Industrial Tribunal–Cum–Labour Court at Dhanbad (two) Bombay (two) one each at Asansol, Calcutta, Jabalpur, New Delhi, Chandigarh and Kanpur; Office of the Chairman Board of Arbitration and office of the Accounts Officer Audit cell at New Delhi. The Autonomous Organisations are : Office of the Director General : Employee's State Finance Corporation, New Delhi; office of the Central Provident Fund Commissioner, New Delhi; the National Council for Safety in Mines, Dhanbad; the National Safety Council, Bombay; the Central Board of Workers Education, Nagpur and the National Labour Institute, New Delhi. The administrative machinery in the field organisation has the responsibility of administering the Labour welfare activities, under the directives issued from time to time by the Headquarters.

[1]*Harish Chandar Sharma : Public Administration in India (1987 ed)*
[2]*Shriram Maheshwari op. cit. p. 55.*

Another example may be quoted : The field organisation of Indian Railways consists of two attached offices viz. Research Design and Standards Organisation, Lucknow and Office of the Railway Liaison Officer with the Director General of Supplies and Disposals New Delhi; five subordinate offices — Railway Rates Tribunal, Madras; Railway Staff College, Baroda; Indian Railways Institute of Advanced Track Technology, Poona; Railway Services Commission, Allahabad, Bombay, Calcutta and Madras and Indian Railways Institute of Signal Engineering and Telecommunication, Secunderabad. The other Field organisations are the Chitaranjan Locomotive works, Integral Coach Factory, Diesel Locomotive Works, and Metropolitan Transport Projects. The entire Railway functions through nine zones — Northern, North-Eastern, Western, Eastern, South Eastern, North-East Frontier, Central, Southern and South-Central. A General Manager heads a zone and the Zonal machinery works under his administrative control. He controls the Zonal administration. The General Manager is responsible to the Railway Board. The Zones are divided into divisions. Under the General manager, the Divisional Superintendents work in the Divisions of a Zone. The Divisional Superintendents supervise and exercise control over the activities of their respective divisions.

Relations between the Headquarters and Field Agencies

The field organisation is mainly concerned with policy implementation. Things decided at the Headquarters — obviously New Delhi — the hub of administration are implemented by the field administration. In the affairs of paramount importance, the field organisation is supervised and controlled by the Headquarters - the Central or supervising office usually in the Capital. The "Headquarters organisation of the Government of India comprises a number of ministeries and Departments". In contrast to head quarters, the offices which seek approval before taking administrative action from the headquarters and are under the control of the latter are termed 'field offices'. In India, the headquarter is synonymous with the Secretariat and the Field refers to attached and subordinate offices.

The main problems emerging out of the headquarters' control over the field are – (*a*) the issue of administrative functional control and the problem of relations between the various levels of field hierarchy itself in case it consists (as not infrequently it does) of more than one tier of authority.

(*b*) Territorial functional dichotomy, i.e., communication and control. Both are considered as major issues involved in the relationship between the headquarters and the field.

Major issues in headquarters and field relationship

Territorial-functional Dichotomy

From the point of view of overhead direction and control, the organisation of field establishment may assume either of the two forms, viz. territorial or functional. Willoughby terms them unitary and multiple. In the unitary or territorial form, the central authority creates regional or area agencies which have over all control of all the activities of the area. The office in charge of the area heads it and the heads of all other specialised units at that level are his subordinates. The entire communication from the field station to the head office and back are made through him and he is responsible for the acts of all other departmental heads. In a functional or a multiple form of organisation on the other hand, the different divisions or branches of the headquarters office have their corresponding field establishments at different area levels and maintain direct contact with them. In this case, a coordinating or integrating authority at the area level is not provided. Each service or agency is considered as an autonomous entity unrelated to either service or agencies and the line of authority runs direct from it to its headquarters office. In France, the Prefect was once the example of the territorial unitary type of field organisation. In case of India, the District Collector, particularly before 1947 was Prefect's counterpart. He was the real executive chief and administrator of the district. His relationship with other specialised agencies at the district level were well portrayed by Montague Chelmsford Report 1918 "as several other specialised services exist with staff of their own, the

District officer influences the policy in all these matters and he is always there in the background to lend his support or if need be to mediate between a specialised service and people". Since independence, the position of Collector has undergone a change. District is today a sub-capital where the district officers of the various technical departments are located. The heads of these departments, being technical persons, are directly responsible to their departmental chiefs at the State headquarters and are independent of the Collector's authority.

The headquarters office of any organisation is subdivided into specialised units, each of which deals with a particular programme of a segment of the total operation. The Railway Management in India, for instance, has a number of functional departments like Civil Engineering, Mechanical Engineering, Electrical Engineering, Operating, Commercial, Signal and Telecommunication, Accounts, Personnel, Stores, Medical and Security. All these Departments have an impact on the working of the Railways. Each of these departments has a field office at the Zonal and divisional levels. Besides, these functional officers, the Railways have Area officers, viz. General manager-over-all in-charge of the Division. The relationship between the functional officials at different levels and the area administrators at these levels as well as their relationship, *'interse* at the same level' form the crux of the headquarters - Field relationships. The Ministry of Railways at the Secretarial levels is organised as a Railway Board which is functional in character. The Railway Board is composed of five members – the Chairman who is in charge of the staff, the Financial Commissioner in charge of finance and three other members, in charge of Civil including Electrical Engineering, Mechanical Engineering and Transport respectively. The Chairman heads the organisation administratively and is responsible for Intra-Board coordination. He can overrule all other members except the Financial Commissioner. The Board members deal with all aspects of technical subjects of which they happen to be in charge. These members are rendered assistance by five additional members in charge of Works, Mechanical, Transport staff and Finance. Besides, the Board is assisted by a number of technical officers, designated as Directors, each heading a Directorate. There are sixteen Directorates viz. Civil Engineering, Establishment, Efficiency Bureau, Finance, Health, Mechanical Engineering, Railway Planning, Railway stores, Railway coordination, Security, Signals and Telecommunications, Traffic, Transport, Statistics and Economics, Wagon production and Vigilance.

Next below the Board in the Field are Zones each headed by the General Manager - a top level official in Railway hierarchy. He is the Chief executive at that level and effects coordination at the zonal level between all Departments. All communications to any Departmental officer are routed through the General Manager except in technical and routine matters. In the latter case, the Departmental officers can correspond directly with the technical officers, i.e. the Director at the New Delhi headquarters. The zones are further divided into Divisions which are under the over-all charge of Divisional Superintendent - a prototype of the General Manager in the Division. The latter is assisted by as many technical officers known as deputies to the Chief at the zonal level.

Communication and Control

Headquarter – Field relationship necessitates a good communication between various levels. Lack of proper understanding of the objectives and purposes of programmes by the field officials is responsible for non implementation or partial implementation of policies and programmes in the country. Neither these officials are taken into confidence while determining policies and preparing of programmes nor have they an appreciation of overall plan or objective. They are not even definite about the methods and techniques they use for executing these programmes. Hence they bank upon Manuals and noting on files while communicating. Communication generally remains one way traffic, i.e. from the top to the bottom, in the form of orders, directions, notifications, circulars and memoranda, and 'sacred manuals' laying down clearly the role of officials at various levels. Feedback from lower to upwards is discouraged if not frowned upon. The field officials invariably hold the view that the procedures and rules laid down in the Manuals are inadequate and do not concur with realities or meet the situation.

Another aspect of this relationship is the exercise of control by the Headquarters over field agencies through commonly accepted techniques and devices. Such techniques appear in the nature of control, before action is taken e.g. prior approval of individual projects before initiation by an operating unit, the promulgation of service standards, budgetary limitation upon the magnitude of operations, approval of key subordinate personnel.[1] Field agencies in the states are handicapped on account of excessive financial control by the Finance Department and also the requirement of prior approval of the departmental Headquarters office before the execution of any programme.

Control after action implies reporting, audit, inspection and investigation. The Headquarters insist on securing information from the field agencies in the form of returns, reports and statistics concerning the progress of field operations. It has, however, been observed that it entails excessive burden on the 'Field' as the reports and returns tend to multiply. The audit prevents embezzlement, fraud, carelessness, errors, unauthorised expenditure, expenditure of excess allotment and non compliance with rules and laws. However, it may be pointed out that audit is a *'post facto'* function and is a sort of postmortem scrutiny. Besides its functions are fairly limited as it is confined to examining compliance with rules and regulations in the financial matters. Inspection ensures that the existing rules, regulations, procedures and practices are observed and instructions are complied with. "What audit is to financial transactions, inspection is to administrative transactions".[2] In the present context of things, the scope of Inspection needs widened. It should play more useful and more effective role. It should not remain confined to observing compliance or rules with the Manuals, it should evaluate performance of the Inspection agency itself. It should develop 'O and M' angle, i.e. it should not simply be a fault finding process but be a guide and instructor to a person working in the inspected agency and suggest improvement in organisational systems, methods and procedures for adding to efficiency. In an ideal Inspection system, the Inspectors act as part of the administrative process and assume responsibility for the successful working of the office or project. Investigation amounts to an enquiry into some alleged or suspected malpractices or abuse of authority. It discovers the guilty and prosecutes them. It is considered as an *ad hoc* basis as it is purely personal and particular in character.

'Methods of Headquarters' Control over Field

L.D. White has suggested important methods of headquarters' control over the field establishment viz. (*i*) From the bureau chief of the agency, there comes the basic general authorisation to act in the field, usually found in the permanent body of the agent's official commission (*ii*) From Headquarters also comes expenditure authority which, in turn, reflects a plan and a specific programme that has received central approval in general or in detail. (*iii*) Specific instructions flow in an endless stream from headquarters to field offices periodically combined into an operation manual which itself is steadily supplemented by new directives. (*iv*) The general flow of field operations is brought to the headquarters' attention in weekly, monthly or quarterly reports. (*v*) In some agencies, certain classes of decisions cannot be made in the field, but must be referred to headquarters. The field offices may ask for advice on difficult or sensitive cases. (*vi*) Headquarters will maintain an inspection service to advise and watch field operations and to report any deviations or poor management. There will always be an examination of fiscal transactions by a bureau of departmental examiners, preliminary to the audit conducted by the Comptroller General. Provisions will be made for a case audit to ensure that the decisions taken in the field office are correct. The assignment and reassignment of important fields are determined in Washington. (*vii*) Some Departments have regular or occasional meetings at which all the field directors confer with the

[1] *Millet, JD : op. cit., pp. 99-107*

[2] *Dr. Avasthi and Maheswari : Public Administration 1992 ed. p. 164*

principal headquarters' officials to clarify policy programmes and operations. The biennial conferences of the staff of the department of Agriculture-headquarters and field-are a model of such meetings. (*viii*) Where the interests of persons are involved, there is an appeal from a field adjudication to headquarters. The authority of the headquarters bureau is undisputed and the actual impact of headquarter's officials is always considerable, "within the channels of accepted policy, close central control tends to obstruct the free flow of business. Much experience suggests that public business is best transacted when field agents of higher competence and character are selected and are given wide responsibility for making decisions. Headquarters bureaus have an obligation as far as possible, to divest themselves of responsibility or doing again what has already been done in the field.[1] Pfiffner also has expressed "......there is both a headquarter and a field way of life, the groups viewing each other with smugness and suspicion. Field workers insist that headquarters does not understand their problems.... Headquarters is characterised by an intellectual or research approach to problems in contrast to the fields' practical approach."[2]

The statements given above are universally recognised. There is a general feeling that the officials posted at Headquarters has a comfortable life, enjoy better amenities, command higher status, draw more emoluments and enjoy good and fruitful contacts. In such a state of affairs, the following suggestions can be of help.

Suggestion for Successful administration of field offices

(*i*) Field offices must be manned by trained and competent personnel who can take sound decisions on matters falling within the purview of their responsibility. (*ii*) The responsibility of the field officer must be clearly defined and their limitation should be made clear to them. (*iii*) There should be free, frank and frequent communication between field officers of different departments in the same area on related problems (*iv*) The powers entrusted to field officers must relieve the headquarters of unnecessary work. (*v*) Special facilities and financial incentives be provided in hardship areas. (*vi*) The tenure system may be further strengthened. Periodical transfers from headquarter to the field and vice-versa is apt to inculcate a balanced outlook on national policies. (*vii*) Informal visits by the headquarter officers should supplement the formal inspections, periodic returns and reports. (*viii*) Training courses and conferences between the headquarter officers and field officers apprise them of each others' problems, make them more competent and build up a community of interests. (*ix*) Both the Headquarter officers and Field officers must be equipped with adequate knowledge of local needs and strive to fulfil them within the frame work of governmental policy and procedure. (*x*) A person posted in the field should be duly briefed by the headquarters regarding problems and issues involved so that he may be able to function adequately in his new job. Likewise debriefing should be done on the completion of his field assignment. It may be in the form of a few terminal interviews with the headquarters personnel to whom he may communicate the operational problems and the difficulties he was confronted with in his task. That would serve as imperative feedback to the headquarters. (*xi*) Effort should be made to create at the headquarters as well as in the field a full appreciation of the particular field station, so that they are fully induced to reach a decision appropriate to the situation.[3]

The use of information technology in public administration has brought the field establishment and Headquarter closer to each other creating therby better harmony between the two and speedy transaction of administrative matters.

---

[1] *L.D. White : Introduction to the study of Public Administration (1958 ed) pp 105-6.*
[2] *John M. Pfiffner Vance R. Presthus : Public Administration p. 221.*
[3] *Avasthi and Maheshwari op. cit., p. 165*

(F)BOARDS AND COMMISSIONS

In a democratic welfare state, public affairs are administered by ministers, departments, boards, commissions and corporate bodies. Mostly, the Government business is conducted through departmental organisations. However, boards and commissions have sprung up to overcome administrative complexities and ease its functioning. There has been a marked preference for a plural executive. In the U.K. Privy Council or Cabinet were vested with executive authority. The American democracy also opted for committee system both for running Government or private business. In our country, the executive authority, since the passage of Regulating Act (1773) rested with the Executive Council. Since 1947, the Cabinet has replaced the Executive Council. The Board and Commission system has been firmly entrenched on our soil as an integral part of administrative institutions. Its dire necessity to serve as an instrument of inquiry or as an administrative-cum-regulatory body has never been questioned.

Both the terms are interchangeably used though they differ. Prof. Willoughby points out the distinction. In his words, "A Board.......is a group of members who are required to act collectively upon all matters falling within their jurisdiction........A commission is a group of members having the duty not only of acting collectively as a Board, but also of serving individually as heads of organisation units that have been setup for the performance of administrative work that has to be done'.[1]

Advantages of Boards and Commissions

The Boards and Commissions are comparatively (*i*) more autonomous and enjoy more flexibility in arriving at quick decisions than the executive agencies i.e. departments. (*ii*) These agencies save the administration from extraneous interference and pressures. The example of UPSC can be quoted to prove the case. (*iii*) A bulk of boards and commissions constitute an admixture of representation and specialisation. It helps in maintaining balance between the two - representation to democratic values and specialised services. Thus administrative requirements are best met : (*iv*) These bodies discharge some quasi-judicial duties and give opinions on issues involving public and private obligations. One person may fail to think that rationally regarding safeguarding of the rights of the people. Plurality of minds may, on the other hand, decide more accurately than one person. (*v*) The organisation of this nature are needed when policies are undecided and joint discussions and deliberations are indispensable.

Hence it may be concluded that whenever it is thought essential to lessen the Central/State Government's burden regarding the day to day conduct of a regulatory function or the provision of a service or the management of a business enterprise, a separate plural body of this type is created.

The Indian Constitution also makes a provision for the establishment of Commissions viz. The Finance Commission[2], Union Public Service Commission[3], Election Commission[4], Backward Commission[5], and Official Language Commission.[6] These bodies do not function under the direct administrative control of any ministry.

The Boards setup under the provisions of statutes passed by the Indian Parliament are : The Railway Board, University Grants Commission, Control Board of Revenue, Atomic Energy Commission etc. These are subjected to general administrative control of the concerned ministry. The bodies which have been established by the Central Governments' executive resolutions are: The Central Social Welfare Board, Central Water and Power Commission, Handicrafts Board, All India Handloom Board. All these are termed as Attached Boards and their existence depends on the willingness of the concerned ministries. Some of the bodies of vital importance are as under.

[1]*W.F. Willoughby : Principles of Public Administration (Indian Edition) p. 109*
[2] *Article 280.* [3]*Article 315.*
[4]*Article 324.* [5]*Article 340.*
[6]*Article 44.*

Finance Commission (Article 280)

Article 280 provides for setting up of an independent agency termed Finance Commission, from time to time, usually after every five years. So far *i.e.*, from 1952 to 1997 eleven Finance Commissions have been appointed. Each Finance Commission is composed of one chairman and four other members. The chairman is appointed from amongst persons having experience in public affairs. The remaining members are selected from amongst persons who (*i*) are or have been or are qualified to be appointed as judges of a High Court or (*ii*) have specialised knowledge of the Finance and accounts of the Government or (*iii*) have had wide experience in financial matters and in administration, or (*iv*) have special knowledge in the field of economics. The members of the commission hold office for such period as may be specified by the President and are eligible for reappointment.

Functions of the Finance Commission

(*i*) To recommend to the President the basis for distribution of the net proceeds of taxes between the Centre and the States. (*ii*) To recommend the principles which should govern the 'grants-in-aid' to be extended to the states out of the Consolidated Fund of India. (*iii*) To tender advice to the President on any other matter referred to the commission in the interest of sound finances. (*iv*) To suggest amounts to be paid to the states of Assam, Bihar, Orissa and West Bengal in lieu of the assignment of system of export duty on jute products.

An analytical study of Part XII of the Constitution with its chapter entitled 'Finance' reveals that the functions of the Finance Commission are not incorporated in Article 280 above. The provisions of the Constitution dealing with the working of the commission are interspersed in the articles referring to financial relations between the Centre and the States. Article 270, for instance, makes it mandatory to divide taxes on income other than agricultural, between the union and the states. However, taxes on income exclude Corporation Tax and Surcharge that may be levied for the coffers of the Union Government. As regards Income Tax, the Finance Commission is charged with the duty of making certain recommendations as "the percentage of the net proceeds of Income Tax excluding the taxes payable in respect of the emoluments of the Central Government that shall be deemed as the proceeds attributable to the Union Territories. The percentage of the net proceeds in any financial year of tax on income other than agricultural income, except insofar as these represent proceeds attributable to the Union Territories or taxes payable in respect of the emoluments of the Centre that shall not be taken to form part of the Consolidated Fund of India but shall be earmarked for the states within which the tax is leviable in that year and the manner in which and the time from which such percentages is distributable among the State Governments.

Besides Article 280 (3) authorises the President to refer any matter to the Commission that he may consider essential in the interest of 'sound finance'. This article has enabled the President to recommend to the Commission the principles that should govern the distribution of the net proceeds among the states in a financial year, regarding the Estate duty on property other than agricultural land, tax on railway fare and the additional duties of excise on mill-made textiles, sugar and tobacco. The President has also asked the Commission to recommend modifications in the rate of interest and the terms of repayment of the loans made to various states by the Government of India.

As a result of the recommendations of various Finance Commissions appointed by the respective Presidents from time to time (so far twelve finance commissions have been appointed) the following substantial steps have been taken — (a) The share of the State Governments in the proceeds of the Income Tax has increased steadily, (b) There is a progressive increase in the amount of the grants-in-aid given by the Centre to the States. The 4th Finance Commission, for instance, recommended (*i*) a new formula for the sharing of taxes between the Centre and the States, based on the enhancement of the Division pool. (*ii*) It ensured incentives for higher revenues realization by the states. The problems of poorer States was taken care of as they were exhorted to maintain a self sustaining fiscal balance.

(*iii*) It suggested the expansion of sharing of Income Tax and Excise Duty with the states by the Centre. (*iv*) It appraised the debt problem of the states. It observed that the borrowing of the states are being utilized to finance current expenditure. Hence, such debt and interest liability mounted to 1,65,000 and Rs 1,600 crores respectively. It was indeed an unhealthy trend. Then the Commission took upon itself to assist all states consistent with the objectives of equality and efficiency and enable them to move towards self-containing and self-regulating fiscal balance. However, the innovative recommendations as above, were made to maintain a correct balance between the resource needs of the state and the finance available with the Centre. The Government accepted all the major recommendations of this Commission for 5 years w.e.f. April 1995.[1]

The 10th Finance Commission was appointed on June 15, 1992 with Shri K.C. Pant as the Chairman, Dr. Debi Prasad, B.P.R. Vithal, C. Rangarajan as the members and Shri M.C. Gupta (Ex-Chief Secretary, Haryana) (as member Secretary). [2] In one of its momentous recommendations to the Parliament on March 14, 1995, it recommended that 77.5 per cent share of the net Income tax receipts (0.927 per cent in case of Union territories) and 40 per cent of the total excise duty proceeds be given to the states. Thus the total share of the states as per Commission's recommendations was to be raised by 29 per cent of the gross receipts of the central taxes. Three per cent of the figure was to accrue from additional Excise duty in the divisible pool under an alternating devolution scheme. The Government later accepted all the major recommendations of the Commission for a period of 5 years to be implemented from April 1, 1995.[3]

The tenth commission was asked to make recommendations on the principles which should govern the grants-in-aid of the revenues of the states out of consolidated fund of India. It also recommended the sums to be paid to the states needing assistance by way of grants-in-aid of these revenues under article 275 of the Constitution. The Commission was required to adopt the population figures of 1971 in all cases where population was regarded as a factor for determination of devolution of taxes and duties and grants-in-aid. The commission was asked to submit its report by November 30, 1993 and asked to indicate the bases on which it arrived at its findings and make available the state-wise estimates of receipts and expenditure. The Commission was also asked to review the present scheme of calamity relief fund and may make appropriate recommendations thereon. The Commission was also required to make an assessment of the debt position of the states at the end of March, 1994 and suggest corrective measures keeping in view the financial requirements of the centre.

The Union Government constituted the 11th Finance Commission to make recommendations on the devolution of the tax revenues and provision of grants to the States for 5 years i.e. April 2000 to March 2005. As a statutory body, the commission will study the same aspects of Centre-State financial relations as its predecessors — the IXth and Xth commissions which tried to see the finances of the states in their totality and made recommendations to take the states towards revenue surplus.. However, it devised a new formula for sharing the central tax revenues determining the question of grants-in-aid to the states and recommend measures to reduce the indebtedness of the states. It has also been asked to suggest ways and means of restructuring the finances of both the Centre and the states to 'restore budgetary balance and main macro economic stability'. However, the crying need of the hour is not to initiate new schemes and programmes to augment the finances of the Union but a true display of political will to avert fiscal deterioration. Basically the Commission will have to examine — (*i*) measures to be devised to augment the pool of state Government resources devolving on the Panchayats and Municipalities (*ii*) to review the formula fixing the states' share of the gross Central Tax revenue at 29%. The Finance Minister in his Budget speech (in February, 1998) promised that the Finance Commission would be asked to review the 29% ratio for the next 5 year period.

[1]*Hindustan Times, November 27, 1994, March 15, 1995.*
[2]*Hindustan Times, June 16, 1992.*
[3]*Ibid : March 15, 1995.*

The 12th Finance Commission was constituted by the President on 1st November, 2002 under the chairmanship of Dr. C. Rangarajan. The Commission submitted its report for 2005-2010 suggesting measures to restructure public-finance, restore budgetory balance, reduce debt burden and curtail fiscal deficit.

It clearly reflects that the states have received the benefits of Cooperative federalism. Thus the "Financial Commission has proved to be an original idea, an innovation of the 20th century. Thus an attempt has been made whereby the units are allowed to partake of the revenues of the Centre to the making of which they themselves do much to contribute".[1] However, if a critical analysis is made of the functioning of the Finance Commissions, one concludes that it has been overshadowed by an extra constitutional authority like Planning Commission. Each Finance Commission has been appointed in view of the requirements of the Five Year Plans. It is required to submit its recommendations in a way and at a time so that the working of the Planning Commission is facilitated. Dr. P.V. Rajamannar — the Chairman of the 4th Planning Commission suggested that the jurisdiction of both — the Planning Commission and the Finance Commission be clearly demarcated so that the latter is not eclipsed by the former. In the words of Dr. Bombwall "When the Finance Commission begins its work, it has to keep in view the requirements of the plan. The result is that it has to function more or less within lines already laid down by the Planning Commission. Over the years, Finance Commission has become a very much devalued institution. The Planning Commission has displaced it as the largest dispenser of largesse."[2]

Despite its somewhat eclipsed position by the Planning Commission, the Finance Commission has set an example of Union-State coordination and cooperation that is unparalleled. Pylee has very well portrayed its importance and striking advantages in the words "The chief merit of the works of the Commission lies in its impartial and objective outlook as a steadying force in the finances of the federal system and its ability to take the question of distribution of finances out of vortex of federal-state political pressures and controversies. In fact the commission acts as a buffer between the Union and the States checking the clamorous, finance-hungry states bent upon applying their political pressures on the Union and at the same time making the latter give as much as possible to the needy states. It will be almost impossible for the Union to go against the recommendations of the Commission."[3]

Criticism

Despite its marked utility, the Commission is vehemently criticised on the following grounds.

(i) Qualifications vague

The critics point out that the qualifications prescribed for the chairman are rather vague. The Chairman of the Commission appointed from time to time did not have the requisite background and did not possess the necessary skill so very essential for handling a specialised subject. Hence the recommendations of the Commission have not been made promptly. In the words of Jhavraj "The qualifications prescribed for the members denote some specialisation, that of the chairman is too vague…Most of the chairmen who have been drawn from the ruling party did not possess the requisite background and skill in handling such a specialised subject. The Commission normally takes more than a year to finalise its recommendations."[4]

(ii) Inter-state equity not possible

The commission relies on the information and data furnished by the states. The states are in

[1] *Hindustan Times dated June 16, 1992.*

[2] *K.V. Rao : Parliamentary Democracy of India Part II, p. 324.*

[3] *Mr. J.K. Jhavraj, Financial Administration of India 1987 2nd ed. p. 109.*

[4] *Mr. J.K. Jhevraj : op. cit, pp. 110-11.*

the habit of exaggerating their problems by presenting wrong figures. There is lack of permanent machinery to cross check the inflated figures. Hence, it leads to wrong assessment and view of situation which eventually leads to non achievement of inter-state equity.

(iii) Accurate assessment of projects not done

The Commission visits all the states but does not get enough time to make an accurate assessment of the projects in operation. Besides, the Commission's tours are limited invariably to visiting of the capitals only.

(iv) Inadequate observation of facts

It is contended that all the members do not present themselves on all the occasions of conducting the hearings in the state capitals perhaps because all are not full-time members and keep themselves occupied in their personal engagements. Hence their observations are inadequate.

(v) Inadequacy of their reports

The Finance Commissions do not quote details of their estimates of 'revenue gap' and 'financial needs' of each state in their reports. This induces the researcher to suspect that the commissions have tried to escape from the criticism of this arbitrary assumptions and estimation methods.[1]

(vi) Planning Commission restricts its role

The Chairman of the Fourth Finance Commission was of the view that the creation of the Planning Commission has circumvented the role of the Finance Commission. In his words "...I think that the relative scope and functions of the two commissions should be clearly defined by amending the Constitution."[2]

Despite these points of criticism, the importance of the Finance Commission cannot be minimised. It is definitely a Centre-state coordinating agency. The Union Government is apt to accept its recommendations on the basis of its meticulous survey of financial conditions of States and Union Territories and its judicious and impartial approach to the economic problems of the country and its component parts.

The Election Commission

The Constitution provides for an independent Election Commission to ensure free and fair elections to the parliament, state legislatures and the offices of President and Vice President. It consists of a Chief Election Commissioner and such other commissioners as the President may decide on from time to time. In 1989 the then Government appointed two Election Commissioners to cope with the enhanced work on account of lowering of voting age from 21 to 18 years.

However subsequently, the National Front Government abolished both these posts and reverted to the old position. Again a multi-member Commission was appointed by the Presidential Ordinance to clip the wings of T.N. Seshan, the CEC on October 1, 1993. Two more Commissioners were appointed despite vehement protests and resentment of CEC. The conflict between the two newly appointed commissioners and CEC was taken to the Apex Court which warned CEC to obey the law and resolve differences between the two newly appointed Election Commissioners by exchange of views and mutual confidence.[3] Even Ex-President Dr. S.D. Sharma expressed concern and anxiety over the unhappy situation in the Election Commission — both the CEC and the Election Commissioners M.S. Gill and G.V.G. Krishnamurthy continued their 'parallel shooting' at each other.

---

[1] *Report of the Fourth Finance Commission Government of India 1965, pp. 58-90.*

[2] *Hindustan Times : November 6, 1993.*

[3] *Ibid November 6, 1993.*

An editorial commented, "The latest escalation of the infighting in the Election Commission has created a situation that is not only unprecedented but also in the extreme".[1] At a later stage, CEC was cut to size though his supremacy over other two commissioners was asserted in a decision by the Apex Court. "...the CEC would remain in complete and overall control of the Election Commission's work and he is not bound by the views of Election Commissioners".[2] The Chief Election Commissioner (CEC) and other election Commissioners are appointed by the President of India for a period of six years. They have to retire at the age of 65 years, whichever is earlier. The tenure of the CEC and other commissioners can be cut down on account of resignation or removal by the President on grounds of proved misbehaviour or incapacity on the recommendation of the Parliament. However, Election Commissioner shall not be removed from office except on the recommendation of the Chief Election Commissioner.

The service conditions and tenure of the Election Commissioners are subject to the provisions laid down by the Parliament. They cannot be changed to their disadvantage during their term of office.

The President or the Governor of a state shall, when so requested by the Election Commission, make available to the Election Commission or to a regional commissioner, such staff as may be necessary for the discharge of the functions conferred on the Election Commission (Article 324).

Functions

The functions of the Election Commission are as under :

(i) To prepare electoral rolls for the elections and suitably revise them after every 10 yearly census and before every General Elections to the Union and State Legislatures. (ii) To supervise the Election machinery throughout the country so that elections are held in free and fair manner. (iii) To appoint and nominate staffs for conducting the elections from time to time and making arrangements of necessary election materials. (iv) To notify the dates and schedules of elections so that nomination papers are filled and properly scrutinised before the elections take place. (v) To appoint officers for enquiring into disputes relating to electoral arrangements. (vi) To request President of India or the Governor of a state for requisitioning of the staff necessary for conducting the elections. (vii) To cancel polls if mass scale rigging or other irregularities are committed. (viii) To play the role of a tribunal for settling matters as giving recognition to a political party or allotting a symbol for the electoral purposes. (ix) To advise the President or the Governor as the case may be, on a matter relating to the disqualification of a legislator. (x) To determine the duration of political broadcasts on radio and television before the commencement of elections and accord equal opportunities to all the political parties in this respect. (xi) To exercise supervision over the Returning officers, Assistant Returning officers and appointing advisers to that effect. (xii) To declare the Election results and appoint Election Tribunals for deciding election disputes. (xiii) To issue a code of conduct to be observed by all parties and people at the time of elections. For instance the Commission warned the State Government against plying of unauthorised vehicles in the Palam constituency during the polling for carrying voters to and from the polling stations. It warned all chief secretaries and Electoral officers that it will monitor violations of Model Code of Conduct on the basis of transfers of officers and payments from discretionary funds by ministers and other authorities. The Governor of Himachal had to relinquish office as he went by official car to Madhya Pradesh to help his son in the elections. (xiv) It can make an appeal to the electorates to elect proper representatives. The CEC on 47th Martyrdom of Gandhiji, for instance, appealed to the electorates of Maharashtra to give lead to the rest of the country by electing representatives having character and values, to the State Assembly. (xv) To curb fraudulent impersonation, (xvi) Political parties which splashed slogans and symbols on private or public walls must get them

[1] *Ibid, November 6, 1993.*

[2] *Ibid, November 16, 1993.*

removed after elections. (xvii) Regulation of hours of the loudspeakers used for election campaign. (xviii) Ceiling on election expenses made effective rigidly. (xix) To decide whether or not situation in a particular state is normal for holding elections. Lyngdoh did not agree with BJP claim regarding conditions in Gujrat being conducive for fair and free elections.

Flaws of the Commissions

Though the Constitution has ensured its independence, some flaws in the sphere of its composition and working are discernible. They are as follows : (i) The Constitution is silent about the qualifications and the term of the Chief Election Commissioner. It is feared that the President on the advice of the Council of Ministers may appoint a person purely on political considerations.[1] (ii) The Constitution does not specify the number of Regional Election Commissioners to be placed under the control of the Chief Election Commissioner and their qualifications, terms and conditions of service, etc. Here also political considerations may weigh on the mind of the President. (iii) The Election commission has been denied the right to recruit and regulate the conditions of service of its secretariat staff. (iv) The 44th amendment Act 1978 has brought the commission into the vortex of politics by empowering the President to seek the opinion of the Election Commission about the possibility of holding elections in a state under President's rule after the duration of six months.

The Election Commission on the whole has observed impartiality and exhibited efficiency in the discharge of its onerous duties. However, its success is very much dependent on the healthy cooperation of the opposition political parties as well as the party in power. The Election Commission has invariably not succumbed to the external pressure or extraneous considerations though the opposition parties have spared no pains in denouncing the former Chief Election Commissioner — T.N. Seshan from time to time. The latter always took a tough stance about the conduct of elections.

However, the supreme court was forced to impose curbs on CEC's powers. In a historic judgment regarding violation of model code of election conduct by a state the Supreme Court held "It was injuncting the Election Commission from taking *suo motto* action against the State Government in cases where it perceived there was a violation of the moral code of conduct...in every such case the Election Commission would have to approach the apex court for directions"[2].

(i) He emphasised audit of accounts of political parties. (ii) He pulled up five State Governments for large scale transfers of officials before elections in violation of code of conduct. (iii) He pulled up central ministers for issuing out of turn LPG and Phone connections. (iv) He put off polls in Bihar citing law and order problems. (v) He put off the hearing of the petition against the BJP about misuse of its symbol till just before elections. (vi) He countermanded elections in five constituencies in Bihar and U.P. and also Patna from where I.K. Gujral, the former Foreign Minister was contesting. (viii) Domicile qualification for Rajya Sabha seats strictly adhered to created problem for certain political favourites who were accommodated in Rajya Sabha without caring for residential qualifications. These reforms constituted a landmark in the Indian political spectrum.

The CEC, T.N. Seshan, during his tenure came in confrontation with the Government on a vital issue — whether or not directive to the Central or State Government be issued by the Commission under Article 324. The Government went to the extent of seeking advice of Attorney General of India who cleared that the Commission could only make a request to the Government. The Commission, in fact, effaced from its mind its earlier stand regarding model code of conduct of election, that it was not legally enforceable. However, it has been issuing directives under the garb of Article 324. The Government, for instance, accepted its contention that Budget would vitiate a free and fair polls and its presentation should be deferred. After the retirement of Seshan, M.S. Gill was appointed as CEC. He pulled on smoothly with his colleagues and had conducted the general elections very successfully. MR Lyngdoh his successor, also has done yeoman service in conducting

[1]*V. Venkatarangaiya : Free and Fair Elections, p. 53.*
[2]*Hindustan Times, April 5, 1995.*

smoothly elections in J & K and Gujrat in the year 2002. However, there developed an unseemly rift between the Chief commmissioner MR. N. Gopal Swami and the Election commissioner MR. Navin Chawla some months before the General Election, 2009 were to be held. The rift snow balled into political issue which adversely affected the image of the Election Commission.

The Backward Classes Commission

The Constitution provides for the appointment of a Commissioner for Scheduled Castes and Scheduled Tribes by the President of India. He commands an independent status. He investigates into all matters relating to the safeguards provided for the Scheduled Castes and Scheduled Tribes. He is to report to the President upon the working of these safeguards at such intervals as the President may direct. Such reports are placed before each House of the Parliament by the President of India. Following are the functions of the Commissioner : (i) To evaluate the progress of the welfare schemes undertaken by State Governments and non official organisations with grants-in-aid received from the Government of India. (ii) To render advice on schemes received for grants-in-aid from the State Governments and non official agencies for the amelioration of the lot of the backward classes. (iii) To serve as a nominee of the Central Government on the Managing Committee of the non official organisations receiving grants directly from the Centre. (iv) To examine the accounts of the non official organisations receiving grants directly from the Centre.

The Commissioner is assisted in his task by eleven Assistant Commissioners. The duties of the Assistant Commissioners are : (i) To investigate cases which may be referred to him by the local residents. (ii) To establish close contacts with the scheduled castes, scheduled tribes and other backward classes. (iii) To submit to the Commissioner periodical reports showing the various facilities available for the scheduled caste and scheduled tribes in his region and the disabilities they are subjected to. (iv) To report on the adequacy of the sources and personnel employed for the various schemes launched by the State Government in the backward class sector. (v) To assist the State Governments to remove the bottlenecks impeding the implementation of the sanctioned schemes and undertaking schemes where necessary to cater to the local needs. (vi) To ensure that cooperation is elicited adequately from the public where public cooperation is involved.

It has been observed by the Study Team on Social Welfare and Backward classes that the Commissioner has exhibited marked independence in the matter of expression of his views, reporting on the findings and evaluation of the working of schemes. Besides, the record of the work done so far by the Commissioner bears ample testimony to the fact that he has been able to attain the purpose of his appointment successfully.[1]

Article 340 of the Constitution provides that the President may appoint a Commissioner to investigate the condition of socially and educationally backward classes and render recommendations regarding the steps to be taken to improve their condition.

The first Backward Classes Commission was established on January 29, 1953. It submitted its report on March 30, 1955. Though Commission's recommendations were wide ranging, it could not come to a unanimous report. It could not work out objective tests and criteria for the proper classification of socially and educationally backward classes. The Government did not implement the Report.

Mandal Commission (January 1, 1979)

A second Commission on Backward Classes was appointed by the President on January 1, 1979. It submitted its report in December, 1980. This report stated "the population of other backward classes both Hindus and non Hindus is around 52% of the total population of India. Accordingly 52% of the posts under Central Government should be reserved for them. But this issue may go

[1]*Report of the Study Team on Social Welfare of Backward Classes, Committee on Plan Projects : Planning Commission (Under the Chairmanship of Renuka Roy).*

against the law laid down in a number of Supreme Court judgments wherein it has been held that the total quantum of reservation...should be below 50%. In view of this, the proposed reservation for OBCs would have to be pegged at a figure which when added to 22.5% of SCs and STs remain below 50%. In view of the legal constraint, the Commission is obliged to recommend a reservation of 27% only, even though their population is almost twice the figure."

Secondly the Commission was of the view that seats should be reserved for OBC students in all scientific, technical and professional institutions run by the Centre as well as State Governments. The quantum of reservation was to be 27% (as in Government service).

Thirdly the Commission opined that separate financial institutions for providing financial and technical assistance be established for backward classes.

Government's Decision

The Government agreed to reserve 27% of the vacancies in civil posts and services under the Government of India and Central Public Undertakings and Banks, in favour of socially and educationally backward classes. An announcement to this effect was made on August 7, 1990 in the Parliament and formal orders were issued on August 13, 1990.

Writs and Decisions of the Apex Court - November 16, 1992

Several writs were filed against the Government's order in the Supreme Court. The Supreme Court gave its verdict on November 16, 1992. (i) The Supreme Court confirmed the Mandal Commissions' recommendations to grant 27% of Government posts to the Other Backward Classes (OBC). (ii) Since objections had been raised regarding inclusion or wrong exclusion of certain communities in the list of OBCs prepared by the Mandal Commission, the Supreme Court directed the Government to appoint a Commission within 4 months to hear and decide such objections and finalise the list of OBCs.

(iii) The Court also held that the 'creamy layer' i.e., the well off among the backward communities should be excluded from the right of reservation (iv) Reservation should be confined to the post of entry into service and should not be extended to the promotional posts.

Committee on Creamy Layer

In pursuance of the apex court's order as stated above, a Committee was appointed to lay down the criteria for the identification of the creamy layer among the socially and educationally backward classes. The Committee excluded from the list of reservations the off-springs of these persons : (i) persons who have held constitutional posts — President, Vice-President, Judges of the Supreme Court and the High Courts, Chairman and members of the UPSC and State Public Service Commission, Chief Election Officer, Comptroller and Auditor General of India, Governors, Ministers and members of legislatures. (ii) Class I officers of Central and State services, Public Sector Undertakings and armed forces (iii) Professional class and persons in trade, business and industry and the property owners provided they had a gross annual income of Rs. one lakh and above. (iv) If both spouses are class II officers then the rule of exclusion would apply; if only one of the spouses is a Class II officer, it would not apply. (v) If a person belongs to a family which owns irrigated land and the extent of irrigated land is equal to or more than 65% of the statutory ceiling area, then the disentitlement would take place.

The Government accepted the recommendations of the aforesaid committee in March, 1993.

National Commission on Backward Classes

On March 26, 1993 the Parliament accorded approval to a Bill seeking to set up a National

Commission for Backward Classes. The Commission would review the list of Other Backward Classes in accordance with directions of the Supreme Court. Its recommendations are to be ordinarily binding on the Government. The Commission possesses the powers of a Civil Court. The Government agreed to undertake a revision of backward classes list after every 10 years.

National Backward Finance and Development Corporation

The Government set up a Finance and Development Corporation for providing financial assistance to Backward Classes for projects aimed at bettering their skills and lot. During 1991-92 a sum of Rs. 25 crores was released for this purpose. An additional sum of Rs. 25 crores was provided in 1992-93.

National Commission for Scheduled Castes and Scheduled Tribes (SCs & STs)

A Commission for the SCs and STs was established in 1978. The 65th Amendment Act (1990) renamed this Commission as National Commission for SCs & STs. It consists of a chairperson, Vice chairperson and 5 other members whose terms and conditions of service shall be such as President may, by rule, determine.

Its functions

(i) To evaluate the working of the safeguards provided for the SCs and STs in the Indian Constitution. (ii) To advise on the socio-economic developments of SCs/STs. (iii) To evaluate the progress of their development under the Union and other States. (iv) To furnish report regarding the implementation of measures for the protection and socio-economic development of SCs/STs to the President of India. It may also recommend measures that shall be taken by the Union and/or any State in this regard. The President is to place the reports before the Parliament. (v) The Commission may discharge such other functions as the President may, by rule, specify.

The Commission possesses all powers of a Civil Court in respect of summoning and enforcing the attendance of any person and examining him on oath. It may requisition any public record from any Court or office. The Commission may receive evidence on affidavits. The Union and the State are required to consult the Commission on all major policy matters effecting the SCs/STs.

The Official Languages Commission

The constitution makes a provision for setting up of a Commission on Official Languages. The President of India was empowered to appoint such a commission, five years after the commencement of the Constitution and thereafter at the expiration of ten years from such commencement. The Commission is composed of a Chairman and such members representing the different languages specified in the Eighth Schedule, as the President may appoint. The procedure to be followed by the commission also will be defined by the President.

Functions of the Commission

The commission is to recommend to the President (a) the progress of the use of the Hindi language for the official purposes of the Union; (b) the restriction on the use of the English language for all or any of the official purposes of the Union; (c) the language to be used for all or any of the purposes mentioned in Article 348; (d) the form of numerals to be used for any one or more specified purposes of the Union; (e) any other matter referred to the Commission by the President as regards the official language of the Union and the language for the communication between the Union and a state or between one state and another and their use. [Article 344 (2)]. However, the Commission while making recommendations under this clause shall take into consideration industrial, cultural and scientific advancement of India and the just claims and interests of persons belonging to the non-Hindi speaking area as regards the public services. The recommendations of the Commission are examined by a committee of Parliament constituted under clause (1). After having considered the report, the President issues directions in accordance with the whole or any part of that report (Article 344-5 and 6).

Besides the commissions cited in the preceding pages, Planning Commission and Union Public Service Commission can be quoted as examples of such other Commissions.[1]

Boards

A few examples of the Boards are : The Central Advisory Board for the Tribal Welfare; the Central Advisory Board for Harijan Welfare; the Central Social Welfare Board and the Railway Board.

The Central Advisory Board for Tribal Welfare

It was constituted in 1956 to associate members of Parliament and other public workers interested in the scheduled tribes, with the matters pertaining to the development of tribal welfare of areas and the welfare of tribal people. The Board is composed of 24 members, including members of parliament. The members of this Board are nominated for one year. The minister of state for social welfare is the Chairman of the Board. In his absence, the Deputy Minister of social welfare presides over the Board.

The Board renders advice to the Government on matters relating to the development of tribal areas and the welfare of tribal people vis. (i) assessment of the requirements of tribal people in the scheduled and other tribal areas; (ii) formulation of welfare schemes for those areas; (iii) periodical review of the working of sanctioned schemes, appraisal and evaluation of benefits derived therefrom with a view to suggesting improvements or changes in the schemes where essential.

Central Advisory Board for Harijan Welfare

It was also constituted in 1956 in order to associate members of parliament and other public workers interested in the welfare of Harijans with matters pertaining to the advancement of Harijans.

The Board is composed of thirty members including M.P.s of whom twenty belong to Harijan community. The members of the Board are nominated for a period of one year. The Minister of state for social welfare is the chairman of the Board. In his absence, the Deputy Minister of social welfare presides over the meetings of the Board.

The Board renders advice to the Government on matters pertaining to Harijan welfare. Secondly, it assesses the requirements of the Harijans and formulates welfare schemes for them. Thirdly, it reviews periodically the working of sanctioned schemes and makes appraisal and evaluation of the benefits derived therefrom in order to suggest improvements or effect changes in the schemes where necessary.

Central Social Welfare Board (CSWB)

The Board was set up in August, 1953 as an autonomous body. It comprised a Chairman and members representing states and U.T.s and some experts. In 1969, it acquired a legal status as it was incorporated as a charitable company under section 25 of the Indian Companies Act. The functions of the CSWB revolve round the improvement and development of social welfare activities. They are as under :

(i) To survey the need and requirements of social welfare organisations periodically through surveys, research and evaluation in such a manner as considered necessary. (ii) To coordinate the

---

[1]*See details in the relevant chapters.*

assistance extended to welfare agencies by the various Ministries/Department of the Union and State Governments. (iii) To evaluate the programmes and projects of the aided agencies. (iv) To promote the establishment of social welfare institutions in places where they do not exist. (v) to extend grants-in-aid to voluntary organisations rendering welfare service to women, children, delinquents, the handicapped, the aged, the infirm and other needy groups. (vi) To subsidise hostels for working women and the blind. (vii) To give technical aid to the deserving institutions or organisations, panchayatiraj institutions inclusive, according to the principles and schemes approved by the Union Government. (viii) To organise and promote programmes of training in social works as and when required and also to organise and work on pilot projects whenever necessary. (ix) To organise through its machinery, emergency relief in case of calamity, national, natural or otherwise, wherever deemed fit.

Its Composition

The CSWB comprises a general body consisting of 44 members headed by a chairman. The chairman is appointed by the Government in consultation with the ministry of Social Welfare Department from amongst prominent women social workers. The General body includes representatives nominated by State Governments, social scientists, representatives drawn from the ministries of Finance, Rural reconstruction, Health, Education, and Social Welfare, one member from the Planning Commission. Besides, three members of parliament, social workers, social scientists, and social welfare administrators also comprise its membership.

The affairs of the CSWB are administered by an Executive Committee nominated from amongst the members of the CSWB. The Executive Committee consists of 12 members including the Executive Director. Some social workers and representatives of the ministers are the members of the Executive Committee.

The General body meets annually whereas the Executive Committee meets about once in two months.

Funds

The Board derives its funds from the Government of India. The allocation for the various programmes as well as non plan expenditure of the Board comprise of Budget of the Department of Social Welfare. There has been substantial increase in the total expenditure on the programme of the Board.

Organisational Structure

The administrative work of the Board is executed through a number of divisions and sections. The chairman is assisted by a secretary who is of the rank of the Deputy secretary or Director, Government of India. There are three joint directors, one financial adviser cum Chief Accounts Officer, Chief Administrative Officer and a Public Relations officer. There are nine Divisions of CSWB viz Socio economic Programme Division, Project Division, Condensed Course Division; Grant Division; Finance and Accounts Division and internal check Division; Field Counselling and Inspectorate Division, Publications Division and Administrative Division; Research, Evaluation and Statistical Division.

Besides, there are three sections — Hindi unit for translating Hindi letters into English; Administrative section dealing with matters pertaining to State Boards; Coordination section for preparing agenda for General Body and Executive committees collecting such other data required for furnishing replies to questions raised in Parliament.

For the implementation of Welfare Extension Projects, Project implementing committees also exist. Each committee has a social worker as the chairman, supported by half a dozen non official women members and local officers like BDOs (Block Development Officers). The non-official members are nominated by the State Board. The committees have their own regular staffs like accounts clerks, peons, drivers, etc. The field staff of these committees consists of *mukhya sevikas*, mid wives, gram sevikas, craft instructors and *dais*.

Its major Activities

(*a*) The CSWB has launched a socio-economic programme viz (a) opening of industrial cooperative societies to enable destitute, deserted women, widows and those belonging to a very meagre income group, to earn a livelihood or supplement their income.

(*b*) Providing financial assistance to voluntary institutions for organising small training cum production units where needy or physically handicapped women could be imparted training and given employment; opening of Dairies for the war widows by supplying them cattle, equipment and the initial amount for funding and other expenses.

(*c*) It has been sanctioning grants to voluntary organisations for providing hostels for working women of low income group.

(*d*) It has been assisting Welfare Centres in urban areas of industrial towns and cities where the activities are directed towards Child welfare, Women's welfare, Recreational and Educational activities.

(*e*) It has implemented the scheme of Creches for children of working and ailing mothers. The scheme is actually meant for the children of migrant labours, working on construction sites and children of sick mothers.

(*f*) It has been launching nutrition programmes for lower strata families children in the age group of 0 to 5 years by making provision for nutritious diet at the Day Care centres and *Balwadies*.

(*g*) It has been organising Family welfare camps in various states for motivating the people through the opinion of the leaders.

(*h*) It has been rendering assistance to low income group women in acquiring higher education and learning material skills to gain employment.

(*i*) It also coordinates with the National Service Scheme (N.S.S.) agencies to carry out the service programmes of the Board during the holidays. They have specially attended to the problems of the urban slums, remote hilly areas, tribal villages and pavement dwellers.

Keeping in view these activities of CSWB, one can afford to agree with the remarks of a former President of India. "The great sub-Continent has awakened from long, deep slumber of centuries and is again regaining slowly and constantly something of its own initiative, strength, vitality and power. The goal before the nation is the attainment of a welfare state. The creation of the Central State Welfare Board is only a small step in the direction of achieving this goal." Pt. J.L. Nehru, first P.M. of India, rightfully remarked, "Social Revolution is the most basic revolution. The Central Social Welfare Board is in the forefront in pushing ahead the social revolution in India." There is no denying the fact that the impact of the Board on the social welfare activities has been quite impressive. However, it has been mostly limited to urban areas and there is ample scope for improvement of its working. It is essential to initiate the measures to improve the administrative machinery, its components and systems e.g. personnel administration and financial administration. Besides, a proper status should be accorded to the Board.

Railway Board

The Railway Board consists of the chairman and five other members. It normally meets twice a week or more frequently to decide policies and other urgent cases which necessitate the Board's consideration. The chairman convenes the meetings of the Board and presides over them. The agenda of these meetings is finalized by the chairman in consultation with the members. The Secretary of the Board circulates the agenda and the memorandum among the members before the meeting is held. He submits minute drafts to the Board for requisite approval, after which necessary action is taken by the concerned officials. The minister holds the meetings of the full Board where policy affairs are discussed and decided.

Functions

The following are the functions of the Board.

(i) To advise the railway ministry on specific issues involved in policy formulation and coordination with other agencies.

(ii) To formulate programmes in a well-planned manner to implement its policies and to supervise and establish effective coordination among the Railway zones.

(iii) To prepare the annual budget of the Railways which is placed before the Parliament by the Minister of Railways.

(iv) To determine the recruitment policy, training and service conditions of its employees and to adopt such measures as are essential to create uniformity with the other ministries and departments in matters concerning personnel management.

(v) To review the trend of expenditure associated with the work performance and take the necessary steps for its appropriate regulation. In fact, all matters related to Railway receipts and expenditure fall within the purview of the Board.

(vi) To frame certain rules for statistical data compilation and set procedures for assessing the works undertaken.

(vii) To accord sanction to those projects/works which do not fall within the purview of powers of General Manager.

(viii) To frame the pay and allowances structure of the Railway staff in order to effect uniformity.

(ix) To accord sanctions for posts, promotions, transfers etc. of the staff whenever these are considered necessary by the Board.

(x) To lay down standards of equipment and rolling stock.

(xi) To formulate rules and regulations for ensuring the safety of the Railway staff.

(xii) To bring out its annual reports showing the performance and accounts.

Recommendations of A.R.C. on the Railway Board

The following are some of the recommendations made by the ARC in its report on Railways :

(i) The relationship of the Railway Board viz-a-viz the Minister of Railways should be patterned on the lines of the relationship as recommended in the reports on public sector undertakings as between a ministry of overall supervision and vigilance, the larger issues involving improved efficiency of the Railway system, and planning and budgeting. The Minister should effectively intervene when matters of public policy or those affecting Government or Board versus other departments are involved.

(ii) For efficient functioning, the Railway Board should be compact in size. The number excluding the chairman and the member Finance, should not exceed six.

(iii) The chairman of the Railway Board should be selected on merit from amongst the members of the Board and the members of the Board should be selected on merit from amongst the General Managers.

(iv) The chairman and the members should have tenure of three and five years respectively. The total tenure of chairman both as chairman and member should be 7 years or above.

(v) All Directors of the Railway Board should be placed in the same pay scale.

(vi) A selection committee constituted by Zonal Railways, including a senior officer of the Board should recommend promotion of officers to the junior administrative grade.

(vii) The Railway Board should prescribe the qualifications, training and job experience required for manning the posts, the specialisation and managerial categories. The Chairman and General Managers should see to the establishment of a career planning cell at the Board level and Zonal level respectively.

(viii) The Railway Board and the Zonal Railways should review the existing training arrangements in the light of requirements and rationalise the training facilities where necessary.

(ix) The Chairman of the Recruitment Board may be appointed by the Railway Board.

(x) The Director General of the Vigilance Organisation at the Board level may work directly under the chairman of the Board and report to him.

(xi) The Railway Board should consider the closure of unremunerative lines where adequate mode of cheaper transport exist and where such closure will not adversely affect the public interest.

(xii) The Research design and standard organisation should function as an autonomous body with a governing Council at the top to guide it. The Chairman of the Railway Board should be the chairman of the Governing Council.

The above recommendations were fairly laudable and some of them have since been duly considered and accepted by the Government.

(G) MINISTRIES

Ministry of Home Affairs

Its origin can be traced from 1843 when the secretariat of the Supreme Government was separated from that of the Government of Bengal. It was then known as the Home Department. It was headed by a bureaucratic head — the secretary — and had six branches, viz General, Revenue, Marine, Legislative and Ecclesiastical. It was considered the residuary legatee in the Government of India, which did not belong to any other department inhered in the Home Department. It was entrusted functions of heterogeneous nature e.g. personnel matters, internal law and order, political matters, police, jail, explosives, explorers, factories, petroleum, education, public works, public health, hospitals, municipalities and local boards. With the growing importance of the subjects, new Departments emerged and these subjects were consequently separated from the Home Department. Public Works Department was the first to be separated from the Home Department, and established independently in 1855. In the recent past it was deprived of personnel subject as the same was created into a full-fledged Department in 1970. In 1973, the Department of Administrative Reforms set up in 1963 as part of the ministry of Home Affairs was merged with the Department of Personnel. Dr. Maheshwari has described ministry of Home Affairs as 'mother ministry' in the Government of India[1]. It is headed by a Minister of Home Affairs — Minister of a cabinet rank.

Functions

(a) In fact every country has such a ministry which plays a pivotal role in the maintenance of Internal Security. India, where terrorist menace and that of anti-social forces is ever on the increase, Internal Security gains paramount importance and that makes the role of ministry of Home Affairs pivotal. It has been described as the nodal agency for law and order which, according to the Indian Constitution, happens to be a state subject and as such is the direct responsibility of State Governments. The primary responsibility for the maintenance of law

[1]*Organisation and Procedure (Maxwell) Committee, Report Delhi G.O.I., 1937 January, Para 23.*

and order lies with the states. However, the ministry of Home Affairs acts as advisory body or coordinating agency. It seeks information from all over the country through its various sources, assimilates it and renders advice to the State Government on the varied problems of Internal Security. The Ministry keeps a vigilant watch on the law and order situation in the country by noting carefully the trends and developments adversely affecting law and order situation in its various states. As regards union territories, the ministry holds direct responsibility for law and order.

(b) Besides maintenance of law and order, the ministry is to keep its grip on the communal situation of the country and deploy central forces if such a situation is likely to creep into a volcanoic disorder. It was recently done to safeguard 400 years old Babri mosque from demolition at the hands of *Kar Sevaks* who had pledged to perform *Kar Seva* on December 6, 1992. Unfortunately, the BJP and VHP who had promised to have 'Bhajans and Kirtans' on December 6 and not damage this disputed structure which is said to be birth place of Lord Ram as well, could not control the situation, and the Mosque was demolished. The Central Forces which were stationed at a distance on the instance of the BJP State Government came into action when the irreparable damage to the Mosque, in fact to our secular fabric, had already been done. This amounted to breach of trust and non fulfillment of promise by BJP Government in U.P. Hence the Chief Minister of U.P. resigned of his own, owning the responsibility. The Centre and the Home Ministry were in the dock for not forestalling things and throwing the country to the throes of convulsions and chaos. The matter is presently before the Supreme Court.

Likewise, agitations by Industrial workers and students are also to be quelled by it. Students' agitation against Mandal Commission Report had very wide ramifications. Hence the Home ministry had to come into picture to restore normalcy and instruct the states to handle the tender minds a bit cautiously. In very recent past, mass killings of *Dalits* in Bihar led to the imposition of President's rule in the State (February 13, 1999). However, the President's rule was revoked on March 8, 1999 as the BJP and its allies were conscious of its disapproval by the Rajya Sabha where the ruling party did not command majority.

Civil Defence also falls within its purview.

(c) It deals with matters pertaining to foreigners and foreign citizenships.

(d) It is to conduct census operation after 10 years and is responsible for holding elections to the parliament and the state legislature.

(e) It is concerned with proper maintenance of Centre and state relations and is responsible for the installation of President's rule in the states.

(f) It administers the Indian Police Service and happens to be its cadre controlling authority. As such, it deals with service matters like appointment to Indian Police Service (IPS) deputation of police officials from states to the Centre, their training, fixation of seniority, pay etc. and other conditions of service. It also administers other para-military services viz Indo-Tibetan Border Police, the Border Security Force, the Central Industrial Security Force, The Assam Rifles and the Central Reserve Police Force.

(g) It exercises control over attached organisations like Intelligence Bureaus, the National Police Academy, the Bureau of Police Research and Development and the Institute of Criminology and Forensic Science etc.

It will not be out of place to point out that prior to 1985, the Home Ministry had wider ramifications. It was responsible for regulating matters of general applicability to all the services and for the maintenance of common standards of recruitment, discipline and conditions of service. In January 1985, it was divested of this job completely as a new ministry was created for the purpose. Likewise, till September 1985, matters pertaining to weaker sections of society were dealt with by this ministry. Thereafter matters concerning the scheduled castes, scheduled tribes, backward classes, communal harmony etc. have been entrusted to ministry of welfare.

The transfer of the above functions to the new ministries has not eclipsed the significance of this ministry. Being the oldest Ministry of the Government of India, and the true legatee of the Government of India, it still retains its stature as 'Mother ministry' and remains custodian of internal security and law and order in the country.

Since 1985, it has four Departments under it viz. Department of Internal Security; Department of States; Department of Home and Department of Official Language.

The Department of Internal Security deals with matters concerning police, law and order, rehabilitation and resettlement. The Department of State is concerned with relations between the Central Government and the State Government, inter-state relations and administration of Union Territories. Later a dynamic leader (Rajesh Pilot) was appointed Minister of Home Affairs for maintenance of Internal Security.[1] However he works under the Home Minister.

The Department of Home deals with population Census, registration of foreigners and rehabilitation of displaced persons as well.

The department of Official Language is required to implement the provisions of the Official Language Act relating to the use of Hindi as the official language of the Union.

The Structure

The Ministry is headed by a Senior Minister of cabinet rank generally assisted by one or two ministers of the level of Minister of State. The level and quantum of such assistance is to be decided by the Prime Minister. Presently the Home Minister is assisted by a Minister of State and a Deputy Minister.

A senior bureaucrat of IAS cadre is the Secretary — the administrative head of the Department. He is termed as Home Secretary. He heads many powerful committees. Experience gained as Home Secretary leads to elevation to the post of Cabinet Secretary. Many Home Secretaries have risen to this coveted post. Quite a few have been assigned Governorships, after retirement.

The Secretary is assisted by Additional Secretaries, Joint Secretaries, Director, Deputy Secretaries and Under Secretaries. The senior positions are invariably held by the IAS and the middle level by the Central Secretariat Services. Some members of Public Service also get a place in the Home ministry. However they are only a handful of the total official cadre.

Besides, a Consultation Committee composed of the members of parliament is attached to the ministry of Home Affairs. It commands only a consultative status. It meets under the Chairmanship of the Home minister to discuss matters pertaining to the ministry.

Conclusion

The ministry of Home Affairs commands respect, known for its uniqueness. It earned the reputation of the *'Sanctum Sanctorum'* of the Government of India. As such, posting in this ministry was the envy of the top bureaucracy. However, presently the ministries dealing with Economic Affairs are more alluring for the civil servants as they can come in the lime light to a greater extent and be more authoritative. Still the importance of the Home ministry does not stand minimised as the custodians of law and order always have an upper hand and cannot remain *incognito*. No doubt its extensive range of functions has been considerably curtailed, due to the emergence of ministry of Personnel, Public Grievances and Pensions and ministry of Welfare in 1985, yet it enjoys pivotal stature in the Union Cabinet.

---

[1] *Hindustan Times dated January 19, 1993.*

Ministry of Personnel, Public Grievances and Pensions

With the fast expansion of civil service in the independent era, the dire necessity of setting up a central personnel agency was felt strongly. The Estimate Committee of the third Lok Sabha also recommended the establishment of a single agency for the effective control on personnel. They did not favour dual control of Ministry of Home Affairs and of Finance on the personnel as it affected adversely efficient functioning of Public services. The Administrative Reforms Commission also urged upon the Government to have a separate Department of personnel under the Prime Minister in order to serve as a nodal agency for the personnel functions of the Government. It stated, "It is necessary to set up a central personnel agency — a central agency with overall responsibility in all important matters and managed largely by specialists will obviously be able to devote concerted attention to formulation of new policies, set new standards and raise the quality of administration".[1] The Central Government accepted its recommendations. Hence the Department of Personnel was set up in August, 1970 and placed under the Cabinet Secretariat.

The functions of the service wing of the Ministry of Home Affairs were transferred to the Department of Personnel. The Ministry of Home Affairs even now determined the method of recruitment and conditions of service of general application to the entire bureaucracy and for the interpretation of existing orders of general application, concreting recruitment or condition of service. It was required to deal with general questions including conduct rules of IAS and central services, except Railway and Atomic Energy service. In a way, general conditions of services except those having financial bearing, were to be looked into by the Ministry of Home Affairs. As regards the Service conditions, such as payscale, fixation of pay, grant of increments, special pay, deputation allowance, compensatory and other allowances of other than IAS services, IPS, Central Secretariat, Economic Service and Statistical Service, it was not imperative to consult the Home Ministry. However, on account of its expertise in service matters, the ministry was even now consulted. This was being done to ensure that similar guiding principles were followed for all the services in general matters and service conditions. In other words, the ultimate responsibility in these matters rested with the Finance Ministry, the Home ministry concerned itself with the general repercussions of these service conditions on the general functioning of the services. Thus to draw a line of demarcation, the function of the Ministry of Finance was to consider the financial implications of these matters and that of the Ministry of Home Affairs to take into account their effects on the efficient functioning of the services in general.[2]

Coming to the Department of Personnel, it was set up as part of Cabinet Secretariat and worked direct under the Prime Minister. Its day to day administration was, however, earmarked to a minister of state in Home Affairs Ministry In February, 1973, the Department of Administrative Reforms formerly located in the Ministry of Home Affairs, was transferred to the Department of Personnel and Administrative Reforms. This was not considered a satisfactory arrangement. The functioning of the Department revealed that it was a trend towards centralization and could enable an assertive Prime Minister to use the new powers to promote his own personal position, impairing the overall efficiency. The checks and balances hitherto used by the Home Ministry got inoperative when the Prime Minister exercised direct control over the Department. The imposition of Internal Emergency made the things worse. The Janata Government on its coming to power transferred this Department once again to Ministry of Home Affairs in 1977.

Conversion to Ministry

In March 1985, the Department was renamed as Ministry of Personnel, Public Grievances

[1]*Report : Administration Reforms Commission on the machinery of the Govt. of India and its Procedure of work (1968), p. 71.*

[2]*S.R. Maheshwari : op. cit. p. 64*

and Pensions and comprised the following three Departments viz. Department of Personnel and Training, Department of Administrative Reforms and Public Grievances and Department of Pensions and Pensioners Welfare. At present the Ministry is headed by the Prime Minister who is assisted by a minister of state.

The administrative Head of the ministry is a Secretary, (Personnel) usually an IAS officer. The junior and middle level positions in the ministry are filled in by the personnel from a number of services. However, senior policy making posts are entrusted to IAS cadre officers. The same criteria as is applying to other ministries and departments, applies to the staffing pattern in the ministry. The officers hold tenure postings and after completion of their stipulated tenure postings the functionaries are transferred and the new officers take their place. The junior staff generally receives some training in one of the state's main training institutions. However, their expertise remains unrecognised and their morale remains low. The Ministry of Personnel is considered the nodal personnel and administrative reforms agency in India. It formulates policies concerning recruitment, training, promotion, employee-employer relations, service conditions etc. in the civil services. It looks after staff welfare, discipline and morale in the civil services and integrity in the administration. It manages the all India services and certain other central services. It chalks out training programmes and lays down policies in the field of public administration.

The Department of Administrative Reforms formulates policy regarding administrative Reforms in India. Besides, it lays down policy and coordinates issues concerning — (i) redress of public grievances, (ii) grievances of Central Government agencies in particular.

The Department of Pension and Pensioners Welfare states the policy, and coordinates matters relating to retiring benefits to Central Government employees.

The Ministry of Personnel is concerned with all administrative matters, concerning Union Public Service Commission, Central Vigilance Commission, Staff Selection Commission, Central Bureau of Investigation, Administrative Tribunals and the Indian Institute of Public Administration. Besides, National Academy of Administration (Mussoorie) and the Institute of Secretariat Training and Management are also managed by the Ministry of Personnel.

Functions of Personnel Ministry

Following are the main functions of the Ministry of Personnel :

(i) To appraise the contingent needs of public services in the context of the developmental goals of the administration.
(ii) Manpower planning.
(iii) Cadre management.
(iv) Job evaluation and position classification system.
(v) Recruitment.
(vi) Training and Development programmes.
(vii) Compensation and remuneration administration.
(viii) Career system planning.
(ix) Conduct, discipline and public service ethics.
(x) Motivation and participation management principles and other welfare programmes.
(xi) Separation and terminal benefits system.
(xii) Developing personnel organisation.
(xiii) Personnel research and other developmental aspects viz establishing broad policies and standardized procedures, developing guides and information, and stimulating best personnel practices through a public reporting and public relations system.
(xiv) Administrative reforms.
(xv) O and M work.

The functions enumerated above reveal that "the Ministry of Personnel" bears a grandiose name but its work does not generally go beyond what may be termed as of 'nuts and bolts' character.[1] "It is argued that vital issues like openness in administration, administrative accountability, ethics in government, democratisation in government" have been just ignored by the reformers in the ministry. Besides, the ministry has not been able to mediate effectively between the Government employees' narrow and sectarian interests and citizen's aspirations. It has always functioned as the custodian of interests of the employees, ignoring the aspirations and happiness of the citizens. An appraisal of its annual reports also reveals that the Ministry has been showing a consistent concern for civil services welfare. In a developing democracy like India, civil servants through their specially created ministry, make the most of the opportunity to ameliorate their lot and consolidate their position and authority. The Ministry has just ignored the citizens' oriented reforms in the country's public administration. The Indian bureaucracy is a bloated bureaucracy. Its number is ever on the increase, more than the actual requirements of the various ministries. Ordinarily, the ministry should have suggested a cut in the strength long ago. It has been realized, in the interest of economy in the administration and reduction in deficit financing, that the Government Departments are having public servants, much in excess of the requirements. In fact, the Departments under this ministry have neither favoured decentralization in the administration nor shown proper concern for the common citizens for whose service they exist in a Welfare state. Hence, the critics feel that the ministry lacks the vision and perspective necessitated for reconciling the citizens' aspirations and employees' self-centered interests.

Ministry of External Affairs

Relations with the foreign countries is a relic of the past. During the rule of East India Company, secret Department of the Supreme Government used to conduct relations with the foreign countries. The Foreign Department was established in 1783. Prior to 1947, two separate departments viz The External Affairs Department and the Commonwealth Relations Department existed and conducted India's relations with the foreign countries. In 1947, when India attained Independence and its Sovereign status, the ministry made its debut again. The two 'Departments' were merged and a single department of External Affairs and Commonwealth Relations emerged out. This Department was renamed as "Ministry of External Affairs and Commonwealth Relations". In 1949, its nomenclature was again changed to "Ministry of External Affairs". Since 1949, the name remains unchanged. Another point worth mentioning pertains to the fact that prior to 1972, it dealt with matters relating to Nagaland besides conducting India's relation with foreign countries. Since May, 1972 the Home Ministry is looking after the affairs pertaining to Nagaland.

The Ministry is headed by Minister of External Affairs of the rank of a cabinet minister. He is assisted by a Minister of State. Jawaharlal Nehru, the first Prime Minister of India, held the portfolio of External Affairs himself. However, his successors have invariably not followed this practice. A.B. Vajpayee, the present Prime Minister had also been holding the portfolio as the External Affairs minister but at a later stage appointed Shri Jaswant Singh (member Rajya Sabha) as the External Affairs Minister. Presently Yaswant Sinha holds the portfolio.

Foreign Secretary is the administrative head of the ministry There are two other secretaries as well to assist him. They are termed as Additional Secretaries — Secretary (EA-I) and Secretary (EA-II). It may not be out of place to point out that till 1964, with a brief break in 1952, Secretary General used to be the administrative head. This was an office of its own kind in this ministry only. Though the post was abolished in 1964, yet from time to time, efforts have been made to revive it. For instance in 1965-66 a committee of the Indian Foreign Service, which was setup by the Government of India under the chairmanship of N.R. Pillai, suggested the resurrection of the post of Secretary General in the Ministry of External Affairs on the plea that the Ministry without this office is rather an unsatisfactory arrangement. It was felt that the conduct of the country's External Affairs cannot be compartmentalised. As such a committee suggested, "it is essential that at the

[1] *S.R. Maheshwari, op. cit. p. 72.*

official level, there should be at the head someone who would not only help in the pursuit of an integrated policy but also speak with authority for the ministry as a whole. This purpose....cannot be achieved under the system that exists at present". Clearly then there is a need such as has been generally accepted elsewhere, to have at the head of the 'Ministry one invested with overall responsibility. We accordingly propose the creation of a post with the designation of Secretary-General'.[1] The committee laid down the following functions of the Secretary General as well :

(i) To act as principal adviser to the Ministry.

(ii) To coordinate activities of the Ministry.

(iii) To ensure the establishment of suitable coordinative arrangements with other ministries and their satisfactory operation.

(iv) To act as the Chairman of the Policy Planning and Review Committee and direct policy planning in the Ministry.

(v) To head foreign service and be responsible for good administration of the service.

There is a Board comprising Foreign Secretary, two Additional Secretaries in the Ministry, the Secretary Ministry of Commerce and the Joint Secretary Administration in the Ministry of External Affairs.

The Ministry is divided into Divisions which at present number 28. There are two types of such Divisions — Territorial and Functional. The Territorial Divisions have been so framed that India's immediate neighbours receive at least, in the organisational structure of the ministry, more concentrated attention.

Important functional Divisions deal with administration, protocol, passport, emigration and consular, external publicity, United Nations and conferences, economic affairs and technical assistance, historical research, legal matters and treaties; policy planning and review, personnel, security, communication and civil defence, overseas Indians, finance, coordination. Some of the important Territorial Divisions are : Africa, America, Bangladesh, East Asia, East Europe, Pakistan, South Asia, West Asia, West Europe, SAARC, Gulf etc., etc.

Besides the prominent Divisions referred to above, the ministry has an Inspectorate which is to review the scales of allowances and amenities in India's diplomatic missions abroad; It was setup in 1954, though it became defunct in 1959, to be revived again in 1964. It has been presently made responsible for the overall assessment of the working and effectiveness of our diplomatic missions abroad. An Additional Secretary ranked as 'Inspector' heads it.

Functions of the Ministry

The Ministry deals with the following functions :

(i) External Affairs;

(ii) relations with foreign states and Commonwealth countries;

(iii) all affairs dealing with foreign, diplomatic and consular offices, U.N. offices and U.N. specialised agencies in India;

(iv) passports and visas and grant of entry visas for Sri Lankan nationals except missionaries;

(v) general administration of Indian Extradition Act 1903 and extra territoriality;

(vi) extradition of criminal and accused persons from India to foreign and Commonwealth countries and vice versa;

(vii) preventive detention in India, due to state connected with External and Commonwealth Affairs;

[1]*Report : Committee on the Indian Foreign Service (1968) p. 23.*

(viii) repatriation of nationals of foreign and common wealth countries from India and deportation and repatriation of Indian nationals in foreign and commonwealth countries to India;

(ix) emigration from India to overseas countries and the return of emigrates; Immigration to India from the Union of South Africa or any other country to which the Reciprocity Act applies.

(x) all consular functions; travel arrangements for traders, porters, pilgrims from India to Tibet region of China;

(xi) liaison work with Education Ministry's cultural scholarship schemes and nomination of private students of Indian origin domiciled abroad to reserved seats in medical and engineering colleges in India;

(xii) matters relating to state of Nagaland transferred to Home ministry;

(xiii) political pensions paid to foreign refugees and descendants of those who rendered services abroad;

(xiv) ceremonial matters concerning foreign and Commonwealth visitors and diplomatic and consular representatives;

(xv) matters regarding Pondicherry, Goa, Daman and Diu involving relations with France and Portugal;

(xvi) relations with states like Sikkim and Bhutan;

(xvii) Himalayan expeditions and permission to foreigners to travel beyond the Inner Line;

(xviii) coordination and development measures in Border areas;

(xix) United Nations specialised agencies and other international conferences;

(xx) Indian Foreign Service;

(xxi) Indian Foreign Branch;

(xxii) External Publicity;

(xxiii) political treaties, agreement and conventions with foreign and Commonwealth countries;

(xxiv) pilgrimages to places outside India including the administration of the Port Haj Committee Act 1932 and rules made thereunder and the Indian Pilgrim Ship Rules 1933 and Pilgrim parties from India to shrines in Pakistan and vice versa, protection of land preservation of non Muslim shrines in Pakistan and Muslim shrines in India in terms of Pant–Mirza Agreement of 1955;

(xxv) recovery and restoration of abducted persons;

(xxvi) evacuation of non Muslims from Pakistan to India;

(xxvii) protection of the rights of Minority communities in India and Pakistan;

(xxviii) non-muslim migration from Pakistan and Muslim migration from India;

(xxix) recovery of advances granted to the evacuees from Burma, Malaya, etc. during 1942-47 and residual work relating to refugees given asylum in India during World War II;

(xxx) notification regarding commencement or cessation of a state of war;

(xxxi) foreign jurisdiction;

(xxxii) piracies and crimes committed on the high seas or in the air, offences against the law of a Nation committed on land or the high seas or in the air;

(xxxiii) inquiries and statistics for the purposes of any of the subjects allotted to this ministry;

(xxxiv) fees in respect of any of the subjects allotted to this ministry;

(xxxv) offenses against laws regarding any of the subjects allotted to this ministry;

(xxxvi) hospitality grants of the Government of India;

(xxxvii) demarcation of the land frontiers of India;

(xxxviii) border raids and incidents on the border's land of India;

(xxxix) diplomatic flight clearances for non scheduled chartered flights of foreign, civil, and military aircraft transiting India;

(xl) matters dealing with the continental shelf, territorial waters, contiguous zone, the question of fishery rights in the high seas, and other questions of international law;

(xli) economic and technical assistance given by India to the Government of Nepal under the Colombo plan for cooperative economic development.[1]

Evidently the ministry is supposed to create a congenial atmosphere for the blossoming of India's friendship with the major powers of the world and also for the cultivation of neighbourly relations with the Asiatic countries. The success of the Government in the international world depends to a greater extent on the dexterity and diplomatic handling of the foreign affairs by the External Affairs minister. Hence the tallest Prime Minister like J.L. Nehru kept the portfolio with himself in order to act tactfully as the cultural ambassador of Spiritual East to the Material West. India gained a prominent place in the U.N. and also Commonwealth of Nations due to his statesmanship.

Ministry of Finance

The origin of this ministry can be traced since 1810 when a separate department of Finance was established in the Supreme Government of India. However, till 1846 it did not requisition the services of full-time secretary. It was in 1947 that the department of Finance was designated as the Ministry of Finance. It comprised three wings — Expenditure, Economic Affairs and Revenue. In 1949, the Ministry of Finance was organised into two Departments : the Department of Revenue and Expenditure and the Department of Economic Affairs. The Ministry of Finance has been holding a pivotal place in every governmental system. The Haldane committee (1918) remarked, "The department of Finance must necessarily have an exceptional position among all the State Departments. The service which it has to perform — that of supervising and controlling all operations of government in so far as they affect the financial position — involves not only the direct administration of taxation and other branches of revenue but also the control of all forms of expenditure including the incurring of obligations or liability to expenditure."[2]

The Finance Ministry consists of three Departments — Revenue Department, Expenditure Department and the Department of Economic Affairs each under a Secretary. The Revenue and Expenditure Departments have three principal Divisions viz Revenue Division; the Civil Expenditure Division and the Defence Expenditure Division. The Ministry is headed by a Senior minister of the cabinet rank assisted by three ministers of State. Secretary is the administrative head. Each Department is headed by Secretary assisted by an Additional Secretary, Joint Secretary, Director, Deputy Secretary and Under Secretaries. The I.A.S. hold these senior positions. The ministry also draws its officers from other services viz Indian Audit and Accounts, the Central Revenue, the Central Customs and Excises and the Indian Railway Accounts. The middle level positions are filled from Central Secretariat Service.

The Revenue Division is concerned with Revenue policy and collection. As such, it deals with matters relating to direct and indirect union taxes. It exercises this control through the Central Board of Direct Taxes and the Central Board of Excise and Customs. The Division also administers and enforces controls and regulatory measures concerning central sales tax, stamp duties, gold control, foreign exchange. It is also responsible for exercising control over production and disposal of opium and its products.

[1] *S.R. Maheshwari : op. cit. 84-87.*

[2] *Report of the Machinery of Government Committee CD 9230 London HMSO 1918, p. 17.*

Through the tax laws and their administration, three main objectives are achieved, viz, creation of atmosphere of mutual trust between the tax collector and the tax payer; solution of problems of tax evasion and reduction of tax arrears and furtherance of socio-economic policies by extending of incentives through proper legislation. The department of Expenditure has two Divisions as follows :

***(i)* The Civil Expenditure Division** deals with the scrutiny and sanction of the expenditure of the various administrative ministries. It determines the pay, allowances, leave and other general conditions of service of Government employees. It has five branches viz. Public Finance; Establishment; Cost Accounts; Organisation of the Comptroller-General of Accounts; Staff Inspection. Each of these branches functions under a Joint Secretary and deals with the scrutiny and sanction of a group of administrative ministers. The Joint Secretary functions as the financial adviser to the various administrative ministries attached to his branch. The Joint Secretary is assisted by Deputy and Under Secretaries. All these officers are empowered to accord sanction to the proposals of the Administrative Ministers with which they deal. The Plan Finance Branch deals with State Government plans and finances and renders advice regarding State Government proposals for investment in industrial enterprises and irrigation, power and flood control projects. It also initiates studies on state taxation and Budgets. The Establishment Branch administers financial rules and regulations and also conditions of service of Central Government personnel.

***(ii)* The Defence Expenditure Division** deals with the scrutiny and control of defence expenditure. It is headed by an Additional Secretary who is designated as Financial Adviser Defence. The Division is concerned with the preparation of the Budget of the Defence Departments. It functions internally from within the Ministry of Defence and is treated as one of its branches.

Department of Economic Affairs

The Department has six main Divisions : viz Economic; Banking; Insurance Budget; Administration; External Finance. A brief account of these Divisions will not be out of place.

(a) **Economic Division** — the nodal wing of the Ministry of Finance — attends to all economic policy matters affecting the country. Primarily it has to play an advisory role. Besides, it oversees the performance of economy in the context of the economic situation, monitors the performance of economy and renders advice to the Government on policy changes to contain inflation and increase the growth. It renders technical assistance to other departments and Ministries in different domains of economic policy.

It prepares annual Economic Survey Report which is placed before the parliament as a background document to the Central Budget. This survey reviews comprehensively significant developments in the economy, analyses recent economic trends and appraises economic policies. It "monitors the state of the economy and prepares background papers on important issues in order to assist the Government in the formulation of economic policies".[1]

This Division maintains proper links with the Reserve Bank of India, the Planning Commission, the Central Statistical Organisation and the Economic and Statistical wings of the other ministries.

(b) **Banking Division**. It is concerned with the formulation of policies concerning commercial banks and term lending institutions. It does not however include the Life Insurance Corporation of India and the Unit Trust of India.

(c) **Insurance Division.** It supervises and controls the activities of the nationalised insurance industry — Life and General. Besides, it formulates policy, administers the Insurance

[1]*Shriram Maheshwari : Op. cit. p. 76.*

Industry, reviews and monitors the performance of insurance companies and determines the policy conditions of Insurance Company employees. It also provides actuarial advice to other ministers and the State Governments.

(d) **Budget Division.** It prepares the Central Budget, submits it to parliament and procures the latter's sanction.

(e) **Administrative Division.** It deals with administrative and vigilance matters concerning the Department and its attached and subordinate offices.

(f) **External Finance Division.** It is concerned with matters relating to financial assistance procured by India from sources abroad viz. International Monetary Fund, the World Bank, the International Development Association, the Asian Development Bank, the United Nations Development Programme and the Commonwealth Fund for Technical Cooperation.

Thus an appraisal of functions of these Divisions makes us conclude that the Department of Economic Affairs reflects economic trends in the country, renders advice to the Government on all matters affecting internal and external economic management, including the working of commercial banks, term lending institutions, investment regulations, external assistance etc. It helps preparing the Budgets of the Central Government and also of the states under President's rule.

Economic Intelligence Bureau

It was set up in September, 1985 under the charge of a Director General, of the rank of an Additional Secretary. The Bureau coordinates and strengthens the activities of the Intelligence Investigation and Enforcement agencies which are concerned with economic offences and the enforcement of economic laws.

Departmental Controlling Officers

The Finance Ministry is said to be the biggest executive authority regarding sanction and control of expenditure. There is a regular hierarchy of sanctioning and controlling authorities composed of administrative officers of various ranks functioning below it. Each of them is vested with sanctioning of a competent authority as specified by the financial rules, manuals and codes.

Subject to the overall control of the Finance ministry, the head of each administrative department is termed as the Controlling Officer in respect of the expenditure occurring in his department. Money is expended by the officers of the administrative departments over the services they provide. These services are spread over the entire country and the officers conducting these functions in the various parts of the country. Evidently, the expenditure of each department takes place at places far away from the capital. Hence, the question arises, how can the Head of Department of the Centre be aware of the expenditure being incurred by the offices at the various places and control such expenses. The placing of the entire allotment of the departments at the credit of its Head in the headquarters bank and withdrawals from it to meet all expenditures can solve this problem. In England, this practice is being adopted. The public funds are kept in the Exchequer account at the Bank of England. The Treasury with the concurrence of the Comptroller and Auditor General is authorised to issue from the Exchequer account the amounts authorised by the Appropriation Act. The Bank at the request of the Treasury transfers sums from the Exchequer to the supply account of the Pay Master General, specifying the services regarding which the issues are to be made. The Heads of the various departments procure the Funds required to meet their Bill by issuing payable orders on the Pay Master General. Departmental officers outside London are provided adequate imprests to meet the expenditure and the imports are recouped from time to time against bills submitted by them to the Ministry to which they belong. In our country, this is not the case. The payments are neither concentrated in the hands of the Controlling Officers nor are they made from one source as is the case in England. Hence the Comptroller and Auditor General of India so remarked, "In India, due to the very large number of treasuries in which Government payments are made, it is impossible under the existing conditions to keep track of up-to-date progress of expenditure either by the Executive or by the Accounts authorities, and excessive over grants inevitably arise." The remedy for this lies in the abolition of the Treasury system of payments, concentrating them at one source as in England and entrusting to the Comptroller and Auditor General the control over issue of money from the Consolidated Fund of India.

Pattern of Ministry's Organisation in brief

After referring to some of the top ministries, it is essential to describe the pattern of Ministry's organisation in general. The Minister of Cabinet rank is invariably a political head. He is assisted by Minister of State and a Deputy minister. Some of our Central Ministers are holding independent charge of the departments as well. The Secretary is the administrative head of the Department, functioning under the Minister and at the top of bureaucracy working within it. He acts as the adviser-in-chief of the Minister regarding policy formulation and administrative affairs. He is to see to the efficient and economical conduct of administration under his control. He represents the Minister before public accounts committee as well. N. Gopalaswami Ayyangar has rightly suggested, "a Secretary should not be immersed in files and burdened with routine, it is essential that he should have time to grasp the overall picture, size up the problem facing government in the field allotted to his charge and think and plan ahead. All these are his proper functions and must be efficiently performed....".[1]

The **ARC has portrayed his role as "coordinator policy, guide, reviewer and evaluator"**. A Secretary may be assisted by Additional Secretaries or a Special Secretary. A Joint Secretary may also be there to deal with personnel and office management. More Joint Secretaries may be added in consonance with the growing volume of work in the ministry. Besides, a Deputy Secretary acts on behalf of the Secretary and holds the charge of a secretariat Division. He has to move in routing work through the Joint Secretary. He submits papers concerning important cases to the latter. Besides, Under Secretaries also are provided. They assist the Deputy and Joint Secretaries in the disposal of governmental business and hold the charge of a branch in a ministry. They exercise control over the personnel in the branch for the dispatch of Government business and maintenance of discipline. The role of under secretary has been well explained by the Maxwell Committee in the words ".....The Under Secretary should dispose of minor cases on his own volition. More important files he should submit to the Deputy Secretary in such a form that in the ordinary course, the Deputy Secretary should be enabled to deal with the case quite briefly. Under secretaries should also attempt to reduce, as far as possible, the number of files to be formally submitted to the Deputy Secretary for taking the latter's verbal orders in appropriate cases ... *one of the great losses in recent years in the working of the Secretariat Departments is the practical disappearance due to various causes of the summary and draft of the efficient Under Secretary*"[2]. What was said by Maxwell committee in 1937 is true till date.

(H) INCOME TAX DEPARTMENT

Income tax is the most significant and potential source of revenue of Indian government. The government is in dire need of money to maintain law and order, safeguard the national integrity both from enemies within and enemies without and above all to promote the welfare of the teeming millions. Since the inception of Independence our Government opted for a socialistic pattern of society and aimed at establishment of welfare state. These dreams could be realized only if frantic efforts were made for the mobilization of finances from varied sources—direct or indirect. Income

[1]*Statement by the Comptroller and Auditor General of India Appendix 1 to the Third Report of Public Accounts Committee 1952-53.*

[2]*Report of the Reorganisation of the machinery of Government 1949 (Ayyangar Report) Government Publication, 1957, Para 14.*

tax, being a direct tax serves as a potent tool for the attainment of balanced socio-economic growth by doling out concessions and incentives for developmental purposes.

Composition of Income Tax Department

The income tax authorities are composed of the following in the hierarchical order :

1. The Central Board of Direct Taxes.
2. Director General or Chief Commissioners of Income Tax.
3. Directors or Commissioners of Income Tax (Appeals).
4. Additonal Commissioners of Income Tax (Appeals), Additional Commissioners of Income Tax or Additional Directors of Income Tax.
5. Joint Directors of Income Tax or Joint Commissioner of Income Tax.
6. Deputy Directors or Deputy Commissioner of Income Tax.
7. Assistant Directors of Income Tax or Assistant Commissioners of Income tax.
8. Income Tax officers.
9. Tax Recovery officers (of ITO status).
10. Inspectors of Income tax

Powers of the Various Functionaries of Income Tax Department

Powers of the Central Board of Direct Taxes

The Central Board of Direct Taxes is the highest authority of the I.T. Department. Its main functions are as under :

1. To frame rules and issue instructions and directions to other income tax authorities for effective administration of Income Tax Act.

2. It can relax the compliance of any requirement (under sections 14 to 59 and 80A to 80U) for claiming deduction if it amounts to avoiding genuine hardship of the assessee.

3. The Board can delegate the authority to any income tax authority below it to enable it to issue orders in writing for the excercise of the powers and performance of the functions by the other income tax authorities subordinate to it.

4. The board can issue general or special orders to (*i*) authorise a Director General or a Director to perform such functions as may be earmarked to him by the Board. (*ii*) to entrust power to the Director General or Chief Commissioenr or Commissioner to issue orders in writing that the powers and functions assigned to an assessing officer may be exercised by any Joint Commissioner or a Joint Director.

5. For proper management two or more Assessing Officers may be assigned functions concurrently. If the Assessing Officer executing concurrent functions are of different classes the authority lower in rank among them, shall excercise powers and perform functions as the authority higher than him will direct.

6. The Board regulates matters concerning jurisdiction for furnishing of returns of Income or the doing of any other thing under the Act by issue of notification in the official gazedte.

7. The Board may, if it considers it expedient to do so (for avoiding genuine hardship in any case) by general or special order authorise any Income Tax authority to admit an application or claim for any exemption, deduction referred or any other relief under the Act.

8. The Board can for avoiding geniune hardshiop relax the compliance of any requirement for claiming deduction. The said order is subject to two conditions: (*a*) the default in compliance with such requirement was owing to circumstances beyond eyind the assessee's control (*b*) the assesse has complied with such requirement before the completion of the assessment in relation to the previous year in which such deduction is claimed.

Jurisdiction of Assessing Officers

1. An assessing officer perform his functions in respect of such area and classes of assessees as are vested with him.

2. Where he has been vested with jurisdiction over any area within the limit of such area he will excercise jurisdiction :

(*i*) *in the case of business assessees* whose business is situated in that area. If the business of an assessee is situated at different places, the principal place of his business will be considered and the Assessing Officer under whose jurisdiction that place is situated shall assess the income of such assessee.

(*ii*) *in the case of any other person living in that area.* An assessee cannot file an appeal against the jurisdiction of an Assessing Officer if he has filed a return voluntarily or after the expiry of one month from the date, he was served with a notice; after the completion of assessment whichever is earlier.

(*b*) Where he fails to file the return after the expiry of the time allowed whichever is earlier.

3. An assessing officer shall be entitled to excercise all the powers in respect of all incomes accruing or arising or received within the area assigned to him.

Special Power of Chief Commissioner or Director General (Transfer of a Case)

The Director General or Chief Commissioner may transfer any case from one assessing officer to another assessing officer subordinate to him. However, he may do so after giving an opportunity to the assessee of being heard and after recording his reasons for doing so.

However, where the Assessing Officer from whom the case is to be transferred are not subordinate to the same transferring authority the case will be transferred with the concurrence of the concerned transfering authorities. If the concerned transforming authorities do not agree, the case will be transferred either by the Board or by any other authority authorised by the Board.

It may not be out of place to point out that the opportunity of being heard to the assessee will not be accorded if the transfer is from one assessing officer to another whose offices are situated in the same city, locality or place. The transfer of such a case may be effected at any stage of the proceeding.

Powers of Joint Commissioner, Assistant Director or Deputy Director Income Tax

The following are some of the most important powers of these officers[1] :

1. All these officers possess the power to seek information under section 133.

2. They can enter any place within their jurisdiction or any place occupied by any person in respect of whom they exercise jurisdiction to conduct survey.

3. They can enter any building or place within their jurisdiction or any place or building in the occupation of a person regarding whom they exercise jurisdiction and collect any information which they consider useful or relevant.

4. They can inspect and take copies of any register of the member debenture holders or mortgagees of any company.

5. The Joint comissioner can hold an enquiry under the Act and is fully equipped with all the powers that an Assessing Officer has under this Act regarding conduct of enquiries.

6. The Assessing Officer is empowered to serve notice U/S 142 for making enquiry before assessment.

7. A Joint Commissioer can send for and examine the record or any proceeding in which assessment is pending. If he deems fit he may issue such directions as he considers essential to the Assessing Officer.

8. The Joint Commissioners or Assessing Officers are equipped with the same powers as are vested with a court under the Civil Proceeding, 1908 while trying a suit under the Act.

9. If the Assistant Director or Deputy Director suspects that any income has been concealed or is likely to be concealed by any person within the jurisdiction he will be competent to excercise all powers under subsection (1) of section 131.

Powers of Commissioner (Appeal)

1. The Commissioner (Appeal) is authorised to excercise the same powers as are vested in a court under the Civil Procedure Code 1908, while trying a suit under the Act.

2. He is empowered to seek any information u/s 133.

3. He may inspect or take copies of any register of member debenture holders or mortgagees of any company.

4. While disposing of an appeal be will excercise the following powers : (*i*) In an appeal against an order of assessment be can annul, reduce or confirm the assessment; (*ii*) in an appeal against an order imposing a penalty he can confirm or cancel such order or change it so as to enhance or reduce the penalty; (*iii*) in any other case he may pass such order in an appeal as he considers fit.

However, in the above cases he will not enhance an assessment or a penalty or reduce the refund till the appellant was accorded a reasonable opportunity of showing causes against such enhancement or reduction. Besides he may consider and decide any matter cropping up during proceedings even if such matter was not raised before him by the Appellant.

Powers of Inspectors

The Income Tax Inspectors who are to be appointed by the Commissioner of Income Tax perform such functions as are assigned to them by the Commissioner or by the authority under whom they are working.

General Powers of Income Tax Authorities

The powers of Income Tax authorities in general are as under :

1. *Discovery and Production of Evidence* : The Income Tax Officers from top to the bottom possess the same powers as are vested in a court under the Civil Procedure Code 1908, while trying a case as regards to—(*a*) discovery and inspection ; (*b*) compelling the attendance of any person and examining him on oath; (*c*) enforcing the production of books of account and other documents; (*d*) issuing commissions.

2. *Search and Seizure* : If the penal and prosecution provisions do not succeed in preventing tax evasion the department can resort to more stringent actions— search and seizure.

3. *Requisition of Books of Accounts* : If the Director General, the Chief Commissioner or Commissioner in consequence of information come to know that books of accounts have been taken into custody by any officer or authority under any other law, the above officers may authorise any Joint Director, Joint Commissioner, Deputy Commissioner or any other Income Tax Officer to requisition such books of accounts or assets or documents forthwith.

4. *Power to seek Information* : The Assessing Officer, the Commissioner Appeals and the Joint Commissioner may (*a*) require any firm to supply him with a return of the name and addresses of the partners of the firm and their shares; (*b*) ask any individual Hindu family to provide him with return of the names and addresses of the manager and the members of the family; (*c*) ask any trustee, guardian or agent to furnish him with a return of the names of the persons of whom he is a trustee, guardian or agent and their addresses.

(*d*) require any person including banking company or any officer to supply such information in relation to such points or matters or to furnish statements of accounts and affairs as will in relevant to any enquiry or proceeding under the Act.

5. *Power of Survey* : The income tax authority can make a survey to (*a*) discover new assessees (*e*) to collect information useful for the assessment; (*e*) to verify that an assessee claiming regular keeping of books of account is in fact doing the same; (*d*) to verify that the assessee who claims not

to maintain any books of accounts is maintaining the books (*e*) No verify that the accounts books so maintained reflect the correct state of affairs; (*f*) to verify independently or by a surprise ckeck, the correctness of the information supplied by assessee.

The surveying Income Tax authority may (*a*) place marks of identification on the books of accounts or other documents inspected by him and get extracts or make copies of them; (*b*) make an inventory of any cash, stock or other valuable articles checked or verified by them (*d*) record the statement of any person useful for any proceeding under the Act.

6. *Collection of Information* : For the purpose of collection of any information useful or relevant for the purpose an Income tax authority may enter into any of the following buildings at which business or profession is carried on : (*i*) any building or place within the limits of the area assigned to such authority; (*ii*) any place or building occupied by any person as regards whom he excercises jurisdiction.

The income tax authority can enter the building or place used for business or profession during the hours it is open for the conduct of business or profession.

7. *To inspect register of companies* : The assessing officer or anybody authorised by him may inspect and take copies of any register of the member debenture holders or mortgagees of any company or of any entry in such register.

***

STATE ADMINISTRATION

These words must be inscribed prominently in every Raj Bhawan, The Governor : Sage or Saboteur."
—S. Sorabjee — an Indian Jurist.

CONTENTS: (A) Governor
(B) Chief Minister
(C) State Secretariat
(D) Directorate

Broadly speaking the pattern of government in the states happens to be the same as that for the Union. The Head of the state, like his counterpart at the Centre, is a mere constitutional ruler who acts on the advice of the Council of Ministers enjoying majority in the lower House of the state legislature.

(A) GOVERNOR

A critical appraisal of the speeches of the members of the Constituent Assembly on the floor of the Assembly reveals the intentions of the Fathers of the Constitution. A proposal that the Governor be directly elected by the people of the state, was rejected on the plea that complications may arise if both the Governor and the Chief Ministers are the elected heads. The former will not like to accept the nominal headship if the verdict of the people had been obtained. Another proposal to elect the Governor by the Legislative Assembly of the state was dropped, apprehending that the Governor would be a suppliant tool in the hands of a single party or a coalition of parties forming a majority. Hence, keeping in view their intentions to opt for a parliamentary set up, it was decided that the Governor might not be elected directly or indirectly. Instead, he should be appointed by the President for a period of five years. So, the Governor is appointed by the President by a warrant under his hand and seal for a period of five years. A common Governor may be appointed for two or more states including some Union Territory or Territories. He holds office during the pleasure of the President. Hence, he can be recalled by the President any time. He is transferable from one state to another and can tender resignation. On March 3, 1999, S.S. Bhandari, Governor of Bihar was transferred to Gujarat.[1] On January 7, 1993 public criticism of P.M. by Maharashtra Governor led to the latter's resignation to avoid embarrassment to the P.M. and in conformity with the codes of public conduct.[2] Likewise in all times and climes political favourites retired Defence Generals/Marshals, and Bureaucrats with strong leakings for the party in power are assigned these covated assignments.

Qualifications

As regards his qualifications, a Governor must be a citizen of India. He must be 35 years of age or above. He must not be holding any office of profit. He is not to be a member of either House of Parliament or a House of the State Legislature.[3] In case any such member is appointed as the

[1]*Hindustan Times, March 14, 1999.*
[2]*Ibid, January 8, 1993.*
[3]*Article 158 (1).*

Governor, his seat in the House is deemed to have fallen vacant from the date of his appointment. A convention has developed that he may not be a native of the state to which he is appointed governor. Dr. H. C. Mukherjee has been an exception.

Salaries and Allowances

He is entitled to such emoluments, allowances and privileges, as may be determined by the parliament. However, to begin with he was drawing Rs. 5500 p.m. as salary. Later his salary was raised to Rs. 11,000/- p.m. In April 1998 it, was increased to Rs 36,000 p.m.[1] Since january 10, 2008 the Union Cabinet raised his salary to Rs 75000 p.m.[2] His emoluments are not to be varied to his disadvantage, during the tenure of his office. He is entitled to free residence and a few other perks.

Powers of the Governor

In the words of D.D. Basu, "The powers of the Governor of a state are analogous to those of the President excepting that the Governor has no diplomatic, military or emergency powers."[3] His powers can be placed in four categories viz., legislative, financial, executive and judicial.

Legislative

Though the Governor is not supposed to be a member of either House of the State legislature, he possesses quite important legislative powers which, in fact, are more or less of formal nature :

(*i*) He summons the Houses or each House of the legislature if it is bicameral. Six months should not elapse between its last sitting in one session and first in the next session for convening of the next session.

(*ii*) He may prorogue the Houses or either House and dissolve the Legislative Assembly (the lower House). For example on March 12, 1967 the Punjab Governor prorogued the State Assembly which was adjourned by the Speaker for two months on March, 7, 1967 before the House could consider the budget. This was a judicious step to solve a constitutional crisis that overtook the State. Dissolution of the Assembly has been a frequent affair. However, this is done when he is so advised by the Chief minister or in case of a coalition government in the state, a faction or a party – a partner in coalition, withdraws support to the government and if there is no majority left at the back of the CM and his Council of Ministers and there is a fear of horse trading, he can take a drastic step-dissolution of the Assembly. If the Party at the Centre is the same as the one which appointed him, and so advises him, he is left with no other alternative. However, if this is not the case and the situation so arises he can use his discretion of dissolving the Assembly, keeping in view the fluid situation in the state politics.

(*iii*) He addresses either or both the Houses where legislative council exists at the commencement of first session each year and first session after each General Elections.

(*iv*) Bills passed by the state legislature are sent to him for his formal consent. He can return the Bill for reconsideration of the House. If the Bill is passed again, he has to accord his assent.

(*v*) He can reserve certain Bills for the assent of the President. For example, Bills providing for compulsory acquisition of property or curtailing the powers of the High Court have to be reserved for the President's assent.

(*vi*) He nominates 1/6th of the members of the legislative councils from amongst the persons who have practical experience in Literature, Art, Science, Cooperative movement and Social service.[4]

---

[1] *Hindustan Times, April 16, 1998.*

[2] *Hindustan Times, January 11, 2008*

[3] *D.D. Basu : Commentaries on the Constitution of India, Vol. II.*

[4] *Article 171(5)*

(*vii*) He nominates some members of the Anglo-Indian Community if the latter is inadequately represented.

(*viii*) On the advice of the Election Commission, he decides questions arising about the disqualification of any member of either House.[1]

(*ix*) He issues ordinances during the recess of the legislature if some eventuality crops up. The ordinances so issued, however, cease to operate at the expiration of six weeks from the reassembly of the legislature. However, the Governor is not authorised to issue ordinances pertaining to the Bills which require prior or final approval of the President of India till President has given instructions to this effect.

(*x*) He may also send messages to the Legislature on a Bill pending in the legislature.

(*xi*) He can get the State Assembly suspended while recommending to the President the taking over of the State administration. This was, for example, done by the Governor of U.P. and the Punjab on June 13, 1973 and October 4, 1983 respectively. On February 13, 1999 President's rule was enforced in Bihar though the Assembly was kept under suspended animation.[2]

Executive

According to the Constitution, the Executive powers are vested in the Governor and his subordinates.

(*i*) His powers, as such, extend to the matters in the State list. He can make laws on the subjects in the Concurrent list as well though subject to the executive authority of the President.

(*ii*) He frames rules for the transaction of business of the Government of the state and for its allocation among the ministers.

(*iii*) He can seek information from the Chief Minister and it is the duty of the Chief Minister as well to keep him informed.

(*iv*) He may instruct the Chief Minister to submit any individual minister's decision for the consideration of the Council of Ministers.

(*v*) He appoints the Chief Minister and on his advice the other ministers. His hands in this respect are fettered. A leader of the majority party or in the case of coalition, of majority group in the House, is to be called for the office of Chief Minister.

(*vi*) He appoints the Advocate General, the Chairman of the State Public Service Commission and other members.

(*vii*) He is consulted for the appointment of the judges of the State High Court.

(*viii*) He acts as the Chancellor of State universities.

Financial

(*i*) No money Bill can be introduced in the State Legislature except on his recommendations.

(*ii*) He can make advances out of Contingency Fund which is at his disposal to meet unforeseen expenditure.

(*iii*) No demand for grant can be made except on his recommendation.

(*iv*) He can ask for supplementary, additional or excess grants from the State legislature.

(*v*) He is to see that the annual financial statement of the budget of the state is placed before the Legislature and passed by it.

(*vi*) Amendments concerning financial matters cannot be moved except on the recommendations of the Governor.

[1]*Article 192 (1) and (2)*

[1]*Hindustan Times, February 14, 1999*

Judicial

(*i*) He is to decide matters concerning appointments, postings and promotions of district judges and other judicial officers.

(*ii*) He has the power of granting pardon to persons convicted by the courts of law or remitting or commuting their sentence. The offence must, however, come under a law relating to matters lying within the executive competence of the State Government. Governor of Bombay exercised his power of suspension of punishment in Commander Nanavati's case. The Bombay High Court justified this action of the Governor on the plea, that he had done so, pending the disposal of his application for leave to appeal to the Supreme Court.

Discretionary

There are certain powers regarding which he does not act on the advice of the Council of Ministers. They are termed as discretionary powers of the Governor. They are as follows :

(*i*) Governor of Assam possesses the discretionary power of administering the tribal areas of the State.

(*ii*) If a Governor is appointed as Administrator of an adjoining Union Territory by the President of India, he has to exercise his functions independently.

(*iii*) The Governor of Nagaland possesses vast discretionary powers to combat violent activities of hostile Nagas.

(*iv*) The Governor may independently appraise the breakdown of Constitutional machinery in the state and may submit his report to the President with his recommendations. In the recent past Romesh Bhandari, Governor, U.P. recommended President's rule in U.P. and the Cabinet made the recommendations for the same to the President. However, K.R. Narayanan, the President asked the Cabinet to reconsider the matter. The Cabinet withdrew the recommendations on September 22, 1998. Governor Bihar recommended invocation of Article 356 for Bihar State.[1] The President did not accord approval and asked Cabinet to reconsider it. The recommendation was withdrawn. It reflects that the Governor can exercise discretion though it is generally done at the instance of the Central Cabinet. In the latter case, the BJP was being pressurised by Samata Party, its coalition partner to topple RJD Government in Bihar. In the former case, the United Front Council of Ministers was pressurising Romesh Bhandari to oust Kalyan Singh's Government (BJP). Thus Governors of U.P. and Bihar exercised discretion dancing to the tune of their mentors at the Centre.

(*v*) He may reserve any Bill for the consideration of the President after it has been passed by the state legislature on the ground that it may conflict with a law or policy of the Union Government.

(*vi*) In certain important matters, he has to seek the advice of the President before promulgating an ordinance. The ministers do not come in the picture at all.

(*vii*) In the event of a conflict between the Union and the State Governments on a matter relating to their respective competence in the exercise of executive authority, Governor can use his discretion.

(*viii*) He may permit intimation of legal proceedings against the ex or present chief minister involved in a scandal or criminal wrong.

(*ix*) In case there is a fractured mandate in the state and no party gets absolute majority, coalitional government becomes inevitable. In such cases, a few parties foge a united front to form Government. Governor can play discretionary role by choosing one of the leaders of coalition partners for the office of Chief Ministership. Governors often made use of such discretionary powers after 1967 when era of coalition governments ushered in the State politics. Earlier than 1967, Orissa provided two such occasions to the Governor in 1957 and 1958 and again on March 1, 1973. Likewise

[1]*Hindustan Times February 22, 1998.*

SVD in Rajasthan and Uttar Pradesh after General Elections in 1967 enabled the Governor to exercise discretionary power. Speaking before Governor's Conference, V.V. Giri (a former President) said, "In appointing a Chief Minister, the judgement of the Governor was decisive and final."[1]

(*x*) In certain circumstances like the ministry losing majority in the legislature on account of defections, but keen to retain power, it advises the Governor to prorogue the Assembly to save itself from the censure motion. The Opposition, on the other hand, may approach the Governor to dismiss the Ministry as it does not retain the confidence of the majority. Thus in such a ticklish situation, Governor can exercise his discretion regarding dismissal of the Ministry. Evidently, Council of Ministers hardly comes in the picture for an advice under such elusive circumstances. In 1967, Governor Dharam Vira (of West Bengal) dismissed the Council of Ministers led by Ajay Mukherjee on the plea that only that ministry had the right to continue which enjoyed the majority in the state legislature. The dismissal of Ch. Charan Singh's ministry in 1970 in U.P. is another example of discretionary power exercised by the Governor. On July 2, 1984, Jagmohan— Governor of Jammu and Kashmir dismissed Farooq Abdulla's ministry though he did not dissolve the Assembly as advised by the outgoing CM. who had lost the majority. Pylee has well summed up use of such a power by the Governor in the words, "*Although these are not normal circumstances yet in a country where democratic institutions are in a stage of evolution and regional, linguistic and other disintegrating loyalties are still reigning supreme...the publicity of such contingencies is not remote. And the Governor is the only person on the spot who can take stock of the situation and initiate appropriate action including the dismissal of the ministry.*"

(*xi*) In the normal circumstances, the Legislative Assembly is dissolved by the Governor only on completion of its tenure yet in a parliamentary government, such a dissolution is possible to appeal to the electorate to end a situation of political instability. He may not be advised by the C.M. to dissolve or not to dissolve the Assembly but in the interest of the State concerned, he may act according to his discretion. Governor of Orissa for instance, dissolved the Assembly on the advice of C.M. Nandini Satpathy in 1973 though Biju Patnaik was to establish his claim of having majority in the legislature and thus form an alternate government. Even Orissa High Court passed strictures against him. The High Court did not challenge his discretionary power but insisted that the Governor must behave in a way so that the *bonafides* of his action remain immune from any possible misgivings.[2] In fact, after 1967 when coalition governments became indispensable in the state politics, Governors —the nominees of the Centre, had been under scathing criticism for partiality and discriminating behaviour towards non-Congress Governments. Hence the Governor's Conference held in December, 1970 decided to lay down possible guidelines in this direction. A committee under Governor of Jammu and Kashmir, was appointed for the purpose and it submitted its report after a year. However, the guidelines were not obligatory. Hence, they could hardly serve any concrete purpose, particularly in vitiated political atmosphere and debased political conditions. The conditions have gone still worse. The Governors are being drawn keeping in view the political background. Hence they act in a partisan manner and become a constant pinprick for a democratically elected government in the state. The examples of a former Governor of U.P. and ex-Governor Bihar are the eye openers. Dr. K.R. Bombwal rightly pointed out, "*The problem is, in fact, the product of India's current political malaise, of the failure of our party system and the prevailing atmosphere of unprincipled politics....No guidelines or code of conduct can restrain the ambitions of unscrupulous politicians.*"[3]

(*xii*) He has discretion to ask the C.M. to place a matter for the consideration of the Council of Ministers if it was decided by an individual minister.

---

[1]*Hindustan Times, November 21, 1971.*

[2]*V.K. Rao : Journal of the Society for the Study of State Government, Nov. 1, 1975, pp. 75-78.*

[3]*K.R. Bombwall : The Constitutional system of Indian Republic, p. 254.*

(*xiii*) He has discretion to seek information from the Chief Minister regarding administrative and legislative matters. Dr. B.R. Ambedkar remarked. "...*It is to enable the Governor to discharge his functions in respect of a good and pure administration that we propose to give the power to call for any information.*"[1]

An appraisal of these discretionary powers reveals that though there is no specific mention about most of these powers in the Constitution yet they are inherent in a particular situation. The provision regarding discretionary powers of the Governor is, couched in general terms. Article 163(2) states "If any question arises whether any matter is or is not a matter in respect of which the Governor is by or under this Constitution, required to act in his discretion, the decision of the Governor in his discretion shall be final and the validity of anything done by the Governor shall not be called in question on the ground that he ought or ought not to have acted in his discretion." The Article quoted above empowers the Governor to be master of the situation. His discretionary powers have been made unchallengable. However, a discretionary power is not to be confused with arbitrariness. It is not to be used capriciously or unjustly. It must be exercised fairly and honestly on judicious grounds and for substantial reasons. Addressing Governors' Conference in November, 1967 Mrs. Indira Gandhi said, *"You can be the guide, philosopher and friend to your respective governments while also discharging your constitutional responsibilities."*[2]

Role of Governor after 1967

Before 1967, Governor in Congress-ruled states played the role of a constitutional head. He acted on the advice of Congress Chief Minister who evidently occupied the seat of authority not only on account of leadership of the Assembly but because of perfect equation with the Congress High Command at the Centre. The same party ruling both at the Centre and in the states did not pose any problem. After 1967, coalitional era ushered in, in the Indian states. The Congress was out of power in these states and SVDs formed the Governments. This brought a radical change in the role of Governors. Unfortunately, coalitional politics was accompanied by opportunism, horse trading, defections and counter-defections, unprincipled alliances and their acting in the spirit of cartels. This led to the rise of unstable governments. The Governors who were till now not assertive and generally danced to the tune of the Central Government, and toed the line laid down by a Chief Minister, became centres of politics in the states. Their confrontation with a Chief Minister of Non-Congress coalition governments was indeed an exposure of the discretionary powers of the Governors which till now were not significantly operative. A high powered Commission rightly remarked, *"The office of the Governor is not meant to be an ornamental sinecure, that the holder of this office is not required to be an inert cipher."*[3]

With the emergence of SVD's[4], the role of the Governor in certain states became more effective. Making use of his discretionary power, he could satisfy himself that the leader of the SVD was the person commanding a stable majority and provided a Government which would be collectively responsible to the Assembly. Further, the Governor was required to see that the Cabinet so constituted, would be stable and not subject to the vagaries of the political groups holding sway in the Assembly.

Likewise, if a coalition Government was confronted with defections and counter defections and a clear-cut majority was not discernible, the Governor had to probe into provisions pertaining to constitutional breakdowns in the state. In the process, he had to face at times, denunciations. The frustrated politicians showed reluctance to part with power, rather frustratingly clung to it even when

[1]*CAD volume VIII, p. 545.*

[2]*The Tribune dated Nov. 11, 1967.*

[3]*Administrative Reforms Commission : Report of the Study Team on Centre State Relationship, Sept. 1967, vol. II, p. 273.*

[4]*A Hindi version of a conglomeration of parties joining hands to form the Government or oppose it.*

they did not have a clear backing of majority. Thus the Governors were faced with conundrums of a new kind. If no party captured majority, whom he should invite for forming the Government? — The leader of the largest party or the leader of some motely group of parties and Independents? Was he to count heads in a parade of M.L.A.s in the Raj Bhavan or use his sense of judgment and ask a leader to test his strength on the floor of the House? Another important question posed a problem when a claim of existing Chief Minister was challenged and he advised the Governor to prorogue the Assembly or adjourn it just to avoid a showdown and doled out more loaves and fishes to win over a few more supporters. The Constitution allows an interval of six months between the two sessions of the legislature. Should the Governor allow the Chief Minister six months for avoiding possible immediate showdown on the floor of the House or should he get the "total supporters of the C.M. counted when the strength of political parties was doubtful and found in a state of constant flux". These were all pertinent questions. All these possibilities enabled a Governor to use his discretion and at times abuse his authority, invariably at the instance of the Central Government. In certain states, President's rule was installed in, on the reports of the Governors supposedly in the best interest of the states. Uttar Pradesh and Andhra are the instances. In certain cases, efforts were deliberately made to find fault with the Non-Congress Ministers and the axe fell on them. If in Haryana, defections and counter-defections induced the Governor to recommend installation of President's rule and oust Rao Birendra Singh's ministry, in the Punjab and West Bengal, the defectionists-in-chief — L.S. Gill and Ajay Mukherjee respectively, were tipped for Chief ministerships of these states.

In some cases, on the advice of the Chief Minister who had lost the majority in the State Assembly, the latter faced a dissolution and the leader of the opposition — a non Congress leader — was not given an opportunity to constitute the Government whereas in some other cases, the process was deliberately reversed. Nandini Satpathy — Orissa Chief Minister's case, is worth quoting. On her advice, in 1973, Governor dissolved the Assembly. The Orissa High Court passed strictures against his hasty action as it deprived the opposition leader under Biju Patnaik of an attempt to form an alternative government. The High Court remarked, "...the Governor must behave in a way so that the *bonafides* of his action remain immune from any public misgivings."[1] In all fairness, the Governor should not have done so. In Rajasthan, under similar circumstances, Chief Minister M.L. Sukhadia lost his majority and recommended to the Governor for President's take over. All this happened when the opposition had actually paraded 92 M.L.A.s out of the total 183 of the Assembly before the Governor, but the latter playing a partisan role did not allow Non-Congress parties to form the Government. In 1977, Governor of Jammu and Kashmir assumed the administration on the advice of the C.M. who had lost the majority and had advised dissolution of the Assembly.[2] In July, 1984, on the other hand, the Governor called Shah to form the Government ignoring the advice of the C.M. to the contrary.

Again J and K state headed for a spell of governor's rule after G.N. Azad led Congress government decided to quit when the CM failed to muster support from non-congress MLA's to make up for the loss of estranged P D P MLA's. On July 7, 2008 he withdrew from the vote of confidence in the 87 membered Assembly after failing to gather the requisite half way majority of the house. After seeking permission of the speaker to withdraw confidence vote, he went to the governor. He said on the floor of the assembly. 'The government was in favour of clean politics' and not horse trading. Thereafter, governor's rule was installed, which ended in December, 2008, after Assembly election. Evidently, Governor accepted the advice of the C.M. of the State.

Examples quoted above can be multiplied to highlight the challenging role of the Governor after the emergence of coalitional politics in the states. Thus he has ceased to be a signing machine or a rubberstamp as was originally conceived. It is not correct to accept the contention of K.M.

[1] *V.K. Rao : op. cit., pp. 70-74.*

[2] *Hindustan Times, March 28, 1972.*

Munshi, "Governor's job is to run a hotel and entertain guests."[1] He toes the line of the Chief Minister so long as the latter belongs to the Party at the Centre and is invariably guided by the directions of the Party High Command. However, if the opposition parties form an alliance and form the Government, he generally indulges in pinpricking and at the behest of the Centre eventually sees to its fall. Farooq Abdulla's fall in July, 1984 is an example worth quoting. Hence it can be concluded that after 1967, the Governor ceased to be a mere ornamental head. He became an important functionary designed to play a decisive role in the State Politics. Addressing Governors' Conference ex President V.V. Giri rightly advised the Governors on December 12, 1969 "to evolve norms and conventions which may facilitate your work and help in laying down popular standards." Again on November 21, 1970 addressing Governors' Conference he observed " A Governor, in spite of the difficult position in which he functions today and in spite of the fact that he may be liable to criticism, has to assert himself in upholding his constitutional duty."[2] It clearly reflects that Governor's role has changed considerably in the changed context of things. Governor C.P.N. Singhi's words at a Press conference on May 18, 1980 are revealing, "He would not allow any irresponsible combination of political groups to form a ministry in Uttar Pradesh, in case no single party secured absolute majority in the ensuing elections". He talked of ensuring a stable majority through a "permutation of political parties which could form such a government "[3] There was a sharp reaction to his statement. It was described as "threat to the opposition parties and indirect support to the Congress." This criticism of the Governor by the opposition confirms our contention that his role is significant and has undergone a sea change. His role is partisan and politically motivated at times. This is so where coalition governments are formed and discordant elements can part company any time and spell uncertanity in political scenario. In such a situation, Governor has to act. Discretion is his. He can be fair or partial. In most cases Governors role has been partisan. Hence there has been clamour against Article 356 which results in imposing of Governors' rule in the state. Hence the question arises can he be an autocrat?

Governor as Autocrat

Keeping in view the vast discretionary authority of the Governor, a question arises whether or not he can assume autocratic powers? So long as he functions within the framework of the constitution, he cannot abuse his authority. There is no denying the fact that neither the Council of Ministers nor the state legislature can control him as far as discretionary powers are concerned. However, his removal by the President, virtually meaning the Central Government, keeps him under proper restraints. In normal circumstances when the party in power in the state is the same as at the Centre, he will act on the advice of the Council of Ministers, enjoying full confidence of the state legislature. Substituting 'decisions' for the 'advice' of the Council of Ministers, will amount to creating political complications, eventually leading to his removal. Under abnormal circumstances i.e., during emergencies, he will act as an agent of the President and his powers will be fairly imposing. In either case, he is not to be considered master of situation himself. He has to dance to the tune of the Centre. In the words of P. Ramamurti (M.P., CPM) *"The Governor's report was made to order. It did not reflect reality."*[4] The reports of Governors in the case of dismissed BJP ministries was described as a commanded performance[5] as the Centre directed them to do so within 24 hours.

However, by virtue of his position as the Head of the State, he has the right to encourage, the right to warn and the right to be consulted.[6] He is to be a general observer of the affairs of the

[1]*As cited by D.C. Parvate : My Days as Governor, p. 9.*

[2] *In 1992 the dismissal of BJP Govt. in the wake of Ayodhya Episode despite their absolute majority in the Assemblies.*

[3]*The Sunday Tribune, November 22, 1970.*

[4]*The Times of India, May 19, 1980.*

[5]*The tribune November 22, 1967.*

[6] *The Statesman, May 20, 1980.*

state, at times encouraging, at times admonishing his government and being kept informed of its activities. He is expected to maintain impartiality and grace by standing above the vortex of party politics. In the words of Dr. P.K. Sen, "*The functions of the Governor shall be to lubricate the machine of the Government to see that its wheels are going on well by reason not of his interference but of friendly cooperation.*"[1]

Besides, he is to play the role of the representative of the Union in the state and as an agent of the President. Pylee remarks "He is the link that fastens the federal state chain, the channel which regulates the Union States relationship. Thus, he is an essential part of the constitutional machinery fulfilling an essential purpose and rendering an essential service."[2] Hence, D.D. Basu, a critic of the constitution, is not prepared to accept him a mere figure head. In his words, if the Governor is an active and good Governor, he could by means of getting in touch with the opponents of the party in power reconcile them to a good number of measures and generally make the administration run smoothly."[3] His position has been very well portrayed by Vishnu Sahay, a former Governor of Assam and Nagaland "*...there will always be a time when he will be able to help as a moderating influence in centre-state relationships, as a rallying point for communities, as a symbol of the continuity of the state or as a standby in an emergency. He does wear two hats and dilemmas will arise in practice. These will be best solved if he acts and appears to act as a creature of the Constitution to which he has sworn loyalty.*"[4] Thus if the Governor tries to be autocratic and ignores the letter or spirit of the Constitution, he is apt to face removal and his political career is likely to be eclipsed at no distant future. Very recently an aged governor of Andhra Pradesh (N.D.Tiwari) had to resign on health grounds as his sex scandle was exposed. It reflects that governor his to maintain dignity of his office and believe inormous of morality as will. A leading jounarlist remakred "However at 86, getting a heavy of young women to his beside one in the master had room of a Raj Bhawan is having like the sultan sulaiman of medieval ages. Some Gandhi was right in sacking him" Thus ends political career of a seasoned politician.

Guiding principles for Governers' office

However there is a necessity of guiding principles so that Governor's office could remain above suspicion and safe from the perennial shafts of the critics. Bhagwan Sahay Committee appointed in 1970 on the instance of President V.V. Giri submitted its report after a year. Its principal recommendations, if kept in view, can go a long way in taking the sting out of the scathing criticism against the Governor :

(*i*) Governor may dismiss ministry if the Chief Minister shirks his primary responsibility of facing the Assembly within the shortest possible time, to test the confidence of the legislature in him.

(*ii*) The test of confidence in the Ministry should be left to vote in the Assembly.

(*iii*) If the formation of an alternative ministry is not possible, the Governor shall be left with no alternative but to make report to the President recommending for the dissolution of the Assembly.

(*iv*) A non member of a legislature and also a nominated member of the House should not be appointed as a Chief Minister.

(*v*) If a constituent party to a coalition government resigns due to disagreement with the Chief Minister, he might not necessarily resign. He should demonstrate his continuing strength in the Assembly by advising the Governor to summon Assembly within the shortest possible time and obtain its verdict in his favour.

---

[1]*CAD, Vol. VIII.*

[2]*M.V. Pylee, op. cit., p. 479.*

[3]*D.D. Basu : op. cit.*

[4]*Vishnu Sahay : 'Governors' role in Administration' an article : The Indian journal of Public Administration, July-Sept. 1970, p. 286.*

(*vi*) The Chief Minister of a Samyukta Vidhayak Dal Government should be formally elected by the parties forming the alliance.

(*vii*) A special cell may be setup in the President's secretariat to supply authentic information regarding political and constitutional developments in the states from time to time.

(*viii*) The Governor is the head of the state. As such, he is not to be treated as an agent of the President.

It may not be effaced from mind that charter of guidelines alone may not be able to solve the problems that are the outcome of current political malaise, the failure of our party system and the emergence of unprincipled politics and cynical opportunism in our body politic. A choice of a right person as a Governor can go a long way in giving true meaning to the office of the Governor. Governorship to be made more meaningful. It should not be made a refuge of retired politicians or loyalist bureaucrats or the seekers of patronage from the party in power. Non-controversial outstanding persons in the social or educational or political domains be assigned Governorship. A dynamic personality does have an impact on the office of such a nature. Moreover, keeping in view the fast-deteriorating administrative standards, the role of the Governors should be enlarged and watchdog functions in specific areas, be entrusted to him. The Governor, being saviour of the Constitution under an oath, should watch the course of political events personally and take action promptly rather than give an impression of dancing to the tune of the Centre or opening his mind after a visit to Delhi. In the present context of things, the Governor serves less as a constitutional head of the State but more as an effective instrument of Central Government, to keep a tight grip on the leaders of State Governments. This is rather unfortunate and uncalled for. Even the Supreme Court of India in a historic judgment in May, 1979 remarked, "*The Governor has an independent constitutional office which is not subject to the control of the Government of India.*" However, Governors till date remain suppliant tools of the Centre. The dismissal of B.J.P. Governments in Rajasthan, Himachal Pradesh and Madhya Pradesh on December 15, 1992 on the basis of commanded reports (almost identical) of the Governor induced a journalist to remark, "the practice of Governors signing on the dotted lines has not come to an end despite past experience."[1] Till date Governor believes in toeing the line of the Centre and issues commanded reports to appease the leaders at the helm of affairs at the Centre. Hence it is being suggested in all rational circles that Governors' post should not be political. It should be apolitical. The opposition parties' demand for the replacement of Governor of Bihar — a staunch RSS man — in March, 1999 reflects that Governor's role has not undergone a sea change as desired from time to time till date. He remains thoroughly partisan, particularly if he has political background. He may dance to the tune of his political mentors even if he happens to be a retired bureaucrat.

Recommendations of Sarkaria Commissions Report (1988)

(*i*) Constitution should formally stipulate that the Centre must consult the C.M. of a State before appointing a Govornor.

(*ii*) A politician from the ruling party at the Centre should not be appointed as the Governor of the state where the government is run by some other party or combination of other parties.

(*iii*) Governor must be from outside the State and should not be too intimately connected with the local parties of the State.

(*iv*) A Governor should be a person who has not been taking active part in politics generally, particularly in the recent past.

(*v*) Too frequent invocation of Article 356 should be avoided.

Most of these recommendations still remain unfulfilled. Hence the Governors office remains under clouds and his suppposedly unimpeachable integreity more of then not unpenchable.

[1]*Editorial Hindustan Times deated December 17, 1992.*

(B) CHIEF MINISTER (C.M.)

The Chief Minister at the state level is analogous to the Prime Minister at the Centre. He is the real executive head of the State Government. Article 164 provides that the C.M. is to be appointed by the Governor and the other ministers on the advice of the C.M. Generally, leader of the majority party is called by the Governor to constitute the Council of Ministers. The Governor is not left with any choice, in case a particular party enjoys a clear-cut majority. In a coalition government also, widely accepted leader of the parties is to be called to act as C.M.. For example E.M.S. Namboodiripad was invited by Governor of Kerala to form his ministry in 1967, A Governor can invite, even the leader of a minority party, to act as the Chief Minister. P.C. Ghosh in W. Bengal and L.S. Gill in the Punjab were invited to form the Government though they were leaders of the minority parties. At times, Chief Minister losing the support of majority in the House, was allowed to hold on to the office without convening the State Assembly. Rao Birendar Singh and once Ch. Bansi Lal of Haryana were allowed to continue without convening the Assembly session. It reflects wide discretion of the Governor in this matter.

The Constitution is silent as to whether the Chief Minister should be a member of the lower House only. In 1952 C. Rajagopalachari was nominated to the Legislative Council (Vidhan Parishad) and was appointed as the Chief Minister. Morarji Desai was nominated to the Legislative Council in 1952 and appointed Chief Minister though he had been earlier defeated at the hustings. Likewise B.P. Mandal in Bihar was nominated to the Legislative Council and then induced as the Chief Minister. However, now by and large, the CM is leader of the majority party or heads a coalition in the coalition era, since 1967.

Powers and Functions

Like his prototype at the Centre, the C.M. has been described as the 'keystone of the Cabinet arch' 'a moon among the lesser stars' the sun around whom the ministers revolve like 'planets'. His powers are numerous and authority onerous at the state level. The following are his powers and functions :

(*a*) *Formation of the Council of Ministers* (C.o.M)

The Chief Minister has been rightly described as the creator, preserver and destroyer of the C.o.M. The Governor appoints the Chief Minister (C.M.) and the rest of the Ministers are appointed by the Governor on the advice of the C.M. However, it is the privilege of the C.M. to choose a team of his liking. Governor may suggest but cannot insist on the inclusion or exclusion of a name. The Governor can drop a minister on his advice. He can dismiss the entire C.o.M. on C.M.'s advice. In fact C.M.'s own resignation means resignation of the entire ministry. On November 25, 1992 C.M. Haryana got dismissed Ch. Birendra Singh, Planning Minister, on the plea of anti-government activities.

J & K C.M. Gulam Nabi Azad was deprived of his coalition partner - PDP's support and he had to seek vote of confidence in the Asssembly Since he was not sure of absolute majority on the floor of the House, he sought the permission of the speaker, withdrew vote of confidence and went to the governor apprised him of the political stalemate and recommended the dissolution of the assembly on July 7, 2008 and tendered his resignation and succeeded in getting governor's rule installed in the state as he did not like horse trading to take place and showed keenness for clean politics in the state. This was a wise decision of a CM who believed in norms of morality.

(*b*) *Allocation of Portfolios*

The C.M. after constituting his team of ministers, allocates portfolios to his colleagues. He can reallocate portfolios as well. Of course, while allocating portfolios, particularly Home and Finance, he has to see to the importance of the individual concerned and his standing with the party and equation with himself. In the recent past, Ch. Birendra Singh, a dissident was divested of Revenue Portfolio by C.M. Haryana, before his final dismissal at a later stage.

(c) Chairman of the Cabinet

He acts as the Chairman of the Cabinet. He convenes and presides over its meetings. These meetings are generally attended by the Cabinet. The Ministers of state also can attend the meetings though the deputy ministers do not attend such meetings.

(d) As a Coordinator

He coordinates the policies and working of all the ministries. He exercises general supervision over the Council and is consulted by the ministers in case of conflict between two or more of them. He is to bring about harmony and elicit cooperation from the ministers as the chief coordinator.

(e) Link between the Governor and C.o.M (Article 167)

The Chief Minister acts as a communicating channel between the Governor and the Council of Ministers. Likewise, the Governor can seek any information from the Council of Ministers through the Chief Minister. If the Governor so requires, he can submit to the Council of Ministers any matter on which a decision had been taken by an individual minister.

(f) Leader of the House

As a leader of the House, he is the chiet spokesman of the House. He helps maintaining discipline in the House. He supports a minister who gets bogged down on the floor of the House while defending his department. His statements carry weight. He can advise the Governor to dissolve the House though such an advice can be rejected by the latter. For instance S.S. Ansari, a former Governor of Orissa rejected the advice of R.N. Singh Deo — the then Chief Minister who had lost majority, to dissolve the Legislative Assembly. At a later stage on his own finding, the Governor advised the President to dissolve the Assembly and the President acted on his advice. The Speaker of the House consults the Chief Minister before fixing up agenda for the House.

(g) Patronage

In theory, the top appointments viz., Advocate General and members of State Public Service Commission, Advocate General etc. etc. are to be made by the Governor but in actual practice they are the nominees of the Chief Minister.

(h) As the leader of the Party

Elections in the state are fought in the name of powerful personalities, aspiring for leadership of legislature after triumph at the hustings. The Chief Minister is the leader of the party before elections and after victory of his party, he issues whips and sees that they are followed by the members. For instance, in the elections of Haryana Vidhan Sabha, Haryana Vikas Party projected Ch. Bansi Lal as its leader and proposed Chief Minister. His party in his name was voted to power. In Delhi Assembly elections Mrs. Sheila Dixit was projected as the Chief Minister by the Congress Party and was elected the C.M. third time defeating Professor V.K. Malhotra the pivotal leader of BJP, in Delhi Assembly elections.

An appraisal of the powers of the C.M. reveals that he is holding pivotal position. He is central to the formation of the Council of Ministers and central to its death. He is more a Captain of the team of ministers and not its boss. In a parliamentary democracy, the head of the Government is not to ride roughshod over the ministers. He is to work with them and not at them. However, he is bound by the dictates of the High Command particularly in case of the Congress ruled states. To what extent he is assertive and can bring round the High Command to his point of view depends, to a great extent, on his dynamic personality, mental calibre, social tangibility and his persuasive ability to keep his colleagues as one folk. A popular leader, commanding towering personality and equipped with administrative acumen, can govern the state more vigorously and comparatively speaking, more independently. Even the High Command will not like to ignore his or her point of view or turn down his recommendations. S. Pratap Singh Kairon in the Punjab, Ch. Bansi Lal ex CM Haryana, and Ch. Bhupinder Singh Hooda the present CM Haryana emerging supreme second time in the coveted CM's assignment, G.B. Pant in Uttar Pradesh, Jyoti Basu in West Bengal, C. B Naidu in Tamil Nadu and Laloo Yadav and now Nitish Kumar in Bihar are some of notable examples of the C.M.'s who dominated the state politics due to qualities of head and heart and strong equation with the High command.

(C) COUNCIL OF MINISTERS (CoM)

Article 164 of the Constitution provides that the Governor shall appoint the Chief Minister and the CoM shall also be appointed by him on the advice of the C.M. In actual practice, Governor can recommend names for inclusion in the ministry but cannot insist on getting anyone included in it. It is the Chief Minister who finalises the list. The Council of Ministers is composed of Cabinet Ministers, Ministers of State, Deputy Ministers and Parliamentary secretaries. However the Cabinet Ministers head the departments generally. The size of the CoM is also determinable by him. There has been a tendency to have oversized ministries in order to give representation to various shades of opinions or save the Chief Ministership from mass defections engineered by political opportunists and turncoats. The ARC also observed, "After the third General Election of 1962, there was a manifest decline in standards at the Ministers' level. The size of the Ministries showed a tendency to expand irrespective of administrative needs in order to accommodate religious and regional claims and satisfy personal ambitions of some of the tall leaders of the party. These trends were more discernible with the emergence of multiparty system and eventually formation of coalition ministries in a number of states after the fourth General Elections. The differences in the ideologies of the parties forming the coalition and the scramble for political power among those left out, led to a wave of defections bringing in its trail further political instability. A recent study reveals that about "14 percent of the total membership in the state since the last General Elections changed political affiliation at least once. The percentage is as much as 23 if the more stable governments are excluded from the total..." The Commission suggested, "Taking a broad view of the needs of the administration in different states we consider that big states like Uttar Pradesh, Bihar, Madhya Pradesh and Maharashtra may have about 20 persons in the Council of Ministers. The middle sized states like Madras, Mysore and Andhra Pradesh may have 14 to 18 ministers and the small states like Kerala, Haryana and Punjab 8 to 12."[1] Despite former P.M. P.V. Narasimha Rao's cherished desire to effect economy in administration by having a CoM equivalent to 10 percent of M.L.A.s of the State, certain states have not been able to effect a cut fearing revolt by unprincipled politicians against the CMs. Haryana State is one such example, well-known for "Aya Ram Gaya Ram" politics. Hence its CoMs have been generally unwieldy. Each minister is to be a member of the State legislature. If he is not, he has to procure this membership within six months.[2] The salaries and allowances of the ministers are determinable by the state legislature from time to time.

Responsibility of the Ministers

The ministers individually and collectively are responsible to the State Legislative Assembly. Article 164(2) states "The Council of Ministers shall be collectively responsible to the Legislative Assembly of the State." The ministers work as a team. 'All for one and one for all' policy works in the functioning of the CoM. A minister cannot dissociate himself from the collective decision. The CoM remains in power so long as it commands the confidence of the legislature. If a no confidence motion is ever passed, the CoM has to tender resignation.

Function of CoM

Following are the functions of the CoM :

(*i*) To maintain law and order and ensure security of life and property of the people in the state.

[1]*Quoted by S.R. Maheshwari : op. cit., The ARC 1970, pp. 86-87.*
[2]*Article 164 (4).*

(*ii*) To formulate and decide the policies of the state and implement them effectively.

(*iii*) To decide the legislative programme of the Legislative Assembly and sponsor all important Bills.

(*iv*) To control the financial policy and decide the tax structure for the public welfare of the state.

(*v*) To chalk out programmes, schemes for the socio-economic changes so that the state makes headway in various interrelated fields.

(*vi*) To make important appointments of heads of Departments.

(*vii*) To discuss disputes with other states.

(*viii*) To advise the Governor on the appointment of judges of the High Court.

(*ix*) To consider state's share of work in the Five Yearly Plans and determine obligations.

(*x*) To frame proposal for incurring expenditure out of State reserves.

An appraisal of the powers of CoM reveals that they are the guides and masters of the legislature. Besides, they are the formulators and executors of policy of the state. However, the State legislature still enjoys the right of passing a vote of no-confidence against a ministry. The ministers are also subjected to severe criticism during the question hour in the State legislature. Besides, the tight grip of the Party High Command and that of the party executive at the state level, are effective checks on it. The individual ministers cannot bypass the C.M. unless they are not worried about retaining their ministership. It is the CM who can shuffle his pack as he pleases.

(D) STATE SECRETARIAT

As already said, Governor is the constitutional head of the state. He is advised by a Council of Ministers headed by a Chief Minister who in fact constitutes the head of the Government. The business of Government is as such conducted by a Minister heading one or two or even more departments – a career civil servant – is the administrative head. The Secretariat as such implies the complex of departments which are administratively headed by the secretaries and politically by the ministers. The Secretary is a senior IAS man. He is Secretary to the Government as a whole and not to the individual minister concerned. The Public Works Department in some states was headed by the Chief Engineer as the Secretary. In practice, more than one department is entrusted to a Secretary. Like his counterpart at the Centre, the Secretary is the principal adviser to the minister. He is responsible for implementing the policies and decisions made by the political Chief. Besides, he also represents his department before the Committees of the legislature. A department comprises officers and the office. The officers comprise a Secretary, a Deputy Secretary, Under Secretary and/or Assistant Secretary. Additional or Joint Secretary also may be provided in big departments. All these officers except those from the secretariat civil service, are appointed to the secretariat for a fixed term. The Chief Secretary is an exception to the tenure system. On the other hand, the office comprises the section officer, assistants, upper division clerks, lower division clerks, stenotypists and typists. The office, however, constitutes the permanent element of the Secretariat system.

The Secretariat departments vary from state to state. Their number varies between 11 and 34. Most of the states cater to the following departments : General Administration; Home; Revenue; Agriculture; Planning; Panchayati Raj; Finance; Law; Public Works; Irrigation and Power; Education; Industries; Cooperation; Transport; Local Government; Food and Civil Supplies; Jails; Labour and Employment; Excise and Taxation.

Besides the Secretariat department are the Executive departments. The Simon Commission defined the Executive department as "an administrative unit, separate from the Secretariat which reaches its apex usually in a single officer like the Inspector General of Police or the Chief Conservator of Forest, outside the Secretariat altogether. Such a head of a department will usually be concerned principally with a single Secretary to Government and a single. Minister for his order and the funds which he has to spend."[1] All departments are not having executive departments attached to them. The Secretariat departments like Finance and Law which are employed for advisory and controlling functions do not have executive department and the Secretary who supervises his work is the Generalist (IAS). The relationship of a generalist and a specialist has been generally a subject of controversy and often of a debate.[2] Certain guidelines can help in smoothening their relationship viz., (*i*) Secretary should deal with the formulation of policy whereas its implementation be left over to the department; (*ii*) the Secretariat should not involve itself in a matter in which its only contribution can be that of delay; (*iii*) the head of the department, subject to certain rules under the conditions of service, be assigned the fullest control over the personnel under him; the Secretariat should provide common services and undertake domestic housekeeping for the Head of the Department concerned e.g., the provision of office accommodation.[3] However, in certain states certain technical departments are also headed by the Generalists *i.e.* IAS.[4]

Functions of the Secretariat

The Secretariat performs the following functions :

(*a*) To formulate Government's general programmes.

(*b*) To prepare the Budget in consultation with the Finance department.

(*c*) To decide the policies and lay down the principles to be employed in the execution of programmes and state the conditions, under which certain aspects of it like grants will be given effect to.

(*d*) To supervise the general progress of the implementation of the Government's programmes.

(*e*) To supervise the incurring of expenditure as per Budget's provision.

(*f*) To modify the programmes and formulate Budget reappropriations within the classifications determined by the Finance department.

(*g*) To appoint Heads of departments to look to the establishment work viz., salary, leave etc., of these officers.

(*h*) To finalise the contents of all proposed legislation.

(*i*) To deal with the questions raised in the Legislative Assembly and Council.

(*j*) To allocate office space and domestic housekeeping both for itself and its attached departments.

(*k*) To nominate individuals to attend meetings convened by the Union Government or other States and also to the training programmes conducted by the Union or the State Governemnts.

Functions of Head of Department

Following are the functions of the Head of the Department :

(*a*) To propose the departmental activities for the ensuing year at the beginning of the Budget framing.

(*b*) To formulate a first draft of the department's Budget.

(*c*) To act as technical adviser to the Ministry.

[1]*Report of the Indian Statutory Commission Vol I Survey p 312.*

[2]*See the details in Chapter XV.*

[3]*Shriram Maheshwari : Indian Administration (Fourth Revised Edition 1989), (reprint 1992) p. 433.*

[4]*In Haryana, for instance, Deptt. of Education is headed by IAS Director.*

(*d*) To carry out the departmental research and experiment programmes and also to improve the department's technique of work.

(*e*) To train the officers working in the departments in these techniques.

(*f*) To inspect the execution of work by the departmental district staff.

(*g*) To allocate grants in accordance with the rules and frame Budget reappropriations within the prescribed limits.

(*h*) To make within approved rules all appointments, confirmations, postings, transfers and promotions of all subordinate officers and also sanctioning their leaves.

(*i*) To exercise disciplinary powers over all subordinate officers according to rules.

(*j*) To advise Public Service Commissions concerning promotions.

(*k*) To advise the Minister on nominations to be made by Government to outside institutions.

(*l*) To sanction the attendance of officers at conferences other than inter-state or government of India conferences.

The powers mentioned above reveal that the Secretariat is an essential agency for policy-making. However, the activities of the Secretariat have been fast expanding. Parliamentary democracy itself has been responsible for arrogation of more and more powers by the Secretariat. The Minister is answerable to the legislature for acts of omission and commission of the Department entrusted to him. Hence he is keen to have a big say in most matters. This leads to the centralisation of functions in the Secretariat. Certain human and psychological factors also are responsible for this monopolization of power. Attempts are therefore, afoot to contain this aggrandisement by the Secretariat. The Rajasthan Administrative Reforms Commission 1963 clearly laid down the functions which are to be performed by the Secretariat. These functions were categorised as General, Financial and those dealing with Service matters. More or less these were the functions we have enumerated above.

Chief Secretary

The Chief Secretary holds a pivotal and coveted position in the state. He is invariably the head of the General Administration Department of which the Chief minister is the Political Head. He is the linchpin of the Secretariat as he exercises control over all other departments. He is in fact the chief of the secretaries running other departments. He is the mentor and conscience keeper of the services in the State. According to a Report "He is the chief of the civil services and all governmental servants look to him to deal with all and every problem concerning their conditions of service and work."[1] He provides desired leadership to the administrative system of the state. He is said to be the Chief Public Relations Officer of the State Government though he is not designated as such. He acts as a channel of communication between his Government and the Central and other State governments.

His office has been excluded from the operation of the tenure system. He either retires after holding this post or is given still more important assignment at the Centre. In the words of Dr. Maheshwari, "In the office of the Chief Secretary, the State Department has an institution the parallel of which does not exist in the Central Government."[2] At the Centre, the amount and nature of work entrusted to him, is interspersed among the Cabinet Secretary, the Finance Secretary and the Home Secretary.

Various committees appointed from time to time have recognized the prominent role of the Chief Secretary in the state politics. The Bengal Administration Enquiry Committee (1945) recogniz-

[1]*Report : Andhra Pradesh Administrative Reforms Committee (1964-5), p. 8.*

[2]*Shriram Maheshwari ; op., cit., p. 437.*

ing the significant position of the Chief Secretary recommended that (*i*) the incumbent of this office should be the civil service head of the Chief Minister's department; (*ii*) he should be Secretary to the Cabinet and the Cabinet Development Committee; (*iii*) he should be chairman of the Development Board; (*iv*) he should be immediate executive supervisor of each District Collector, regarding developmental activities of the state.

The Rajasthan Administrative Reform Committee (1963) also recognized the pivotal position of the office. It so reported, "By virtue of his unique position as head of the official machinery and advisor to the Council of Ministers, the Chief Secretary has an extremely important role to play in the State Administration. Apart from attending to the work of the departments which are directly under him, he should be in a position to effectively coordinate the work of different secretariat departments and ensure that there is a certain degree of uniformity in the policies adopted by the State Government with respect to different departments."[1] The committee went to the extent of recommending that the Chief Secretary should invariably be consulted by the Minister-in-charge in all important cases involving adoption of new principles or new schemes and proposals suggesting deviation from existing rules and practice and also in all cases of appointments, confirmations, promotions, transfers and postings of officers of the Deputy Head of department rank and above.

Functions of the Chief Secretary

An analysis of all reports since 1945 enables us to conclude that the Chief Secretary is the keystone of the administrative arch at the State level. His functions can be summed-up as under :

(*i*) To act as the principal adviser of the Chief Minister. (*ii*) As a Secretary to the Cabinet, to prepare agenda for its meetings, make requisite arrangements for such meetings and maintain minutes of its proceedings. (*iii*) To exercise general supervision and control over the entire secretariat. (*iv*) As head of the civil service in the state, to effect transfers and postings of government personnel. According to Woodruff, "The Chief Secretary was the Channel through which the orders of the Government were conveyed to their officers. He was traditionally the source of postings and transfers to most district officers. He was in fact the Government."[2] (*v*) To act as Secretary by rotation to the Zonal Council of which the State concerned is the member. (*vi*) To exercise administrative control over the secretariat buildings, including allocation of rooms in them. (*vii*) To control the staff attached to the Minister. (*viii*) To exercise control over the central record branch, the secretariat library, the conservancy and watch and ward staff of the secretariat. (*ix*) As head of all Secretaries, to preside over a large number of committees, most of which he is the member. (*x*) To serve as a nerve-centre of the State during emergencies or crisis. (*xi*) To look after all other matters, not falling within the purview of other Secretaries.

On account of high significance of the office, since 1973, only the senior most Secretary in the state is elevated as the Chief Secretary. Prior to that, he was not necessarily the senior most. In the Punjab, for example, he was junior to the Financial Commissioner and in U.P., he was junior to the members of the Board of Revenue. In 1973, Chief Secretary's post was equated with that of the Secretary to the Government of India. His emoluments were also kept at par with that of the Secretary of Government of India.

In general, political interference in the states is attaining climax. Even Chief Secretaryship is sometimes offered to a political favourite, by compelling comparatively a senior officer to seek transfer to the Centre or manage long leave so that the highest administrative seat could be offered to a "Yesman of the Chief Minister." This is detrimental to the State administration and

[1]*Report : Rajasthan Administrative Reforms Committee, 1963 p. 46.*

[2]*Woodruff Philip : The Men who ruled india : The Guardians 1963, p. 274.*

impairs objectivity and impartiality expected of head of state administration. It has been suggested that national roster of senior officers be prepared and out of it Chief Secretaries for different states be appointed. Besides, tenure of a Chief Secretary should be sufficiently long, so that he could leave impact on the state administration by effective functioning during a long period of his chief secretaryship.

(E) DIRECTORATE

In India, the work of the Union as well as state governments is divided into a number of ministries. A ministry generally consists of a single department or of a number of departments grouped together. A typical ministry of the Union Government as well as that of the State Government is like a three storeyed building comprising : (*a*) the Minister in charge who is the political head and is invariably assisted by 'minister of state', Deputy Minister and a Parliamentary Secretary, (*b*) the secretariat organisation and the attached offices of the ministry headed by the Secretary — a senior permanent IAS official. (*c*) the executive organization of the department or departments within the ministry. The official head of the department is usually designated as the Director, Director General etc. In the state, the Department at the lower level i.e. level below the secretariat, is termed as Directorate. Secretary heads the department whereas the Director heads the Directorate.

The Directorate, as said above, is headed by a Director who may be a technical head as in case of Health Directorate in Haryana, Director Health Services is the senior most CMO (Chief Medical Officer) whereas an IAS officer, is Director of Higher Education as well as School Education in Haryana. The practice varies from state to state, and department to department in the case of the latter. In Rajasthan, U.P. and Punjab for instance, the seniormost educationist — Principal of Government College or an educationist holding the post of Joint Director or Deputy Director Education is promoted for the assignment of Director whereas in Haryana a young IAS officer may be transferred to the Directorate from the field appointment of a D.C. as the Director. In Haryana, in directorate of Health department, a technical man (senior most CMO) holds the post of Director whereas in Department of Education, IAS officers head the Directorate of Higher and School Education as the Directors.

Further instances in Haryana : Director of Education is assisted by a Joint Director Colleges, the senior most in College Cadre of Class I status, two to three Deputy Directors of Class I status and ADPI's (Assistant Directors) of Class II status. Besides there are three superintendents concerning government colleges, non-government affiliated colleges and administration respectively. They are gazetted officers, promoted from the clerical cadre. The Director is also assisted by an Administrative Officer who deals with the establishment and general administration and is H.C.S. officer class I, and an Accounts Officer (Gazetted) to maintain financial meticulousness of accounts. A Caretaker, taking care of the maintenance of the Director's and other officers' offices, (an assistant rank officer), a Registrar dealing with the leave, pay bills etc. of the rank of deputy superintendent; auditors, assistants; stenos; upper and lower division clerks, personal assistants to the Directors are other personnel comprising the Higher Education Directorate to be controlled by the Director. Likewise, there is a separate Directorate for School Education, headed by Director Public Instructions — an IAS officer. The Director is assisted by ADO - H.C.S. officer Class I, additional Director Primary Education and Joint and Deputy Directors. Besides there is a regular staff as said above to assist him in running the department. The District Education Officers (Class I officer) run the administration concerning schools at the district level. In school Primary Education headed by additional director of school Education was also created in they are He was a require most education officer in school cadre.

As in the case of Department of Higher Education and School Education, we find similar

Directorates in the other departments. A specialist/technocrat heads the Directorate in some cases whereas an Indian Administrative Service official functions as the Director in the other non technical Departments. The officials to assist the Director are more or less of the same level as described above in the case of Directorate of Higher and School Education. The functions of the Director of a Department are mainly to act as technical adviser to the ministry. Hence in the fitness of things, a technocrat/specialist should head the Directorate.

Second, he exercises disciplinary powers over subordinate officers according to rules.

Third, he is to render advice to the Public Service Commission concerning promotions.

Fourth, he makes *ad hoc* appointments if a vacancy occurs.

Fifth, he effects confirmations, transfers and appointments of subordinate officers within prescribed rules. In fact, this is done on the recommendations of Public Service Commission regarding certain categories of services and Subordinate Selection Board, in case of lower appointments of prescribed category.

Sixth, he recommends to the minister the persons to be sent on deputation to outside institutions, through the Secretary of the Department concerned.

Seventh, he organises, with the assistance of subordinate officers, in-service training courses for departmental officers, in order to update their knowledge and keep them abreast of the latest techniques pertaining to the Department.

Eighth, he has to carry out departmental research and experiment programme in order to effect improvement in department's technique of work.

Ninth, he has to accord sanctions to the officers for the attendance of conferences other than inter-state or Government of India.

Tenth, he has to earmark grants in accordance with the rules and make Budget reappropriations within the prescribed limits.

Eleventh, he is responsible for formulating first draft of the Directorate Budget.

Twelfth, he has to spell out departmental activities for the ensuing year at the time of formulation of Budget.

Thirteenth, he has to conduct inspections of the field agencies personally or through his Joint or Deputy Directors. For instance, the Director Higher Education, Haryana had earmarked Government Colleges for inspection purpose and comprehension of their problems on the spot to Joint, Deputy and Assistant directors (the latter only for insignificant colleges). A questionnaire used to be prepared at the Directorate and sent to the Principals in advance. Thus a full fledged account of the activities, the number of students or staff on rolls, the vacancies existing, the achievements of the 'staff and the students' during the preceding year and the problems confronting the institution could be prepared. Such visits of the officials were not treated as 'fishing trips' to embarrass the principals but as fact-finding and problem solving missions. It was a commendable device to develop rapport between Headquarters and Field agencies and help out the latter in sorting out problems on the spot or at least bringing them to the notice of the Director without unnecessary correspondence and adoption of 'through channel' dilatory procedures.[1]

Fourteenth, he gets organised Conferences and Seminars etc., for portraying the plans and projects for the uplift of the department and its renovation. The Directorate of Education in various states organised series of seminars in colleges and also conferences at university level to discuss New Education Policy during Rajiv Gandhi's era. The findings of such conferences and the outcome of deliberations in the seminars were consolidated in a report which was submitted to the Government. The Government's point of view on the New Education Policy was thus communicated to the Centre, with

[1]*The author retired as Joint Director Colleges Education, Haryana in 1987. Hence the above fact is quoted through personal knowledge and experience.*

modifications incorporated by the Secretary Education in the Directorate's Report.

Lastly, the Director looks into the Annual Confidential Reports submitted by the Field officers and endorses them if he agrees, and reverses or lowers the gradation, if he differs.

The functions enumerated above reveal that the Directorate plays a pivotal role in maintaining the efficiency of the department and providing an effective feedback. Proper implementation of the Departmental policy depends to a great extent, on conscientious and efficient functioning of the Directorate.

It may not be out of place to point out that some of the departments like P.W.D., Forests and Police do not have Directorates as such. They have technical persons or specialists as the heads of the departments. A Chief Engineer heads the P.W.D. Department. He is assisted by technocrats like Superintendent Engineers, XENs and SDOs. Likewise department of Forests is headed by the Chief Conservator of Forests. He is assisted by Direct Forest Officers. To quote another example, Director General of Police, heads the Police Department. He is assisted by Inspector Generals of Police, Superintendent of Police and Assistant Superintendents of Police. He functions directly under the Home Secretary. The officers of the latter department are however IPS personnel duly selected by the UPSC and trained in special Police Academy. They develop in the academy expertise to tackle the baffling law and order problems. However, they do not fall in the category of technocrats or specialists as is the case with those manning the department of P.W.D. (Public Works Department) or Directorate of Health and Education.

***

Centre-State Relations

The principles underlying our Constitution are a compromise between the demands of regionalism and local patriotism and the requirements of unitarianism. As a result, our Constitution has in it some of the characteristics both of federalism and unitarianism...it is federal in form with a pronounced unitary bias in certain circumstances." — ***D.N. Bannerjee***

CONTENTS: (A) Legislative Relations
(B) Administrative Relations
(C) Financial Relations

As already analysed in Chapter 1, Indian federal system is a unique mixture of the Federal and Unitary models. In the words of R.S. Gae, former Law Secretary of the Government of India, "Broadly speaking the structure of the Constitution of India is so unusual and so unique in itself that it is very difficult, if not impossible, to describe it concisely and at the same time precisely. However, it may legitimately be said that our constitution is neither purely federal nor unitary in character but is really a cross section or a mixture of the two structures though it leans more in favour of the federal rather than the unitary structure."[1]

The essence of federalism lies in the division of powers between the National Government and the State Governments. Within their respective spheres, both the Governments are supreme and their authority is coordinate. The conflicts of jurisdiction are to be resolved by the Supreme Court – an independent judicial tribunal. An analytical appraisal of various federations of the world reveals that the division of powers in each federation was envisaged in accordance with the peculiar political conditions prevailing in the country concerned. In USA for example, the sovereign states which were keen to federate did not like the Central Government to arrogate to itself superior position. Hence, they entrusted subjects of common interest to the Central Government retaining the rest with themselves. The framers of the American Constitution thus enumerated a list of legislative powers which were to rest with the Central Government and the Residuary powers were left to the states. The Canadian Constitution followed an antithetical policy feeling conscious of the Civil War in America in 1861. They opted for a strong Centre. They divided the subjects in two lists — Federal and Provincial, and the Residuary subjects were entrusted to the Centre. In this respect, Indian Federation bears close resemblance to the Canadian Federalism.

(A) LEGISLATIVE RELATIONS

The framers of the Indian Constitution followed the Canadian pattern though we have an additional list of 'concurrent subjects'. Article 246 of the Constitution divided the legislative authority between the Union and States in three lists — Union, State, and Concurrent. The Union list now comprises 99 (formerly 97) items and is the longest of the three. The Union Parliament alone makes

[1]*R.S. Gae : "Administrative Relations betweel the Union and the States". Jain, Kashyap and Srinivasan (eds): The Union and the States, p. 297.*

laws regarding these subjects in the Union List. Foreign Affairs, Defence, Banking, Currency Coinage, Union Taxes and Duties fall in this category. The State list comprises 61 (formerly 67) subjects. These subjects are of local interest and envisage diversity of legislation. Some of the more important subjects included in this category are — Public Order and Police, Local Government, Public Health and Sanitation, Agriculture, Forests and Fisheries, Education and Land Revenue. Though the Constitution entrusts exclusive jurisdiction to the State legislatures to make laws regarding the subjects enumerated in the State list, yet Articles 249-53 authorise the parliament to legislate on the State subjects. Articles 249 states, "if Rajya Sabha passes a resolution by a majority of all and 2/3 of the members present and voting that it is expedient in national interest that Parliament should make laws regarding a particular State subject, then Parliament will be empowered to legislate on the State subject, though maximum for one year. If however, the situation so persists, by another resolution, the period may be firther extended".

Article 251 specifies that the Union Law shall prevail over any State Law in the event of conflict between the two. Article 250 enables the Parliament to legislate regarding any matter in the State list during the operation of the proclamation of Emergency under Article 352 (1). The maximum period for which such a law can be in force is the period for which the Emergency lasts, and maximum six months beyond that period. Under Article 356 which relates to the breakdown of Constitutional machinery in the state, Parliament can legislate on the matters enumerated in the State list.

Article 252 specifies that if the legislature of two or more states pass resolutions that it is desirable to have a parliamentary law regulating any of the matters in the State list, it becomes lawful for the Parliament to make laws regarding that matter. Such laws can be made applicable to the other states as well if they pass resolutions to this effect. However, such laws can be amended and repealed as well but only by the Parliament. Article 253 authorises the Parliament to make any law for the whole or any part of the territory of India for the implementation of treaties and international agreements of which India is a party.

The above facts make it clear that the states are not vested with exclusive jurisdiction over the subjects assigned to the states in the State list.

As regards Concurrent list, it originally consisted of 47 items of common importance viz., Marriage, Divorce, Civil and Criminal law, Newspapers, Books and Printing Presses, Adulteration of foodstuffs etc., etc. The 42nd Amendment Act 1976 inserted four new entries : 17A, 17B, 20A and 33A. Thus forests, protection of wild animals and birds, population control, family planning, weights and measures were further added in this list. Presently, there are 52 items in this list. Both the Parliament and the State legislatures are empowered to make laws regarding matters in the Concurrent list. In case of a conflict, the will of the Centre prevails. If the law passed by the state legislature on a Concurrent subject had already received the assent of the President of India on being so reserved, it will prevail over the Central law unless the parliament passes a new law overruling the provisions of such a state law. According to Pylee, *"The Concurrent list is like a twilight zone as it were, for both the Union and the States are competent to legislate in this field without coming into conflict."*[1] No doubt, the possibility of encroachment is reduced to minimum by providing for a Concurrent list incorporating matters over which conflicts of jurisdiction are likely to arise. The Concurrent list comprises matters having varying degrees of local and national interests. Pylee has rightly portrayed the concurrent list as a "*shock absorber which enables both the Union and the States to go beyond their own exclusive legislative spheres, as necessity arises so as to meet exigencies without transgressing the boundaries of each other.*"[2] The Concurrent list was devised to serve as a device to avoid the excessive rigidity of a two list distribution', which created two watertight compartments.

[1] *M.V. Pylee : op. cit., p. 257.*

[2] *Ibid.*

The Residuary subjects not specifically mentioned in the three lists, have been vested with the Centre, a clear departure from the practice prevalent in USA, Switzerland and Australia. This reflects leanings of the Fathers of the Constitution towards a strong Centre.

Thus an analysis of distribution of powers between the Centre and the states reveals that a strong centre was envisaged with a capacity to thrust its will on its units by means of its qualified legal sovereignty. The state legislatures have been entrusted a truncated area of authority and even that has been further truncated by empowering parliament to make more and more encroachments upon the legislative domain of the states. Besides, comparatively unimportant subjects have been put in the state list. V.K. Rao remarks, "a mere glance at the State list shows how important the subjects are and also how ambiguous and blurred."[1] In fact the plan of the distribution of legislative powers clearly reflects a strong tendency towards high degree of centralisation — a product of realism and a general tendency towards centralisation in all conspicuous federations. Besides, under exceptional circumstances, the parliament can encroach upon State subjects. This is done in keeping with the national interests or during the Emergency when Parliament is empowered to enact legislation regarding the state subjects when treaties and international agreements are to be implemented. The critics denounce it as a 'deviation from a strictly federal pattern and attempt to embody unitaryism in a federal form.'

The Centre has unreluctantly taken recourse to the encroachments through invocation of the various articles strengthening it at the cost of the states. Through special resolution, the Rajya Sabha exhibited the keenness of the Centre to meet acute food shortage problem by adding a new item in the Concurrent list through 'third constitutional Amendment Act 1954. The item is "trade and commerce and the production, supply and distribution of (*a*) the products of any industry where the control of such industry by the Union is declared by a law of the Parliament to be expedient in the public interest; (*b*) foodstuffs including edible oil seeds and oils; (*c*) cattle fodder; (*d*) raw cotton and cotton seeds and (*e*) raw jute.

The provision of Presidential Veto on state legislation is also an impairment of states' autonomy. In fact, when a Bill already passed by the state legislature is scrutinized by the Government of India and does not become an act till President accords his assent, the whole federal system seems to be in jeopardy. Pandey has rightly expressed his apprehensions thus, "*the whole frame of the federal constitution falls if the President is pleased to take a more active part in the consideration of State Bills.*"[2] In fact the Centre has been dictating its policies to the states though President has not been frequently resorting to the device of withholding his assent to the Bills. Thus the scheme of distribution of legislative powers reflects a strong tendency towards a high degree of centralisation. It is apprehended by the well-meaning critics that *excessive centralisation may sooner or later lead to apoplexy at the centre and anemia at the circumference.*

(B) ADMINISTRATIVE RELATIONS

Though the areas of administrative/executive authority of the Union and the State have been clearly defined, the latter have become subservient to the former on account of colossal power of direction, superintendence, direction and control entrusted to the Central Government. Hence, the myth of the so called state autonomy stands exploded. D.D. Basu opines, "*...the success and strength of the federal polity depends upon the maximum of cooperation and coordination between the governments.*" The framers of the Constitution incorporated detailed provisions to avoid clashes between the Centre and the States in the administrative domain and meet all possible eventualities for the smooth functioning of federal mechanism of government. Coordination between the Centre and the States was envisaged through (*a*) Techniques of Union Control over the States and (*b*) Inter State Comity.

[1]*V.K. Rao : Parliamentary Democracy of India (Ed. 11), p. 318.*

[2]*R.P. Pandey : The Presidential veto over State legislation in SAH Haqqi (ed.) Union State Relations in India, p. 101.*

Techniques of Union Control over States

During emergencies, Government of India exercises complete control over the states and virtually reduces them to mere political appendages. Even in the normal circumstances, the Centre possesses adequate authority over the states. Its control over the states is exercised through various agencies and varied techniques as under : (*a*) Governor; (*b*) Directions to the State Governments, (*c*) Grants-in-aid (*d*) Inter State Councils, (*e*) Inter-State Commerce Commission, (*f*) Immunity from Mutual Taxation.

Through the Governor

Governor — a nominee of the Centre — heads the State. He is to keep the President informed of constitutional functioning of men and matters in the state objectively. In fortnightly reports to the President, he makes an assessment of various events in the State and furnishes his views on various matters. After 1967, when coalitional era dawned in the states and political stability became the *sine qua non* of the state politics, Governor's report to the President was meaningful. His report formed the basis of decision about the future of the state. The Centre could improve deteriorating administration of the states through his assessment of the situation, eventually leading to the takeover of the state's administration by the President under Article 356. In certain cases, Governor acted as a tool of the Central Government, often indulged in undue pinpricking and ultimately manoeuvred the end of the popular rule in the states. Examples of Haryana, Kerala, West Bengal, Gujarat and Tamil Nadu can be cited to prove the case. The example of former Governor of U.P. (Shri Romesh Bhandari) recommending President's rule in October 1998 and President K.R. Narayanan turning it down by asking the Cabinet to reconsider it and in September 1998, the ex-Governor of Bihar (Shri Bhandari) recommending invocation of Article 356 in the State and President turning it down eventually, shows the Governors' high handedness and virtually dancing to the tune of Central Cabinet. It is thus evident that the Governors acting as the agents of the Centre have enabled the latter to maintain its supremacy over the states. On December 15, 1992, the end of BJP Governments in the states of Himachal Pradesh, M.P. and Rajasthan through the commanded acts of the Governors at the instance of the Centre confirms this contention.[1]

The annual conference of the Governors with the President provides an occasion to the Centre to get a candid report on the conditions prevalent in the states and to discover the impact of the Central policies at the State level. However, Governor can play the right role when Delhi stops treating Raj Bhavan as Central outposts and Governors look for guidance from the Constitution and not from the Union Home Ministry. In the words of Vepa, "*Such conferences may not be productive of any immediate policy decisions but none the less they enable the Central and State administrations to take stock of each other and to evolve policies in the light of such knowledge ... and apart from the purely formal conferences much is gained at the social 'Get together' that invariably attend such a conference through informal talks and discussions.*[2]

Directions by the Union

The idea of Union conveying the directions to the States was adopted by the framers of our Constitution from the Government of India Act 1935 "in view of the peculiar conditions of this country and particularly circumstances out of which the federation emerged."[3] According to Article 256 the executive power of every state is to be exercised in a way as to ensure compliance with the laws made by the Parliament. Besides, the Union Government can give such directions to the States

[1]*Hindustan Times dated December 16, 1992.*

[2]*K. Ram Vepa : Administrative Consultation Formal and informal — an article in Journal of Public Administration July-Sept., 1970, p. 423.*

[3]*D.D. Basu : Introduction to the Constitution of India, p. 263.*

as it deems fit. Dr. B.R. Ambedkar was of the view that without this power vested with the Centre, the proper execution of the laws passed by the Parliament would be impossible. Article 257 specifies that every state is called upon not to impede or prejudice the executive power of the Union in the State. If a Union agency fails to function within a state, the Union Executive can issue proper directions to the State Government to remove all obstacles. In two specific matters, Union power of issuing directions extends to — (*i*) the construction and maintenance of means of communication which are of national or military importance; (*ii*) the protection of railways within the state. It may not be out of place to point out that this power of giving directions does not, in any way, affect the power of the Parliament to declare highways or waterways or the power of the Union to construct and maintain means of communication as part of its functions with respect to travel, military or air force works. The states are, however, compensated for the extra cost incurred by them for following the Centre's directions.

The Constitution prescribes a coercive sanction for the enforcement of such directions through Article 356 which empowers the President to proclaim Emergency, dismiss State Governments and assume to himself functions of the state. This has been repeatedly done by the Governors on the instance of the Central Government.

The 42nd Constitution Amendment Act 1976 empowered the Centre to deploy its forces to maintain law and order in any state by inserting Article 257-A. The forces were to act on Centre's direction and not the State Governments. The 44th Constitution Amendment Act 1978 omitted this article though entry of 2A in List of the VIIth schedule was still retained. Entry 2 A dealt with the deployment of any armed force of the union or any other force, subject to the control of the Union, in any state, in aid of the civil power. In the course of discussions on this Amendment Bill, the then Home Minister Giani Zail Singh stated, "even in the event of communal riots and atrocities on Harijans the Union Government would be competent to deploy armed forces of the Union without awaiting the request from the State Governments." This further tightens the noose of the Centre around the State Government's neck. The forces were deployed in Ayodhya by the Centre to save the Babri Mosque from demolition at the hands of *Kar Sevak*s on December 6, 1992 though the latter suceeded in their union.

Delegation of Union's Function

Article 258 empowers the Union Executive with the consent of the State Governments to entrust to that Government or its officers functions which fall within this purview of Union Executive's functions. Parliament also can entrust powers to or impose duties on state officers through any of its laws which are applicable in a state. However, the Union Government is required to foot expenses on the postings of such officers. According to Article 255A inserted in the Constitution by the Amendment Act 1956, the Governor may, with the consent of the Government of India or its officers, function in relation to any matter to which the executive power of the State extends. In a way, the Constitution makes a provision for inter-level delegation of functions.

Article 355 empowers the Union Government to protect every state against external aggression and internal disturbance and to ensure that the Government of every state is carried on according to the Constitution.

All India Services

Though two separate services, one for the Union and the other for the states exist, yet there are certain services common to both. They are termed as All India Services. Indian Administrative Services and Indian Police Services are common services to the Union and the States. Article 312 enjoins upon parliament to create more of such services even when it deems it expedient. Recruitment to these services is made by UPSC — a central body which lays down minimum uniform standards of recruitment for All India Services. Their conditions of service are also regulated by the Central rules and regulations and their ultimate responsibility lies with the Government of India. Dr. B.R. Ambedkar remarked, "*The Constitution provides that without depriving the states of their right to form their own civil services there shall be an All India Service recruited on all India basis with common qualifications, uniform scale of pay and members of which alone could be appointed to these strategic posts throughout the Union.*"

Up to 1967, a few IAS officers could not adjust with the State leaders. Some of them were prone to maladministration as well, but majority of them justified the objectives for which they were created viz., to foster national integration and combating parochial and local needs. After 1967, political scenario changed, coalition era ushered in. It was strongly apprehended that the IAS, "*may fail to adjust well to the fast changing political landscape of the state especially where coalition Cabinets are collapsing like house of cards.*"[1] In such a situation they can play moderating role as well by projecting the justified demands of the States before the Centre and likewise convince the State that the Centre will not tolerate more than the specified limit. They can smoothen the work as negotiators and coordinators of Centre and State relations. Besides, they constitute a device to exercise control over the State Government in a manner that they do not run in flat contradiction to the spirit of the Constitution or the important national policies."[2]

Grants-in-aid

Article 275 of our Constitution empowers the parliament to extend such grants-in-aid as it deems necessary. Such grants-in-aid to the states help the Union to remove inter-state disparities in financial resources which obstruct the all-round development of the country and welfare schemes of the states on the national scale. Such grants are chargeable on the Consolidated Fund of India. The Constitution provides for specific grants on two matters viz., (*a*) schemes of development for the Welfare of Schedules Tribes and for raising the level of administration of Scheduled Areas as may have been undertaken by a state with the approval of the Government of India; (*b*) for the state of Assam for the development of Tribal Areas in that state. Grants-in-aid serve as a political source of Central control and direction. However, these grants-in-aid have apronstrings attached to them which curb the already truncated economy still further.

Inter State Council

The President of India has been empowered to establish an Inter State Council in the public interest and define its nature of duties. Such councils as per constitution, have following important duties : (*i*) To enquire into and advise upon the disputes which may occur among the States; (*ii*) to investigate and discuss subjects of common interest between the Centre and the States or between two or more States *inter se*, eg., research in such matters as agriculture, forestry, public health; (*iii*) to make recommendations for coordination of policy and action relating to such subjects. A Central Council of Health and Central Council of Local Self Government have already been established by the President for effecting coordination of policy amongst the States. An Inter State Council was established in April, 1990. It was composed of six Union Cabinet ministers and the Chief Ministers of all the states. The Council had its second meeting on October 6, 1996. In fact it could not do anything substantial. However, in this meeting it proposed to the Government to amend the controversial Article 356 as suggested by Sarkaria Commission. Such a Council can smoothen the relations between the Union and the States or between the two or more states. The main recommendations of this Council were : (1) More freedom to the states — financial and functional. (2) Constitutional amendment of Article 356. (3) Demand for greater autonomy for Jammu and Kashmir. (4) Reorientation of Planning Commission. (5) Provision for institutional framework for

[1]*C.P. Bhambri : Indian Federalism and Indian Administrative Services — an article in Indian Journal of Public Administration, July-Sept., 1970, p. 327.*

[2]*Amal Ray : Inter Governmental Relations, pp. 10-31.*

Centre-State consultations and conflict resolution.

Inter State Commerce Commission

Article 37 of the Constitution empowers the Parliament to set up such an authority as it deems appropriate for enforcing the provisions of Constitution with regard to inter-state trade and commerce and entrust to it such duties as it thinks fit. Such an authority in India is analogous to the Inter-State Commerce Commission of the U.S.A.

Immunity from Mutual Taxation

The smooth working of a federal form of government necessitates the immunity of the property of one Government from taxation by another. The mutual immunity from taxation saves, to a large extent, fruitless labour in assessment, calculation and cross accounting of taxation between the two governments. Article 285 (1) specifies that the property of the Union shall be exempt from all taxes imposed by a state or by an authority within a state. In case of the property of the state, it is specified that not only the property but also the income of a state is exempted from Union Taxation. Parliament is, however, authorised to tax the income of a state derived from a commercial activity.

Inter-State Comity

The federal Constitution generally lays down certain rules of comity which the units take into consideration while dealing with each other. These rules relate to — (*i*) Recognition of the public acts, records and proceedings of each other; (*ii*) extra judicial settlement of disputes, coordination between states; (*iii*) freedom of inter-State trade, commerce and intercourse. A brief explanation of these matters will not be out of place.

(*i*) *Recognition of Public Acts.*

Article 245 (1) states that jurisdiction of each state is to be confined to its own territory. Obviously, it created apprehensions that the acts and records of a state might not be recognized by another state. Hence a provision for compelling such recognition was incorporated in the Constitution. Article 261 (1) provided, "Full faith and credit shall be given throughout the territory of India, to public acts, records and judicial proceedings of the Union and the State." Article 301 too, specifies that final judgments or orders delivered or passed by the civil courts in any part of India are executable in all parts of India according to law.

(*ii*) *Extra Judicial Settlements of Disputes*

Article 131 provides for the judicial determination of disputes between states by empowering the Supreme Court with the exclusive jurisdiction in the matter. Article 262 provides for the adjudication of such disputes by an extra-judicial tribunal. Parliament may, by law, provide for the adjudication of any dispute or complaint regarding the use, distribution or control, of the waters of or in any inter state river, or valley and also provide for the exclusion of the jurisdiction of all courts including the Supreme Court to entertain such disputes. Inter-State Water Disputes Act 1956, establishes an *ad hoc* Tribunal for adjudication of any such dispute. Article 263 provides for the prevention of inter-state disputes by the establishment of Inter State Councils. The President can establish such a council in the public interest, whenever he deems fit. The President exercised this power by establishing the Central Council of Health and Central Council of Local Self Government. The States Reorganisation Act, 1956 established Zonal Councils for advising on matters of common interest to each of the five Zones in which India had been divided. They discuss matters of common concern of the states and territories comprising each zone. For example, economic and social planning, border disputes, inter-state transport, matters cropping up out of reorganization of states are taken up by these councils. The River Board Act 1956, provided for the establishment of a River

Board for advising the Governments interested in relation to the regulation or development of an inter-state river or valley.

(*iii*) *Freedom of inter-state trade, commerce and intercourse.*

Article 19 guarantees freedom of movement and residence throughout the territory of India. Articles 301-307 provide for free flow of commerce and intercourse as between different states without any barrier. The provisions of these articles deal with both inter-state and intra-state freedoms. In other words, subject to a few exceptions provided in these articles, no restrictions are imposed upon the free flow of trade and commerce and intercourse between one state and the other or in between any two points within the territory of India. Article 307 authorises the Parliament to establish such authority as it considers fit for enforcing the provisions of the Constitution regarding inter state trade and commerce and entrusts to it such duties as it considers necessary.

Constitutional Arrangements for Consultation

The National Development Council is the highest institutional arrangement for consultation between the Central and State governments. It consists of all the chief ministers of the States and the heads of the Union Territories, the Union Cabinet ministers and also the Prime Minister who is the *ex-officio* chairman of the Council. It is the forum of the highest level for discussions on all vital matters affecting the Centre and the States. It helps the Centre and the States' executives to have face to face discussions on problems of great importance. In the case of states where the ruling party is different from that at the Centre, it serves as the only forum for such discussions.

Group discussions at Party Conferences

Party conferences or meetings comprise another forum for consultation as far as the Chief Ministers of the ruling party are concerned. Most of the C.M.s are on the Working Committee or Parliamentary Board of the Congress Party and all are on A.I.C.C. The meetings of these party bodies provide an opportunity for discussions of problems affecting individual States. Some specific matters viz., a river water dispute or a border quarrel between two or more states are discussed in such meetings and settled then and there. The P.M. and other ministers of the Central Government have been unreluctantly taking interest in settling the issues which fall in the jurisdiction of the State Governments. In the words of Santhanam, "*The Indian Republic started with a contradiction. While the Constitution established a federal system of government, all the political parties existing at the time, it came into force, were unitary and highly centralised. This was particularly the case with the Congress.*"[1] Nehru's leadership and the hegemony of a single party both at the Centre and in the states in the initial decade were responsible for Centre's dominating control over the States. The Kamraj Plan which prompted the Chief Ministers of the States to place their resignation in the hands of the Prime Minister illustrates the overwhelming influence of Pt. Jawahar Lal Nehru upon the regional leaders.

Planning Commission

National planning reinforces centralization of the Central Government over that of the States. Planning Commission of which P.M. is the *ex-officio* chairman and a Deputy chairman who has the status of Cabinet minister, constitutes an important vehicle through which broad policies are translated into administrative schemes and are incorporated in state plans. Through frequent consultations with the state officials and the concerned ministers, it reviews the implementation of the plans and takes into consideration the bottlenecks and problems encountered in practice and endeavours to

[1] *K. Santhanam : Political Parties of India, The White Star, Vol. VI, July 1969.*

find suitable policy solutions for such problems. It results in a constant, two-way dialogue to be maintained between the Centre and the States and between political and administrative cadres.

Ad hoc Commissions

The ad hoc Commissions are appointed from time to time for specific matters concerning both the Centre and the States. For example, Finance Commission which is appointed once in 5 years, renders advice to the Union Government on the allocation of revenues between the Centre and the States. The Administrative Reforms Commission appointed in mid-sixties touched almost every aspect of Centre-State relationship. The States Reorganization Commission earmarked administrative boundaries of the constituent states. The Sarkaria Commission announced by PM. Mrs. Indira Gandhi on March 24, 1983 was appointed to review the existing arrangement between the Centre and the States. If its report submitted on October 20, 1987 is implemented fully and sincerely, it can smoothen the relation between the Centre and the recalcitrant states. In view of its recommendations, Inter State Council was established in the recent past,[1] The Sarkaria Commission recommended that the whole country be divided into six zones and each should have its Zonal Council. The North Eastern Council set up under the North Eastern Council Act should be converted into the Zonal Council for the area. All the Zonal Councils should have same functions and powers.

Another important recommendation of the Sarkaria Commission pertained to the appointment of Inquiry Commission. No commission should be setup against a former state minister on charges of the abuse of authority unless both the Houses of Parliament by a majority of vote requires the government to do so. The Commission could be appointed if the minister concerned requested in writing for its appointment. It also suggested that appropriate safeguards should be incorporated in the Commission of Inquiry Act, 1952 against the public misuse of power in the appointment of Commission of Enquiry.

It recommended that the State Governments should be dissuaded from using their power of transferring, promoting, posting and suspension of All India Officers just to discipline them. They suggested appointment of an Advisory Council for personnel administration of the All India services with the Union Cabinet Secretary as its Chairman, to advise the Union and the State Governments and suggest solutions to the problems referred to by the Central and State Governments.

It went to the extent of suggesting that invocation of Article 356 should be resorted to, very rarely. Further, Planning and its implementation should be a cooperative process between the Centre and the States. S.B. Chavan – the then Home Minister of India – in Question Hour before Lok Sabha, assured that the Sarkaria Commission's, recommendations will be taken after the Inter State Council sub-committee renders its final report....the Government's intention was very clear and it was very serious about implementation of the Commission's recommendations.[2]

Ministerial Committees

Each of the administrative ministries has a committee or a Board consisting of ministers and senior officials of the states and the Centre. The representatives of the states express their opinions candidly. Since such meetings are held under the chairmanship of the union ministry, the views of the ministers of the state are heard by those in charge of national policies. For example, Land Reforms and small Industries Development are in the domain of the State Governments but the Centre is required to intervene as the latter is keen for allotment of land to the landless and create new fields for their employment through the development of small scale industries. Hence the existence of ministerial committees can ensure healthy growth of the national economy.

The critics are, however, of the view that with the passage of time, the already limited autonomy

---

[1]*Article 263 also makes a provision for such Council.*

[2]*Hindustan Times dated December 4, 1992.*

of the states is being jeopardised by usage and sufferance. Hence the dismal prophets predict that if the centralising trends persist, the states' autonomy will be completely eroded and they would no longer be in a position to re-assert or regain their constitutionally conceived authority. Hence there have been currently cries for devolution of authority. The urge for 'greater say' in local affairs is reflected through the mounting demands, not only of state governments run by the opposition parties, but also the Panchayat Institutions.

Delivering the Maulana Azad Memorial Lecture on May 7, 1992 Ex President R. Venkataraman took note of divisive forces and growing demand for devolution of power and authority by the states. He suggested that the states be "accommodated if we were to hold in check the divisive forces in society." He emphasised, "*The Constitution of the country has to grow with the changing needs of society and absorb progressive trends so as to reflect the will of the people.*"[1]

In recent past, a political resolution moved by L.K. Advani at Antyodayanagar, Gandhi Nagar, on May 3, 1992 denounced the Congress Government at the Centre for creating a mess in Kashmir, Punjab, Assam and North Eastern States and suggested the appointment of a National Commission to study the decentralisation of political and economic powers. The Non Congress Chief Ministers also from time to time have been grouping to pressurise the Centre for more legislative and financial autonomy. The U.P. chief minister had time and again sounded a note of warning to the Centre for threats of unposing Presidential rule under Article 356 on frivolous pretexts as it would entail dire consequences. Very recently, Bihar Chief Minister took the same plea when President's rule was recommended. Even President K.R. Narayanan asked the Central Cabinet to reconsider the recommendation. Finally the recommendations were withdrawn on September 22, 1998.

It is therefore prudent to take stock of the situation, note carefully the fast changing moods of the people in the various parts of the country and take steps to restore faith in the minds of the people of the States who are fully conscious of ever rising hegemonic role of the Centre. However, the erring states which strike at the roots of fundamental principles of secularism, national integrity or peace and amity should not be given so long a rope that the foundations of our hard won independence are shaken. The dismissal of BJP Government in U.P. on December 6, 1992 for its failure to protect the Ram Janambhoomi Babri Masjid structure from extensive damage and causing a severe blow to the concept of secularism is an instance of State Government's deliberate inaction.[2] A prompt action by the Centre in the crying need of the hour and reflect an apt use of central intervention for controlling the erring state Similar action was contemplated in Bihar in February, 1999 when law and order seemed to be repeatedly at stake. Even the Lok Sabha accorded approval to the President's Rule but the Bill could not be taken to Rajya Sabha for want of the requisite majority. Hence President's rule was revoked. It raises a question mark as to whether or not Article 356 will be used impartially and if invoked even rightly, will it get the approval of the opposition if it commands majority in either of the two Houses. In fact, this article has been mostly invoked by the Centre whenever political expediency so necessitated. L.K. Advani, ex President of BJP described non intervention of the Article in U.P. despite barbarities at Muzzafar Nagar on October 2, 1994 as 'constitutional double-standard'.[3]

(C) FINANCIAL RELATIONS

There is no denying the fact that if the legislative and administrative authority of the states is to be a reality rather than a formality, they must be autonomous financially as well. However, this principle of federation remains only a figment of imagination in most of the existing federations of the world U.S.A. being no exception. D.D. Basu comments "*No system of federation can be successful unless both the union and the states have at their disposal adequate financial resources*

[1]*Hindu (New Delhi) May 8, 1992.*
[2]*Hindustan Times dated December 7, 1992.*
[3]*Ibid, October 9, 1994*

to enable them to discharge their respective responsibilities under the Constitution." In case of India, the framers of the Constitution recommended the retention of the existing distribution of resources of revenue as laid down under Government of India Act 1935 for initial five years after which Finance Commission was required to review the position. The Constitution made a provision for the appointment, within two years of the inauguration of the Republic or thereafter at the expiration of every fifth years or earlier of a Finance Commission. The Commission was to recommend to the President the requisite changes to be effected in the distribution of taxes between the Union and the States and also define the principles on which the Union Government was to extend Grants-in-aid to the states. In a way, the Constitution introduced a unique element of flexibility while tackling the distribution of public revenues. In fact, the provision of a Finance Commission for this purpose is an innovative step in the Indian Federation. The first Commission was setup in November, 1951 and the second on April 2, 1956. The recommendations of both these Commissions were accepted by the Government. The Third Finance Commission asked for enhancement of its functions so that the total financial assistance to the states could be augmented. It is being increasingly realized that political autonomy of the states is next to impossible if fiscal autonomy is negated. Financial decentralization is as important as political autonomy. In fact, both supplement each other. In the words of Adarkar, "*Freedom of operation must be extended to both the federal and state governments in order that they do not suffer from a feeling of cramp in the discharge of their normal activities and the achievements of their legitimate aspirations for the promotion of their social and economic achievements.*"[1]

So far, Twelve such Commissions have been appointed. It may be pointed out that the Finance Commission makes recommendations to the President who is required to place such recommendations before each House of the Parliament. The recommendations are not, however, binding upon the Government though their non-implementation can result in gross dislocation in the states as the latter might be tempted to spread in anticipation of flow of money from the Centre as per Commission's report. Such a situation can cause embarrassment. The operational period of the 12th Finance commission is, 2005 to 2010. These commissions are brought into existence to (*a*) make recommendations on the devolution of the tax revenues and provisions of grants to the states for 5 years; (b) tø study the various aspects of centre-state financial relation as done earlier; (c) to determmine the question of grants-in-aid to the states and to recommend measures to reduce the indeletedness of the states; (d) to review the formula fixing the states share of central tax reserves at 29 percent.

The Centre and State Relations in the domain of finance are evident from the following factors : Allocation of Revenues, Grants-in-aid, Borrowing authority, Financial emergencies and the office of Auditor and Comptroller General.

Allocation of Revenues

The distribution of sources of revenue between the Centre and the States is based on the scheme laid down in the Government of India Act 1935. The States and the Union, possess exclusive jurisdiction over the proceeds of taxes enumerated in the State and the Union Lists. The Concurrent List does not include any tax. While the proceeds of the taxes within the State List are exclusively retained by the states, the proceeds of some of the taxes in the Union List are or may be earmarked wholly or partially for the states. Four Union Taxes which can be wholly or partially assigned to the states are as under :

(*i*) Duties levied by the Union but collected and wholly appropriated by the states such as stamp duties in respect of bills of exchange, cheques, promissory notes, bills of lading, letters of credit, policies of insurance, transfer of shares, debentures, excise on medicines and toilet preparations containing alcohol.

[1] *B.P. Adarkar : The Principles and Problems of Federal Finance, p. 219.*

(*ii*) Taxes levied and collected by the Union but whose net proceeds are wholly assigned to the states, such as duties in respect of succession to property other than agricultural land, estate duty in respect of property other than agricultural land, terminal taxes on goods and passengers carried by railway, sea or air; taxes on railway fares and freights; taxes other than stamp duties on transaction in stock exchanges and future markets; taxes on the sale and purchase of goods in the course of inter-state trade and commerce.

(*iii*) Income tax is levied and collected by the Union but is shared between the Union and the States, after deduction of sums attributable to the Union Territories and to the Union emoluments.

(*iv*) Taxes which are levied and collected by the Union but whose net proceeds are shared between the Union and the States. Union Excise duties other than those on medicinal and toilet preparations fall in this category. This division of taxing power has made the states dependent upon the Centre and lean heavily on the latter. In the words of Chanda, *"...But whatever be the reason, the distribution has given the Centre the resilient and expansible sources of revenue and given the states the inelastic and even eroding sources of revenue."*[1]

Grants-In-Aids

The constitution provides for three types of Grants-in-aid to the states from the Union resources:

(*i*) The States of Assam, Bihar, Orissa and West Bengal are extended grants in lieu of export duty on jute and jute products.[2] The amount of such grants is earmarked by the President. These sums were payable to the states till the export duty on jute and jute products continued to be levied by the Government of India or till the expiry of 10 years after the installation of the Republic, whichever is earlier.

On July 2008 Dr. Manmohan Singh P.M. released a thrilling document 'North Eastern Region vision 2020' emphasising that the capitals of all North Eastern State would be linked by rail. Air ports are being modernized and new ones are being built. 31,000 Rs. crores is being invested in 2008, 11th Plan Period (2007-12). This is a big financial assistance by the Centre for the development of the road which is indispensable part of Infrastructural development in the region. The financial involvement of the centre in the North Eastern states, infrastructural development is thus self evident. Besides rural and agricultural development in these states is envisaged. He stated : a second green revolution specific to the region' is required."

To quote a recent example, the P.M on August 26, 2008, reviewed the issues concerning the development, security and welfare of the people of Assam and announced a package of measures for all round development of the state – (a) The Centre will provide additional assistance of Rs. 250 crores for the proposed integrated development of the Bodoland territorial council. Flood control measures for integrated development of Majuli will be given high priority and adequate finds will be given Rs. 20 crores additional central assistance for Matuli was made available. (b) The Centre promised to provide assistance for setting up a centre of the Rajiv Gandhi Institute of Petroleum Technology in Assam and a National Institute of Design in Guwahati on the pattern of NID in Ahmedabad (e) Financial assistance was promised for the inception of state level University of Technology and a Law school and Judicial Academy.

Likewise P.M announced Rs. 1010 crore package for Flood hit Bihar on August 28, 2008. In addition on september 15, 2008 the Union Rural Development ministry announced assistance package of Rs. 1600 crores for the flood affected people of Bihar. Rs. 11, 200 crore project was sanctioned by the Centre for. connecting Kashmir with the rest of the country. On October 11, 2008 Kashmir was put on the rail map of India when PM flagged off the first ever train in the Kashmir valley at Nowgam station in the outskirts of Srinagar.

---

[1] *Institute of Constitutional and Parliamentary Studies : Union-State Relations in India, p. 138.*

[2] *Article 273.*

Exemption from taxation

In this respect also, Government of India Act 1935 was the guiding factor for the framers of the Constitution. The Act exempts the property of one Government from taxation by another. According to Article 285 unless the Parliament otherwise provides, Union's property is not subject to taxation by the state. Article 287 prevents a state from imposing tax on electricity supplied to the Government of India or a Railway unless permitted to do so by the Parliament. Article 288 specifies that without the consent of the President, a state may not tax water or electricity supplied or controlled by the authority established for regulating or developing any inter-state river or river valley. Article 289 exempts the property and income of a state from Union Taxation. Such an exemption does not extend to trade or business carried on by the Government or state, unless Parliament by law declares such trade or business incidental to the ordinary functions of the Government.

Power of Borrowing

The Union is equipped with unlimited power of borrowing upon the security of the revenues either within India or outside it, subject to such limits as may be fixed by Parliament from time to time.[1] The borrowing power of a state is subjected to certain limitations viz., (*i*) It cannot borrow from outside India; (*ii*) It can borrow within the territory of India, upon the security of the revenues of the state subject to conditions as under. (*a*) Limitations may be imposed by the state legislature. (*b*) If the Union has guaranteed an outstanding loan to the state, no fresh loan can be raised by the State without the consent of the Union Government. (*c*) Government of India itself may sanction a loan to the State under a law made by the Parliament. So long as such a loan or any part thereof remains outstanding, no fresh loan can be raised by the state without the consent of the Government of India.[2] The Union Government can wave the loan or increase its limit for any section of people in the country. On May 23, 2008 loan package was increased by 20 per cent to give relief to the farmers. The scheme was implemented by end of June, 2008.

Financial Emergency

Article 360 refers to Financial Emergency powers of President of India. While proclamation of Financial Emergency is in operation, the President may direct that for a period not exceeding 'beyond the expiration of financial year in which the proclamation ceases to operate, all or any of the provisions concerning the division of taxes between the Union and the States and grants-in-aid shall be suspended'.[3] During the course of such an order by the President, the States will have to bank upon their narrow resources from the revenues under the State List, without any financial assistance from the Centre.

Secondly, during the proclamation of Financial Emergency, the Union Government will be competent to give directions to the states to (*a*) observe such canons of financial propriety and other safeguards as may be specified in the directions; (*b*) reduce the salaries and allowances of all persons serving in the state, including the judges of the High Courts; (*c*) reserve for the consideration of the President all Money Bills after they are passed by the legislatures.[4] The critics denounce Article 360 as a means of establishing Centre's hegemony over the states. H.N. Kunzru feels that these provisions would lead to the "financial autocracy of the centre."[5] Biswanath Das remarked, *"the States might be treated like charity boys of the 'North block of the Secretariat."*[6]

[1]*Article 292.*
[2]*Article 293.*
[3]*Article 354.*
[4]*Article 360.*
[5]*Constituent Assembly Debates, Vol. IX, Part 13, p. 510.*
[6]*Ibid Part 6, p. 210.*

Control by the Comptroller and Auditor General of India

The Comptroller and Auditor General of India is appointed by the President of India and is entrusted such duties and vested with such powers in relation to the accounts of the Union and the States and of any other authority or body as Parliament may prescribe by law.[1] The accounts of the Union and the states are to be maintained in such form as the President may, on the advice of the Comptroller and Auditor General of India prescribe.[2]

1967 and Its Aftermath

As already said, 1967 General Elections ushered in the coalitional era in some of the states putting an end to the dominance of the Congress in these states. The Union and Non-Congress parties run states' relations got strained. The core of the disputes has been mostly the meagre resources kept at the disposal of the states. Before 1967 also, some of the chief ministers of the Congress too had felt the crunch and often subdued whispers used to be heard about the inadequacy of their financial resources. However, they could not be courageous enough to protest loudly. The 1967 General Elections shook the monolithic Congress rule in the states. The Non-Congress Governments in these states ceased to feel subservient to the Centre. They refused to agree on national priorities and laid down socio-economic programmes of their own, caring not the least for the paucity of their resources. Namboodiripad raised the banner of revolt in Kerala and sought redefinition of Centre and state relationship. DMK did not lag behind in Madras and the United Front in West Bengal followed suit. The Rejamannar Committee appointed by Non Congress Tamil Nadu Government in 1971 made drastic recommendations for effecting financial devolution in India. It suggested that major part of the Union Government's power of taxation should be transferred to the states and the states should be vested with the power of individual licensing, except for industries of national importance or of all India character or which have a capital of Rs. 100 crores. It also recommended the reduction of the Central control over the planning programme in the states. The Central Government, however, ignored the report of this committee.

Surprisingly, some of the Congress Governments in the states also asked for the revision of financial provisions. The Administrative Reforms Commission in its report submitted on June 19, 1969 also stated that the main grievances of the states in the Indian federation lay in the financial field and recommended that Finance Commission instead of Planning Commission — an extra constitutional body — established by an executive order of the Centre, should be entrusted the responsibility of formulating the principles governing the allocation of plan grants. Besides, they stated that the excessive dependence of the states on the Centre has tended to produce irresponsibility and operational inefficiency. Hence, in the interest of smooth relations between the Centre and the states, the degree of financial dependence of the states on the Centre should be reduced to the minimum. Chanda remarks, "Union-state relations have now reached a stage in which intermingling of resources and functions will no longer work smoothly. It is best to have a clear cut division. This will insulate the Centre from demands and compliance and give the states freedom to shape their own destinies on an assured quantum of devolution and such resources as they themselves are prepared to mobilize. They will not be able to point a finger at the Centre as now for their lapses and they will be fully accountable to their people for their performance — good, bad or indifferent."[3]

It may, therefore, be suggested that the states may be assigned by the Centre 95 percent of the Income Tax and 70 percent of the Excise Duties. The Grants-in-aid system which has been the main source of pinpricking should be dispensed with. That may bring the states on sounder financial footing and conflicts between the Centre and States may come to an end. Besides, a more balanced,

[1]*Article 149.*

[2]*Article 50.*

[3]*The Institute of Constitutional and Parliamentary studies – Union and State Relations in India (1969 ed) p.143.*

rational and mature approach by the political parties holding power at the Centre and in the states can be useful in redressing the grievances of the states run by parties other than the one in power at the Centre.[1] The Centre should also shed the display of strongmanship when a state assumes deliberately a recalcitrant attitude.

Conclusion

An analytical appraisal of relations between the Centre and the states in the Indian Federation makes the critics conclude that the Indian states have been reduced to mere glorified municipalities. In case of the rule of the same party both at the Centre and the states, the government of the latter dances to the tune of the former. In case of two different political parties being at the helm of affairs at the Centre and in the states, pinpricking and occasional conflicts occur, eventually resulting in triumph of the overpowering Centre and a curb on the autonomy of the states. It induced Mr. Rao to remark, "We were a unitary state with the states functioning as agents of the Central Government as was the case under the British rule.. I know of no federation where its constituent units are so heavily, dependent on the federal Government as they are in the so called Indian Federation."[2] Whatever the case, movements in the directions of more and more autonomy for the states need not be encouraged as they would lead to dismemberment of a united India at no distant future and history may repeat itself. We may become playthings of the foreign invaders. Hence, the crying need of the hour is to achieve national integration and avoid divisive and fissiparous tendencies so far as possible. Cries of Bodoland in Assam, perpetual struggle for liberation and independence of Kashmir,* recently camour for Telengana dismembering Andhra and Centres" cemdnod it resulling in demands for many small states like surkha land voderline are the eye-openers and a constant deterrent against weak and unstable Centre or its fluctusting policies ponibly resulting in disintegration of the country at no distant fuline. The growing trend towards a more perfect union may not be impeded, keeping in view the fast changing conditions in social, economic and political spheres which play a prominent role in tilting the federal balance definitely in favour of the centre and standing as a formidable mark of the evolution and establishment of a lasting and perfect union."[3]

The union/government is not, however, oblivious of the cravings of some of the states. The Raja-manaar committee report of 1971, the Anandpur Sahib Resolution of 1973, the West Bengal resolution of 1977, the proceedings of the Regional Council attended by southern non-congress chief ministers and also proceedings of 17 opposition partis conclaves all have made a number of proposals for restructuring the union-states relations. A former Home Minister affirmed in the Lok Sabha that more powers should be given to the states. He expressed seriousness of the Union Government regarding implementation of the Sarkaria Commission's recommendations. He categorically stated that 120 out of 247 recommendations of the Commission had already been processed by the sub committee (composed of Chief Ministers and Central Ministers) and its report will be placed before Inter State Council.[4] This statement before the House was reflective of the intentions of the then Government.

The dismissal of the BJP Governments in Rajasthan, Himachal Pradesh and Madhya Pradesh, on December 15, 1992[5] by procuring more or less identical reports in 24 hours from the Governors not only looked as a commanded performance[6] but a clear violation of the guidelines laid down by

[1] *Ibid p. 144.*

[2] *V.K.R.V. Rao : Journal of Constitutional and Parliamentary Studies, Vol. VIII, No. 4 October, December 1974, p. 537.*

* *Demand of Uttarkhand resulting in violence at Muzaffarnagar on October 1-2, 1994, Hindustan Times, Oct. 2-3, 1994.*

[3] *J.D. Duchacek : Comparative Federalism : The territorial dimensions of Politics, p. 343.*

[4] *Hindustan Times dated December 4, 1992, p. 9.*

[5] *Hindustan Times, December 16, 1992.*

[6] *Ibid dated December 17, 1992 (Editorial).*

the Sarkaria Commission. The latter wanted Article 356 to be used in the event of political crisis, internal subversion, physical breakdown or non compliance with the directives of the Union Government. None of this happened in these states. It has been a big setback to Centre-State relations particularly when two different political parties ruled at the Centre and in the States. "It is difficult to accept the contention that there was a breakdown of constitutional machinery in these states."[4] Dismissing the State Governments on the plea that the chief ministers of these states had links with banned R.S.S. organisation and as such their sincerity in enforcing the ban order was doubtful, makes the mockery of the whole issue as "to dismiss governments on the basis of mere suspicion is to go against constitutional propriety."[1]

This unfortunate episode though motivated with an idea to protect our secular fabric of polity proved assertions of the then Home Minister rather exaggerated and contrary to the noble intentions of the Union Government expressed before an august representative body of the nation on December 4, 1992. In the coalitional era of United Front Government, the sinister article was not misused except once and that too proved to be a futile attempt on account of President's bold intervention. The BJP Government has been vehemently opposed to the imposition of President's rule by invoking article 356, due to the persistent pressure of its coalitional partners. But its attempts in Bihar were foiled once by the President of India and second time due to the lack of BJP majority in the Rajya Sabha. Let us hope, the popularly elected governments in the states are not toppled down and democracy is no longer strangulated as per the whims of the Central Government or its attempt to save its own sinking ship.

Sarkaria Commission on Centre and State Relations

The Sarkaria Commission appointed a June 9, 1983 by Prime Minister Indira Gandhi submitted to the Government on October 31, 1987 and summary released on January 29, 1988 stated :

(*i*) A strong Centre is indispensable to preserve the unity and integrity of the country.

(*ii*) It advised the Centre to make sparing use of powers under Article 356. It denounced dismissal of State governments in 1977 and 1980 and recommended that justifying factors should be mentioned in the Proclamation of President's Rule.

(*iii*) The Centre must consult the Chief Minister of the state before appointing a Governor.

(*iv*) The Centre should consult the State before deploying the army.

(*v*) It recommended a process of consultation by the Centre in all concurrent subjects.

(*vi*) An Inter-State Council under Article 263 be set up.

(*vii*) Constitution be amended for providing sharing of Corporation Tax between the Centre and the States.

(*viii*) An expert committee be set up to examine taxation reforms and revenue mobilisation.

The Home Minister, in course of debate in the House, expressed willingness to examine the Report and set up Inter State Council. He also assured the House to reactivate the Zonal Councils for resolving inter state disputes. He described the report as "document based on mature judgement". During Narasimha Rao's tenure as P.M. (till 1996) Article 356 was not misused to destabilize and scrap the ministries formed by the opposition. AB Vajpayee, the NDA P.M. led by BJP refused to oblige its political ally — AIADMK's supremo Mrs. Jayalalitha by refusing to dismiss DMK Government in Tamil Nadu. Thus the atmosphere seemed quite ripe to amend the article to avoid its misuse. In the words of eminent lawyer and former union minister of Urban Affairs (Ram Jethmalani) "Its misuse can only be prevented by amending it."[2]

---

[1]*Ibid.*

[2]*Hindustan Times, July 9, 1998.*

On December 19, 1998 the Standing Committee of Inter State Council failed to arrive at a consensus on providing safeguards against the misuse of contentious Article 356 of the Constitution. Hence it appointed a four member sub-committee to make an indepth appraisal of this vital issue.[1] The sub-committee comprising C.M.s of Andhra Pradesh, Orissa, U.P., and West Bengal, under the chairmanship of Defence Minister was required to appraise deliberations of the previous meeting of the committee. The Inter State Council deliberations were, however, useful, valuable and constructive.[2]

The UPA Government had in its Common Minimum Programme (CMP) promised to set up a panel on centre-state relation in 2004. In September 2006 under the chairmanship of a retired Judge of the Apex Court the panel was set up. It had few other members, former Home Secretary Dharmendra Singh being its secretary. The Panel was asked to appraise the complexities which cropped after the ushering in of coalitional era in the country. The challenges were posed to healthy relationship due to Naxalism described as sub nationalism, liberalised market economy and a plethora of WTO and intellecutal property issue. Hence the panel was exhorted to furnish its report with in two years after due consultations with the institute of socio-economic change, Institute of Public Finance, the National Council of Applied Economic Research. They were told togather the suggestions of cross section of society viz Industry Association, NGO, media representatives and Central and State Government functionaries[3]. All these steps reflect the great concern of the Centre for the welfare of even for flung states which have remained backward and seek emergent development and security safeguarding them from the menace of terroristic attacks by the Naxalities and the terrorists, the infiltrators and so called Jehadis" for the liberalism of state like J & K.

***

[1] *Ibid, December 20, 1998.*

[2] *Ibid, Home Minister's remarks after the meeting of the Inter State Council and also its sub-committee.*

[3] *Hindustan Times September 26, 2006. p.13.*

PUBLIC SERVICES

The civil servants are partners in a joint enterprise and one has only to consider what would happen without either of them. Without the official element being there, the representative element would be futile and actually ineffective to carry out its views. Without the representative element, the official administrators would turn out to be aimless." — ***W.A. Robson***

CONTENTS:
(A) Historical Background of Public Services in India
(B) All-India Services
(C) Central Civil Services
(D) State Services
(E) Local Civil Services
(F) Public Service Commission
(G) Training of Civil Services

Public Administration is management of public affairs by civil servants who constitute public services or civil services. No well thought-out and well-planned policies can succeed without competent public services to execute the work. Even the best organisations based on scientific principles are liable to have breakdown without them. In fact, no activity of public administration can be performed without civil servants. The days of *laissez-faire* are gone now. Under the impact of science and technology, the activities of the State have multiplied. At every step, the citizen comes into contact with the civil servant who is the "sovereign factor in public administration." In the words of Prof. Robson, "*The Civil Servants are partners in a joint enterprise and one has only to consider what would happen without either of them. Without the official element being there, the representative element would be futile and actually ineffective to carry out its views; without the representative element, the official administrators would turn out to be aimless.*"[1]

(A) HISTORICAL BACKGROUND OF PUBLIC SERVICES IN INDIA

The history of public services in India may be tracked back to the 'Rule of the Company Bahadur' which had been granted a charter by Queen Elizabeth in the year 1600 giving to it the exclusive rights of trading to all parts of Asia, Africa and America, beyond the Cape of Good Hope and eastwards to the Straits of Magellan. India, at that time, was being governed by the Mughal rulers. The Company gradually acquired territories and its position changed from that of the tenants of factories, owing obedience to the Mughal Emperor, to one of the practical and independent sovereign. The civil servants of the Company who used to run the trade of the Company, became administrators when the Company acquired territorial possessions and the authority to govern them. The term 'civil servants' was used to make a distinction between those engaged in trade overseas and others performing duties in naval or military spheres. The condition of the civil servants under the Company's rule was quite bad. They were not well-paid which was the cause of several abuses.

[1]*Quoted by C.P. Bhambri, "Public Administration in India", p. 57.*

The services were classified as 'covenanted' and 'uncovenanted' and were manned by the Europeans. The 'covenanted' services denoted the higher services created by a law of the Company, whereas the 'uncovenanted' referred to 'inferior posts' created otherwise. By the first quarter of the 19th century, Indians practically occupied no post in the public service.

The Select Committee of the British Parliament was convenqed in 1831-32, to investigate into the East India Company's affairs and the Indian administration. The Committee observed that the exclusion of Indians from higher posts was not "so warranted" on the score of incapacity for business or the want of application or trustworthiness. The Committee further said, that admitting Indians to higher services, "*would have a beneficial effect in correcting the moral obliquities of their general character, would strengthen their attachment to British domination, would conduce to the better administration of justice, and would be productive of a greater saving in the expenses of the Indian Government.*"[1]

Accordingly, the Charter Act of 1833 included a clause which read, *"No native of the said territories shall be, by reason only of his religion, place of birth, descent, colour, or any of them, be disabled from holding any place, office or employment under the Company."* The Macaulay Committee, appointed in 1853, strongly recommended the open competition system for recruitment to civil services. It recommended the age of 18-23 years for admission to the tests. The examination was to be held in London. Consequently, the first examination under the new system for recruitment to Indian Civil Services was held in 1855.

With the assumption of direct responsibility for the Government of India by the Crown in 1858, the Secretary of the State-in-Council was empowered to regulate appointments to the Indian Civil Service. In 1886, a Commission headed by Charles Aitchinson, the then Lieutenant Governor of the Punjab, was appointed "to devise a scheme which may reasonably be hoped to possess the necessary elements of finality, and to do full justice to the claims of the natives of India to higher and more extensive employment in the public service. It may be remarked that prior to 1886, the maximum age for admission to the Indian Civil Service examination was reduced thrice — in 1860 it was lowered to 22 years; in 1864 it was reduced to 21 years and in 1878 it was further reduced to 19 years. Obviously, it was not practically possible for the Indians to appear in the said examination at such a lower age, go all the way to London for the purpose and stay there to satisfactorily complete the period of probation in England. This led to the demand for the Indianization of services. The Aitchinson Commission, in its report submitted in 1888, recommended that the services should be divided into three categories — Imperial, Provincial and Subordinate. The recruitment to the first category was to continue, as before, in England; however, recruitment to the other two categories was to be made by the provincial governments; partly through recruitment and partly through promotion from the subordinate services. It recommended that the age be raised to 23 years. The Commission did not favour the idea of holding the competitive examination simultaneously in London and India.

The Islington Commission (1912-1915) recommended the amalgamation of the Imperial and Provincial sections in central departments into a single service divided into two classes, a higher and a lower one. The Montford Report, 1918 recommended that the association of Indians in the administration should be increased and the examination should be held simultaneously in England and India. It also laid down that 33 percent of the higher Indian Civil Services be filled by the Indians and this should follow an increase of one and half percent. As regards other Services, the same procedure was to be adopted.

The Government of India Act, 1919 decentralized administration by transferring certain subjects to the provinces placed under popular control, described in political parlance as 'dyarchy'. At that time, there were nine All India Services viz., Indian Civil Service, Indian Police Service, Indian

[1]*Parliamentary Papers, Volume 8 of 1031-32, p.2.*

Forest Service, Indian Educational Service, Indian Agricultural Service, Indian Civil Veterinary Service, Indian Forest Engineering Service, Indian Medical Service (Civil), and Indian Service of Engineers. Appointments to these services were made by the Secretary of State. The Act provided for the establishment of the Public Service Commission to conduct examinations in India for recruitment to the All-India and Central Services. However, with the transfer of power to the provinces, the propriety of All India Services was questioned. Accordingly, the Royal Commission on the Superior Services in India, under the chairmanship of Viscount Lee of Fareham, was appointed in 1923 to examine the issue of All India Services and other matters like Indianisation of services.

The Lee commission submitted its report in 1924 and made the following main recommendations :

(1) No further recruitment should be made for provincial Governments, particularly in the transferred fields, namely, the Indian Educational Service, the Indian Agriculture Service (Civil), the Indian Veterinary Service, The Roads and Building Branch of the Indian Service of Engineers and Forest Service in Bombay. The personnel required for these services should in future be recruited and appointed by local governments.

(2) The other All India Services viz., Indian Civil Service, Indian Police Service, Irrigation Branch of the Indian Service of Engineers, Indian Medical Service, Indian Forest Service (except Bombay) should be retained and controlled by the Secretary of State.

(3) Twenty percent of the superior posts should be filled by promotion from the Provincial Service. Direct recruitment should provide equal share to Indians and Europeans so that a 50:50 cadre should be produced in about fifteen years. For the Indian Police Service, direct recruitment was to be made on the basis of 5:3 among Europeans and Indian, respectively, and the remaining 20 percent were to be obtained by promotion from the Provincial Service. For the Indian Forest Service, it was to be in the ratio of 75 and 25 percent respectively, and, for irrigation it was to be in an equal ratio of 40 percent each, with the remaining 20 percent to be filled by promotion from the Provincial Service.

(4) The British officers should have the freedom of retirement on proportionate pension if at any time the Department in which they had been employed should be placed under the control of the concerned ministers.

The recommendations of the Lee Commission were accepted by His Majesty's Government though the Commission did not fully operate in its recommendations the principle that responsibility should be matched by authority. The retention of Indian Medical Service and the Indian Service of Engineers as All India Services was clearly in violation of this principle since medical matters and PWD were provincial subjects. A section of Indian public opinion was opposed to the retention of the institution of All India services. R.K. Shanmukham Chetty, a member of the Central Legislative Assembly observed that "*An all-India Service with extraordinary privileges is an anachronism in any system of provincial responsible government, and, we could add, is a violation of the spirit of the Government of India Act of 1919.*"[1]

So, now onwards, the main issue and the subject of controversy was the question of retention of All-India Services. The nationalists considered the institution of All-India Services an anachronism in the emerging political set up wherein the provinces had come to possess a measure of self-government, though limited. The nationalist members of the Reforms Enquiry Committee, set up by the Central Government in 1924 'ventured' to think that "*under the present system the entire constitution, the methods of recruitment and control of the services are incompatible with the situation created by the Reforms (of 1919) and the possibility of their further developments.*"[2] Likewise, the nationalist members of the Indian Central Committee (1928-29) constituted by the Central Government to liaison with the Indian Statutory Commission, pressed for provincialisation

[1]*Legislative Assembly Debates, Vol. IV, Part V, p. 3261.*
[2]*Report of the Reforms Enquiry Committee, p. 163.*

services are provincialised and all officers are placed under the Ministers." The Committee appointed in 1929 by the United Provinces Legislative Council to cooperate with the Indian Statutory Commission remarked, "...we hold that the retention of these (*i.e.*, all-India) services in a system of full provincial autonomy would unnecessarily complicate matters."[1] The retention of all-India Services was also opposed by some Indian members of the Sub-Committee constituted by the first Indian Round Table Conference. Hafiz Hidayat Hussain argued, "The great objection, which to my mind seems to be insuperable, is that we are going to have provincial autonomy, and if every subject is going to be transferred to the administration of the Legislative Council, the retention of the Indian Civil Service and the Indian Police Service is, to my mind, fraught with considerable difficulties and inconveniences." It may be of interest to know the views of Dr. B.R. Ambedkar, who said, "*We are framing a Constitution in which we propose to give as large a degree of provincial autonomy to the provinces as possible, and it seems to me that no province can be deemed to have provincial autonomy if it has not the right to regulate the civil service that is going to work in its area.*"[2]

However, the Joint Committee on Indian Constitutional Reform did not accept the viewpoint of the Indian nationalists. It recommended the retention of Indian Civil Service, the Indian Police Force and Indian Medical Service as all-India Services. The Government of India Act, 1935 accepted the recommendations which found expression in section 244 of the Act which read, "(1) as from the commencement of Part III of this Act, appointments to the Indian Civil Service, the Indian Medical Service (Civil), and the Indian Police Service (which last mentioned service shall hereafter be known as "The Indian Police") shall until (British) Parliament otherwise determines, be made by the Secretary of State." The Act also provided for the establishment of a Federal Public Service Commission, Provincial Commissions and a Common Commission for two or more Provinces and continued the protection which the civil servants had enjoyed earlier.

At the time of transfer of power in 1947, there were only two All India service viz., the Indian Civil Service and the Indian Police Service as recruitment to other all India services viz., Indian Medical Service, Indian Forest Service and Indian Service of Engineers was suspended when Provincial Autonomy was provided under the Act of 1935. Besides, there were various Central Services divided into Class I and Class II, subordinate and inferior. In the provinces, the classification was between Provincial Service Class I and Class II and the subordinates (sometimes divided into upper and lower), and the inferior.

The question of having all-India Services again became a matter of controversy when in 1946 the independence of India appears to be in sight. The national leadership which had earlier opposed the retention of All India Services under the Government of India Acts of 1919 and 1935, now favoured the continuance of the old pattern of Civil Services. The arguments advanced were the obvious importance of maintaining the highest possible standards of efficiency, of giving the civil service 'experience at the centre leading to efficiency, and administrative experience of the district' of serving as 'a liaison between the provinces and the Central Government,' and of introducing, both in the provinces and in the Centre, 'a progressive and wide outlook, and freshness and vigour of administration.' However, it was not easy for Mr. Vallabhbhai Patel, the Home Member in the Indian Government, to get the approval of the provinces for the proposed All-India Services, the Indian Administrative Service which was to replace the Indian Civil Service and the Indian Police Service. The Unionist Party in Punjab under the leadership of Sir Khizar Hayat Khan declared "Punjab is one of the provinces which would prefer to have a superior service of their own instead of the all India administrative service under contemplation for this purpose".[3] Sind and Bengal also

[1]*Report of the Committee, pp. 104-105.*

[2]*Report of the Joint Committee for Indian Constitutional Reform, Vol. I, (Part I), para 296.*

[3]*The Hindu, 25 October, 1946, p. 4.*

of the all India administrative service under contemplation for this purpose".[3] Sind and Bengal also expressed similar views. Even Govind Ballabh Pant opposed the idea of all-India services with unusual force. A 'consensus' however, at the Provincial Premiers Conference was reached at for having these services for the first five years. But, soon events led to the partition of the country which cleared the way for the acceptance by all of the all-India services.

The drafting committee of the Indian Constituent Assembly did not originally provide a constitutional base to the all-India services. Explaining its view, the committee observed : "*The committee has refrained from inserting in the Constitution any detailed provisions relating to the services; the committee considers that they should be regulated by acts of the appropriate legislature rather than by Constitutional provisions, as the committee feels that the future Legislatures in this country, as in other countries, may be trusted to deal fairly with the services.*"[1] Vallabhbhai Patel wrote to Nehru on 27 April, 1948 : "*The draft Constitution does not provide for an all-India service. We will, therefore, have to make provision for these services...in the new Constitution.*"[2] Accordingly, the draft was amended and a new Article 282C was inserted providing for all India Service. Dr. B.R. Ambedkar addressing the Constituent Assembly said "...it is recognised that in every country there are certain posts in its administrative set-up, which might be called strategic from the viewpoint of maintaining the standard of administration...there can be no doubt that the standard of administration depends upon the calibre of the Civil Servants, who are appointed to these posts "*The Constitution provides that there shall be an all-India Service, the members of which alone could be appointed to these strategic posts throughout the Union.*"[3] The dominance of the Indian National Congress in the Constituent Assembly led it to accept the povisions relating to All-India Services without demur.

The public services in India are presently classified as below :

1. the All-India Services,
2. the Central (Union) Services, Class I
3. the Central (Union) Services, Class II
4. the Provincial (State) Services
5. the Specialist Services
6. the Central Services, Class III, and
7. the Central Services, Class IV,
8. the Central Secretariat Services, Class I, II, III and IV.

(B) ALL-INDIA SERVICES

As discussed above, the issue of All India Services has been a subject of controversy in the administrative history of India. With the establishment of responsible government in the provinces under the Government of India Act, 1919, the propriety of All India Services was questioned, but the Lee Commission did not favour the idea of abolition of these services. The nationalist leaders including even Dr. B.R. Ambedkar had also opposed their retention. However the Joint Committee on Indian Constitutional Reform did not accept the viewpoint of the Indian nationalists. After India gained independence and a new Constitution was being drafted for the country, the idea initially was to abolish the All India Services, yet the Constitution which ultimately emerged from the Constituent Assembly not only embodied reference to all India services, but also included provision for the creation of new All-India Services.

Articles 309 to 314 of the Constitution of India relate to the Services under the Union and

[1]*Draft Constitution of India, p. xi.*

[2]*Shiv Rao (ed.) The Framing of India's Constitution, Vol. IV, p. 332.*

[3]*Constituent Assembly Debate, Vol. IX, pp. 116.*

the States. Of these Articles, Article 312 needs special mention. The Article reads as under :

(1) Notwithstanding anything in Part XI, if the Council of States has declared by resolution supported by not less than two-thirds of the members present and voting that it is necessary or expedient in the national interest to do so, Parliament may by law provide for the creation of one or more all-India services common to the Union and the States, and, subject to the other provisions of this Chapter, regulate the recruitment, and the conditions of service of persons appointed to any such service.

(2) The services known at the commencement of this Constitution as the Indian Administrative Service and the Indian Police Service shall be deemed to be services created by Parliament under this article.

Need for All India Services

The all-India services are common to the Union and State governments and these are composed of the officers who are said to be in the exclusive employment of neither but who, at times, may be at the disposal of either. In a Federal polity, the Central Government and the Governments of Constituent States have usually separate services for the administration of subjects falling within their respective spheres of jurisdiction. The creation of all-India Services in our country is, therefore, something peculiar. The arguments advanced for continuance of these services are as under :

1. The members of All-India Services possess an all-India outlook which helps in national integration.
2. Being based on all-India recruitment, they attract the best talent in the country.
3. The members of all-India services are immune from local pressures and influences which reinforces their impartiality and integrity in administration.
4. They being common to both the Union and State Governments facilitate liaison between the two.
5. They can give independent advice to the ministers of the State Governments which the members of State services would hesitate to do.
6. In times of the failure of the constitutional machinery in a State, they would carry out the President's policies more effectively because they are under the direct control of the Union Government.

The above arguments, however, do not stand the scrutiny of examination. The argument that members of all-India service possess an all-India outlook is neither supported by logic nor borne out by actual experience. There is no necessary correlation between the recruitment to a particular service and an individual's outlook. All-India outlook is a cultural trait which is not peculiar only to the members of all-India Service. The three hours written examination and half an hour's interview can hardly find out the personality traits of the candidates. Personality is a complex phenomenon which cannot be so easily judged. To say that by merely being recruited on an all-India basis, a person comes to possess an all-India outlook is highly conjectural. Further, the members of State Services are also recruited on all India basis as the Constitution prohibits any discrimination on grounds of place of birth or residence in respect of any employment or office under the State.

On the other hand, experience shows that the members of all-India service, especially of the Indian Administrative Service, are very conscious of their separate identity, too conscious of their status and privileges and too resistant to sharing their privileged position with members of other services which has led to Generalist vs. Specialist controversy in the country. They are not prepared to visualise their role against the totality of operations. They are the victims of 'elitism' and do not show much emotional cohesion with the Indian culture. They are no less succeptible to regional, linguistic and other pressures than the members of State services.

The question arises what about the national outlook of the members of State Services promoted to all-India Services ? Would it be fair to brand them as parochial or provincial in their outlook on the ground that they were not initially recruited on all-India basis? National outlook is a positive process which depends more on one's education, cultural background, national ethos and various other social factors. To say that members of all-India service possess an all-India outlook vis-a-vis the members of state services is sheer ignorance. Again, an all-India outlook is of little avail when members of the all-India services are required under ministerial pressure to join in Centre-State or inter-State disputes, and prepare briefs and memoranda claiming for their State something under dispute — an oil refinery, or a public sector undertaking.

For leadership in administration, it is the State Civil Service which has to be depended upon more than the all-India Service. The members of all-India Service remain at the middle level positions for a short period only and this also at the start of their career. The considerable number employed at junior and middle level positions do not come into direct contact with the top men of the all-India services. It is the members of the State Civil Services who remain at the middle and supervisory levels for a long period and come in frequent contact with the majority of employees. It is, therefore, these members of State services that have to be utilised, if at all, for leadership purposes in administration.

It may also be pointed out that a large number of members of all-India services have aligned themselves with different political parties and pressure groups having lost thereby the so called all-India outlook. Otherwise, how do we explain the phenomenon of large-scale transfers of these members whenever political power changes hands. There is no denying the fact that cliques, caste, community, provincialism and parochialism play considerable part in the actual administration run by the bureaucrats of all-India services.

The second argument that all-India services attract the best talent available in the country is a myth. A majority of the candidates joining the all-India services are of average abilities, having graduated in the second division. Only a very small percentage who come at the top are among the best products of Indian Universities. Then, the candidates selected from the reserved categories are ordinary candidate without any merit except their caste character. The persons promoted from state services also form a part of all-India service. Thus, if we take into account the academic merit of the majority of 'general category' candidates, the candidates for reserved posts, and those promoted from state services, we could find the argument that all-India services consist of the best talent in the country to be factually unsound. Moreover, if the all-India Services are abolished, the available talent would be diverted to state services in preference to other forms of employment on account of the charms of government service as a career. The country's administration will not, therefore, suffer from want of talent if all-India services disappear.

The third argument that the members of All-India Services are immune from local pressures and influences which enables them to be impartial and independent is hardly tenable, as the Central Government is not free from political pressures and pulls. The political rulers of the Central Government come from the same source from where the political rulers of the state government come, and, therefore, it would be incorrect to ascribe political manipulations to the state level only. One of the serious charges against Indian bureaucracy is that it has become politicised and committed to the party in power. The concept of neutrality is today under great strain. There is large volume of empirical evidence to support the view that, in India neither civil servants strictly adhere to its principles; nor are the politicians intent on maintaining it.

There are other criticisms levelled against all-India services which are as follows :

1. These services are a hangover from the days of the British colonial rule and ought to have no place in independent India.
2. The States ought to have the right to recruit and control the civil service for the

performance of tasks which have been allotted to them under the Constitution. An All-India service violates the spirit of federation and curtails the autonomy of the states. At present, the Centre-State relations are under great strain, and the states are demanding more autonomy.

3. The all-India service System creates a sense of inferiority among the personnel of state services and has a demoralising effect on them. They are allotted lesser roles and get lower scales of pay. The senior positions in a State are held by I.A.S. people, the State personnel function in subordinate positions.
4. A person selected to an all-India service may not know the language of the adopted state which may make him an ineffective administrator and create a chasm between him and the masses.
5. In the present political setup when the monopoly of Congress rule in the states has broken down and a number of states are being governed by Non-Congress governments, the all-India services have become suspect in the eyes of such states. E.M.S. Namboodripad, the former Chief Minister of Kerala, once openly questioned the validity of the all-India services, the members of which 'are recruited and trained by the Congress Government at the Centre and posted to states in many of which there are non-Congress Governments.'
6. The I.A.S. officers feel both psychologically and emotionally closer to the Central Government, though they are borne on a state government's cadre. The disciplinary authority vests in the Central Government and prospects for better posting through deputation or otherwise lie within its competence. They are keen to go to Centre, unless they are residents of the states. Thus, their loyalty to the state always remains under suspicion.
7. The payscale of the All-India Services is higher than that of the State Civil Services. This not only creates discontent among the ranks of State Civil Services, through whom they discharge their functions, but also imposes heavier financial burden on the states, leaving them with correspondingly less resources for development tasks. Moreover, their payscales are revised by the Central Government which a state government has to enforce while it may not be able to raise the payscales of its own services. The state services get alienated from the All-India Services.

From the foregoing analysis, it is clear that the institution of all-India services has now lost its primacy. The arguments advanced in favour of their retention are not held valid both on the basis of logic and experience. The politicisation of these services and the idea of a 'committed' bureaucracy have made them suspect in the public eye. At a time when with the growth of a large number of regional political parties, and the emergence of regional leaders, the issue of Centre-State relations is getting hotter and hotter every day and the country is faced with the problems of regionalism and national integration, it may be useful to review the institution of all-India services. The federal structure of the country during the last four decades has suffered heavy strains, there is a demand for total revision of the Constitution. It would, therefore, be appropriate at this time to explore if the abolition of the All-India Services will cause any significant damage to the total administration of the country, if such an abolition can make our federal polity stronger and safer.

It may, however, be mentioned that Sarkaria Commission has opposed the move to disband the All-India Services and has rather emphasized the need for creation of more of them.

Indian Administrative Services

Article 312 of the Indian Constitution has specifically mentioned the Indian Administrative Service and the Indian Police Service to be the All-India Services and has further empowered the

Parliament to create one or more All-India Services on a resolution passed by the Council of States by not less than two-thirds majority of the members present and voting. The new All-India Services added are Indian Service of Engineers, Indian Forest Service, Indian Medical Service, Indian Foreign Service, Indian Economic Service and Indian Statistical Service. Of these various all-India services, the Indian Administrative Service is the most prestigious and attractive both from the point of social status and of promotional avenues right up to the administrative top. Although the present I.A.S. is the successor to the old I.C.S., however, there are some major differences between the two. First, the I.C.S. was a generalist, omnibus service. Its members used to man superior positions in all branches of the government, including, the judiciary. The I.A.S. has a limited area of operation. The technical departments are headed by members of technical services while the judiciary consists of members of judicial services. Second, there is no reservation of posts in the Central Secretariat for the I.A.S. people as it used to be for the members of the I.C.S. Third, the talent recruited to the I.A.S. is comparatively lower in merit than that in the I.C.S. In the I.A.S., even third divisioners have been recruited. The reservation on caste basis has caused a certain amount of qualitative decline in the I.A.S.

The Indian Administrative Service consists of the following according to Article 3 of the I.A.S. (Recruitment) Rules of 1954.

1. The former members of the I.C.S., excluding those permanently allotted to the judiciary. (The last member of the Indian Civil Service retired in 1979);
2. Those recruited to the I.A.S. through ad hoc selection after termination of the Second World War, hereafter referred to as 'War Service Candidates';
3. The candidates recruited during 1943-44 but who had not been selected because of a small number of vacancies during the said period, which is also described as "War Service";
4. Those who had been recruited from I.A. & A.S., Indian Police Service etc., on the assumption that they might have been selected to the I.C.S., through competition and had continued after 1943, also herein-after referred to as "War Service";
5. Those who had been selected under the Emergency Recruitment Scheme 1947-49 and the Special Selection Scheme of 1956-57, hereinafter called "I.A.S., (E.S.)",
6. The candidates selected from the Civil Executive Services under the Emergency Recruitment Scheme 1947-49, and through the Special Selection Scheme 1955-57 hereafter called "I.A.S. (P.E.)",
7. Those officers promoted from the State Civil Services through the criterion of 25 per cent reservation provided for them in I.A.S. quota. It would also include those who were from other than the executive services comprising 15 per cent of the 25 per cent promotion quota, hereinafter called "I.A.S. (P.P.)", and
8. Those who have been recruited through annual competitive examination since 1947, described as the direct recruits, hereinafter called "I.A.S. (D.R.)."

The entire strength of the Indian Administrative Cadre is now constituted by I.A.S. (D.R.) and the I.A.S. (P.P.). The selection for promotion from the State Civil Services to the Indian Administrative Service is made by a Committee constituted for each state, which consists of the chairman or a member of the Union Public Service Commission and other members drawn from the seniormost officers of the State Cadre of the Indian Administrative Service. They prepare a list of officers of the State Civil Service suitable for promotion to the I.A.S. The list is made on the basis of "merit and suitability in all respects with due regard to seniority." Eight years minimum service qualifies for selection, but a junior officer may be placed in the list over a senior one, if he has exceptional merit. The list is forwarded by the State Government to the Union Public Service Commission for approval. Promotions are made from this approved list as vacancies occur.

As the I.A.S. is an all-India service, it is under the joint control of the Centre and the states and its members are divided into State Cadres. The ultimate control rests with the Central Government but immediate control is exercised by the State Government to which a member has been assigned. The strength of each State Cadre is fixed in such a way as to include a reserve of officers who can be deputed to the Central Government under the tenure system. While fixing the strength of a State Cadre, consideration is given to the number of superior administrative posts above that of the district Collector/Deputy Commissioners (Divisional Commissioners, Members of the Board of Revenue and Secretaries in administrative departments), all posts of district Collectors/Deputy Commissioners, and those of heads of offices with provision made for a reserve of officers for deputation to the Central Government. The strength and composition of each of the Cadres is determined by the Central Government in consultation with the State Governments. It need hardly be mentioned that the I.A.S. cadre has been continually expanding because of the increasing activities of the state to accelerate socio-economic development.

Recruitment

The direct recruitment to the Indian Administrative Service is made through a competitive examination held annually by the Union Public Service Commission. Any citizen of India holding a graduate degree of any of the Universities incorporated by an Act of the Centre or State Legislature in India or other Educational Institutions established by an Act of Parliament or declared to be deemed as a University under Section 3 of the University Grants Commission Act of 1956 or possessing an equivalent qualification can appear in the examination. The age limit is 21 to 28 years (raised to 30 years w.e.f. the 1999 recruitment), with four attempts being allowed, which is relaxable up to a maximum of five years if a candidate belongs to a Scheduled Caste or a Scheduled Tribe.

Prior to June, 1979 examination, a single competitive examination was held. The syllabus consisted of three compulsory papers, viz., Essay, General English and General Knowledge, each carrying a maximum of 150 marks. Out of a number of optional papers, three papers of 200 marks each and two additional papers (I.A.S. and I.F.S. only) out of another list of subjects carrying 200 marks each were to be offered. The candidates who qualified in the written examination, were called for interview which carried 300 marks.

The candidates who failed to secure a minimum of 33% of qualifying marks in the interview were declared a failure, no matter how high they might have scored in the written test. In 1958, however, the system of minimum qualifying marks at the interview was done away with. Whatever marks a candidate secured in the interview, began to be added to the marks obtained in the written examination. Thereafter, the Commission recommended the list of the selected candidates in order of merit to the government.

There had been a growing dissatisfaction with the above method of recruitment. To suggest changes in the methods of recruitment, the Union Public Service Commission appointed in 1974 a Committee on Recruitment and Selection Methods under the chairmanship of D.S. Kothari. The Committee submitted its report in March, 1976. The main features of Kothari Report are:

1. A preliminary examination to screen the candidates for the main examination;
2. The main examination to select candidates for entry to the National Academy of Administration (Mussoorie) for a foundation course of about 9 months;
3. Post-training test of 400 marks to be conducted by the UPSC on completion of the foundation course to assess personal qualities and attributes relevant to the civil services. In this test, the trainees will be interviewed by a board constituted by the UPSC and marks assigned to each candidate.
4. Assisgnment to a particular service to be done on the basis of the total marks obtained in

the main examination and the post-training test, taking into account the candidate's preference for the services.

5. The candidate to be allowed to answer all the papers, except of the language one, in any language listed in the eighth schedule of the Constitution, or English.

In December 1978, the Government accepted the examination scheme recommended by the Kothari Committee. The U.P.S.C. conducted the 1979 examination according to the new scheme. Thus the examination for recruitment to the Indian Administrative Service is now conducted in two stages (i) Preliminary examination, and (ii) Main examination.

The **Preliminary examination** consists of two papers of objective type (multiple choice Questions) and carries a maximum of 450 marks. The two papers are :

Paper I	General Studies	150 marks
Paper II	One subject to be selected from the list of optional subjects.	300 marks

The optional subjects are Agriculture, Animal Husbandry and Veterinary Science, Botany, Chemistry, Civil Engineering, Commerce, Economics, Electrical Engineering, Geography, Geology, Indian History, Law, Mathe-matics, Mechanical Engineering, Philosophy, Physics, Political Science, Psychology, Public Administration, Sociology, Statistics and Zoology.

The question papers are set both in Hindi and English. The course content of the syllabi for the optional subjects is of the degree level. Each paper is of two hours duration.

The purpose of preliminary examination is to weed out candidates who are not competent enough for the main examination for it is through a device like this that the main examination can be made manageable and meaningful. Today, more than one lac candidates apply for the Civil Services and obviously it is senseless to administer the main examination to such a large number when only about 600 are to be selected. The screening test can only be of an objective type so that it is quick and easy to identify those who have the capability for the main examination.

A Critical analysis Delhi High Court Decision Sept 3, 2008. The candidates who failed to pass preliminary exam have been feeling restive on UPSC system of concealing the marks of the candidates. The UPSC in fact published the list of candidates who qualified for the Main Examination. Thus, the rest of the applicants were automatically declared as failure. It was highly disgusting for the candidates who used to fail and who even did not know their marks. The candidates invoked Right to Information. The UPSC did not agree to reveal the marks. The case went up to Central Information Commission (CIC). The latter decided in favour of the students. They held 'The candidates had the right to know the marks secured by them in the Preliminary Test of the Civil services. The UPSC filed an appeal against the decision of CIC asking the former to disclose the marks scored by 100 candidates (who had moved CIC in Novermber 2006) in the Delhi High Court.

The Delhi High Court rejected the contention of the UPSC which argued that details like cut off marks, individual marks and model answers were top secret and their revelation would amount to violation of intellectual property rights". It also expressed apprehension that I A S coaching academies/centres *would misuse such information'*.

The Division Bench of High Court on September 3, 2008 rejected the contention on the plea that the 'answer papers were not of such a nature that can be categorised as secret or of a type the disclosure of which would not be in public interest. It also held that scoring methodology was already in the public as the UPSC in an affidavit to the Apex court had already done so. Hence, UPSC fear that it will compromise the merit was unfounded. They remarked "the whole procedure having preliminary, main and then interview is to ensure that only meritorious candidates are selected for government services." Justice B. D. Ahmed also observed UPSC being a public body was required to act and conduct itself in a fair and transparent manner. Access to information ought to be provided by a public authority even when it is otherwise entitled to withhold the same if public interest in disclosure outweighs the harm to protect interests. The appeal of UPSC was then dismissed. This is a land mark judgement and enable the candidates to know where they stand.

The **main examination** consists of two parts : a written examination and an interview. The written examination consists of the following papers :

Paper I	One of the Indian languages to be selected from the languages included in the Eighth Schedule of the Constitution.	300 marks
Paper II	English	300 marks
Paper III & IV	General Studies	300 marks
Paper V	Essay	200 marks
Papers VI, VII VIII, IX	Any two subjects from the list of optional subjects, each subject has two papers.	300 marks for each paper.

The papers on Indian languages and English are of matriculation or equivalent standard and are of qualifying nature; the marks obtained in these papers are not counted for ranking.

The paper on General Studies and optional subjects of only such candidates are evaluated as attain such minimum standard as may be fixed by the Commission in their discretion for the qualifying papers on Indian Languages and English.

The optional subjects for the Main examination are : Agriculture, Animal Husbandry & Veterinary Science, Anthropology, Botany, Chemistry, Civil Engineering, Commerce and Accountancy, Economics, Electrical Engineering, Geography, Geology, History, Law, Management, Mathematics, Mechanical Engineering, Philosophy, Physics, Political Science and International Relations, Psychology, Public Administration, Sociology, Statistics and Zoology, Literature of one of the following languages — Arabic, Assamese, Bengali, Chinese, English, French, German, Gujarati, Hindi, Kannada, Kashmiri, Marathi, Malayalam, Oriya, Pali, Persian, Punjabi, Russian, Sanskrit, Sindhi, Tamil, Telugu, Urdu. Thus it will be seen that while the list of optional subjects for the Preliminary examination consists of 21 subjects, that for the Main examination consists of 25 subjects. The three additional subjects of Anthropology, Management and Literature are not included in the list of optional subjects for Preliminary examination. For the students of Public Administration it will be interesting to know that Public Administration was included as a full subject at the Preliminary test and the Main examination in 1987 only.

The candidates are not allowed to offer the following combinations of subjects :

(a) Political Science and International Relations and Public Administration;

(b) Commerce and Accountancy and Management;

(c) Anthropology and Sociology;

(d) Mathematics and Statistics;

(e) Agriculture and Animal Husbandry & Veterinary Science;

(f) Management and Public Administration;

(g) of the Engineering subjects, viz., Civil, Electrical and Mechanical not more than one subject.

The question papers for the examination are of conventional (essay) type. Each paper is of three hours duration. Candidates have the option to answer all the question papers, except the language papers vis. Paper I and II above in any one of the languages included in the Eighth Schedule to the Constitution or in English. The question papers are set both in English and Hindi. The Commission has the discretion to fix qualifying marks in any or all the subjects of the examination.

Candidates are allowed four chances at the examination. Scheduled Caste and Scheduled Tribe candidates are however, allowed to take the examination without any restriction on the number of chances, subject, of course, to the prescribed age limits. The number of attempts for OBC candidates is seven.

The number of candidates to be admitted for the Main examination is about ten times the total number of posts to be filled up. These candidates who obtain the minimum marks as are fixed by the Union Public Service Commission in the Preliminary examination are allowed to appear at the Main examination.

The candidates who obtain such minimum qualifying marks in the written part of the Main examination as may be fixed by the Commission are called to an interview for a personality test. The **interview** carries 300 marks (with no minimum qualifying marks.) The candidates are interviewed by the Board. In order to expedite the process of recruitment, four/five Boards are setup for interviewing the candidates. To ensure uniformity, the membership of each Board is changed from time to time, so that each member of the Board could participate in the deliberations of the different Boards setup for the interview.

The object of the interview is to assess the personal suitability of the candidate for a career in public service. The test is intended to judge the mental calibre of a candidate. In broad terms, it is really an assessment of not only his intellectual qualities but also social traits and his interest in current affairs. Some of the qualities to be judged are mental alertness, critical powers of assimilation, clear and logical exposition, balance of judgement, variety and depth of interest, ability for social cohesion and leadership, intellectual and moral integrity. The technique for the interview is not that of a strict cross-examination but of a natural though direct and purposive conversation which is intended to reveal the mental qualities of the candidate. Candidates are expected to have an intelligent interest not only in their special subjects of academic study but also in the events which are happening around them both within and outside their own state or country as well as in modern currents of thought and in new discoveries which should a rouse the curiousity of well-educated youth.

After the interview is over, the rank-order list is prepared on the basis of the total marks secured in the Main examination and the interview, by the successful candidates. The allocation of the candidates to different services is made on the basis of their rank in the test and preferences. The list is submitted by the UPSC to the Department of Personnel for further necessary action.

Criticism of the New System

The new system of recruitment to the Indian Administrative Service introduced in pursuance of the Kothari Commission's Report is not without defects. *First,* the conduct of all-India examination in 18 regional languages will result in gradually impairing the national unity which already stands on last legs. Communalism, provincialism and linguism are raising their ugly heads. The crying need of the hour is unity and solidarity. The introduction of regional languages as the media of examination will aggravate linguism and provincialism. At the all-India level, the national language along with English ought to have been the only medium of examination. *Second,* uniformity of standard of marking is not possible. It involves the appointment of about 13,000 examiners as 30 optional and compulsory subjects are to be answered in 18 different languages. Even if these examiners remain impartial it is not possible to achieve uniformity in assessment and evaluation of the answers. A mediocre or average answer in one language may be considered as excellent in the other. *Third,* regional and linguistic rivalries are apt to play their nasty role. The language enthusiasts in order to push their languages may not be objective in the evaluation of answer books. *Fourth,* mobility of the officers selected through the media of these languages may be curtailed defeating thereby the purpose of all-India services.

However, the new scheme of examination is definitely an improvement upon the previous system which was urban-oriented. The introduction of regional languages may enable the candidates from rural schools to compete favouraly with those from public schools. Secondly, the undue importance given to personality test in the previous system has been lessened as there are no minimum qualifying marks for viva voce. An urban-bred candidate had an advantage under the old system but now the candidates from rural background can hope to get into the coveted Indian Administrative Service if they work hard and do well in the written examination.

Satish Chandra Committee Report

Satish Chandra Committee comprising of six members, was set up by the Union Public Service Commission in August, 1988 under the chairmanship of the former U.G.C. chairman – Dr. Satish Chandra to recommend possible changes in the Civil Service examination. The Committee submitted its report in August 1989. Its recommendations were studied by the U.P.S.C. in consultation with the Personnel Ministry. The recommendations accepted are as follows :

1. No departure from the present practice of holding a common examination for Civil Services.
2. An essay paper carrying 200 marks to be reintroduced in the scheme of examination from 1993 and the candidates to be allowed to answer this paper in English or in any one of the language included in the eight Schedule of the Constitution.
3. The marks for the personality test to be increased from 250 to 300 from 1993 examination. Thus in conjunction with the decision to introduce an essay paper, the total marks for the written examination and personality test would be raised from 2050 to 2300, in the Civil Service (Main) examination.
4. French, German, Chinese and Russian to be deleted from the list of optional subjects for the examination from 1993 onwards. In addition, Arabic, Persian and Pali also to be deleted, as very few candidates opt for them.
5. Medical Science to be included as an optional subject from 1994 both for the preliminary and the Main examinations.
6. The syllabi of the optional subjects for the examination to be spelt out comprehensively and steps taken to periodically revise the syllabi of various subjects included for the optional papers.

Some of the other recommendations of the Committee on post-examination matters which have been accepted are :

1. Allotment of service should continue to be on the basis of the candidate's rank and preference to service. Allotment of service after a common foundational course is not feasible.
2. The National Academy, Mussoorie, should be developed into a high level professional institution. Development of the faculty and infrastructural facilities should be paid adequate attention.
3. Research or development, regulatory and social aspects of administration should be a regular activity of the Academy. Comparative national studies should be undertaken, taking lessons from both the developing and developed countries.
4. Functioning of the training institutions for central services, should be studied in depth. In all these institutions, adequate infrastructural facilities and proper staffing with inter-disciplinary faculty should be ensured.
5. U.G.C. may review the scheme of providing coaching classes in selected institutions to persons belonging to the minority communities to enable them to compete in various competitive examinations.

The recommendations of the Committee, which have not been accepted by the Government of India, are as follows :

1. That some of the Group 'A' and Group 'B' services and posts which are at present being filled through the Civil Services Examination should be delinked from this system.
2. That the lower and upper age limits for the Civil Services examination should be 21 and 26

years respectively. The Government has decided to keep the upper age limit at 28 years.

3. That the candidates who qualify for the interview on the basis of an earlier Civil Services Examination should be exempted from taking the Preliminary Examination in the following years.
4. That there should be a system of negative marking for objective Type Tests at preliminary Examination. They had proposed that for each wrong response 50 percent marks allotted to that question should be deducted.
5. That Group Discussion should be made an adjunct to the interview tests.
6. The committee had suggested the introduction of three optional subjects, namely (i) Education (ii) Electronics and Telecommunications, and (iii) Medical Science, both for the Preliminary and Main Examinations.

It has been decided that while Medical Science will be included from the year 1994 onwards as an optional subject in the scheme of both the Preliminary and Main Examinations, the other two optional subjects, viz., Education and Electronics and Telecommunications need not be included as optional subjects.

It is observed that enhancement of marks for personality test and introduction of essay paper are likely to make a better judgement of a candidate's level of articulation and leadership potential — two crucial qualities in a good administration. The proposal to drop a large number of foreign or antiquated languages from the list of optional papers is also a welcome step. According to an editorial, "*Even if belatedly the Satish Chandra Committee has made a valiant attempt to correct the imbalances unnecessarily introduced in the selection process for civil servants during the late 1970s. With the traditional values greatly restored it is to be hoped that the quality of administration too will improve significantly over the coming decades.*"[1]

As referred above, the all-India services consist of Indian Foreign Service, Indian Police Service, Indian Service of Engineers, Indian Medical Service, Indian Economic Service, Indian Statistical Service and Indian Forest Service, besides the prestigious Indian Administrative Service. The examination for Indian Police Service, Indian Foreign Service, Indian Administrative Service and allied is common and has been described above. For other services, there are separate examinations since these services are of a technical nature and call for specific technical qualifications. The scheme of written examinations and interview for these technical all-India Services is naturally different for different services.

(C) CENTRAL CIVIL SERVICES

The Central Civil Services are those services which are under the exclusive control of the Central government and are recruited to administer the subjects allocated to the Union Government under the Constitution of India. These services are classified into Class I and Class II. The Central Civil Services, Class I are : Archaeological Science; Botanical Survey of India; Central Engineering Service; Central Electrical Engineering Service; Central Health Service; Central Revenues Services; Chemical Service; Central Water Engineering Service; Central Secretariat Service; General Central Service; Geological Survey of India; Indian Audit and Accounts Service; Indian Defence Accounts Service; Indian Foreign Service; Indian Meteorological Service; Indian Postal Service; Indian Post and Telegraphs Traffic Service; Indian Revenue Service; Indian Salt Service; Mercantile Marine Training Ship Service; Mines Department; Overseas Communication Service; Survey of India; Telegraph Engineering Service; Zoological Survey of India; Central Legal Service; Railway Inspectorate Service; Indian Foreign Service Branch B; Indian Inspection Service; Indian Supply Service; Central Information Service; Indian Statistical Service; Indian Economic Service; Telegraph Traffic Service; Railway Personnel Service.

[1] *The Hindustan Times, Dated October 28, 1992.*

The Central Civil Services, Class II are : Botanical Survey of India, Class II; Central Electrical Engineering Service, Class II; Central Secretariat Service, Section Office Grade (II); Central Secretariat Service, Grade IV; Central Secretariat Stenographers' Service, Grade I; Central Secretariat Stenographers Service (Combined); Central Engineering Service, Class II; Central Health Service, Class II; Indian Meteorological Service; Labour Officer's Service, Class II; Postal Superintendents Service, Class II; Post Master's Service; Central Excise Service, Class II; Customs Appraisees Service; Customs Preventive Service, Class II Chief Inspectors; Custom Appraisee's Service, Class II, Customs Preventive Service, Class II inspectors; Income Tax Service, Class II; Telegraph Engineering and Wireless Service, Class II; Telegraph Traffic Service, Class II; General Central Service, Class II; Indian Salt Service, Class II; Survey of India, Class II; Geological Survey of India, Class II; Zoological Survey of India, Class II.

Thus, in all there are 34 Class I and 25 Class II, Central Civil Services. Class I comprises posts of high rank the work of which is mainly administrative, Class II in many cases is entrusted with work similar to that of Class I, but it is lower in salary range and status.

Apart from the above mentioned Class I and II Central Services, there are also Class III and Class IV services. Class III (the former subordinate services) consist of posts carrying clerical, ministerial, executive for outdoor duties while Class IV services (the former inferior services) are at the lowest rung consisting of employees such as peons, sweepers, chowkidars, laboratory attendants etc.

Of the above central civil services, a special mention may be made of the Central Secretariat Service. The old name — Imperial Secretariat Service was replaced by the name Central Secretariat Service in 1948. The Central Secretariat Service is organised as follows :

1. Selection Grade	Joint Secretary Director Deputy Secretary
2. Grade I	(Under Secretary or equivalent)
3. Section Officer's Grade	
4. Assistant's grade	

Appointment to the Selection Grade is made by promotion on the basis of merit of permanent officers of Grade I having five years Service in that Grade. For the purpose of promotion, a select list is prepared from which appointments are made as and when vacancies arise. Appointments to Grade I is likewise made by promotion from amongst the Section Officers having at least ten years experience in that Grade on the basis of merit. In this case too, a select list of Section Officers is prepared. So far as appointments to the Section Officer's grade are concerned, usually one-third of the vacant posts are filled through direct recruitment and the remaining by promoting the Assistants already serving in the Central Secretariat. These Assistants with eight years service appear in the departmental competitive examination. Assistants are appointed through direct recruitment and partly through promotion, the ratio being 3 : 1. The examinations for direct recruitment of Assistants are conducted by the Staff Selection Commission while direct recruitment of Section officers is conducted by the UPSC.

The Union Public Service Commission makes recruitment to the Central Civil Services Class I and Class II (Grade A and B). Recruitment to Group C (Class III) is made by the Staff Selection Commission. The UPSC holds a common examination for the following All India Services and Central Civil Services.

(i) Indian Administrative Service

(ii) Indian Foreign Service

(iii) Indian Police Service

(iv) Indian P & T Accounts and Finance Service, Group 'A'

(*v*) Indian Customs and Central Excise Service, Group 'A'
(*vi*) Indian Revenue Service, Group 'A'
(*vii*) Indian Postal Service, Group 'A'
(*viii*) Indian Civil Accounts Service, Group 'A'
(*ix*) Indian Information Service (Junior Grade)
(*x*) Central Trade Service, Group 'A'
(*xi*) Posts of Assistant Commandant, Group A in Central Industrial Security Force
(*xii*) Indian Railway Traffic Service, Group 'A'
(*xiii*) Indian Audit and Accounts Service
(*xiv*) Indian Railway Accounts Service
(*xv*) Indian Railway Personnel Service, Group 'A'
(*xvi*) Indian Defence Accounts Service
(*xvii*) Indian Ordnance Factories Service, Group 'A'
(*xviii*) Posts of Assistant Security Officer, Group 'A' in Railway Protection Force.
(*xix*) Indian Defence Estates Service, Group 'A'
(*xx*) Central Secretariat Service, Group 'B' (Section Officer's Grade)
(*xxi*) Railway Board Secretariat Service, Group 'B' (Section Officer's Grade)
(*xxii*) Armed Forces Headquarters Civil Service, Group 'B' (Assistant Civilian Staff Officer's Grade)
(*xxiii*) Customs Appraiser's Service, Group 'B'
(*xxiv*) Delhi and Andaman & Nicobar Island Police Service, Group 'B'
(*xxv*) Delhi and Andamans & Nicobar Islands Civil Services, Group 'B'
(*xxvi*) Posts of Deputy Superintendent of Police in C.B.I., Group 'B'
(*xxvii*) Pondicherry Civil Service, Group 'B'

For the other Central Civil Services like Archaeological Service, Central Health Service, Central Engineering Service, Indian Meteorological Service, Survey of India Services etc., the U.P.S.C. conducts separate examinations, written/oral or both.

The Ministry of Personnel, Public Grievances and Pensions is the managing authority for two all-India Services, namely the Indian Administrative Service and the Indian Forest Service. It also manages the Indian Economic Service and the Indian Statistical Service. It is also the controlling authority of the Central Secretariat Service (Selection grade and Grade I). The Indian Police Service is managed by the Ministry of Home Affairs. The other Services are managed by the respective Ministries of the Central Government. Thus, the Indian Foreign Service is managed by the Ministry of External Affairs, the Indian Revenue Service by the Ministry of Finance, the Indian Defence Accounts Service by the Ministry of Defence and so on. It may, however, be noted that the general policies relating to personnel in all the Services are determined by the Ministry of Personnel.

The class II civil services are managed by the respective Ministries of the Government. As regard class III and class IV services, these are departmentally managed.

The IInd ARC Report

The Moily Commission known as the Second Administrative Reforms Commission in its tenth report under the title. Refurbishing of Personnel Administration – Scaling New Heights, has recommended wide ranging reforms to make the administrative system more responsive. In regard to recruitment eligibility age for entry to the civil services should be 21-25 for general candidates and not 21-30 years as it is now. The advantage of lowering the entry age is that the young mind is malleable and can be moulded as desired. Requisite value system and attributes and sense of responsiblity can also be gradually inculcated with the advancement, a person develops a personality of his own, a fixed mind set and moral value criterion. With pre conceived vision and ideas he may not be inconsonance with what is needed of him in the service. On conducting the examination the ARC subjects should be on the Constitution, the legal system, economy, polity, history and culture but it should have no optional subjects. That means specialists like doctors, engineers and others stand ruled out. The Moily Committee has not favoured automatic entry from state civil services into I.A.S. or the I.P.S. It says "Let them take an exam". All those who have completed 8 to 10 years of service in grade 'A' posts be made eligible. A maximum of two attempts should be allowed and that the upper age limit be fixed at 40 years for entry.

On selecting people for specific specialised posts the ARC wants that all officers of the All India Service and the Central Civil service, who have completed 13 years of service should be eligible to apply for specific posts that require knowledge of a particular domain, for example, finance, urban development, rural development, infrastructure, agriculture, revenue generation, taxation etc.

The ARC has recommended the setting up of Civil Services Authority consisting of five members and appointed by the President. The Authority will interview the applicants on the basis of their work. The candidates selected for a specific domain will remain posted in that field only. Further, the ARC suggests that the rules be clearly defined for recruiting at each level so that there may not be any scope for misuse.

Regarding the conduct of civil services examination the ARC has said."The Civil Services Examinations as they are usually conducted by the Union Public Service Commission have become elaborate affair and take almost a year to complete. The long period taken is a national loss because this detracts from the Civil Services career by that extent of time The Indian Institutes of Management that select candidates for the MBA degree do not take more than three months to complete, even though they also handle very large numbers of candidates". The ARC is of the view that both the preliminary Examination and the Main Examination be administered at one stage, oneafter the another on consecutive days. The Preliminary Examination paper could be evaluated first and the evaluation for the conventional type of papers for the main Examination could be undertaken for only those candidates who have secured a threshold level of marks. This would reduce the time taken for completing the examination and would also benefit the candidates as it would not be necessary for them to fill up forms twice and also travel twice for appearing in the examinations. The Moiley committee has cited the example of CBSE which handles a much larger number of candidates in more diverse subjects having conventional descriptive papers and completes the examination process within three months.

(D) STATE SERVICES

The Constitution of India provides for a federal type of government wherein the powers have been divided between the Union and the States. In order to manage and administer the matters assigned to the States, the State services have been constituted. Thus the State services include those services and posts which are concerned with the administration of state subjects such as education, agriculture, transport, cooperation, health, maintenance of law and order, industries, prisons, forests, fisheries, etc. The recruitment and the service conditions of these services are regulated under the Act which may be adopted by the State Legislature. In the absence of a legislation, the Governor has been empowered to issue rules and regulations for the said purpose.

It may be pointed out that the senior posts in the State are manned by the officers of Indian Administrative Service and Indian Police Service. These officers, although operate under the administrative control of the State Government to which they are allotted, the conditions of their service are regulated by the rules made by the Union Government. The State Government does not have any power to take any disciplinary action against them. It can only request Union Government to take such an action against an officer for his acts of omission or commission. Normally, all superior administrative posts of district Collector/Deputy Commissioner and above (Commissioners, Directors, Members of the Board of Revenue, Managing Directors of public undertakings, Secretaries to the Government, Chief Secretary etc.) are held by I.A.S. officers and those of Superintendent of Police and above in the police department are held by members of the Indian Police Service. Thus, the State services operate in a position of subordination to the officers of the all-India Services, who occupy inferior positions in the administrative hierarchy and get lower pay scales. The members of the State services can be promoted to the all-India Services to a certain percentage reserved for them.

The State Services are constituted department wise and are divided into Class I, Class II, Class III and Class IV. Thus there are Education Service, Police Service, Industries Service, Prison Service, Cooperative Service, Agriculture Service, Veterinary Service, Medical Service, Forest Service, Engineering Service, Public Health Service, Irrigation Service, Judicial Service. But the most important service is the State Civil Service which commands the greatest prestige, prospects and also power. Similar is the position of State Police Service. A certain percentage of the I.A.S and I.P.S. cadre is filled-up by promotion from both these services respectively.

Class I Services generally include a number of posts on a common time-scale of pay and a smaller number of posts carrying salary above the ordinary time-scale. Ordinarily, each departmental service has a Class I cadre, but there is no uniformity of pay scales for all Class I officers. In some services, better pay scales are provided viz., medical, engineering, health, etc. than those of education, cooperation, agriculture, etc. Generally, Class I posts are filled up by promotion, but in some cases these may be filled up by direct recruitment by the State Public Service Commission. Direct recruitment may be made on the basis of an open competitive examination or by selection at interviews held by the Commission. In some departments the recruitment is both through promotion and Direct recruitment in the ratio of 50 : 50.

Class II Service consists of the posts which are of lower status and responsibility than those in Class I service. Recruitment to these posts is made partly by promotion and partly by direct recruitment. The State Public Service Commission holds open competitive examinations for filling up Class II posts of the general administration, judicial and police services. For other posts of specialised nature, the Commission makes selections on the basis of interviews. The percentage of promotion differs from one State to another. In some States it is fifty, whereas in others it is sixty. Traditionally, promotions are made on the basis of seniority, provided the confidential roll has been up to the mark.

It may be pointed out that promotion to the I.A.S. is restricted to State Civil Service only and promotion to I.P.S. is from the State Police Service. There is no provision for promotion to all-India or Central Services from amongst the officers of the other State services. The only State services entitled to promotion to the all-India service are the State Civil Service and State Police Service.

Class III and Class IV Services. Each department has Class III and Class IV services. The class III services are of two types — subordinate executive and ministerial or clerical. The subordinate executives class III service consists of the posts like Naib-Tehsildars, Sub-inspectors of Police, Co-operative Inspectors, Excise Inspectors, Sales Tax Inspectors, Food and Supply Inspectors, Assistant Inspectors of Schools, Teachers, Assistant Sub-Divisional Engineers (overseers), Patwaris, etc. The ministerial or clerical class III consists of Clerks, Cashiers, Accountants, Junior Auditors, Assistants, Deputy Superintendents, Superintendents, Laboratory Assistants, Pharmacists, Restores in the libraries, etc. Recruitment to these posts is made by the Subordinate Services Selection Board through competitive examinations or interviews. A percentage of posts is filled through promotions also. The posts of Assistant, Deputy Superintendents and Superintendents are partly filled by promotion from among the immediately preceding junior posts. Patwaris are promoted to the posts of Kanungos who are later promoted as Naib-Tehsildars. Teachers are promoted to the posts of Headmasters. The Head-Constables are promoted as Assistant Inspectors of Police eligible for promotion as Sub-Inspectors of Police later on. The promotion quota differs from State to State and from department to department. In case, a State does not have a Subordinate Service Selection Board, recruitment is made by a departmental Committee or departmental heads. The district level posts are filled up by the district head of the department concerned either on ad hoc or regular basis.

Class IV Services include posts like peons, orderlies, watchman, carpenters, drivers, khalasis, duftaries, laboratory attendants, and sweeper etc. These persons are engaged in manual work – unskilled, semi-skilled or skilled. The appointment to these posts is made by the head of the office through the State Employment Exchanges. There is no state cadre of class IV services, nor these employees are transferable.

Domicile Requirements for State Services. Until 1957, the State services were open to such candidates only who fulfilled the domicile requirements as laid down by the State Government concerned. This provision existed in most of the States — the philosophy underlying being that a State has a moral duty to provide employment to its 'sons of the soil' and that 'outsiders' with little knowledge of local culture and environment would not be welcomed by the people of the State. This practice of the States, notwithstanding the prohibition of such practice under the Constitution, was criticised by the States Reorganisation Commission (1953-55). Consequent to the recommendations of the Commission, the Central Government disallowed, from 1957 this kind of discrimination by enacting the 'The Public Employment (Requirement as to Residence) Act'. The State services are now open to all the citizens of India irrespective of their place of residence.

Although the state services are legally open to all, yet in practice, the 'sons of the soil' have an edge over outsiders. The element of 'localism' does play its part in a fully enfranchised democracy. The people's representatives elected with the votes of the local people cannot ignore their constituents. Moreover, the adoption of the regional language as the State's official language also discourages the outsiders. The State Civil Services have now become more or less "provincialised."

Reservation for Backward Classes

In view of the recent anti-Mandal agitation a word may be said about reservation of posts on caste basis. The Constitution under Article 16 (4) allows both the Central Government and the State Government to make any provision for the reservation of appointments or posts in favour of any backward class of citizen which, in the opinion of the State, is not adequately represented in the services under the State.

Article 355 of the Constitution provides that the claims of the members of scheduled castes and scheduled tribes shall be taken into consideration, consistent with the maintenance of efficiency of administration, in making appointments to posts and services, in connection with the affairs of the Union or the State. Thus, there is reservation of posts in civil services for scheduled castes, scheduled tribes and other backward classes. For the scheduled castes, reservation is 15 percent of the vacancies for which recruitment is made on all India basis by open competition and 16.66 per cent of the vacancies in which recruitment is made on all India basis otherwise than by open competition. For the Scheduled Tribes, the reservation is 7.5 percent in both cases. For the State Services also there is a similar reservation. Besides the Scheduled Castes, and Scheduled Tribes, there is a constitutional provision, as earmarked above, for reservation for other backward classes in terms of Article 16(4). All the states have provided reservation in State Services for the backward classes, though the percentage varies from State to State. In Kerala, it is 40 percent, in Karnataka 48 percent, in Bihar 20 percent, in Andhra Pradesh 25 percent, and in Tamil Nadu 50 percent, 5 percent in Punjab, 15 percent in Uttar Pradesh, 10 percent in Haryana and 5 percent in Himachal Pradesh. It may be noted that there is no reservation in All-India and Central Services for other backward classes; but such reservation exists in the State services only.

As the backward classes have a powerful lobby and high political value in terms of votes on account of their numerical strength, they have been asking for reservation in Central Services. The main difficulty in providing reservation to backward classes at the central level is that of identifying these classes and preparing a list thereof. The Kalelkar Commission appointed in January 1953 had listed 2,399 castes as backward, but the Kalelkar's Report was not accepted by the then Government. In 1978 the Janata Government appointed the Second Backward Classes Commission headed by B.P. Mandal. The Mandal Commission identified 3,743 backward castes and recommended 27 percent reservation for them, though they constituted 52 percent of the total population. But since there was already 22.5 percent reservation for the Scheduled Castes and Scheduled tribes, so more than 27 percent for other backward classes could not have been recommended, as according to a judgment of the Supreme Court, the total quantum of reservation should not exceed 50 percent. The Report was presented to the Government on December 31, 1980. It was presented to both the houses of the Parliament on April 30, 1982. But the then Government did not consider it advisable to implement the Report as it was fraught with adverse consequences for the social fabric of the country.

V.P. Singh, leader of the National Front Government, announced, all of a sudden the acceptance of the Mandal Report on August 7, 1990 in the Parliament. The announcement led to a violent agitation particularly by the student community which ultimately, brought down Mr. Singh's government. The Rao government went further and announced on September 25, 1991 through a notification that it would give 10 percent reservation to economically weaker candidates of all other communities over and above 27 percent reservation stipulated in Mr. Singh's order. The matter went to the Supreme Court. The apex court by majority judgments delivered on November 16, 1992 held that reservations in government service on the basis of caste are permissible under Article 16(4) of the Constitution. However, the "creamy layer" of backward classes should be excluded from enjoying the benefit of reservation. Also there should be no reservation for the higher civilian posts of scientific, technical and professional nature including the Professors. The Supreme Court has also again declared that reservations could, in no circumstances, exceed 50 percent of the total number of jobs. It has also been held that reservations will not apply to promotions in services.

The Supreme Court judgement in the Mandal Case has been criticized on numerous grounds, more on the ground that it has ensured a fresh lease of life to the canker of casteism for a long and indefinite future. From the viewpoint of efficiency in administration, reservation on caste basis undermines the efficiency of the civil service by inducting candidates of sub-standard quality in administration. The reins of power pass from meritocracy to mediocracy. Reservation of jobs on caste basis means shutting the doors of employment to meritorious students belonging to higher castes. In a society like India with limited job opportunities, reservation of 50 percent jobs for certain classes of society is truly a great handicap for others who do not have the benefit of reservation. Kaka Kalelkar's own letter forwarding his Report to the President said, *"I am definitely against reservation in government services for any community for the simple reason that the services are not meant for the servants but they are meant for the service of the society as a whole."*[1] Jawaharlal Nehru once said, "I dislike any kind of reservation more particularly in service, I react strongly against anything which leads to inefficiency and second-rate standards...But if we go in for reservation on communal and caste basis, we swamp the bright and able people and remain second rate or third rate. It has amazed me to learn that even promotions are based sometimes on communal or caste consideration. ......Let us help the backward group by all means, but not at the cost of efficiency." It is sad to note that the wise words of Nehru have not been heeded and the present day political leaders are clammering for reservation for more and more categories — obviously the caste vote-bank. It is also debatable if reservation for OBC would help to bring these classes into the mainstream of national life. In the case of scheduled castes certain caste groups have monopolised the constitutional benefits provided for these castes. The majority of scheduled castes still lead a

[1]*Quoted by N.A. Palkhivala in his article 'Mandal Perpetuate Casteism'. The Tribune, Nov. 30, 1992.*

life of utter deprivation and poverty. If all out efforts are not made to educate their children and raise their economic system for a proper living, the job reservation for OBC people is rather a doubtful proposition. What the people belonging to weaker sections require is special attention and help, not charity. Instead of putting a permanent mark of second rate citizenship on SCs/OBCs, they should be given the confidence to match their intelligence and mix up with those who are better placed caste wise in society.

Union Cabinet approval for highter ceiling for creamy layers (Oct, 2008): On october 3, 2008 the Union Cabinet approved raising the income criteria for the creamy layer among the OBC from 2.5 Lakh to 4.5 Lakh a year. This was done with an idea to accommodate more people under the reservation category. The states had demanded that the new ceiling be fixed between 4 to 6 Lakh.

In services and admissions in educational Institutions this ceiling is to be taken in view.

Apex Court Observation (Oct. 22, 2007): Amidst raging controversy on reservation the Supreme Court five judges Constitutional bench headed by Chief Justice of India Y. K. Sabharwal held "Reservation is necessary for transcending caste and not for perpetuating it. It has to be used in limited sense otherwise it will perpetuate casteism in the country. If the extent of reservation goes beyond cut off point them it results in reverse discrimination. They however held "It was important to find a stable eqilibrium between justice to the backwards, equity for the forward and efficiency for the entire system ". The Court for the first time referred to the creamy layer among the Scheduled Castes and Scheduled Tribes and kept them out of the purview of reservations.

(E) LOCAL CIVIL SERVICES

The local civil services comprise the services of both the urban local government and rural local government. The urban local government in India is divided into five categories : Municipal Corporations, Municipal Committees, Notified Area Committees, Town Area Committees and Cantonment Boards. The rural local Government is known by the name of Panchayati Raj which consists of Zila Parishads, Panchayat Samitis and Gram Panchayats. Local Government is a State subject under the Constitution; hence the power to regulate and determine the mode of recruitment, training and other conditions of service of local government employees rests in the State Government.

Urban Local Services

The States in India have adopted different personnel systems in the organisation of urban local government. The integrated system is followed in Tamil Nadu and other southern States wherein officers serving municipal governments are transferable horizontally between municipalities and also vertically between national, State and municipal government. The Unified Personnel System is in vogue in the States of Rajasthan, Uttar Pradesh, Punjab and Haryana where municipal services have been unified up to the supervisory and clerical levels but the lowest level of employees continue to be recruited separately and controlled at the municipal level. The States of West Bengal, Maharashtra and Gujarat have adopted the Separate Personnel System whereunder the municipal committees possess exclusive jurisdiction to recruit and control their personnel. Generally, in these States, rules are framed by the State government to control certain aspects of the management of municipal personnel, but in hiring and firing their personnel, full authority is vested in a municipal committee. Thus personnel system of urban local government in our country differs from state to state and even in the same state as therein Unified Personnel System operates so far as higher municipal services like those of Executive Officers, Health officers and Engineers are concerned and Separate Personnel System operates in the case of services at lower levels.

The local services consist of (*a*) superior staff such as Executive Officers, Secretaries, Superintendents, Accounts Officers, Accountants, Engineers, Medical Officers, Health Officers, Chief

Sanitary Inspectors, Fire Station Officers and Town Planners; and (*b*) subordinate staff viz., Clerks, Fire Fighters, Sanitary Inspectors, other Inspectors like Octroi, Tax, Food Adulteration, etc. Draftsmen, Drivers, Assistants, Cashiers and class IV employees.

Provincialisation of Municipal Services. The term 'provincialisation' implies :

(*a*) creation of state-wise cadre for different categories of municipal employees;

(*b*) transferability of municipal employees from one municipality to another;

(*c*) recruitment by a state level agency and fixation of conditions of service by the State Government;

(*d*) day-to-day control by the municipal bodies; and

(*e*) payment of salaries out of municipal revenue by the municipal committees.

Provincialisation of municipal services has been stressed and emphasised by various forms of committees from time to time. The first conference of Local Self Government Ministers held in August, 1948 had adopted the following resolution :

"In view of the fact that provincial cadre would facilitate recruitment of suitable personnel from a wide field and provide a more efficient and contended service, this conference is of the opinion that there should be provincial cadres for the higher executive and technical staff employed by local bodies."

The second conference of Local Self-Government Ministers held in 1954 had reiterated the same suggestion. The Central Council of Local Self Government in conjunction with the Fourth Conference of Ministers of Town and Country Planning held in 1963 had recommended the provincialisation of administrative, health, engineering and town planning services of the municipalities in the interest of better and more efficient administration. The Rural-Urban Relationship Committee (1966) had observed that it would be more convenient and advantageous to have a combined integrated service for public health engineers, town planners, medical and health officers as also of accounts and audit officers.[1] The Task Force on Management of Urban Development appointed by the Planning Commission (1983) in its report held that personnel development had been the weakest aspect of urban management in India and suggested the formation of State cadres for key posts in municipal management like executive officers, engineers, accounts officers, revenue officers, and opined that separate personnel system would be of a greater advantage in respect of lower levels.

In pursuance of the above suggestions and recommendations, various state governments had provincialised municipal services by making necessary amendments in their Municipal Acts. The Punjab Government amended Punjab Municipal Act, 1911 in 1973 and provincialised (*i*) Punjab Service of Municipal Executive Officers; (*ii*) Punjab Service of Municipal Engineers and Section officers; (*iii*) Punjab Service of Municipal health officers; (*iv*) Punjab Service of Municipal Secretaries; (*v*) Punjab Service of Municipal Accountants. Later on, more services such as Town Planners, Section Officers, Accountants, Superintendents, Sanitary Inspectors, Draftsmen, Assistant Divisional Fire Officers were also provincialised. The State Government has thus provincialised the municipal services from the post of an Assistant and above and also laid down rules regarding their recruitment, promotion and conditions of service.

Appointments to the superior municipal services in the States where these have been provincialised are made by the State Government concerned on the recommendation of the Selection Committee appointed by the Government or the State Public Service Commission. In those States

[1]*Bombay and Sind had a joint Commission as also Punjab and NWFP. Bihar, Orissa and Central Provisions also had a joint Commission.*

where separate personnel system has been adopted, appointment is made by the Municipal Committee concerned. In all the States, appointment to the junior level posts such as clerks and class IV staff is made by Municipal Committees.

Municipal Corporations have been set up in big cities like Bombay, Calcutta, Madras, Delhi, Kanpur, Lucknow, Varanasi, Allahabad, Agra, Gwalior, Indore, Jabalpur, Jalandhar, Amritsar and Ludhiana etc. The Chief Executive Officer of a Corporation is designated as Municipal Commissioner. He is assisted by an Assistant Commissioner. Both the Commissioner and Assistant Commissioner are appointed by the State Government from amongst the I.A.S. officers, though senior officers from the State civil services can also be appointed to these posts.

The State Government in the Punjab makes appointments to the municipal corporation services such as those of Executive officers, Secretaries, Municipal Engineers, Municipal Health officers, etc. also on the recommendations of the Public Service Commission. For the recruitment to lower posts, the Corporation and the commissioner have to abide by the rules and regulations which may be framed by the state government. The Commission has no hand in the selection of officers to be appointed against posts in the provincialised cadre. The Calcutta Corporation has setup a Municipal Service Commission for appointment to the posts in the junior scale of pay while the posts carrying a senior scale are filled on the recommendations of the State Public Service Commission.

Rural Local Services

These services comprise the officials of the Zila Parishad, the Panchayat Samiti and the Panchayat. The official in charge of a Zila Parishad is the Secretary or Executive officer. There are also other officers viz. Taxation officers, Accountants, Assistants, Stenos, Clerks and Class IV employees etc. The Panchayat Samiti works under the overall control of the Block Development and Panchayat Officer who is a member of the Provincial Civil Service. He has under his control the other employees of the Panchayat Samiti like Social Education and Panchayat Officer, Mukhya Sevikas, Gram Sevikas and the ministerial Staffs of the Samiti. At the Panchayat level, there is a Panchayat Secretary or Gram Sachiv. In Kerala State, each Panchayat has an Executive officer who belongs to the State cadre of service, a Panchayat Assistant and a Bill Collector to assist him. Some states like Maharashtra, Gujrat, Rajasthan and Andhra Pradesh have created Panchayati Raj Services. Sometimes, the State Governments also send their officers on deputation to the Panchayati Raj institutions. Andhra Pradesh has classified the Zila Parishad and Panchayat Samiti posts into State, District and Block cadres.

The Panchayati Raj personnel are of two categories, i.e., the government staffs and the Panchayati Raj staffs. The first category includes the key personnel who are the employees of the State Government but are deputed to work with the Panchayati Raj bodies, such as BDO, Extension Officers, Gram Sevaks, etc. The other category includes Panchayat secretaries, local clerks, accountants, tax collectors, peons, etc. who are appointed by the Panchayati Raj bodies for their respective units.

(F) PUBLIC SERVICE COMMISSIONS

The Government of India Act, 1919 provided for the establishment of a Public Service Commission in India, but no action was immediately taken thereon. The Lee Commission, 1924 gave particular attention to the matter and observed. "Wherever democratic institutions exist, experience has shown that to secure an efficient civil service it is essential to protect it as far as possible from political or personal influence and to give it that position of stability and security which is vital to its successful working as the impartial and efficient instrument by which Governments, of whatever political complexion, may give effect to their policies. In countries where the principle has been neglected, and where the 'Spoil System' has taken its place, an inefficient and disorganised civil service has been the inevitable result and corruption has been rampant. In America, a Civil Service Commission has been constituted to control recruitment to the services, but for the purposes of India it is from the Dominions of the British Empire that more relevant and useful lessons can perhaps be drawn. Canada, Australia and South Africa now possess Public Civil Services Act regulating the position and control of the Public Services and a common feature of all of them is the constitution of a Public Service Commission. It was this need which the framers of the Government of India Act had in mind when they made provision in Section 96(C) for the establishment of a Public Service Commission.[1] It was only in October, 1926, that a Public Service Commission was established at the Centre in 1929. Madras established its own Public Service Commission.

The Indian Statutory (Simon) Commission recommended the establishment of Public Service Commissions in all the Provinces. It was, accordingly, suggested that, if any Provincial Legislative Council did not pass within a prescribed period an Act for the establishment of a Public Service Commission, with a Constitution and functions approved by the Secretary of State in Council, the Provincial Government shall be required:

(1) to conduct its recruitment through the agency of the Central Public Service Commission;

(2) to submit appeals from members of the provincial and subordinate services to the same body; and

(3) to accept and apply the same convention in regard to the Commission's recommendations as are accepted by the Government of India.[2] The Government of India Act, 1935, accordingly provided that "there shall be a Public Service Commission for the Federation and a Public Service Commission for each Province." Provision was also made whereby two or more Provinces could have a joint Commission.

The Commission was purely an advisory body. Appointments to the Commission were made by the Governor-General or Governor, as the case might be, acting in his discretion. At least half of the number of members of a commission were to be from the services who had held office under the Crown for ten years or more. The tenure of office of the members and conditions of their services were determined by regulations made by the Governor General or Governors. The Governor-General and Governors acted in their discretion.

The Constitution of India, following the passage of Act of 1935, has provided for a Public Service Commission for the Union and a Public Service Commission for each state. The provisions in this regard are on the lines of those in the Government of India Act, 1935. The Parliament may establish a Joint Commission for two or more States if the legislatures of such States pass a resolution authorising the Parliament to do so. The Union Public Service Commission also may perform the functions of a State Public Service Commission at the request of the Governor of a State, and with the consent of the President. The Union Territories are served either by the Union Public Service Commission or by the Public Service Commission of an adjoining State.

Appointment and terms of office

The Constitution of India does not prescribe the strength of the members of the UPSC or the State Public Service Commissions. It is determined by the President in the case of UPSC and in the case of State Commissions by the Governor by regulations. At present, there are ten members — one chairman and nine members of the UPSC.

There are usually 3 to 6 members of a State Commission. The chairman and the members of the UPSC are appointed by the President and in the case of a State Public Service Commission by

[1] *Lee Commission Report, para 24.*

[2] *Report of the Indian Statutory commission, Vol. II. para 39.*

the Governor of the State. One-half of the members of a Commission, Union or State, must have held office for at least ten years either under the Government of India or under the Government of a State. A member holds office for six years or until he attains, in the case of a Union Commission the age of sixty-five years and in the case of a State Commission the age of sixty-two years whichever is earlier. A member of a Public Service Commission is, on the expiration of his term of office, not eligible for reappointment to that office. The Chairman of the UPSC is ineligible for further appointments either under the Government of India or under the Government of a State. But a member of the UPSC is eligible for appointment as chairman of the UPSC or a State Commission. The Chairman of a State Commission is eligible for appointment as chairman or a member of the UPSC or chairman of any other State Commission. A member of a State Commission is eligible for appointment as chairman or a member of the Union Commission or as chairman or that of any other State Commission. None of them is, however, eligible for any other employment either under the Union Government or under the Government of a State.

Employment under the Government has been interpreted to mean employment which is paid by the Government. The universities and public corporations are independent legal entities with their own independent financial resources and, accordingly, employment under such bodies is not employment under Government. The Governorship also is not considered as employment under the government as the salary of the Governor is paid out of the Consolidated fund. A.K. Kidwai, a former chairman of UPSC was appointed as Governor of Bihar in 1978.

The chairman or any other member of Public Service Commission may be removed from his office by order of the President on the ground of misbehaviour after the Supreme Court, on reference being made to it by the President has, on inquiry held in accordance with the procedure prescribed under Article 145 of the Constitution, reported that the chairman or any such other member, as the case may be, ought on any such ground be removed. The President in the case of the Union Commission and the Governor in the case of a State Commission may suspend from office the chairman or any other member of the Commission pending Supreme Court's opinion on such reference.

The President may by order remove from office the chairman or any other member of a public Service Commission if the chairman or such member (*a*) is adjudged as insolvent; or (*b*) engages during his term of office in any paid employment outside the duties of his office; or (*c*) is, in the opinion of the President, unfit to continue in office by reason of infirmity of mind or body.

It may be noted that the power of removal belongs only to the President even in the case of a State public Service Commission. The Governor or the High Court has no say in this matter. The Governor, of course, possesses the power of suspension.

Functions of Public Service Commissions

The Public Service Commissions are constitutional bodies. Their functions have been mentioned in Article 320 of the Constitution. According to this Article, the following are their functions :

(1) It shall be the duty of the Union and the State Public Service Commissions to conduct examinations for appointments to the services of the Union and the services of the State respectively.

Recruitment to Group A and Group B gazetted services under Central Government is done by the UPSC.

(2) It shall also be the duty of the Union Public Service Commission if requested by any two or more states so to do, to assist those states in framing and operating schemes of joint recruitment for any services for which candidates possessing special qualifications are required.

(3) The Union Public Service Commission or the State Public Service Commission, as the case may be, shall be consulted as under.

(*a*) On all matters relating to methods of recruitment to civil services and for civil posts.

(*b*) On the principles to be followed in making appointments to civil services and posts and in making promotions and transfers from one service to another and on the suitability of candidates for such appointments, promotions or transfers.

(*c*) On all disciplinary matters affecting a person serving under the Government of India or the Government of a State in a civil capacity, including memorials or petitions relating to such matters.

(*d*) On any claim by or in respect of a person who is serving or has served under the Government of India or the government of a State that any costs incurred by him in defending legal proceedings instituted against him in respect of acts done or purporting to be done in the execution of his duties should be paid by the Government.

(*e*) On any claim for the award of a pension in respect of injuries sustained by a person while serving under the Government in a civil capacity and any question as to the amount of any such award.

It shall be the duty of a Public Service Commission to advise on any matter so referred to them or any other matter which the President or the Governor may refer to them.

Normally, a Public Service Commission must be consulted on all the matters referred to above, but the Constitution also empowers the President and the Governors to make regulations specifying the matters in which, either generally or in particular circumstances, the Commission at the Central and State level may not be consulted. No reference need be made to the Public Service Commission on matters relating to the reservation of appointments of posts in favour of Backward classes, Scheduled Castes and Scheduled Tribes.

In 1961 an amendment was made which provided, "It shall not be necessary for the President to consult the Commission in any case where he proposes to make an order of dismissal, removal or reduction in rank after being satisfied that such action is necessary in the interest of the security of the State." In 1962, following the proclamation of Emergency, similar amendments were made curtailing the advisory functions of the Commissions. All regulations made by the President or Governor specifying the matters in which it is not necessary to consult the Commission are to be laid before the appropriate legislature and are subject to legislative control and modifications.

Under Article 321, the functions of the Union or State Public Service Commission may be extended by an Act of Parliament or the State legislature in respect of the services of any local authority or any body corporate.

Independence of the Commissions

The various constitutional provisions to ensure the independence of the Commissions in the discharge of their functions are — (1) The Public Service Commissions are constitutionally created; (2) the term of office is fixed and none is eligible for reappointment to that office on the expiration of his term; (3) removal or suspension of a member can take place only for the reasons laid down in the Constitution; (4) the conditions of service of a member cannot be altered to his disadvantage after his appointment; (5) bar on re-employment under Government except under certain cases; and (6) the salary and other emoluments are charged on the Consolidated Fund of India or the State and the same are not votable by the parliament or the State legislature concerned. But in actual practice, the independence of the Commissions has suffered, more particularly in the states. Appointments to the Public Service Commissions have been made on political considerations thereby lowering their prestige in the public eye. At the Union level, except for Shivashunmugam Pillai, who was a former speaker of the Madras legislative Assembly, no politician has been appointed to the Commission. (He was a member of the UPSC from 1955 to 1961). The Law Commission of India in its fourth Report has observed, "*We are constrained to state that the personnel of the Public Service Commissions in some of the States was not such as could inspire confidence from the points of view of either efficiency or impartiality. There appears little doubt that in some of the States appointments to the Commissions are made not on considerations of merit but on grounds of party and political affiliations.*"[1] An ex-chairman of the Mahdya Pradesh Public Service Commission said, "*The constitutional independence given to the Commission is largely vitiated by vesting the appointment of members in the hands of the Governor, (i.e. the Chief Minister in actual practice.) The Chief Minister often appoints persons on political, communal, regional and other grounds, and not solely on merit. Such persons usually find it difficult to resist ministerial pressure and influence in carrying out their duties in an independent and impartial manner.*"[2] In Maharashtra, a Deputy-Minister was appointed a member of the Commission from the quota reserved for civil servants. According to B.A.V. Shrama, "*Although the appointment serves to fulfil the legal niceties, it was clearly against the spirit of the Constitution. There cannot be a worse example of a party government ruthlessly seeking to promote its interests and that of a party member in total disregard of constitutional propriety.*"[3]

The Union Public Service Commission does continue to enjoy independence but, the situation in regard to State's Public Service Commission is shocking and gloomy. There is undue political pressure and interference to influence their decisions. What is worse is the widespread public belief that money factor is one of the major criteria in the selection of candidates. The recent Punjab scandal in- volving the chairman is an eye-opener. Nothing can be more shameful than his acts of public betrayal by selling off jobs for huge amounts. The members are selected on the basis of political and personal considerations ignoring the qualifications requisite for such posts. The members of the Commission are just not exhibiting integrity and intellectual capabilities expected of the incumbents of such office. They probably cannot come upto the expectations till the State Governments stop treating the Commissions as their appendages.

Role of the Public Service Commissions

The Public Service Commissions in India play a limited role in regard to both their administrative and advisory functions. So far as administrative functions, relating to recruitment to all civil services and posts under the Union Government or the State Governments are concerned, the Constitution empowers the Government to exclude any service and post from the purview of the Commission. Further, Class III and Class IV posts are recruited either through a Subordinate Services Selection Board/Commission or departmentally. As regards senior posts too, there are several agencies like Atomic Energy Department, Council of Scientific and Industrial Research, Life Insurance Corporation, General Insurance Corporation, State Bank of India, Indian Council of Agricultural Research, University Grants Commission, NCERT, and a number of other quasi-government institutions entirely or substantially financed by the Government which have been authorised to directly recruit their Class I and Class II staffs. Thus, the Public Service Commissions have only a limited role to play in recruiting personnel partly or fully paid by the Government directly or otherwise. Their jurisdiction extends to a very limited number of posts.

Second, the Public Service Commissions are only advisory bodies. Their advice may or may not be accepted by the Government concerned. In regard to the Union services for instance the Union Government has had to consult the Union Commission every year on more than seventy-five thousand cases and the number of cases in which the Commission's advice was not accepted, was 57 times between 1950 and 1985. But it increased to 92 times between 1985 to 1990. The annual average thus shot up to 18.4 cases as against 1.6 cases in the first 35 years. The UPSC noted that what was

---

[1]*Law Commission of India, Fourth Report, Vol. 1, p. 171.*

[2]*Rege. D.V., "The Public Service Commission. Its powers and Functions – A critical Assessment in Studies in State Administration, Edited by G.S. Halappa, p. 134.*

[3]*Sharma, B.A.V., "Public Service Communications in India". Studies in Indian Democracy Edited by Aiyar, S.P., and Srinivasan, R.P. 227.*

"particularly disturbing" was that in several cases the Government did not give the reasons for the rejection of the Commission' advice. In the States, the picture is more gloomy. The State Governments do not show adequate respect to the recommendations of the Commissions. Sometimes, the Commissions are asked to recommend a panel of names for a particular post out of which the Government makes its own selection without adhering to the priority recommended by the Commission. Further, the practice of making adhoc appointments and extending their period from year to year and then legalising such appointments after two/three years of adhoc service negates and considerably curtails the role of the Public Service Commissions.

It may, however, be pointed out that under Article 323, it is the duty of both the Union and the State Public Service Commission to present annually to the President/Governor a report indicating the cases where the advice of the Commission was not accepted and also the reasons for such non-acceptance. The report is discussed in the Parliament/State legislature as the case may be. This provision ensures that the recommendations of the Commission are not rejected without sufficient justifications. As such actions are liable to be censured by the legislatures of the Union and the States.

Third, the Public Service Commissions play a negative role only, i.e., 'to keep the rascals out'. The Constitution does not envisage any wider or positive role for the Commissions in personnel administration. It is a recruiting body with a purely advisory role. Personnel development, in the sense of the term, is not its concern.

A.R.C.'s Recommendations

The Administrative Reforms Commission (1965) made certain recommendations regarding the composition and powers of Public Service Commissions which are as under :

I. (*a*) In appointing members of State Public Service Commission the Governor should consult the Chairman of the U.P.S.C. and also the Chairman of the State Public Service Commission. (*b*) In appointing members of the UPSC the Chairman of the UPSC should be consulted (even when the appointment deals with his own successor). (*c*) Not less than two-thirds of the members of the UPSC should be drawn from among the Chairmen and members of the State PSCs. (*d*) At least one of the the members of a State PSC should belong to a different State. (*e*) The minimum academic qualifications for a member of the Commission should be a Graduation degree. (*f*) Only a Secretary or head of a department or person holding a post equivalent to this rank or a comparable post in the institution of higher education should be eligible for selection out of government officials (*g*) Members selected from non- officials should have practised at least for 10 years in any recognised profession vis. Law, Medicine, Engineering, Science, Technology, Accountancy or Administration.

II. (*a*) The Commission should be consulted by the Government before keeping certain matters regarding consultation with it beyond its purview. (*b*) The UPSC should be associated with the selection of personnel and their promotion within the quasi-government bodies entirely or substantially financed by government. (*c*) State Public Commissions should be equipped with similar powers over quasi-government institutions falling within the jurisdiction of their respective State Governments. (*d*) Research cells should be setup in the UPSC to appraise the effectiveness of recruitment by follow-up studies and to analyse trends in the skill market and in the educational sphere and to provide data for determining the recruitment policies.

(G) TRAINING OF CIVIL SERVICES

Prior to the attainment of independence, a coordinated and well-conceived plan of training of public services both at the Centre and in the provinces did not exist. The only cases in which a training course was provided after entry into service, were in some of the technical departments or in some of the highest grades, ie. the All India Services. The Indian Civil Service recruits were given an initial general training of 1 to 2 years at Oxford or Cambridge Universities, the subjects taught being Indian History, Indian Criminal Law and procedure and some Indian languages. On their arrival they were assigned to the different provinces. The Chief Secretary of the province assigned them for training to experienced District Officers. In the course of their training in the districts, the new officers were required to pass two departmental examinations. On passing the first examination, the new officer became a deputy magistrate and on passing the second, he was made a first class deputy magistrate. An officer was given independent charge of a district after he had put in 6 to 7 years of service and acquired sufficient experience working in different capacities e.g., Deputy Magistrate, Extra Assistant Commissioner, Joint Magistrate, etc.

There also existed some Central training schools e.g. Telegraph schools, Police Training schools in some departments. Departmental examinations were held for officers in the technical department i.e., Audit and Accounts Department, Income Tax Department etc. The clerical and subordinate employees learnt the job by experience.

With the dawn of independence, the Government of India decided to pay some attention to the problem of organisation and training of the civil services. An officers' Shortage Committee was appointed in November, 1947 to go into the matter. The Committee recommended for the establishment of a Directorate of Methods, Organisation and Training at the Centre with a view to supervise the training programme of various departments. It also recommended the establishment of a training school for I.A.S. In 1951, A.D. Gorwala also made a similar recommendation in his report on Public Administration. He suggested the creation of such a Directorate with two branches — one for the Organisation and Methods and the other for Training. Dr. Paul Appleby — a visiting American Professor — also recommended the same in his report on Public Administration submitted to Government of India in 1953. Even the Planning Commission remarked, "Next to recruitment, the training of personnel has considerable bearing on adminsitrative efficiency."[1] The Commission also recommended the appointment of a Director of Training for training programmes.

The I.A.S Training school was established at New Delhi in March, 1947, where all the probationers were imparted training for a period of one year. In 1957 a Refresher Centre at the I.A.S. Staff College, Simla was started. In September 1959 the I.A.S. Training School, New Delhi and I.A.S. Staff College, Simla were merged and a National Academy of Administration was setup at Mussoorie which is now known after the name of Lal Bahadur Shastri since 1972.

Lal Bahadur Shastri National Academy of Administration, Mussoorie

The L.B.S. National Academy of Adminstration provides training to those who are directly recruited to the All India Civil services and non-technical central services under Group A. The Academy arranges Foundational courses of 16 weeks duration for them. The Foundational course has the following main objectives :

(*i*) to promote *esprit de corps* among the probationers of different services emphasising the interdependence of various services as part of the higher civil services; (*ii*) to motivate probationers towards developing certain basic professional, administrative and human values; and (*iii*) to impart a basic understanding of the constitutional, political, social, economic, legal, historical, cultural and adminsitrative framework within which the services function."

During the Foundational course, the probationers are taught basic Economics for Administrators; Law; Public Administration (including Social Administration); Management and Behavioral Sciences; Indian History and Culture; and Political Concepts and Constitution of India. This course is covered through lectures, tutorials, case studies, management games, guest lectures and films, etc. Each probationer has to prepare a 'term paper' which has to be based on independent study and investigation. Hindi is compulsory for all probationers. There is also a 'Village Visit Programme' of about ten days duration to acquaint the probationers of the rural problems. An eight

[1]*Planning Commission, Administration and Public Corporation, p. 121.*

day trekking programme is also organised.

After the completion of the four months Foundational course and Professional course of two months, the I.A.S. probationers are sent for one year of district training in the State to which they have been assigned. The probationer is sent to a training school, if there is any in the state, for institutional training for a certain period. He then goes to a district and works as an understudy in various administrative capacities. In the district, he gets an opportunity to study institutions, policies and programmes. Thereafter, the probationer comes to the State Secretariat to get adequate knowledge of the working of the Headquarters.

There is a counsellor at the Academy with whom the probationer remains in constant touch during the course of his district level training and communicates with him about his experiences, problems and impressions, etc. The probationer is also required to prepare reports on various subjects, primarily concerning district administration, allotted to him at the Academy before the district training begins. These reports are evaluated at the Academy and are taken into account for his final evaluation.

After the district training, the probationer returns to the Academy for the second phase of training. During the second phase, which lasts three months the probationers discuss the administrative problems they were confronted with and they observed during their training period in the state. Training at this stage is more problem-oriented. At the end of the training, the probationer appears at an examination held at the Academy by the UPSC. Every probationer is required to secure at least 50 per cent marks in each subject to pass the examination. After he passes the examination, he becomes an officer and is sent to the state of his posting. After being shuttled at various posts in the district and Secretariat for six or seven years, he becomes ripe for the senior post of Deputy Commissioner/ District Collector or any other post of equivalent responsibility.

Training Arrangements for other Services

The L.B.S. National Academy of Adminstration also provides 4 months' educational course in Foundational subjects to the direct recruits in other all-India Central Services besides I.A.S. for which the UPSC holds a common examination. These services are Indian Foreign Service, Indian Audit and Accounts Service, Indian Revenue Service, Indian Posts and Telegraphs Service, Indian Customs and Excise Service, Indian Defence Accounts Service, etc. (It may be noted that the direct recruits to the Indian Police Service do not attend the Foundational course taught at the Academy). After Foundational courses, these recruits leave the Academy and go to their respective institutions for further training.

Indian Foreign Service (I.F.S.)

The I.F.S. recruit has to undergo a training programme for a period of three years. He is attached to a district for sometime to enable him to understand the practical work and undergo a period of secretariat training after receiving educational course in the foundational subjects at the National Academy. He also undergoes training for learning of some foreign languages, subjects related to diplomatic techniques and procedures as well as international affairs. For this purpose he is sent to an Institute of Foreign Languages abroad.

Indian Police Service

The Central Police Training college, Mount Abu, in the State of Rajasthan established in 1948, was shifted to Hyderabad during the Emergency period. The college is under the charge of a Commandant, assisted by appropriate staffs. It imparts training to the new entrants to the Indian Police Service. The general lines of training are similar to those at the National Academy but the subjects of instruction do not include economics or administration, emphasis is placed on criminal law and procedure, crime psychology, scientific aid in detection of crime, physical training, shooting, methods of combating corruption and emergency relief. After the completion of training, the probationer has to take an examination conducted by UPSC. Thereafter, he undergoes a year's programme of field training which means doing the work of various subordinate officers under the guidance of the District Chief. After the field training, he is posted as Assistant Superintendent of Police.

Central Services

The recruits to the Income Tax Service and the Indian Audit and Accounts Service receive educational course in Foundational course at the National Academy of Administration and department training at their respective schools. Thus for the recruits to I.A.A.S. there is the Departmental School at Shimla. The training imparted has a direct relation with the job of the trainees. For practical training they are attached to the Accountant General's office, the divisional accounts offices and the district treasuries. After passing the departmental examination, he is appointed as an Assistant Accounts officer.

The probationers of Income Tax Service get training at the Income Tax Training School, Nagpur after completing Foundational courses at Mussoorie.

Railway Staff College, Baroda imparts training to the recruits in the Railway, Traffic, Personnel and Accounts Services.

The Customs and Central Excise Training School, New Delhi imparts training to the recruits in the Customs and Central Excise Service.

The Institute of Secretariat Training and Management, New Delhi, previously known as the Secretariat Training School, trains the entrants to the Central Secretariat Services — Section Officers Grade, Assistant Grade and Lower Division Grade — in the field of organisation and methods, office procedures, financial rules and regulations etc. On the completion of training, the official has to work for a short term as an Assistant, before he becomes a Section Officer. The Institute also organises refresher courses for officials working as Section Officers and Assistants.

Moiley Committee Report

The Moily committee is of the opinion that the present training modules are too generic and do not inculcate greater domain knowledge in civil servants. According to it suitable measures be put in place for mandatory training of officers periodically at all levels, senior, middle and lower in addition to the induction stage in view of the rapidly changing environment and the increasing demand for improved governance. The quality of training should improve. It should seek to impart to the officer better functional knowledge, skills, aptitudes necessary for performing their assigned tasks more diligently. At the cutting edge level. the focus should be citizen centric and service oriented.

The commission is of the opinion that the expertise which most officers acquire during training goes waste as it is not put to use by the governors. They are not given the fields in which they specialize during training. According to it, the aquisition of domain knowledge has become imperative for All India Services officers in view of the changing context of governance and globalisation. Suitable, relevant and intelligent modules should be devised for the purpose and efficiently taught.

10th report of IInd ARC– Appraisal of transfer of Top service January 2009: In the 10th report of 2nd Administrative Reforms Commission the frequent transfers of civil services on the basis of past data were resented. It held "Unfortunately frequent transfers of civil servants continues to be one of the most vexatious governance problems still facing India. It adversely affects governance because civil servants are not allowed to stay in a position long enough to acquire adequate knowledge and experience of their job, the understanding of the milieu and culture in which they have to function and the problems they need to redress. They are unable to build the required mutual confidence and understanding which take time to develop and is necessary for administrative leadership.[1] They pointed out the shortcomings of frequent transfers as under:

(i) It restraints civil servants to institute and sustain essential reforms

(ii) It is demoralising and demotivating for the civil services not to see personally the fruitful outcome of their hard lobour which could be the source of satisfaction to dedicated souls.

(iii) Frequent transfers and postings against different assignments may lead to lack of accountability and corruption.

(iv) In the state governments the situation was still worse. In order to curb such tendencies and curtail such possibilities leading to demeaning and eventually denigration of civil services a Central Civil Services Authority should be constituted and given the responsibility of fixing tenure for all civil services under the Union Government.

(2) Presently, the functions of the Authority are envisaged as more advisory as per Draft Public Services Bill 2007. It needs to be changed.

(3) As regards fixation of tenure of civil services is concerned the decision of Authority should be binding on the Government.

(4) The Authority be vested with the responsibility to monitor postings and place before Parliament, a periodic evaluation of the actual average tenure for each post and also for the central government as a whole.

It may be the pointed out that the data collected by the ARC for the 10th Report was not only characteristic of the administration of the lower echelons but also pertains to higher Civil services including IAS and IPS.

State Services

Prior to Independence, the training of State Government employees of various categories, including the Provincial Civil Service used to be largely in-service. However, most of the provinces had their own police training schools/colleges to impart training to both the gazetted and subordinate police officers. In Uttar Pradesh, there was a training school for Patwaris and Quanungos, the linchpin of revenue administration. In 1962 Mr. V.T. Krishnamachari in his Report on the Indian and State Administrative Services, recommended the establishment of training schools in all States.

Many States have made institutional arrangements for imparting training to the new recruits to State Civil Services. U.P. was the first State to set up in 1950, a Staff College at Allahabad. It was, however, disbanded in 1962 under the plea of Emergency and later, of economy. It was revived in 1971 and is at present located at Nainital. Today, almost every State has a training school or Institute like State Institute of Public Administration for imparting training to the members of State Civil services. There are also Secretariat Training Centres and Institutes which provide knowledge of the Secretariat work, to enable the State Civil servants to perform their duties efficiently.

Local Services

The local services, as discussed above, consist of Urban Municipal Services and Panchayati Raj Services. Before Independence, some universities (Nagpur, Allahabad and Lucknow) had instituted Diploma courses in Public Administration and Local Self-Government. Besides, there was an All-India Institute of Local Self-Government which was established in Bombay in 1927. For some years after Independence, the Government of India took no interest in regard to Local Self-Government and its development along new lines in the country. It was only in 1963 that the Government of India appointed Nur-Uddin Committee on the training of municipal employees. The

[1] Hindustan Times: January 12, 2009, Frequent transfers trouble ARC.

Committee recommended the setting up of training institutes at the central level and also observed that "it should be one of the central institute's major responsibilities to prescribe the standard of training and research and it should serve as a model in this respect." The Committee did not rule out the need for setting up State institutes but it was felt that lack of adequate resources, equipment and facility might stand in the way of simultaneous development of a number of state institutes in different parts of the country.[1]

Rural-Urban Relationship Committee (1963-66) also emphasised the need for setting up training and research institutions in the field of municipal administration. As a sequel to these recommendations, the National Centre for Training and Research in Municipal Administration, New Delhi, setup earlier in pursuance of Nur-uddin Committee's recommendations was attached to the Indian Institute of Public administration and now known as Centre for Urban Studies. Four Regional Centres were also setup at Lucknow, Hyderabad, Bombay and Calcutta. The Municipal employees in upper and middle grade of pay undergo orientation courses normally of six weeks duration at these centres. Another central institution setup by the Ministry of Works, Housing and Urban Development, Government of India is the National Institute of Urban Affairs.

In the North Western region of the country including Punjab and Haryana, there is no regional institute to impart training to municipal employees. Both Punjab and Haryana are of the view that their personnel can be imparted training in their respective Institutes of Public administration and at the Indian Institute of Public administration, New Delhi. It is, however, desirable that a regional Centre to serve the needs of the States of Jammu and Kashmir, Himachal Pradesh, Haryana, Punjab and Rajasthan may be setup on the pattern of the other Regional Centres in the country.

The rural local services comprise officials of the Zila Parishad, the Panchayat Samiti and the Panchayat. The key functionaries of these bodies are the Executive Officers of the Zila Parishad, the Secretary of the Panchayat Samiti and the Panchayat Secretary. Besides, there are field workers like *mukhya sevaks, gram sevaks*, extension officers, supervisors and clerical staff. The higher officials are trained at the National Institute of Rural Development, Hyderabad, Tata Training Institute of Social Sciences, Bombay and other training centres situated at Wardha, Allahabad, Lucknow, etc. For other officials, there are state level training institutions. In Punjab, the Block Development and Panchayat Officers, Extension Officers, Accountants, *mukhya sevaks, gram sevaks* etc. undergo training organised by Sardar Vallabhbhai Patel Community Development Training Centre at Batala and Gram Sevak Training School Nabha. In Haryana, there is a training centre at Nilokheri to meet the training needs of the rural local personnel in the State.

It may be pointed out that the training arrangements for local services are quite inadequate keeping in view the complexity of ubran and rural problems and the general apathy of the local people. Not only the number of training institutions is insufficient, the content of training also leaves much to be desired. Much of the training is archaic and not directly related to the changed conditions and requirements of both the urban and rural areas.

In-Service Training

Training is not one-time affair. It is a life long process.

Refresher courses at suitable intervals must be provided to help the employee to bring his knowledge of the work up-to-date and adjust his attitude to the fast changing social environment. The training imparted to an officer at the time of his initial appointment loses its content value after ten years or so. It is, therefore, desirable to organise a variety of mid-term courses for civil servants

[1]*Report of the Committee on the Training of Municipal Employees, New Delhi, Ministry of Health, 1963, p. 7.*

to update their knowledge in the new technique of administration and acquaint them with the latest changes in various fields like Information Technology, management and public relations.

The various Institutes/Colleges/Academies have been set up by the Government of India to provide initial and in-service-training to public administrators. These are :

1. Administrative Staff College of India, Hyderabad.
2. National Institute for Educational Planning and Administration, New Delhi.,
3. Central Emergency Relief Training Institute, Nagpur.
4. Customs and Central Excise Training School, New Delhi.
5. Family Planning Training and Research Centre, New Delhi
6. Indian Audit and Accounts Staff Training College, Simla.
7. Indian Institute of Foreign Trade, New Delhi.
8. Indian Institute of Mass Communication, New Delhi.
9. Indian Institute of Public Administration, New Delhi.
10. Indian Revenue Service Staff College, Nagpur.
11. Institute of Applied Manpower Research, New Delhi.
12. Institute of Secretariat Training and Management, New Delhi.
13. L.B.S. National Academy of Administration, Mussoorie.
14. National Institute of Rural Development, Hyderabad
15. National Institute of Health Administration and Education, New Delhi.
16. National Institute for Training in Industrial Engineering, Bombay.
17. National Police Academy, Hyderabad.
18. Railway Staff College, Baroda.
19. Small Industries Extension Training Institute, Hyderabad.
20. Vaikunth Mehta Natinal Institute of Cooperative Management, Poona.
21. Management Development Institute, Gurgaon.
22. National Institute of Urban Affairs, New Delhi.

Of the above institutions, special mention may be made of Administrative Staff College, Hyderabad, Indian Institute of Public Administration, New Delhi, and Lal Bahadur Shastri National Academy of Administration, which are the apex organisations for training of all categories of higher civil services.

The Administrative Staff College, Hyderabad

This college was established in 1957 to bring together experienced executives of proved administrative capacity and provide them an opportunity of examining different administrative practices in order to prepare them for still higher responsibilities in future. It also facilitates the maximum interchange of ideas and experience and thus enriches the personality of the participants. There is no formal teaching, although some lectures by competent persons on economics, planning, management, accounts, Indian Constitution etc. are arranged. For the rest, the method of training through group discussions and syndicate study is followed. The college does not admit or train new recruits. It also conducts courses for industrial personnel, educational heads and Trade Union Management.

Indian Institute of Public Administration, New Delhi

The Indian Institute of Public Administration has been in the forefront of in-service training for civil services in India. The civil servants belonging to different services viz., All-India, Central and State-have participated in the various Refresher Courses conducted by the Institute from time to time. Some of these courses have been techniques of Administrative Improvement, Financial Control, Administrative Leadership, Development Administration, Modern Aids to Management, Material Planning, Performance Budgeting, Personnel Administration, Project Formulation, O & M Techniques in the Government, Social Policy and Administration, Economic Decision-Making etc. Besides, conducting Refresher courses, the Institute has also organised various seminars, conferences and workshops for different categories of Government employees.

As regards **in-service training for I.A.S. officers,** the Ministry of Personnel has drawn up the programme, keeping in view the pertinent training needs at four stages, vis. 6-9 years service; 10-16 years service; 17-20 years service and above 21 years. The course designed for the group of 6-9 years is for a period of four weeks and covers environmental analysis, interpersonnel skills, project management, rural and urban development programs, management of public enterprises, education, water and health services and decision-making techniques. This course is arranged by the Indian Institute of Public Administration.

For the second stage, comprising 10-16 years Service, the main thrust is on the aspects of modern management concepts and decision analysis, with particular focus on management in Government as well as in the public sector. For this course, the officers are sent to an Indian Institute of Management. So far as the training for 17-20 years service groups is concerned, it is for a period of four weeks and it relates to policy planning and analysis. This course is conducted by the National Academy of Administration and the Indian Institute of Public Administration. The officers with 21 years or more of service experience are deputed to Administrative Staff College, Hyderabad where there is no formal lecture work but the officers interchange their experience and carry group discussions and syndicate study. The distinguished persons in different fields and disciplines are called to deliver talks.

It may also be mentioned that a number of officers from various services, Centre as well as State, are also now being sent abroad for in-service training for varying period.

Conclusion

While India, after Independence has become training-conscious, it cannot be said that our training arrangements including in-service training are fully adequate or above criticism.

Firstly, the present training facilities are more concentrated at the middle and senior levels, the junior and lowest part of bureaucracy (e.g. the clerks, inspectors and others) stands neglected despite the fact that it is these employees who come mostly in contact with the citizens and who desperately need training in office procedures, in expeditious performance of tasks, in public relations etc. Likewise, the instruments of decisions sorely stand in need of training because implementation of policies and programmes is the weakest link in the chain of Indian administration in general, and planning in particular.

Secondly, the refresher courses are neither well planned nor well imparted. Although, the titles of the courses do suggest sharply differentiated individual contents, one can discover wide component of themes included in most of the courses which signify that a course title has not yet acquired a well-defined or standard vocabulary, and perhaps cannot be offered as a self-contained unit. Moreover, the duration of the course is not given proper thought. A too short or too long duration may defeat the very purpose of refresher course as a too short duration course may not impart adequate knowledge and a too long duration course may make training monotonous and boring.

Further, sometimes, a training programme comes to be organised not because there is any need of it, but because either the theme is in fashion or some one occupying a vantage position is interested in it for extraneous reasons. For example, the courses on Computers, Performance Budgeting, Environmental Pollution attended by officers belonging to a service like Education Service and Police Service for whom these courses have no value from their career point of view or their work-efficiency.

Training must be organised for the enlightenment of the trainees. Concentration on themes which are not being presently practised nor are to gain acceptance in the immediate future may generate disrespect and disillusionment towards the whole training system. A trainee from public services in India who is to work within the Indian social milieu and has necessarily to employ existing tools of work should not be unnecessarily subjected to Western jargon. Training courses should be realistically planned and effectively communicated in the Indian context unless they are to become dysfunctional.

Thirdly, most of the departments send for training only those employees who are likely to receive only minimal benefits because they are the ones who could be spared for training. In many cases, departments even do not send nominations for various training and development courses on the grounds that their limited manpower did not enable them to do so. Sometimes, the same individuals are nominated to different courses in quick succession. It is necessary that departmental heads should develop a positive attitude towards training and development of their personnel.

Fourthly, there is an absence of regular follow-up of the trainees. When the course is over, the participants disperse. No effort is made by the Training Institute to be in constant contact with the trainee and learn the efficacy of training imparted to him. After the course is over, the organisers heave a sigh of relief.

Fifthly, the training program is mostly academic in nature consisting of class-room lectures, seminars, discussions and library study. Field training is miserably lacking in the in-service training program for civil servants. The country-side and the most backward areas of the North-East needs to be studied first hand as most of the bureaucrats are urban-dwellers. During such training period, the officers should stay away from the district headquarters and spend their time in the villages and stay in the village to get first hand knowledge of the multifarious problems faced by the people in these areas. The directive of the Ex-Defence Minister George Fernandes to the Defence Minister officials to proceed to Ladakh and get to know the state of affairs there first hand, aptly points out the need for field training.

Lastly, the success of any training programme depends upon the attitudes and interests of the trainees. The reading habit in our country is generally weak and the bureaucracy is no exception. Additionally, the security of employment and promotion tend to create an apathy towards training which the employees do not consider directly relevant or meaningful either to their lives or their careers. If a person lacks inherent zeal for knowledge and individual striving for excellence, no training will be able to get him off the ground.

***

MACHINERY FOR PLANNING

> *"The undefined position of the Planning Commission and its wide terms of reference have gradually led to its growth as economic Cabinet not merely for the Union but also for the States."*
>
> ***— Ashok Chanda***

CONTENTS:

Ever since Dada Bhai Naoroji published his paper on *Poverty of India* in 1876, Indian leaders had urged the necessity of coordinated action in the economic field as a means to the economic development of the country. As the struggle for national independence progressed, its social and economic aims became more definite. In 1936, Dr. M. Visvesvarayya, the veteran engineer-economist published a paper underlining the desirability and feasibility of planning for industrial growth of the country. He had suggested a 60 member advisory body and Planning Commission of 5-7 members for the formulation and implementation of the plans. However, it was an intellectual exercise only and the Government did nothing in this regard. In 1938, a National Planning committee under the chairmanship of Sh. Jawaharlal Nehru was setup by the Indian National Congress. The committee considered all aspects of planning and produced a series of studies on different subjects allied with economic development of the country. However, the work of this Committee was interrupted due to the outbreak of the second World war during which many of its members went to the jails. Besides this, eight industrialists conceived of a ' A Plan of Economic Development', popularly known as Bombay Plan. There was also a Gandhian Plan prepared by Shriman Nayar. M. N. Roy formulated the People's Plan. These three plans were published by the Department of Planning and Development setup by the Government in 1944.

An interim Government was appointed in 1946 as a part of the process of transfer of political power from Britain to India. An Advisory Planning Board was appointed by the Interim Government in October, 1946 with K.C. Neogy as chairman which recommended the appointment of a Planning Commission to devote continuous attention to the whole field of economic development and to suggest methods and means to rebuild the shattered economy of the country.

The Board also suggested that the proposed Planning Commission should be mainly advisory in character, the final decision resting with the Government. It was like a non-political and permanent body whose membership would not fluctuate with the change in political power.

(A) PLANNING COMMISSION

The Planning Commission was setup as an extra constitutional and nonstatutory body in March, 1950 by a resolution of the Government of India with the following functions:

1. To make an assessment of the material, capital and human resources of the country, including technical personnel, and to investigate the possibilities of augmenting such of these resources as are found to be deficient in relation to the nation's requirement;

2. To formulate a Plan for the most effective and balanced utilisation of the country's resources; which would initiate a process of development raising the living standards and opening more opportunities for a richer and more varied life.

3. To define the stages in which the plan should be carried out and to propose the allocation of resources for the due completion of each stage on a determination of priorities;

4. To indicate the factors which are tending to retard economic development, and determine the conditions which, in view of the current social and political situation, should be stabilised for the successful execution of the plan;

5. To determine the nature of the machinery which would be necessary for securing the successful implementation of each stage of the plan in all its aspects;

6. To appraise from time to time the progress achieved in the execution of each stage of the plan and to recommend the adjustments of policy and measures that such appraisal might show to be necessary; and

7. To make such interim or ancillary recommendations as might be appropriate on a consideration of the prevailing economic conditions, current policies, measures and development programmes, or an examination of such specific problems as may be referred to it for advice by Central or State Governments or for facilitating the discharge of the duties assigned to it.

To be brief, the functions of the Commission are assessment of resources, determination of priorities, priorities for the allocation of resources, formulation of the development Plans of both the Central and State Governments, determining the machinery required for the implementation of the plan, appraisal of the progress achieved in the execution of each stage of the plan, perspective planning, and publication of the journal 'Yojna'.

The main function of the Planning Commission is to prepare a National Plan which means the five year plan broken into annual plans.

Composition

The organization and composition of the Commission has undergone several changes since its inception in 1950. Since the Planning Commission is not a statutory body, its composition can be changed by the Government any time. That's why, a major reshuffle takes place in the composition of the Planing Commission with the take over of every new government. To begin with (1951-52) it consisted of four members in addition to the Chairman and Deputy Chairman. In 1951 the hitherto Deputy Chairman was appointed the Minister of irrigation and power but he continued to be the Deputy Chairman till 1953 when the Minister of Planning was appointed its Deputy Chairman.

In March 1964, there were six full- time members Tarlok Singh, T. N. Singh, Ashok Mehta, P.C. Mahalnobis, M.S. Thacker and V.K.R.V. Rao. The Administrative Reforms Committee in its interim report of April, 1967 recommended that the number of whole time members should not exceed seven. But the Government decided to keep the number of full-time members, including the Deputy Chairman at five. The Planning Commission in 1973 consisted of the Chairman, the deputy chairman, the Minister of Finance and four other members – G. S. Pathak, B. Sivaraman, B.S. Minhas and S. Chakaravarty. The total membership of the Commission as on July 1975 was six – Indira Gandhi, Prime Minister and Chairman, P.N. Haksar, Deputy Chairman, C. Subramaniam, Minister of Finance,

S. Chakravarty and S. Sivaraman as members. The composition of the Commission again underwent a change under Janta Government. The total membership of the Commission was eight with prime Minister as Chairman, Deputy Chairman, D.T. Lakadawala, three full -time members and three part-time ex- officio members — the Minister for Finance, Home and Defence despite the recommendation of the A.R.C. against their inclusion. Mrs. Indira Gandhi on resumption of power in January, 1980 reconstituted the Planning Commission and appointed the Minister of Planning as its Deputy Chairman. Under Rajiv Gandhi, the Planning Commission consisted of the Chairman, Deputy Chairman, four Ministers of home, Finance, Defence and Human Resources as part-time members with Minister of Planning as an ex- officio member, and five full time members. The Minister of Planning ceased to be its Deputy Chairman. Under the Rao Government, the Planning Commission consisted of the Prime Minister as Chairman, a Deputy Chairman, four ministers as part-time members and eight full time members. The successive coalition Governments did not show any active interest in the composition of Planning Commission except to put their own men as Deputy Chairman and include the ministers of their choice as part-time members.

Three things may be noted in the composition of the Planning Commission. First, the Planning Commission does not have any fixed tenure. Any of its members including the Deputy Chairman can be replaced any time. Since the Prime Minister is its Chairman, therefore, any change in the Central Government leading to change of the Prime Minister means the change of the Chairman of Planning commission. The Prime Minister has always been its Chairman. Second, some union ministers have been its part-time members. While the Minister for Finance and Planning have been its ex- officio/ members, the other ministers such as those of Home, Defence and Human Resources have been appointed in their individual capacity at the sweet will of the Prime Minister. Third, the states at no stage now or before, have been represented in the Commission.

The inclusion of Prime Minister and other Ministers in the Planning Commission has not been commended by a section of expert opinion. The Administrative Reforms Commission in its report (1967) had suggested that the Prime Minister should cease to be the Commission's Chairman. The Commission observed, "Ever since the inception of the Planning Commission, discussion has gone on whether the Prime Minister should be its Chairman. Although the practice all along has been for the Prime Minister to be the Chairman of the Commission, there is a view that the association of the Prime Minister with the Commission in this manner has not been healthy. One of the grounds for criticism against this practice is that, taking advantage of the Prime Minister's Chairmanship, the Planning Commission has steadily added to its functions and personnel and has stepped into the areas of executive authority of the Central and the State Governments. The Commission has been sometimes called a parallel Cabinet and sometimes a super Cabinet. It has been strongly criticised on the grounds that, it has proved to be another level in the making of executive decisions and consequently, responsible for the extension of " red-tape methods."[1]

The A.R.C. did not also favour the appointment of minister as members of the Commission. In this regard, it observed: " Experience so far gained, however, show that Ministers, busy as they are with their governmental and parliamentary work, are unable to find time to make a significant contribution to the planning process. Their membership of the Commission has only provided a ground for critics. If Ministers are members of the Commission, the Commission is likely to be committed to Minister's stand with regard to executive matters relating to the implementation of the plans. They will affect its capacity to make a critical appraisal and evaluation of the implementation of the plan by the executive. Further, as the Commission has to formulate plans for the whole country, the inclusion of some Central Ministers as members thereof is likely to expose the Commission to the criticism that the States which they are interested in are placed in a favourable

[1] *Interim Report on the Machinery for Planning, A.R.C., 1967, para 14.*

position and the other States suffer neglect. Such a criticism becomes particularly serious if the parties in power in some of the States are different from the party in power at the Centre."[1]

The exclusion of the States from the membership of the Commission has added to the estrangement of relations between the Centre and the States. Economic planning visualizes a significant state role in the implementation of the plans. The structure of Indian polity is such that most of the development plans are to be carried by the State Governments. More than 60 percent of the total expenditure of planning is on the State subjects. But the role of the State in the plan formulation has been subsidiary. The approval of the National Plan by the National Development Council — a representative body of the State`s Chief Ministers — is only formal. It has neither the time nor the expert knowledge to scrutinise the plan as formulated by the Planning Commission. The Sarkaria Commission also has observed that planning should be a cooperative process between the Centre and the States.

The Planning Commission is a collegiate body. The full Planning Commission meets periodically to review the work and indicate policy guidelines. These meetings are presided over by the Prime Minister as Chairman of the Commission. But the day to day work is carried on by the full-time members among whom the work of the Commission has been divided. Thus one member looks after agriculture, rural development, irrigation, village industries, multi-level planning, etc. The second member deals with industry, labour, transport etc. The third one is in charge of finance and economics. The fourth one looks after education, scientific research and social services, environment etc. The fifth one attends to perspective planning, irrigation, power resources etc. The full-time members remain in close touch with the concerned ministries at the Centre.

Its Internal Organisation

The present internal organisation of the Planning Commission is based on the principles laid down by a group which the Commission setup in September, 1971. These are:

1. There should be a more coherent grouping of the Divisions in the Planning Commission, with a clear delineation of (a) the division lines dealing with various sectors and their inter relationships, (b) the plan formulation and coordination divisions, and (c) the servicing divisions.
2. The division lines need to be strengthened in order that they are fully equipped to (a) undertake the long-term sectoral planning, (b) participate in the preparation and evaluation of projects and programmes, (c) monitor plan performance, and (d) make improvements in the information content of their work.
3. Necessary expertise should be provided in the servicing divisions to provide back-up support for project appraisal, monitoring and evaluation and information.

The internal organization is built around two hierarchies- administrative and technical. The administrative hierarchy is headed by a Secretary who is assisted by Joint Secretaries, Deputy Secretaries, Under Secretaries, senior and junior research staffs, junior administrative and clerical staffs, and miscellaneous staffs. These functionaries are drawn from the I.A.S. and other Central Services like the Indian Audit and Accounts Service, Indian Revenue Service, Central Secretariat Service, etc. The Commission has a staff of more than 2,000 out of which about 800 are officers.

The technical hierarchy begins with the Programme Advisors who report directly to their respective members depending upon the allocation of work among them. They have the status of ex-officio Additional Secretaries to the Government of India. These Advisors have considerable experience of administration in the States and they help the Commission in keeping close touch with the progress of planning and its implementation. The main advisors are :

[1] *Ibid.*

Principal Adviser (Agri); Principal Adviser (State Plans); Principal Adviser (SP); Adviser (SP); Adviser (V and I); Adviser (V & S.); Adviser (Education); Adviser (I & M); Adviser (Perspective Planning); Adviser (Transport); Adviser (LEM); Adviser (Social Development and Women's Programme); Adviser (PAD); Adviser (I & M); Adviser (Evaluation); Adviser (Rural Energy); Adviser (Irrigation); Adviser (Health); Adviser (Energy Policy); Adviser (FR); Economic Advisor (Fiscal and Monetary Policy Modelling); Economic Adviser (Urban and Social Sector Planning). In addition, there were Additional Adviser (I & M) and Additional Adviser (FR). There was also a Joint Secretary (SP), officer on special Duty (I & M) and a Consultant (Employment Policy).

Under the Programme Adviser comes the Chief. The Chief is the head of a Technical Division. There are 26 technical Divisions which are

1. Agriculture and cooperation.
2. Backward classes.
3. Communications, Information and Broadcasting.
4. Education.
5. Health and Family Welfare.
6. Industry and Minerals.
7. Irrigation and Command Area Development.
8. Labour, Employment and Manpower.
9. Plan Information and Publicity.
10. Power and Energy.
11. Rural Development.
12. Housing and Urban development.
13. Science, Technology and Environment.
14. Social Welfare and Nutrition.
15. Transport.
16. Cottage and Small Scale Industries.
17. Rural Energy.
18. International Economics.
19. Financial Resources.
20. Monitoring.
21. Perspective Planning.
22. Plan Coordination.
23. State Plans.
24. Development Policy.
25. Administration.
26. Project Appraisal.

The Chief is assisted by Directors, Joint Directors and other staff. It is also possible that there may be no Chief or Director and the Adviser may have directly under him a Joint Director. Each Division consists of research staffs like senior Research officers, Research officers and Investigators and some Secretariat Staffs. It is in these Divisions that various types of data are collected and processed and put in shape to help in the formulation of plan programmes and policies. These Divisions are responsible for scrutiny and analysis of schemes and programming to be included in the plan, preparation of material for and reports of the Plan, conduct of technical studies and research, follow-up on Plan recommendations, examination of references from Central Ministries, State Governments and voluntary agencies with regard to plan programmes and projects.

Programme Evaluation Organisation

There are no attached or subordinate offices under the Planning Commission. However, there are two organizations, viz., the Programme Evaluation Organisation and Committee on Plan Projects which function in the Planning Commission.

The Programme Evaluation Organisation (PEO) functions as an independent unit of the Commission. It was originally setup in 1952 for making a systematic and periodic assessment of the methods and results of the Community Development Programmes and National Extension Movements. The functions of the organization were later extended so as to cover the field of rural development and to act as the eyes and ears of the Planning Commission in rural areas. The organization is assisted in technical matters by the Programme Evaluation Board. The Headquarters consist of a Director and two Deputy Directors, a number of research officers and other staffs. There are seven regional offices at Calcutta, Bombay, Madras, Hyderabad, Lucknow, Jaipur and Chandigarh. A regional evaluation office is headed by a Deputy Director and has under it a number of Project Evaluation Offices.

The original functions of the Programme Evaluation Organisations were:

1. to make a systematic recurring evaluation of the methods and results of the Community Development Programme by keeping all concerned appraised currently of the progress being made towards accomplishing the programme objectives;

2. to point out those extension methods which are proving effective and which are not;

3. to furnish an insight into impact of the Community Development Programme upon the economy and culture of India;

4. to help explain as to why some recommended practices are adopted while others are rejected.

Over a period of years the Programme Evaluation Organisation's functions have undergone a change and at present its functions are :

1. to carry out evaluation of programmes and plans as contained in the five year plan;

2. to organise training courses in evaluation methodology;

3. to undertake documentation of work done by the Central as well as the State evaluation agencies;

4. to maintain liaison between the Centre and the States in the field of evaluation of programmes;

5. to participate in the annual plan discussions pertaining to evaluation of programmes;

6. to render advice to States in regard to evaluation of programmes.

The P.E.O. has brought out Annual Evaluation Reports making a general review of the programmes and giving a detailed description of its work in certain specified evaluation centres. It also makes an objective test of finding out as to what is actually occurring in the field.

Committee on Plan Projects

The Committee on Plan Projects (CoPP) was setup in 1956 in pursuance of a decision of the National Development Council for exploring the possibilities of achieving economy consistent with efficiency in the projects included in the Second plan. The functions of the committee were:

1. to organise investigations, including inspections in the fields of important projects both at the Centre and in the States through specially selected teams;

2. to initiate studies with the object of evolving suitable forms of organisations, methods, standards and techniques for achieving economy, avoiding wastes and ensuring execution of projects;

3. to promote the development of suitable machinery for continuous efficiency audit in individual projects and in agencies responsible for their execution;

4. to secure the implementation of suggestions made in reports submitted to the committee on projects and to make the results of studies and investigations available; and

5. to undertake such other tasks as the National Development Council may propose for the promotion of economy and efficiency in the execution of the Plans.

Although setup in the background of the Second Five-year plan, the COPP now devotes its main attention to studies relating to management and administration and to economise the construction costs. It works through several teams and groups, which are composed of technical personnel and eminent public men with experience of the subjects detailed for study.

Research Programme Committee

For the purpose of undertaking research in economic, administrative and social problems, the Planning Commission has setup a special organization, viz., the Research Committee. The Committee consists of the Deputy Chairman of the Planning Commission and most eminent social scientists. It invites research projects from interested research workers, gives necessary technical guidance to research workers and provides them with financial assistance. It organises research on problems of social and economic growth.

Besides, the Planning Commission is also assisted by a number of Advisory and Associated bodies such as Advisory Committee on Irrigation; Flood Control and Power Projects; Co-ordination Committee for Planning Forums; National Advisory Committee on Public Cooperation; Foreign Agreements Committee, Rural Industries Planning Committee, Land Reforms Committee etc. the Reserve Bank of India and the Indian Statistical organization are also closely associated with the work of the Planning Commission.

The system of appointing a number of working groups at the stage of the formulation of a Plan is also a very important part of the Indian Planning procedure. In connection with the formulation of a plan, a number of working groups are setup. Some of the important working groups are on Resources, Agriculture, Steel, Industry, Community Development, Fuel, Education, etc. The reports of these working groups form the basic material for the formulation of the Plan.

The Planning Commission also consults the representatives of some of the important organizations in the private sector such as Federation of Indian Chambers of Commerce, the Associated Chambers of Commerce of India, All India Manufacturers Association, etc.

(B) NATIONAL DEVELOPMENT COUNCIL

India being a federal Constitution, it is imperative that there should be a close cooperation between the Planning Commission and the States. As seen above, the States have no representation in the membership of the Commission. However, to make the Plans effective and successful, it was important to have close cooperation between the Planning Commission and the States. The first Five Year Plan (Draft outline) observes: "In a country of the size of India, where the States have under the Constitution full autonomy within their own sphere of duties, it is necessary to have a forum such as a National Development Council at which from time to time, the Prime Minister of India and the Chief Ministers of the States can review the working of the Plan and of its various aspects,"[1] Even earlier, the need of a consultative body representing the provinces, the princely states and some other interests to advise the Planning commission was pointed out.

Accordingly, the National Development Council was setup as an adjunet to the P.C. on August 6, 1952 with the main objective of securing the cooperation of the States in the execution of the plan. The cooperation extended by the states included the following steps : (*i*) to mobilize the

[1]*First Five Year Plan, A Draft outline, p. 253.*

resources and efforts of the country for the implementation of the plan, (*ii*) to evolve common policies in all vital spheres and (*iii*) to ensure balanced development of all regions of the country.

Its Functions

The functions of the National Development Council as set out in the Resolution are :

1. to review the working of the national plan from time to time;
2. to consider important questions of social and economic policy affecting national development, and ;
3. to recommend measures for the achievement of the aims and targets set out in the national Plan, including measures to secure the active participation and cooperation of the people, improve the efficiency of the administrative service, ensure the fullest development of the less advanced regions and sections of the community, and, through sacrifice borne by all citizens, build up resources for national development;
4. To ensure balanced and rapid development of all parts of the country.

As per the recommendations of the Administrative Reforms Commission, the functions of the NDC were revised in 1967. These are (i) to prepare the guidelines for the formulation of the National Plan including assessment of its resources, (ii) to consider the National Plan as formulated by the Planning Commission, and (iii) , (iv) and (v) as set out in the Resolution, setting up the Council.

Thus, the NDC has been evolved as an administrative agency to achieve the fullest cooperation and coordination in planning between the Central Government and State Governments and to bring about uniformity of approach and unanimity in the working of the National Plan. It plays an important role in the preparation and finalisation of National Plans. The Plan as prepared by the Planning Commission is placed before the NDC for its approval. It is here that the Union and State Governments are involved in the decision-making process. The Plan is presented to the Parliament for its final approval after it is passed by the NDC.

Its Composition

The NDC, constituted initially, had the following members — the Prime Minister of India, the Chief Ministers of all the States, all members of the Planning Commission, those Ministers of the Central Government whose cases were being considered, Ministers of State Governments concerning the Ministries of Finance and Planning, and Ministers of Central and State Governments specially invited to attend the meeting.

The National Development Council was reconstituted in 1967 on the recommendations of the Administrative Reforms Commission The reconstituted Council includes the following members — the Prime Minister, all the Cabinet Ministers of the Central Government, the Chief Ministers of all the States, and all the members of the Planning Commission. The Central Ministers whose subjects are being discussed in the Council, also participate in its meetings. The prime Minister is the Chairman of the Council. The Secretary of the Planning Commission performs the duty of the Secretary of the Council.

The Council generally meets once or twice a year to review the Plan programmes. It may constitute *ad hoc* committees to undertake detailed investigation of specific problems.

Evaluation

The National Development Council has served as a good forum for discussions and free exchange of ideas and has created a sense of high responsibility on the part of the State governments for making the Plans a success. It has also served as a useful link between the Central Government, the Planning Commission and the various State Governments. In the words of V.T. Krishnamachari, one of its former Deputy Chairmen, "*It provides a forum in which the Union Ministers and Chief Ministers of States discuss the Plans at important stages in their formulation. Plans are also approved at its meetings after completion and before they are presented to the Parliament and State legislatures. The council also considers social and economic policies affecting the country from a national point of view so that where necessary, uniformity may be secured. In this way, it gives a lead to the country on local issues of policies and promotes collective thinking and joint action on matters of national importance.*"

The National Development Council during the course of its working has gradually acquired powers which has raised questions about its advisory and federal character. Some critics are of the opinion that the NDC has become a "super cabinet" and relegated the Planning Commission. "to the status of a research arm". H.M. Patel has observed, "*Among the advisory bodies to the planning Commission is included the NDC. This is surely inaccurate, as is clear from its composition. The NDC is a body obviously superior to the Planning Commission. It is indeed, a policy making body and its recommendations cannot but be regarded as policy decisions and not merely as advisory suggestions.*"[1] Brecher writes in the biography of Pt. Nehru, "The National Development Council was established as a supreme administrative and advisory body on planning. It lays down policy directions invariably approved by the Cabinet. Since their inception, the NDC and its Standing Committees have virtually relegated the Planning Commission to the status of a *research arm.*"[2]

K. Sanatham is a little more unsympathetic when he says, "*The position of NDC has come approximate to that of a super Cabinet of the entire Indian Federation, a Cabinet functioning for the Government of India and the Governments of all the States.*"[3]

Late A.P. Jain, ex-Food Minister, in an article, charged the NDC for acting arbitrarily. According to him, it encroaches upon the functions which constitutionally belong to other bodies, Council of Ministers at the Central and State levels. In his opinion, it was incompetent, both by law and by the nature of its composition, to take high-level decisions.

Opposed to the above view is the view that the real centre of authority is the Planning Commission. The basic decisions are taken by the Commission which are just formalised in the meeting of NDC. The real authority is the Prime Minister who gives a shape to the proposed Plan first in the cabinet meeting and then in the Planning Commission presiding over both. The approval of the Plan by NDC again presided over by the Prime Minister is just a formality, for the voice of the Prime Minister cannot be defeated by a few Chief Ministers belonging to the opposition parties. During the lifetime of Pt. Nehru and Indira Gandhi, the power of the NDC was more apparent than real. The Chief Ministers do not evince any interest in the meetings of NDC, They are too preoccupied with political machinations to give any deep thought to the Plan priorities and programmes. The National Development Council is more a debating shop than a deliberative body. It's not in a continuous session and is also devoid of expertise except that the members of the Planning Commission due to its small size and expertise is better fitted to understand the problems of country's development and devise suitable strategies and programmes. It is, therefore not correct to say that the NDC "has relegated the Planning Commission to the status of a research arm."

Regarding its federal character, doubts have been expressed whether it has fulfilled the desired purpose. The position of the Chief Minister had a natural setback when this body was reconstituted in 1967 so as to include all Union ministers as per the recommendations of the Administrative Reforms Commission that subserved the purpose of the Prime Minister under the changed political conditions. The infrequent meetings of this body and these also for two/three days do not afford the time necessary for the ventilation of all sorts of grievances that dissident rulers of the State

[1]*Patel, I.I.P.A. Journal, Oct-Dec., 1959, p.466.*
[2]*M. Brecher, Nehru – A Political Biography, p. 521.*
[3]*Sanatham, K., Union-State Relations, p. 47.*

government long for. However, as more and more States are coming under the rule of the opposition parties, the National Development Council is steadily emerging as a more effective federal body to give the States a greater say in the formulation of National Plans.

To conclude, it may be noted that the National Development Council is neither a constitutional nor a statutory body, rather it is a creature of the Union Cabinet and as such its role is only advisory and its recommendations have no binding character. But considering the fact that the Council consists of the Prime Minister , all the Union Cabinet Ministers and the Chief Ministers of all the States, it occupies an outstanding position in the Indian federal structure and its advice, though not backed by any legal sanction, is no less than a popular mandate.

(C) PLAN FORMULATION

The Planning Commission has evolved a certain planning procedure which may be briefly described as under.

In the light of the basic political, social and economic objectives of the Government of India, the Planning Commission lays down tentatively certain general goals to be achieved over a relatively long period, say, 15 or 20 years, after a careful survey of the economic resources of the country and in the light of various technical possibilities. It may be noted herein that every political party has its own particular social and economic objectives, therefore, whenever there is a change in political power , the plan outlook also undergoes a change. After the tentative long-term objectives are approved by the Government of India, the Planning commission formulates certain broad five-year targets, keeping long-term picture in view. These broad five year targets are simply guidelines and are given for detailed discussions to various working groups, one for each important sector. These groups consist of economists, technicians and high-level administrators who work out the details of the policies and programmes needed for achieving these targets. On the basis of the reports of these working groups, the Planning Commission prepares a short memorandum of the Five Year Plan which it places before the Cabinet and the National Development Council. After the approval of the Cabinet and the NDC, the outlines of the Plan are prepared and published. The Draft outline of the plan which lays down the objectives, aims and estimates of the resources is placed before Parliament for approval. The draft is also widely discussed in the press and other forums. At the same time, the Planning Commission invites comments from the State Governments and the Central Ministries. In the light of these discussions, details and comments, the Planning Commission re-drafts the plan and submits it to the Cabinet, National Development Council and the Parliament for final approval. At the same time, the States, districts and the blocks prepare their own plans keeping in view the Draft outline. These are modified later in the light of the final plan approval by the Parliament. The Plan as approved by the Parliament becomes the Final Plan, and is sent to all concerned authorities and organisations for implementation.

As five-year term is a relatively long period, it is a practice in India to break up the five year plan into a series of annual plans. After each year of the plan, the Planning Commission along with the Central Ministries and the State Governments reviews the progress of the Plan during the previous years, reassesses the resources and formulates an annual plan for the next year. This links the plan with the Budget. "An annual plan", as remarked by S.R. Sen, "*Introduces on the one hand, a much needed flexibility in the implementation of the Five Year Plan and, on the other, sets out the programme of development to be implemented every year with sufficient details.*"[1]

The process of a particular Plan starts about three years before the commencement of the plan.

During the period 1951 to 2007 the country has had ten Five Year Plans. The period 1966-69 was a period of plan holiday due to the situation created by the Indo-Pakistan conflict, two successive years of severe drought, devaluation of currency and erosion of resources available for plan progress.

[1]*S.R. Sen, "Planning Machinery in India" published in the journal of I.I.P.A., July-Sept. 1961, p. 221.*

Therefore, the Fourth Five Year Plan was formulated for the period 1969-74. The Fifth Five Year Plan (1974-79) was terminated in between at the end of the financial year 1977-78 by the Janata Government. The Sixth Plan was similarly formulated for the period 1978-83, but with the fall of Janata Government in 1979, the Congress Government which came to power in January, 1980 terminated the Sixth Five Year plan and put up another new plan for the period 1980-85. Thus, there were two Sixth Five Year plans for the period 1978-1985. The Seventh Plan was formulated for the period 1985-90. After the seventh plan was over, there was again a gap in the planning period due to the political changes in the country. There were two Annual Plans for the year 1990-91 and 1991-92, one formulated by the National Front Government and the second by the Rao Government. The Eighth Five Year plan was formulated for the period 1992-1997. The Ninth Five Year plan (1997-2002) envisaging a public outlay of Rs. 8,59,200 crore was approved by the National Development Council on February 19, 1999 — two years behind schedule. The Tenth Five Year Plan 2006 (2002 - 2007) was approved by the National Development Counsil on 21st December, 2002. The Eleventh Five Year Plan also (2007-2012) has got the approval of National Development Council.

(D) PLANNING COMMISSION — AN EVALUATION

Ever since its inception, the composition and working of the Planning Commission has been a subject of great criticism for several reasons.

Firstly, the Planning Commission looks like an agency of the Prime Minister. It is he who appoints members according to his individual judgement. There is no mention in regard to the qualifications and experience of the members of the Planning Commission. The strength of the Commission may vary as per the convenience of the Prime Minister. Moreover, the term of the members is also not fixed. The Administrative Reforms Commission has not favoured the inclusion of both the Prime Minister and Union Ministers in the Planning Commission.[1]

Secondly, the Planning Commission has lost its character as a 'staff agency' in so far as it is getting on an authoritarian pattern. Whatever it recommends is taken for granted not only by the Centre but also by the State Governments.

As one critic has observed, " In fact, the Planning Commission has almost dethroned the Finance Commission, the latter is now restricted to the non-plan sector of State budgets... And given the dominant role of the Planning Commission, the independence and even the usefulness of the Finance Commission, is severely circumscribed. Indeed, the *modus operandi* of Central planning in India precludes the Finance Commission from playing the role destined for it by the architects of the Indian Constitution. Hence, the *raison d'etre of* a separate statutory body like the Finance Commission under the existing circumstances may be seriously questioned."[2] P.J. Rajamanner, the chairman of the Fourth Finance Commission (1965) in his separate note appended to the report, wrote: " It is the setting up of the Planning Commission that has in practice restricted the scope and functions of the Finance Commission."[3]

Thirdly, from a federal point of view, the Planning Commission has seriously affected the autonomy of the States and reduced them to the status of 'doles receiving corporations'. The State Governments rely increasingly on the Commission for economic advice and financial assistance. The Planning Commission not only formulates the Plan of the Central Government but also puts its seal of approval on State Plans. The State governments are called by the Commission one by one to justify their plan projects and the amounts allocated to them. The Commission may reject any development project of a State and refuse grants for it. The Central Government gives assistance to the States either by way of grants or loans for plan projects on the recommendations of the Planning Commission.

[1] *See ante.*

[2] *A.T. Eapen, "A Critique of Indian Fiscal Federation" in Public Finance, Vol. XIV, No. 4, 1969, p. 537.*

[3] *The Indian Journal of Public Administration, Oct.-Dec. 1959, p. 460.*

Fourthly, most of the employees of the Planning Commission are government officers on deputation. They do not welcome their posting to the Commission. It has become a dumping ground for bureaucrats fallen in favour with the government since the posting in the Commission which does not carry that prestige and authority which a posting in the line agency brings, they are always eager to go back to their parent departments. This definitely adversely affects their loyalty and proper adjustment in the Commission. Further, the Commission is a victim of Parkinson's Syndrome. Its staff strength has been continuously increasing without any proportionate increase in the volume of work. The number of personnel working in the Commission is around 2,000 and the total expenditure on it has been around Rs. 8 crores annually. Being a staff- agency, it should have kept itself free from over-staffing.

Fifthly, what is really anomalous is that the Planning Commission is not at all accountable to the Parliament, and any member having a difference of opinion with the Chairman is required to submit his resignation. It is an extra constitutional and non - statutory body, yet it enjoys the supremacy to the extent that it has been called a 'super cabinet,' without any responsibility for its failures to the people. It is 'New Despotism' in the economic garb.

Sixthly, the working of the Planning Commission is defective. The targets prepared by it are un-realistic, divorced from ground realities. The targets are set too high which are seldom achieved. The availability of resources is miscalculated. It has been called "a starry - eyed organisation manned by persons who are fanatically applying text book maxims." Planning is sectoral rather than spatial. The Planning machinery is divorced from operational responsibilities. Plans have failed to realise the targets because of defective and half-hearted efforts of an inadequate plan implementation machinery. The most cherished goals of full employment, eradication of illiteracy and poverty and creation of a more equal society are as distant today as they were when we set out on the road to planned development.

Lastly, since the Planning Commission was setup, there have been global changes in the economic scenario. In the light of the changing situation — economic liberalisation, growing importance of the private sector, disinvestment in the public sector and globalisation and plugging of the Indian economy into the world economy, a creditable case is made out for revamping the Planning Commission. Instead of spending its time and resources on relatively small project files and doling out grants to the states it should develop the policy prescriptions for the many ills that plague the Indian economy and suggest a framework for effective implementation to achieve these objectives. Details of schemes and projects should be left to the Central Ministers and State Governments.

Recommendations of Administrative Reforms Commission

The ARC examined the functions, composition and working of the Planning Commission and made the following recommendations:

1. The Prime Minister has to be closely associated with the working of the Commission but he should not be its Chairman. He may be regularly informed of the matters coming up for discussion at the meeting of the Commission. He may also attend its meetings and address it whenever he considers it necessary. The Prime Minister will preside over the meetings of the Commission when he attends them.

2. The Finance Minister will also be kept informed of the matters coming up for discussion at the meetings of the Commission and he may attend its meetings. But he also will not be a member of the Commission.

3. Ministers should not be appointed as members of the Commission.

4. The Prime Minister or the Finance Minister as the case may be, should deal with matters

of importance of a general or administrative nature relating to the Planning Commission for which the Government would be answerable to the Parliament. Matters pertaining to specific subjects allocated to different Ministers should be dealt within Parliament by those Ministers.

5. The number of members should not exceed seven. They should be selected on the basis of their expertise and experience. Part-time members from among the experts may also be appointed. One of the full-time members should be its Chairman.

6. The members may be appointed for a fixed term of five years. Reappointments may be made in exceptional cases.

The above recommendations of the Commission have not been accepted by the Government of India.

The recommendations accepted by the Government are:

1. The Planning Commission should be divested of its executive functions and decisions so that it confines itself to the formulation of the plans — the long term perspective Plan, the five year Plan and the annual Plan and the evaluation of Plan performance.

2.The Planning Commission should be a non-statutory advisory body having close relations with the Union Government.

3. Long-term research activities should be taken away from the Planning Commission. Primary research work should be got organized through other official and non-official agencies. The operating and field agencies of the government should be used for the collection of data.

4. Allocation of work may be made among the members keeping in view their special knowledge and expertise.

5. Decisions on important questions should be taken by the Commission as a whole and not by individual members.

(E) PLANNING MACHINERY AT STATE LEVEL

In March 1962, the Planning Commission suggested to the State Governments to setup State Planning Boards on the lines of the Planning Commission for the formulation of the plan in the light of the resources and needs of the State. It also suggested that the State Planning Boards should have Chief Ministers as the Chairman and the Minister of Finance as its member. In addition to them, there could be two/three full-time members possessing special knowledge and experience in planning and economic problems. The Planning Commission felt that the Board would be able to carry out the task of planning in a more comprehensive manner than the individual departments which are mainly concerned with the implementation of specific projects. It was felt that the setting up of Boards would improve the quality of planning by way of bringing about expert knowledge and close collaboration with the Planning Commission .

In 1966, the Administrative Reforms Commission also recommended the constitution of State Planning Boards. The Commission observed, "in our view, the basic reason for the absence of temporal, spatial and insectoral phasing of State Plans is the absence of adequate planning machinery at the state and lower levels. In the absence of such a planning agency, the work of project and programme planning could not be taken up in a scientific manner and on a continuous and systematic basis, and planning had to be largely confined to financial planning with very little attention paid to the actual results of plan investment."[1]

The ARC noted that about eight states, viz. Bihar, Gujarat, Jammu and Kashmir, Kerala, Orissa, Punjab, Rajasthan and West Bengal had organised State Planning Boards and Councils, but according to it, " they have best served as, "Public Relations Committee." The appointment of the Boards or other similar bodies have thus not helped in the past to strengthen either the planning machinery or

[1]*The A.R.C. Report on Machinery for Planning, p. 92.*

the process of planning in the states."[1]

The ARC accordingly recommended a three-tier machinery - a state agency, sectoral (departmental) planning agencies and regional and district planning agencies. The functions of the State Boards would be :

1. to make an assessment of the state resources and formulate plans for the most effective and balanced utilisation of these resources.

2. to determine plan priorities of the State within the framework of the priorities of the National Plan';

3. to assist the district authorities in formulation of their development plans within the spheres in which such planning is considered to be useful and feasible and to coordinate these plans with the State Plan.

4. to identify factors which tend to retard economic and social development of the State and determine the set of conditions for successful execution of the plans, and

5. to review the progress of implementation of the plan programmes and recommend such adjustments in policies and measures as the review may indicate.

Accepting the recommendations of the ARC, the Planning Commission again instructed all the States to setup Planning Boards and strengthen the Planning machinery in general. Following the Planning Commission's frequent suggestions, a number of States such as Gujarat, Maharashtra, Tamilnadu, West Bengal, Orissa, Assam, Rajasthan, Uttar Predesh, Punjab, Harayana, Bihar, Kerala, Nagaland, set up State Planning Boards in the late sixties or early seventies.

State Planning Boards

The State Planning Boards are composed of a Chairman, Vice Chairman and some other members. Like the Prime Minister at the Centre, the Chief Minister is the Chairman of the State Planning Board. The Post of Vice/Deputy Chairman is generally occupied by the Finance Minister of the State concerned. It is only in a few States that this post is filled up by a non-official expert.

The number of members of the Planning Boards varies from state to state. It ranges from 1 in Nagaland to 40 in Maharashtra. These members include ex-officials, non-officials and part-time members,. The ex-official members include generally Chief Secretaries to Government, Planning Department Secretaries, Finance Secretaries, Development Commissioners etc. Among the non-officials are included economists, scientists, administrators and State professionals. The Secretary Planning Department generally is the Member-Secretary of the Board. The part-time members are generally appointed on the basis of their eminence in public life and their academic background.

In a number of States, the Planning Boards do not have an independent Secretariat. The Planning Department or the planning wing in the Secretariat of the State Government provides the necessary secretarial assistance. However, some states likes Assam, Bihar, Kerala, Tamilnadu etc. have full-fledged independent Secretariats for Planning. The Secretariat in these States is divided into different divisions like perspective Planning division, Plan Monitoring and Information division, Man Power planning division. Each division is headed by a Director/Deputy Director. In addition, there are various working Groups on separate subjects like — Agriculture, Industry, Irrigation, Science and Technology, Power and Rural Electrification, Financial Resources etc. Committees are also setup for plan review and evaluation, monitoring and plan coordination.

Every State Plan is the product of a compromise between state and Centre, worked out through discussion with the Planning Commission but it is the State's own Planning handiwork that provides the basis for discussion. The Planning Commission after working out the details for both the Central Sector and the State Sector in the light of the Government policies — industrial, agricultural, social

---

[1]*Ibid.*

and economic, and plan priorities, communicates them to the States. At the State level, each department prepares its own plan. The plans prepared by the different departments are consolidated in the Draft form by the Planning department of the State Government which is presented to the Cabinet sub-committee and is subsequently discussed by the State Planning Board. After the approval, the plan becomes a Draft Plan and its copies are sent to the Planning Commission and the Union Ministries. The Planning Commission discusses the State plans with the Chief Minister, the Planning and Finance Ministers of the state concerned where a lot of bargaining goes on, some projects are excluded while others get partly included and financial projections are reduced. Thus, the final State Plan is the outcome of a compromise between the Union Government and the State Government. After the State Plan has been cleared by the Planning Commission, it is placed before the State Cabinet and later before the State Legislature for its approval.

As mentioned above, it is only in few States that the Planning Boards have been provided with separate Secretariat. In the absence of such Secretariats, it is the planning department which is responsible for the formulation of the State Plan and its evaluation. Further, the Planning Boards setup by the States have not been constituted on the lines of the Planning Commission. These Boards have inadequate or untrained staffs. Personnel working in the State planning machinery lack training in planning techniques. Besides, there is a preponderance of official elements in the composition of the Boards. The Vice Chairman is either the State Finance Minister, who is already too preoccupied with his ministerial duties or political manipulations to devote any time to look after the work of the State Planning Board, or a politician accommodated in the ruling hierarchy. The criterion for resource allocation is based on political considerations. It has been rightly pointed out, " In most States, the Planning Boards, like several 'autonomous' corporations have been made sanctuary for disgruntled, defeated or troublesome politicians who tend to treat plan funds as discretionary grants - inevitably, such political accommodation has led to the minimum involvement of economic experts who alone should comprise State Planning Boards"[1].

(F) PLANNING MACHINERY AT DISTRICT LEVEL

The concept of decentralised district level planning has, for a long time, been considered an idealistic approach to planning in India. The Community Development Programme launched in 1952 was a step in the direction of socio -economic development through the involvement of local people. In 1954 the Planning Commission issued guidelines for planning at local levels in regard to agriculture, small-scale industries and corporations. During the period of Second Plan, an effort was made to not only decentralize the administration at the District and Block levels but also to promote the establishment of a three tier system of village, block and district panchayats. In 1969, the Planning Commission issued another set of guidelines for the formation of District Plans. In 1977, the Ashok Mehta Committee was appointed by the Janata Government to inquire into the working of Panchayati Raj institutions and to suggest measures to strengthen them so as to enable an effective decentralized system of planning and development. The Committee was of the view that the district level was broad enough to consider policy options and was immediately below the State – a strategy level for economic planning.

The planning machinery at the district level comprises the officers of the various development Departments and other non -official representatives. The Collector or Deputy Commissioner is the chief coordinator who gets the district plans prepared with the help of other district level officers. The concerned officials assess their resources and formulate the programmes for development in their related fields in consultation with the block and village level officers. Some States have setup District Planning and Development Councils /Boards headed by District Collector or Minister from District. These Councils/Boards are empowered to formulate plans in some States like Maharashtra,

[1]*The Tribune, Aug. 1, 1979.*

Uttar Pradesh, Rajasthan, Tamil Nadu and West Bengal while in other states like Haryana, Gujarat, Kerala, Punjab, Nagaland, these are advisory in nature.

Although, District Planning Boards/Councils have been setup in some States, yet the planning at district level continues to be a unit within the framework of state planning. District outlays are allocated from the divisible outlays provided for in the State Plan. The national leaders have time and again emphasized the role of decentralised planning. However, the machinery of planning at the district level continues to remain weak. The ARC did not consider the need for any elaborate machinery in a district. "At the operational level, the planning cannot be divorced from implementation. A district plan would necessarily have to be in the nature of identifying the particular potentialities of development of the district, and assessment of its crucial needs and formulating of specific measures to exploit the local resources and meet the local needs. The best arrangement, therefore, would be that the same set of persons who are responsible for implementation are also made responsible for planning. We would, therefore, like the work relating to planning at the district level to be handled by the development set -up in the district."[1] The subject of Block planning and district planning was also examined by the Dantwala Committee and the Hanumantha Rao Committee which opined that the Block- level planning was not to be viewed as an isolated exercise but as a link in a hierarchy of levels from a cluster of villages below the block level to the district, regional and state level.

To conclude, planning machinery at the district level continues to be weak and district planning has not become effective despite the tall talk of decentralised planning. The district planning, as practised in an Indian district, is primarily a process of data collection at lower levels. Final decision-making power is not delegated to lower levels. Planning in India is highly centralised. The grassroot Planning has not yet acquired any significance.

***

[1] *A.R.C. Report on Machinery for Planning.*

9

PUBLIC UNDERTAKINGS

"However the weight of the considerations... has led us to the conclusion that the form of public corporation is the one that is best fitted for the commercial and industrial sector in the public sector. ***—Study Team on Public Sector undertakings (A.R.C.)***

CONTENTS: (A) Forms of Public undertakings
(B) Management of Public undertakings
(C) Control of Public Undertakings
(D) Problems of Public Undertakings

The *Laissez -Faire* view of state activity gave place in the 20th century to socialistic view leading to expansion of state functions in the economic and industrial fields. The state is no longer a law and order maintaining and revenue collecting organ, it is now more concerned with the economic welfare of its people. The newly independent states in order to overcome their economic stagnation and the poor rate of growth during colonial rule had to enter the field of industrial and commercial enterprise to ensure better utilization of available resources and build the essential infrastructure for national development. This led to the setting up of public undertakings and creation of a large public sector. In India both the Central and State governments have setup a number of enterprises in the public sector. This sector has seen phenomenal growth during the five decades, spanning seven Five Year Plans from 1951-56 to 2005-2006. The total number of central public undertakings as on 31st March, 2006 was 239 with total investment of Rs. 3, 93, 057 crores. In 1951, the number was five only. Of the 239 public sector emterprises, the government has identified nine as Navratna PSES. These are BHEL, BPCL, GAIL, HPCL, IOC, MTNL, NTPC, ONGC and SAIL. These have been given enhanced power and autonomy.

The major reasons for state intervention in economic activity are: to build up an industrial infrastructure and raise productivity; to increase employment and general standard of living and promote balanced regional development by accelerating national growth and development; to render needed services and cater to public utilities like power, transportation and communication which are capital heavy investments and strictly unprofitable under private enterprise; to provide sources of credit to finance agricultural and industrial production and trade; to prevent/reduce concentration of private economic power and to reduce dependence on foreign capital and aid in the long run.

(A) FORMS OF PUBLIC UNDERTAKINGS

There are three principal forms into which our public undertakings have been organized, namely, departmental undertakings, government companies and statutory public corporations. In addition, there are other forms also such as holding company like, Steel Authority of India Limited and Coal Authority of India Limited; Commissions like, Tariff Commission; Control boards like Bhakra-Beas Management Board; Public Trusts like Port Trusts, Unit Trust of India, Commodity Boards like Tea Board, Coffee Board, etc.

Historically, the *departmental form* has been the oldest, but has now fallen into disuse for economic and financial enterprises due to its inherent features of rigidity and delays. The two big departmental undertakings are Railways and Posts and Telegraphs, though there are others also like All India Radio, Doordarshan, Defence Production, etc. The main characteristics of a departmental enterprise are:

(1) The enterprise is financed by annual appropriation from the Consolidated Fund of India and is a part of the annual Budget (However, Railways in India have their own separate budget).

(2) The enterprise is subject to the Budget accounting and audit controls applicable to other departmental activities.

(3) The staff of the enterprise are civil servants. Their service rules are guided by Civil Service Rules.

(4) The enterprise is subject to the direct control of the head of the department. He is fully accountable through his ministers for the activities of the enterprise.

(5) The enterprise can be sued only through the State. It is not a legal entity.

(6) It is created by an executive resolution. Its creation does not require any prior parliamentary approval.

The second form, i.e. *government company* has been defined under the Indian Companies Act as that company in which not less than 51 percent of the paid up share capital is held by the Central Government and by any State Governments or partly by the Central government and partly by one or more State Governments. The main features of a government company are;

1. It has most of the features of a private limited company.

2. The whole of the capital stock, or 51 percent or over, is owned by the government.

3. All the directors, or a majority of them, are appointed by the government, depending upon the extent to which private capital is participating in the enterprise.

4. It is body corporate created under a general law, i.e,. the Companies Act.

5. It can sue and be sued, enter into contract and acquire property in its own name.

6. It is created by an executive decision of the government without parliament's specific approval having been obtained, and its Articles of Association, though conforming to an Act, are drawn up.

7. Its funds are obtained from the government and in some cases from private shareholders, and through revenues derived from the sale of its goods and services.

8. It is generally exempt from the personnel, budget, accounting and audit laws and procedures applicable to government departments.

9. Its employees excluding the deputationists are not civil servants.

The government company may be wholly owned, partially owned and joint-sector company. A wholly owned Company is one in which the entire share capital is invested by the government itself without any participation from the public. A partially owned company is one in which the government invests at least 51 percent of the share capital, the remaining part coming from the public. A joint sector-company is one in which both the public and private investment has taken place and where the State takes an active part in direction and control. It is a mixed enterprise of government and some other private entrepreneur, the government reserving the power to control and supervise while the private entrepreneur carries on the work of production and management.

The company form is the most acceptable form of organization of public enterprises. A. D.Garwala favoured it for substantial commercial functions.

Some of the government companies are Bharat Heavy Electricals Limited, Hindustan Machine Tools Limited, National Fertilizers Limited, Rashtriya Chemicals and Fertilizers Limited, Bharat Electronics Limited, Hindustan Cables Limited, Hindustan Shipyard Limited, Maruti Udyog Limited, Indian Telephone Industries Limited, Indian Oil Company, etc.

The third form of the organization of public undertakings is *statutory public corporation*. A public corporation may be defined as a legal entity created by the government, but exterior to the government organization, hence financially independent for the purposes of carrying out the activities specified in the law creating it . Its main features are:

1. It is a legal entity capable of suing and being sued, entering into contracts, acquiring and owning property in its own name.

2. It is incorporated under a special statute of the legislature which lays down its purpose, powers and functions etc.

3. Its functions are primarily of a business or industrial nature.

4. It is run on business lines and not in accordance with the departmental procedures and practices. It is possessed of the flexibility and initiative of private enterprise.

5. It has its own budget and finance separate from the national Budget and finances. It holds funds in its own name and enjoys complete autonomy in the management of these funds.

6. It enjoys complete administrative autonomy from the control of the chief executives.

7. Its personnel do not form part of the civil services but are recruited independently with separate conditions of service.

Some of the Corporations constituted by the Central Government are:

Damodar Valley Corporation, Life Insurance Corporation, Industrial Finance Corporations, Indian Airlines Corporation, Air India International, Reserve Bank of India, Central Warehousing Corporation, Rehabilitation Finance Corporation and Employees State Insurance Corporation.

The important corporations within the purview of State Governments are Transport Corporations, Finance Corporations, Power Corporations, etc. It may be noted that the State legislature can create state Corporations only under an Act of the Parliament.

After having described the essential features of the three main forms of organization of public undertakings, the question arises as to which of the three forms is the best for public undertakings in India. The matter has been considered by various committees and commissions such as A. Gorwal Committee, Estimates committee (Second Lok Sabha), Krishna Menon Committee and Administrative Reforms Commission. In this context, the observations made by the study team on Public Sector Undertakings (ARC) deserve special mention. The Team observed:

"To sum up, of all the three forms in which public undertakings have been organized, the departmental form is one that is generally regarded suitable only for undertakings that provide services affecting the totality of the community or the security of the country. The flexibility and autonomy that are needed for commercial and industrial enterprises can not be provided by a departmental form. Such undertakings require a high degree of freedom, boldness and enterprise in management, and must be free from the circumspection and cumbersome, time consuming and vexatious procedures of departmental administration. Both the company form and the public corporation form can provide for this flexibility and autonomy. It is not, therefore, possible to prescribe one of these forms as applicable for all types of undertakings and under all circumstances. The choice will have to depend on the nature of the undertaking, its importance, its magnitude and investment and the role that it is expected to play in economic development, capital formation and provision of goods and services. What is crucial is the vigilance and responsibility with which autonomy is exercised and the meticulousness and spirit of cooperation with which autonomy is respected".

"The Articles of the Association of the Company or the statutes of the Corporation can provide for autonomy and operational flexibility. The Company form gives greater freedom to the executive to determine the structure and autonomy of the undertaking and to decrease or increase the autonomy by revising the Articles of the Association. The Corporation is setup by an Act of Parliament. It is the embodiment of an expressed desire of Parliament to setup a new agency. It is , therefore, setup, after a full and informed public debate on the need, objectives, financial and economic obligations and structure and autonomy of the new agency. Such a debate in parliament and decision that follows it invests the corporation with the sanctity of national approval for its objectives, obligations and structure and undertaking that is created by heavy investments from the scarce resources at the command of the exchequer. While the company form may have all the other advantages that a corporation may have, the sanctity and individuality that a corporation alone can acquire are essential in democracy that nurses and depends on the efficiency of the public sector. Nor can the company form be discarded altogether as useless and unprofitable under all cirumstances."

However, the weight of the considerations... has led us to the conclusion that the form of public corporation is the one that is best fitted for the commercial and industrial sector in the public sector. We are convinced that the public corporation form has distinct advantages over that of the government company. We, therefore, recommend that the government should implement the declared intention of the Industrial Policy Resolution in this behalf and adopt the form of public corporation as the general rule for the industrial and commercial undertakings in the public sector in India."[1]

The ARC in its Report of 1968 recommended that —

1. The form of statutory corporation should, in general, be adopted for public sector projects in the industrial and manufacturing fields.

2. The government company form of organization may be adopted for projects in which there is a measure of private participation.

3. Promotional and development agencies should, as far as possible, be run as statutory corporations or as departmental undertakings.

4. Undertakings which are predominantly trading concerns or which are setup to improve and stabilize particular areas of business, may have the company form of organization.

The government's decision on the above recommendations was that "For certain enterprises providing public activities which are primarily intended to develop the basic infrastructural facilities, the statutory form of management may be preferable. For other enterprises including those operating in the monopolistic field but where the commercial aspect is predominant, the present form of a company may allow more flexibility. The government, therefore, does not consider that the form of statutory corporations should in general be adopted for public enterprises." Thus, the government has continued its earlier policy of having company form of organization for manufacturing and commercial activities, corporation form for infrastructural and big industries and departmental form for service undertakings.

(B) MANAGEMENT OF PUBLIC UNDERTAKINGS

Departmental Undertakings

As said earlier, the departmental form of organization has been the oldest but has now fallen into distinct disfavour so far as the management of public undertakings is concerned. The Posts and Telegraphs and the Railways are the most important departmental undertakings, Department form has been adopted in other areas also like ports, docks, atomic energy projects, printing press, ordnance factories, Mints, security and Currency, Integral Coach Factory, All India Radio, Doordarshan. At the state level fisheries, dairy and milk schemes, forestry and irrigation etc are managed departmentally.

1. *Report of the ARC Team on Public Undertakings, pp. 20-21.*

To illustrate the management of departmental undertakings, we may describe briefly the management of the Railways and Posts and Telegraphs.

The administrative management of Railways is under the charge of Railway Board consisting of the Chairman, Financial Commissioner and four other members. All of them are appointed by the Union Government on the recommendation of the Appointment Committee of the Cabinet. The Board is constituted for a period of five years subject to superannuation on the normal date of retirement. The Chairman of the Railway Board enjoys the status of a Principal Secretary while the other members function as ex-officio Secretaries to the Government. To assist the members, additional members were appointed in 1974 to look after different subjects like commercial, engineering, vigilance, staff, and finance. They used to attend the meetings of the Board without having the right to vote. But now these posts have been abolished and Advisers to the Board have been appointed. At present there are 18 Advisors and Two Directors-General, 62 Executive Directors, one Financial Commissioner and 5 members.

All the members of the Board are responsible to the chairman. He may overrule them but in cases of disagreement, the matter can be referred to the minister. The minister can overrule any decision taken by the Board.

The Railway Board has powers regarding regulations, construction, maintenance and operation of railways. It formulates policies and gets them implemented. It prepares the railway budget and allocates the budgetary grant to the administrative units. It keeps a watch on the operational efficiency, and directs and coordinates the different activities. It gives sanctions to development works and new posts. The posting, transfer and promotion of senior railway officers are made by it. The Board frames various rules and regulations for the efficiency of railway service.

The top management comprises Directors-General: security, railway, health services, and an officer on special duty The railways are divided into nine zones each headed by a General Manager. There are also General Managers of production units: Chitaranjan Locomotive Works; Diesel Locomotive Works; Integral Coach Factory; and Wheel and Axle Plant. To look after research and design, there is a Director-General.

Posts and Telegraphs is the second largest state owned undertaking and public utility service in India. This undertaking is managed by a Directorate-General headed by a Director-General who is assisted by a Board. It may be noted that this department is now known as the Ministry of Communications. The Directorate-General is primarily responsible for the postal, telegraph, telephone and wireless communications in the country. Since December 31, 1984, under the Ministry of Communications, there is a separate Department of Telecommunications which has its own separate Telecommunication Board.

The Board is an internal arrangement and does not have any statutory recognition. It is headed by a Director-General who is also the Secretary of the Department of Posts. In addition, there are senior members and members who look after finance, posts, postal development and agency functions and administration. The senior members are also the Additional Secretaries while the other members are ex-officio Joint Secretaries in the department of Posts. The senior member Finance functions as principal advisor on all financial matters, rates and tariffs, staff establishment matters relating to the postal and railway mail service branches and is responsible for operational matters, rates and tariffs, staff establishment matters. The senior member Posts is in charge of all matters relating to the postal and railway mail service branches and is responsible for operational matters, rates and tariffs, staff, establishment matters and planning. The member Postal Development and Agency Functions is in charge of agency functions concerning banking and insurance. The member Administration is in charge of staff and establishment and service matters, vigilance, organisation and methods, publicity, petitions and welfares.

The Board and the Directorate- General between them exercise all powers of the Department of posts in administrative matters, with the approval, where necessary, of the Minister for Communications. The Board normally meets once in a fortnight, but the chairman may call its meeting any time, he considers necessary. The decision is generally taken unanimously. In case of irreconcilable differences, the matter may be referred to the minister for decision.

The Telecommunication Board which was created in 1984, has the Secretary, Telecommunications Department as the Chairman and four other members entrusted with Services, Production, Technology and Finance. In addition, there are a number of Deputy Directors-General and advisors.

For administrative convenience, the country has been divided into territorial postal units and functional telephone units. There are 15 territorial postal circles viz., Andhra Pradesh, Assam, Bihar, Gujarat, Jammu & Kahmir, Kerala, Maharashtra, Madhya Pradesh, Mysore, Orissa, Punjab, Rajasthan, Tamil Nadu, Utter Pradesh and West Bengal. Each circle is headed by the Post-Master General who is assisted by Deputy Post-Master and Assistant Post masters General who are the senior officers of Indian Postal Service. In a district there is a Senior Superintendent Post Offices, a member of Indian Postal Service, assisted by Superintendents and Post- Masters of Head Offices.

For telecommunication purposes, the country is divided into telephone districts such as Ahmedabad, Bangalore, Bombay, Calcutta, Patna and Poona etc. The telephone district of Delhi is looked after by MTNL (Mahanagar Telephone Nigam Ltd.).

The departmentally managed undertakings are under the complete control of the Minister concerned who is directly responsible for the efficient functioning of the departmental undertaking. For the purpose of administrative convenience some special bodies are setup. Otherwise, the administration does not differ much from the administration of general department. It may also be mentioned that the Posts and Telegraph Board is weaker in authority than the Railway Board. Thus while the latter is the ministry in itself, the former is only a directorate with the status of an attached office in the Ministry of Communications.

Government Companies

India has made great use of company form for the management of its enterprises, such as Bharat Electronics Ltd, and Hindustan Cable Ltd. etc. The government company is setup under the Indian Companies Act and its management is vested in a governing board which is known as Board of Directors or Board of Governors or Management Board. Such Boards include not only full -time functional Directors but also part-time Directors. As a general rule, there is a full- time Chairman of the board. However, on occasions he may be part-time only. Generally , no officer of the ministry is made Chairman of the Board nor is the Secretary to a ministry included in the Board. The chairman is appointed by the government and the members of the Board are appointed by the government in consultation with the Chairman. The tenure of the Chairman and full-time Directors is five years. Two government representatives are appointed as ex- officio members of the Board. In addition, there are two or three part- time members on the Board from outside the government. In order to ensure workers' participation in the management of the company, a representative of the workers working in the undertaking is also included.

The general policy of the company is laid down by the government. The Board exercises general supervision over the affairs of the company. The Board meets periodically and gives directions and sanctions to the management. The Board is free to manage the enterprises subject to certain limitations, for instance, for capital investment beyond certain limits and where the government has to provide funds or government approval is necessary. In matters of foreign exchange, licences and reservation of posts for weaker sections etc. also the government comes into the picture. As said above, the government can give directions in regard to matters of general policy in the fields of purchase, production and marketing.

The number of Directors and the mode of their appointment is laid down in the Articles of Association. In a fully government owned company, all the directors are appointed by the government, while in the case of a mixed company or a company setup with foreign collaboration, one or two Directors may be the representatives of such other interests. The Board exercises two types of powers — general and specific. The general powers are those which are laid down in the Indian Companies Act, while the specified powers are provided in the specific context of the related company. The Chairman of the Board may also be its Managing Director. In case the Chairman is a part-time one, the Managing Director should be a full-time one. The full- time Directors share among themselves the various assignments pertaining to the affairs of the company. Thus one of them may look after matters dealing with presonnel management, another may be the in charge of finance, the third one of production, and so on. Below the Directors in the hierarchy are the General Managers and chief engineers and so on. The General Managers are the heads of various executive departments who report to their director.

The Chairman and Managing Director being the chief executive of the company, presides over the meetings of the Board and inter-alia, ensures the company's accountability to the government, presents the unified image of the company and initiates the activities of different units.

It may be noted that the word 'corporation' has been added with the names of some of the government companies which creates confusion about their nature. The Dairy Development Corporation, The Indian Tourism Development Corporation, Shipping Corporation and Fertilizer Corporation are government companies but do not use the word 'limited' in their nomenclatures.

Public Corporations

As told earlier, a public corporation is setup by an Act of legislature which defines the organization and functions of the corporation. The idea behind establishing a corporation is to secure "a combination of public ownership, public accountability and business management for public ends. "A corporation is free from the ministerial control in respect of its managerial decisions and multitudinous routine activities. The government takes policy decisions and leaves the rest for management and administration to the corporation. Of the various public corporations setup by the government of India, the management of Damodar Valley Corporation may be described by way of illustration.

The Damodar Valley Corporation was setup by the Government of India in 1948 for the development of the Damodar Valley in the states of Bihar and West Bengal. According to the preamble of the D.V.C. Act the functions of the corporation are " the promotion of the schemes for irrigation, water supply and drainage, generation, afforestation and control of soil erosion and finally the promotion of public health and the agricultural, industrial, economic and general well being of the Damodar Valley and its area of operation". Thus it is a multipurpose project. The corporation is also required to cooperate with the participating governments, railway authorities and local bodies in order to reduce to the minimum the inconvenience caused to the public by submersion of roads and communications.

In order to enable the corporation to perform the above functions, it was given powers to acquire movable and immovable property, to construct dams, barrages, reservoirs, powerhouses, canals, etc. to divert and close any road or open space after giving due notice to the persons affected or to the general public, to supply water in bulk to state governments for irrigation, industrial and domestic purposes, generate and sell electricity and to make rules and regulations with the previous sanction of the central government, for carrying out its functions.

The corporation is financially autonomous. Its capital was subscribed by the union and the two state governments concerned. It is empowered to borrow money subject to the approval of the union government. It prepares its annual budget and annual report which is presented to the three governments. The accounts of the corporation are audited in consultation with the Comptroller and Auditor General of India. In policy matters, the decision of the Union Government is final and if there is some dispute between the corporation and the concerned state this has to be referred to an arbitrator appointed by the Chief Justice of India.

There is a Board of Directors to look after the affairs of the corporation which consists of a Chairman and two members appointed by the government of India, after consulting the Bengal and Bihar governments The Union government also appoints a financial adviser to assist the corporation in financial matters. He may attend the meetings of the Board but without the right to vote. To seek the advice on technical matters, the corporation appoints a Board of Consultants. The Director and the Financial Adviser are appointed for a term of five years, however, they may be reappointed. The Act disqualifies a member of the central or state legislature to become a member of the Board. There is also a Secretary appointed by the Union government given the additional title of General Manager. He holds his office for five years but is eligible for reappointment. The other officers are Deputy Secretary, Director of personnel, purchase officer, chief information officer, etc. The corporation appoints its personnel directly according to the provisions of the D.V.C. Act.

The Indian Airlines has been very much in the news on account of the frequent strikes by its employees, hence, its management may also be described. The Indian Airlines till recently was managed by a corporation established on June 15,1953 under the Air Corporations Act, 1953. The Ministry of Civil Aviation issues the necessary guidelines to run the affairs of the corporation. There is a Board of Directors headed by a Chairman. The members of the business community, Director General of Civil Aviation, Air Force, and International Airports Authority are also given representation on the Board. All of them are appointed by the Union government. The Chairman and Managing Director of Air India are also its members.*.

Immediately below the Chairman of the Board, there is a Managing Director who is the chief executive of the corporation. Under the managing Director are two Deputy Managing Directors, Director Finance, Secretary, Chief Vigilance officer and Chief Audit officer. One Deputy Managing Director is assisted by the Directors of Engineering, Operations and Commercial fields while the other has under him the Directors of Training, Planning, Support services and Controller of stores and purchases. The corporation has its headquarters at New Delhi and is divided into northern, southern, eastern and western regions. Each region is headed by a regional Director, who is, in turn, under the direct control of the Managing Director. The regions have been divided into stations.

The regions have also a number of departments viz., commercial, engineering, operation, administration and personnel, stores and purchases, audit, finance, planning, public relations, vigilance and medical The commercial department deals with the passengers and is divided into sections. This department remains in constant touch with the passengers from the time the tickets are issued and till their baggage is unloaded and handed over to them. The engineering department is concerned with the over hauling and maintenance of aircrafts, construction and maintenance of airport buildings and run ways, etc. The operations department is responsible for ensuring proper operation of the aircraft, in flight schedule, in-flight services to the passengers, maintenance and operation of the communication system. The administration and personnel department is vested with recruitment, promotion, transfer, appraisals, grievances, discipline, retirement, joint consultation, handling of disputes, enforcement of labour laws, implementation of awards, welfare services, training arrangements etc. The finance department exercises control over expenditure, arranges finances, allocates funds, collects and records revenues and makes payments. The audit department audits the accounts to ensure their accuracy and proper observance of rules and procedures regarding purchases and expenditures, the air safety department probes into the accidents and mishaps and suggests suitable ways to avoid accidents. The public relations department tries to maintain and enhance the image of the Airlines.

Both the Air India and Indian Airlines Corporations have been converted into Public Limited Companies.

According to Air Cooperations Act, the functions of the Corporation are to meet the needs of reliable, economic and efficient air transport service; to maintain essential and strategic communications in the country during national emergencies; to improve passenger (cargo) services and facilities for consumer satisfaction; to increase contribution to the national economy through a reasonable return on capital consistent with social goals; to foster international tourism in India so as to improve the national balance of payments; to stimulate domestic tourism and internal trade by air for the purpose of developing the Indian market; to provide a share in promoting the social, cultural and emotional Indian values and to participate in the process of minimizing regional economic imbalance; to take part in developing national aircraft and ancillary industry; to encourage employees' participation in the activities of the corporation; and to contribute in promoting the good image of the public sector in consonance with the national ambition.

With regard to the management of corporations, three things may be noted. *First*, there are some corporations like Industrial Finance Corporation and the Industrial Employees State Insurance Corporation in which the governing body or the Board of Directors is distinct from the general body corporate. Thus the Industrial Finance Corporation consists of the various kinds of shareholders, governmental and non- governmental, while its Board of Directors is a smaller body of 12 members. In the same way, the Industrial Employees' State Insurance Corporation consists of the nominees or representatives of the central government, state governments' employers, legislatures, and the medical profession while its governing organ is a smaller body. In the case of the other corporations, the governing body or the board of directors itself constitutes the corporation and there is no general body distinct from it. *Second,* in the case of the Industrial Finance Corporation, Rehabilitation Finance Corporation and the Employees State Insurance Corporation, the Board of Directors consists of the representatives of non-official interests also either nominated by the government or elected by these interest groups themselves. *Third*, in some cases 'local or area boards' are established in order to decentralize the administration, as in the case of the State Bank, Rehabilitation Finance Administration, Industrial Finance Corporation, Employees' State Insurance Corporation, Life Insurance Corporation.

(C) CONTROL OVER PUBLIC UNDERTAKINGS

Public Undertakings in the modern welfare states are considered to be one of the principal instruments of the state to bring about socio-economic development. Since vast public funds are invested in these undertakings and also since these undertakings relate to the strategic core of the economy, it is but imperative that adequate control should be exercised over them in order to ensure their efficiency and enable them to serve social goals and objectives.

Departmental Undertakings

Out of the three forms in which the public undertakings in India have been organized, the control of the government and the parliament is total so far as departmental undertakings are concerned and is justified on the ground that their operations e.g. the Railways, Posts and Telegraphs and Defence undertakings directly or indirectly affect the entire community. The departmental undertakings are more of the nature of service organizations rather than profit earning enterprises. A departmental enterprise is like a division, bureau or section within a department and is a part of governmental organization subject to the control of a minister. It is financed out of the Consolidated Fund and is a part of the annual Budget. It is subject to the same accounting and audit controls as are applicable to other departmental activities. Its staff is a part of the civil service guided by Civil Service Rules. It is directly under ministerial control and accountable to the parliament. Whatever goes wrong, the minister concerned is answerable, though he may not be personally responsible for the wrong caused. The minister can be asked to explain the poor catering arrangement on the railway platforms or the cause of late departure/ arrivals of the trains; though these are routine matters. Thus, in the case of departmental undertakings, there is not much problem so far as control over them is concerned.

Non- Department Undertakings

But, other forms of public undertakings viz., company and corporation enjoy a large measure of operational autonomy. Hence they are free from detailed ministerial or parliamentary control. The problem of control arises only in the case of government companies and statutory corporations. In these cases the ministerial control is exercised through the following measures in the administrative field.

1. The government is empowered to appoint the Chairman and members of the board of management and the Managing Director. The government can remove the members for reasons specified in the Act. This power of appointment and removal gives to the government sufficient authority to exercise effective and strict control, formally as well informally, over the affairs of public enterprises.

2. If a particular board of management fails to carry out the purposes for which it was set up and if it fails to carry out the directives issued by the government, the latter can supersede it and appoint a new board. The supersession is, however, to be reported to the Parliament. It may be noted that this provision does not exist in the case of government companies which are governed by the provisions of the Indian Companies Act. Since supersession is normally not resorted to, therefore, this measure is not an effective measure of ministerial control over public enterprises.

3. The government is authorised to frame the rules and regulations to facilitate the working of these enterprises. Besides, it has the power to issue general policy directions. It is the duty of the board to implement the government policies and rules and regulations communicated to it. Such power is given to the government by the Articles of Association in the case of government companies and by the Enabling Acts of public corporations.

4. The government can institute enquiries into the working of a corporation. Such an enquiry was made by Mr. Chagla in the investments made by the Life Insurance Corporation in Mundhra firms. Similar enquiries can be held in the case of government companies.

5. The government can ask any enterprise to submit information or report on any matter it likes. Every public enterprise submits to the government its annual report of working.

Ministers exercise control over the working of public undertakings in the financial field as follows :

1 Ministers are authorised to appoint a financial adviser in the board of a corporation. Such adviser exercises a sort of veto affecting expenditure and financial policy of the government.

2. The sanction of the government is necessary to (i) incur capital expenditure above a certain amount, (ii) for approving variations in estimates of over 10% and (iii) for matters connected with borrowings, investments, securities, distribution of profits, etc. The Articles of Association and the Controlling Acts of the Public Corporations do have such provisions. For instance, in the case of the Hindustan Steel (Private) Limited, approval of the central government is necessary for increase of capital, issue of new shares, reduction of capital, borrowing of money, issue of bonds, debentures and securities. Similarly, the Air Corporations Act, 1953 required the two Air Corporations to take the previous approval of the government for undertaking any expenditure for the purchase of any immovable property at a cost exceeding a particular limit.

3. The audit of the accounts of public enterprises is done by the auditors appointed by the government. The audit of the departmentally managed undertakings like any other department is done by the Comptroller and Auditor-General. In the case of government companies the statutory auditors of the company audit the company's accounts according to the principles of commercial audit and the Comptroller and Accountant General conducts the audit of the same accounts more or

less on the principles of financial audit applicable to government departments. Under the Indian Companies Act, the company auditors are appointed by the union government. A copy of the audit report of the company auditor is sent to the C- AG who has the right to comment upon the audit report. The audit of statutory corporations is conducted by an independent authority but these corporations are required to submit their annual reports and accounts to the parliament.

Department of Public Enterprises

(Formerly Bureau of Public Enterprises)

The governmental control over public enterprises is decentralized among various ministries according to their functional areas. In order to provide an effective centralized coordinating unit for providing policy and overall guidance to public enterprises and for undertaking a continuous appraisal of the organizational set-up, personnels' requirement, etc. of the public enterprises, a Bureau of Public Enterprises, located in the Ministry of Finance, was setup in 1969 and assigned five specific functions: to provide a central point of reference and consultation and to deal with matters of general interest; to explore avenues of economy in capital costs of projects; to devise steps for improving productivity and profitability; to undertake appraisal and evaluation of selected areas in the performance of public enterprises; and to prepare an annual report on the working of industrial and commercial undertakings of the central government for presentation to Parliament. As a result of the recommendations of the Administrative Reforms Commission, the Bureau was assigned more functions viz. assist the ministries in making an expert scrutiny of feasibility studies and project reports; act as a data bank and a clearing house of informations in respect of important matters of common interest including informations about organizational structure and pricing policies in public enterprises in other countries; to function as the Secretariat of Public Enterprises Selection Board and assist the enterprises in making other selections, and to arrange training programmes and to advise the public enterprises on management development. The ARC was of the view that the Bureau should become the main, if not the sole central agency. It will act as a staff agency but will not undertake any critical evaluation of performance of public enterprises.

The Bureau ceased to exist in September, 1985 and became instead the Department of Public Enterprises under the Ministry of Industry.

Parliamentary control over public enterprises is exercised through the methods of questions, debates / discussions and parliamentary committees

Questions. Under a parliamentary system of government, the first hour of every day parliamentary session is devoted to questions and answers. The questions to be asked by the members of the Parliament are scrutinized by the Speaker with regard to their admissibility. The Speaker examines the admissibility of the questions in the light of certain principles and guidelines. Questions relating to routine administration, personal grievances, or prejudicial to the safety of the state are generally not admitted. The Starred questions are replied orally by the Minister concerned on the floor of the house; the unstarred ones are replied in writing. The questions should pertain to matters of policies or public interests. The members can put questions relating to the acts of commissions or omissions by a public enterprise, its policy and functioning. The Minister under whose functional jurisdiction the enterprise falls, is required to reply the question. Supplementary questions can also be asked. However, the minister may refuse to disclose the informations on grounds of public interest. Since the government companies and corporations possess autonomy in matters of internal administration, the Question Hour in the Parliament keeps the administration alert and circumspect in their actions.

Debates and discussions. Through debates and discussions the Parliament examines and scrutinizes the activities and efficiencies of the public undertakings. The inaugural address of the President, the Budget Speech, enactment or amendment of a law, introduction of Motions or Resolutions, provide an occasion for debates and discussions. Among the various motions are included no Confidence Motion, Adjournment Motion, Censure Motion and Call Attention Motion. In addition, there can be held half-an-hour discussion and two hours debate on any enterprise. The half-an-hour discussion follows the Question Hour when the member feels dissatisfied with the reply given to his question and requests the chair to allow half-an-hour discussion on the subject of his Question. Two hours discussion may be held on a matter of urgent public importance if so allowed by the Chair. The debates and discussions expose the weak points of administration and compel the Government to explain and defend the particular policy or action of the public enterprises.

Reports. Every Statutory Corporation and Government Company prepares an annual report on its policies, activities and programmes during the previous years, and indicates the nature of activities and programmes to be undertaken next year. A copy of such report together with the report of the auditors is placed before each House of Parliament which provides an occasion for it to discuss the acts of omissions and commissions of the enterprise.

Parliamentary Committees. The appointment of the committees by the Parliament from among its membership is a very important method of exercising parliamentary control over public undertakings. The three important committees are Public Accounts Committee, Estimates Committee and Committee on Public Undertakings. Since the establishment of the Committee on Public Undertaking in May, 1969, the role of the Public Accounts Committee and Estimates Committee relating to public undertakings has been taken over by the Committee on Public Undertakings.

Committee on Public Undertakings. In India many members of parliament during the course of a debate on the parliamentary control over public corporations held on 10th and 11th December, 1953, demanded the appointment of a Select Committee on the lines of British Select Committee to keep a watch over the financial working of public corporations. Dr. Lanka Sundaram, who initiated the debate, said, "The Public Accounts Committee is there, but it comes into the picture and holds an inquest perhaps one or two years after the money is spent. There is neither the time nor the opportunity for either the Public Accounts Committee or the Estimates Committee to take a grip of the problems involved here. The basic position is that these committees are already overburdened with work and they have neither the time nor opportunity to go into these questions fully - so each of the corporations in India today has become a monopoly without competition. Each one has become an *imperium in imperio* — small kingdoms, completely assigned to ...the overlordship of the officer who happens to be the Managing Director or Chairman. But in the national interest something must be done immediately to ensure that (a) the control of the minister becomes effective, and (b) the authority of the House is maintained". To achieve this purpose, he proposed the creation of a Parliamentary Committee, apart from the Public Accounts Committee and the Estimates Committee to sit all the year round, specifically charged with the task of looking into the affairs of the various corporations.

The proposal of Dr. Lanka Sundaram was, however, not accepted by the House. The Finance Minister Mr. C.D. Deshmukh, expressing his inability to accept the proposal said, "Is it necessary for Parliament to be informed from day-to-day or session to session as to how a particular corporation is being run? Is it not better to enable the executive to manage these, and then to call the executive to account. That is a consideration which Parliament will have to bear in mind, before they take a decision on this matter".

The Krishna Menon Committee (1959), a subcommittee of the Congress Party in parliament suggested the desirability of a separate committee on public undertakings in view of the fact that the existing methods of parliamentary control over public undertakings were not adequate to bring enough parliamentary criticism to bear on them. As a sequel to the recommendations of this Committee, the Lok Sabha resolved to form a committee on November 20, 1963, and the Committee on Public Undertaking was constituted on May 1, 1964. It consisted of 15 members, 10 elected by the Lok Sabha from among its members and 5 from the Rajya Sabha. These members are elected according to the principles of proportional representation by means of a single transferable vote system. The Chairman of the Committee is nominated by the Speaker from among the members elected from the Lok Sabha. The terms is five years, one fifth of the members retire by rotation every year. Such members are those who have been longest in office. A minister can not be elected as a member and in case a member of the committee becomes a minister, he ceases to be a member of the Committee. There is no bar to re-election of the same members. The committee was setup to examine the working of the following undertakings: Air India International, all government companies, Bharat Electronics, Central Warehousing Corporation, Damodar Valley Corporation, Garden Reach Workshop, Hindustan Aircraft Ltd., Insurance Corporation, Life Insurance Corporation, Mazagon Docks, Oil and Natural Gas Commission.

Of these undertakings, the Committee every year selects six or seven undertakings for detailed study. The public sector outlay in the Seventh Plan turned out to be Rs. 2,22,169 crores. In the eighth five year plan, public sector outlay was Rs. 3,35,000 crores (i.e. 45% of the total). It includes Rs. 2,80,000 crore of fresh investments and Rs. 65,000 crores of revenue expenditure. Thus the actual increase in the public sector outlay was 52 percent over the revised public sector outlay of the Seventh Plan. All this necessitated the institution of a Committee of Parliament in order to examine the working of public undertakings, including, of course, their accounts and finances and enable the parliament to exercise control over their expenditure. The functions of the committee clearly reflect its significance in this direction, particularly when all public undertakings except nationalized banking institutions and those departmentally organized, fall within its purview.

Its functions (*i*) It examines the reports and the accounts of the public undertakings, as earmarked for the committee.

(*ii*) It examines the reports, if any, of the Comptroller and Auditor General on Public Undertakings in the context of autonomy and efficiency.

(*iii*) It examines as to whether or not the affairs of public undertakings are being managed according to sound business principles and prudent commercial practises in the context of autonomy and efficiency.

(*iv*) it can undertake such other functions as may be entrusted to it by the speaker from time to time.

Its Working : The work of the Committee commences with the beginning of the year. The Chairman ascertains full details of the requisite informations from the undertaking concerned. The informations revolve round : (*i*) preliminary and detailed information submitted by the concerned undertakings regarding subjects to be examined; (*ii*) memoranda on the subjects of study submitted by nonofficial organizations; (*iii*) evidence produced by the officials of the undertaking; (*iv*) commercial audit reports and the 'Memorandum of important points' submitted by the C-AG.

Thereafter the Draft of the Committee is communicated to the concerned Ministry, Department, Ministry of Finance, C-AG and the undertaking for verification of the facts. On the basis of the factual information received from these agencies, the report is finalized. The final report is submitted to the parliament. Conventionally, the report is not discussed in the House. However, the action taken on the report of the committee is discovered from the examined undertaking. At the final stage, a 'consolidated Action Taken Report' prepared by the committee is submitted to the Parliament. After presentation of the report a communication is sent to the concerned undertaking and Ministry for furnishing within six months replies to the observations made in the report indicating the action taken thereon. After the receipt of the replies, 'Action Taken Report' is prepared and presented to both the Houses of the Parliament. This Report incorporates comments of the committee on some of the important recommendations regarding which the Government replies have not been found satisfactory by the Committee. It also comprises recommendations accepted by the Government, recommendations regarding which replies have been received but not accepted by the Committee and the recommendations regarding which the government's final replies have not been received.

Besides, the government's replies in respect of recommended action not received by the time of submission of an Action Taken Report are placed before the Parliament, after their actual receipt. Regarding an undertaking examined for the second time, the Committee exhorts the government to indicate the position as to whether or not the recommendations already made have been implemented.

The Committee brought out its first report in April, 1965 and since then it has published over 150 reports, more than half of which are 'Action Taken Reports'. The horizontal study of some aspects of all the enterprises keep all the undertakings under the scrutiny of the committee in some form or the other. The procedure of these studies is welcomed both by the government and the undertakings.

The working sphere of the committee is fairly limited as there are 244 public undertakings out of which ten to fiteeen only come under the examination conducted by the Committee. The committee examines each undertaking practically after every ten years. It does not probe into technical matters and pricing policy of the undertakings. The critics, however, do not attach much importance to scrutiny by this Committee, as its members are neither equipped with expertise and knowledge nor adequate experience for analyzing the working of the selected undertakings. Despite this vehement criticism, it has been observed that the committee has proved to be an effective instrument of control and has contributed towards greater efficiency and economy in the management of public undertakings on account of its constructive and valuable recommendations made from time to time.

(D) PROBLEMS OF PUBLIC UNDERTAKINGS

Public undertakings in India have come to occupy an important role in the socio-economic development of the country. The investments in these undertakings have been increasing at an accelerated rate in the Five Year plans, but despite the huge investments, the performance of public sector has been disappointing. It has belied the hope that it would be an effective instrument for achieving the socio-economic objectives which the country has set for itself. The return on the colossal investments in the public enterprises have been very low and their contributions to the growth of the economy have also not been very significant. The present government, taking a serious note of the poor performance of public sector, has embarked upon the policy of liberalization and is considering the closure of many such public sector units. Recently, a part of the shares of some government companies have been sold out to financial institutions to overcome the problem of resource scarcities. The poor performance of the public sector has naturally invited attention to the problems being faced by it. Among these problems, we may consider the three main problems viz. (*i*) problem of control and accountability, (*ii*) organizational problems including personnel, and (*iii*) problem of profitability.

Problem of Autonomy and Accountability

One of the advantages claimed in favour of public undertakings, as we have seen above is the flexibility and freedom of action in their operating activities. The need for autonomy has been emphasized by various committees and commissions. Thus the Second five Year Plan observed, "These enterprises have to fulfil business criteria and standards and have to meet obligations similar to those expected in the private sector. The general policy, therefore, is to confer upon their managements the largest measure of financial and administrative autonomy".[1] The Third five Year plan emphasised, "If an enterprise does not have real autonomy, it is not likely to be effective."

But, on the other hand, it is also imperative to ensure their accountability. The government is

[1]*Second Five Year Plan, p. 130.*
Third Five Year Plan, p. 267

to see that the public undertakings fulfil the economic and social objectives for which they are setup and that the funds invested in them are not wasted or misused. Likewise, it has also to ensure that the interests of consumers and labour are properly protected.

We have described the methods of ministerial control over public enterprises. While a departmental undertaking is under the full control of the minister, companies and corporations are free from detailed ministerial or parliamentary control. The usual distinction made in this regard is between the 'matters of policy'; and 'matters of daily affairs'. While 'matters of policy' are decided by the government, the undertakings enjoys autonomy in regard to 'matters of daily affairs'. Likewise, questions, adjournment motions or discussions in the parliament are not allowed on internal and routine matters of public corporations. But it is not a simple task to differentiate between 'matters of policy'; and 'matters of daily affairs'. There does not exist any convenient line of demarcation between the two. Mr. A.H. Hanson says, *"As an administrator knows, the process of policy formulation takes place at a number of different levels and therefore it becomes almost impossible to say where 'the general' ends and the 'day-to-day' begins. General principles of policy are not always specifically formulated at the highest level, but may quite often arise from a host of small decisions of the day-to-day order, which collectively constituted something of genuine public importance."*[1] A command can only be relatively more general or more particular than another. Sometimes, the so-called small matters may involve such important matters as might demand the direct attention of the legislature.

In actual practice, a tendency of transgressing their limits and encroaching upon the jurisdiction of the other is observed in both the corporation and the minister. In 1951 on the working of Damodar valley Corporation, Mr. Gorwala observed, "The history of the corporation since then appears to have been a series of unedifying episodes in which, so far as one can make out, the corporation has had to use a great deal of its energies in attempting to maintain its autonomy and sections of government therein attempting to reduce the corporation to the position of a department subordinate to the secretariat". The Estimates committee of the House of People in 1955 remarked, "the autonomous character of DVC has been taken to extreme limits. The DVC has developed strange conceptions of its autonomy and tried to bypass the authority or the advice of the government. Government, in their turn, have failed to keep it within limits although necessary power is vested in them under the Act to do so."

As a consequence of the recommendations of the various enquiry committees, DVC Enquiry Committee, 1952, Chhagla Enquiry Commission, 1958 and the reports of the A.D. Gorwrala and Appleby, the quantum of autonomy of public undertakings in the fields of personnel, finance and administration has been increased by the government.

The ministers have tried to exercise control more through informal methods than through the methods provided for in the Statutes or Articles of Association. The informal control takes the form of consultations between the minister and the Board behind closed doors. The members of the Board do not want to come into clash with the minister. The minister does not give written directives. The ministerial advice is taken as a directive. This kind of informal control has destroyed the autonomy of the public undertakings. The power of the government to appoint members of the Board of Directors and other topmost officials, has been used to appoint 'trustworthy' and 'dependable' persons who look more to the government than to the public undertaking. The result is that there is neither autonomy nor control. Commenting on the nature of relationship between the ministers and public undertakings Robson observed, "It may be due, in some instances, to a minister not wishing to make himself liable to accept the blame or public odium for a particular policy which may turn out badly. In others, it may be because the corporations have not the courage to tell a minister point blank that they refuse to adopt policy he is urging on them unless he gives them a direction in writing to that

[1]*Journal of Public Administration, Jan. 1951, p.*

effect. Whatever the reasons may be, the tendency to rely on influence or pressure rather than formal discussions is misplaced in the relations between minister and the nationalized industries. Ministers must be prepared to face up to the responsibilities they have assumed."[1]

The success of any public sector undertaking depends ultimately upon how far it has been able to harmonize its relations with the government . In the case of public sector, a minister stands on a dangerous ground because while, on the one hand, he does not hold the administrative control over the undertaking, on the other the undertaking by its unwise acts may involve his future. There is a great need of establishing a just balance between autonomy and control through appropriate conventions and understandings. The ministerial power should not be misused for political purposes. The attitude of a minister towards a public undertaking should be that of a friend, philosopher and guide, and not of an unnecessary director. The questions asked in the parliament should be pertinent and policy oriented and its debates / discussions should be objective based on correct informations and proper data. Unnecessary prying into the affairs of the public undertakings may dampen their initiative and enterprise. The parliament should safeguard public interest and simultaneously protect the public undertakings from excessive ministerial interference.

Organizational Problems

The form of organization has an important bearing on the success of an enterprise. The Estimates committee (second Lok Sabha) in its eightieth report, April 1960, observed that no well-defined principles had been followed in determining the form of organization of public undertakings and haphazard decisions had been taken. The committee proposed the setting up of an expert committee to advise the government in the matter. The Krishana Menon Committee and the study team on Public Sector undertakings (ARC) had recommended the adoption of the corporation form for commercial and industrial undertakings. The government has not made much use of the corporation form. It has been adopted in a limited matter only.

In the field of personnel administration, no scientific manpower planning exists in public enterprises. As in the case of departments, the manpower is far in excess than the actual requirements in most of the public enterprises. The problem of reducing the strength has become complicated due to the vested interests having developed. The government has recently offered a number of benefits to the employees who opt to quit the service in order to bring down the excess strength.

Recruitment of top management personnel in public enterprises is mostly based on 'political acceptability' rather than professional competence. Senior civil servants or retired military officers have been deputed in some public enterprises to man the key posts. The Industrial Management Pool constituted in 1957 could serve only a limited purpose and was eventually abolished in 1973. The Public Enterprises Selection Board constituted in 1974 has now improved its position. However, the government has reserved to itself the full privilege of appointing the Chairman, Managing Directors and members of the Board of directors. It also plays a major role in the appointment of full-time executive and functional directors and the General Managers as the members of the Public Enterprises Selection Board are its appointees. However, so far no All-India Public Sector Service has been constituted, which would be a desirable step.

As a result of technological development, and new techniques of production and management, proper training of employees is essential. But training and development of manpower is the weakest link in the management of public enterprises. The Arjun Sen Gupta Committee (1984) observed that "*One of the most vital but neglected areas in public enterprises has been the training or re-training of workers and supervisors, managerial development at the induction and middle levels, as well as the succession planning for the top post*". It was observed by the Head of the Bureau of Public Enterprises in 1979 that "*a critical appraisal of the training efforts often show that they do*

---

[1]*Robson, W.A. Nationalized Industry and Public Ownership, pp. 151-62.*

not improve significantly the trainee's ability. The shortcomings are often accounted for by (i) theoretical orientation of trainers; (ii) ill planning of courses; (iii) duration, (iv) choice of value; (v) improper selection of trainees without adequate linkage to successive plans; (vi) varying culture and background of a group of trainees; etc."

But this is the weakness of training programmes for civil services also. The training programme both for senior and junior level officers/ employees should become an integral part of the management process in public undertakings. A multiplicity of trade unions, owing allegiance to different political parties, have emerged in different enterprises. This had the effect of politicising the public sector. As the sector became more politicised and more politically controlled, it became financially unviable. The government through its ministers and administrators intervenes in all the major decisions regarding contracts to be awarded, technologies to be selected, supplies to be procured, services to be brought and managers to be appointed. The politicisation of public sector led to corruption and the inevitable financial losses.

The financial performance of public enterprises is not of a desired satisfaction. Their poor performance has not only thrown over the national planning process out of gear but at the same time has resulted in higher doses of taxation year after year. In order to overcome the resource constraint, equity shares of some public sector enterprises have been recently sold to the financial institutions. The public sector lacks cost consciousness and is guilty of extravagant expenditure in the shape of purchasing, hiring and furnishing palatial guest houses, providing luxurious vehicles and paying high travelling allowances.

Problems of Profitability

Of the 244 central public undertakings, 98 are in the 'red'. Of the loss making units, 50 were "chronically sick". There is little which suggests that the public sector has turned the corner and launched itself into self-sustaining growth on the basis of internal resource generation. Over 80 per cent of the net profits of public undertakings is based on the performance of petroleum, steel and coal sectors through occasional price increase. The non-petroleum sector has not shown any creditable performance.

The financial losses are partly due to poor operational performance, low capacity utilization, excessive overheads, poor technology, defective pricing policy and political and administrative corruption.

Changing Role of the Public Sector in the Context of Liberalisation: As said earlier India after independence started on the road to economic development through the policy of socialism. But after the dismantling of communism in the Soviet Union it became evident that excessive state control of economy does not necessarily lead to more productivity and greater economic welfare. India also realised that massive investment in public enterprises did not bring in satisfactory profit. Even a return of 5 per cent was not earned. Public enterprises became loss making unit, and a burden on the economy. The Narasimha Rao Government announced New Industrial Policy on July 1991 wherein he affirmed that while India would continue to support the mixed economy, there would be no more nationalisation of private sector industries. Also such public enterprises would have to fed for themselves without additional funding from the government. In other words, henceforth the policy of liberalisation was to be the main plank of Indian Industrial development which implies delicensing, deregulation, disinvestment, privatisation, removal of subsidies and price supports. The first step in the direction of liberalisation was to be partial disinvestment of public enterprise shares. The Government appointed a Disinvestment Commission in 1996 to draw up a comprehensive long term disinvestment programme. The government has decided to list profitable CPSES on domestic stock exchange and to selectively sell small portions of equity on listed CPSES other than the Navratanas. The total proceeds from disinvestment between 1991-92 and 31st March 2007 amounted to Rs 51,608.58 crore.

Another plank of the new economic policy relates to the closure of sick and loss-incurring public enterprises. The government has been under heavy pressure from trade-unions and the leftist political parties in the matter of sick public enterprises to sell them or to revive them. Through an amendment in 1991 of the Sick Industrial Companies Act, 1985 it was made mandatory to refer the cases of sick public enterprises to the Board for Industrial and Financial Reconstruction (BIFR). In Feburary, 1992 a National Renewal Fund was set up to provide social safety to the sick public enterprises.

In India, though the policy of liberalisation has been adopted through delicencing, deregulation and disinvestment methods, yet public enterprises continue to play an important role in economic development. Public enterprises occupy a key position in core sector like steel, iron, fuel, energy and fertiliser. However, there is need for restructuring public enterprises which include modernisation, rationalising of capacity, improvement in management and technical upgradation. It may also be mentioned that in the present global economic recession PSUS have become the favourite choice of the candidates from the reputed business Institutes for placement. PSUS have been able to face the global recession much better than private sector counterparts.

***

Control of Public Expenditure

> *"The public and parliament should be satisfied that somewhere or other in the government there is a guarantee for financial order; that there is some authority which will watch the progress of expenditure, the obligations which the different departments are incurring and will give timely warning if that expenditure or those obligations are either outrunning the revenue provided for the year or engaging the nation too deeply in future years".*
>
> ***—Durell***

CONTENTS :

A well-conceived system of control over public expenditure is necessitated to ensure fidelity of public personnel and to accomplish set tasks economically within the limited period. Hence it has become an integral ingredient of Indian financial administration. Control of public expenditure in Indian democracy is exercised by the parliament through the parliamentary committees, the Finance ministry and the Comptroller and Auditor General. We discuss below these controls which vouchsafe for sound financial administration.

The parliament exercises control through three committees viz., the Estimates Committee, the Public Accounts Committee and the Committee on Public Undertakings.

(A) ESTIMATES COMMITTEE

The Estimates Committee was constituted in April, 1950. To begin with, it was composed of 25 members and its membership was raised to 30 in 1956. Its members are elected every year by the members of the Lok Sabha from amongst themselves according to the principle of proportional representation based on single transferable vote system. Conventionally, since 1956, 2/3 of the members have been re-elected for another year. The ministers cannot seek the membership of the Committee. The Chairman of the Committee is a nominee of the speaker from amongst the members of the Committee. If per chance, the deputy speaker happens to be a member of the Committee, he acts as the Chairman.

Functions of the Committee

The vital task of the Committee is to suggest economies in the expenditure. Hence some critics portray it as 'continuous economy committee'. However, it has not to deal with policy matters. It ensures within the framework of the policy laid down by the Parliament that a bare minimum expenditure is incurred for the fulfilment of objectives of the government. The main business of the committee is to suggest as "to how the policy and objectives of the government could be carried out with the least expenditure of public resources".[1]

[1] *C.P. Bhambri: op. cit. p. 215.*

Second, the committee examines the estimates referred to it by the Lok Sabha or its Speaker with a view to : (*i*) report what economic improvements in organization, efficiency and administrative reforms consistent with the policy underlying estimates, may be effected; (*ii*) suggest alternative policies in order to bring about efficiency and economy in administration; (*iii*) examine whether the money is well laid out within the limits of the policy implied in the estimates; (*iv*) suggest the form in which estimates can be presented to the parliament".[1]

Third, the Committee makes use of estimates as sources of information to avoid waste and extravagance in expending public funds. In a way, the Committee pays close attention to those aspects of governmental activity where men and material are either wasted or underutilized. "In actual practice, the Committee examines current governmental activity in the light of what it costs the public".[2]

Inaugurating the Estimates Committee in May, 1959, the Speaker remarked, "The fundamental objectives of the Estimate Committee are economy, efficiency in the administration and ensuring that money is well-laid out; but if on close examination, it is revealed that large sums are going waste because a certain policy is followed, the Committee may point out the defects and give reasons for the change in policy for the consideration of the House".

Working of Committee

The Committee after its constitution, prepares its programme duly based on the specified estimates which are to be examined. It gathers and collates the required material for necessary examination. The Committee issues questionnaires and holds interviews of the officials of the concerned ministries and departments. It is authorised to call any official to produce relevant papers, records and files for evidence and witness. If disclosure of any document is insidious to public interest, the matter is referred to the Speaker for his guidance. The Committee appoints study groups to conduct on the spot study of the selected projects. On the basis of findings, the Committee formulates its recommendations. However, nothing is to be incorporated in the report unless it is thrashed out with the Ministry concerned. A copy of the Report is communicated to it in advance for verification of facts contained therein. The Report embodying Committee's recommendations is then submitted to the Lok Sabha. No regular debate is initiated on the Report though the members frequently refer to it in the course of discussions on the Budget and the demand for Grants. The Speaker of the third Lok Sabha elucidated that 97 percent of its recommendations had been accepted. What was said there is almost true even today though a seminarian remarked, "In fact, sometimes one gets the feeling that the Estimates Committee merely gives a big list of advices".[3]

However, this is an exaggerated view. The recommendations of the Committee have been invariably judicious and useful.

(B) PUBLIC ACCOUNTS COMMITTEE

It is a relic of the past. It was constituted at the Centre in 1923 and was composed of 12 members — 8 non-officials duly elected by the Assembly and 4 nominated by the Governor General. The Finance member was its Chairman. The Auditor General assisted the Committee. After the attainment of Independence, the Committee became truly a Parliamentary Committee, as it did not have official elements in it. In the initial stage, it consisted of 15 members, all drawn from the Lok Sabha. Its strength was raised to 22, to accord representation to the Rajya Sabha. Thus 15 members are drawn from the Lok Sabha and 7 from the Rajya Sabha. The Committee is elected annually in accordance with the principle of Proportional Representation. To ensure continuity, two years tenure

[1] *Rules of Procedure and Conduct of Business in Lok Sabha.*

[2] *R.N. Aggarwal : Financial Committee of the Indian Parliament in Aspects of Administration, p. 183.*

[3] *Report of the Seminar on Administrative Problems of State Enterprises in India, 1957, p. 10.*

is usually allowed to the members. It is headed by a Chairman who is nominated by the Speaker from amongst its members. Generally, the Chairman belongs to the ruling party. However, on two occasions, opposition parties headed the Committee. Its functions reveal, as to how it helps the Parliament in controlling the expenditure.

Functions

(A) The Committee is to ensure that (*i*) the moneys shown in the accounts as having been disbursed were legally available for and applicable to the service or purpose for which they have been applied or charged; (*ii*) the expenditure conforms to the authority which governs, (*iii*) every re-appropriation has been effected according to the provisions made in this behalf under rules framed by the competent authority.

(B) It is required to examine, in the light of the report of the Auditor General the statement of accounts showing income and expenditure of state corporations, trading and manufacturing schemes and projects together with the balance sheets and the statements of profit and loss accounts which the President may have required to be prepared or are preferred in accordance with the statutory rules regulating the financing of a particular corporation, trading concern or project.

(C) It examines the statement of accounts showing the income and expenditure of autonomous and semi-autonomous bodies.

(D) It considers the report of the Comptroller and Auditor General in cases where the President may have directed him to conduct an audit of any receipts or examine the accounts of stores and stocks. The report is considered ministry-wise and the Committee is authorised to send for persons, papers and records. The Secretaries of the ministries concerned appear before the Committee to clarify the points raised in the audit report. In the words of Asok Chanda, "*the effectiveness of the Committee is largely determined by the thoroughness with which the audit examination has been conducted; likewise, the value of audit criticism depends on the support that it receives from the Committee. Not only are the functions of these two authorities inter-related, but there is a measure of interdependence in their relations*".[1]

(E) The Committee examines the report of the C&AG in order to find out whether the money voted by Parliament has been properly utilized by the authority concerned. In other words, it sees that - (*i*) public expenditure does not exceed the appropriations granted by the parliament without its prior approval, (*ii*) the grant is utilized for the purpose for which it was sanctioned by the parliament, (*iii*) the nature of items of expenditure compiled against a demand should justify their being so compiled.

(F) It also undertakes a review of the form and details in which the estimates are composed.

Working of the Committee

The Committee finalises its recommendations after the witnesses are examined and the report of the CAG is perused. Conventionally, the recommendations of the committee are invariably accepted by the government after they are discussed in the Parliament. In case of any difference of opinion, the government explains reasons for non-acceptance and suggests to the Committee to modify or reconsider them. The committee may either reconsider in the light of the government's view or hold to its own. The differences are resolved by arriving at an agreement. Though the Lok Sabha can discuss the reports of the Committee, in actual practice it is rarely done.

An Appraisal

The critics call it a postmortem committee. Once money has been mis-spent, the loss cannot

[1] *Ashok Chanda : Indian Administration (1958 ed.) p. 175.*

be made good of. It is felt that postmortem is also not devoid of significance. The Committee's scrutiny of accounts is a continuous process. As such, it looks at the present as well as the future. It serves as a deterrent against slackness or negligence on the part of the executive. "The examination, thus leads to general efficiency of the administration. The examination by the Committee may also be useful as a guide for both future estimates and future policies".[1]

Evidently, the Public Accounts Committee plays a vital role in the country's financial administration. It keeps the executive accountable to parliament, thereby lending new dimensions to the nation's fiscal policies and programmes. The Committee, being a nonparty body, has been exposing the irregularities of expenditure incurred on the various departments of the government. In fact, with the increase in the expenditure, the waste and misuse of funds had also been coming to light. Hence it was essential to restrain such tendencies, by imposing a check on waste and misuse of funds. The Committee could unmask such cases where parliamentary authority on the administration of tax laws had been diluted by the executive fiat. The government has been cooperating with the Committee and its reports have been given due recognition. Hence, it was remarked by Asok Chanda, "*It may be claimed that the traditions established and conventions developed by the Public Accounts Committee conform to the highest traditions of a parliamentary democracy*".[2]

It may therefore be concluded that the control exercised by the Public Accounts Committee over the financial matters is fairly significant. It has invariably acted as a Sword of Damocles for the executive. However, recurrence and ever-changing patterns of official neglect or default reflects that the committee's deliberations have not been very fruitful. The critics blame the government for reducing the committee to a toothless watchdog and in general treating all parliamentary committees as sinecures and their reports as documents to be consigned to dust-gathering morgues of Secretariat shelves.

Rajiv Gandhi, the Prime Minister addressing Chairman of Public Accounts Committee on September 10, 1986 observed, "The Public Accounts Committee has been a failure; not that they have failed to do their job well—they cannot be accused of this—but that they have not been able to take the result of their labour to its logical conclusion. Unless parliament asserts itself and tells the Government to mend its ways in the light of suggestions and proposals from expert panels, the Estimate Committee and Public Accounts Committee will be reduced to the status of powerless bodies composed of back benchers in quest of minor perks of office".[3] According to Mr. Amal Dutta, M.P., a former chairman of P.A.C., "Over the years, the expenditure and revenue collection has gone up considerably and the P.A.C. is totally inadequate to perform its task.[4] Further, the committee members do not have the expertise to question the officials about technical matters like atomic energy, space and defence equipments and there is no provision to invite experts to brief the committee members. It is also pointed out that the attendance of the members in the meetings is very low. Ministers do not appear before the committee to explain the reasons for any policy decision. According to T.N. Chaturvedi, a former CAG, "The follow up action on the PAC report is lackdaisical and evasive. The government has the support of the ruling party and they consider any criticism to be a fault of the party instead of the administration. Therefore, the PAC and other parliamentary committees are losing their edge".[5] However, one cannot ignore the fact that, through this Committee regularity and economy in expenditure has been ensured. The Committee has ensured that expenditure does not exceed the grants made by the Parliament and that money was spent for the purpose for which it was sanctioned.

---

[1]*G.V. Mavalankar : Speeches and Writings. Speech to the PAR April, 1950, p. 97.*

[2]*Ashok Chanda : op. cit. pp 179-180.*

[3]*The Tribune, September 11, 1986, P. 4.*

[4]*Times of India, March 19, 1995.*

[5]*Times of India, March 19, 1995.*

(C) ROLE OF FINANCE MINISTRY

The Finance ministry is the custodian of all public revenues. As such, it ensures that the tax-payers money is best protected through its effective control over the spending ministries and departments. The Finance ministry exercises control over public expenditure at three stages : according approval to programmes and policies in principle; accepting provisions in the budget estimates; and giving prior sanction to incurring of expenditure, subject to such powers as have been delegated to the administrative ministries. The control exercised at the last stage, impinges on the day to day working of the administrative ministries. Through three instrumentalities viz. rules of business, internal financial advisers and internal audit, control is exercised.

Article 77(3) accords a special position to the Finance ministry in the management of financial matters of the government. No department, without the prior concurrence of the Finance ministry can issue orders involving : (*i*) any abandonment of revenue or expenditure for which no provision has been made in the Appropriation Act; (*ii*) any grant of land or assignment of revenue or concession, grant, lease or licence of minerals or forests, rights or a right to water power or any easement or privilege relating to such concession; (*iii*) the number and grades of posts or the strength of a service or the pay or allowances of governmental officials or any other conditions of their services having financial implications, (*iv*) any matter otherwise having financial bearing whether involving expenditure or not.

The Finance ministry has also been made responsible for reasonable distribution of the total sum amongst the programmes and activities of the government within the plan framework. Obviously, its control at the stage of approving a programme and subsequently at the stage of making of the budget provision for it, is important.

Scrutiny of proposed expenditure by the Finance ministry serves best the interests of purposeful and proper control of finance. The Budget Division in the Department of Economic Affairs of the Finance ministry conducts scrutiny and examination of expenditure on standing charges, consisting of pay, allowances, honoraria of permanent establishments and office contingencies.

Besides, the administrative ministries are required to submit estimates on the continuing schemes. The same are scrutinised by the Department of Expenditure of the Finance ministry. The Finance ministry also examines thoroughly the expenditure to be incurred on the new schemes. The Department of Economic Affairs after consulting the Planning Commission, conducts and considers the screening, taking into consideration the resources available and the priority of each item among the competing demands and suggests their inclusion in the budget. Thus the Finance ministry as a whole, in the capacity of financial representative and adviser to the Government, is to convince itself of the advisability and soundness of the proposed expenditure before according sanction to the administrative ministry to go ahead.

Thereafter, the Finance ministry is to act as watchdog over the progress of expenditure being incurred by the administrative ministries. The spending administrative agencies submit their periodic reports and the Finance ministry issues the necessary directives to caution them. It also sanctions reappropriations beyond the competence of the controlling officers of the spending departments. It has also to see whether the spending ministries and departments surrender the unspent balances before the closure of the financial year. It acts as a guide and adviser to the administrative ministries as well, wherever the need arises.

The Finance ministry has been introducing schemes from time to time to control expenditure to be incurred by the administrative ministries. In May, 1956, an internal financial adviser of Deputy Secretary rank was appointed in the ministry of Power and Irrigation, to scrutinise all financial proposals of the multipurpose projects and render assistance to the Secretary of the ministry in all financial matters.

To effect reform in financial administration, the Central Government adopted a new scheme of delegation of financial powers. Since August 20, 1958, the administrative ministries were provided with Finance officers designated as Financial Advisors who were to deal with budgetary and financial matters and helped the ministry to exercise control over expenditure. If their advice was not accepted by the concerned ministry, the matter was referred to the Finance Ministry and the CAG for information.

Another scheme introduced on June 1, 1962 conceived of a financial adviser as an integral part of the Ministry. He was required to oversee the preparation of budget estimates, tone up financial administration through reporting and test checks and to see that specified procedures and requisite norms pertaining to expenditure are followed. The Heads of the ministries could, however, overrule the advice tendered by the internal financial advisers. However, the condition of referring to the Finance ministry and CAG (according to 1958 scheme), the cases of non-acceptance of advice of the Internal Financial Advisor was waived by 1962 scheme. The Secretary of the administrative ministry was the real authority to deal with matters of administrative and financial nature.

Another scheme was introduced on October 18, 1968 by the Finance ministry. It delegated more financial powers to the ministries, authorised them to have their own internal Financial Advisers and organize their financial cells. The Internal Financial Advisers were made overall in-charge of the internal Finance section, the Budget and Accounts section. They were to be consulted by the Secretary of the ministry concerned before they exercised financial powers. The Secretary could ignore their advice by an order in writing.

In 1975-76, the Central government introduced another scheme of integrating Financial Advisers to all ministries. The financial adviser, according to this scheme, had been made responsible both to the Administrative and Finance ministry. A double role had been envisaged for the financial advisers. The administrative ministry exercises delegated powers with the assistance of financial advisers. The latter also functions under the general guidance of the Finance ministry so far as delegated powers are concerned. The advice tendered by them regarding delegated powers can be overruled by the Secretary.

To sum up, it may be said that the financial advisers are required to conduct reviews so as to be acquainted with the progress of expenditure. It enables the Finance ministry to appraise performance at regular intervals.

Departmental Control over Expenditure

Each Head of the department is to act as the controlling officer regarding the expenditure to be incurred in the department. He has to see that money is spent by the officers of the department as per sanctioned grants for specific purposes. The field officers submit periodic returns and reports concerning the expenditure to the superior officers and to the Head of the department. The Finance ministry lays down an elaborate procedure for the purpose as under :

(*i*) A disbursing officer maintains a special register showing each minor head of account. On the third day of each month, he sends a copy of the entries made in the prescribed register to the controlling officer or to the Head of the department concerned.

(*ii*) The returns framed by the disbursing officers are examined by the controlling officer who is required to see that, (*a*) the classification of accounts has been correctly imparted, (*b*) the expenditure showing progress has been correctly noted and the available balance worked out cautiously, (*c*) the expenditure does not exceed the grant sanctioned, (*d*) the disbursing officer has duly signed the returns, (*e*) in case of discrepancy, the controlling officer prepares a statement duly leased on returns submitted to him and the same is sent to the Head of the department, (*f*) the Head of the department prepares a statement on the basis of the returns received by him. The statement depicting the exact expenditure out of grant at his disposal up to the end of the preceding month, is placed before the Accountant General.

From the above analysis it is, therefore, clear that the Finance Ministry plays a very important role in the field of Government expenditure. Not a single penny can be spent without its being included in the budget formulated by the Finance Ministry. It is one of the ministries mostly sought for by the politically powerful member of the Cabinet. It ensures economy in public expenditure and brings about coordination among the various ministeries so that administration of public affairs may be conducted smoothly, economically and efficiently.

In the monetary and fiscal fields also, the Finance Ministry has an important role to play. The major objectives of monetary policy are to induce saving, provide for profitable, investment of savings, regulate rate of interest on loans and advances, maintain monetary equilibrium between supply and demand of money; remove disequilibrium in the balance of payments, ensure price stability in the market and achieve high economic growth. There are serveral instruments to control and regulate the volume of currency and credit like bank rate, open market operations, variable reservation, credit lending rates and regulation of consumer credit.

Although the Reserve Bank of India as the controller of currency and credit is responsible for the formulation and implementation of monetary policy, however, it acts in consultation with the Finance Ministry and there lies its role in the field of monetary policy making. Both of them in unison go to achieve high rate of economic growth. In the crisis created by global recession, both the Reserve Bank and Finance Ministry were seen making important announcements to check economic slow down and achieve 9% growth rate.

Fiscal Policy refers to government spending, taxing, borrowing and debt management. It is a process of shaping public taxation and public expenditure so as to maintain a progressive and high employment economy free from excessive inflation or deflation. There are three constituents of fiscal policy, *i.e.* taxation policy, public expenditure and public debt policy. As described earlier the annual budget of a country is formulated by the Finance Ministry, hence it is the main organ of the government to determine the fiscal policy for a particular financial year.

(D) COMPTROLLER AND AUDITOR GENERAL

The office of Auditor General was established in 1857. An Audit Board comprising the Auditor General and the Chief of the Military Finance Department was setup in 1860 in order to conduct a monthly appropriation audit. The Board was abolished in 1865 in order to centralise the administration of the entire public account in the Comptroller General. In 1882, the Comptroller General was redesignated as the Comptroller and Auditor General and was assigned the supervision of the accounting system and conduct of an appropriation audit. The Act of 1919 changed the nomenclature. He was, henceforth, to be termed as the Auditor General. The office was accorded statutory recognition and an independent status and authority. He was to be appointed by the Secretary of State-in-Council. The Act of 1935 specified his duties and added to his status. The Constitution of India lays down his powers and states his method of appointment and his position in Article 148.

The Comptroller and Auditor General is appointed by the President by warrant under his hand and seal. He is removable from office only on an address of each House of Parliament as in the case of judges of the Supreme Court. His emoluments are chargeable on the Consolidated Fund of India. His conditions of service are not variable to his disadvantage, during his term of service. He is not eligible for any further office whether under the Union or the State governments. All this has been done to make him independent and impartial and free his office from any kind of extraneous influence and pressure. Even the administrative expenses of the office of CAG are chargeable upon the Consolidated Fund of India.

Powers and Duties

The Constitution of India states, "The Comptroller and Auditor General shall perform such duties and exercise such powers in relation to the accounts of the Union and of the States and of any other authority or body as may be prescribed by or under any law made by parliament......."

According to the 44th amendment of the Constitution (passed in 1978) the accounts of the Union and the States shall be kept in such form of accounts as the President on the advice of the CAG of India may prescribe. The reports of the CAG concerning the Accounts of the Union are to be submitted to the President, who shall see that the following necessary conditions have been complied with : (*i*) that the expenditure is covered by sanction, whether special or general, accorded by competent authority, (*ii*) that it conforms to the relevant provisions of the Constitution or law thereunder and with the financial rules and regulations framed by the competent authority, (*iii*) that it is covered by provision of funds authorised by the competent authority and is within the purpose for which the grant was intended to provide, (*iv*) that the demand is supported by voucher in proper form, the person to whom the payment has been made and the fact of payment has been so recorded as to make second claim on the government impossible; (*v*) that the expenditure has been incurred with the observance of general principles of financial propriety.[1]

Audit against Rules and Orders

The C&AG has to see that expenditure conforms to the constitutional provisions, laws and rules made under it as well as the rules, regulations framed and orders given to the competent authority.

Audit against Propriety

A propriety audit is conducted to detect cases involving extravagance and waste, although the expenditure has formally been conformed to regularity and legality. Such audits are discretionary and are to be conducted tactfully.

Formerly (i.e. before 1976) the CAG was performing both the audit and accounting functions, regarding all financial transactions of the Central and State governments. With the separation of audit from the accounts, the CAG was relieved of the functions concerning the compilation and maintenance of accounts. Since 1976, he has been entrusted with audit responsibility only.

Audit of Public Enterprises

The audit of public enterprises is more or less on the same lines as in the case of the government departments. The findings of the audit related to public enterprise also form part of the C&AG report.

The audit of Employees State Insurance Corporation and National Cooperative Development Corporation and test audit of government companies also falls within the purview of the C&AG. The C&AG is empowered to direct and prescribe the procedure through which the company's accounts would be audited by the auditors appointed by the Government. He can comment upon or supplement the audit reports of the professional auditors. The CAG is to conduct audit in the field which remains uncovered by the internal auditor or the professional auditors. He is empowered to conduct efficiency cum performance audit as well just to appraise whether or not the public enterprises fulfil the objectives for which they were established, whether fruitful results have been achieved commensurate with the money spent, whether there has been expending of money extravagantly and discern weaknesses in the management of affairs, resulting in unavoidable delays impeding the progress.

In the recent past, on the recommendations of the Administrative Reforms Commission, an Audit Board consisting of a Chairman and two members to be appointed by CAG was setup. The report of the Board is included in the audit report which is presented to the parliament.

---

[1]*C.P. Bhambri, op. cit. p. 156.*

Keeping in view the functions of CAG, it can be concluded that the Auditor General serves as custodian of revenues and servant of the legislature. He assists the legislature in seeing that its wishes and decisions expressed in the budget are respected. In the U.K. the CAG is considered a parliamentary officer and the audit conducted by him is on behalf of the House of Commons. So is the case in India. However, Indian audit is primarily a legal audit. The CAG has "to ascertain whether moneys shown in the accounts as having been disbursed were legally available for and applicable to the purpose to which they had been applied and whether the expenditure conforms to the authority which governs it". However, this does not mean that Indian audit is precluded from investigation into or commenting upon the *impropriety,* wastefulness or extravagance of expenditure if a *prima facie* case exists for the same.

The C&AG thus plays a vital role and acts as an extended arm of the parliament in controlling the public expenditure. In the words of Sitaramayya, "the C&AG today has been installed as a supreme master who has his own judgment to look to and who has no frowns or favours to be guided by from outside". Durell has also well-explained his role. "The CAG is the agent of the parliament. He is parliament. Parliament only works through him". T.G. Bowls portrays him, 'the acting hand of the Committee of Public Accounts'. Osber Peaks describes him as the "guide, philosopher and friend".[1] However, the C&AG report is sometimes denounced as 'stage-managed' and 'politically motivated' when it points out an accusing finger at a powerful political leader. Such denouncement of C&AG report is not in the best traditions of the parliamentary system.[2]

Professor Appleby has been very critical of the role of C&AG. His main points of criticism are :

(*i*) The system is in a large measure an inheritance from colonial rule.

(*ii*) The parliament and public give undue importance to the audit rule.

(*iii*) Auditing is highly a pedestrian function with a narrower perspective and very limited usefulness.

(*iv*) Audit of public undertakings is not done in a fashion which may fit the nature of operation of each enterprise.

(*v*) Auditing is strictly negative and aggressive. It does not suit the needs of a welfare administration.

However, Professor Appleby's criticism is not wholly valid. A.K. Chanda, a former CAG has refuted most of these points of criticism raised by Professor Appleby. He states that colonial rule did not have analogous office and such an office was indispensable in a democratic form of government where public accountability of administration is to be secured.

As regards the charge of 'pedestrian function' Chanda opines, 'Dr. Appleby seems allergic to audit which he describes as a highly pedestrian function. This attitude of mind has obviously coloured his observations on the Indian audit organisation'. The role of AG has been widely recognised by democratic countries like the U.S.A. and U.K. and the continental democracies.

Regarding disapproval of auditing of public enterprises Chanda remarks "this suggestion ignores the basic difference between the structure of public and private enterprises", while in the case of private enterprises, those in control have a significant financial stake in the concern and are also vitally interested in its financial operations, there is no such incentive in the case of state undertakings. These are managed by officials without any direct financial interest". A public auditor responsible for the audit of commercial enterprises is primarily concerned with the certification of the profit and loss account and the balance sheet but the audit by the C&AG is much more

[1] *For details on Audit see Chapter 43 of "Public Administration" by the same authors.*

[2] *R.J.D. President Laloo Prasad Yadav termed the CAG Report for the year ending March 31, 1997 as mlafide, full of vendetta and sinister campaign against him. Reported in the Tribune, July 20, 1998.*

comprehensive in scope. It has not only to ensure that the "appropriations made by parliament have not been exceeded without a supplementary vote or that the expenditure conforms to rules but also is to be satisfied as to its wisdom, faithfulness and economy". Hence Chanda so remarks the CAG's office is one of the essential ingredients of a parliamentary democracy "whose role is to uphold the Constitution and the laws in the field of administration". He defines this role as "to maintain the dignity, independence, detachment of outlook and fearlessness necessary for a fair, impartial and dispassionate assessment of the executive in the financial field".

It may, however, be accepted that our audit system needs reorientation so as to meet the requirements of social ideology and objectives of a national government. The administration and the audit should not be treated as two water tight compartments. They must understand each others' point of view, clarify issues and take remedial measures. In Chanda's words, "It must be recognised that the purpose of a plan or project and the manner in which it is being implemented are far more important than mere technicalities".[1]

The audit and administration should be brought closer. They should develop commonness of purpose, of endeavour and of achievement. Each of them should comprise a component of the machinery of government. These components should be properly synchronized in operation so that the optimum result is achieved.

The separation of audit from accounts in March, 1976, through two ordinances of the President of India effected remarkable improvement in the financial management. At a later stage these ordinances were replaced by an amending Act. Commenting on this amending Bill, C. Subramaniam remarked, "We are trying to improve our financial management....we want to be a little more modern and get away from the colonial method of financial management".

We may thus come to the conclusion that public expenditure is to be kept under three pronged control if the country's economy is to be safeguarded. The Finance minister is a valuable instrument of balancing the budget and securing coordination of the activities of the government. The parliamentary committees are the most effective tools in the hands of Parliament to expose the administrative extravagance and wastefulness. The Auditor General and his department serves as a means of enforcing accountability and determine the process of ascertaining whether the administration has spent or is spending its funds in accordance with the terms of the legislative instrument which appropriated this money.[2]

A full fledged system of vigil and whetting by standing committees has also been provided in April 1993. There are seventeen such committees, each consisting of 30 members of Lok Sabha (ministers are kept out) and 15 of Rajya Sabha to scrutinize the demands for grants contained in the Annual Budget. It is thus evident that "from now on the House will not only have the opportunity to discuss the details of every grant of every ministry or department but also have the committee's report to guide them".[3] These committees will scrutinize the proposals and send the Inspection report to the House. Evidently many demands for grants are likely to be guillotined without a detailed discussion. That will save the time of the House as well. Besides, the level of discussion will no longer be parochial or regional but also national. The political parties will have to nominate to such committees M.Ps with right aptitude to get the best results.

* * *

[1]*Ashok Chanda : op. cit. pp. 244-45.*

[2]*C.J. Charlesworth : Governmental Administration p. 344.*

[3]*Editorial, The Tribune, dated March 31, 1993.*

ADMINISTRATION OF LAW AND ORDER

> *"Next to the blessings which a nation derives from an excellent constitution and the system of general laws, are those advantages which result from a well-regulated and energetic plan of police, conducted and enforced with purity, activity, vigilance and discretion".*
>
> **— Colquhoum**

CONTENTS : (A) Historical Background
(B) Role of Central Agencies
(C) Role of State Agencies

Maintenance of law and order is the primary condition for the socio-economic development and successful working of the polity of a country. Of late, there has been a disturbing trend as regards the law and order situation in India. Large scale mass violence and anti-authority agitations have become the order of the day. A saddening aspect of the affair is that even the guardians of law and protectors of the public order do not hesitate in disturbing the maintenance of law and order through agitational demonstrations. The policemen of many states have on occasions defied laws and started public agitations to seek redressal of their grievances. During the past few years group clashes, political agitations, industrial strikes, peasant uprisings and students' unrest, besides the problems of terrorism, insurgency, extremism and caste wars have put to test the ingenuity, skill and imagination of all those who have the responsibility for administration of the state. Religious intolerance is on the increase and the secular character of the Indian polity stands threatened.

(A)HISTORICAL BACKGROUND

The police is the main agency of the administrative setup for maintenance of law and order. The word 'police' signifies an organised body of civil servants engaged by the government for the enforcement of laws to regulate different aspects of public life — order and safety. Since people learnt to live in society, there has always been some functionaries to execute the laws and regulations. The indigenous system of police in India was organised on the basis of land tenure and collective responsibility of the village community. The Zamindar in ancient India was found to apprehend all disturbances of peace and make good the loss. The kings had their own network of secret intelligence and kept themselves well-informed about the nature and incidence of crimes. Kautilya's Arthasastra written about 310 B.C. gives a graphic account of the investigation patterns, punishment agencies and control devices during the Mauryan period. In the literature following Arthasastra, we come across Thirukkural written by Thiruvalluvar describing the principles and practices of criminal administration of that period. Although the ancient writers had special knowledge about the administration of law and order during that period, yet there was no independent police department with the exclusive functions of detection and control of crimes. There existed several agencies for the maintenance of law and order in society.

After the decline of the Hindu kingdoms, the country slipped into a state of disintegration and chaos. The police functions were exercised by a number of functionaries like superintendents of roads and buildings, excise, treasury, royal household and all kinds of spies.

During the Mughal period, the empire was divided into *Subas* (provinces) under the charge of *Subedars* (Governors) who had a number of *Fauzdars* under him to administer the sub-divisons. The sub-divisions were divided into *Thanas* (Police Station) under the charge of *Thanedars* (Station House Officers). The *Fauzdar* was a combination of the modern collector and the superintendent of police. His duties in the fields of revenue and criminal administration overlapped and so was the situation in the case of *Thanedar* also, who was not an exclusive police officer. In the cities and large towns the *Kotwal* had the responsibility of maintaining law and order and arranging night patrolling. Abul Fazal in his *Ain-i-Akbari* calls him "a fairly important man of the town who had to be present at all royal *darbars*". He was a magistrate, a prefect of police and a municipal officer, all rolled into one. The Mughal system of the administration of law and order could not, however, bear the stresses and strains of political instability which followed in the wake of disintegration of the central authority of Mughal empire.

When the East India Company took over the reins of administration from the Mughals, the law and order situation in the empire was at a very low ebb. The company rulers evolved a concrete policy of gradual but piecemeal reforms in the organization and working of police machine in India. They retained the village system but relieved the *Zamindars* of their liability for police duties. The company administration appointed magistrates and *Darogas* and put the latter under the administrative supervision and control of the former. The *Darogas* had specific jurisdiction in regard to police stations and about thirty armed *Burkundazas* and the village watchmen were sanctioned for an average police station in Bengal. The cities continued with the system of *Kotwal*, who had a number of *Darogas* to assist him. In some sub-divisions the medieval institution of *Fauzdar* was not only retained but systematically strengthened.

The mutiny of 1857 shook the very roots of the administration of law and order in India which led the British into serious rethinking about introducing an effective institution for the restoration of law and order in India. The Government of India appointed an all-India Police Commission in 1860 to inquire exhaustively into the police needs of the country. The recommendations of the Commission were incorporated into the Police Act (V of 1861) which continues to govern the basic structure of the police organisation in India till today.

The main recommendations of the Commission were :

1. Adoption of military police;
2. Retention of village police;
3. Constitution of a single homogeneous police force of civil constabulary for the performance of all police duties;
4. A police system on provincial basis with an Inspector General as the head of the provincial police organisation.
5. A district based police system headed by a Superintendent police who was to function under the general direction and supervision of the District Magistrate;
6. A subordinate police force which was to consist of inspectors, head constables, sergeants and constables;

The police reforms of 1860 remained a matter of debate and controversy for the rest of the century. Different provinces allowed different control mechanisms to operate. The reforms did not alter the situation materially and the total scheme remained in abeyance for one reason or the other in various provinces of the country.

Lord Curzon appointed another Police Commission in 1902 to examine the present setup of police organization and its strength, recruitment and pay-scales etc. Some of the main recommendations were :

1. The recruitment to the Indian Police Service to be made entirely in England through examination and for the Provincial Police Services in India by direct nomination and promotion from the ranks.

2. An officer of the rank of the Superintendent of Police should be placed in charge of the police of a district.

3. The village police system should be retained.

4. A central department of criminal investigation was to be established to collect, collate and communicate informations obtained from the provincial C.I.D. or otherwise and to secure full information regarding the commission of crime from the police of the native states.

5. The province was to be divided into several ranges and each such range was to be controlled by a D.I.G. of Police.

6. A separate and independent police organisation to be known as Railway Police Force was also to be constituted.

7. An armed police force was to be constituted at the headquarters of each district to serve as a reserve police force to handle emergent situations.

The obvious objective of these recommendations was to strengthen the district police and to make it serve as a bulwark for the sustenance of the gigantic structure of the British Empire.

The recommendations of the committee were accepted by the Government of India which later on served as the basis for the reorganisation of the police machine in the provinces. The C.I.D. and the Railway Police Force were created. The English rulers laboriously built a structure to suit the colonial needs of the imperial government. It also served the cause of peace and order without which no political structure can survive for long.

The post-independence police organisation in India retains the basic structure of the colonial period. The Constitution of India has retained the Indian Police Service. Likewise the pre-Independence central agencies like the Central Reserve Police, the Special Police Establishment, the Central Intelligence Bureau, the Railway Protection Force have also been retained. In the states also, the *status quo ante* has been maintained in police administration. Although the various State Police Commissions and the National Police Commission (1977) were setup to study the problems of police administration, there has been no comprehensive review at the national level of the police system. The Indian Police organisation more than its other counterparts in Indian administration is basically a prisoner of its history. It is even now exploited by the political masters to serve their personal interests and is hated by the people for its tyranny and arrogance. The dawn of Independence has neither changed the outlook of the Indian police nor improved the system.

The Mumbai terrorists attack on November 26, 2008 has put the Indian police to shame. Its officers and coops were fighting the terrorists with their crude and antiquate firearms and weapons which were no match to those used by the terrorists. They did not even have bullet proof jackets on their body and necessary gadgets to locate the terrorist movements inside the building under attack. Although some of our brilliant and brave police officers and coops lost their lives, however, the inadequacies of our security system to meet the challenge were widely criticized.

(B) ROLE OF CENTRAL AGENCIES

India has developed a complex network of police organisation for the maintenance of public order. 'Public order' and the 'police' are state subjects according to items 1 and 2 of the State list in the Seventh Schedule of Article 246 of the Constitution. According to List 1, item 2, the Union Government can raise naval, military and air forces as also other armed forces. The Union Government is not empowered to raise any police force. The Border Security Force, the Central Reserve Police Force, the Rapid Action Force and the Indo-Tibetan Boarder Police fall in the category of "other armed forces of the Union", and the word 'police' in the title of CRPF and the ITBP is a misnomer. These "other armed forces of the Union" are more commonly known as paramilitary forces. The 42nd Amendment of the Constitution in 1976 has inserted a new article (257 A) authorising the Union Government at its own volition to "deploy any armed force of the Union or any other force subject to the control of the Union for dealing with any grave situation of law and order in any State". The police administration of the Union Territories is an exclusive responsibility and concern of the Union Government.

Role of the Union Ministry of Home Affairs

The role of the Central Government in the working of the police administration in the states is largely played through the Ministry of Home Affairs. The ministry has a special function of giving guidance and assistance to its counterparts in the states in important matters pertaining to criminal administration and specialized problems of law and order. It can provide special assistance to state police organisations by arranging for deputation of extra forces, either from central reserve or from other states. The specific aspects of the role of the Ministry can be mentioned as follows :

1. There are several Acts enacted by the Central Government which govern police action and behaviour at the state level and delimit its internal and inter-state activities in a uniform manner. Such laws are the Indian Penal Code, Code of Criminal Procedure, Indian Evidence Act which are to be followed by the police in the prevention, investigation and punishment of crimes. Similarly, the Central Acts like the Indian Arms Act, Motor Vehicles Act, Preventive Detention Act and the Suppression of Immoral Traffic Act govern police action in the states.

2. The Ministry of Home Affairs is directly responsible for the administration of law and order in the Union territories. The administrative agencies of these territories are specially manned by regular cadres separately recruited.

3. The Indian Police Service is under the control of the Union Ministry of Home Affairs. Though most of the IPS officers serve under State Governments for most part of their careers, yet the State Governments have virtually no control over their recruitment, promotion, training and matters concerning discipline and punishment.

4. The Union Home Ministry plays an important role in the co-ordination of police work and providing a framework on the coordination of police administration. For this purpose, meetings and conferences of State Home Ministers and Senior police officers are called by the Union Home Ministry in order to know their problems in the field of administration of law and order and find solutions through mutual discussions.

5. The Union Home Ministry awards several kinds of police medals and national awards for outstanding police service rendered by policemen in the states.

6. The Union Home Ministry arranges the supply of modern and sophisticated arms, ammunitions, wireless equipments and vehicles for police use at the state level. The efficiency of the police depends largely on the quality of arms possessed by them. One of the reasons for the failure of our police force to counter the militants and terrorists' activities is the better quality of weapons possessed by the latter.

7. The Union Ministry of Home Affairs owes to the States to come to their assistance and rescue, in case the police administration in the states need its specialised help and guidance. For the purpose, the ministry maintains an extensive network of auxiliary agencies like Forensic Institutes, Directorate of Police Wireless and Internal Security Academy and reserve units like C.R.P.F., B.S.F., R.P.F., C.I.S.F., the Assam Rifles and the Rapid Action Force.

8. Lastly, the 42nd amendment to the Constitution has empowered the Union Government to induct its armed forces into a state without the state government's requisition. The control of such forces would remain with the Central Government.

Deployment of Central Forces

The deployment of paramilitary forces by the Central Government without any request from the state concerned has in the past given rise to misgivings, especially in the states where the ruling party was not the same as the party in power at the Centre. The flurry of protests by the Uttar Pradesh Government against locating the forces at Faizabad at the time of Kar Seva by the B.J.P. volunteers in Ayodya in December 1992, caused considerable political furore. The Constitution recognises the responsibility of the Central Government in meeting threats to internal security and ensuring that the government of every state is carried on in accordance with the provisions of the Constitution. When paramilitary forces are sent in aid of a state government, such deployment is at the request of the state government concerned. The operational control in such cases remains with the state government. But when these forces are deployed without any request from the state government, the central government in that case assumes the responsibility for law and order which is a state subject.

The relationship between the state authority and the paramilitary forces deputed by the Centre is a sensitive issue, and they cannot afford to work at cross-purposes. There must be a unified, clear-cut operational control. Otherwise, in a surcharged atmosphere even a small misunderstanding can have disastrous consequences. The central government is absolutely competent to station its forces anywhere in the country. Keeping in view the sensitive nature of this issue, the National Police Commission in its third report remarked, "it is for the consideration of the central government and the state governments whether the central government should be constitutionally facilitated to coordinate and direct police operations in situations which threaten internal security. In our view, the addition of Entry 2A in the Union List of the Seventh Schedule following the 42nd amendment Act, 1976, recognises the need to some extent. We understand that no law has yet been enacted governing the jurisdiction, privileges, and liabilities of the armed forces of the Union deployed in a state in accordance with Entry 2A. We recommend that appropriate law, rules, regulations for this purpose be enacted soon".[1]

Despite the recommendations of the National Police Commission (1977), the Government of India has not detailed out the rules/regulations regarding the liabilities and jurisdiction of the armed forces when deployed in a state. The situation still remains fluid and controversial. It need not be re-emphasised that the central forces and the state police should not work at cross-purposes and that there should be a unified, clear-cut operational control. Otherwise, under the present strained federal-state relations, there may ensue more chaos and disorder.

Central Forces

Prior to independence, the British Government in India managed serious threats to law and order with the help of the Army, which was located in cantonments to assist the civil powers. The use of the Army in Jallianwala Bagh incident is a case in point. Provinces were asked to look after law and order themselves, and the civil police had the District Armed Reserve and Special Armed Police Battalions to assist them. To help the princely states, the British Government created the Crown Resrve Police.

After independence when insurgency erupted in the Northeast and communist uprising took place in the South, the CRP was expanded and Indian Reserve Battalions were raised. International borders were looked after by the respective states. The Chinese aggression highlighted the need to intensively police the Indo-Tibetan border and the Indo-Tibetan Police was created. Later, to strengthen the Indo-Pak border, the Border Security Force was established. Similarly as and when the need was felt, the National Security Guards, the Central Industrial Security Force, Railway Protection Force, Rapid Action Force, etc. were created to deal with specific problems. Although these forces were raised to play a particular role, they have nevertheless been deployed by the Central Government to control serious law and order situation in the States.

The management of para military forces is the responsibility of the Ministry of Home affairs.

[1]*National Police Commission Report, paragraph 14.12*

Below we give a brief descriptive profile of these forces.

1. The Central Reserve Police Force (C.R.P.F.)

The Central Reserve Police Force had its beginning in 1939 as "Crown Representative Police". The primary task of the Force was to help the Princely States to preserve law and order. It was also utilised for other duties like guarding of German and Italian detenues, tackling of the Hur menace, anti-dacoity operations in Madhya Bharat etc.

After independence the CRPF was renamed as 'Central Reserve Police' by an Act of the Parliament. In the succeeding years, the force grew in size with the ever increasing demands on it. The force today is more than 1.5 lakhs strong spread over 129 Battalions including 5 Signal Battalions, 1 Special Duty Group, 19 Group Centres, 7 Training Institutions, 3 Base Hospitals and several other ancillary elements. It has also a Mahila Battalion. The Rapid Action Force was formed in 1992 by conversion of 10 standard battalions of the CRPF to deal specially with riots and riot-like situations.

The CRPF is a reserve establishment for emergencies. It is sent by the Government of India to those troubled sports where the Central Government has a special responsibility to discharge and the situation warrants the use of armed police. The state administration also can in times of special crisis requisition its services. It has today become the most hard-worked force in the land. It has to rush about from place to place– fighting communalism, rushing to help every state which sends an S.O.S. to the Centre, helping during natural calamities, fighting insurgency and terrorism, assisting election authorities in the peaceful conduct of polls and helping out in wars. In the present circumstances when the country is faced with the problems of militancy and insurgency and there are occasional internal disturbances, the CRPF remains in operation perpetually.

2. Border Security Force (B.S.F.)

The B.S.F. was raised in 1965 to check incidence of crime on the borders. Its functions are : (*i*) to police and patrol the India-Pakistan and India-Bangladesh borders and give a high sense of security to the people living in border areas by providing special protection to their persons and property against depredators from across the border; (*ii*) to deal effectively on the spot with incidents of minor intrusions, illegal infiltrations and transborder smuggling in the sensitive areas of the border; and (*iii*) to coordinate the activities of various law and order agencies involved in the detection and prevention of crime in the border areas. The BSF is headed by a Director-General.

3. Railway Protection Force (R.P.F.)

The Railway Police are divided into Government Railway Police and Railway Protection Force. The former is a special branch of the State Police and is normally controlled by a Deputy & Inspector-General of Police. This force is responsible for preventing and investigating crimes committed on the railways. The Railway Protection Force is a Central Government Force to guard and protect railway property, tracks and property entrusted to railways. It has replaced the railway watch-and-ward staff of the British days. It is headed by an independent Director-General in the Railway Board.

4. Central Industrial Security Force (C.I.S.F.)

CISF was created in 1969 to provide security in the major industrial undertakings of the Government of India in the public sector. It is meant to prevent violence and labour unrest which sabotage work and retard production in public sector units. The force is posted to selected industries on the basis of need and convenience. It is headed by a Director-General of Industrial Security.

5. Indo-Tibetan Border Police (I.T.B.P.)

The ITBP's functions are similar to those of Border Security Force. It checks crime on the Indo-Tibetan Borders and illegal infiltration from across the border and provides security to the people living in the border areas.

Keeping in view the alarming law and order situation caused by the assassination of Smt. Indira Gandhi and Rajiv Gandhi and the communal violence in the country, the Government of India has recently created specially trained forces like 'commandos' and 'Rapid Action Force' to provide security to the VVIP's and quell disturbances.

In times of grave crisis, army is sometimes called to restore law and order and maintain peace, for example, in the wake of anti-Mandal agitation. The frequent use of army for law and order duties has not, however, found favour with citizens. According to them, it unnecessarily exposes the army to civilian culture of corruption and indiscipline. Further, the need for restructuring and reorganising the para-military forces with clear-cut responsibilities has also been felt.

Besides the above line agencies, there are other auxiliary and staff units created and maintained by the Government of India which variously assist in the investigation of crimes and providing informations useful for maintenance of internal security. Such units are Central Intelligence Bureau (CIB), Central Bureau of Investigation (CBI) and Central Forensic Institutes.

Of these three agencies we may briefly describe the role of Central Intelligence Bureau and Central Bureau of Investigation. The Central Intelligence Bureau came for severe criticism for its failure to gather advance information about the impending attack and timely diseminate it to the proper authorities at the time of terrorist attacks in Mumbai on November 26, 2008. The Central Government had to cut a sorry figure for the incapacity of the 1.B to come up with intelligent information. As a matter of fact every major security event has been throwing up an outcry of the failure of intelligence. Intelligence is the bedrock on which police effectiveness rests, whether one is dealing with a terrorist, a criminal or a political situation.

The country needs effective hard intelligence which cannot be generated by the existing skeletal intelligence network. The intelligence agency should collect hard facts that anticipate an event. The intelligence apparatus should be strengthened both at the centre and in the states and adequately furnishesd with technology based infrastructure. It is strange that much of the information presented by the IB is already available earlier and in greater detail in the media. The setting up of National Investigation Agency is the first step taken by the Central Government in this direction.

The role played by Central Bureau Investigation (CBI) has also come for public criticism during the last three decades. It has lost its autonomy and functions through political pressure to serve political ends. Recently (February 12, 2009) it was severly indicrated by the Supreme Court for having acted on the directions of the centre in the disproportionate assets probe against Samajwadi Party Chief Mulayam Singh Yadav and his family members. The Supreme Court remarked "You (CBI) are acting at the behest of the central government and law ministry You are not acting on your own". The senior advocate Mr. Salve said, "The agency had lost all credibility and was being used to target political adversaries. Another advocate observed "The CBI has lost its soul".

Earlier on January 6, the court had observed that it did not want the CBI to act as the government's hand maid. In a key judgement on December, 18, 1997 the court had observed that the CBI should operate under the superintendence of the Central Vigilance Commission. It had also mandated the creation of a prosecution agency similar to that of the United Kingdom's Director of Prosecution which will, among others, fix responsibility on individual officers in cases where poor investigation leads to acquittal. It need not be said that crime at high levels can be investigated effectivley only when the CBI becomes truly autonomous and free from political influence.

The above description makes it clear that the central government plays a significant role in terms of coordination, special responsibilities and staff unit of professional nature. The powers, responsibilities and specialised services of the central government provide framework within which the law and order administration in the states have to operate. The framework is fairly tight and is gradually becoming too rigid to allow any scope for the state police administration to assert its autonomy and freedom. The Central Government may also invoke Article 356 and dismiss the State Government in case the administration of a state fails to maintain law and order.

(C) ROLE OF STATE AGENCIES

Administration of law and order is a complex phenomenon which includes many activities, such as protection of life and property, enforcement of multifarious laws, internal security, detection and prevention of crime etc.

As pointed out earlier, public order and police are state subjects. Therefore, the primary responsibility for maintenance of peace and order falls on the state governments. To perform their responsibility, the states maintain a police department which consists of both line and staff agencies.

The major functions and responsibilities of the police in the field of law and order are as follows :

(I) Prevention of Crime

The primary duty of the police is to prevent the commission of a crime and to control the dangerous criminals. The costs of crime are staggering. It impairs the joy of living. Lives and property are rendered insecure, and peace is frequently disturbed. Direct economic losses to criminals amount to tremendous sums. Further, the cost of detection, investigation and trial of the crime and the expenses on the upkeep of the prisoner are heavy drains on the public exchequer. All this is unproductive expenditure. Therefore, prevention of crime is of utmost significance for ensuring social development. In this field the police performs the patrol duty, maintains crime records, and enlists public cooperation.

(II) Investigation of Crime

The first step in the investigation of crime is registration of the case. Section 154 of the Criminal Procedure Code lays down : "Every information relating to the commission of a cognisable offence if given orally to an officer in charge of a police station, should be reduced to writing by him or under his direction and be read over to the informant; and every such information, whether given in writing or reduced in writing as aforesaid, shall be signed by the person giving it, and the substance thereof shall be entered in a book to be kept by such officer in such a form as the state government may prescribe in this behalf". This is called F.I.R. which plays an important role in the investigation of crime. For the investigation of crime and detection of the criminal the police employs various methods wherein it takes the services of detective agencies, forensic laboratories, medical experts and the people who depose at the time of the trial. The deposition by witnesses is a vital part of the trial.

(III) Maintenance of Order

Under Article 19(1) (b) of the Constitution of India, all citizens have the right to assemble peaceably and without arms. It also includes the right to hold meetings and take out processions. But this is not an absolute right. It is subject to public order which in other words means that the assembly should be peaceful, without arms and should not pose threat to public peace and order. It is, therefore, the responsibility of the police to see that such assemblies do not disturb public order. For this purpose, the authorities may deny permission to hold an assembly and use force considered necessary if the assembly indulges in damage, loot of property, assault, arson and violence. It is obvious that the nature and quantum of force used should be warranted by circumstances. The services of state intelligence wing are used to collect prior and timely information and prepare a plan of action to meet eventualities.

Organisational Set-up

Maintenance of law and order is primarily district based and district oriented. The state level officers are too far from the scene of activity to matter and play effective role as line officers. The role of these officers tends to be more of an advisory and assisting nature. The police organisation at the state level consists of two organisational wings – (*i*) the civil, and (*ii*) the professional.

In the civil wing may be included the Home Minister and the Home Secretary who are not professionals. The Home Minister is the political head of the police department and is concerned with policy decisions regarding police administration. He maintains general and overall control and supervision over the department for which he is answerable to the legislature. The Home Secretary aids and advises the Minister in the discharge of his duties. He is usually a senior civil IAS officer who is a generalist and coordinates, controls and supervises the varied aspects of police administration in relation to the directives of the Union Government and the activities of the district officials below.

The professional wing consists of the IPS and the state police officers. At the headquarters, there is the Director-General or Inspector-General of Police who is the seniormost IPS officer of the state cadre. He is operationally in charge of everything that goes on in the police department. The responsibility for the command of the police force, its recruitment, discipline, equipment, internal security, training etc. lies with him. Several high ranking officers like Inspector-General, Deputy Inspector-General, Assistant Inspector-General and Senior Superintendent of Police etc. assist him in his line and staff functions. His primary functions are (*i*) to serve as a principal advisor to the state government in matters concerning police administration, (*ii*) to act as administrative head of the state police organisations and to execute the policy decisions and directives of the state government, and (*iii*) to ensure efficient functioning of the police forces in the state.

The Inspectors-General of Police now perform staff functions and look after functional responsibilities of specialised nature like training, intelligence, telecommunications, technical, rules, crimes, modernization and welfare etc. In these areas they may be assisted by Deputy Inspectors-General or Assistant Inspectors-General.

In the line hierarchy, the Director-General is assisted by the Deputy Inspectors-General of Police who holds the charge of a police range. Each police range generally consists of 6 to 7 administrative districts depending upon the size and population of the districts concerned. The line functions of a DIG include maintenance of serviceability and efficiency of his force by periodical inspections, frequent consultations, calling of reports and returns and despatch of instructions to his subordinates. He is responsible for the enforcement of discipline among the ranks under his control and command.

As mentioned earlier, the administration of law and order is state based and district oriented. The state is divided into ranges, a range is divided into several districts, a district is divided into circles which are further sub-divided into police stations. The district is placed under the charge of Senior Superintendent of Police or Superintendent of Police who is an IPS officer. A circle is under the charge of a Circle Inspector while the police stations are managed by Sub-Inspectors of police. Of course, to assist these officers there are junior level officers like Deputy Circle Inspectors or Assistant Sub-Inspectors. Head Constables, Constables, etc. In a large district, the S.S.P. may be assisted by Additional Superintendents of Police.

The SSP/SP is the head of the district police organisation who wields a great amount of power and prestige in the district. Working under the overall supervision of the district magistrate, he looks after the problems of law and order and of administration of crime in the district. As the chief intelligence officer of the district, he collects information from the lower levels and can communicate his assessment of the same to his superiors. He also looks after the service conditions of his staff and is responsible for their efficiency, morale and discipline as policemen. In the districts which have bigger cities, the SSP has additional responsibilities such as regulation and control of the traffic, collection of special intelligence and handling of political and communal conflicts.

In the field of maintenance of law and order, the SP is empowered to take all sorts of preventive measures, if a breach of peace is apprehended in the district. He may advise the District Magistrate to impose prohibitory orders and even curfew. In the event of actual breach of law, he makes adequate police arrangements to meet the situation. Crowd-control during fairs, religious festivals, VIP visits, election campaigns and political meetings are his special concerns.

Prevention of crime, even if it does not immediately involve breach of public order and peace, is necessary in the larger public interests. The SP of a district has special responsibilities in his district through (*a*) effective patrol by his fleet, (*b*) close watch over the movements and activities of bad characters, and professional criminals and (*c*) investigation of grave crimes, and (*d*) arrest of criminal characters before they indulge in law-breaking activities.

Role of District Magistrate

The District Collector/Deputy Commissioner represents the state administration in the district and heads the district administration in all its aspects. When he acts in the field of law and order, he is designated as the District Magistrate. As District Magistrate, he exercises numerous police, executive and magisterial functions.

The District Magistrate is the head of the criminal administration in the district. He can inspect the Police Stations and ask for any information, statement, record and register dealing with crime. He can ask the incharge of any police station to come personally and explain matters. The police officials are duty-bound to obey his orders. He can ask the SP to supply him the crime and intelligence reports so as to keep himself in touch with the law and order situation in his area. It is the legal responsibility of the SP to inform him of any apprehension of breach of peace and order.

On the executive side, the District Magistrate grants licences for explosives and can order any enquiry into an accident caused by explosion. He may order the prohibition of the performance of an objectionable play, seize the material and arrest the persons who try to violate the prohibitory orders. He grants licences for possession and sale of all types of poisons and poisonous substances. He can issue warrants for the arrest of a suspected offender under Dangerous Drugs Act, and arrest of a fugitive criminal. A person may be detained by him if there is any apprehension of breach of peace. He can call for armed forces to aid the civil administration to deal with any abnormal situation. He can put restrictions on the movement of any person for a month to reside or enter his area if he is satisfied that the person may cause danger to the maintenance of peace and security of the state. He can ban the assembly of five or more persons if it is likely to cause danger to peace. He may also impose curfew in a particular locality or localities for a specific period.

As Executive Magistrate, the District Magistrate has the power to disperse unlawful assemblies, remove public nuisances and issue orders under Sections 144 of the Criminal Procedure Code. He can bind the people for keeping peace under Section 107 of the Cr. P. C.

Relationship between the District Magistrate and Superintendent of Police

The administration of law and order in India, as seen above, is of a dyarchical nature. The Union Ministry of Home Affairs maintains a wide network of agencies which constitute para-police forces and variously play a domineering role in the maintenance of law and order. At the district level, the police organisation is subject to the control of the District Magistrate. The Administrative Reforms Commission observed: "In the maintenance of law and order, all regular powers of law are vested in the police officers in England. The same practice was adopted in the Presidency towns of Calcutta, Bombay and Madras even in British times and have since been extended to certain other areas also. Promulgation of orders under Section 144 Cr. P.C. is an exclusively executive function. All such executive functions should be entrusted to police officers thus relieving judicial magistrates of them except in grave emergencies in the absence of appropriate executive officers. Since orders under this section are passed primarily for the preservation of public peace and averting serious situations, it is only too proper that the power to pass such orders should be given to the police on whom rests the principal duty of maintaining law and order and averting the breach of peace".[1]

Those who suggest that law and order should exclusively be subject to the control of state police hierarchy in the district, argue as under :

(*i*) That the present system of dual control leads to delay and inefficiency.[2]

(*ii*) That the District Magistrate is so heavily overloaded with developmental and welfare activities that he cannot do justice with police functions.[3]

(*iii*) That the District Magistrate's control over the district police is against the principles of unity of command. The chain of command from the Director General of Police to the District Police has been broken by putting the district police under the general control and direction of the District Magistrate.[4]

(*iv*) That the District Magistrate is not well equipped to discharge his responsibilities of supervising police administration effectively for lack of special training.[5]

(*v*) That the District Magistrate's control is indicative of want of confidence in the district police force.

(*vi*) That the office of the District Magistrate is being held in low esteem by the public at large. He is more a political stooge rather than an impartial administrator.[6]

Those who favour the existing arrangement advance the following arguments.

(*i*) That the District Magistrate only acts as a coordinating agency. The SP continues to be the operating agency and there is no erosion of his powers.[7]

(*ii*) The police does not enjoy a good image in the public eye. The abolition of the control of District Magistrate would tantamount to making India a police state.

(*iii*) The District Magistrate acts as a shock-absorber between the police and the public. The police is used to repressive methods which makes people hostile.

(*iv*) The present system has stood the test of time and has functioned satisfactorily.[8]

(*v*) The present system has promoted integrated system of field administration and the removal of control would lead to deadlocks and conflicts in district administration.

The question of relationship between the Superintendent of Police and District Magistrate has been examined by various State Police Commissions.[9] All have supported the basic position about the general control and direction of the District Magistrate over the Police. However, the National Police Commission in its eighth report has suggested the enactment of a new Act to replace the century old Police Act which could meet the needs and compulsions of the present day world. The Commission has proposed that the police should be made solely responsible for the maintenance of law and order to the exclusion of the District Magistrate.

---

[1] *Report of the Working Group of Police Administration, Chapter III Para 56.*

[2] *Ibid, Chapter IV, Para 29.*

[3] *Ibid, Para 3b.*

[4] *Ibid, para 3.*

[5] *David M. Bayley, "The Police and Political Development in India". p. 354.*

[6] *Report of the working Group of ARC Para 34.*

[7] *Haridwar Rai "Dual Control of law and order Administration in India", article published in I.J.P.A., vol. Xiii, No. 1, p. 61.*

[8] *Report of the Administrative Re-organisation and Economy Committee, Govt. of Kerala, 1965-67, p. 39-40.*

[9] *These commissions were appointed in Uttar Pradesh, West Bengal, Bihar, Punjab, Maharashtra and Kerala.*

Conclusion

Maintenance of law and order is a critical function of the state. The role played by both the Central and State agencies in this field has not been commensurate with the gravity of the law and order situation. The Union Ministry for Home Affairs has converted itself into a special kind of national police department with increasing powers of direction, supervision and control over police administrations in the various states of the country. The State machinery has lost its credibility. Instances are not rare when CBI investigations have been demanded and conceded to pacify public misgivings of serious nature. But as stated above, the role played by the union agencies has been considered a direct intervention in the affairs of the State by some state governments, a violation of the federal nature of the Constitution and an encroachment of the State's rights. The institution of Governors through whom the Union Government judges the efficiency of the state police machinery is often misused for political ends. Designed as an aid or a tool to strong governments in the states, the role of the Union Government in maintenance of law and order has restrained the openness, autonomy and accountability of state police administration.

The criminal justice system also has failed to control crime and disorder. The judiciary has distanced itself so completely from public weal and woe that it appears to be totally unconnected with the maintenance of law and order. Cases in the courts go on indefinitely. The worst cases of violence and corruption can drag on for years. Known gangsters cannot be booked. Mafias move freely. The political offenders come out on bail, after defrauding the nation of crores, like national heroes to the acclamation of rented crowds. No one seems to be accountable for decline in justice. It is well said that "justice denied invites street law". The whole criminal justice system has been weakened due to corruption, lethargy, deliberate evasive attitude, lack of purpose, lack of faith in law and sense of irresponsibility.

The state police machinery is stagnant and stationary. Its methods of investigation are archaic and crude. It does not have hi-tech equipment and tools needed for scientific investigation. Complaints of beating, physical torture, maltreatment and harassment by police officers are not wanting. Untrained in modern sophisticated methods of handling public disorders, the officials of the Indian police know very little about the anatomy and pathology of various kinds of violent disorders, ranging from students' rampages to communal carnage and works in non-professional manner. Six decades after independence was too long a period for us for implementing the police reforms suggested by various commissions and committees. The role played by the politicians has aggravated the law and order problem. Furthermore, they care more for their political survival than for maintaining public order and peace. The criminalization of politics or the politicization of criminals has added a new dimension to the maintenance of law and order in the country. There are political leaders, communalist groups, high caste oppressors, notorious outlaws and angry youngmen who provoke and precipitate the breakdown of law and order administration in the country. The Bombay riots, descretion of idols at Gaya in January, 2003,[1] massacre of Dalits in Bihar, murder of Christian missionaries and rape of nuns, burning of train carrying Kar Sewaks at Godhra in (Gujrat) by mischief mongers to ignite communal violence and increasing cases of rape, kidnapping and killings are the recent examples in this score. The Telgi case involving stamp scam at national level speaks volumes of corruption in police establishment. The police has become an instrument of political manipulation misused for partisan ends. In public perception its image is very poor. There is crisis of leadership in the Indian Police. The police and magistracy today face an uphill task in the present political

[1]*Hindustan Times January 11, 2003 -10*

scenario. The gradual disappearance of moral values and disintegrative forces have brought about a situation in which violence and conflict among various sections of society are more frequent, generally tense and acute. The crime graph is on the rise and we have all the ingredients for a big explosion that can shake us to our foundations. The law and order administration in India must equip itself with the requisite perspectives to face and counteract the impending challenges of the coming decades boldly and with firm determination.

National Investigation Agency

The terrorist attack in Mumbai on 26th Nov., 2008 and similar attacks at different places earlier have highlighted the serious danger to our security, flawed intelligence system and weak police administration. The fire power and weapons of the Mumbai police were no match for those wielded by the terrorists. The intelligent authorities ultterly failed to gather advance information about the impending attack and inform the concerned offices for taking necessary measures. The country suffered a grave shock and there was alround condemnation of the security agencies. The law and order situation as described above, is at its lowest ebb and now the threat of the terrorist attacks has further added to the problem of maintenance of peace and protection of the life and property of the people of India.

In order to bolster security and help combat terrorism in speedy and effective manner the Central Government has now set up National Investigation Agency. The NIA will be a super body with far reaching and country wide powers. It will control and investigate everything connected to terrorism, counterfeiting of currency, threat to atomic installations and energy, maritime security, hijaking, sedition and waging war against the nation, among other crimes. Its officers will have over-riding powers over state police forces when dealing with designated crimes falling under its jurisdiction. The NIA will be backed by special courts, provision for in camera proceedings and protection of witnesses. It will also over-ride the provisions of the Police Act 1861 when investigating the crimes.

***

DISTRICT ADMINISTRATION

> *"District administration is that portion of public administration which functions within the territorial limits of a district".*
> —*S. S. Khera*

CONTENTS :

District is the basic unit of administration in India. It is a "sub-division of a division". The Oxford dictionary defines it as a "territory marked off for special administrative purposes". From the stand point of government, district is "a sufficiently large territory with an overall unity, governed by common historical, geographical, social and economic conditions".[1] For the purpose of administrative convenience, a country is divided into numerous administrative units such as provinces/ states, divisions, districts, sub-divisions, etc. Therefore, district is an administrative unit in the hierarchy of administration which consists of a number of territorial areas – villages, towns and cities. A district is generally named after the largest town / city of the territorial area of the concerned district.

The word 'District Administration' means the management of the tasks of government so far as it lies within an area legally recognised as a district. According to Khera, "District administration is the total management of public affairs within this unit".[2] In other words, "District administration is that portion of public administration which functions within the territorial limits of a district".[3] As a district is considered the most viable geographical unit where the total apparatus of public administration can be concentrated, the district administration deals with management of numerous public affairs. Here we find a number of functionaries belonging to various departments of the state government, such as Superintendent of Police, District Medical Officer, District Education Officer, District Agriculture Officer, etc. It may be noted that the administration of some departments may not be district based, for example the unit of administration of the department of Public Works is circle which is not co-terminous with the district, and may include a number of districts.

(A) EVOLUTION OF DISTRICT ADMINISTRATION

The present form of district administration in India is a mixed creation of Mughal and British rulers, but as a unit of administration it goes back to early times : In Manu's times, about a thousand villages formed a district which was under the charge of a separate official. Under the Mauryans, Guptas and other Hindu rulers of North India, the kingdoms were divided into provinces and

[1]*Shastri, KNV : "Principles of District Administration in India", p. 73.*
[2]*Khera, S S : "District Administraiton in India", (1964) p. 21.*
[3]*Ibid, p. 76.*

provinces were divided into districts. The provinces were governed by governors and the districts were under *Sthanikas* or *Rajjukas* under the Mauryans and under *vishvapatis* during the *Guptas*"[1]. These officers enjoyed comprehensive powers of judicial as well as of executive nature. Their most important position was in the field of revenue administration. They were assisted by a number of subordinate officers who had the charge of smaller divisions of a district.

During the Mughal period, the head of the district was *Faujdar* a military officer who worked under the direct control of a Subedar (Governor). The work of revenue collection was carried by an officer known as *Amil* or *Amulguzar* who also exercised certain police and judicial powers. However, he did not hold a dominant position, because similar functions were also assigned to the *Zamindars.*

With the fall of the Mughal Empire, the institution of *faujdar also* suffered an eclipse. The East India Company which had acquired the *diwani* rights from the Mughal emperors, appointed its own officers to collect revenue. Warren Hastings created the office of the Collector in 1772 for the dual purpose of collecting revenue and dispensing justice. The appointment of collectors reduced the position of *Zamindars.* Cornwallis (1786-1793) made certain reforms. He disapproved the policy of concentration of executive, revenue and judicial powers in the hands of one individual and the collector ceased to be a judge of the Civil and Revenue Courts and became the Magistrate-Collector as the district head. In 1872, the then Lieutenant Governor of Bengal, Sir George Campbell wrote, "*It is the Lieutenant Governor's wish to render the head of district no longer the drudge of many departments and master of none, but, in fact, the general controlling authority over all departments in each district. He has, though striven to make the Magistrate-Collector of a great Bengal district the real executive chief and administrator of the tract of the country committed to him and supreme over everyone and everything except the proceedings of the Court of Justice*".[2]

When the Bengal Local Self-Government Act was passed in 1885, the Collector became the Chairman of the District Board. At the time of the report of the Royal Commission on Decentralization (1909), the village area of district was 4430 sq. miles and the average population 9,31,000 [3]. At the head of each district was the District Magistrate "who in the old regulation provinces is styled the collector and elsewhere the deputy commissioner. He has assistants and deputies varying in number, title and rank and his district is sub-divided for administrative purposes into charges which bear different names in different parts of the country".[4]

With the introduction of dyarchy, district administration underwent some changes. The local government institutions were given more powers and functions than before. One result of division of political powers and the strengthening of local government was that "the former overall cohesion of the district administrative apparatus began to be increasingly intermeshed with separate departmental levels, leading also in some cases to a sense of departmentalism, and working in mutual isolation".[5] The post-dyarchy developments made the office of the collector more coordinating rather than the unifying agency for the different departmentalised and other components of district administration".

However, the Indian Statutory Commission (1930) made the assertion that the District Collector is "*in the eyes of most of its inhabitants the Government*". *Ramsay Macdonald went a step further and compared the collector with that tortoise on whose back stood the elephant of the Government of India.*

The introduction of provincial autonomy under the Government of India Act 1935 weakened the position of the District Collector. The responsible governments in the provinces had appointed

[1]*DC Potter : "Government in Rural India – An Independent Contemporary District Administration, p. 8".*
[2]*Stevens, GW : In India, p. 57.*
[3]*Misra, BB "District Administration", p. 153*
[4]*Ibid*
[5]*Khera, S.S., op. cit., p. 83-84.*

various heads of development departments like health, education, social welfare, public works, etc. who acted independently. The district collector was concerned mainly with public order, prompt collection of revenue and correct maintenance of land records. The increase in the powers of the local bodies also affected his position, however, he was given the general power of supervision over the rural development, cooperative movement and the village panchayats. After the resignation of popular ministries and the start of the Second World War, the district magistrate gained greater powers and prestige. One of his main responsibilities was to suppress the national movement for independence and augment war efforts.

After independence the district administration continues to be the hub of Indian administration. Almost all the activities which touch the welfare of the people, are performed at district level. The district administration is now more complex and comprehensive than in the past. Just as the British rulers refined and developed the system they found, to meet the needs of British Raj, so in post-independent India new developments and refinements in district administration are currently taking place in order to satisfy the elected representatives of the area and meet the fast emerging needs of of populous country having global recognition as the largest democracy having sound economy even in the global recession.

(B) ROLE AND IMPORTANCE

District administration has a very important place in the hierarchy of Indian administration. It is this tier of administration that touches the people more directly and more strikingly. An ignorant Indian villager may not know anything of the structure of state government, but the collector is a living reality to him. Almost all the departments of state government have their field agencies in the district which come close to the people. There are Food and Supply Officers, Agriculture Officers, Medical Officers, Education Officers, etc. who almost affect every citizen in one way or the other. The citizen, therefore, finds in the district administration, the actual working of the state administration. The responsibility for the people's comfort and satisfaction of their needs lies primarily on the district administration. The people approach the district for redressal of their varied grievances. Very few of them go to the state capital for the said purpose. Thus, for an average citizen, the district administration is the Government. The DC is still the *Mai-Bap* of the semi-literate and administration may get a set back if the head of the district is unresponsive to the needs and utterly ignorant of their aspirations.

The state government, on the other hand, also depends upon the district administration for the successful implementation of its policies. It receives feedback from the district officers in the light of which it revises its policies and programmes. There is nothing wrong with our policies, the fault lies at the implementation level. And it is the officers in the field who are actually involved in the task of policy implementation. Therefore, the success of any state government depends on how its policies are implemented by the district administration. An honest and people-oriented district administration may earn a good name for the state government while a corrupt and an autocratic may result in its un popularity. The responsibility for maintenance of law and order and protection of the life and property of the people devolves upon the district administration which can create chaos by inept handling of public affairs. The district administration acts as the eyes, ears and arms of state government. Hence, its efficiency and integrity are of vital importance.

According to Potter, district administration means to (*i*) maintain the district in a state of law; and order; (*ii*) ensure that justice shall be done and rule of law shall prevail, (*iii*) assess and collect a number of taxes e.g., land revenue, irrigation rates, agricultural income tax, etc.; (*iv*) ensure that the land which is the major source of the people is properly administered; (*v*) exercise various regulatory and control functions of the government and (*vi*) take immediate action in case of a calamity or disaster and the like.[1]

[1]*Potter,: DC., op. cit., p. 15-20.*

There has now come about a radical change in the fundamental aims of the district administration which is being remodelled in all the states to enable it to carry out the new responsibilities. In the new order of things, the district administration will have an even more vital role to play than in the past. The Planning Commission expressed its views in the First Five Year plan as follows :

"In brief, from now, the primary emphasis in district administration has to be on the implementation of development programmes in cooperation with the active support of the people. The reorganisation of district administration has to provide for : (*a*) strengthening and improving the machinery of general administration, (*b*) integration of activities of various development departments in the district and the provision of a common extension organisation, (*c*) linking up, in relation to all development works, of local self-governing institutions with the administrative agencies of the state government, (*d*) regional coordination and supervision of district development programmes".

Thus, new dimensions have been added to district administration which is a well-tried form of field administration adapted to the needs of the country. As a practical unit of field administration, it has stood the test of time and may well continue to be the principal pattern of field administration throughout the country for a long period. The district administration as said earlier, provides the principal points of contact between the citizen and the process of government and is truly the cutting edge of the tool of public administration. In the development and refinement of this tool, new changes may be brought about in order to fulfil the changing needs.

Type of Districts

District Administration as pointed out above, constitutes a convenient method of performing the functions of Government in a district. There are several types of districts :

(*i*) The largest number is that of Rural districts as the average district in India continues to be on the whole a rural district.

(*ii*) There are districts where the local administration concentrates more on urban areas and on urban population. Delhi may be cited as an example.

(*iii*) Next, there are industrial districts which are found in heavily industrialised areas. Such districts are in Kanpur, Jamshedpur, Calcutta, Surat, Bombay, Ludhiana, etc.

(*iv*) Backward districts constitute another type. They are those districts where the local people do not enjoy those opportunities or advantages, which are the monopoly of more developed areas.

(*v*) Lastly, there are hill districts where the pattern of living and that of local administration, differs from those of the districts which are situated in the plains.

Features of District Administration

The following features of district administration may be noted :

(*i*) It is at district level that government comes into contact with the people.

(*ii*) The problems at this level are local relating to the district.

(*iii*) District administration is a field work as opposed to staff or secretariat functions.

(*iv*) At district level, policy formulation ends, implementation begins.

(*v*) The District Officer is the last agent of state government and the 'man on the spot'.

(*vi*) At the district, there is functional aggregation of units. A large number of departments have their field agencies located in the district.

(C) DISTRICT COLLECTOR

The District Collector also known as Deputy Commissioner (Haryana, Punjab, Assam, Jammu and Kashmir and Karnataka) and District Magistrate (Uttar Pradesh and West Bangal) is the head of district administration. He is a generalist, normally an IAS officer or a promotee from state civil service. The direct recruit is naturally of a younger age than the promotee. He performs multifarious functions, hence the District Officer is called the pivot of the entire district administration. His principal duty today, as it has always been, maintenance of law and order in the district. Collection of revenue and upkeep of land records is his another duty of significance. In the post-independent India direction and fulfillment of tasks relating to the socio-economic development has been added to his functions. Besides these three main functions, he also performs numerous other functions which make him the pivot of district administration.

1. Land Revenue

The origin of the institution of District Collector in its present form goes back to the period of East India Company when it acquired the 'Diwani' rights from the Mughal emperors and appointed its officers to collect revenue. Warren Hastings, the first Governor-General of India had created the office of District Collector for the dual purpose of collecting land revenue and dispensing justice. The District Collector is the head of the revenue department of the district. In this capacity, he possesses the power of general supervision and control of the land records and their staff. He is responsible for collection of land revenue, canal dues and the Government dues; distribution of *taqavi* loans; recovery of *taqavi* dues; distribution of *distress taqavi* during losses to crops caused by natural calamities; relief to fire sufferers; payment of Zamindari Abolition compensation and rehabilitation grant remission of revenue in case crops are destroyed due to flood havocs or droughts or crops being infested with locusts in the harvesting seasons; managing government properties and courts of ward estates; assessment and realisation of agriculture tax; supervision of Treasury and sub-Treasury; enforcement of Stamp Act; ensuring proper administration of land and proper sale and mortgages of land; submission of periodical reports to higher authorities and seeing that the rights in land are held and enjoyed and passed from one party to another within the jurisdiction of law and in a peaceful manner. He also looks to land acquisition work and all matters relating to land records.

2. Law and Order

In the earlier chapter on 'Administration of law and order' we have already described the role of district magistrates in the maintenance of law and order in the district and his relationship with the superintendent of police. As a district magistrate, he promulgates orders whenever there is any danger of breach of public order and peace. He can inspect police stations and ask for any information, statement, record and register dealing with crime. He can ask the incharge of any police station to come personally and explain matters. It is the legal responsibility of the SP to inform him of any apprehension of breach of peace and order. He grants licences for explosives and fire arms. He may also order enquiry into an accident caused by explosion. He can issue warrants for the arrest of a suspected offender. A person may be detained by him if there is any apprehension of breach of peace. Thousands of workers of Bharatiya Janata Party were arrested by the district administration in order to prevent them from going to attend the rally at the Boat Club, New Delhi on Feb 25, 1993. The district magistrate can call for armed forces to aid and assist the civil administration to deal with any abnormal situation. He may impose curfew in a particular locality or localities for a specific period. He has the power to disperse unlawful assemblies, remove public nuisances and issue orders under Section 144 of Cr. P.C. He can bind the people for keeping peace under Section 107 of the Cr. P.C.

He makes jail inspections, disposes the cases of undertrial prisoners, grants superior class to prisoners, orders premature release of prisoners, release of prisoners on parole, deals with mercy petitions from prisoners, submits an annual criminal report to the government, appoints village chowkidars, deals with labour problems, strikes etc., initiates prosecution of offenders under Factories Act, Trade Mark Act, Cinema and Entertainment Tax. He takes necessary action for eviction under Public Premises (Eviction) Act and Rent Control Act. He hears petitions and general complaints received from the people against any matter relating to district administration. He makes necessary arrangements for the holding of fairs and exhibitions during festivals in order to ensure peace.

3. Developmental Functions

With the dawn of independence, India has embarked upon a new era of welfare state and community development. Hence the developmental functions of the district collector include dispelling of illiteracy, eradication of superstitions, control of population growth, spread of cooperative institutions, successful implementation of Panchayati Raj, seeking people's participation in Community Development Programme, strengthening local government institutions, involvement of voluntary agencies in social welfare work, promotion of small savings scheme, ensuring adequate provision of social services and public amenities by different agencies and effecting coordination in the work of all the district level officers.

In regard to the developmental functions of the district officer, states have followed different patterns. In Maharashtra and Gujarat all the development functions have been brought under the administrative control of the Zila Parishad. A separate officer, Chief Executive Officer, has been appointed who has administrative control over all the officials of Zila Parishad. In Tamil Nadu, Rajasthan and other states, the Collector looks after both the regulatory and development functions. As a matter of fact, prior to the introduction of the Panchayati Raj in 1959 in consequence of the recommendations of the Balwant Rai Mehta Committee (1957) the Collector was closely connected with all development activities in the district, including Community Development and National Extension Service. Since the introduction of the Panchayati Raj, however, developmental activities have been handed out to the elected bodies and the role of the Collector in this respect differs from state to state. Balwant Rai Mehta Committee had recommended, "*At the district level, the Collector or the Deputy Commissioner should be the captain of the team of officers of all development departments and should be made fully responsible for securing the necessary coordination and cooperation in the preparation and execution of the district plans for community development*".[1]

Although Maharashtra and Gujarat states have appointed separate officers in charge of developmental work who work independently of the district collector, yet the prevailing practice in many of the states is to make the district collector the coordinator of development functions and appoint an officer in the form of Additional District Collector-cum-Chief Executive Officer to assist him. Since the District Collector has the final authority in regard to all district affairs and is in a better position to get the cooperation of other district functionaries, he is the appropriate person to look after the developmental activities in the district. It may, however, be emphasised that his role in regard to development functions is more of an adviser, guide and coordinator. The actual implementation of different development programmes is carried by officers of the concerned departments who work under the direct control of their respective heads of department.

It has been opined that the District Collector has not been able to emerge as an effective coordinator. Lal Bahadur Shastri, the successor Prime Minister to Jawaharlal Nehru opined thus :

"In regard to development activities, the difficulty at the present moment is that there is no proper coordination. Formerly, the District Collector used to be the coordination authority. He was in overall charge of every activity in the district. The District Collector is there but there are also at the district level officers of different departments, like the PWD, agriculture, cooperation, education, etc. There is also someone in charge of community development work. These different units function

[1] *Report of the Team for the Study of Community Projects and National Extension Service, Vol. I, pp. 39-40.*

in a district but they are not under the district collector or supervision of the district collector. They have their direct connections with the respective heads of department sitting in the state secretariat, or in some cases with the Departmental Officers at the divisional level. The result is that there is no proper coordination".[1]

So, the need for effective coordination in development activities is of crucial importance. The need is all the more important in terms of our commitment to decentralised planning and Panchayati Raj institutions.

Other Functions

In the preceding account we have described the functions of District Collector in the fields of land revenue, law and order and development. Besides these important functions he performs numerous other functions of varied nature which may be listed as follows :

1. Postings, transfers and leave of the land revenue officers working under his control;
2. Appointment of Punishing Authorities in respect of ministerial and inferior servants of collectorate and tehsil staffs and other allied offices.
3. Dealing with pension cases of his staffs.
4. Controlling, drawing and disbursing officers of the district.
5. Submitting annual budget estimates.
6. Preparing estimates of works in respect of revenue building and responsibility for maintenance of all government buildings under the charge of revenue department.
7. Issuing tour programmes of Ministers and VIPs.
8. To act as a Protocol officer in the district.
9. To make arrangements for stay of VIPs at Circuit Houses.
10. Compiling and submitting annual administration reports of the district.
11. Supervising the proper conduct of civil suits in which the state is a party.
12. Attending to character verifications.
13. Interviewing members of the public and the officials.
14. Training junior officers in official procedures and administrative works.
15. Attending to public grievances and presiding over District Grievances Committee in the absence of minister-in-charge.
16. Enforcement of Press Act.
17. Issue of certificates of domicile, scheduled and backward classes, guardianship of political sufferers etc.
18. To act as the Returning Officer for elections to Parliamentary and Vidhan Sabha constituencies.
19. Conduct of census operations once in ten years.
20. Civil defence work.
21. Supervision of local government institutions.
22. Superintendence over all other branches of district administration.
23. To take prompt action in case of calamities, disasters and the like.
24. To keep liaison with military authorities and look after the welfare of the armed forces - serving and retired both in the district.

[1] *The Indian Journal of Public Administration, Vol. X, no. 4, Oct.-Dec. 1964, pp. 595-6.*

25. Management of Government estates.

26. Administration of *Nazul* lands.

27. To provide famine and flood relief to those affected adversely.

28. To execute government policies on new schemes like National Savings and population control.

29. Allotment of government houses.

30. Supervision of local bodies.

31. Effecting co-ordination in the work of all other district officers.

Rural Development

Various rural development programmes such as the Integrated Rural Development Programme, Drought Prone Areas Programme, National Rural Employment Programme, Rural Landless Employment Guarantee Programme, Command Areas Development Programme, Minimum Needs Programme etc., meant for the amelioration of the weaker sections of the rural society are being implemented by the District Rural Development Agency established in each district, under the chairmanship of the District Collector. He presides over the meetings of the Agency consisting of district officers belonging to different development departments and coordinates their activities.

The *Integrated Rural Development Programme* assists the families below the poverty line in rural areas by encouraging them to take up self employment ventures. The *Drought Prone Areas Programme* aims at an integrated area development on a mini and micro watershed basis to bring about optimal development of land, water, livestock and human resources for restoration of ecological balance so as to mitigate the effect of drought. Under this programme, activities such as afforestation, soil conservation, efficient utilization of scarce water, conservation of scanty rainfall, introduction of dryland farming technology are taken up. The *National Rural Employment Programme* launched in October, 1980 seeks to provide supplementary employment opportunities to work-seekers during the lean periods of the year, besides creating durable community assets. The objectives of *Rural Landless Employment Guarantee Scheme* are to maximise both direct and long-term employment opportunities through investment made under the programme and to help in stabilising the market wage rates. *The Command Area Development Programme* aims at bridging the gap between potential created and its utilization. Under this programme activities like construction of field channels, land levelling and "*Warabande*" are undertaken. The *Special Livestock Production Programme* provides financial assistance to small/marginal farmers, and agricultural labourers for rearing crossbred calves and for establishment of sheep, poultry and piggery production units. The *Minimum Needs Programme* seeks to provide arrangements for the satisfaction of the minimum needs of the rural people such as drinking water, health care, sanitation, housing facilities etc.

Recently, *Jawahar Rozgar Yojna* has been launched to guarantee employment to atleast one person in a rural family living below the poverty line, for 50 to 100 days a year at a workplace near to his or her residence. The existing rural employment/wages schemes, such as *Indira Awas Yojna,* R.L.E.G.P., I.R.D.P., were merged into the Yojna. The yojna is being implemented through the Panchayats.

Position of District Collector

Having had an overview of the functions of the District Collector, it may be said that he occupies a pivotal place in the district administration. His authority is onerous and powers enormous. William Hunter's description of the powers of the District Collector hold good even today. According to him, "the District officer is the fiscal officer charged with collection of land revenue, is also a revenue and criminal judge both of the first instance and appeal.....police, jails, education, municipalities, roads, sanitation, dispensaries, local taxation and the Imperial revenue of the district are to him matters of daily concern. He is expected to make himself acquainted with each natural aspect of the country".

Even today most of his functions are similar to those of the British days; rather they have increased with the addition of developmental functions. He is the sole chief agent and representative of the state government in the district. He serves as a channel of communication between the government and the inhabitants of the district. Palande rightly called him, "*the eyes, the ears, the mouth and the hands of the provincial government in the district*". He is a prop to the needy and the distressed. People run to him for succor and redress in times of calamity and oppression.

With the ushering in of independence era in India and the growth of democratic institutions, the halo of glamour which surrounded him in the British days, has considerably warned. Instead of being an agent of the oppressive alien rule, he has become a public servant of a popularly elected government. As such, he is required to be persuasive and not coercive in his approach to the people. He no longer keeps himself aloof from the people, rather he mixes with them freely and meets them daily to listen to their grievances. With the emergence of the concept of welfare state, he, like all other officers, has become the custodian of the welfare of the people in his district. He has changed his lifestyle and working in accordance with the changed circumstances. He can no longer treat the people as mere abstractions. He can no longer create awe and fear in their mind. He is to win their cooperation and goodwill through persuasion, appeals and humble requests. The elected legislators from the area are viz the MLAs and the MP have markedly influenced his position. They being the representatives of the people and nearer to the seat of political power carry greater weight with the government. There is a '*durbar*' at their residences where the people of their constituencies cluster to seek favours and redressal of their grievances including the highhandedness of the District Collector. An influential MLA/MP can get him transferred, even suspended, in case he is *negligent*, corrupt autocratic and partisan.

The District Collector is today an overburdened officer. Comparing the present position of the District Officer with that of his predecessors in British days, it has been observed by a senior Indian Civil Service officer that in those days, district work was essentially automatic involving very little consultation. But, today, the expansion of his responsibilities, the change in emphasis and quality — from the regulatory to the development — and the altogether different context of work in a free and democratic system, combine to make him one of the most harassed and hardpressed of all government employees.[1] He is under heavy political pressures and has sometimes to do acts favouring the ruling party. The local political leaders pressurise him to seek favours for themselves and their supporters. Paul H. Appleby has portrayed the District Collector as follows :

"...no Ministry knows how much of his time it is entitled to and none has any capacity for ensuring that it receives that portion of his time and energy".

"...overburdening, understaffing, and lack of stringent administrative evaluation of performance are generally characteristic of the Collector's situations. The Collector is so broadly responsible and overburdened that one of his two primary functions has suffered seriously. One sits in his office only to hear him receive, alongwith streams of citizen visitors, telephone calls from all of the state ministers who lay their most pressing problems at his door; he is responsible to every body for everything, though with varying degrees of clarity....He struggles valiantly in an outmoded structural situation."[2]

Dubhashi rightly observes, "The position of the Collector is under strain. According to some observers, symptoms of a general weakening of district administration have appeared. Functional

---

[1]*J.C. Kakkar, "Role of District Collector in India : Changing Perspectives", (in A. Avasthi and Ramesh K. Arora (eds) Bureaucracy and Development : Indian Perspective, p. 92.*

[2]*Appleby, Paul H. "Public Administration in India" pp. 21-22.*

specialization in the wake of new planned programmes have naturally increased the burden of work. On the other hand, the emergence of the several government authorities at the local level has made breaches in what was traditionally an impregnable authority of the district officer. A simple 'unity of command' no longer obtains. Apart from the vertical commands of the technical hierarchy, there are now the cross-commands of the elected representatives. The local pressure groups have grown in strength. The easy accessibility to the policy makers at the state headquarters has eroded the finality of the decision of the officer on the spot. It is feared by many that sometimes even in small matters, the collector has no say. For redressal of grievances, genuine or imaginary, direct approach to the state government through local political leaders has become easy. *Thus while the responsibilities have grown, the prestige of the District Collector has declined and function without power has become the privilege of the District Collector*."[1]

However, the District Collector (*i*) will continue to be responsible for the maintenance of law and order in the district; (*ii*) will retain the powers of control, superintendence and supervision over the local government bodies; (*iii*) will continue to be head of the district revenue administration; (*iv*) will function as the 'eyes and ears' of the state government at the district level; (*v*) will be the chief source to supply independent reports on any matter concerning district administration, and (*vi*) execute the directions of the government. He is also to be conscious of the fact that he is the public servant. Hence bureaucratic ego is to be kept aside.

(D) DISTRICT ADMINISTRATION AT LOWER LEVELS

The District Collector is the head of the administration in the district and for the performance of his functions he has a well-knit hierarchy in the district which may be described as follows:

Sub-Division

Most of the districts in India are divided into two or more sub-divisions, each of which is under the charge of an assistant to the collector called a Sub-Divisional Officer/SDM/Asst. Collector/Sub-Collector/Revenue Divisional officer/Prant officer. A sub-division helps to further decentralize authority as well as to provide field training to recruits to the IAS. The SDO is either a newly recruited member of the IAS or a member of the state civil service. Thus like the District Collector, the SDO is a generalist administrator. He speaks out with the voice of the government in his own sub-division. His duties are similar to those of the Collector. Apart from his law and order duties and the case work which generally consists of a 'mix of revenue and criminal cases', he shares with the Collector, but subject to the latter's control, responsibility for the regulatory functions of maintenance of maps and records of his sub-division and assessment and collection of land revenue. His judicial duties comprise of decisions of cases pertaining to land rights, enhancing, abating or commuting a rent, ejecting illegal sub-letting and deciding the question of the rightful ownership of a disputed land. As a first class magistrate, he tries cases falling within his jurisdiction. He commits cases to sessions court. His quasi-judicial duties pertain to liaison and cooperation with the police in the sub-division, special precautions during actions in emergencies, appointments of *mukhias*, recommendations to the collector for grant or arms licences etc.

Supervising the police, deciding disputes of non-criminal character, appointing, promoting or transferring functionaries of the revenue department, maintaining closer contact with the public are his important executive duties. He also performs developmental functions within his subdivision.

In short, the SDO is an integral part of the district administration and a valuable field aide to the District Collector. He is a link between the District Collector and the Tehsildar in revenue matters and the District Magistrate and the Station Officer (police) in matters relating to law and order.

---

[1]*PR Dubhashi : "Leadership Role of the Collector". IJPA Vol. XI, no. 3, p. 620.*

Tehsil

Each sub-division is divided into two or more administrative areas called *Tehsils* in Andhra Pradesh, Jammu and Kashmir, Punjab, Rajasthan, Haryana, *Talukas* in Gujarat, Kerala, Madhya Pradesh, Tamil Nadu, Maharashtra and Karnataka.

Each tehsil is under the charge of Tehsildar (Mamaltdar) who is an officer with gazetted status and is subordinate to the SDO. He acts as an assistant collector and is responsible for revenue collection. He is the sub-treasury officer. He recommends remissions or other concessions to the district collector in times of distress. The tehsil is the basic unit for purpose of general administration, treasury, land revenue, land records and other items of work. It is not necessary that all departments are represented at Tehsil level. He is also responsible for the maintenance of law and order within the area of Tehsil. In big towns he has to look after all important visitors — official and non-official. He has to submit numerous reports on every conceivable subject, he has to hear the grievances of and generally keep in touch with the people of his Tehsil. He also extends cooperation and help in development work. He is assisted by Naib-Tehsildars to whom he may delegate his powers.

Pargana

The next lower unit in revenue administration is known as pargana in Uttar Pradesh, circle in Maharashtra and Punjab and *firku* in Tamil Nadu. The head of this unit is called *Kanungo* in U.P. and Punjab, Circle Inspector in Maharashtra and the Revenue Inspector in Tamil Nadu. He is entrusted with supervision and compilation of land records. He is the first line supervisor in the chain of revenue administration in the states. The work of the *Kanungo* is periodically inspected and checked by the *Sadar Kanungo*, *Naib Tehsildar*, Tehsildar and SDO. He supervises the work of the *Patwaris* and reports to the higher authorities from time to time.

Village

The *Tehsil* periphery comprises between 200 - 600 villages. The population of the village varies from state to state. On an average, approximately 68 percent of the total rural population lives in very small villages (less than 500 persons). The village is the lowest unit for all administrative and fiscal purposes in all the states of the Indian Union, and its main functionary is called *Lekhpal/ Patwari* in U.P., *Patel* in Maharashtra and *Karnam* in Tamil Nadu. He is the most powerful government representative, connected with land records at the village level and looks after one or more villages. He performs a multitude of functions including maintenance of land records and statistical data, land measurement, helping other departments in the discharge of their functions, report to the higher authority any serious breach of peace and order, cases of illegal distilling and violation of Arms Act. He has been called the 'king-pin' of revenue administration in the district.[1]

With the inception of Panchayati Raj institution under the 73rd Constitutional Amendment Act, 1993 and devolution of important powers and developmental functions to such institutions at the Zila, Block and Village levels, the role of bureaucratic administration has lessened. Like the M.P. or M.L.A., the Sarpanch or the Panch is an important political leader with direct access to the Chief Minister who has to meet his demands in order to keep his vote-bank safe and secure.

(E) OTHER FUNCTIONARIES AT DISTRICT LEVEL

A brief account of the functions of other functionaries in the district may not be out of place. The District and Sessions Judge, Civil Surgeon or Chief Medical Officer, Superintendent of Police, Executive Engineer, District Education Officer, District Food and Supply Officer, District Development Officer and District Social Welfare Officer are some of the important district Officers of the concerned departments.

[1]*S S Khera, op. cit., p. 38.*

The *District and Sessions Judge* heads the judicial organization of the district. He constitutes the highest court in the district. As such he is equipped with both original and appellate jurisdiction. In the former capacity he tries the murder cases which are committed to his court by a first class magistrate. In his capacity as an appellate authority, he hears appeals in both civil and criminal cases from the courts of magistrate and subordinate judges in the district.

The *Civil Surgeon or the Chief Medical Officer* is in charge of government hospitals and dispensaries in the district. He advises and assists the District Officer in matters pertaining to health and sanitation. He also issues medical certificates to government employees and conducts their medical examination prior to entry in government service.

The *Superintendent of Police* is the in charge of the police force in the district. He assists the District Officer in the maintenance of peace and order in the district. He gets assistance from Deputy Superintendent of Police and other police officers in his work. We have already described his role in an earlier chapter entitled 'Administration of law and order'.

The *Executive Engineer* heads the Public Works Department in the district. He deals with the construction and maintenance of government buildings, roads, bridges, etc.

The *District Education Officer* or Inspector of Schools supervises and inspects the working of educational institutions upto Higher Secondary level in the district. He makes recommendations regarding extension of grants-in-aid to these institutions. It may be noted that there is no District Officer to supervise the functioning of colleges and other higher educational institutions. The chain of command in their case passes from the heads of these institutions direct to their head offices.

The *District Food and Civil Supply Officer* is in charge of rationing department in the district. He regulates the supply of essential commodities like sugar, wheat, rice, etc. according to the instructions of the State Food department.

The *District Development Officer* looks after the developmental activities being carried in the rural areas of the district. He is more a coordinating and monitoring officer rather than an executive officer.

The *Social Welfare Officer* looks after the welfare of the weaker sections of society particularly the Scheduled castes and backward classes. He assists the students belonging to these classes in getting scholarships and other financial assistance for higher education and others to get loans from banks for self-employment.

All these officers work under the control and supervision of their respective departmental heads; the District Collector only supervises and coordinates their work who are under an obligation to keep him informed of their activities and report to him any serious matter likely to disturb public peace and order. The annual confidential reports of all these officers are either written or a column is to be filled up by the DC regarding social tangibility and reputation of the officer, holding a particular post.

***

PANCHAYATI RAJ

> *"One of the tasks of nation building and development is to bring members of the national community into a network of relationships and institutions which enable them to participate actively in decisions affecting their individual and group welfare."* ***— Million, J. Esman***

CONTENTS:

(A) REVIVAL OF PANCHAYATI RAJ

A Brief History

Restoration of Panchayats to their pristine glory had been accepted as an article of faith during our incessant struggle for political emancipation. With the ushering in of independence era, the establishment and promotion of village panchayats was apt to be given top priority. A permanent status was accorded to the panchayats in the political framework of the country through incorporation of the Directive Principles pertaining to panchayats in the constitution. Article 40 of the constitution ran as follows: "The state shall take steps to organize village panchayats and endow them with such powers and authority as may be necessary to enable them to function as units of self-government." The significance of this article had been very well-defined by Dr. Jain in the words : "It is rather an embodiment of the most cherished dream of the constitution-makers and an objectification of the most widely held consensus. So long as the constitutional tradition remains alive in the mind of the citizens and respected by their leaders, this would continue to guide the course of Panchayati Raj in this country and endow every step in the progressive realization of the idea with the necessary sanctity and sanction."[1]

Article 40 did not remain a mere ideal. Within four years of the framing of the Constitution of India, Madras, Travancore-Cochin, Jammu and Kashmir, Hyderabad, Madhya Bharat, Saurashtra, PEPSU, Mysore, Punjab, Rajasthan, and Himachal Pradesh established village panchayats on statutory basis whereas Assam, Bihar, Uttar Pradesh and Madhya Pradesh, introduced amendments to further consolidate them.

The pattern of legislation varied from state to state. However, the basic principles — village panchayats to be popularly elected bodies with an elected President, representation to scheduled castes, vesting them with a wide range of municipal, judicial and developmental functions, assigning them a distinct source of income and specifying a large measure of central control over them — were adopted practically by all these Acts. A trend towards increased democratization and autonomy was discernible in all the states. The structural variations were, however, quite evident. The population

[1] *Jain, SC, Community Development and Panchayati Raj in India, p. 129.*

per Panchayat varied between 500 and 10,000. The size of Panchayat membership varied between 30 and 51 in U.P. and 5 and 9 in Punjab and erstwhile PEPSU. In most of the states, membership ranged between 5 and 15. The tenure of the Panchayats was three years in most of the states. The term of Panchayats in Mysore and Bengal was four and five years respectively. The system of nomination was replaced by direct election. Nomination and co-option were provided only for scheduled castes and women. The mode of election of the President to the Panchayats also differed from state to state. Rajasthan, Saurashtra, Travancore-Cochin opted for direct election by the electorates. Assam, Bihar and Delhi stood for direct election by Gram Sabha. In the rest of the states, more or less indirect election by Panchas was adopted.

Another significant variation in the constitution of the Panchayats related to the pattern of Nyaya Panchayats. West Bengal did not form any Nyaya Panchayat at all. In Madras, Bombay, Punjab, Jammu and Kashmir, Rajasthan and Mysore, the village panchayats performed the function of judicial panchayats. In Madhya Pradesh, there was one judicial Panchayat for eighteen Gram Panchayats. In other states, the Nyaya Panchayats were distinct bodies but their jurisdiction and mode of constitution comprised of three to five village panchayats. The general mode of constituting the judicial panchayats was through indirect election amongst the Panchas. In Travancore-Cochin, the members were nominated by the government on the basis of selection by the villagers themselves. In Delhi, the Gram Sabha sent representatives for panchayati adalats directly.

A considerable improvement was effected in the powers of the judicial panchayats. They could try civil suits involving a subject-matter between Rs. 50 and Rs. 200. However, this power could be increased to Rs. 500. Punjab, Delhi, P.E.P.S.U. and Madhya Bharat enjoyed the maximum power whereas Hyderabad, Travancore-Cochin, U.P. and most of the Part C states empowered the panchayats to hear civil suits of value of Rs. 100 with a provision for extension up to Rs. 500. In Bihar and Rajasthan, this power was restricted to Rs. 50 whereas in case of Bombay up to Rs. 25. The Panchayats could impose fines ranging from Rs. 25 to Rs. 100.

During this period, specific functions were assigned to the Gram Panchayats and independent sources of income were earmarked for them. The State Governments supplemented these resources by their grants.

In order to avoid confusion and disparities of standards caused due to diversities of pattern, the Congress Village Panchayat Committee laid down guidelines in 1954 for working out the future pattern of the panchayats.

Recommendations of the Congress Village Panchayat Committee, 1954

The recommendations of the said committee were as follows :

1. As far as possible, the panchayats should be kept out of politics. Unanimity of election should be encouraged by providing incentives as bestowing of greater powers and authority upon those units which return their *panchas* unanimously.
2. The size of panchayat unit should be 1500 to 2000 heads of population.
3. Adult franchise should be the basis of constituting the Panchayats. If adults are too many in a village, representation according to the family might be accepted.
4. Panchayats must be vested with social and economic functions besides civil and judicial already entrusted to them.
5. The judicial panchayats should be separated from the village panchayats.
6. Panchayats should be allowed share of land revenue to the extent of 13 to 20 per cent of the total revenue. They should be assigned revenue collection work. They should be allowed to levy labour tax.
7. Panchayats and village co-operatives should be kept separate.

The local self-government ministers at a meeting in Simla endorsed all these recommendations. During the next five years, there was a rapid expansion of the Panchayats and creation of the conditions necessary for proper working of the new institutions. The question of augmentation of finance of panchayats was accorded expert attention. The Local Finance Inquiry Commission's Report (1951) and the Taxation Inquiry Commission's Report (1953-54) had great impact on the pattern of local finances till 1959.

Panchayats and Five-Year Plans (1954-59)

During this period, the panchayats were associated with the rural-Community Development Programme. They were represented on the Block Development committee. They were made the agency for implementing local development works costing up to Rs. 300. The Bombay government, for example, made the provision of Rs. 415 lacs for water supply works to be executed through the panchayats in its first five-year plan. The panchayats were deemed as the base agency for implementation of social and economic transformations. According to the Draft of the First five-year plan, "*Unless a village agency can assume responsibility and initiative for developing the resources of the village, it will be difficult to make an impression on rural life, for only a village organization representing the community as a whole can provide the necessary leadership.*"

The Second five-year plan reiterated the significance of the panchayats in bringing about a more just and integrated social structure in rural areas and in developing a new pattern of rural leadership.

There is no denying the fact that the vigorous drive for increasing association and participation of village panchayats in development work started bearing fruits. However, despite rapid expansion of panchayats and marked improvement in their administrative setup and allocation of resources on a more liberal scale, the rural bodies could not be considered to be on a sound footing as yet. Paucity of finances was, in particular, a serious malady of rural local bodies.

(B) INAUGURATION OF PANCHAYATI RAJ (1959)

In 1959, Panchayati Raj was inaugurated. The Panchayats which formerly acted in advisory capacity to the Community Development Programme now undertook to assume full responsibility for carrying it ahead. The Balwant Rai Mehta Committee was set up by the National Development Council in 1957 to enquire into the questions of economy and efficiency and suggest measures for the review and re-organisation of Community Development Programme, National Extension Service. The committee suggested a three-tier system of rural local government. It was termed as "*Democratic Decentralization*" *which ultimately begun to be called as "Panchayati Raj". In the words of Waghmare, "Panchayati Raj is the three-tier structure of the rural local government at the village, taluka and district level based on democratization and devolution of powers and resources for the specific purposes of planning and implementation of Community Development Programme with the active, spiritual, spontaneous participation of the rural people.*"[1] The following were the main recommendations of the Mehta Committee:

Recommendations of Mehta Committee

1. There should be a three tier structure of local self government from the village to the District level with the intermediary link if institution are organically related to each other.

Besides genuine transfer of power and responsibility to the local institutions was envisaged. Adequate resources were to be transferred to these bodies so that. they can discharge their responsibility effectively.

[1] *Waghmare, S K : Administrative Organisation in Community Development Programme, (1977 ed.) p. 45.*

2. The development work within a local area was to be entrusted to a statutorily constituted body known as Panchayat Samiti.

3. The Panchayat Samiti was to be constituted of the President of the Panchayat and some co-opted members from scheduled castes and women etc. Every state could evolve its own mode of constituting the Panchayat Samiti. The M.P.s and M.L.A.s from that constituency were to be associate members. The SDO was to be the Chairman of the Samiti till the elected Chairman took over.

4. The Zila Parishad was to consist of all the Chairmen of the Panchayat Samities and MLAs and MPs from the District and some co-opted members. They were to elect their own Chairman. The Collector was to be a member of the Parishad. The Zila Parishad had to act as an advisory, coordinating and supervisory body though more functions could be devolved upon it.

5. The budgets of the Panchayat were to be scrutinized by the Panchayat Samiti and those of panchayat samities by the Zila Parishad.

6. The functions of the Panchayat Samiti were to comprise of all the functions performed by the NES block and those of the District Board.

7. The Panchayat Samiti was to enjoy independent sources of revenue.

8. The SDO had to work as the Executive Officer and Secretary of the Panchayat Samiti.

9. At the village level, the Panchayats served as the main agency of development work.

10. The village level worker was to be the development secretary of the panchayats.

11. The State Government was empowered to exercise control over these bodies. It could suspend them.

12. The entire social and economic development formulated through the network of planning should be channelized through the (above mentioned) local institutions.

13. The committee also visualised the devolution and dispersal of power and responsibility and resources in future.

Keeping in view the variations in different states, it was recommended that the broad patterns and fundamentals of the Panchayati Raj, institutions should be uniform though rigidity in the details of pattern may not the permitted in view of the vastness of country and complexities of the procedure. A genuine transfer of power to the people to be ensured. Hence varying of patterns in different states do not matter.

The Mehta Report is considered a historic document. It is described as the 'master blueprint' and a sort of 'Bible of Panchayati Raj'. In the words of R L Khanna, "It is a bold and imaginative attempt to inaugurate valuable and virile rural self-government, an earnest effort to transfer into four square reality– Mahatma Gandhi's dream of the Panchayati Raj. It envisaged a revolutionary experiment in democratic decentralizaiton. It is a testament of faith in democracy, a grassroots approach to administration".[1]

Rajasthan and Andhra were the first states to opt for democratic decentralization. By the end of 1963, Panchayati Raj was established in most of the Indian states. It was hoped that by 1964-65 all the states of India would have enacted legislation for the introduction of panchayats in their areas. However, the target could not be hit within the stipulated time. The legislations regarding the Panchayati Raj were in accordance with Mehta Committee's report, but as expected, inter-state variations in the unit of devolution and structural design were discernible. An analysis of the legislations reveals that there were two broad issues regarding the constitution of the bodies — (*i*) Should district or Block or both be adopted as units of decentralization?; (*ii*) should the members be directly elected or the membership be indirect or should they be elected in both ways? Maharashtra and U.P. favoured the district as the unit of devolution whereas Gujarat, Bihar, Punjab and Andhra opted for a mixed system. Madras and Rajasthan stood for panchayat samities as the supervisory,

[1]*Khanna, R L, Panchayati Raj in Punjab, p. 69.*

co-ordinating and grant distributing agency. Madhya Pradesh, Mysore, Orissa and Assam followed the Rajasthan pattern. Regarding the modes of constituting these bodies, there were three patterns adopted by the states. In some, indirect election method was preferred due to its inherent simplicity, convenience and building up of organic link with the base tier. The Direct Election was the favourite in some other states due to the key element of responsibility, responsiveness and peoples' interest contained in it. The mixed system claimed to embody merits of both without the flaws of any. Mysore adopted Direct Election method whereas Rajasthan, Andhra, Assam, Madras, Madhya pradesh, Punjab and Gujarat stood for indirect system. Maharashtra opted for a mixed system, though with a bearing towards the Direct system.

Though Panchayati Raj legislation and its implementation came like an emotional upsurge yet crisis of village panchayats did not come to an end. According to Balwant Rai Mehta Committee's Report, "The number of Panchayats which are torn by faction or in which squabbles are rampant is large. Panchayat elections have resulted in creating or aggravating rivalries in about one-third of the villages in which there is a contest — separatism arising out of caste distinction is on the increase. In practice economically weaker sections have no voice in the affairs of the panchayats. In some cases, they are in debt to a Sarpanch who is often a man of influence." Unanimity of selection remained a far cry on account of prospects of power at Panchayat Samiti and District level. Political parties exploited local factious to find a foothold in the rural areas. Three most important problems pertaining to panchayats started haunting the minds of the Indian politicians — the paucity of finances, spread of factions spirit and the character of emerging leadership. A study team was appointed by the Ministry of Community Development in June, 1962 to go into these questions. The team recommended the statutorization of Gram Sabha and earmarking of distinct functions of control regarding budget, taxation, annual programme and construction projects of the Panchayats, to it. It also recommended that Gram Sabha meetings be attended by some responsible officials and non-officials from the Samiti and the Gram Sabha should take up planning production programme.

Another study team was deputed to make an appraisal of Panchayat Raj finances in July, 1962. The committee submitted its report in 1963. Its recommendations pertained to :

1. Resources of the Panchayats.
2. Expenditure of the Panchayats.
3. Resources of the Panchayat Samitis.
4. Zila Parishad.
5. Loans to Panchayat Raj bodies.
6. Budget, Accounts and Audit.
7. General

Before we make an analytical appraisal of the Panchayati Raj in India, it is essential to explain political organization of the three-tier system, commonly known as Democratic Decentralization or Panchayati Raj.

(C) POLITICAL ORGANIZATION OF THE PANCHAYATI RAJ

Though there is a basic similarity of structure in the Panchayati Raj legislation introduced throughout the country yet some variation in the pattern on account of peculiarities of the historical evolution of the Local Self-Government institutions and differences in rural setting cannot be denied. Most of the states have adopted the three-tier system as recommended by the Mehta Committee Report. The village Assembly or Gram Sabha has been statutorily recognized in all states except Kerala, Madras and Mysore. In Bengal the panchayat unions constituted for a group of panchayats have been retained as an intermediate tier, between village panchayat and Panchayat Samiti. In other words, in Bengal four-tier system prevails. The intermediate tier in Andhra, Bihar, Maharashtra, Orissa, Punjab and Rajasthan is termed as Panchayat Samiti. In Assam, it has been named as "Anchalik Panchayat" and in Bengal "Anchalik Parishad". In Gujarat, Mysore, Madhya

Pradesh, U.P., Madras, it is named as "Taluk Panchayat", "Taluka Board", "Janapada Panchayat", "Kshetra Samiti" and "Panchayat Union Council" respectively. Likewise the District level body also has been differently named. In Gujarat and Madhya Pradesh it is known as "Zila Panchayats", in Madras and Mysore it is termed as "District Development Council" and in Assam it is named as "Mohkuma Parishad". In rest of the states "Zila Parishad" is the accepted nomenclature.

The Gram Sabha (Village Assembly)

The Gram Sabha or village assembly lies at the base of Panchayati Raj superstructure. It consists of all the adult citizens who have been entitled to vote. According to the laws of most of the states, Gram Sabha is called at least twice a year usually after *Rabi* and *Kharif* crops are harvested. In Jammu and Kashmir and Orissa, it meets only once a year. In some other states its meeting can be convened if certain proportion of voters (1/5 in most cases) requisition it.

The village Panchayat owes responsibility to the Gram Sabha. It presents its budget accounts of the last year and annual administrative report before Gram Sabha. Projects of local development, proposals for taxation and village production plan have to secure the approval of Gram Sabha before it is implemented by the Panchayat. In Punjab, Bengal, Gujarat and Assam, village Panchayat is elected by Gram Sabha. In Bihar, Gram Sabha elects 50 of the members of the executive council and its President.

Evaluation of the Working of Gram Sabha

In the initial stages, the Gram Sabha has not been an active body. Its attendance is generally thin, probably because of low level of political education of the members and too much diffusive character of its membership. Proposals are afoot to strengthen the working of Gram Sabha so that it could effectively control the Panchayati Raj leadership. Giving it right to recall and making its meetings more effective and attractive are some of the important proposals which may be given due consideration. In fact, Gram Sabha is as yet in an infant stage and necessitates constant nurture before it can develop into a base organ of Panchayati Raj. Through the political education of the masses, larger participation in development programmes, more effective control over panchayat leadership and better mobilization of resources, Gram Sabhas can be made more effective centres of political energy. As expected the panchayats heed the advice and suggestion of the Gram Sabha without reducing themselves to mere executive bodies. Likewise, Panchayat Samiti lend dignity to Gram Sabha if Pradhan, Vikas Adhikari or some other senior officers attend its meetings and render advice to it.

The Panchayats

Prior to the launching of community projects and till the end of the First plan, Panchayats were primarily institutional devices entrusted with functions of minor importance — settling of minor disputes and restraining wasteful litigation in the city courts, looking after sanitation, maintaining drinking water wells and repairs of community works. The panchayats undertook to stimulate and sustain the tempo of local development activities when community project administration emerged out. It was not realized that a permanent agency alone can mobilize local citizens for a specific project. At a later stage *i.e.* 1959 onwards, the Panchayats assumed new role of increasing agricultural production by laying down village uplift plans and seeing to their implementation with the assistance of the village level worker and the Block Agency. In order to enable them to concentrate on development work, judicial functions were vested with Nyaya Panchayats.

Composition of the Panchayats

A Panchayat was to be the lowest rung of the three-tier system and consists of elected representatives of the people. Its structure and composition differs from state to state. Its membership varies from five to thirty-one. In U.P. the Panchayats consist of 16 to 31 members. In Orissa, the number goes up to 25. In Gujarat, the maximum number has been 31 whereas minimum is 15. In rest of the states membership ranges between 5 and 15, depending upon the size of the Panchayats. In addition to elected members, seats have been kept reserved in the Panchayats for the Scheduled Castes, Scheduled tribes and female citizens. These seats are filled by co-option as otherwise, on account of their small number, and other social reasons, they may remain unrepresented. Panchayat is headed by a Sarpanch who may be elected directly or indirectly. In certain states like Rajasthan, Bihar, Assam, U.P. and Himachal Pradesh, the Sarpanch is elected directly either by the Gram Sabha through the show of hands or by the electorates through secret ballot. In other states, the Panchas elect the Sarpanch. A directly elected Sarpanch can prove more effective. In fact, direct election of the Sarpanch is essential to enforce popular responsibility and ensure responsiveness. Moreover, direct election method is comparatively, though not fully, immune from corrupt and blackmailing practices.

Direct election of the Sarpanch does, however, curb the initiative and curtails considerably the controlling power of Panchayats.

Size

The average population per Panchayat on all-India basis is approximately 1,400. Inter-State variations regarding the population, size of the village Panchayat get evident from the following table.

Population Size	*States*
Less than 1000	Punjab, Delhi, and U.P.
Less than1501-2000	Madhya Pradesh, Maharashtra, Gujarat, Madras, Andhra, Rajasthan.
Less than 2001-3000	Himachal Pradesh, Mysore
Less than 3001-4000	Assam, West Bengal, Bihar, Jammu and Kashmir.
Over 4000	Orissa, Kerala.

Kerala is at the top from the population per panchayat standpoint and Uttar Pradesh is at the bottom. A different picture emerges regarding the number of villages per panchayat. The table given below stands witness to the fact.

No. of Villages per Panchayat	*States*
Less than 2 Villages	Andhra, Gujarat, Kerala, Madras, Punjab, U.P., Delhi.
Less than 2 - 3.9 Villages	West Bengal, Madhya Pradesh and Maharashtra.
Less than 4 - 5.9 Villages	Mysore, Rajasthan.
Less than 6 - 8 Villages	Assam, Bihar, Jammu & Kashmir
Over 8 Villages	Himachal Pradesh, Orissa

Kerala is at the bottom in terms of villages per panchayat whereas Orissa, Himachal Pradesh have the largest number of villages per panchayat.

Term

The Panchayat is elected generally for a period of five years, but some variations are there. It is four years in Assam, Karnataka, and West Bengal, whereas in Andhra Pradesh, Rajasthan and Orissa it is three years and in Kerala, Madhya Pradesh, Tamil Nadu, Punjab, Haryana and Uttar Pradesh, it is five years. It may be pointed out that Panchayat elections are not held regularly with the result that the Panchayats far outlive their normal term. The Panchayat can also be superseded. Ashok Mehta Committee had recommended a uniform term of four years for all the elected tiers of Panchayati Raj and suggested that elections to all bodies should be held simultaneously.

Committees of Panchayats

No doubt, a few bodies like Vikas Mandals, Youth Clubs, Mahila Mandals, coexist with Panchayats in some of the states but they are not organically linked up with the Panchayat Structure. A sound committee system is conspicuous by its absence. The Panchayat should evolve a functional and territorial committee system. The former should take up production programmes and social services while the latter may be ward or village development committees. These committees will have to be delegated some sources. Dr. Jain correctly opined: "The virtual absence of the committee system, however, does come in the way of the people. The situation must be remedied in time."[1]

A ward or village development committee appointed by the Gram Sabha can be entrusted the function of drawing up the development plan for the ward of the village in consultation with the families and local organizations. It can seek assistance from the Panchayat Secretary, village level worker, Patwari, teacher, block technicians and the Sarpanch concerned for co-ordinating the thinking on the village plan. The said committee may supervise the execution of work and serve as the proper agency for channelising the grants. It may also perform conciliative function in certain disputes.

Functions of the Panchayats

Statutorily two types of functions — obligatory and optional were entrusted to the Panchayats. With the passage of time and occurrence of new developments, such a division of functions became obsolete. The functions of the Panchayats were divided into following groups :

1. Municipal

Municipal Functions can be further sub-divided into :

(a) Public Health.

(b) Social Education.

(c) Public Safety.

(d) Public construction.

Thus these functions include lighting, sanitation, medical relief, refuse disposal, safe drinking water supply, street drainage, public recreation, registration of births, deaths, control of epidemics, registration of cattle, maintenance and repair of public roads, inns and buildings, tree plantations, celebration of public festivals, providing reading rooms and other items of further education, public latrines and allotment of manure pits.

2. Development and Production Planning

It comprises of two broad functions :

(a) Construction of amenities.

(b) Preparing village plans regarding the development of agriculture, animal husbandry, cooperatives, cottage industries, small savings, etc. and watching their execution, maintaining grain funds and purchasing agricultural tools for common use.

3. Physical Planning of the Village

Control over common land and control over the site land fall in this category of functions.

4. Social Welfare

Social Welfare functions include famine or emergency relief, aid to the handicapped, children, women and youth welfare programmes and also welfare programmes for the backward classes. The enforcement of Early Child Marriage Prohibition Act or of similar other social laws can also be included in this group.

[1] *Jain, S.C. Op. cit., p. 274.*

5. Representational

Airing local grievances, representing constituents in Panchayat Samiti through the Sarpanch, expressing opinions upon the cases of loans and grants-in-aid to be distributed by the Panchayat Samiti and associating in the execution of land legislation comprise this group.

6. House-keeping

It includes electing up-Sarpanch, collecting Panchayat revenues, budgeting, accounting, appointing and controlling staffs, maintaining records, supervising schools, managing Panchayat enterprises, and disposing case work concerning municipal disputes.

7. Conciliative

The Panchayats have been empowered to conciliate the disputes before they are sent to the Nyaya Panchayat, of course with the mutual consent of both the parties.

8. Civil Defence and Others

The Panchayats may undertake the organization of village volunteer force and also the maintenance of watch and ward services.

9. Agency Functions

They may be entrusted agency functions such as small savings, insurance and revenue collection.

It will not be out of place to point out that some of the development functions have also been entrusted to Panchayat Samiti. This overlapping of functions has caused confusion to the voters regarding area of responsibilities.

Powers of Panchayats

In order to enable the Panchayats to perform these functions, they have been given some specific powers which are as follows :

(a) Regulatory

1. The Panchayat may prevent the use of water from a well or a tank which is considered unhealthy by it.

2. It may order the resident or the owner of a house to remove a nuisance from a public road or drain or remove a danger arising from the bad conditions of a house.

3. It may regulate the refuse disposal and deepen a water channel.

4. It may punish the defaulter by imposing a fine not exceeding Rs. 15 which may further rise by Re. 1 per day for continued defiance.

5. It may reserve a well or a tank exclusively for drinking purposes.

(b) Judicial

Where Nyaya Panchayats have not been kept separate from the Vikas Panchayats, Panchayats hear civil and criminal suits.

1. They can impose fines up to Rs. 50.

2. The power to hear civil suits to a certain extent varies from state to state. The panchayats in Rajasthan for instance hear civil suits up to Rs. 250.

3. They can impose fines up to Rs. 15 for committing the breach of their execution regulation.

4. In some states, they have other powers of a court of law as well *viz.*, summoning witnesses, calling for records, maintaining dignity of court, judicial immunity, etc.

(c) Fiscal

Panchayats can levy taxes prescribed under the statute with due regard to rules and regulations framed by the State Government.

(d) Administrative

1. The Panchayat appoints its own Secretary in concurrence with the Panchayat Samiti, conforming with the standards of the qualifications laid down by the State Government.
2. It may take disciplinary action against the Secretary.
3. It has full control over class IV staffs.

The separation of Nyaya Panchayats from the Panchayats has very adversely affected the capacity of the Panchayats in obtaining local contributions though it has helped in removing the feeling of suspicion and distrust against the Panchayats equipped with too many coercive powers.

Working of Panchayats

Panchayat holds its meetings once a fortnight at a fixed place. One-third of its members constitute the quorum. Sarpanch or in his absence, Up-Sarpanch presides over the Panchayat meetings. A Secretary maintains the records of the decisions and communicates the agenda along with other relevant informations. Decisions are arrived at by the majority vote, though a special majority of 2/3 of the members is required when some decision regarding the construction of amenities is to take place. The village level worker usually attends its meetings. He communicates to the members the new scheme transmitted to him by the Block headquarters. He can suggest fixing of targets for the various items of village plan, or place before them the progress of work for review or point out shortfalls against the planned targets. There is a lot of informalities regarding the transaction of business. The order of business generally is reading of minutes; municipal case work; forwarding of some loan application or application for grants-in-aid; discussion of some circular sent by the Block or a matter initiated by the village level worker; approval of some house-keeping matter such as panchayat budget accounts or an application from a Panchayat employee.

Sarpanch

Sarpanch holds a pivotal position in the panchayat. He combines in himself the functions of a Chairman, executive, chief judge and representative. He presides over the meetings of Panchayat and announces decisions on behalf of the Panchayat. He serves as a spokesman of the Panchayat in the Panchayat Samiti. He is responsible for the safe custody of Panchayat funds. Accounting for all receipts and payments is authenticated by him. He maintains panchayat records under his safe custody and gets all reports prepared as required by the various lawful authorities. He supervises and controls the employees of Panchayat and discharges duties as authorized by the State Government. He is the ex-officio member of the Panchayat Samiti. He participates in the election of the Pradhan and the members of the other standing committees. As a member of the Panchayat Samiti he participates in decision-making.

The multifarious functions of the Sarpanch have not only made the Sarpanch very dominant but have resulted in the apathy and inactivity of Panchas. The process of his removal in most of the states has also contributed a great deal in strengthening his position. Three-fourth majority of total members of Gram Sabha, is required to remove him from the office of Sarpanch. Such a majority is not easily obtainable. Hence, practically speaking, he is not removable till of course the State Government itself takes the initiative of ousting him for the gross misuse of powers.

Panchayat Budget

The Panchayat Acts allocate large number of taxes, and other sources of income for the panchayats. The sources of income of panchayats can be classified as follows :

(a) Raised by Panchayats

1. **Taxes**

They include house tax, land cess, sanitary cess, lighting rate, vehicle tax, grazing tax, labour tax, octroi, water tax, marriage tax, tax on trade and callings and tax on commercial crops.

2. **Fees and Fines**

Proceeds or shares of fees and fines from case works, registrations of animals and cattle pools.

3. **Other Revenues**

Income is derived from the management of common land, disposal of panchayat property, fruit trees, fisheries, tanks and sale of Abadi land.

(b) Government and Panchayat Samiti Grants

Matching grants, ad hoc lumpsum grants or per capita grants constitute this source of income.

(c) Other sources of Income

Income from agency functions, donations and other types of voluntary contributions comprise this source of income.

It will be relevant to point out that in some states, certain taxes are obligatory whereas in others, they are optional. For example, Professional tax is compulsory in Andhra, Madhya Pradesh, Madras, Mysore and Kerala. Likewise, House tax is compulsory in all the above States as well as in Maharashtra and Punjab. In Gujarat, Assam, Rajasthan, Uttar Pradesh, Jammu and Kashmir, all taxes are optional.

The income of the Panchayat varies from state to state and from Panchayat to Panchayat within the same state. The average income of Panchayat in Bihar and U.P. is about 25 paise per capita whereas in Gujarat it is Rs. 3 and Rs. 4 per capita. The highest per capita income was recorded at Rs. 17.86 per capita in Takhatgarh Panchayat of Rajasthan whereas the lowest percapita income was recorded at Rs. 0.80 in some Panchayats of Bihar.

Heads of Expenditure

The paucity of funds leads to incurring of low expenditure on obligatory and discretionary functions and high ratios of administration costs to the total expenditure. The expenditure level also varies from state to state, from year to year and from Panchayat to Panchayat. The heads of expenditure are administration, civic amenities, social welfare, construction, maintenance and miscellaneous.

A study team on Panchayati Raj finances recommended an expenditure of Rs. 5 per capita as an immediate target. Keeping in view the civil developmental functions of the Panchayats this is hardly an ambitious target. The panchayats are apt to lose prestige, if they do not perform all these functions satisfactorily. At present, the highest chunk of the Panchayat income is spent on administration. Less than 5% is spent on Education, Social Welfare and Public safety. Only one-ninth of the total expenditure is incurred on public health, sanitation and water supply. Public works receive approximately one-fourth of the total. It is estimated that in majority of the Panchayats not more than 60% of the total (Panchayats) expenditure is devoted to municipal and developmental functions.

How to Improve Panchayat Resources

The paucity of panchayat funds poses a big problem. The following methods can be adopted for improving the resources of the panchayats :

1. Further utilization of the existing sources of self-raised income can augment panchayat income. An independent agency may be setup for assessing the liabilities, toning up collection machinery, plugging the leakages and punishing the defaulters, *i.e.*, the evaders of taxes.
2. Panchayats should man their resources a bit more vigorously. Through common land, common grazing grounds, small irrigation works and fisheries considerable additional income is possible.
3. Steps should be taken to have panchayat undertakings and panchayat utilities. For example, construction of or letting out of residential houses, markets, hotels, cinema houses, shops, etc. can be fairly fruitful enterprises for the Panchayats. Loans on liberal terms can be procured to build up the panchayat enterprises. They may purchase tractors, bore-well units, thrashers, etc., to be hired out or initiate small-scale undertakings for processing agricultural or animal husbandry produce. Once they are built up, the returns which are apt to be substantial can be utilized to pay off the principal and the interest.
4. Government grants must be enhanced.

If the sources suggested are tapped and the government also extends grant liberally, the per capita income of panchayat will certainly go up. Lofty expectations from the panchayats might be frustrated if sincere efforts to raise per capita income are not made.

State Control Over Panchayats

The state Government exercises quite effective supervision and control over the panchayats in the following ways :

1. It can annex, separate or transfer a particular area under the Panchayat according to due process of law.
2. It can frame rules and bye-laws in pursuance of the provision of the Panchayati Raj Acts particularly regarding creation of Panchayats, administration, maintenance and control of public property; appointment and control of panchayat personnel; settlement of assets and liabilities in case of merger or dissolution of the panchayats; accounting and auditing procedures and other such matters.
3. If a Panchayat fails to execute any legal obligation the State Government, after getting its explanation in writing, gets it done by an official appointed for the purpose and charge the cost to the Panchayat fund.
4. The State Government might direct the Panchayat to carry out lawful duty under an emergency and charge the expenses from the Panchayat fund.
5. In the event of gross misuse of powers, illegal excesses, or persistent neglect of duties, the State Government after giving an opportunity for hearing supersedes a Panchayat. However, a superseded panchayat is to be reconstituted within six months from the date of supersession.
6. The government may ask for records and reports. It may inspect Panchayats whenever it likes.
7. Panchayat accounts are to be audited by the Government auditors.
8. It can suspend or restrain the implementation of Panchayat's resolution which endangers public life, health or property or hinders or annoys a lawfully appointed person.

9. Some of the State Governments are empowered to suspend and remove a Sarpanch or Panch after proper enquiry. If the Sarpanch or Panch has already retired, the State Government might declare him ineligible for election for three years after recording the adverse findings against him.
10. While extending grants to the Panchayats, the State Government can impose restrictions upon the Panchayats as regard the utilization of these grants.

It may, however, be said that the State Governments have been vested with rather excessive controlling authority over the Panchayats. The power of reconstitution, supersession and suspension is liable to be politically misused. No doubt such an action can be taken after proper enquiry and consultation with Panchayat Samiti and Zila Parishad. Yet a revengeful politician at the helm of affairs can play havoc with local autonomy. Hence it is suggested that an impartial machinery may be devised to conduct enquiry against Panchayats for gross misuse of power, before any action is taken against them.

Nyaya Panchayats

As already said, with the ever-increasing developmental role of the Panchayats, it was realized that their judicial functions should be assigned to a separate body. Moreover, in the interest of equitability and impartiality of justice, separation of judicial functions from the executive was thought indispensable. This resulted in the emergence of Nyaya Panchayats as separate entities.

Composition and Constitution of Nyaya Panchayats

The Nyaya Panchayats cover a jurisdiction between five and seven Panchayat circles of the old pattern or according to the local situation. The officer in charge, generally the collector, is responsible for demarcating the jurisdiction. He is assisted by Tehsildars and Naib Tehsildars and Vikas Adhikaris in discharging his duties. Each Panchayat within the jurisdiction of Nyaya Panchayat, elects a member for the latter. The member so elected must be a registered voter in the Panchayat electing him. He must not be less than 30 years of age. He must be literate enough as to read and write the state language fluently and legibly. He must not suffer from any disqualification which ordinarily debars a Panch from being elected to the Panchayat. A Nyaya Panch is disallowed from holding an office of Sarpanch or that of member of Samiti, Parishad, State Legislature or Union Parliament simultaneously. The elections of the Nyaya Panchayats are regulated by the same rules as those of the elections of Vikas Panchayats. The members from amongst themselves elect a Chairman of the Nyaya Panchayat. One-third of the members retire by rotation every second year. The Chairman constitutes bench of the three members each for dealing with the civil and criminal cases coming before the Panchayats. The member hailing from a circle in which the case arises is not allowed to sit on the Bench. Likewise if a member of the Bench is a direct party to the suit or is personally interested in it, he is not allowed to sit for hearing of such a case. The members of the Nyaya Panchayat when on duty, enjoy the same protection as is enjoyed by public servants under law.

Powers

The Nyaya Panchayats possess civil and criminal jurisdictions. Their criminal jurisdiction extends to offences under the Indian Penal Code *viz.*, possession or use of false weights or measures, negligence or deliberate doing of acts which endanger public health, life and property, or cause public inconvenience such as fouling of water meant for public use, rash driving on public ways, obstructing or damaging public ways, failure to repair a dangerous building, causing hurt with or without provocation, misappropriation where the value involved is not more than Rs. 25, mischief, trespass, using coercion to wrongfully confine a person; injury to public property, insult, criminal intimidation, uttering words or making gestures intended to insult the modesty of a woman. Besides this, the Nyaya Panchayats are empowered to deal with offences under the Cattle Trespass Act, Public Gambling Act, Primary Education Act, Prevention of Juvenile Delinquency Act, Prevention of Cruelty to Animals Act and offences under the other Acts as may be declared by the State Government to be taken by the Panchayats.

The criminal jurisdiction extends to the trial of cases dealing with offences against public servants. These cases include refusal to answer questions, refusal to give information, refusal to produce documents, refusal to sign a statement and refusal to take an oath where a person is duty bound to act in that manner under the orders of a public servant. The Nyaya Panchayats can impose penalty prescribed by the statute upon the persons convicted for deliberately obstructing or insulting a public servant. The Nyaya Panchayats can impose penalty between Rs. 25 and Rs. 100. They may discharge young and juvenile offenders by fining or by issuing admonition to the offenders.

The civil jurisdiction of the Nyaya Panchayats extends to suits for damages, breach of contracts not affecting immovable property, suits for compensation for wrongfully taking or injuring movable property and suits for specific movable property the value of which does not exceed the ceiling prescribed by the statute. Such value generally ranges between Rs. 100 and 500. The Nyaya Panchayats do not exercise jurisdiction in cases where the suits may be brought before a Revenue Officer under any of the existing laws, against the Chairman or any member of Nyaya Panchayat, against a Sarpanch or Panch of the Panchayat, against a minor or person of unsound mind.

The Nyaya Panchayat is empowered to pass a decree with or without interest or instalment. It may give *exparte* judgement if the other party does not appear after getting due notice. It may dismiss complaint or application if there is not a '*prima facie*' case against the defendant. It may issue *summons,* cause appropriate documents to be produced and require the presence of a particular person for evidence. It may conduct local enquiry and make a report if directed by a magistrate to do so regarding an offence committed within its own circle.

Evaluation

Though the judicial activity of the Nyaya Panchayats has not been subjected to searching examination, yet on the basis of performance of these Panchayats in some of the states, it can be concluded that their services to the village community have been fairly commendable. The villager's fondness for these Panchayats has got accentuated due to quick, cheap and easily accessible justice rendered by the Nyaya Panchayats. On an average, a Nyaya Panchayat devotes approximately ten hours a month for case work and takes about two hours on an average to get the case disposed of.

The Panchayat Samiti

The emergence of Panchayat Samiti as a new unit of rural local self-government and its blending with the unit for area development and planning is a remarkable achievement of Community Development Programme. "Its architecture incorporates some of the bold administrative innovations of our times namely co-ordinated team work between the specialist and general administrator, multipurpose worker strung with the functional specialist, official agency wedlocked with the non-official workers."[1]

The acceptance of the Mehta Committee's recommendations by the National Development Council in 1958 and the passage of the Panchayat Samiti and Zila Parishad Acts by Rajasthan in 1959 ushered a new era in the evolution of relationship between the officials and non-officials. The Panchayat Samiti was established to share the responsibility of Community Development at local level.

The Panchayat Samiti is variously known. It is called *Anchalik Panchayat* in Assam, *Anchalik Parishad* in West Bengal, the *Janpada Panchayat* in Madhya Pradesh, *Panchayat Union Council* in Tamil Nadu, *Buluk Development Board* in Karnataka, the *Kshetra Samiti* in Uttar Pradesh and *Panchayat Samiti* in Punjab, Haryana, Andhra Pradesh, Bihar, Orissa, Rajasthan and Maharashtra. In Arunachal Pradesh it is known as *Anchal Samiti*. In Punjab the Panchayat Samities stand abolished.

Size

The area of the Panchayat Samiti is generally co-terminus with an N.E.S. Block or a Tehsil or Taluka which comprises of 112 villages. In Maharashtra the Panchayat Samiti consists of an area equivalent to two or three Blocks. The average area covered by Block works out to be 566 sq. miles though the usual range varies from 105 sq. miles to 2,837 sq. miles. The number of Panchayats per Block also varies from state to state e.g. from 8 per Block in Kerala to 80 in U.P.

Composition

The constitutional pattern of the Panchayat Samiti varies from state to state. Co-option of scheduled castes and tribes and the female members is a common feature. Special representation to co-operative societies, co-operative banks and progressive farmers is also accorded. The M.L.A.s and M.P.s are *ex-officio* members of the Panchayat Samiti in most states except Maharashtra. They are associate members having right to attend Samiti's meetings but are not allowed to exercise right to vote or get elected to the office of Pradhan or Chairman of the standing committee. In Karnataka M.L.A.s and M.P.s are full-fledged members of the Samiti.

Methods of Election

The members of Samiti are directly elected in Karnataka and Assam. Direct election method ensures direct responsibility of the elected representatives to the electorate and safeguards Samiti from local pulls and pressures. The system has its defects too. It snaps the organic link with the Panchayats and creates the problem of co-ordination.

Indirect election method prevails in rest of the states. It is of two kinds :

1. The Samiti is constituted of Sarpanchas as *ex-officio* members and
2. Indirect election through an electoral college, composed of *Panchas* and *Sarpanchas*. In Andhra, Bihar, Tamilnadu, Rajasthan, Orissa and Uttar Pradesh, the former method prevails. The system maintains organic links with Panchayat though makes Sarpanch as very powerful. "It blurs the sense of responsibility regarding Panchayat Samiti issues before the electorate and subjects the system to local pressure." The latter method has been adopted in Punjab and Madhya Pradesh. The system enables the Panchas to participate more vigorously in Samiti affairs than is possible in the former method. Moreover, it allows a certain measure of independence. It is apprehended by the critics that organic links with the panchayats cannot be maintained under this system. It gives rise to problems of coordination of plans and programme.

Tenure

The tenure of the Panchayat Samiti in most states is the same as that of Panchayats. This avoids the possibility of structural strains which might crop up if the social and political complexion of Panchayat Samiti undergoes a change while that of Panchayat remains the same. The absence of synchronisation of the terms of the two bodies may result in the emergence of two different political groups. In these two seats of authority at local level the local government may be converted into an arena of political conflicts. Obviously this may have serious repercussions on the development of local government in the country.

The Pradhan

The Pradhan is the linch-pin of the new set up. He plays a vital role in enthusing the people and controlling the chief executive. He is elected by the members of the Panchayat Samiti and is removable by a vote of no-confidence by a special majority. The indirect election of the Pradhan

---

[1]*Jain, S.C., op. cit., p. 200*

has resulted in worst type of blackmailing, corruption and questionable underhand practices. In his absence, ailment or disability or during the interregnum caused by Pradhan's removal or resignation, Up-Pradhan acts as Pradhan.

Functions of Pradhan

The following are the statutory functions of Pradhan :

1. Convening and conducting the meetings of Panchayat Samiti as its President.
2. Exercising administrative control over Vikas Adhikari and his staff regarding implementation of the decisions and resolutions of the Panchayat Samiti and standing committees.
3. Encouraging the growth of initiative and enthusiasm in the Panchayats and guiding them in making plans, carrying out production programmes and helping the growth of cooperatives and other voluntary organisations.

Powers of Pradhan

In order to enable him to discharge his functions satisfactorily the Pradhan has been vested with powers recognized by the statute as well as conventions. They are as follows :

1. He has full access to all the records of Panchayat Samiti.
2. He writes confidential report of Vikas Adhikari which is later on transmitted to the Collector.
3. He grants leave to the members of Samiti, subject to review by the Samiti and possesses other incidental powers of a presiding officer.
4. He is vested with emergency powers which he exercises in consultation with Vikas Adhikari under such powers. He can direct the execution of any work which normally necessitates the sanction of the Panchayat Samiti or its standing committees but the immediate execution of which is in his opinion, essential for the maintenance of services and safety to the general public. He can pass stay orders for the execution of any work, stating reasons for doing so. He can alter any programme of the Panchayat Samiti subject to the ratification of Zila Parishad. However, these emergency powers are subject to two limitations :
   (a) The act so directed should not contravene any orders of the State Government.
   (b) The action so taken must be reported to the Panchayat Samiti or the Standing committee at its next meeting.
5. He is an *ex-officio* Chairman of the standing committee if he happens to be its member.
6. He is an *ex-officio* member of the Zila Parishad as well. In this capacity, he can influence the opinion of the Collector and district level officers regarding Vikas Adhikari and the extension staffs.
7. The transfer of Vikas Adhikari and extension officers requires prior consultation with Pradhan.

Position of the Pradhan

The Pradhan plays a vital role in the new set up. On account of support of a stable majority and the trust he enjoys of the ministerial benches Pradhan has become a very powerful functionary. He is not easily removable as 2/3rd majority is required to oust him. He can even unnerve a Sarpanch with the assistance of a few of his loyal colleagues. Through his administrative powers, he can make his position envious. The support or hostility of Pradhan may affect the chances of a standing MLA to a considerable degree.

Since he exercises administrative control over Vikas Adhikari, he can compete with Vikas Adhikari regarding the latter's authority over his staff.

On account of his political links and his prominent place in political hierarchy, he can help the Panchayat Samiti in procuring financial assistance from the State Government and Zila Parishad and get over its financial and subsequently administrative difficulties.

The role of Pradhan as a President is also fairly important. A permissive Pradhan well aware of committee and meeting procedure can encourage the members to express their views freely and can bring about a true integration of view in arriving at a decision. The quality of decisions and the productivity of meetings depends to a great extent upon the balanced role of Pradhan.

Since the Panchayat Samitis and the standing committees meet only for a few hours once or twice a month, they can hardly consider the action report thoroughly. The Pradhan supplies standing vigilance on behalf of the samiti and its standing committees, and sees that their resolutions and decisions are carried out properly. An unsatisfied Pradhan may distort it into an instrument of interference which results in undermining administrative discipline, moral unity and efficiency. An indifferent and non-vigilant Pradhan may fail to discharge the duty of supervising and controlling the Vikas Adhikari properly. We can conclude that a Pradhan with progressive outlook, having a firm grasp over procedure supported by a solid and stable majority can prove to be a powerful functionary who can tone up the Panchayat Samiti business and Panchayat Samiti administration. A Pradhan devoid of these qualities can hardly inspire the members of Panchayat Samiti and administration with the requisite zeal and high standards of service.

The Committee System

A sound committee system provides opportunity to a large number of individuals to partake in decision-making. It helps in prompt disposal of cases and very thorough appraisal of issues. The Panchayat Samiti is not only an unwieldy body but also meets for a brief spell of time. Hence during its interregnum, committees alone can look into broad details.

In Panchayat Samiti, the members of committees range from three to seven. However, in case of need, the Samiti can constitute more committees as well. Every committee consists of usually not more than seven members. The Panchayat Samiti is entitled to coopt not more than two persons to a standing committee from outside the membership of Panchayat Samiti from amongst the experienced and knowledgeable persons. The committee possesses only delegated jurisdiction. The Panchayat Samiti can ask for any of their records or proceedings. It may withdraw, reduce or increase the powers of a committee. It is thus evident that the committee's position depends upon the confidence the Panchayat Samiti reposes in it and the status of its Chairman and the members, in the eyes of the other members.

Conduct of Business

The State Government prescribes the rules for the conduct of business. The Vikas Adhikari in consultation with the Chairman, prepares the agenda. Decisions are arrived at by majority with a casting vote for the Chairman. The Vikas Adhikari or some senior official on his behalf, participates in the proceedings though does not possess the right to vote. Members exhibit keen interest in loan applications or other applications for aid or procurement of a scarce commodity. Discussions generally take place on Government circular or any scheme which the concerned officer might read and explain.

Functions of the Panchayat Samiti

The functions of Panchayat Samiti can be divided into the following groups :

(1) Social Services

Following functions are included in this group.

(a) **Education** : Opening and running of primary schools, conversion of primary schools into basic schools, extending scholarships and stipends to the children of scheduled castes, scheduled tribes and other backward classes. Adult education, provision of library services, community centres, youth organisation etc. are also the set tasks of the Samiti.

(b) **Health and Sanitation :** This function comprises vaccination and control of epidemics, providing portable drinking water facilities, inspection and setting up of Ayurvedic dispensaries and primary family planning health centres, conducting health campaigns, imparting education in nutrition, maternity, child health and control of communicable diseases, regularisation of obnoxious and offensive trade and reclamation of healthy localities.

(c) **Social Welfare :** Management of hostels of scheduled castes and scheduled tribes, the strengthening of voluntary social welfare organizations, service of backward classes, propagation of prohibition, child and women welfare, inspection of poor houses, asylums and orphanages, rural housing for low income groups comprise social welfare functions.

(d) **House-keeping functions :** Collection of statistics, publicity, supervision and guidance of Panchayats, collection of Panchayat Samiti revenues, budgeting, record maintenance, reporting, administering trusts for furthering the purpose of Samiti are its house-keeping functions.

(e) **Emergency Relief :** It is expected to provide relief against fire, flood, famine, epidemics or other widespread calamities.

(f) **Communication :** Maintenance of inter-Panchayat roads and culverts are included in this function.

(g) **Miscellaneous :** Rural insurance agency, representation of the area interests and agency for small savings are also important functions of the Samiti.

(2) **Community Development**

In this category, it can be included organisation of village institutions and striving for increasing production, employment and amenities so as to promote self-help and community feeling.

(3) **Production Programmes**

In this category, the following functions can be included :

(a) Construction and maintenance of irrigation works.

(b) Development of co-operatives by promoting co-operative societies, providing credit and other facilities, encouraging investments in small savings and insurance.

(c) Development of village forests and rotational grazing.

(d) Development of cottage and small-scale industries, establishment and maintenance of production-cum-training centres, effecting improvement in the skills of the artisans and craftsmen and popularizing improved tool.

(e) Development of agriculture and animal husbandry by popularising improved seeds, use of manure, fertilizers, improved implements, improved methods of cultivation, castration and fruit and vegetable gardening.

(f) Organising services and supplies, catering to agricultural and animal husbandry development. It implies the establishment and maintenance of seed multiplication farms, artificial insemination centres, stock breeding farms and veterinary dispensaries. It also implies purchases, manufacture and distribution of improved implements, grading of wool, provision of insecticides to control plant and animal diseases.

Besides these functions, the State Government may confer more functions upon the Samiti.

Panchayat Samiti Finances

There are four main sources of income of the Samiti :

1. Self-raised resources.
2. Grants-in-aid by the state and other bodies.
3. Resources available under transferred scheme and departmental schemes.
4. Funds available under schematic budget.

1. Self-Raised resources

In this category, we include the following :

1. Taxes

The Samiti is empowered to levy the following taxes under the statutes of the various states.

(a) Local taxes at the prescribed percentage of the rent payable by the owner or rent received by a landholder or the assumed rental value of such land if no tax is payable on such land, share or entire proceeds of land. These rates vary from state to state. In Rajasthan, it is 5 paise, in Andhra 25 paise and in Tamilnadu 45 paise per rupee.

(b) Tax on trades, professions and industries.

(c) Primary education cess.

(d) Share of surcharge on stamp duties.

(e) Tax leviable on the Panchayat Samiti fairs and cattle fairs.

(f) Surcharge on local cess.

2. **Contributions**

Contributions can be made by private individuals and also the Panchayats and town committees. The latter pay between 6 paise and 12 paise per rupee of their income.

3. **Non-taxation sources**

In this group, following sources can be included :

(a) **Fees and fines :** Fees are procured from issuing licences, registration of animals, service of bulls, marketing fees on the use of Panchayat Samiti property, fees from schools and dispensaries. Fines are collected while exercising administrative jurisdiction and from hearing of the appeals.

(b) Income through the toll charges and entertainment tax.

(c) Sale proceeds of movable and immovable property.

(d) Revenue receipts from Panchayat Samiti undertakings.

(e) Income from the lease of ponds, ferries and fisheries.

(f) Income from agency functions, *viz.*, Insurance schemes, small saving agency, income from endowments and forfeitures.

(g) Income from unclaimed deposits and forfeitures.

(h) Share of profit from state trading in any commodity. With the sanction of the State Government, it may also raise the loan.

4. **Grants-in-aid**

The grants-in-aid are also important source of revenue. Grants are extended to the Panchayat Samitis in various ways :

(a) **Adhoc grants.** In Punjab, for instance, a sum of Rs. 6,000 was extended to each Panchayat Samiti with specific instructions from the State Government as to the way it is to be expended. Rajasthan Government also adopted the same system of extending Rs. 2,000 per Panchayat Samiti as the ad hoc grant.

(b) **Matching grants.** The Tamil Nadu Government advances matching grants to the Panchayat Samitis, from 75% to 150% of the sums raised by the Samitis through surcharge on land cess depending on the class of Samitis.

(c) **General grants.** These grants are not tied to specific schemes or purpose. They are given to the Samitis to be spent in the manner determined by them within a specified broad framework. Andhra, for example, gives 25 paise per capita, as general grants to the Samitis. Gujarat credits 25% of its land revenue to the Panchayat Samiti fund whereas Karnataka gives 20%.

(*d*) **Specific purpose grants.** These grants are given for specific purposes and are not available otherwise.

5. **Finances under Schematic Budget**

Of the total available income of the Panchayat Samiti, the Schematic Budget under Community Development contributes a sizable amount from Rs. 1.5 to Rs. 3.5 per capita depending on the stage of the Block. However, the schematic budget which was expected to place nucleus funds at the disposal of the Block agency, has suffered substantial alterations, as regards overall quantum, composition and method of administering the same. In the initial stages a project area approximating the size of three Blocks was allocated 65 lakhs for a period of three years. In 1953-54 the said allocation of funds was reduced from 21. 6 lacs to 15 lacs for three years. The provision for the newly started N.E.S. Blocks was fixed at 7.5 lacs. In the Second Five Year Plan, the C.D. and N.E.S. Blocks were constituted at the rate of Rs. 12 and Rs. 4 lacs respectively for three years. During the Third Five Year Plan period the I stage and II stage Blocks were allocated Rs. 12 lacs and 5 lacs respectively for five years. The amount of annual income accruing from the schematic budget was Rs. 2.4 lacs and Rs. 1 lac respectively for I and II stages Blocks and was less than 50% what it was during the First Five Year Plan.

Such allocations have been progressively increased from plan to plan and from state to state.

6. **The Transferred Schemes and Department Sources**

The State Government pays the Samiti for the transferred liabilities such as primary education, primary health centres, irrigation works, inter-Panchayat link roads, social welfare schemes and demonstration farms. Panchayat Samiti's funds are further augmented due to the departmental schemes for seed multiplication, inoculation of animals, schemes of Khadi and Village Industries Board.

Though the income figures seem fairly impressive yet the freedom of the Panchayat Samiti to take initiative in planning and programming is very much restricted. The schematic budget, the departmental schemes and the various grants hardly have any scope for initiative. The self-raised sources are so meagre that freedom to plan their use is hardly of any practical utility. However, the Panchayat Samitis have full freedom to frame their own budgets and formulate their own annual plans of development within the framework of State plan.

Heads of Expenditure

1. **Management**

A large slice of income is , however, eaten up by the management in most of the States. The expenses on this account are approximately 0.80 lacs per year in the I stage Block and nearly 0.52 lacs in the II stage Blocks. In U.P. in particular, 56% of the budget is spent on the management.

2. **Agriculture, Animal Husbandry, Irrigation**

Agriculture was given top priority by the Samiti, in the initial stages. However, during the Second Five year Plan, a drastic cut was effected in the allocation meant for agriculture, animal husbandry and irrigation. During the Third Five Year Plan, cut was restored to a great extent. The amount on irrigation was, however, cut down by 50%.

However, in the rest of the 5 yearly plans, Agriculture and Irrigation have been given priority over many other heads of expenditure.

3. **Social Services**

The Samiti incurs expenditure on the social services as well though the provision on the social services suffered a great cut. In this category we include health services and social education.

4. **Education and Social Welfare**

Education is the most important item which distinguishes the Panchayat Samiti of one State from that of the other. The Samitis having control over primary education as in Tamilnadu, Andhra and Rajasthan have fattened their budgets considerably. Hence they spend lavishly also on education. In pursuance of Directive Principles of State policy, primary education was to be made free and compulsory for all children upto the age of 14 till 1970. Obviously more and more expenses were apt to be incurred on primary education.

The provision on social welfare is generally not made in the budgets of most of the States. However, Rajasthan and Andhra do make a provision for social welfare in their respective budgets.

5. **Housing and Communication**

In the early stages, communication was an important item of the Block budget. Due to higher emphasis on production programme rather than amenities, expenditure on this item has suffered a sharp decline.

6. **Provision for Industries** (Rural Arts and Crafts)

There has been a sharp fall in expenditure on this item, as well. For instance, the provision of 0.41 lacs a year for Rural Arts and Crafts during the First Five Year Plan was cut down to 0.16 and 0.13 lacs during the Second and Third Five Year Plans respectively.[1]

The Zila Parishad

The Zila Parishad is mainly an advisory, coordinating, fund distributing and supervisory body in Rajasthan, Tamilnadu, Assam, Madhya Pradesh, Orissa and Bihar whereas in Gujarat, Andhra, Maharashtra, Punjab and U.P. It is equipped with executive functions like health, education, social welfare etc. In the rest of the states, the Zila Parishads have inherited numerous executive functions from the former district boards and district school boards. In 1987 there were 297 Zila Parishads. The number has since gone up.

Composition of Zila Parishad

There are two methods of constituting Zila Parishad. Directly constituted pattern prevails in Gujarat, Punjab, U.P. and Maharashtra. According to this pattern, some elected members are also included in the membership of the body. In Gujarat, Maharashtra and U.P. some of these elected members are elected from the electoral constituencies consisting of 35,000 people. In the Punjab the members of Panchayat Samiti constitute an electoral college to elect five members of Zila Parishad from amongst primary members. Similar provisions exists in U.P.

A Committee recommended direct election of the Zila Parishad stating "...Consequently we are convinced that district Councils (Zila Parishad) which will exercise the functions of the state as proposed by us should be broad-based, should be directly responsible to the people and have the requisite political stature and, therefore, substantially directly elected."[2]

The other pattern, which prevails in Rajasthan, Andhra, Tamilnadu, Assam, MP., Orissa and Bihar, Zila Parishad comprises of all the Pradhans of Panchayat Samitis in the district, all the members of the Legislative Assembly elected from the district, all the members of the Lok Sabha elected from a constituency which forms part of a district, all the members of the Rajya Sabha living in the district and the President of the Central Cooperative Bank. These members co-opt two women if no woman happens to be a member of the Zila Parishad. They co-opt one woman in case one is already the member of the Zila Parishad. Likewise a member of scheduled caste and also a scheduled tribe is co-opted if none out of them is a member of the Zila Parishad and if the population of the scheduled castes and scheduled tribes exceeds 5% of the total population of the district. Besides, two other members whose experience in administration and public life or rural development might be of benefit to the Zila Parishad are also co-opted. The Collector is the *ex-officio* member of the Zila Parishad. He does not possess right to vote. Chairman of the Central Co-operative Bank and Chairman of the District Co-operative Union are the associate members.

1. *See Appendix ix p. 542.*
2. *Maharashtra Committee on Democratic Decentralization (1981), pp. 78-80.*

The members or Zila Parishad elect the Pramukh and Up-Pramukh from amongst themselves. The Pramukh or Up-Pramukh is removable by a vote of no confidence carried out by a majority of 2/3rd of the total members. The term of the Zila Parishad is five years.

Function of Zila Parishad

The Zila Parishad performs executive, co-ordinative, advisory, appellate, supervisory, declaratory, house-keeping and joint servicing functions. The Asoka Mehta Committee (1978) emphasised the transfer of major powers to Zila Parishad. However, these powers should be supervisory and coordinative and not executive where effective Panchayat Samiti at Block level exists. Following these recommendations, the States assigned only coordinative and supervisory functions to it. The Naik Committee assigned executive functions as well. Following are the functions of the Zila Parishads.

1. **Executive**

In Punjab, Andhra, Gujarat, Maharashtra and U.P., the Zila Parishad has been endowed with executive functions which were formerly vested with district local boards, district school boards, district development committees and Panchayat Samitis. For example, the Zila Parishads in the Punjab have been entrusted agricultural credit, agricultural promotion, animal husbandry, inter-village roads and communications. In U.P. the Zila Parishads look to the development of animal husbandry and village and cottage industries, medical and public health, education and culture of the residents of the area and public works. It performs relief works, looks to planning, statistics and administration. In Maharashtra, the Zila Parishad is responsible for performing all functions covered within the ambit of "local sector". Such functions pertain to agricultural development, minor irrigation, animal husbandry, development, health and rural sanitation, water supply, primary and secondary education, development of cottage industries and social welfare programme.

2. **Supervisory**

The Zila Parishad supervises the activities of the Panchayat Samiti with regard to the promotion of agricultural production, construction and employment programmes. It can seek information from any local body within its jurisdiction regarding its activities and possesses right of inspection. It can ask for and review the administrative reports of the Samiti before forwarding them to the State Government. Through the distribution of ad hoc grants amongst the Panchayat Samitis, it can exercise control over delinquent Panchayat Samitis.

3. **Co-ordinative**

Co-ordination of the work of Panchayats and Panchayat Samitis is another important function of the Zila Parishad. Its power of examining the budgets of the Panchayat Samitis enables it to effect co-ordination.

4. **Advisory**

The Zila Parishads tender advice to the State Governments on matters concerning the activities of Panchayats and Panchayat Samitis, the implementation of any statutory or executive order as might be referred to them by the State Governments and executing the plan projects in the districts.

5. **Appellate**

The Zila Parishad settles disputes between a Panchayat and Panchayat Samiti within the same district or between two different Panchayats or two different Panchayat Samitis within the same district. An appeal can be carried by the Zila Parishad staff to the Zila Parishad, against the disciplinary action taken against them by the Secretary or the standing committee on finance, taxation and administration of a Panchayat Samiti, amounting to withholding of an increment of the member of Panchayat Samiti or Zila Parishad services.

6. **Joint Servicing**

Where Zila Parishads have not been entrusted executive functions, their jurisdiction has been confined to establishment functions as joint training, organisation of camps, conferences, seminars and training institutes, selection and promotion of Panchayati Raj personnel (class III), hearing appeals regarding disciplinary action against such personnel, execution of a project concerning two or more Panchayat Samitis with their consent and framing rules regarding use and maintenance of such works.

7. **Declaratory**

The Zila Parishads have also been assigned the duty of declaring the "progressive farmers", the best Block and the best village level worker. They can also classify fairs, festivals and roads as having village, inter-village or district character.

8. **House-keeping**

The house-keeping functions of the Zila Parishad comprise of publication of statistics, secretarial work, budgeting, reporting to state governments. The indirectly constituted Zila Parishads are empowered to examine the budgets of the Panchayat Samitis, make nonbinding observations thereon and call for the records and other informations. They may, however, be assigned other functions by the State Governments.

We can afford to conclude that though the Zila Parishad is chiefly a supervisory, advisory and co-ordinative body, it also examines and approves the budget of Panchayat Samitis under it. It also performs important administrative functions. It can also assume the role of a real intermediate power. Much, however, depends upon the State Government which may fully respect the advice of the Zila Parishad. Dr. Jain has well portrayed the authority of Zila Parishad in the words : "The real authority of Zila Parishad, however, has to be moral. It is woven with its ability to accommodate and do justice to the differing viewpoints and claims which arise inevitably in co-ordination work of the lower bodies, stimulating productive activities and developing and disseminating creative ideas and solutions with regard to administration and technical problems."[1]

Functions of Pramukh

1. The Pramukh presides over the meetings of the Zila Parishad and conducts its meetings.
2. He pays visit to the Panchayats and Panchayat Samitis to enthuse them and to inspect their work. He places his report regarding their work before the Zila Parishad.
3. He sends a report to the Collector regarding the work of the Secretary of the Zila Parishad.
4. Where Zila Parishad is executive body, he possesses considerable administrative powers to deal with emergencies.
5. He supervises the Chief Executive Officer for implementing the resolutions and orders of the council.
6. He submits confidential report to the Commissioner.
7. He can pass remarks on confidential reports of class I and II officers as submitted by the Chief Executive Officer.
8. He can have access to the records of the council.
9. In emergency, he can direct the execution of any work pertaining to the district body.

It is thus evident that the Parmukh combines in himself the role of a leader and supervisor. His appraisal of the work of a Pradhan might affect the political fortunes of the latter. His inspections also are fairly rewarding. However, much depends upon his own personality, his competence as a leader, his objective outlook and his human relationship skills. If he adopts an authoritarian attitude,

[1]*Dr. Jain, S.C., op. cit., pp. 240-45.*

the Pradhan of different political complexions might embarrass him not only by indulging in criticism in the meetings of Zila Parishad but also by actively campaigning against him in the election.

The role of a Collector

The Collector's position in the Zila Parishad has entailed lot of criticism. The Balwant Rai Mehta Report had recommended :

"At the district level, the Collector or the Deputy Commissioner, should be the captain of the team of officers of all development departments and should be made fully responsible for securing the necessary coordination and cooperation in the preparation and execution of the district plans for community development. Where he is not already empowered to make the annual assessment of the work of the departmental officers in regard to their cooperation with the department, their speed of work, their dealing with the people and their reputation for integrity, he should be invested with such powers."[1]

In practice, the District collector's association with the Panchayati Raj system and the role assigned to him vary from state to state, as indicated below :

1. In Maharashtra, Gujarat, West Bengal and M.P. he is kept out of the Zila Parishad.
2. In Uttar Pradesh and Bihar he is entitled to attend the meetings of the Panchayat Samiti and its standing committees but without a right to vote.
3. In Assam, Punjab and Rajasthan, the collector is a non-voting member of the Zila Parishad with which he is associated in a purely advisory capacity.
4. In Tamil nadu, he is the Chairman of the district Development Council as well as of Zila Parishad.
5. In Andhra Pradesh, he is not only the member of the Zila Parishad, but also the Chairman of all standing committees in whom is vested executive authority in most matters.

Thus, there is a lot of variation in the Collector's powers and functions with regard to the Panchayati Raj institutions. However, leaving Maharashtra, Gujarat, West Bengal and M.P., all other states have granted the following powers to him :

1. He co-ordinates the work of various development departments of the state government at the district level.
2. He examines the extent of progress achieved in the execution of various schemes and implementation of decisions and resolutions of the Zila Parishad and suggests improvements.
3. He is to see to the proper utilization of funds by the Panchayat Samitis and their maintaining minimum standards of service.
4. He is to see that Vikas Adhikari and his staffs play their role properly.
5. He can inspect and call forth any record, report or information from the other local bodies.
6. He can ask the Samiti or Parishad to consider any objection or information which he considers essential to be taken into account.
7. As a watch-dog of the State and Central Government at district level, the Collector exercises regulative powers on behalf of the state government except the powers of supersession, dissolution, rule-making power of revision and review under exceptional circumstances and the amendment of schedules.
8. He is responsible for the maintenance of law and order in the district. Hence Panchayat Samitis' and Zila Parishads' areas come under his purview for this purpose.
9. He has been vested with special responsibilities regarding the election of the President and Vice-President of the Samiti or Parishad, co-option of members and administration of oath.

[1]*Report of the team for the study of community Project and National Extension Science, VMI, pp. 39-40.*

10. He presides over the extra-ordinary session of the Panchayat Samiti specially convened to consider no-confidence motion against the Pradhan.
11. He is to see that the technical assistance is made available to the extension officers by the corresponding departments of the State Government.
12. He assists the Panchayat Samitis in the early recovery of dues.
13. He is to see that adequate provisions are made by Panchayat Samitis to recover and repay the loans advanced by the state government to the Panchayat Samitis.
14. He is to see and report to the State Government whether the priorities in the Plan are being adhered to and whether the general pattern of work is in conformity with the policies laid down by the State and the Central Governments.
15. He can suspend the resolution of a Panchayat Samiti or a Panchayat in the event of immediate threat to human life, health, safety or public order.
16. In an emergency he can provide for and direct the execution of any work which is essential for public safety.

Thus it is obvious that his powers as guardian of law and order and district development officer are fairly imposing. However, since Zila Parishads have been vested with executive powers and a senior I.A.S. officer is their Executive Officer, the Collector's powers of inspection, suspension and direction have been transferred to the Commissioner. Still the Collector is allowed certain emergency powers and to make a report to the Commissioner if he feels that the situation necessitates action on his part. Besides, he is the head of revenue and general administration at district level. Hence his contribution is apt to be of immense importance for the harmonious functioning of the Panchayati Raj institutions with the Zila Parishad, as its spearhead.

Zila Parishad Finances

The income and expenditure of the Zila Parishad to a great extent, depends upon the status of this body in the three-tier system. In Rajasthan, the budget of Zila Parishad varies between Rs. 20,000 and Rs. 30,000. The entire income of the Parishad accrues from the grants made by the State Government. The major part of the income is expended on the salaries and allowances of the staff and members. However, a minor part of it is spent on publicity and member education programme. In U.P., Punjab, Maharashtra, Andhra, where executive functions are also entrusted to the Parishad, the resources are considerably large. An overall comparative assessment of the finance of the Zila Parishads reveals that the financial position of the Maharashtra Zila Parishads is the strongest, as they spend approximately 1/3 of the total income of the State. This income is derived mostly from Government's grants and loans. Only very meagre income is derived from the self-raised resources. The same tale is to tell in U.P. In Andhra, the self-raised resources constitute the major part.

As regards the expenditure pattern, expenditure on education is the maximum. It is nearly 50% of the total income. Nearly 1/4 of the income, with the exception of U.P., is spent on local works. Medical and public health services also consume fairly sizable portion of the income. A part of revenue is spent on agriculture though in U.P. percentage of such expenditure is woefully small. The expenditure on General management is very meagre total expenditure. This favourably compares with the same in the Panchayat Samiti, which is over 20% of the total.

Relation between Zila Parishad and Panchayat Samiti

The Panchayat Samiti is organically linked with the Zila Parishad. The Pradhan of the Samiti sits as a member in the Parishad's meetings and participates in the election of Pramukh. If the political composition of both the organs is not homogeneous, the problems of co-ordination are conspicuous by their absence.

The Panchayat Samiti sends its budget to the Zila Parishad which possesses only advisory jurisdiction except in U.P. and Maharashtra where it possesses mandatory powers. The Panchayat Samiti banks upon Zila Parishad for the distribution of matching or adhoc grants. The Zila Parishad possesses the power of supervising the activities of the Panchayat Samiti. It can ask for the latter's records and seek any information it deems essential. It even advises the State Government regarding the development work in the district and can exercise influence on the opinion of the latter about the work of the Panchayat Samiti.

The Zila Parishad can institute an Establishment Committee or Selection Board, which regulates the mode of temporary appointment or appointments by promotion or transfer and renders advice to the Panchayat Samitis on all disciplinary matters concerning the employees employed in Panchayat Samiti and Zila Parishad Services.

Besides the supervisory powers, the Zila Parishad can exhort the district technicians to respond to the needs of the Samitis and effect coordination in their activities through the Collector or Chief Administrator.

It may, however, be said at the end, that unless large amounts of ad hoc grants are extended through the Zila Parishad and district technicians are effectively subordinated under it, it cannot force the Panchayat Samiti to observe its own notions of propriety. If, however, the Parishad is held in confidence by the State Government, it can exert indirect pressure but its utility chiefly lies in its being a "forum for the exchange of views and experiences, operational coordination, expression of grievances and learning from the experiences of elderly statesmen."

Possibility of tension between Zila Parishad and Panchayat Samiti cannot be ruled out if both are dominated by leaders of different parties embracing contrary views. However, on account of expectations of procuring grants which are to be distributed amongst the Samitis through the Parishad, the Samitis cannot displease the latter. The Parishad's assistance in mobilising technical support at district level and solving administrative difficulties through the Collector or Commissioner can also prove substantial allurement for the Samitis to abide by the directions of the Parishad. Likewise, the Parishads have to depend upon the Samitis for the execution of development projects within the district. Hence a strong bond of interdependence automatically helps in resolving their differences and relieving the tension between the Parishads and the Samitis.

The Committee Systems in Zila Parishad

Before we come to the close of this chapter, it is imperative to say a few words about Committee System in Parishads. The composition, functions and powers of the committees of the Parishads differ from state to state according to status of the Zila Parishad in the three-tier system. The statutory committees of the Parishad do not exist in Rajasthan except of course a District Establishment Committee which makes appointments and effects transfers and promotions within the District. In actual practice, various other committees on production programme, social services, finance and administration have come into existence. In the states where Parishads are equipped with executive powers, standing committees have been constituted to probe into each major group of functions. A few standing committees dealing with planning, community development and communications, cottage and village industries, small-scale industries, women and children welfare, social welfare, education, public health and medicine, taxation and finance, food and agriculture, animal husbandry, forests, irrigation and power exist in Andhra. The Collector is the Chairman and the Pramukh is the ex-officio member of these committees. These committees meet comparatively less frequently than their counterparts in the Panchayat Samitis, probably because they are concerned with review and overall supervision rather than with execution. In Maharashtra, the committee system of the Parishads is of more vigorous type. Six statutorily prescribed subject-matter committees *viz.*, finance, agriculture, works, cooperative, education and health exist in Maharashtra. Besides these committees, there exists another standing committee consisting of the President and seven other members elected by the council from its own members. The President is the *ex-officio* Chairman of the standing committee. The Vice President happens to be the *ex-officio* Chairman of the two subject-matter committees. The secretarial and executive assistance is provided by the Chief Executive Officer and the heads of the technical departments for their respective subject matter committees.

Each subject-matter committee is responsible for the development schemes within its subject-matter competence. It not only sanctions the estimates prepared under various schemes but supervises their execution as well. It is concerned with periodic review of the progress, formulation of budget estimates for area of its own subject-matter, responsibility, supervision of the budget execution in the field assigned to it, acquisition, sale or transfer of immovable property, sanctioning execution of schemes and contingent expenditures.

Besides these subject-matter committees, there are Block committees on territorial basis for each N.E.S. Block. These committees consist of members of the District Council, elected from the area of the Block and other co-opted members of the District Council, two Sarpanchas elected by Panchas, Chairman of agriculture co-operative society of the Block, Chairman of Taluka purchase and sales union, one member each from scheduled castes, scheduled tribes and women of the area. The Chairman of the Block committees is selected by the members of the area and is *ex-officio* member of the district samiti. These committees execute and supervise the schemes and works of the Council in the Block area and execute any other work on behalf of the Council or its committees. They can submit development plans of their Block to the District Council. They also propose increase in local cess on land revenue, taxes, fees to the District Council.

The standing committees supervise and control the inspection and collection of taxes and other dues of the Council. They regulate the investment of district funds, pass monthly accounts of receipts and expenditure and review progress of the programmes periodically. They can sanction leave to the Chief Executive Officer up to one month and to other Class I or Class II officers up to four months. They in consultation with the appropriate selection body possess revision authority against the orders of the Chief Executive Officer, in regard to Class III and Class IV employees of the Council. Commenting on the committee system, Dr. S.C. jain remarks, "This remarkable system is designed to combine principles of administrative efficiency with the necessary political control and allow wide scope for the exercise of local initiative with full assurance of a high order of legal, technical and administrative advice."

(D) ASSESSMENT OF PANCHAYATI RAJ

An analytical survey of the three-tier system reveals that Panchayati Raj is a dull echo of its former self. Scholars are of the view that India is on the way to have a strong rural administration, rather than an effective rural government. The three-tier system has been working in the different parts of the country for the last many years but certain glaring shortcomings are still discernible viz., lack of clear and scientific distribution of functions at the various levels; domination of higher structure over the subordinate structures; undue interference of the state governments and curtailment of autonomy of these institutions; lack of adequate finances; scant attention to the views and aspirations of people by the officials; parochial thinking on account of politicization of the Panchayati Raj Institutions; indirect election of the Panchayat Samitis and Zila Parishads, absence of democratic principles; tight control of the government over the Panchayati Raj Institutions.

Ashok Mehta Committee

Keeping in view these facts, a committee on Panchayati Raj Institutions under the Chairmanship of Ashok Mehta was appointed in December, 1977 by the then Janata Government. It submitted its Report in August, 1978 making about 132 recommendations. The main recommendations pertained to (a) functional necessity for decentralization of administration though under democratic supervision; (b) two-tier system of Panchayati Raj viz., the revenue District assuring the technical expertise of high order required for rural development and the Mandal Panchayat to be constituted by grouping a number of villages; (c) The Panchayati Raj Institutions to have compulsory powers of taxation and mobilize their own resources, thus reducing their dependence on diversion of funds from the state government. Certain taxes collected from the area such as provision tax, entertainment tax and special tax on land and building be transferred to Panchayati Raj Institutions; (d) Open participation of political parties in Panchayati Raj affairs; (e) The creation of certain monitoring forums to safeguard and promote the interests of vital social and economic groups in the villages; (f) A regular social audit by a district level agency as well as by a committee of legislators to check whether funds earmarked for these social and economic groups are actually spent on them; (g) The State legislators will have a committee on Panchayati Raj with adequate representation for scheduled castes and tribes to cater to their needs and mitigate grievances of the weaker sections; (h) The State Government must not supersede the Panchayati Raj Institutions on partisan grounds. In case of an imperative supersession, election must take place within six months; (i) Provision of urban amenities such as roads, potable water, medical care, employment and education in rural areas to neutralise craze for immigration to urban centres.

These recommendations were quite laudable as they were designed to revitalize Panchayati Raj Institutions and accord them constitutional status but they were not without pitfalls; *firstly*, Ashok Mehta Committee conceived of Panchayati Raj in very narrow terms. It reduced Panchayati Raj into mere administrative contrivance whose justification lies in terms of rural development. Panchayati Raj should have been considered a system of government enjoying a certain measure of autonomy in the matter of its functions and existing in its own right.[1] *Secondly,* the committee did not give proper recognition to the elective participative organism at the village level. Such a view makes the village too conspicuous by its absence.[2] *Thirdly*, the present structure is not that inadequate as painted by it. The proposed two-tier system and the exact location of two-tiers are structural manifestations of an overall sensitivity to technology and an under-reaction to democracy at the grass roots. *Fourthly*, the Panchayati Raj institution lacks inherent power of taxation. The committee also failed to suggest a list of local taxes. *Fifthly*, the committee did not suggest making Panchayati Raj a part of the organic law of the land. A constitutional base, if suggested, could have imparted both a sanctity and stature to the grassroot democracy. *Sixthly,* election on party basis will pollute the rural atmosphere. The villages will become hotbeds of intrigues and animosities. Comparing the Balwant Rai Mehta report with that of Ashok Mehta, an eminent social scientist remarks, "Both are easily the two landmarks in the history of local government in India though each has its distinctive conceptual framework of analysis and examination. In certain respects the second builds upon the first but in many other seeks a deliberate departure from his predecessor."[3]

With the fall of Janata government, these recommendations of the committee remained in the tantalizing realm of unfulfilled aspirations. Hence the rural local bodies maintained *status quo.* Their financial resources remained meagre. Their supersessions were too frequent. The State Governments have been too domineering. They have not shown sustained enthusiasm for Panchayati Raj. The formidable challenges to democracy necessitated a changed attitude to Panchayati Raj. Democracy at higher levels is apt to have a weak base unless there is its habitual practice at the local level.

Attempts to revitalize the System in not too distant past

In July-August 1989, the Congress (I) Government under Rajiv Gandhi introduced the 64th Constitutional Bill with a view to revitalise and rejuvenate the Panchayati Raj Institutions. However, the Bill was defeated in the Rajya Sabha. The 64th Amendment Bill had sought to strengthen centralization through holding Panchayati Raj Institutions' elections under the supervision of Election Commission, appointment by the Centre of Finance Commission to regulate taxes and grants-in-aid and introduction of auditing of the Panchayati Raj Institutions's accounts by the Comptroller and

[1] *Dr. A. Awasthi and Dr. S.R. Maheshwari, op. cit. p. 169.*
[2] *Ibid, p. 170*
[3] *Maheshwari, S.R. op. cit., p. 508.*

Auditor General of India who was to submit his report to the Governor. Thus in all matters wings of the State Governments were clipped and the rule of the Centre was perpetrated. Since, the Bill was vehemently opposed by the opposition it could not be passed.

In November 1989, the National Front Government soon after assuming power announced that it would grant powers to the rural democratic institutions to make them effective bodies. In two days conference of Chief Ministers held in June 1990, Panchayati Raj Institutions and urban local bodies were discussed. The Government showed welcome promptness in proposing legislation to give constitutional status to Panchayati Raj Institutions, guaranteeing devolution of powers for developmental decision making to villages. On December 3, 1989, V.P. Singh in his first broadcast to the nation declared that he would "bring forward legislation for genuine Panchayati Raj which will respect the imperatives of our federal structure." The Chief Ministers' conference decided that each state shall appoint its own Election Commission to supervise elections and have its own finance commission. The government aimed at granting constitutional status to Panchayati Raj Institutions, reservation of seats for women and weaker sections and the provision of safeguards to make supersession of local bodies difficult. The thrust of the reforms was to make Gram Sabha the base of rural set up. However, the fall of the government resulted in shelving the proposals of National Front Government.

The Congress (I) government under Narasimha Rao introduced 72nd Amendment Bill on September 16, 1991. It proposed to add a new section for regular elections and adequate representation to the scheduled castes, scheduled tribes and women in Panchayati Raj Institutions. It provided for 1/3 reservation of seats for women and fixing tenures of the panchayats for five years. In the event of supersession of the Panchayats, elections were to be held within six months. The elections would be conducted by the election commission which would be independent of the Election Commission in Delhi. A Finance Commission will also be appointed to allocate sources of revenue independent of state control. The Panchayats would get 29 clearly defined subjects like sanitation, drainage, veterinary services, ponds and tanks, vital statistics, maintenance of community places, welfare of the weaker sections, primary education, village planning, public distribution system etc. to function on their own. The Bill was passed by the Parliament in its winter session, in 1992 and was supported by all the parties represented in both Houses of Parliament.

73rd Amendment Act 1993 – Its Salient features

The Constitution Act 1992, known as 73rd Amendment Act, came into force on April 24, 1993 after ratification by the requisite number of states and the President's assent. It laid the foundation of a strong and vibrant Panchayati Raj Institutions in the country. The salient features of the Act were as follows: (i) All the states (wherever applicable) would amend their Panchayati Raj Acts in accordance with the new constitutional provisions within the stipulated time by April 23, 1994, (ii) Establishment of Panchayats at the village, intermediate and district levels, (iii) Panchayati Raj Institutions to function as institutions of self-governance and to be endowed with powers and authority to formulate and implement schemes of economic development and social justice, (iv) Regular elections after every five years, (v) Direct elections of village chairperson and indirect elections of chairpersons at Block and District level, (vi) Reservation of seats for scheduled castes/scheduled tribes in proportion to their population, not less then 1/3 are to be from women (vii) Reservation of 1/3 seats for women, including scheduled caste quota in the same ratio of 1/3 (viii) Similar reservation in respect of the office of chairperson, (ix) Constitution of State Election Commission. The superintendence direction and control of the preparation of electrol rolts and conduct of all elections to the panchayat are vested with the election commission. The conditions of service of the State Election Commission are not variable to its disadvantage after its constitution. The state legistature as per constitution makes the provisions relating to elections to the Panchayat. (x) Constitution of State Finance Commission every five years to review the financial problem of the panchayat. (xi) States empowered to provide the reservation in favour of backward classes of citizens. (xii) The most distinguished feature of the Act was that it granted constitutional status to the Panchayati Raj institutions.

After the inception of Panchayati Raj Institution, the states were required to equip their Institutions with adequate powers, autonomy and authority so that they may be able to function efficiently, as institutions of local self government and discharge their constitutional responsibilities of preparing and implementing programmes of economic development and social justice.

After the passage of 73rd amendment Act almost all the states and Union Territories (NCT Delhi being an exception) have enacted legislation. Almost all have held the elections. Consequently 234676 Panchayats at village level, 60 97 Panchayats at Intermediate level and 537 panchayats at the district level have been established. Approximately 21.93 Lakhs representatives at all levels are manning these Panchayats. This is said to be the broadest representative base in a democratic country.

Although the new Panchayati Raj system as conceived in the 73rd Amendment Act has been ushered in, there is a feeling that the new system, barring a few exceptions, could not become a vibrant system of rural self governance due to lack of political will and also committed support of the bureaucracy. The objective of empowerment of people at the grass root level does not seem to have been achieved. Further, the successful working of the new Panchayati Raj lies in the harmony of castes and prevention of clash of factional egos. During Panchayat elections many states witnessed violence and political warfare. People with criminal records entered the Panchayati Raj institutions. The money received by the Sarpanch under the rural development schemes is misappropriated by him like other functionaries of state administration. It is also being doubted if the Panchayats are in a position to undertake the developmental projects concerning drinking water supply, irrigation, health care and community welfare. Unless those who work the new system do so with honesty, integrity and concern for the rural community and inspire people's participation, and unless these institutions are equipped with adequate powers, sufficient funds and sizable authority, the new system may fail to usher in the era of rural development through self-governance.

No doubt the revival of Panchayati Raj has been a laudable step towards establishment of a grassroot democracy but unfortunately certain prerequisites of such a revival have been conspicuous by their absence as is evident from the following facts (a) unhealthy relationship between the local bureaucracy and the elected representatives should have been taken care of. Hence it is doubtful "whether the problem of relationship between local level bureaucracy and elected representatives of Panchayati Raj institutions will be properly attended or smoothened by the state legislatures (b) A firm committment to Panchayati Raj as a political value and also political will to establish[1] it (c) Necessity of a perpetual reminder that revival of Panchayati Raj is an attempt to reconstruct Indian polity entailing decentralisation of genuine power from Union to the States and from states to rural and urban government bodies. Still it is heartening to note that the Panchayati Raj institutions at the local level are ensuring greater peoples representation and their involvement in development work. Besides granting of constitutional recognition to the Panchayati Raj and effecting unformity in its structure throughout. India has led to the awakening of the rural masses and has considerably reduced the overwhelming influence of the affluent section of society in their affairs.[2]

July 9, 2001 conference. On July 9, 2001 the Union Rural Development minister convened conference of the state ministers to appraise the working of Panchayati Raj Institutions. The

1. Professor B. L. Fadia and Dr Kuldeep Fadia: Public Administration 2008 edition pp 894 and 895 Figures as on April 2005.

2. S. N. Mishra : Panchayat Raj institutions 73rd ammendment and after – Employment New – august 14–20, 1993

conference observed (a) that some states were working against the 33% reservation for women in panchayats by moving no confidence motion against women chairpersons in Gram Sabhas and replacing them by men (b) A majority of state governments possessed power to dissolve or supersede panchayats for abuse of power and remove President or vice President for misconduct in discharge of duties. In most cases the collectors were vested with powers to remove chairpersons or members of gram panchayats. Excessive controls are counter-productive (c) Panchayat Raj elections have not been conducted in states like Andhra Pradesh, Assam, Pondicherry, Delhi, Jharkhand and Uttaranchal. In Punjab, Gujarat and Chandigarh elections were held partially (d) The Union Home minister asked the State Government of Jammu and Kashmir to extend the provision of the 73rd Amendment Act to the state as well. (e) Only eleven states have so far taken initiative to constitute District Planning committees which are indispensable for decentralised Planning. (f) The conference took up the issue of extension of the provisions of the Panchayats Act 1996 (extension to the scheduled Areas) to the states of Andhra Pradesh, Jharkhand, Maharashtra, Gujrat, Himachal Pradesh, Orissa, Chattisgarh and Rajasthan.

Reservation of women raised to 50% in Pancheyats – august 27, 2009. On august 2009 the Central Government approved a proposal to raise reservation for women in Panchayats from 33 to 50 per cent. A constitution amending Bill embodying this proposal was proposed and accepted in the totality. Article 243 will thus be amended and women empowerment will further get a boost at the grass root level. Five states *viz* Bihar, Uttarakhand, Himachal Pradesh, Madhya Pradesh and Chhatisgarh have already given reservation to that extent to women. Rajasthan and Kerala also have decided to implement the reservation up to 50% to women by 20%.[1]

(1) Pursuant to 73rd amendment Act 1992 "With the exception of Jammu and Kashmir the National capital Terrority of Delhi and Uttaranchal, all the states have enacted the necessary legislation for establishing strong viable and responsible panchayats at different levels in their respective States and Union Territories except Arunachal Pradesh, NCR of Delhi and Pondicherry.

(2) In all the states, panchayats have been established.

(3) The state governments are gradually transforming administrative and financial powers to the Panchayati Raj institutions. The government has appointed an empowered sub-committee of National Development Council on financial and administrative empowerment of PRIs to appraise the whole gamut of issues relocated to devolution of powers, functions and financial resources to PRIs.

(4) Through State Acts, Gram sabhas have been vested with responsibilities and functions.

(5) The states have been requested to empower the Gram Sabha to ensure that Gram Sabha should meet at least once on Republic day, Labour day, Independence day and Gandhi jayanti.

(6) Vest powers in Gram sabhas entrusting the ownership, management and control over natural resources under the provisions of the Panchayat Act, 1996. Gram sabhas are to determine principles for various programmes;

(7) panchayats are; to be accountable to the Gram Sabhas

(8) Members of Gram sabhas have to ensure mass participation of SCs/STs and women;

(9) Gram sabhas should involve own procedures to preserve their resources.

(10) The provision of 1996 Act extends panchayats to Tribal areas of nine states, assumes control over their own destiny to preserve and conserve.[2]

***

1. India 2008 (Government of India Publication Division)

2. Competition Success Review: October, 2009 India

URBAN LOCAL GOVERNMENT

> *"Democracy was no exotic growth in India and centuries before the advent of the British or Mughal rule, the stress was on self-governing institutions or corporate life."*
>
> **— Frank Moraes**

CONTENTS: (A) Evolution of Urban Local Government
(B) Features and Norms
(C) Municipal Administration in India
(D) Autonomy of Local Bodies

Municipal government in India has its roots in prehistoric times.[1] The epoch-making excavations at Harappa and Mohenjodaro reveal that a highly developed urban civilization existed in the ancient past. The cities had their councils with elected bodies. In the words of Havell — "*The administrative council of the city was modelled upon that of village communities and it may be assumed that like the latter, it was an elected body though certain matters were reserved for the control of imperial officials.*"[2] India can thus rightly be a claimant of the hoariest traditions of local government in the world. Frank Moraes, a biographer, supports this contention. He writes, "*Democracy was no exotic growth in India and centuries before the advent of British or Mughal rule, the stress was on self-governing institutions and a corporate life.*"[3]

Though the existence of elective city councils in ancient India cannot be denied yet there is no doubt that the foundations of modern system of municipal government were laid by the British particularly after the transfer of power from the East India Company to the Crown in 1858. The dominant consideration which prompted the British to establish local government institutions in India were (a) paucity of finances of the Imperial power, (b) administrative problems due to the large size of the country,[4] and (c) the need of providing relief to the District Officer from some of the details of his work.[5]

(A) EVOLUTION OF URBAN LOCAL GOVERNMENT

Some of the landmarks of the evolution of urban local government in India are as follows :

Lord Mayo's Resolution, 1870

The policy of decentralization, which started during 1860-70 found full expression in Lord Mayo's resolution of 1870. The resolution embodied the first systematic attempt to make provincial governments responsible for the management of their own local finances. It was hoped that,

---

[1] *Calder, Richie : The Inheritors, London, 1961, p. 99*
[2] *Havell, B.B. : The History of Aryan Rule in India, pp. 77-80.*
[3] *Moires, Frank : Jawaharlal Nehru – A Biography, p. 407.*
[4] *Report : Rural Urban Relationship Committee, Vol. I, p. 6.*
[5] *Argal, R..: Municipal Government in India, 1967, p. 1.*

"The operation of this resolution in its full meaning and integrity will afford opportunities for the development of self-government, for strengthening Municipal institutions and for the association of natives and Europeans to greater extent than heretofore in the administration of local affairs."[1]

In pursuance of this policy, several Acts were passed which not only extended the elective system [2] but also enlarged the powers of the municipal bodies to some extent. Besides, the resolution marked the beginnings of the system of local finance. In fact local self-government as a conscious process of administrative devolution dates from this Resolution.

Lord Mayo's policy on local self-government was revived in 1881. On 18th May, 1882, Lord Ripon, who is acknowledged as father of local self-government in India, issued a historic resolution. It aimed at fulfilling the national urge for self-government, meeting the growing demand for political and social justice and making local self-government an instrument of political and popular education.[3] Three broad principles were laid down for the guidance of provincial government; (a) that they should maintain and extend throughout the country a network of local government institutions; (b) that they should introduce into these bodies a large preponderance of non-official members — the number of official members being not more than one-third of the whole; and (c) they should exercise control over these bodies from without and not from within.

The underlying intention of the Resolution was evidently to give the people more real and meaningful share in the management of local affairs. The emphasis was laid on self-government aspect. An Indian historian has rightly remarked —

"*Lord Ripon's Reform of Local Self-government laid the basis of local and municipal self-government which soon took firm root in India and became the groundwork of democratic institutions in higher spheres.*"[4]

Following the passage of this Resolution, impressive progress in the field of local self-government was made during the decade. The percentage of elected members rose from 22.5 to 53.1, municipal income registered an increase from Rs. 1.28 crores to Rs. 2.05 crores, and expenditure from Rs. 1.26 crores to Rs. 2.06 crores.[5]

However, Lord Ripon's reforms were impeded by a conservative administration wedded to the cult of administrative efficiency. The head of the district administration, i.e. the Deputy Commissioner, dominated the local self-government and the official control was meticulous and rigid. The election principle was not based on adult franchise. Financial autonomy was hardly conceded to municipal bodies. In other words, the success of Lord Ripon's reforms fell short of the expectations raised in the minds of the enlightened nationalists.

Lord Ripon was succeeded by Governor-Generals who did not prefer political education to efficiency. The official tutelage thwarted the growth of self-governing institutions and civic consciousness. Thus the urban local self-governing bodies could not strike roots in India even after a hundred years of their existence.

Besides, the caste-ridden Indian people did not develop loyalties to the assemblages. They showed more allegiance to their respective caste or religious groups than to the local community. Hence they were not keenly interested in making a success of the local self-governing institutions of the modern type which were super-imposed upon traditional social institutions.

[1]*Resolution No. 3334 of 14th December 1870, also Mayo's Minute, July, 1870.*

[2]*Principle of election was introduced in four towns of Madras, three of Bengal, a number of towns of N.W. Provinces. In other provinces about 50% members were elected – The Imperial Gazetteer of India, Vol. IV (1909), p. 287.*

[3]*Para 5 of the Resolution.*

[4]*Panikkar, K.M. : A Survey of Indian History (1957 ed.), p. 211.*

[5]*Imperial Gazetteer, Vol. IV (1909), p. 306.*

Decentralization Commission, 1906

In 1907-1909, the subject of local self-government was considered by the Royal Commission on Decentralization. Its main recommendations were: (a) the Chairman should be an elective non-official; (b) a majority of the members should have freedom to increase any branch of taxation and exercise full control over their budgets; (c) municipal executive should be strengthened by competent chief officers; (d) all cities with a population of 1,00,000 and above must have executive officers; (e) all towns with a population of 20,000 and above should have qualified Health Officers; and (f) large municipalities should be given greater powers.

These recommendations were given consideration by Lord Harding's government, which issued a Resolution in 1915, favouring changes in the structure and functions of local bodies. The Resolution indicated the broad lines on which advance should be made. It was, however, realized that the Government of India could not press their views upon Provincial governments, because the latter alone possessed the requisite knowledge to foster and develop local institutions. Yet the initiative lay with the Government of India, which controlled the resources and reserves of taxation. This dichotomy was resolved through the introduction of Montford reforms.

It may not be out of place to point out that the introduction of communal electorates[1] as the basis of election to municipalities as well, impeded the healthy development of local self-government on secular lines. It proved a serious hindrance to the development of self-governing institutions.[2] It was in fact a negation of secular democracy.

The Resolution of 1918

The authors of the Montford report (which embodied Montagu Chelmsford reforms) were guided by the principle that "*there should be, as far as possible, complete popular control in local bodies and the largest possible independence for them from outside control.*"[3] In pursuance of this principle, the Government of India issued a comprehensive resolution.[4] It embodied certain basic principles calculated to establish, wherever possible, complete popular control over local bodies. Prof. Rushbrook rightly contends that this resolution : "*placed in the forefront of the subjects of local self-governing the training of the people in the management of their own affairs and laid down in clear-cut form the doctrine that political education must take precedence over departmental efficiency.*" [5]

Government of India Act, 1919

With the introduction of Dyarchy, after the passage of the Government of India Act, 1919, the local self-government department was transferred from bureaucratic hands to those of an elected minister in all provinces. As a result, the overall responsibility for the functioning of the local bodies was no longer to rest with the district officers and they ceased to be the Chairmen, though they still retained general supervisory control over them. The popularly elected ministers established elected councils and gave executive authority to the elected Chairman. Thus the approach was more liberal and there was a deliberate attempt to give the local bodies greater freedom from outside control.[6]

---

[1]*Communal Electorates were introduced by the Govt. of India Act, 1909 though they were extended to local bodies later on.*

[2]*Report : Montagu-Chelmsford, paras 227-232.*

[3]*Ibid., p. 123.*

[4]*Indian Education, Resolution No. 41 of may 16, 1918, p. 191.*

[5]*Report : Rural-Urban Relationship Committee, Vol. I, p. 10.*

[6]*Report : Simon Commission, Vol. II, p. 306.*

However, the working of urban local bodies during this period of Dyarchy (1921-1937) was neither a complete failure nor unqualified success. According to Simon Commission — "In every province, while a few local bodies have discharged their responsibilities with undoubted success and others have been equally conspicuous failures, the bulk lies between these extremes."[1]

In fact, laws passed during this period failed to prescribe an effective administrative structure based upon administrative efficiency and public accountability. Deliberative and executive functions were combined in the hands of the elected representatives, but proper organization of municipal employees into well-trained and properly recruited services was not attempted.

Communal bickerings and caste-dissensions had a marked impact on municipal administration during this period. They not only impaired the efficiency of municipal administration, but also tended to prevent the employment of suitable persons in administrative posts and obstructed the development of a sense of common citizenship, so very essential for a healthy civic life. Besides, the two main requisites of successful local government, viz., "a high sense of duty among elected members and proper civic spirit among those who elect them were more often absent than present."

According to Jawaharlal Nehru, many of the failings of municipal bodies were due to the hybrid framework within which they had to function. It was neither democratic nor autocratic. It was a cross between the two and had the disadvantages of both. Lack of administrative experience in elective members, untrained managerial personnel and want of expert guidance also contributed to the failure of municipal bodies during this period.

Provincial Autonomy and After

The inauguration of provincial autonomy on April 1, 1937, under the Government of India Act, 1935, gave further impetus to municipal government, though temporarily. Dyarchy was abolished and the popularly elected ministries were entrusted full responsibility at the provincial level. Local Government was classified as Provincial subject. Popularly installed ministries were expected to fare better, but conspiracy of circumstances, *viz.,* the occurrence of world war and keenness of the Congress to absolve itself from the responsibility of fighting for others, forced the ministries in the Congress dominated provinces to resign after the lapse of two years. It gave a setback to the development of local government both in the urban and rural areas.

By the time, the constitutional machinery was restored in the provinces, much water had flown down the Ganges, and India freed herself from the shackles of imperialism.

Independence and After

With the dawn of independent era, and the establishment of a democratic constitution, new hopes were pinned on the Indian leadership for establishing popularly elected governments at the local level. Under the new Constitution, which was enforced on January 26, 1950, local self-government became a state subject. It was realized that the local self-government would play a vital role as the chief architect of community making and the base of the democratic pyramid in our country. A universal desire to make local institutions not only a training ground for democracy, but also an effective agency to shoulder the onerous responsibilities envisaged in the Five-Year Plans was discernible in the initial stages. An appraisal of local self-government during the last few decades reveals that the rural areas have been involved in national planning and development during the succeeding Five-Year Plans, but the urban areas have been kept out of the mainstream of the development process to a great extent.

Some sporadic attempts have been made to reorganise the structure of urban local government institutions in the various states through laws. The main trends and features of these legislative enactments can be summed up as under :

[1]*Keith, A.B. : A Constitutional History of India, (1937 ed), p. 279.*

(a) Adult franchise has replaced limited franchise in local bodies in all the states; (b) communal representation has been done away with. Joint electorates have been substituted for separate electorates; (c) the Uttar Pradesh Amendment Act of 1952 and the Madhya Bharat Act of 1954 provided for direct election of the Chairman of the Municipal Board by the primary voters. However, the system failed and both the States returned to the old practice of indirect election of the Chairman/President of the Board; (d) attempts were made to strengthen the Chief Executive by vesting him with specific powers under the Acts or rules, and by providing for the appointment of Executive Officers where there was none; (e) attempts have been made to regulate the appointment, promotion and disciplinary control of the municipal staffs and to adopt the practice of making certain appointments on the recommendations of the Public Service Commission; (f) there is an increasing tendency to make provisions in Municipal Act for creating state cadres of municipal employees, particularly for Executive Officers, Engineers, Accountants, Health Officers, etc.

Another notable feature of this period is the emergence of various associations which have attracted the attention of the government and of the masses to the problems of local bodies. The Central Council of local self-government which was set up, on the recommendations of the second Local Self-Government Ministers' Conference in 1954, was perhaps the most important of such associations. It was required to consist of Union Minister for Health as its Chairman and the Local Self-Government Minister of all the states of India as members. It reviewed the work done by the state governments in the field of local government and gave suggestions for improvement from time to time. In the words of Dr. Agral—

"*The conferences and discussions of these associations have been helpful in awakening the consciousness of the people and governments to the problems of local bodies.*"

The Ministry of Health looked after both rural and urban government until 1950 when the former was separated from it and put under the charge of the Ministry of Community Development. In January, 1966, a part of local government namely Urban Development was made the responsibility of the Ministry of Works and Housing which was renamed the Ministry of Works, Housing and Urban Development. In 1967, the subject of urban development was transferred to the Ministry of Health which was designated as Ministry of Health, Family Planning, Housing and Urban Development. In February, 1973, the subject of Urban Development was transferred to the Ministry of Works and Housing. In 1985, the Government of India decided to set up a separate ministry of urban development and entrusted to it the responsibilities of broad policy formulation and monitoring programmes in the area of housing, urban development, urban poverty alleviations, urban water supply and urban transport.

The state governments have set up Departments/Directorates of urban local government in conjunction with other departments of allied nature or as separate departments.

Besides, a number of central committees and commissions have been set up from time to time to suggest ways for streamlining the local government structure in the country. These included the Local Finance Enquiry Committee (1949) to recommend steps for the improvement and stabilization of local finances, the Taxation Enquiry Commission (1953), for making recommendations on municipal taxation, the Rural-Urban Relationship Committee (1963) for defining the structure and functions of urban local bodies and their relationship with Panchayati Raj institutions as well as for making recommendations for the more efficient and effective functioning of urban local bodies. A Central Committee for the Augmentation of Financial Resources of (urban) Local Bodies has also been appointed for effecting improvement in urban local government.

In the states also, various committees and commissions have been appointed for looking into the problems of municipal administration and recommending measures for its improvement. Some of the Committees/ Commissions have been : Delhi Municipal Corporation Enquiry Committee 1948; Gujarat Municipal Rationalisation Committee 1961; Haryana Resource Committee (Local Bodies)

1988 and the Municipal Grants Commission 1969; Kerala Municipal Grants Enquiry Committee 1965; Madhya Pradesh, Urban and Local Self Government Committee 1959; Maharashtra, Committee for the Unification of Acts relating to Municipalities in Maharashtra State 1963; Orissa, Local Body (urban) Administration Enquiry Commission 1963; Punjab, Local Government (urban) Enquiry Committee 1957. Committee of Ministers on Augmentation of Financial Resources of urban Bodies (1963), committee on service condition of Municipal Employee 1965-68; committee on Budgetary Reform in Municipal Administration (1974) National Commission urbanisation 1985–88.

However, the Indian states have not been enthusiastic about effecting substantial improvements in urban local government despite occasional proddings by the Central Government. The onus for stimulating the municipal bodies and animating them to grow as local self-government institutions falls primarily on the state government.

The latest Landmark – 74 Amendment Act

The latest landmark in the evolution of urban local government was the setting up of National Commission on Urbanisation by the Government of India in 1985 to make a comprehensive study of the rapidly growing phenomenon of urbanisation and of the problems caused by it and to suggest measures to combat them. The Commission submitted its seven volume report in 1988. The Government has since accepted most of its recommendations and incorporated them in the constitution (73rd Amendment Bill) which was introduced as Nagarpalika Bill in August, 1989. It was passed by the Lok Sabha but was defeated in the Rajya Sabha by a narrow margin of three votes. The Narasimha Rao's Government again introduced the Bill in the form of Constitution 74th Amendment Bill on 16th September, 1991 which was passed in the winter session, 1992. The Act was portrayed as the greatest landmark which aimed at removing the deficiencies which the urban local governments have been suffering from for the last one hundred years and strengthening them so that they could ensure their efficient and effective functioning in the best interests of the urban residents.

The 74th Amendment Act aimed at decentralising the responsibility for urban management by increasing the participation of the people and accountability in the administration. In the 10th five year plan, sincere effort was made to assist the local bodies to grow organisationally so as to fulfil the demands of urban residents for a quality life at par with world standards. Substantial steps have already been taken to upgrade the infrastructure. The urban development authorities have attained substantial skills in planning and executing of project with the help of state and central government. Mega city projects for five selected cities, the integrated development of small and medium towns and the accelerated urban water supply programme have to some extent met some of the urban needs. The parastatals and development authorities are designed to play supportive role to the elected bodies of the urban local government.

Efforts are afoot to improve the financial conditions of the Urban local bodies The 12th Finance commission recommended Rs 5000 crores for local bodies as grants in aid for the period 2005 to 2010. To ameliorate the financial position of the urban local bodies, steps have been taken to implement the recommendations of the State Finance Commission and also distribution of proceeds between the state and the urban local bodies.[1]

(B) FEATURES AND NORMS

Urban local government, as seen above, means the administration of an urban area by the people through their elected representatives. With the phenomenal increase in the process of urbanisation and consequent spurt in the emergence of urban problems like those of slums, pollution, insanitation and housing, municipal government and administration is no longer a simple affair.

1. India 2008 Govt. of India Publications division ministry of Information and Broadcasting. p.695

The chief features of urban local government in India are : *First,* that its jurisdiction is limited to a specific area and its functions relate to the provision of civic amenities to the population living within its jurisdiction. *Second,* it functions within the provisions of the statute which has created it. The Municipal Corporation is created under a Corporation Act, whereas the Municipal Committees and other bodies are created under the Municipal Act of the State concerned. *Third,* local government is a state subject. The state government is fully empowered to demarcate its territorial area into different kinds of local bodies and define their powers and functions. *Fourth,* the urban local government has the power to raise finance by taxation in the area under its jurisdiction. *Fifth,* the local body is subject to the control of the state government which can supersede or dissolve it. It is not sovereign and can exercise such powers only as are conferred by the state government. *Last,* the state government has created certain special uni-purpose or multipurpose agencies to perform functions which legitimately belong to the domain of urban governments. Such agencies are Improvement Trusts, Water Supply and Sewerage Boards, Housing Boards, Pollution Control Boards etc.

Forms

There are five types of urban local bodies in India, *viz.*, Corporations, Municipalities, Notified Area Committees, Town Area Committees and Cantonment Boards. It may not be out of place to point out that the Cantonment Boards are governed by the Cantonment Act, 1924 which is a Central legislation. They are still controlled directly by the Central Ministry of Defence. Each such Board consists of partly elected and partly nominated members. Its key officials are drawn from forces on an *ex-officio* basis.

The Notified Area Committees exist in areas which are fast developing as new urban areas but which are not yet ripe for municipalisation. At the moment they function in eight states and one Union Territory in the country. The members of these Committees are all nominated by the state governments which vest them with specific powers in accordance with the provisions of the prevailing Municipal Acts.

In six states and one Union Territory, there are Town Area Committees, the members of which are usually nominated or partly nominated and partly elected. Generally, such committees are established in small towns and are entrusted with limited local functions. However, the Town Area Committees have been abolished and converted into Class-III Municipal Committees.

The Municipal Corporations, which are usually found in the principal cities, enjoy wider powers and more autonomy than other municipal councils. A distinctive feature of an Indian Corporation is the statutory distribution of powers among three co-ordinate authorities, the Corporation Council, the Commissioner and the Standing Committees. The council consists of popularly elected representatives. The commissioner who heads the executive administration is appointed by the state government. The standing committees derive their powers either from the Act itself or through delegation by the council. The Mayor is only the ceremonial head of the corporation, having no executive powers. The Commissioner who is the chief executive officer of the corporation supervises the day-to-day administration of the corporation.

Another distinctive feature of the bigger municipal corporations, *viz.*, Calcutta, Delhi and Madras, is the existence of sub-municipal units viz Borough committees in Calcutta, Zonal committees in Delhi and Circle committees in Madras. Many of the purely local functions such as vaccination, registration of births, cleaning of streets and other local improvement works are entrusted to them.

It is evident from the facts stated in the preceding paragraph that the corporation system bifurcates the deliberative and executive functions. The council constitutes the deliberative wing and the Commissioner is the chief executive. All the municipal corporations in India enjoy uniformity in this respect.

The municipal councils which are commonly found in urban areas possess an integrated structure. The Chairman who is the head of the deliberative wing—the Council— is also the chief executive. The trend in almost all the states is towards making statutory provision for the appointment of executive officers who are made responsible for day-to-day administration.

It is being increasingly felt that the urban local bodies in India have, in general, failed to fulfil the aspirations of the people. In the words of Dodwell — "*The advent of freedom even has not very materially substantially improved matters in the field of local self-government which does not at all measure up in efficiency and honesty to either the central or state government standards.*"[1]

(C) MUNICIPAL ADMINISTRATION IN INDIA

With the rapid growth of both urban and sub-urban populations, more and more urban local bodies are being set up in all states. However, the expansion has been quantitative rather than qualitative.[2]

In the next few pages, role, organisation and management, resources and financial management and government control over the local bodies will be discussed in brief in order to apprise the reader of the functioning of urban local bodies in India.

1. Role and Functions

Local bodies constitute a vital step towards decentralisation of powers and promotion of democratic values. They contribute to the efficiency of government by enabling the bigger officials of the districts to rid of local tasks, and entrust them to locally elected representatives and the officials attuned to the performance of such tasks. They prove effective instruments of social and cultural development of urban committees by inculcating civic sense and neighbourhood consciousness amongst them.

Their functions at a glance

A bulk of municipal Acts lay down specifically two types of functions, *viz.*, Obligatory and optional. These functions comprise medical and public health services, sanitation, water supply and drainage, education, municipal trading, housing, town improvement and planning, etc.

The expenditure pattern reveals that functioning of local bodies has been inadequate in almost all towns except in a few cities where per capita expenditure exceeds Rs. 40 per year. In about 50 per cent of the Municipal bodies, per capita expenditure on public health and sanitation is less than Re one. Most of the medium and small towns do not have sewerage system. Even in larger towns, open drainage system exists whereas 40 per cent towns lack proper drainage facilities. The same tale is to tell regarding water supply to inhabitants of the towns. The analytical surveys reveal that some of the obligatory functions even have not been adequately performed by the urban local bodies — both big and small.

2. Organisation

The urban local bodies like the rural are subject to the state legislation. Hence the local bodies in the different states differ widely regarding their organisation, powers, functions and resources although in recent years, some states have adopted concrete steps for the rationalisation and simplification of their municipal bodies. Some of the common characteristics of these urban local bodies and also their common problems are as follows :

[1]*Dodwill, H.N.F. Cambridge History of India, Vol. V.P. 476.*

[2]*In 1994 Faridabad Complex Administration in Haryone was converted into Faridabad Municipal Corporation.*

Franchise and Constituencies

In India, as already said, after dawn of independence, adult franchise was adopted. Separate Electorate system was replaced by Joint Electorate system. At the later stage, multi-member constituencies were replaced by single member constituencies. The single member constituencies have proved more compact and wieldy. However, they have given rise to communal feelings and caste considerations in some of the towns.

It is felt that in larger constituencies, a caste or a particular community may not succeed in dominating the elections. Besides, the various communities and castes may aspire for an electoral alliance, cutting across sectional, caste or community interests. Hence some scholars have suggested the adoption of single member constituencies in general though they strongly feel that multi-member constituencies may be adopted at certain places in order to foster integration between different castes or communities, or for according representation to weaker sections of the community. This will avoid the necessity of having reserved constituencies.

Term of Municipal Council

The tenure of Municipal council should be ordinarily long enough so that it can yield concrete results through its policies and actions. In the initial stage, the tenure of the council was three years. Some state governments raised it to four and five years. The third conference of the Municipal Corporations convened in 1962, after careful deliberations, suggested a five year term for the Municipal Corporations and expected that their election won't conflict with parliament or state legislature elections. The Rural-Urban Local Bodies Relationship Committee also recommended that the term of the Corporations and Municipal Councils should be five years. Now by and large the tenure is 5 years.

Aldermen

In some Cørporations, Aldermen who enjoy the privileges of elected councillors are selected. They are experts and specialists, fully aware of the technicalities of the local administration. Besides, women and special interests not represented in the council get a place in the Corporations. In actual practice the system has failed to achieve its objective as party considerations weigh heavily when Aldermen are chosen. Hence Bombay and Madras Corporations have abolished the institution of Aldermen. The Corporations of Ahmedabad, Hyderabad and Poona do not have Aldermen and that has not adversely affected their functioning. The Rural Urban Relationship Committee had also recommended the abolition of institution of Aldermen. However, they did suggest co-option of experts and citizens of eminence.

Mayor/Chairman

The Mayor is the Chairman of the Corporation whereas President is the Chairman of the Municipal Council. The Mayor is not vested with the executive authority. In fact, in smaller and medium sized Councils, dichotomy of deliberative and executive powers is not possible though in Corporations, separation of these functions is possible and essential. It is suggested that in the interest of proper functioning of the Councils, having population of 2 lakhs or more, separation of policy-making functions from executive should be progressively achieved. The small and medium sized municipalities should opt for a full time paid executive officers in order to assist the elected Chief Executive.

Mode of Election of the Chairman/President

In Madhya Pradesh and U.P., the system of direct election of the Chairman was adopted but it proved to be a dismal failure. There were constant bickerings between the councillors. This led to the rise of the weak Presidents/Chairmen, impairing seriously the efficiency and continuity of Municipal administration. Hence there is a dire necessity of devising a mechanism of legislative accountability to ensure stability to the office of the Chief Executive without divesting Council of its inherent authority of control.

The Urban Local Bodies Relation Committee had recommended that the Chairman or the President of the Council should be elected by the Municipal councillors and hold office for full tenure unless removed earlier by a vote of no confidence. This resulted in emergence of weak Presidents which adversely affected the efficiency and continuity of Municipal activities.

Committees of the Council

In order to cope with the complexity and enormity of work, the corporation and the municipal councils are finding it hard to pull on without the active assistance of experts. Who could share their burden ? Hence it has led to the emergence of committee system. These committees handle relatively less important matters. In some cases, they possess the final authority of arriving at decisions while in others they play the role of advisory bodies to the council. Though the committee system is in vogue since long, yet no uniform pattern has been evolved for the inception of such committees. It will not be out of place to point out that the committee system in our municipalities has not been successful as the Municipal Councils have been reluctant to delegate powers to the committees.

The Executive

The Chief Executive is at the apex of the hierarchical pyramid. He is to implement the policies formulated by the popular representatives. He exercises disciplinary control over the departmental heads and the subordinate staffs. Besides, he co-ordinates their activities to maintain efficiency. Hence it is expected that the Chief Executive must be an official immune from factional politics and free from undue interference. However, he must owe allegiance to the deliberative body and carry out its decisions faithfully.

The various types of Chief Executives exist in the world. In U.K. the Mayor functions as the effective Chief Executive. The committee system exists in England. A permanent civil service headed by the Town Clerk assists the Chief Executive. In the U.S.A. two distinct types of managerial system have been adopted, *viz.,* Strong Mayorship system resembling presidential system of government and City Managerial system in which executive functions are vested with professionally trained managers appointed on permanent basis. Likewise in French system, deliberative and financial powers have been decentralised. They are entrusted to elected local bodies whereas executive powers are vested with the officers of the Central Government working in the Departments and Communes. In our country all these types of Chief Executives are found in varying degrees in different states. However, nowhere a satisfactory system of Municipal management has emerged so far. Hence a question of vital importance has arisen as to what type of managerial system should be adopted in Municipal Government? Whether the system of Chief Executive in Metropolitan cities, non-metropolitan cities and small towns differ ? In Indian states, where the provincial cadres of municipal executive officers have been constituted, a question has cropped up — what should be the relation between the Municipal Chairman and the Chief Executive Officer? To some extent such a problem arises in an Indian Municipal Corporation also where municipal commissioner is appointed by the State Government and the Mayor is elected by the Corporation Council.

3. Personnel Administration

We lack a well organised and effective system of personnel administration. An ever-growing imbalance between the people's aspirations and needs on the one hand and the actual performance of municipal administration on the other hand has been discernible, owing to lack of capable and honest Municipal Officers. No organisation can yield results unless competent personnel are attracted to it. The paucity of resources and the inability to utilise the existing sources properly can also be attributed to the inadequacy of administrative and technical personnel. Hence to meet the challenge of rapid urbanisation and development tasks inherent in it, we need to acquire high degree of administrative and technical skills.

In most of the municipalities, the municipal personnel with the executive officer at the apex of administrative hierarchy, may be classified into two categories — technical and non-technical — on the basis of nature of job entrusted to them and the technical qualifications that they are expected to possess to perform such duties. Both these categories of personnel may further be classified as top management (high), middle management (middle) and manual (low level) personnel. The middle level employees may further be divided into upper and middle, upper comprising supervisory staff and lower middle class comprising clerical staff and their equivalents performing operational duties. The top management generally consists of Municipal Medical Officer, Health Secretary and Municipal Engineer. In the upper middle category of officials, the heads of the other branches *viz.*, Accountant, tax superintendent, octroi superintendent, office superintendent, chief sanitary inspector, fire superintendent, etc., who have been entrusted supervisory powers, have been included. The lower middle class consists of assistant octroi superintendent, octroi inspectors, sanitary inspectors, clerks, drivers, firemen, etc. The manual class comprises sweepers, scavengers, octroi peons, vaccination dispensers, etc.

As regards their recruitment, procedures differ from state to state. However, in general, appointments of employees getting certain amount of salary are made by the Municipal councils. The top categories are now appointed through State Public Service Commissions. For instance, in Punjab and Haryana, after the passage of Public Service Commissions (Additional) Functions Act, appointments of officers are made by the State governments on the recommendations of the Public Service Commission. This has brought in merit principle in the recruitment of these top services. The lower categories of employees, are to be appointed by the majority of the Municipal councils. However, Employment Exchange is the source through which names of candidates are to be entertained as per Employment Exchange Act, 1959. Thus the junior employees remain to a great extent on the mercy of the municipal councillors. The Calcutta Corporation has set up a Municipal Services Commission for appointments to junior and middle level posts. The posts carrying salaries higher than Rs. 1500 p.m. are to be filled by the recommendations of State Public Service Commission. In Andhra Pradesh, Madras and a few other states, executive and technical posts are recruited from local government services or by deputationists from the state services. In four Southern states, statewise cadres of Executive Officers, Engineers, Health Officers and Tax Superintendents etc. exist. In order to have a proper personnel system a proper balance is to be struck among a number of considerations like the need for the state government to have a control over the local bodies and their personnel, the need for local bodies to have a measure of local autonomy and also probably the need for the non-officials of the local bodies to have a feeling that they have an element of patronage, the requirement of the job and the feasibility of forming viable local government service.[1] In fact, "*an optimum advantage can accrue from a synthesis of these systems, viz., a unified local government service, a separate municipal personnel system and an integrated system.*"[2]

According to unified local government service, the Municipal Officers are recruited exclusively for the municipal bodies. They can be posted to local bodies and are transferable only between the municipal authorities in the state. Such a system prevails in Ceylon, Ireland and Western Nigeria. The administrative and revenue services of municipal bodies which necessitate a special type of

[1]*Section 4th E..O. Act 1431.*

[2]*Bhagwan, Vishnoo, 'Municipal Government and Politics in Haryana', (Ph.D., Thesis) p. 142.*

knowledge and expertise, different from that required for work in the government department, fall in this category. Recruitment for such posts should be made both directly *i.e.*, on the basis of merit from an open selection and indirectly, *i.e.*, on promotion basis. A satisfactory personnel system should be an amalgam of both the systems. An integrated cadre will be advantageous for the combined recruitment of the municipal bodies and the state governments. The posting of the services under this category would be inter-changeable between the state and the local bodies according to availability of the posts, the security of the incumbent and the needs of the different departments. Municipal Engineers, M.M.O.H. and Superintendent Water Works fall in this category. Already in Andhra Pradesh and Tamilnadu, the Municipal Medical and Health Officers belong to an integrated service. In U.P., Orissa, Bihar and Karnataka, Medical and Health Officers (M.M.O.H.) are drawn from the state Public Health Services.

The separate personnel system should be adopted for the municipal committees of the State to make appointments of lower middle and the upper middle employees not covered under first two categories. Alternatively, the Municipal Service Commission should be empowered to recommend three names in order of merit leaving it to the Committee to make the final choice itself. This amounts to combining both the principles of merit and that of local control together.

If the above system of recruitment, *i.e.*, integration of three systems is adopted, the evils of the recruitment system that prevail at present, are likely to be considerably removed. The recruitment system will not be a tool in the hands of the faction-ridden municipal councillors. Moreover, persons having proper qualifications will be appointed.

Training

The Municipal employees are not imparted any in-service or post-entry training which is so very essential for technical employees as they are to be acquainted with the latest techniques in their respective vocations. In-service training at the initial stage and post-entry training at a later stage is essential for such types of employees. The existing municipal employees in the municipal bodies should be sent to the Training Centres or Institutes for short-term courses so that they are in a position to keep pace with the fast-changing concept of town development. Such trainees may be given leave with pay so that they do not feel financially handicapped. Extra increments for acquiring up-to-date knowledge for running municipal administration should serve as incentive to the working employees. It has been rightly said, *"Properly trained employees cannot only improve prospects of their promotion but prove an asset to the administration. The old employees, keeping abreast with the latest developments in the domain of administration are also saved from a general ridicule which they have otherwise to face at the hands of their better qualified subordinates."*[1]

Disciplinary Control

Disciplinary action for misdeeds is a negative reward for improper, inefficient or dishonest employes. The powers of disciplinary action *viz.*, reduction in rank, removal and dismissal from service are generally vested in the appointing authority. However, right to appeal is allowed. It has been noticed that the officials and its staff curry favour with the councillors for improving their prospects and saving themselves from disciplinary action. That involves them in factional politics, impairing efficiency of administration. In certain cases, they lose drive and initiative. They get identified with groups in the council, and subsequent changes in the complexion of the council following the election adversely affect their position. Thus the existing system of discipline and control is defective. It keeps the morale of the employees low.

The adoption of a system of unified and integrated municipal services will solve the problems as regards high and revenue officials. The state government will be the punishing authority in the

[1]*Ibid, p. 153-154.*

case of integrated services. In the case of state wide unified cadres, the state governments should set up a Directorate of local bodies to deal with disciplinary matters relating to the personnel. This will prevent direct or corrupt officials from bringing indirect influence to save themselves. All this will help in maintaining local autonomy without impairing the efficiency of municipal administration. As regards menials, authority of removal and dismissal should be delegated to the Executive Officers or Municipal Chief Officers as the case may be. However, they should exercise their authority on the recommendations of the head of the department concerned.

A regular code of conduct should be drawn for the Municipal councillors as well. Interference in the administrative and official matters by the Municipal councillors should be considered as a breach of conduct entailing first a warning and then their removal from the membership of the Local Bodies Department, after proper investigation by the Directorate of Local Bodies.

Employees and Incentives

The Municipal employees, in general till date, constitute a disgruntled lot. In most cases their emoluments are inadequate. In certain other cases, injustice has been done in the revision of grades. Seniority has been ignored many a time. Chances of promotion are not only bleak but are meant only for the favourite few. The retirement benefits are not alluring. The gratuity has not been instituted in many cases. The privileges of disability leave, sick leave and study leave are conspicuous by their absence in many municipalities, particularly at lower levels. There is rampant corruption. Dr. Robson is of the opinion : "If the leading officers were given opportunities of this kind and the elected councillors themselves persuaded to follow suit, almost unimaginable improvement in certain departments of civil affairs might be affected as a result."[1]

The working environments are largely dull and unhealthy. Medical facilities also exist only in name. Hence, the municipal employees are, in general, dissatisfied with their working conditions. They do not take work as worship. Instead, they take it as drudgery and try to shun it or do it half-heartedly. This undermines efficiency of municipal administration and hampers the urban development. It is suggested that adequate measures for staff welfare should be adopted as early as possible. Staff welfare officers should be appointed to appraise inadequacies of the conditions of the service of the municipal employees and suggest ways and means to improve them. If proper conditions of service are provided, the employees may be "aflamed with the desire to imbue our municipal institutions with some of the majesty, the colour and the conviction which they now lack." The local government services must be organised into proper cadres and they should enjoy the esteem and prestige in the eyes of the community and successfully compete with other Public Services. Provision of State cadres for municipal services as already done in Rajasthan, M.P., Karnataka, Punjab, Maharashtra and U.P. can-go a long way in boosting the sagging morale of municipal employees. It is heartening that in some of the states like U.P. and Karnataka, integrated Health Services have been provided for the states and the municipalities. In Orissa deputations from State Engineering, Public Health and Administrative Services are being frequently allowed.

Municipal Finances

Sound fiscal policy at municipal level is the crying need of the hour. Imprudent financial management not only brings bad name to the government but also alienates it from the people. Hence, investigations have been instituted from time to time by the Government of India, to appraise the financial position of the local bodies and recommend measures for their augmentation. The Local Finance Enquiry Committee (1951), the Taxation Enquiry Commission (1954), Committee of Ministers for the augmentation of Financial Resources of Urban Local Bodies (1962), were specially appointed for the purpose though their recommendations have not been fully implemented.

[1]*Robson, W.A., The Development of Local Government, p. 368.*

Sources of Revenue

The sources of Municipal Revenue may be described as follows :

(a) Revenue from taxation by the municipal bodies.

(b) Revenue from non-tax sources under the control of municipal bodies.

(c) Assignment of shares of taxes levied and collected by the state governments and grants-in-aids.

(a) Taxes levied

The urban bodies levy, in general, following taxes :

(*i*) Taxes on property; rates on buildings and lands; duties on transfer of properties, (*ii*) Personal taxes, terminal taxes on passengers including pilgrim tax; (*iii*) taxes on vehicles and animals, (*iv*) theatre or show tax.

(b) Non Tax Sources

Revenue from non-tax sources comprises fees, fines, rents of municipal properties, income from investments and revenue from commercial undertaking etc. Urban bodies in India derive about 1/5th of their revenue from non-tax sources.

Grants-in-aid

The percentages of grants-in-aid varies from 0.4% in Jammu and Kashmir to maximum of 42.0% in Orissa. In Assam and Bihar in particular grants-in-aid are insignificant. In most cases, the grant is a fixed uniform proportion of expenditure on specified terms of service. It does not take into account their different needs and resources. No state except M.P., Gujarat and Kerala has opted for a grant-in-aid code embodying simple and well defined principles. The main purposes of grants are as follows :

(a) Ad hoc, non-recurring grants to meet partially the capital cost of water supply, drainage schemes and slum clearance and housing.

(b) For maintenance of primary schools.

(c) For payment of occasional instalments of Dearness Allowance to employees.

(d) To meet expenditure on the construction of secondary schools, medical centres and anti-malaria measures.

(e) To meet the pay of Health Officers and Engineers.

(f) General purpose grants.

Revenue from sharing of Taxes

In some states like Andhra, Tamilnadu and Karnataka the state entertainment tax is shared with the municipalities and corporations. In Orissa 50% of the proceeds of motor vehicles tax is earmarked to local authorities, keeping in view mileage of the roads maintained by them. In Gujarat and Maharashtra 15% of the land revenue is given to the municipalities by the State government. In Assam 25% of the land revenue goes to the municipal exchequer, in Maharashtra and Gujarat 75% (approximately) of the non-agricultural assessments is paid to the municipal bodies.

A close analysis of the Municipal finances reveals that they are not adequate enough to enable the urban local bodies to perform nation-building activities properly and make our towns worth living. Mismanagement of municipal finances has been one of the main causes for dismal state of affairs in urban local bodies. The collections have been generally low, taxes have been running in arrears, municipal councillors have been reluctant to reimpose new taxes for fear of losing their vote-bank, the officials have been either negligent or made to act as delinquent by the councillors. Even the citizens of the towns have not been cooperative and law abiding. What the Simon Commission said about our municipalities in 1930 is true even today. It said, "It is a common place of administration in India that financial resources are generally inadequate and this is specially true of local self-government. Undoubtedly one of the reasons for the failure to develop trained municipal personnel is the poverty of the municipality. But it is not only actual poverty which cramps these sources but the reluctance of the elected members to impose local taxes." Hence, there has to be a general toning up of the municipal administrative machinery and the municipal councillors should exhibit a greater sense of selfless devotion to the town community. The citizens of the town should also emulate them and avoid all attempts at evading the payment of taxes. Moreover, some new sources of income like entertainment tax, property tax and part of the vehicle tax should be earmarked as a source of financial adjustment between state and municipal bodies rather than as an instrument of state control.

The loan policy of the state government in relation to the municipality requires re-thinking as it is not based on a consistent, logical and rational basis. The state government should earmark loan for the municipalities on a rational and consistent basis in the initial year of the five-yearly local plans which too should be launched. We agree with Dr. Tripathy who opined, "*In order to stabilise the basis of Indian democracy, it is necessary that the finances of the municipal bodies be placed on an even keel. In order to achieve this, it is important that their resource potentials should be fully utilized and the flow of resources from State Government to the municipal bodies be related to the implementation of Municipal Five Year Plan.*"[1]

Heads of Expenditure

In the words of Dr. Finer, "*the local authorities supervise, direct and control our lives, awake and sleep at work and at play; they provide for all citizens a common minimum of health, education, welfare services, roads, peace and security of environment*."[2] The efficient performance of municipal services not only creates congenial milieu for healthy and comfortable living but the municipal government also shares the burden of the state governments for promoting the welfare of the people. The main services performed by a municipal committee are generally grouped as medical and public health, public works, public safety and convenience, education and social welfare, town planning, water supply and other miscellaneous works. The 'miscellaneous' category comprises mainly of preparation of annual and other reports, general administration, maintenance and development of municipal property, defining of boundary marks, etc.... A glimpse of expenditure pattern on municipalities in various states will reveal the amount of significance, they are attaching to public welfare services. In Assam, Karnataka and West Bengal, municipalities spend about 50 per cent of their ordinary expenditure on public health, in Gujarat and M.P. about 20 per cent, while in U.P. only 9 percent. Municipalities in Punjab, Karnataka, Rajasthan and Delhi incur about 25 per cent of expenditure on general administration and collection of revenue. In Gujarat, Jammu and Kashmir and Orissa about 15 per cent of expenditure is incurred on public health whereas the municipalities in Kerala and Andhra Pradesh spend about 24 per cent of their funds on public safety and convenience, though Bihar and Karnataka municipalities spend only 5 per cent. Miscellaneous expenditure consists a sizeable proportion in some of the states. In M.P. it is as high as 25 per cent of the total expenditures.[3]

(D) AUTONOMY OF LOCAL BODIES

The local bodies are intra-sovereign bodies created by the state governments, hence the latter has the power to determine their structure, functions and financial resources. Ever since the inception of statutory institutions of local government, the state government has reserved the right to regulate

[1]*Tripathi, R.N., Municipal Finance in a Developing Economy – A paper in Seminar on Municipal amendment in India.*

[2]*Finer, H, English Local Government, p. 2.*

[3]*As quoted in Tyagi, A.R., op. cited., p. 289-90.*

their structural autonomy, functional jurisdiction and financial powers. Hence, the autonomy of local bodies only implies the degree of self-government within the ambit of their functions. It does not, in any case, mean unlimited authority and freedom. Thus it has to be conceded that state control over local bodies is justified as it is conducive to the maintenance of a reasonable degree of efficiency, wean away the local bodies from vested interests, ensure stability and uniformity in administration, prevent financial mismanagement and facilitate socio-economic development.

However, the state control over the local bodies has been excessive. Both the Union and the State Governments have a negative approach towards this problem. They feel that curbing the initiative, restricting the discretion and over-aweing the local bodies, perhaps amounts to control over them. Techniques of government supervision and control, if remain confined to giving of directions, calling for information and reports, review of local action, conditional grants-in-aid, will not earn denunciation at the hands of the critics. Unfortunately, the governmental control has been drastic. Annulment of local decision, prior approval of local action, suspension and removal of elected members, dissolution and supersession of the municipal/corporation councils, overriding powers of the Deputy Commissioner, approval of the municipal budget and the power to cut any expenditure or tax are some such measures of governmental control as are resented and considered as a great curb on local autonomy. A re-orientation of relationship between the state government and municipalities in the context of changing political and socio-economic milieu is the crying need of the hour. The local government is to be recognised as a part of the responsible governmental system of the country and allowed to play its role as such, in the development of the lives of the people and promotion of their welfare. The Taxation Enquiry Commission (1953) had observed :

"The state government constituting the representative authority in a state has a vital role to play in ensuring the proper functioning of local bodies. It is its responsibility to see that local bodies are effectively organised, that they perform their functions properly and that they take adequate part in the development of the country. The role of the State Government is therefore not merely of a negative nature, viz., the prevention of the misuse of power by local bodies through audit and periodical examination but has a positive aspect, viz. active encouragement and development of local bodies. Government control and help should, however not be so meticulous or minute as to destroy the autonomy or self-reliance of local bodies. **The goal of state efforts as well as the purpose of state control should be the development of local self governing institutions into efficient instruments of administration, capable alike of formulating policies and of executing them.**"[1]

In other words, the conception of government role must change from that of a controller to that of an adviser, guide and helpers. The state control should facilitate rather than restrict the functioning of municipal institutions.

The nagarpalika Bill passed by the Parliament in December, 1992, aimed at rectifying the defects, deficiencies and inadequacies in the structure and organisation of urban local government and to revitalise and strengthen them. The strong points embodied in the Bill are : (i) setting up of three types of Nagarpalikas — the Nagar Panchayats for transitional areas, Municipal Councils and Municipal Corporation for urban areas; (ii) setting up ward committees and zonal committees to enable the local bodies to prove to be training ground for democratic institutions in the country; (iii) giving power to the people and placing responsibility on them at various levels so that a new leadership emerges; (iv) empowering Election Commission to conduct local bodies' elections so that these may be held periodically in a fair and impartial way; (v) reserving thirty three percent of the seats for women. The Scheduled Castes and tribes have been given representation in proportion to their population in the area concerned; (vi) appointing Finance Commission to look into the fiscal needs of the local bodies and empowering the Comptroller and Auditor General to audit the accounts and (vii) granting constitutional status to the urban local bodies by amending Article 40 of the

[1]*Report of the Taxation Enquiry Commission, p. 374*

constitution. These provisions, it was hoped, would strengthen the urban local bodies and usher in an era of properly organised and suitably re-invigorated local government system which constitutes a vital factor for the success of a democratic system of government to which India is committed. It is, however, sad to note that the concept of grass root democracy at both the rural and urban levels has not flourished in the country. From the functional point of view the local bodies have failed to deliver goods–adequate and clean drinking water, proper sanitation and drainage, satisfactory health and medical services, planned growth, recreation facilities and housing for the poor. From the organisational point of view the elections to local bodies carry all the evils like bogus voting, booth captures, intimidation of voters, corrupt electoral practices and political groupism leading to violence and also frequent supercessions. From the financial point of view, most of the taxes and dues are not collected, resources are inadequate to provide even the basic facilities to the citizens, corruption is rampant and virtually there is no effective and efficient administration. In short, the Local Government is afflicted with all the evils, the state government suffers from – the politicisation of administration, the entry of criminal elements in the elected bodies, rampant corruption, mal-administration, poor resources, lack of people's participation, caste and group divisions, priority to self-aggrandisement over public welfare and electoral malpractices.

Forum of urban local bodies prior to the passage of 74th amendment act.

In 1989 there were 73 corporations, 1770 muncipalities and 229 town area committees and 717 notified area committees. Thus in all there were 2789 urban local bodies. In other urban areas there existed Nagar Panchayats Cantonement Board, Industrial notified areas etc. Thus presently six types of urban bodies exist at local level. They are as follows:

(1) Muncipal Corporation
(2) Muncipalities
(3) Notified area committees
(4) Town Area Committees
(5) Cantonment Boards
(6) Improvement Trusts

Problems of Urban Bodies that still persist

(1) Financial paucity. They still have limited resources and bank upon state governments financial assistance. There is dire necessity of synchronizatin between municipal functions and resources. Greater dependence on State governments grants or loaves impairs local autonomy.

(2) Urbanization on ascendence. The urbanization is gradually on the ascendence. the municipal services have failed to cope with the necessary population both qualitatively and quantitatively.

(3) Executive system fragmented. Separation of executive powers from legislative particularly in corporations has led to fragmentation of the executive system. The elected Mayor is only a presiding officer over the corporation deliberation and the Commmissioner a government officer of IAS cadre holds the key position and exercises administrative powers. The executive thus remains under the grip of the state government.

(4) Encroachment on Municipal Powers. Since the late fiftees despite tall talks of equipping them with more powers the state Governments have encroached upon Municipal functions like Planning, water supply, sewage drainage and development of urban areas particularly in big cities. That has led to the minimization of Municipal authority.

(5) Functional decentralization as per 12th schedule of no use. The 12th schedule of 74th amendment Act added few functions for the local bodies but dil not ear-mark adequate resources.

It has demigrated the position of the urban local bodies as they are dubled incompetent by the populace because of poor output. It leads to demoralization of the local exceutive and in councillors.

(6) Alternate mechanism of service not suggested in the 74th amendment Act. The 74th amendment Act suggests amendments in Municipal law but no proposal has been made regarding alternate mechanism for effecting improvement in local public services. Some institutional arrangement viz public private partnership privitasiation in managing some services should have been provided. This way the local bodies would have been enabled to make choice of the most appropriate mechanism for delivering goods.

(7) Widening of operative sphere, a deprivation of earlier essential functions. The 12th Schedule of the Act widens the operative sphere of the urban local bodies by entrusting them – (i) Social and economic planning (ii) care of the weaker section of the populace (iii) Poverty alleviation. Instead of encouraging the local bodies to take care of human development activities, they have been exhorted to take up environmental control, physical planning, provision of shelters maintenance of roads and manage water supply efficiently. In a way, the muncipalities are being reoriented from carler more meaningful preoccupation like public health, elementary education, sanitation and environmental control. They are apt to be failure in the new fields of operation.

(8) Municipal Management structure left untouched. The 74th amendment Act has laid stress on the Municipal Councils regular elections but has not paid adequate attention to municipal management structure or cared for local political accountability.

Besides the opt quoted pressing demands of the urban local bodies to the contrary the hegemonic role of the State government and district administration is remains firmly entrenched at the grass root democratic level. The regulatory activities which are managed by the district administration ensures the predominance of the state government over the urban local bodies. Hence the substance of urban governance remains a dream.

***

ADMINISTRATION FOR WELFARE

"The core idea of social welfare is the human well-being in its each and every respect and a welfare state must ensure minimum opportunities for the physical and social well- being of all citizens."
—***Jawaharlal Nehru***

CONTENTS:

(A) BRIEF HISTORY OF SOCIAL WELFARE IN INDIA

The concept of social welfare has been an integral part of the Indian tradition. In the past, people in distress were rendered assistance by the rulers, the rich and also by individual members of the community. Religion emphasized charity and religious institutions such as temples, *maths, dharamsalas,* became the centers of social service on an extensive scale. Further, social institutions like the joint family, the caste organization and the panchayats catered to the needs of the aged, the ill and the handicapped.

These traditions gradually began to be influenced by the new social and economic forces released in the country during the 19th century. As a result of increasing industrialization and urbanisation, the compact rural community began to show signs of stress and disorganization. At the same time, the Christian missionaries began their religious and welfare work in various parts of the country. They tried to eradicate the evils of Hindu society, viz., child marriage, polygamy, female insecticide, sati and restrictions on widow remarriage. Most of the early welfare institutions were established in the country by Christian missionaries.

As an effective counterpart to services provided by the Christian missionaries, Indian religious and social reformers also established a number of welfare institutions to revitalize the Indian social structure. Among these reformers Swami Dayanand Saraswati and Raja Ram Mohan Roy were the first to make a significant contribution in breaking down the barrier of caste and removal of untouchability. A roll call of the pioneers in this field would also include such names as Dwarkanath Tagore, Devendranath Tagore, K.C. Sen, Justice M.G. Ranade, Jyotiba Phule and Sir Syed Ahmed Khan. In 1905, Gopal Krishna Gokhale founded the Servants of India Society which was the first secular organization dedicated to social service in the country. Important women's organizations were also established in the country such as Women's Association of India, All India Women's Conference and the National Council for Women.

It was Gandhiji, however, who revitalized the work began by the early social reformers. He championed the cause of the downtrodden classes whom he called 'harijans' and the women. He established Harijan Sewak Sangh, Adivasi Sewa Mandals and the Kasturba Gandhi National Memorial Trust for raising the social status of these classes. He himself preferred to live in 'Harijan Basti' and also started a newspaper 'Harijan' to highlight the pitiable conditions of the depressed classes and build opinion for securing improvements in the tenor of their social life.

The British Government on its part had done very little by way of providing social welfare benefits as such for the disadvantaged and underprivileged sections of society like the scheduled castes, scheduled tribes and backward classes except for the provision of educational facilities for them and that too as late as 1944 when the central government had made a distinct provision for the education of backward communities. Hardly any attention was paid to the amelioration of the economic lot of other deprived sections of society. The poor led a wretched life of utter poverty exploited by the landlords. They lived in deep ignorance afflicted by many social evils.

It was after the attainment of independence that social welfare was given its due place in the Constitution of India. The fathers of the Constitution had come to appreciate the role of the state in the promotion of people's welfare particularly of the disadvantaged section of society. The constitution contains several provisions for the welfare of scheduled castes, scheduled tribes, backward classes, women and children. The preamble clearly enunciates the resolve of the people to commit themselves to the ideals of a welfare state. The fundamental rights prohibit social discrimination and seek to create an egalitarian society. The directive principles aim to bring about a non-violent social revolution to change the oppressive structure of our society. In pursuance of the aims and objectives as laid down in the Constitution, the Government of India has enacted various legislative measures to protect the weaker sections of society against social injustice, appointed various commissions/ committees to study their problems and make recommendations for their solution, convened conferences and seminars of eminent persons in the field of social welfare to provide forum for discussion, exchange of views, sharing experiences on the working of various schemes and programmes of social welfare, and setup Ministry of Social Welfare and the Department of Women and Child Development for the formulation of social welfare policies and programmes and ensuring their implementation. The development of social welfare in the post-Independence period has been phenomenal in terms of provision of administrative machinery, financial outlays and expansion of social welfare programmes for numerous sections of disadvantaged, downtrodden and underprivileged people.

(B) UNION MINISTRY OF WELFARE

India being a federal polity, the responsibility for administration of welfare schemes for the deprived / disadvantaged sections of society rests with both the centre and the state governments. Social planning and social security are concurrent subjects. The Union Government formulates the nation's policy for social welfare and coordinates, guides and assists the states in the implementation of welfare programmes for the weaker sections of society including the women. The initial organized efforts towards the creation of an organization for welfare at the Union level was the establishment of Department of Social Security in June, 1964 to look after the subjects relating to social welfare pooled together from different ministries like Education, Home Affairs, Labour, Health, Commerce and Industry. In January 1966, the Department of Social Security was redesignated as Department of Social Welfare which was elevated to the status of a Ministry in August, 1979 and known as Ministry of Education and Social Welfare. In 1984, it was redesignated as Ministry of Social and

Women Welfare. It was on 25th September, 1985 that the Ministry of Welfare was formed by transferring subjects relating to welfare of the scheduled castes, scheduled tribes, minorities and other backward classes from the Ministry of Home Affairs and the welfare of the disabled and programme of social defence from the Ministry of Welfare w.e.f. 6th January, 1986.

The Department of Women and Child Development was placed under the Ministry of Human Resource Development. Thus, at present the welfare of scheduled castes and scheduled tribes and the backward classes is the responsibility of the Union Ministry of Welfare, and the welfare of women falls under the jurisdiction of Department of Women and Child Development placed under the Ministry of Human Resource Development.

Organization

The Ministry of Welfare is headed by a Cabinet Minister who is assisted by a Deputy Minister. At the secretariat level, there are one Secretary, one Additional Secretary, five Joint Secretaries and one Financial Adviser. The Joint Secretaries look after the different wings into which the work of the Ministry has been divided. These wings are Handicapped Welfare, Minorities Welfare, Scheduled Castes Development, Social Defence, Tribal Development, and WAKF wing. The Financial Advisor looks after the Financial wing. The ministry also has a consultative committee of the Members of Parliament which reviews the matters relating to the Ministry and advises the Ministry on matters relating to general welfare as well as that of the sectoral groups. There are a number of subordinate organizations, National Commissions and National Institutes over which the Ministry exercises administrative control. These are Central Social Welfare Board; National Commission for Scheduled Castes and Scheduled Tribes, Minorities Commission, National Institute of Social Defence, National Institute for the Visually Handicapped, National Institute for the Orthopaedically Handicapped, National Institute of Rehabilitation, Training and Research, National Institute for the Hearing Handicapped, National Institute for Mentally Handicapped, Commission for Scheduled Castes and Scheduled Tribes; Commission for Linguistic Minorities, Artificial Limbs Manufacturing Corporation of India, National Scheduled Castes and Scheduled Tribes Financial Corporation and Tribal Cooperative Marketing Development Federation of India Ltd.

Activities of the Ministry

The Ministry of Social Welfare has been assigned various subjects relating to social welfare of different sections of society – the most important ones being: social welfare planning, project formulation, research, evaluation, statistics and training; education, training, welfare and rehabilitation of the physically and mentally handicapped; all matters relating to prohibition, drug addiction, social and moral hygiene, probation of juvenile offenders, beggary, juvenile delinquencies and after care programme; welfare of scheduled castes, scheduled tribes, denotified nomadic and seminomadic tribes and other backward classes and their development; supervision, administration and control of different National institutes setup for the handicapped; all matters relating the Minorities Commission and the Commission for Scheduled Castes and Scheduled Tribes; and matters relating to wakf.

The main activities of the Ministry of Social Welfare are:

(*i*) *Welfare of various sections of society* : The ministry has over the years focussed attention on the issues relating to the welfare of weaker sections of society including the handicapped, minorities, scheduled castes, scheduled tribes, drug addicts act. It also looks to the matter of social defence, social security and social welfare.

(*ii*) *Policy, Planning and Coordination of Programmes* : The ministry of Welfare is the nodal ministry of overall policy, planning and coordination of programmes of development for various sections requiring developmental inputs.

(*iii*) *Operation of central and centrally sponsored schemes* : The ministry operates some central and centrally sponsored welfare programmes. The central schemes include socio-economic programmes, administration of National Institutes for handicapped, social education work and training, planning and research, evaluation and monitoring, grants-in-aid to voluntary organizations by the Central Social Welfare Board.

The centrally sponsored schemes include services for integrated development of the physically handicapped, scheduled castes, Scheduled tribes and other backward classes.

(*iv*) *Guidance and Direction to the States* : The Ministry of Welfare provides policy guidelines and directions to the states in consonance with the national objectives of social welfare such as reduction of poverty, inequality and increasing self-reliance.

(*v*) *Association with Planning Commission* : The Ministry associates with the Planning Commission for discussion of its plans and allocation of funds for their execution as also for the five year plans and annual plans, thus availing of an opportunity to review programmes implemented in the states.

(*vi*) *Convening of conferences of state ministers/secretaries of social welfare* : The ministry convenes conferences of state social welfare ministers and secretaries from time to time to evaluate the current welfare programmes, discuss the field problems and modify the welfare plans accordingly.

(*vii*) *Constitution of Commissions, Committees /Study Teams* : The Ministry constitutes various committees, study teams, working groups. etc. to study current programmes and emerging trends and to make recommendations for improvement of social services and formulation of better policies. The Ministry has some standing committees as well viz Advisory Committee on Social Welfare.

(*viii*) *Assistance to Voluntary Organizations* : the Ministry provides financial assistance to voluntary organizations engaged in providing services to the underprivileged groups. The role of voluntary agencies in the field of social welfare and removal of social distinctions cannot be minimized.

(*ix*) *Information and Mass Education Activities* : The Ministry has setup an Information and Mass Education Cell to create awareness about its various social welfare programmes, to mobilize public opinion and encourage voluntary action against social evils and to promote positive social attitudes.

(*x*) *Publications* . The Ministry had started the publication of Handbook on Social Welfare Statistics in 1974 which provided data base to social welfare programmes and policies through the statistical compilations. These statistics provide an integrated picture of the programmes and achievements of the Ministry in a miniature form.

(*xi*) *Research, Evaluation and Documentation.* The ministry sponsors research and evaluation studies in the areas allotted to it. It need not be emphasized that Research and Evaluation studies provide useful informations on different dimensions of social problems to facilitiate effective planning, policy formulation and implementation of programmes for weaker sections of society. It also provides financial assistance to various Universities, Institutes and Organizations conducting action reoriented research and evaluative studies in the fields of social welfare, social policy and social development to faciliate planning and policy formulation and effective programme implementation. Since social welfare activities are mostly carried out by the state governments, therefore, the main activity of the Union Ministry of Welfare is policy formulation, research, evaluation, monitoring, guidance and assistance in the field of social welfare.

The activities of the Ministry of Welfare as mentioned above, however, do not represent exhaustively the wide spectrum of its engagements, which has over the past few years increased and is bound to increase further due to the increase in the strength of its clientele in the wake of population explosion, poverty, atrocities on weaker sections of society, scheduled castes and other backward classes in particular and spurt in the number of victims of political violence.

(C) CENTRAL SOCIAL WELFARE BOARD

Its Organization

The Central Social welfare Board was constituted by the Government of India through a resolution in August, 1953 to administer a sum of Rs. 4 crores provided in the First Five year plan "as grants-in aid to voluntary social service organizations for strengthening, improving and extending the existing activities in the field of social welfare and developing new programmes and carrying out pilot project." Later, it was registered as a charitable company under the India Companies Act, 1956 with effect from April 1, 1969. It has a governing body which comprises of all chairpersons of state and union territory boards, five professionals, one each from the fields of law, medicine, nutrition, social work, education and social development, three eminent persons with extensive experience in social work, one representative each of Ministries of Welfare, Rural Development, Health, Education, Labour, Finance and the Planning Commission, two members of the Lok Sabha and one of the Rajya Sabha, Chairman of the Board and Executive Director of the Board as Member Secretary all nominated by the Ministry of Welfare. It is a policy making body. It meets every year to pass the budget, to discuss the annual report and reports of the Executive Committee, etc.

The administration of the affairs of the Board rests with the Executive Committee which comprises 15 members nominated by the Government of India from amongst the members of the Board. It includes Chairman of the Board, Chairpersons for State Advisory Boards and one Chairperson of Union Territory by rotation, representatives of the Ministers of Welfare, health, Finance, Rural Development and Education, two professionals and Executive Director. It meets once in two months.

The Chairman of the Board is its Chief Executive. The Executive Director functions directly under him. He is responsible for all aspects of the working of the Board and performs many managing and advisory functions.

The work of the Board is divided into five divisions each headed by a Joint Director responsible to the Executive Director. These divisions are :

(*i*) *Industrial Programme Administrative Division* deals with socio-economic programmes of the Board which are meant to provide opportunities to needy women and physically handicapped to engage themselves in production activities and thus to enable them to become economically rehabilitated.

(*ii*) *Welfare Programme Administrative Division* deals with the programmes of general welfare. It has three sections : (*i*) General Grants Section; (*ii*) Child Welfare Section; and (*iii*) Condensed Course Section.

(*iii*) *Administrative Division* is meant to manage, supervise and administer a variety of personnel functions such as recruitment, placement, transfers, promotion, conduct rule and discipline, motivation and incentive and service functions such as record management, property management, transportation, and advisory functions such as identifying long and short range personnel needs of the Board, procedural changes etc.

This division also deals with the reconstitution of State Welfare Advisory Boards, their budgets and annual reports. It also carries out public relations work and publications work.

(*iv*) *Finance and Accounts Division* is headed by an internal Financial Advisor-cum-Chief Accounts Officer. It is responsible for maintenance of proper accounts, budget formulation, release of funds for different purposes and exercising supervision and control over various financial transactions of the Board.

(*v*) *Planning, Monitoring and Coordination Division* is concerned with overall planning of social welfare programmes in consonance with the objectives of the Board, supplying necessary information about determining priorities in the implementation of various programmes, conducting research and surveys in the field of social welfare, evaluating the efficiency of various welfare programmes, examining the function of voluntary organizations aided by the Board, assessing the needs of the weaker sections of the society in different regions of the country ad suggesting projects and programmes to meet them and assisting the overall coordination of welfare activities of different agencies, departments and ministers. For the performance of these activities, the Division is divided into numerous sections.

The Board also has a field level machinery comprising welfare officers and project officers to ensure proper utilization of funds and to provide guidance to grant receiving organizations for the proper implementation of projects and programmes.

The organizations and structure of the Board described above reflects that the Board is fully under the control of the Union Government and virtually functions as any other government department. It follows government procedures of work and lays more emphasis on observance of the prescribed rules and regulations. It thereby creates rigidity in administration and centralization of authority which defeats the spirit behind a social welfare institution which should have flexibility in its organization and autonomy in its functioning. It has therefore been suggested that the Board should be formed into a statutory corporation.

Objectives and Activities

According to the Memorandum and Articles of Association of Central Social Welfare Board, its main objectives are:

To study the needs and requirements of social welfare organizations from time to time through surveys, research and evaluation and to evaluate the programmes and projects of the aided agencies; to coordinate assistance extended to social welfare activities by various ministries in central and state governments in the programmes entrusted to the Central Social Welfare Advisory Board; to promote the setting up of social welfare organizations on a voluntary basis in places where no such organizations exist and to promote additional organizations wherever necessary; to render technical and financial aid, when necessary to deserving institutions or organizations including Panchayati raj institutions in accordance with the scheme/principles approved by the Government of India; to promote social welfare activities intended for the general welfare of the public such as welfare of the family, women and children, and the handicapped and assistance in cases of unemployment, under-employment, old age, sickness, disablement, etc; to organize or promote programmes of training in social work as and when required and also to organize and work in pilot projects wherever necessary; and to organize through its machinery emergency relief in cases of calamity, national, natural or otherwise, whenever deemed fit or necessary.

In pursuance of these objectives, the Board has been formulating and implementing various welfare programmes. Its main programmes and activities consist of : (*i*) general grants-in-aid to voluntary organizations engaged in the welfare activities for childeren, women, physically handicapped, aged and infirm; (*ii*) welfare extension projects to provide minimum services to women and children through Mahila Mandals, (*iii*) supplementary nutrition programme with the object to provide supplementary food to children in the age group of 3 to 5 years belonging the low-income families through Balwadis/Day Care centres; (*iv*) holiday camp programmes to assist the voluntary organizations organizing camps for the children of the group of 10 to 16 years coming from economically backward classes and also from the physically handicapped children, (*v*) hostels for working women, (*vi*) awareness generation projects for rural and poor women, (*vii*) condensed courses of education for adult women and vocational education, (*viii*) socio-economic programmes for women and disabled with a view to create income generation activities and opportunities for women and the disabled, and (*ix*) Family Counselling Centres and Voluntary Bureau to help in the cases related to family discord, maladjustment and exploitation of women and children.

The Central Social Welfare Board is a unique and pioneering organization outside the government framework, integrating the governmental and non-governmental resources and skill for planning and administration, manpower and finance for creating a network to deliver welfare services to women, children and other socially and physically handicapped sections of the society. It functions as the focal and apex agency in the voluntary sector. As pointed out earlier, it would be conducive to its working with flexibility and enable it to function with greater efficiency if it is given autonomous character in order to relieve it from the rigours of government procedures.

State Social Welfare Advisory Boards

The State Social Welfare Advisory Boards have been constituted by the State Governments in pursuance of the recommendations to that effect by the Union Government and Central Social Welfare Board for purpose of better coordination between the institutions in the State, State Governments and the Central Social Welfare Board and also for a wider coverage and intensive study of the working of the institutions in the states and to follow up frequently their programmes and activities.

The State Social Welfare Advisory Boards follow the pattern of membership of the Central Social Welfare Board. They comprise non-official women members having experience of social work in voluntary organizations and officers representing the government in the department of social welfare, Directorate of Women's Programmes, Development Commissioner, Directorate of Education and Directorate of Health. The non-official members are selected both by the State Government and the Central Social Welfare Board each nominating 50 percent of the members. The Chairperson of the State Boards is the chief Executive authority. He is supported by the Secretariat headed by a Secretary and the subordinate staffs, inspectorate staffs, functional committee at the Block level and the project staffs. There is no fixed term for the Chairperson and the members of the Board.

Functions of the Boards

As laid down in the Memorandum and Articles of Association of the Central Social Welfare Board, the State Social Advisory Boards are to perform such functions as are assigned to them by the Central Social Welfare Board. And as they were primarily established as advisory bodies, they function as such and tender advice to the Central Board in respect of welfare programmes of voluntary organizations and other institutions in their respective States. Generally speaking, the functions of the State Boards comprise : to invite and scrutinize the applications from registered voluntary organizations for grant-in-aid and recommend their cases to the Central Board, to supervise the working of the grant receiving voluntary organizations and to report to the Central Board; to advise and assist the Central Board, sponsoring new welfare programmes and activities; to encourage and promote the growth of voluntary social welfare organizations; to assist the Central Board in providing field counselling services for aided voluntary organizations; to achieve coordination among voluntary organizations, between voluntary organizations and statutory agencies at the State and local levels and between the various departments of the state government; to implement the programmes on behalf of the state government; to implement the programmes on behalf of the Central Board and to undertake with the concurrence of the Central Board such programmes as may be entrusted to them by any Department of the Central or State Government.

In short, the State Boards assist the Central Social Welfare Board in the discharge of its functions and carry out all such activities as are assigned to them by the latter. As is evident in their nomenclature, the State Boards advise the Central Board in sponsoring and supervising the welfare programmes in their respective jurisdictions, recommending grants-in-aid to the voluntary organizations. They have no rigid or independent functions of their own. They are the advisory and assisting bodies of the Central Board and do not possess a statutory or judicial status.

(D) SOCIAL WELFARE ADMINISTRATION AT THE STATE LEVEL

The state governments/union territories have setup departments concerned with social welfare under one nomenclature or the other to carry out their welfare obligations and programmes. Andhra Pradesh, Arunachal Pradesh, Assam, Haryana, Jammu and Kashmir, Karnataka, Madhya Pradesh, Manipur, Meghalaya, Nagaland, Punjab, Rajasthan, Sikkim, Tamil Nadu, Uttar pradesh, West Bengal and Union territories of Andaman and Nicobar Islands, Chandigarh, Dadra and Nagar Haveli, Delhi, Daman and Diu, Lakshadweep have designated them as Departments of Welfare; Gujarat as the Department of Social Welfare, Cultural Affairs, Sports and Tourism, Orissa carries out several welfare programmes through the Community Development Department; Tripura through its Education Department. In Pondicherry, a Department of Social Welfare was established in 1969. Thus all the States and Union Territories have created Departments for the formulation and implementation of social welfare schemes and to provide welfare services in their respective jurisdictions to the socially and economically weaker sections of the society—women, children, scheduled castes, scheduled tribes, backward classes, disabled and others.

Administrative Organization

The Department of Social Welfare is headed by a Minister. The Secretary is the administrative head of the department who may be assisted by Joint Secretaries and Deputy Secretaries. The Secretary is a senior IAS Officer. He assists and advises the minister in the formulation of the policies of the department and supervises the execution of the policies and programmes formulated by the government.

The execution of the policies and programmes is the responsibility of the Directorate which is headed by a Director who is assisted by Additional Director, Joint Director, Administrative officers and supporting staffs. These officers operate at the Headquarters.

In the field, there are Divisional and District Social Welfare officers who execute the various welfare programmes in their respective jurisdictions. At the local level, Taluka / Tahsil / Block also social welfare officers are appointed. The Divisional and District Social Welfare Officers, as pointed out earlier, are the employees of the Central Social Welfare Board, though they work under the administrative control of the State governments concerned.

The administrative and staffing pattern in all the states is more or less the same and so are the kinds of welfare services provided in each state except for some minor variations.

The activities of the social welfare department generally include child welfare, welfare of women, welfare of the aged and the infirms, welfare of the handicapped and general welfare. The women welfare programmes consist of financial assistance to widows and destitute women, homes for widows and destitute women, state protection homes to prevent women against immoral traffic, Nari Niketan for deserted women and unmarried mothers. The general welfare programmes consist of grants-in-aid to voluntary organizations working in the field of social welfare.

At the local level, the Panchayati Raj institutions and urban local authorities have been assigned welfare functions including programmes for the welfare of women and children, disabled persons, beggars, destitutes and the disadvantaged sections of society. But since the local government bodies live in a state of perpetual financial crisis, their contribution in the field of social welfare has been disappointing.

[1] *India 2008 India Publication river the 878-80*
(A reference 2. Child p 890-3)

(E) COMMISSIONER FOR SCHEDULED CASTES AND SCHEDULED TRIBES

Article 338 of the Constitution of India provides for the appointment of a special officer for the scheduled castes and scheduled tribes to be appointed by the President. It shall be the duty of the special officer to investigate all matters relating to the safeguards provided for the scheduled castes and scheduled tribes under the Constitution and report to the President about the working as incorporated in those safeguards at such intervals as the President may direct those. The President shall cause all such reports to be laid before each House of Parliament. In pursuance of this provision, a special officer, known as Commissioner for scheduled castes and scheduled tribes is appointed by the President from time to time . The Commissioner performs the following functions :

(*i*) evaluating the progress of welfare schemes undertaken by state governments and non-official organizations with grants-in-aid received from the Government of India; (*ii*) giving advice on schemes received for grants-in-aid from the state governments and non-official agencies for the amelioration of the conditions of backward classes; (*iii*) serving as a nominee of the Central government on the managing committees of the non-official organizations receiving grants directly from the Centre; (*iv*) examination of accounts of the non-official organizations receiving grants directly from the Centre.

Duties of Assistant Commissioner

The Commissioner is assisted by a number of Assistant Commissioners appointed for different regions. The duties of an Assistant Commissioner are:

(*i*) to investigate cases referred to him by the Commissioner or which may be brought to his notice by the local residents ;

(*ii*) to establish close contacts with the scheduled castes, scheduled tribes and other backward classes, with a view to gaining first hand knowledge of the disabilities under which they live and to educate them about the measures that they should adopt for their welfare;

(*iii*) to submit to the Commissioner periodical reports, showing the various facilities available for the scheduled castes and scheduled tribes in his region and the disabilities under which they live;

(*iv*) to report on the progress of expenditure and of the achievement of the prescribed physical targets from time to time and to investigate and advise on how best the collection of statistical data can be improved;

(*v*) to report on the adequacy of the resources and personnel employed for the various schemes by state governments in whom the responsibility for the implementation of sanctioned schemes in backward classes sectors is vested;

(*vi*) to help the state governments to remove the bottlenecks as may be noticed in the actual implementing of the sanctioned schemes and undertaking new schemes, where necessary in the light of local needs; and

(*vii*) to ensure that cooperation is forthcoming in an adequate measure from the public where the schemes involve public cooperation.

However, from the very beginning there has been controversy regarding the status of the Commissioner. His status and position are not laid down in the Constitution as in the cases of Chief Election Commissioner or the Chairman of Union Public Service Commission. The status of the Commissioner is that of a Secretary to the Government of India. Although the Constitution empowers the special officer to investigate only matters relating to the safeguards provided in the Constitution, but, over the years, the office of the Commissioner has assumed the role of an executive agency by associating himself with the examination of the schemes for grants-in-aid under various state governments and non-official agencies for the development of scheduled castes and scheduled tribes.

Commission for Scheduled Castes and Scheduled Tribes

Considering the magnitude of the problem of welfare of scheduled castes and scheduled tribes, the Government of India had been of the view that in addition to the special officer, there should be setup a high level Commission to look into the matters relating to these classes. Accordingly, a Commission was setup in 1978 which was to consist of a Chairman and not more than four members, including the Special Officer appointed under article 338 of the constitution. The term of the Commission was fixed at three years. The functions of the Commission were laid down as under. [1]

(*i*) To investigate all matters relating to safeguards provided for scheduled castes and scheduled tribes in the Constitution. This should inter alia include a review of the manner in which reservations stipulated in public services for scheduled castes and scheduled tribes are in practice implemented.

(*ii*) To study the implementations of protection of Civil Rights Act, 1955 with particular reference to the objective of removal of untouchability and individual discrimination arising therefrom.

(*iii*) To ascertain the socio-economic and other relevant circumstances accounting for the commission of offences against persons belonging to scheduled castes or scheduled tribes with a view to ensuring the removal of impediments in the laws in force and to recommend appropriate remedial measures including measures to ensure prompt investigation of the offences.

(*iv*) To enquire into individual complaints regarding denial of any safeguards provided to any person claiming to belong to scheduled castes or scheduled tribes.

The Commission was required to submit an annual report to the President detailing its activities and recommendations which was to be placed before each House of Parliament.

On 1st September 1987, the Commission was reconstituted as the National Commission for Scheduled Castes and Scheduled Tribes[2]. Its functions were to be as follows :

(*i*) to study the extent and ramifications of untouchability and social discrimination arising therefrom and effectiveness of the present measures and recommend further measures to be taken;

(*ii*) to study socio-economic and other relevant circumstances leading to the commission of offences against persons belonging to scheduled castes and scheduled tribes; and to recommend appropriate remedial measures to ensure prompt investigation of such offences;

(*iii*) to make studies on different aspects of development of the scheduled castes and scheduled tribes with a view to ensuring integration of these groups with mainstream of the society in all aspects. These would include studies in the fields of socio-economic development, education, commerce, trade, art, literature, language, housing, communication, agriculture, forestry, horticulture, fisheries, rehabilitation, pollution and environment, and

(*vi*) Such other functions as may be entrusted to it in evolving general policies relating to any aspect to development of the scheduled castes and scheduled tribes as may be thought proper by the Central Government.

The Commission consists of a Chairman and five other members. The term of office is three years. It is assisted by a Secretariat with headquarters at New Delhi. The Secretariat is headed by a Senior IAS officer. It functions through field offices located in the sates. The Commissioner for Scheduled Castes /Tribes is no longer its ex-officio member who functions separately. The National Commission is an advisory body on broad issues of policies and levels of development of the Scheduled Castes and Scheduled Tribes. It is not an executive agency. As pointed out above, the Commissioner is not an independent authority as the chief election commissioner is and does not have enough powers in respect of state governments and the various departments of the central

[1] *Vide Resolution of the Ministry of Home Affairs, Dated 21 July,1978.*

[2] *Vide Resolution of the Ministry of Welfare, Dt 1 Sept. 1987.*

government. On the other hand, the National Commission has no statutory powers as it has been created by a Resolution of Welfare Ministry. A proposal to merge the office of the Commissioner with the Commission and give it statutory powers is under the consideration of the Government of India. This proposal, when implemented, may go a long way in improving and streamlining the functioning of the institution charged under the Constitution with the duty to investigate all matters relating to the safeguards for the scheduled castes and scheduled tribes.

(F) WELFARE PROGRAMMES

The Constitution of India has provided the following safeguards to scheduled castes and scheduled tribes :

(*i*) the abolition of untouchability and the forbidding of its practice in any form (Art. 17);

(*ii*) the promotion of their educational and economic interests and their protection from social injustice and all forms of exploitation (Art. 46);

(*iii*) the throwing open by law of Hindu religious institutions of a public character to all classes and sections of Hindus (Art. 25 Ab);

(*iv*) the removal of any disability, liability, restriction or condition with regard to access to shops, public restaurants, hostels and places of public entertainment or the use of wells, tanks, bathing ghats, roads and places of public resort maintained wholly or partially out of state funds or dedicated to the use of the general public (Art. 15(2));

(*v*) to curtail the rights of general citizens to move freely, settle in and acquire property (Art. 19(5)), in the interest of any scheduled tribe or scheduled caste;

(*vi*) the forbidding of any denial of admission to educational institutions maintained by the state or receiving grants out of state funds (Art.29 (2);

(*vii*) permitting the states to make reservation for the backward classes in public services in case of inadequate representations and requiring the state to consider the claim of the scheduled castes and scheduled tribes in the making of appointments to public services (Art. 16 and 355);

(*viii*) special representation in the Lok Sabha and the State Vidhan Sabhas to scheduled castes and tribes till 25 January, 2000 (Art. 330, 332, and 334);

(*ix*) the setting up of tribe advisory councils and separate departments in the state and the appointment of a special officer at the Centre to promote their welfare and safeguard their interests (Art. 164 and 338);

(*x*) special provision for the administration and control of scheduled tribe areas (Art. 244 and Fifth and Sixth Schedules) and

(*xi*) prohibition of traffic in human beings and forced labour (Art. 23).

In pursuance of these provisions, seats have been reserved for scheduled castes and scheduled tribes in the Lok Sabha and State legislative Assemblies and reservations have been provided in public services and educational institutions.

A number of centrally sponsored schemes have been started for the welfare of scheduled castes and scheduled tribes. Among such schemes, mention may be made of : (*i*) Pre-matric Scholarships for the children of those engaged in unclean occupations. (*ii*) Post-matric scholarships for scheduled castes and scheduled tribes students. (*iii*) Book Banks for scheduled castes / tribes students studying in medical and engineering colleges; (*iv*) Girls Hostels scheme for scheduled tribes. (*v*) Coaching and allied scheme for scheduled castes and scheduled tribes. (*vi*) Scheduled castes development corporations. (*vii*) National overseas scholarships. (*viii*) Liberation of Scavengers Scheme. (*ix*) Central assistance scheme to voluntary organizations of All India character who are engaged in the welfare of scheduled castes and scheduled tribes.

In the Union Budget of 2002-03 the allocation for the welfare and uplift of scheduled castes was increased from 792 crores to 879 crores for the the year 2003.

At the state level, the welfare programmes comprise. (*i*) Educational and Training Programmes. (*ii*) Economic uplift programmes and (*iii*) Health, Housing and other programmes.

The **twenty point** economic programme lays special emphasis on the development of scheduled tribes. The tribal sub-plan is the main instrument for the development of tribal people and tribal areas.

Mention may also be made of the reservation in the educational institutions and public services recently provided to other backward classes in pursuance of the Mandal Report. Although the issue created heated controversy, leading to unprecedented violence in the country, the issue has, however been now finally settled after the judgment of the Supreme Court which upheld reservation policy of the Government in public services on the basis of caste as permissible under Art. 16(4) of the Constitution.

(G) WOMEN WELFARE PROGRAMMES

"To awaken the people it is the woman who must be awakened. Once she is on the move, the family moves, the village moves, the nation moves", said Jawaharlal Nehru. Women represent almost half of the total population of our country. According to the 1991 census, there were 927 females per 1,000 males in the country. In 2001 the figure went up to 933 females as against 1000 male. In 1991 the average literacy among women was 39.29 per cent as against 64.13 per cent among men which in 2001 census oroze to 54.16% as against 75.05 respectively. No schemes of economic and social development can be successful unless women play their constructive role in such programmes. In spite of the social imbalances, there has been considerable improvement in the status of women in India. There is nothing astonishing in it if only one looks through the pages of Vedic history when women used to be learned, cultured and enjoyed an equal rather higher status in society. It was an old Indian saying 'Where women are honoured there Gods reside'. Unfortunately, due to social, economic and political factors, women lost their coveted position in the later centuries. Evil customs like *Sati*, *Purdah*, Child marriage, enforced widowhood, dowry system crept in, and women's status in home and outside declined. During the past few years, new dimensions have come to be added to the problems of women. Rape, dowry deaths, misuse of the tests to determine the sex of the child in the womb and the termination of pregnancy in the event of female foetus convey an indication of the horrible behaviour patterns. Despite social legislation, there has been little change in the social outlook, in the perception of women's role and support services. The overall situations is still distressing. The struggle for equality, justice and parity between women and men and also for their identity continues.

The Department of Women and Child Development

As pointed out above, functions relating to welfare of different weaker sections of society prior to 1964 were looked after by different Ministries like Education, Home Affairs, Labour, Health, Commerce and Industry when a Department of Social Security was setup in June, 1964. In 1966, with the transference of certain subjects to other ministries, it was designated as Department of Social Welfare. The Department was raised to the level of Ministry in 1979. In 1984, it was redesignated as Ministry of Social and Women Welfare. In September, 1985 when the central ministries were restructured, a separate department for women and child development was created and placed under the ministry of Human Resources Development.

The Department of Women and Child Development is headed by a Minister of State who is assisted by a Secretary, two Joint Secretaries and one Financial Adviser. There are two bureaus in the department, namely, Nutrition and Child Development and Women's Welfare and Development, each under the charge of a Joint Secretary. The department has two organizations viz. The National Institute of Public Cooperation and Child Development and the Central Social Welfare Board to assist in its functions including those connected with the implementation of some of its programmes. The department also enlists in its activities active cooperation and involvement of voluntary organizations in the field of women/child development.

The bureau of women's welfare and development has the responsibility of formulating policies and implementation and execution of schemes and programmes of women's welfare and development in consultation with Central ministries/departments concerned, women's voluntary organizations and central social welfare board. The subjects dealing with women's welfare and development assigned to the department include : family welfare, women welfare and coordination of the activities of other ministries and organizations in connection with this subject; references from the United Nations Organizations relating to traffic in women; nutrition education of women; charitable and religious endowments pertaining to subjects allocated to the department; promotion and development of voluntary efforts on subjects allocated to the department; attached or subordinate offices or other organizations concerned with any of the subjects specified herein; administration of Suppression of Immoral Traffic in Women and Girls Act, 1956; Dowry Prohibition Act, 1961; Planning, Research, Evaluation, Monitoring, Project Formulation, Statistics and Training relating to the welfare of women, Central Social Welfare Board and National Institute of Public Cooperation and Child Development.

The department has been making concerted efforts to bring women into the mainstream of national development through various socio-economic programmes. A significant step in this direction was the drawing up of the national perspective plan up to 2000 A. D. for women which is a long term policy, guided by the principles and directives relevant to the development process. The plan is linked to the national targets determined for the end of the century in respect of certain basic sectors such as those of health, education and employment. A National Research Centre is also in the process of being established as a national level apex body to extend research, training and information services.

The department has set up a women's division in the National Institute of Public Cooperation and Child Development, to identify the problems of women and utilize the services of reputed consultants in the field to guide in the preparation of programmes. The department has been covening National Conferences on Women and participating in international programmes such as SAARC Women's Handicrafts Exhibition (Dhaka), SAARC Technical Committee on Women Development (New Delhi), SAARC Year for the Girl Child, International Conference on Women in Development Process (West Berlin, 1989), Expert Group Meeting on Equality in Political Participation and Decision making (Vienna) etc. The department has been observing international women's week from March 1 and Women's Day on March 8 every year. The year of 1990 was observed as the Year of the Girl Child. During the year, India hosted many conferences and symposia that deliberated on the age old trials and tribulations of the girl child. A great achievement of the year was the increase in the number of adopted girls. Statistics compiled by the voluntary coordination agency, Bombay under the auspices of Indian Association for the Promotion of Adoption show that more parents are taking to adoption and they prefer girls. Another achievement of the year was banning amniocentesis, though the sex determination tests are still carried under the garb of determining the health of the foetus. Greater awareness has led to more cases of dowry and atrocities on women being reported.

The major programmes/schemes for the welfare and progress of women are mentioned below:

Social Legislation

In our country, each community has its own personal laws based on religious codes. Thus Parsi, Christian and Muslim women enjoyed a comparatively higher status while Hindu women suffered from many legal disabilities. The Constitution of India, as adopted in 1950, accorded complete equality of rights to women with men. All women now enjoy political rights equal with men. They have the right to vote and get elected at the proper age, and have the right to hold public offices. In Panchayati Raj bodies, seats are reserved for them. The recent 73rd and 74th Amendment

Bills, dealing with Panchayati Raj and Urban local bodies respectively, have provided 30 per cent reservation of seats in the elected bodies for women. The Bill providing 33 per cent reservation in Parliament and State Legislatures to women was introduced recently. However, it still awaits parliamentary approval. The Hindu Marriage Act and Divorce Act, 1955; the Hindu inter-state Succession Act, 1956, and the Hindu Guardianship Act, 1956 have removed the several disabilities women suffered from. No Hindu can now marry a second time unless the wife or husband is dead or divorced. Divorce is recognized and allowed for women. The daughter has an equal right of share in the self-acquired property of the father. The widow and daughters inherit the property as equal partners. The women have acquired the right of adoption. A daughter can be adopted in the same manner as the son. The Supreme Court has recently held that mother is as much the legal guardian of the child as the father is. The child marriage has been prohibited. The Child Marriage Restraint Amendment Act, 1978 has raised the age of the marriage for girls from 15 to 18 years and for boys from 18 to 21 years. The Marriage Laws Amendment Act, 1976, provide for the right of the girl to repudiate before attaining majority, the marriage as a child, whether the marriage has been consummated or not.

The Dowry Prohibition Act 1961 has been made more stringent by the Amendment Act, 1984. The Factories Amendment Act, 1976, provides for the establishment of a Creche where 30 women are employed as against 50 hitherto. The Maternity Benefits Act, 1961, was amended in 1976 to cover women who do not fall within the purview of the Employees' State Insurance Act, 1948. The Equal Remuneration Act, 1976, provides for the payment of equal remuneration to men and women workers. All these legislative measures have gone a long way in developing awareness among women and removing social prejudices and social inequalities.

Education Programmes

Lack of education has been a great hindrance to women's progress. Therefore, special efforts are underway to raise the literacy rate among women and promote girls' education in the country. The Central Government gives financial assistance under the plan schemes to the educationally backward states for establishing schools and colleges exclusively for girls. Incentives are provided to states at different administrative levels for encouraging girls to enrol in larger numbers. Loans and grants are given for construction of women hostels buildings. The scheduled castes/tribe girls receive higher rates of post-matric scholarships as compared to boys. Other incentives to girls include free clothing and free tuition.

Special programmes have been started for women in adult education centres, providing education in subjects like health, nutrition, child care and family planning. The curriculum also include skills like teaching, sewing, embroidery and knitting etc. The Ministry of Welfare has launched functional Literacy Programmes for Adult Women. The Central Social Welfare Board gives grants to voluntary organizations to conduct courses of two to three years duration for passing matric/ secondary/middle/primary examinations and one year duration for failed girl candidates for passing matric/secondary level examinations for women of 15 plus age groups under the Scheme of Condensed Courses of Education. In order to encourage the entry of large number of women into scientific profession minimum 100 scholarships a year are to be provided to women scientists and technologists.[1]

To create awareness among women, the Central Social Welfare Board is implementing the Awareness Generation Scheme since 1987-1988. The scheme provides a platform for the rural and poor women to come together, exchange their experiences and ideas and in the process, develop understanding of their problems and also ways to tackle those problems and fulfil their needs. The scheme seeks to impart knowledge and analysis of the socio-economic conditions of the local areas

[1] *Union Budget 2002-03 as incorporated in World Competition April 2002. p. 10*

in relation to the status of women, technical information on subjects ranging from relevant legislation to health and hygeine and strategies and plan of action to organize women towards development and against injustice.

Employment and Income Generating Programmes

The government is giving greater attention to the training of women in vocational courses. More women polytechnics are being opened where girls are provided training in instrumentation technology for repair and maintenance of electronic equipments, manufacturing of readymade garments, handloom weaving, food preservation, typing and stenography, etc.

Employment and Income Generation Production Programme was started in 1982-83 to train women belonging to weaker sections of society and provide them employment on sustained basis. The various trades in which training is imparted are electronics, watch assembly and repair, Computer programming, printing and binding, handloom weaving, handicrafts, weaving and spinning, toy-making, doll-making etc. The programme is implemented through Public Sector Undertakings / Corporations/Autonomous Bodies/Voluntary organizations. Assistance for the programmes comes from the Norwegian Agency for International Development.

For the rehabilitation of women in distress, a scheme was launched in 1977 to provide vocational training-cum-employment and residential care so that women in distress such as young and old widows, unmarried mothers, victims of kidnapping, deserted women could become economically independent. This scheme envisages training of short duration not exceeding one year. The scheme is a centrally sponsored scheme. Voluntary agencies registered as societies/trusts, district rural development agencies, Panchayats and other local bodies are eligible for assistance under the scheme.

A new omnibus scheme known as STEP to render support to women's employment in various sectors such as agriculture, dairying, animal husbandry, fisheries, khadi and village industries, handlooms, handicrafts and sericulture, where women are preponderantly engaged in work, was formulated at the beginning of the seventh plan. The scheme focuses on the poorest, the most marginalized poor assetless women including wage earners, unpaid family workers, migrant labourers, tribals, and other dispossessed groups. Under this scheme, proposals from various agencies, organizations, women cooperative societies etc. are considered for financial assistance by a project sanctioning committee in the department.

The Women's Development Corporations are playing an important role in providing better employment avenues to women so that they may become economically independent and self-reliant. The functions of the corporations include identification of potential areas of employment, assistance for project formulation and raising required finances, arranging raw material for working women, providing training facilities and infrastructure for marketing the products. These corporations have been setup by the State Governments and Union Territories. The Union Government has provided funds to states through equity participation. The Department of Women and Child Development has given, up to 49 per cent of the paid up capital as financial assistance.

The corporations release loans at highly subsidised rates of interest to promote entrepreneurship amongst women. They also arrange loans through banks and allow benefit of interest subsidy.

In order to prepare women for self-employment by making full use of the financial assistance arranged / made available to them, the corporations also organize training and orientation camps in different trades such as rearing of crossbred cows, raising of poultry farms, training in knitting, soap making, fruit preservation and a few others independently as well as in collaboration with departments and organizations connected with particular activities. The corporations have also setup handicraft centres where women learn traditional and non-traditional arts, embroidery as well as cutting and tailoring of clothes.

Since all women are not able to take up independent economic activities for various reasons, the corporations have undertaken a number of assured and guaranteed employment programmes. For example, the Punjab women and children development and welfare corporation has setup a readymade garments unit at Mohali which has trained more than 200 women workers. It has been declared as an approved source for the supply and stitching of government uniforms and office linen. It also gets quota for export of garments to foreign countries. Similarly, it sponsors women for training in electronics to Electronics Units of Punjab State Industrial Development Corporation where they get a stipend during training period and after training all are absorbed as employees of these units.

The corporations also provide marketing assistance by procuring orders from export houses, emporiums and other organizations. These orders are passed on to the women entrepreneurs for execution on payment. Regular sale counters have also been opened at State Emporiums for sale of articles manufactured by them.

Hostels for Working Women

One of the main difficulties faced by working women is lack of suitable accommodation in a healthy and wholesome environment. Keeping in view the difficulties faced by such women, a Central Scheme of Assistance for construction of Hostel Buildings for working women was started in 1972. The scope of the scheme was widened in 1980 by including a provision for Daycare Centres for children. Financial assistance to the extent of 50 per cent of the cost of land and 75 per cent of the cost of construction of the Hostels is given to voluntary organizations. Assistance on the same pattern is also provided for the purchase of building to start hostels.

The population criteria for setting up hostels and child care centres was initially fixed at 10 lakh which meant that only big cities and towns could be benefited. This criteria was lowered to a population of two lakh and later a decision was taken to sanction hostels at any place where a minimum of 25 working women needed this facility. An Advisory Committee on working women's hostels has been setup under the chairmanship of the Minister of State for Women and Child Development to review the functioning of the programme and advise the government on the measures for its improvement and expansion.

The Department also gives financial assistance to voluntary organizations for establishing and running short stay homes to protect and rehabilitate those women and girls who are facing social and moral danger because of family problems, mental strain, exploitation or any other reasons. Such Homes have an average of 30 residents at a time. Under the scheme services/facilities of medical care, psychiatric treatment, occupational therapy; social facilities of adjustment, and education, vocational and recreational activities are provided. In the Union Budget of 2002-03 the allocation for the Department of Women and Child Development was increased by 33% to Rs. 2200 crores.[1]

Mahila Mandals

The Scheme of Welfare Extension Projects started in 1954 to provide basic minimum services to women and children comprising Balwadis, maternity and health services, literacy and social education for women, arts and crafts centres and recreational facilities in the rural areas was handed over to voluntary organizations known as Mahila Mandals in 1961. The Social Welfare Board bears the expenditure up to 75 per cent, and the remaining 25 per cent is to be raised by the Mahila Mandals/Voluntary organizations themselves. This programme is now being administered by the State Boards.

Family Life Institute

The Association for Social Health in India runs the Family Life Institute in Delhi. The major functions of this institute are counselling services and family life education for the maladjusted

[1]*Competition World, April 2002 Issue, p. 10.*

spouses, parents, unmarried youths, teenagers of unsettled and depressed mind, child dropouts, etc.

The Association also generates public opinion against trafficking and elevation of moral standard in general. It is given financial assistance by the Department of Women and Child Development.

The voluntary organizations working for women uplift and social betterment and carrying out education work for the prevention of atrocities against women through propaganda, publicity and research work are given assistance to the extent of 90 per cent to meet the expenditure on any of their programmes/activities which may comprise production and publication of educative journals, articles, books and other publicity material like pamphlets, booklets, posters, etc. depicting themes of violence against women, dissemination of information or material in the form of films, books and other material; holding of seminars/conferences/meetings/exhibitions etc.; training camp for social workers and performance of street plays, puppetry shows to raise awareness related to violence against women.

Appointment of Commissions and Committees

The Government of India in order to study the problems of women and invite suggestions and recommendations for their solution with a view to ameliorate their lot and provide facilities for their welfare has been appointing various committees and commission from time to time and accepting their recommendations to the extent possible. Among these committees and commissions, the important ones have been : National Committee on the Status of Women (1974); National Expert Committee on Women Prisoners (1986); National Committee on Women (1980); National Commission on Self-employed women and women in the informal sector (1987). A National Commission on Women — a statutory body for protecting the rights of women on the pattern of National Commission for scheduled castes and scheduled tribes and the minorities commission was set up in 1992. Its main task is to study and monitor all matters concerning legal and constitutional and to review the existing Acts and advise amendments. A national Plan of Action was formulated in 1998 to combat trafficing and commercial sexual exploitation of women. Necessary guidelines were sent to the state governments for implementation of the National Plan.

The important voluntary organizations working in the field of Women Welfare and Development are Women's Action for Development, Delhi; Indian Red Cross; Rotary Club and Lion's Club; Indian Prostitutes Welfare Society; Family Planning Association of India; Indian Council for Women Welfare; Indian Council of Social Welfare; National Federation of Indian Women; Human Rights Organization; Mahila Mandals; Kasturba Gandhi Trust; Kamla Nehru Memorial Trust; Indira Gandhi Trust; All India Women's Conference; Bharatiya Grameen Mahila Sangh; Association for Social health in India; Young Women Christian Association, Bharat Sevak Samaj and a number of local organizations besides the religious organizations like Arya Samaj, Ramakrishna Mission. Recently South Asian Women in International security (SAWIS) has offered academic leave for professional women working in subcontinent to engage in research at John Hopkin University, USA.[1]

From the above analysis of the measures taken for the development and welfare of women, it is clear that today's woman in India has better opportunities and avenues in all spheres of national life — social, economic and political. She has come to occupy a better status partly due to the legal, economic and social measures and partly due to the change in social attitudes and upsurge. She has now become liberated from many of the age old evils and complexities. There is a large number of woman entrepreneurs, high civil service officers, political leaders, social reformers, religious preachers, teachers and voluntary workers who are playing an important role in the task of national development. However, the Feminist movement in India is confined to the cities and towns only; in the villages not many of the voluntary agencies exist. The schemes initiated for improving the economic status of rural women seem to have failed as there are not many women headed enterprises

[1]*Hindustan Times January, 2003, p. 11*

in the countryside. Exploitation of women labour both in the formal and informal sectors still continues. The rural women are ignorant about provisions of law protecting them against atrocities. As a matter of fact, the task of women welfare and development is multi-faced for which regulative and promotive measures have to be initiated not only by the Department of Women Welfare and Development but by several ministries and agencies in a well-coordinated manner. In addition, the feudal mindset of male dominated Indian society needs to be changed. No amount of social legislation and welfare measures will bear fruit, if the patriarchal social system and its values and attitudes do not experience any major change. However, in the ultimate analysis, with all the concern that is reflected in the policy of government and the massive programmes undertaken by it for women welfare and development, the woman in independent India has a bright future.

(H) Child welfare programmes

Children constitute about 40 per cent of India's population. They number over 300 million more than the children of all the 46 countries of Africa put together. Of these 6.2 crore are slum dwellers. Nearly 48 per cent suffer from malnutrition, about one lakh succumbing to it every month. India's mortality rate of 120 per thousand put it in the 27th position from the top in a list of 120 countries. For every seven children born, one dies before the age of five, over 30,000 children go blind, five every year. Nine out of every 1000 school going children suffer from rheumatic heart disease because of nutritional anaemia. Over 4.6 million in the age group of six to eleven years are illiterate.

Over 16 million children work as labour comprising 5 per cent of the work force. Most of them are exploited. The hundreds of children are kidnapped every year and many of them are sold or forced into beggary. The girl child is doubly deprived. She is discriminated against because of her sex. The various schemes for the child welfare carried on in India are the following:

(1) Constitutional Provisions

The national concern for children is reflected in the constitutional and legislative provision which govern the rights of children. Article 24 lays down that no child below the age of 14 shall be employed to work in any factory or mine of hazardous nature. Article 39 of the Directive Prionciples of State Policy requires the States to ensure that children are not forced by economic necessity to enter vocation unsuited to their age and strength. It further stipulates that children are given opportunities and facilities to develop in a healthy manner in conditions of freedom and that childhood and youth are protected against exploitation and against moral and material abandonment. Article 45 requires the State to endeavour to provide free and compulsory education for all children upto the age of 14 years.

The State has enacted various legislations in pursuance of the above provisions for the welfare of children. These include laws prescribing minimum age for boys and girls, appointment of guardian for a minor child's person or property, the Hindu Adoption and Maintenance Act, 1956, Women's and Children's Institutions (Licensing) Acts 1960, State Children Acts, Factories Act of 1948, plantation labour Act of 1951. The mines Act of 1952, Shops and Establishment Act prohibiting the employment of children in hazardous occupations, Juvenile Justice Act, 2000, Prohibition of Child Marriage Act 2006, Commission for Protection of Child Rights Act, 2005.

India is a one of the very few developing countries in the world to translate its commitment to the cause of child into a National Policy on children adopted in 1974. The first major step towards implementing this policy was taken with the introduction of multi-sectoral Integrated Child Development Services (ICDS) programme in October, 1975. This programme as also other measures taken in pursuance of the National Policy for Children by the Government of India, State Governments, Union Territory Administrations, Voluntary Agencies and National association are discussed as follows:

---

[1] *Prohibiton of child act 2006, Commission for Protection of child Right Act, 2005*

Integrated Child Development Services (ICDS) scheme – The Integrated Child Development Services (ICDS) Scheme was introduced on October 2, 1975 in the country. Its main objectives are: to improve the nutrition and health status of children in the age group of 0-6 years; to lay the foundations for proper psychological, physical and social development of the child; to reduce the incidence of mortality, morbidity, malnutrition and school drop outs; to achieve effective coordination of policy and implementation amongst the various departments to promote child development, and to enhance the capability of the mother, through proper nutrition and health education, for looking after, the normal health and nutritional needs of the child.

The Scheme covers children below the age of six years, expectant and nursing mothers and other women in the age group of 15–44 years belonging to the poor families. It aims at the delivery of package of services such as : supplementary nutrition, immunization, health check-up, referral services, non-formal pre-school education and health and nutrition education to all women.

The focus point to provide the ICDS package of services is an anganwadi in every village, or a ward of an urban slum area. Generally, there is one anganwadi for a population of about 1000 in rural and urban areas and 700 in tribal, hilly and sparsely populated areas. However, the number of anganwadi can be increased according to local needs, depending on the number of inhabited villages, population of the project area, topography etc. The anganwadi is run by an Anganwadi Worker (AWW), who is an honorary voluntary women worker from the local community. Her work is supervised by a Mukhyasevika (MS)/Supervisor. The administrative unit of an ICDS project, is a block/taluka in rural/tribal areas and a group of wards/slums in urban areas. A Child Development Project Officer (CDPO) is incharge of an ICDS project and he/she has a numebr of AWWs and MSs under him/her. When the number of Anganwadi is 150 or more in a rural project or 100 or more in tribal/hill project, one or more Assistant or Additional CDPOs are sanctioned to assist the CDPO. Health infrastructure in the project area is strengthened according to the national norms laid down by the Ministry of Health and Family Welfare.

ICDS places great emphasis and relies greatly on the involvement of local communities and the coordinated efforts of different Ministries/Departments and Organisation at all levels. Co-ordination Committee are envisaged at the Central, State, District and Project levels.

The All India Institute of Medical Sciences (AIIMS) and through it, several Medical Colleges in the country are associated with the training and orientation of medical and nutritional status of children and mothers in them. Baselines and repeat surveys conducted by the AIIMS and Medical Colleges have shown that there have been better utilization of supplementary nutrition, Vitamin "A" iron and Folic Acid and Immunizatin services among the pre-school children, pregnant women and nursing mothers in the ICDS project areas, compared to that by the beneficiaries in the non-ICDS areas.

In order to study and monitor the benefits of the social components of the ICDS, a Central Technical Committee is constituted in the AIIMS and a Monitoring and Evaluation Division exists in the National Institute of Public Cooperation and Child Development (NIPCCD), New Delhi, Eleven Technical Institutions, like Home Science College and Colleges of Social Work are associated with the monitoriong and evaluation of the social components of the ICDS namely health and nutrition education, per school education and community participation.

(2) Other Programmes

The other important activities and programmes of the welfare department for child welfare are: Creches/Day Care Centre for children of working and ailing women, early childhood education Centre, Ananad pattern Integrated Family Welfare Programme, National Award for child welfare, celebration of Children's Day, public awareness programme through mass media agencies like radio, television, children's films, public exhibitions and other measures of publicity, and Mid Day Meal Scheme for school-going children. Adequate emphasis in being laid on cultural and recreational activities of children, also children's park, co-curricular activities in school, games and sports tournaments. Painting competitions, cultural programmes, children's publications. Shankar's weekly,

Doll's Museum, Children's Film Society, Bal Bhawans, Children's Libraries, Children's Fair, Holiday hours for children, Children's Book Trust etc. are all meant to provide cultural and recreational facilities for children.

The Welfare Department gives grants in aid to the institutions engaged in the field of child and women welfare.

Children Acts have been enacted by the State to wean away the children from crime. Reformatory institutions and children's homes have been opened.

An Indian Council for Child Welfare has been set up to formulate and monitor the child welfare programmes.

The National Institute of Cooperation and Child Development set up in 1975 is an autonomous body with three regional centres at Bangalore, Guwahati and Lucknow. Its main functions are: research and evaluation studies in public cooperation, women and child development, training of personnel engaged in social development; women and child development and allied activities ; dissemination of information pertaining to women and child development ; technical advice and consultancy in promotion of and implementation of policies and programmes for women and child development and liaison with international and regional agencies, research institutions and universities and technical bodies engaged in the activities similar to those of itself.

The efforts made by the Government and non-Government agencies for the welfare of children have touched only a fringe of the problem as yet. While central and state Government have allocated thousands of rupees for the welfare schemes of children yet only a paltry amount of 5 paisa out of a rupee is spent the rest going into the pockets of schemes operators. Corruption has eaten up the roots of Indian administration and not even spared the children welfare programmes. In order to accelerate the pace of child welfare and development, the plethora of legislation needs to be examined with a view to removing their lacuna. Their honest implementation in both letter and spirit is also imperative to give justice to children. Ground realities should not be swept under the carpet manipulative figures produced for political gain and media publicity should be condemned. Financial constraints, lack of adequate administrative organisation and shortage of qualified and trained personnel which constitute the other weakness of the child welfare programmes need be rectified to ensure better services to children. It is hoped that the movie *Slumdog Millionaire* winning eight Oscar Awards would stir the conscience of the government to save the children from leading a life of miserable poverty and despair.

Child Labour

An essential part in the study of children welfare programmes is the study of the problems of child labour. Hence we may now briefly look into this aspect of child welfare programmes.

At the outset it may be noted that the definition of "child" has kept changing from time to time and there is different age fixation for different types of work and also for getting benefit under the child welfare programmes. The Factories Act, 1948 defined child as a person who has not completed 12 years of age and prohibited the age of employment of children below the age of 14 in factories. The Constitution of India under Article 25 states; "No child below the age of fourteen years shall be employed to work in any factory or mine or engaged in any other hazardous employment. Thus it may be said that child is a person who is below the age of fourteen years.

Causes of Child Labour

The causes of child labour are mainly related to the problem of poverty in India. There are said to be 44 million child labourers of whom 7.5 million are below the age of 14. Though the Constitution contains provisions to protect such children against exploitation and provide them facilities to develop in a healthy manner yet these children live their childhood under inhuman conditions and virtual captivity. Thirty percent of people in India are living below the line of poverty.

Most of them do not get two square meals a day. They go to sleep hungry and sleep on the foot paths without any roof over their head. The parents can not afford to send their children to schools nor can they provide them nutritious food, healthy entertainment and joyful atmosphere. They live in congested area and dingy huts. The parental income is too meagre to support the family. Naturally, they have no option but to send their children to earn whatever they can in order to supplement the family income necessary for a living-half starved and half clothed.

Another cause of child labour may be abandonment of or loss of family. Sometimes parents themselves abandon their children and leave their home on account of family disputes. The girl child is often abandoned, even sold. The children in some cases suffer the loss of their parents on account of their death with no relative to support them. Under the circumstances they have to seek some job for their existence. In some cases the children may of their own on run away from their homes because their parents scolded or beat them.

Urbanisation has also played a role in increasing the number of child labour. On the one hand the growth of demand for cheap labour to meet the needs of industries mainly located in urban areas and on the other, the allurements of urban life have attracted the rural children to join the labour force in the cities and enjoy the pleasure of urban life.

It need not be emphasised that the working conditions of the child labour are very humiliating and depressing. They get meagre wages, sometimes they are paid no wages but are provided food and clothing only, are subjected to beating and atrocities, live in dark and dingy makeshift dwellings, get no facilities for entertainment and made to work for long hours, provided poor food including left overs, and are even sexually abused. The child labour particularly the girl child working in the household are open to cruelty and sexual exploitation. The child labour is cheap labour, hence much in demand by wayside eating shops, workshops and small factories, retail shops and households, hotels and restaurants, entertainment houses and film studios. In India a child labour can be seen working anywhere and every where – the railway station, the bus stops, the guesthouses and hotels wayside street shops, households, workshops, business houses and industrial establishments. The International Labour Organisation reports that India has 44 million working children, the highest in any country of the world. It constitutes one third of child labour in Asia and one-fourth of the world's working population. Whether it is a matter of pride or shame for us, let our leaders say.

Although it is illegal to employ children below a certain age, yet they are employed on quite a large scale as described above. The problems of child labour may be listed as follows:

(*i*) Longer hours of work and inadequate wages.
(*ii*) Lack of education
(*iii*) Lack of proper amenities and entertainment
(*iv*) Unhygienic and rigorous working conditions.
(*v*) Poor food lacking wholesome balanced diet.
(*vi*) Dark and dingy dwelling places.
(*vii*) Physical torture and cruelty.
(*viii*) Sexual abuse and exploitation
(*ix*) Employed mostly for menial and manual work with no bright prospects.
(*x*) Sooner or later fall in bad habits leading to criminal activities.

Remedial Measures

It is unfortunate that budding children aspiring to blossom in their childhood should be condemned to manual labour under sub-human conditions and suffer atrocities committed on them by their employers. It is a blot to their parents, community and the country. It is therefore, desirable that necessary measures be taken to enable the children to grow into happy, healthy and useful citizens. Following remedial measures can be suggested to meet the challenge:

(1) Alleviation of poverty: Since poverty is the root cause of child labour it needs to be eradicated. Various programmes of "Garibi Hatao" and for " Aam Admi' have been started, but there has been no marked improvement. Thousands of crores of Ruppes have been allegedly spent on these programmes, the situation on the ground remains the same. Corruption has entered into the soul of our leaders, rulers, administrators and programme implementers who have masqueraded a large portion of allocated money for various poverty removal programmes. Unless and until something substantial is done to remove the evil of corruption from the Indian political and administrative system, 'Aam admi' will never become 'Khas Adami'.

(2) Provision of free and compulsory Education: As the parents are poor, therefore they are perforced to send their children to find job in order to supplement the family income. They cannot afford to spend on the education of their children. It is therefore, necessary that the state should take effective measures in this direction. Article 45 of our Constitution states that the state should provide within a period of 10 years from the commencement of the constitution free and compulsory education for all children until they complete the age of 14 years. It is regrettable that even after six decades this provision of the Constitution has not been enforced effectively though the 86th amendments has made it a mandatory duty of the parents to send their children to a school. The government has implemented various schemes like Mid-Day meals or free food to the students in order to ensure their continuation in studies and has launched 'Sarva Shiksha Abhiyan just to encourage children to attend school yet a lot remains to be done to achieve the targets in real sense and not produce paper figures. To what extent the recently enacted "Right to Education Act" will help in this direction is yet to be seen.

(iii) Effective Enforcement of the constitutional Provision: Our Constitution specifically provides in Article 24 that no child before the age of 14 years should be employed to work in any factory or mine or engaged in any hazardous employment. Article 39 states that the health and strength of workers, men and women and the tender age of the children are not abused and the citizens are not forced by economic necessity to enter a vocation unsuited to their age and strength. As already referred the 86th amendment to the Constitution has made it mandatory duty of the parents to send their children upto the age of 14 years to the school for education. Child Labour Prohibition and Regulation Act, 1986 was enacted. A National policy on child labour was announced in August 1987. The government has also prohibited the employment of children as domestic servants and in tea shops and dhabas etc. A National Commission under Protection of Child Rights Act was set up in March 2007 to ensure proper enforcement of children rights and effective implementation of laws and programmes relating to children rights.

To conclude, it is the basic right of a child to get education and it is the statutory duty of the parents to send him to school for education. The poverty of the parents, however, becomes a compelling reason for them to send the child to earn a penny for survival of the family. It is evident that unless and until poverty is not eradicated the poor children of the country may not have a bright future.

(I) Welfare Measures for the Minorities: The National Commission of Minorities Act 1992 have notified five religious communities viz muslims, christian, sikhs, buddhist and zoroastrians (Parsies). Those minorities form 18.47 percent of the country's population. The Government has taken certain substantial measures for the welfare of the Minorities.

National Commission for Minorities (NCM): The NCM – a statutory body was set up in 1993 through the passage of National Commission of Minorities Act 1992. In November 2004 the NCM was granted constitutional status. A constitutional Amendment Bill (103rd) was introduced in the Lok Sabha on December 2004 for this purpose. The NCM stands for the protection of the rights and the interests of the minorities. Broadly the complaints of the minorities relate to atrocities of the police, service matters, minority educational institutions and disputes of religious places. The complaints are preused and reports are called for from the concerned authorities. On the receipt of the reports the Commission makes necessary recommendations to the authorities concerned.

Keeping in view the welfare needs of socially and economically backward sections of religious sections and linguistic minorities the Government of India constituted a National Commission for

Religious and Linguistic minorities. The NCRLM suggests (i) criteria for identification of socially and economically backward sections among religious and linguistic minorities.

(ii) Recommends measures for welfare of socially and economically backward sections among religious and linguistic minorities including reservation in education and government employment (iii) Suggest the necessary legal, constitutional and administrative modalities for implementation of their recommendations. (iv) and finally to present a report of their deliberations and recommendations:

Since, March 21, 2005 the commission has been functioning quite effectively.

Welfare of persons with disabilities: By 2005 National Policy for persons with disabilities was finalised. The policy focusses on the prevention of disabilities and the economic and physical rehabilitation measures for disabled persons. The Government and the other agencies are required to implement the policy for the welfare and amelioration of the lot of the disabled persons.

Persons with Disabilities Act, 1995-96: The Persons with disabilities Act was passed in Feburary 1996. The Act aims at prevention and promotional aspects of the rehabilitation of disabled persons. As such their education, employment, vocational training, creation of free environment, provision of rehablitator services for disabled persons besides, institutional services are to be rendered and supportive social security measures viz. unemployment allowance and grievances redressed machinary are to be adopted by both the central and the state governments.

Rehabilitation Council of India 1992: It is a statutory body which was set up under the Rehabilitation Council of India. Act 1992. The Council regulates the training policies and programmes for various categories of professionals in the areas of general rehabilitation and special education. Following are its main functions: (i) To standardise and regulate training courses at different levels in all the training institutes of the country (ii) to recognise the institutions and universities which act as training centre in the area of rehabilitation of the disabled within and outside the country on reciprocal basis. (iii) To promote research, in rehabilitation and special education.

(iv) To maintain a Central rehabilitation Register for professionals equipped with rehabilitation qualifications in the area of rehabilitation. (v) To encourage continuing Rehabilitation programme with collaboration in the areas of disability.

National Handicapped Finance and Development Corporation: The NHFDC is the apex level financial institution which extends credit facilities to persons with disabilities for their economic development. The disbursement of funds is done through the channelising agencies authorised by the state government, UT administration and non governmental organisations (NGOs). It also advances loans for pursuing education at undergraduate and higher levels. It also renders assistance in the upgradation of technical and other skills to enable the beneficiaries to manage their production units efficiently.

National Policy for Older Persons (NPOP) January 1999: The NPO announced in January 1999 to take care of the aged and their spouse. The main objective was (i) to encourage and exort the families to take care of their older family members (ii) to extend support to voluntary and NGOs to supplement the care provided by the family (iv) to provide health care facility to the elderly (v) to provide research and training facilities to the organisers of services to the aged (vi) To create awareness regarding elderly persons to develop themsleves into non-dependent citizens.

Inception of National Council for older persons: The government reconstituted the NCOP for older persons to advise and assist the government on framing policies and programmes for older person's. It in fact provides feedback to the government on the recommendation of NCOP. The NCOP is the highest body to render advice and coordinate with the Government on the formulation and implementation of policy and programmes for the welfare of the old the senior citizens.

Integrated programme for older persons: Under this scheme financial assistance upto 90 percent of the project cost is extended to the NGOs for establishing and maintaining old age homes, Day care centres, Mobile Medicine Units, and to make provision of non-institutional services to older persons.

***

[1] *India 2008 (A Reference manual) Govt. of India publication pt 900-902*

Major Issues in Indian Administration

> ......"*There is nothing more difficult to carry out, nor more doubtful of success, nor more dangerous to handle than to initiate a new order of things. For the reformer has enemies in all those who profit by the old order*".
> — ***Michiavelli***

CONTENTS : (A) Relationship between Political and Permanent Executive
(B) Generalist vs. Specialist
(C) Values in Public Services and Administrative culture
(D) Corruption in Public Services
(E) Redressal of Citizens' Grievances
(F) People's Participation in Administration
(G) Impact of Information Technology or Public Administrator
(H) Symbolic atom-impact or public administrator

India has opted for a parliamentary system of democracy. The ideas of democracy—progress, prosperity and protection of the common man—can be attained only through impartial, honest and efficient administration. An administrator should honestly serve the people without indulging in the game of political power. He should possess an agreeable personality and the ability to go along with the people. He should become the public's servant in the true sense of the word. The concept of welfare state has made increasing demands on public administration.

"Administration is a moral act and administrator is a moral agent" observed White. Such a thinking is the very base of transformation which is imperative in public administration in order to turn it into an effective instrument for ushering in an era of democratic welfare state. It is sad to note that public administration in India is baffled with various problems such as undue intervention of politicians in administration, lack of integrity among civil servants, widespread corruption in administration, peoples' apathy, absence of any effective machinery for redressal of citizens' grievances and the archaic structure of administrative machinery. In this chapter we propose to discuss some key issues of Indian Administration.

(A) RELATIONSHIP BETWEEN POLITICAL AND PERMANENT EXECUTIVE

It is an era of welfare states. Gone are the days when states were either instruments of tyranny or mere custodians of law and order. Nowadays the states not only protect and restrain but also foster and promote. As such, the role of the ministers, who work for the states has become of vital importance.

The ministers may not necessarily be embodiment of knowledge and competence. Anybody 25 years of age can get elected to the Parliament or state legislatures and thereafter if fortunes smile at him, become a minister. A socially tangible person, clever in art of canvassing or manoeuvering can sweep the polls. Administration requires expertise which a minister does not possess. Hence he banks upon his secretaries who have seen the tides of times and on account of rigorous training after their recruitment and vast experience, are fully acquainted with the ins and outs of the department. A minister being a layman cannot run the department entrusted to his care. The secretaries and other top services in the department give him or her judicious counsel. In fact, they lay down the policy, the minister in most cases signs the dotted line. An experienced minister goes a step further. He/She himself lays down broadlines of policy though the secretaries chalk out the details. The execution of policy also requires tact, courage and skill which of course the civil services possess in an ample measure. If they find a particular policy unworkable, they may point out flaws to the minister unreluctantly and suggest modifications in the policy. The minister will be judicious enough to accept their mature counsel as he/she is fully conscious of his/her limitation and the responsibility of efficient administration that he/her owes to the electorates. He/she won't unnecessarily reject their advice just to show his/her superiority knowing it fully well that his/her future prospects will be bleak if his administration earns denunciation at the hands of electorates.

Ramsay Muir has given a very analytical portrayal of relationship between ministers and civil services in these words, "Think of a newly appointed minister taking command of a great public department such as Ministry of Health or the colonial office. He has obtained the position because of his achievement in the general field of politics, because he is a good platform speaker or a good parliamentary debator or commands a great deal of social influence or is a prominent trade union organiser. In majority of cases he has no special knowledge of the immense and complex work of the department over which he is to preside. He has to deal with a body of officials who may be and often are men of far greater natural ability than himself. They bring before him hundreds of knotty problems for his decisions but of most of them, he knows nothing at all. They put before him their suggestions supported by the most convincing arguments and facts. It is obvious that unless he is either a self important ass or a man of quite exceptional grasp, power and courage......he will in 99 cases out of 100 simply accept their views and sign his name on the dotted line. In the 100th case, some question of party principle, some promise that has flourished on the platform may be involved. The officials, of course, know this. They perhaps point out the practical difficulties in the way of limited fulfilment of the pledges. They suggest to him a plausible compromise....They know that with one type of minister, they will have to go slow and that with the other types of minister they can suggest bolder devices....on the whole the policy of the office will nearly always prevail; its powers of quiet persistence and of quiet obstruction and its command of all the facts are irresistible except to a man of commanding power".

Ramsay Muir's analytical approach of relationship between the ministers and the civil services is very apt. A minister of exceptional grasp over the situation can alone ignore the advice of the civil services, otherwise in general he toes the line laid down by his secretaries. A dynamic personality like Jawaharlal Nehru could make the secretaries dance to his tune. Nobody had the courage to dictate terms to him. Shastriji, the next Prime Minister, had to bank upon his secretariat advice quite a great deal because of his limitations when compared with his predecessor. Mrs. Indira Gandhi in the initial stages leaned too heavily on L.K. Jha and later P.N. Haksar, her secretaries, as she did not muster clear majority in Lok Sabha and was shaky in administering national affairs. With the passage of time, she emerged to be a very dominant leader. She no longer got dictation from her secretaries in political or administrative affairs. Rather, she made them blow her trumpet. Rajiv Gandhi, her illustrious son being a politically novice banked upon bureaucrats to a great extent. Mrs. Sarla Grewal was one of such bureaucrats. The successive Prime Ministers were weak Prime Ministers or they did not have sufficient majority in the Parliament or headed a coalition government. Since the death of Rajiv Gandhi in May 1991, there have been five Prime Ministers during a period of twelve years. Thus no hard and fast line can be drawn regarding the extent of dependence of a minister over the civil services. However, it is wrong to presume that ministers are always subservient to the civil services on account of their limitations. The competence and calibre of the concerned

Prime Minister or a minister matter a lot. It will be indeed a sad day for democracy if the civil power represented through the ministers, is subordinated to the civil services.

The civil services are quite conscious of the fact that the ministers are cross examined on the floor of the House. A wrong advice by them can land a minister in difficulties. Evidently, they won't be able to save their skin if the minister is exposed on the floor of the House. They will be subsequently fired. Mr. Kaul, ex-Secretary of Lok Sabha, rightly points out, "When the minister is questioned on the floor of the House, the heart of the secretary is under constant palpitation in the lobbies". Thus, it is not correct to presume that civil services can become arbitraric and arrogate the authority to themselves or misguide the ministers. They know their place. They have to remain *incognito*. They cannot come in the lime-light. They are aware of ministers' leadership and also support by the majority party. If the Council of Ministers acts as a team, no minister can be defied or bypassed by his secretary. It is, therefore, rather an erroneous view to hold that in a social welfare state, democracy is misnomer, it is bureaucracy that rules. Both the ministers and the civil services have to work as a team for the socio-economic uplift of the masses. A.D. Gorwala has rightly remarked, "The relationship between the ministers and the official of whatever rank and between officials of various ranks is not that of master and servant but rather of senior and junior colleagues engaged on the same beneficial tasks".[1]

The Maxwell Committee (1937) observed, "We are emphatically of the opinion that the machinery of administration will not function smoothly unless the relations between a Minister who will be the political head of his department and the Secretary, who will be the chief of his staff for administrative purposes, are relations of mutual confidence and trust".

It is, however, sad that there has not yet fully developed a body of well-crystallised conventions regarding the relationship between the Minister and Secretary in India. While everyone agrees that there must exist a close and cooperative relationship between the two for the optimal efficiency of the ministry, in practice it has not been so possible. As a matter of fact, the history of confrontation between the Minister and Secretary goes back to the era of Montague-Chelmsford Reforms introduced under the Act of 1919. Prior to the Act, there was the Governor-in-Council in the provinces and there were no ministers popularly elected by the people. The Act of 1919 introduced the scheme of Dyarchy in the provinces under which the provincial subjects were divided into 'Reserved' and 'Transferred' subjects. The 'transferred subjects' were placed under the control of Ministers selected by the Governor from amongst the elected members of the state legislative council. There was no office of Chief Minister; the Governor acted as Head of the Government. He was the head of his Councillors as well as of his Ministers, the Ministers expected the civil servants to faithfully obey and implement their orders, for the civil servants as they belonged to the Indian Civil Service were not reconciled to their changed status. They did not show sincere loyalty to the provincial ministers. What was more depressing was that the ministers were humiliated by the members of the Indian Civil Service by their insubordinate and even defiant attitude in many matters".[2] They bypassed the Ministers and directly communicated with the Governor. Sir C.Y. Chintamani, who was a minister of Education in the United Provinces complained before the Reforms Enquiry Committee (1924) about lack of cooperation on the part of the Secretary. He even resigned on the issue. One of the reasons for the failure of Dyarchy in the provinces was the unwillingness on the part of the Indian Civil Service to cooperate with the ministers.

Under the Government of India Act, 1935, parliamentary system of government was introduced for the first time in the provinces. The ministers were selected by the Premier belonging to the majority party in the state legislature. He distributed portfolios among his colleagues. The Ministers, however, faced opposition from the civil services. The superior civil services were under the control

[1]*Report of the Committee on Organisation and Procedure, 1937, para 9.*
[2]*Pylee, M.V., "Constitutional History of India", pp. 66-67.*

of the Secretary of the State for India and, as such, their incumbents hardly cared for their new ministers. The civil servants were given special safeguards and the Governors in the provinces and the Governor-General at the Centre were there to protect their legitimate interests. When the new constitutional experiment started functioning in the Indian provinces, some of the senior public servants tendered their resignations. Most of the civil servants desired to create troubles for the popular ministers so that the new experiment would not last long. Thus, the Chief Secretary of United Provinces at his own instance issued a circular to the administrative officers that no order of a minister should be executed until it was countersigned by him or any one of the Secretaries. This situation could not be altered until Premier Pant called an explanation of the Chief Secretary and charged him with act of insubordination and incompetence.

During the early days of independence, the Ministers had to face problems as the civil servants, particularly of the higher rank, had entertained some strange views about their own position and wanted to run the administrative affairs according to their own directions. They found it difficult to adjust themselves to the changed political setup. Even the Prime Minister had difficulty in keeping these civil servants in check and getting his policies implemented.[1] But as things went by, the civil servants gradually found it advantageous to change their attitude and function as the Prime Minister wanted them to do.[2] They thought that it would be to their advantage if they are on the right side of the Prime Minister. Whatever cooperation the Ministers could get, was due to their own personality and position in the political hierarchy. Some Ministers being new to the administrative job preferred to follow the decisions of their Secretaries rather than to pick up quarrel with them and create a situation of confrontation. Some new officers also wanted to adjust themselves in the new positions acquired by them and followed the directions of their Ministers. Exceptions apart, the senior bureaucracy soon became a tool in the hands of political rulers and started serving the interests of their political masters rather than the public interests. There are also instances of shabby treatment being meted out by the Prime Minister / Ministers to the senior officials who failed to carry out the dictates of the former and tried to act independently. The treatment meted out by Sh. K. Hanumanthaiya, the Railway Minister in 1971 to Shri B.C. Ganguli—the then Chairman of the Railway Board and by Sri Rajiv Gandhi to the Foreign Secretary Sh. A.P. Venkateswaran are the instances of the worst kind in the history of Minister-Secretary relationships.

In short, relations between the Ministers and the Secretaries have not been as good as they should have been. The Administrative Reforms Commission remarked, "There is a disinclination among quite a number of Ministers to welcome frank and impartial advice from the Secretary or his aides and an inclination to judge him by his willingness to do what they wish him to do. Instances are not wanting of Minister preferring a convenient subordinate to a strong one and thereby making the latter not only ineffective but a sulky and unwilling worker. This has also bred a tendency on the part of an increasing number of civil servants to attempt to anticipate the minister's wishes and proffer their advice accordingly. A further development of this unhealthy trend is the emergence of personal affiliations leading to an element of "politicisation" among the civil servants. All these cut at the root of the healthy relationship".[3]

The reasons for the deteriorating relations between the Minister and the Secretaries are the following :

(*i*) The frequent changes in the portfolios of the ministers do not provide adequate time to both the minister and the secretary to develop proper trust and understanding.

(*ii*) Ministers do not often appreciate the value of independent advice and when the same has been unpalatable to them they feel the civil servants are putting hurdles in their way.

---

[1] *Sri Prakasha, Early Days in Pakistan – II : Public Men and Permanent Officials, The Hindustan Times, March 17, 1963.*

[2] *O.P. Motiwal (Ed) 'Changing Aspects of Public Administration in India', p. 67.*

[3] *Report on the Machinery of the Government of India and its Procedures of Work", ARC Report, 1968, para 56.*

(*iii*) Some of the officers are in the habit of exposing themselves and criticise the individual ministers or their respective policies in private and social circles which transpires to the political bosses who strongly react to the criticism.

(*iv*) Both the Minister and the Secretary lack proper understanding of their respective roles. Sometimes, ministers interfere in petty matters of day to day administration of the department, while the Secretaries on their part put through 'half baked' proposals before the ministers and important matters are not brought to their notice. Some bureaucrats have developed a nexus with the business magnates and shape their advice to their ministers accordingly.

(*v*) Ministers have often blamed their secretaries for their failures to give the impression that they were willing to do a certain thing but they were helpless because the officers of their department put unfavourable comments.

(*vi*) The group politics has filtered down to the civil services and some bureaucrats have come to be identified with a particular political party or a minister. Such bureaucrats ascend or descend the ladder of fortune the way as the political wind blows in the country. They have lost their impartiality, neutrality and credibility.

On account of the above reasons, the relations between the Minister and Secretary have not been smooth and the civil servants have to a great extent been demoralised. There is reluctance among them to offer advice without fear or favour. Even the officers known for their honesty and integrity have been subjected to shabby treatment. The Administrative Reforms Commission held that proper relations between the Minister and Secretary can be regulated, if on the part of the political executive there is "a proper understanding of administrative functions and recognition of its professional nature, with as little interference as possible in service matters, e.g. postings, transfers, promotions, etc. and discouraging officers of the department to see him personally for redress of service grievances; and there should be no requests for departures from declared and approved policies to suit individual cases" either as a result of political considerations or other considerations, which cannot be reduced to general principles of action."[1] So far as the services are concerned, the Commission has asserted that there must be a sincere and honest attempt to find out what the political head wants and the necessary adjustment in policies and proceedings may be made to suit his wishes; if a secretary holds an opinion different from that of his Minister, he should politely indicate the dissent and if he is over ruled in writing, he should willingly carry out his orders.

La Palombera has observed that 'the distinction between the political and administrative rolls must be understood and adhered to by both the minister and secretary.[2] The civil service is not concerned with policy. Its duty is to implement the policy and to act legally within the limits of power conceded to it. It is a neutral instrument of power.[3] The minister should refrain from involving the civil servants into political affairs and should play a constructive role. In the views of the ARC the Secretary should be loyal to the Minister and the latter should have confidence in the former. In the recent Past, the Urban Development Minister, Mr. Ram Jethmalani came into clash with his Secretary, Ms. Kiran Agarwal (September 1998) and divested her of all her responsibilities for refusing to implement the minister's decision by showing the rule book. In the Defence Ministry, indigenous air defence ship programme cleared by Mr. George Fernandes got struck because a note of dissent was appended to it by a Secretary-level officer, countering the logic of AD Ship. It is also reported that a group of bureaucrats misrepresented the facts and got passed a self-serving ordinance on the appointment of the Central Vigilance Commission. These instances are bad enough for smooth relations between the Ministers and the Secretaries.

---

[1]*Ibid, para 59.*

[2]*Joseph La Palombera (Ed) – Bureaucracy and Political Development, p. 24.*

[3]*B.B. Majumdar "Problems of Public Administration in India", (ed), p. 147.*

(B) GENERALIST VS. SPECIALIST

In the recent past, Generalist versus Specialist controversy has reached its climax. The specialists commonly termed as technocrats strongly feel that they are not being given due place in administration though on account of their expertise and technical qualifications, they happen to be superior to the so-called generalists. Hence, we find brain drain. The technocrats prefer to take up assignments abroad. They do not relish being ridden roughshod by bureaucrats who are non-specialists or non-technocrats though they claim to be 'Sir Oracles when they speak let nobody open his lips'. Before we come to any conclusion as to whether or not their claim is worth consideration, it is essential to explain the meaning of the terms 'specialist' and the 'generalist' and reveal the background which accorded the latter a higher status in our democracy.

Meaning of the Terms

These terms are well understood terms in science and technology. Generalist is one who has a bird's eye-view knowledge of science and technology. He takes a comprehensive view of the problem in science or technology and can render advice in general. He is in a position to provide the bridge between the various branches and sectors of science or technology as a whole.[1] In the words of Dr. White, "A generalist is a career person within the executive branch who by the breadth of this experience and the quality of his mind is competent to deal effectively with complex problems of relationship among agencies or officials and to apply judgement of a high discriminating character to difficult and obstinate problems....."[2] A generalist is not a policy-man as a rule but is concerned with the higher coordination and facilitating of operations. He is in a position to command detail while avoiding responsibility for detail and seeing far beyond it. Generally, he functions in the higher levels of middle management or in the lower levels of top management. In Great Britain, such a class of services is called Administrative class. In U.S.A. there is no special category of such officers though they are scattered through all the large departments. Occasionally, some of these administrative generalists may rise to political positions. Generally, they remain firmly anchored in the career service.

A specialist, on the other hand, is equipped with knowledge of science or technology in depth in one particular branch or sector. He is generally probing in depth in his limited field. He is not bothered about the place of his work in science or technology as a whole. In other words, the specialist by the nature of his work is myopic. His interest lies only in a small sector of science or technology and he persistingly probes into that sector in depth. He does not look at science or technology from a broad angle at all. He can see problems only from his limited angle as an Engineer, Doctor or Scientist. Unlike that of a Generalist, he cannot go down from the whole to the part. "The specialist has been described in somewhat derogatory terms as a man who knows more and more about less and less".

Neither description would be appropriate, although each contains a kernel of truth.[3]

Difference of their approach

The approach of the generalist, though in the expanding fields he is in touch with a broad sector of the field, is always comprehensive. He goes down from the whole to the part. His training is in overseeing and not in specialisation. He has to see the interplay between several sectors that is to be developed to utilise the finding in any one of the sectors. Thus the approach of the generalist is co-ordinative as against the intensive approach of the specialist. The generalist may occasionally

---

[1]*Sivaraman, B., "Generalist and specialist in Administration", an article in Indian Journal of Public Administration, July-Sept. 1971, p. 383.*
[2]*White, L.D., op. cit., (1968 ed.), p. 91.*
[3]*While, L.D., op. cit,. p. 91.*

take to the study in depth of some particular sector of his field but that does not affect change in his normal approach.[1]

The approach of the specialist, on the other hand, is intensive and not co-ordinative. Some of the specialists who possess an inborn aptitude to keep abreast of the world around them may acquire co-ordinative approach of the generalist. However, this branch of specialists is a rarity.

Background of controversy in India

The controversy over the role of the generalist and the specialist in administration is as old as administration itself. However, the generalist administrator is generally considered as the legacy of the British who used to employ youngmen of aristocratic families equipped with liberal education which could help them to lend wholehearted support to the imperial rule. The youngmen belonging to Indian Civil Service were thus the guardian of the Empire in its remotest corner. They were trained to be autocrats and keep up the dignity of their prestigious positions. The ICS (Indian Civil Service) cadre of the British days has been succeeded by the IAS (Indian Administrative Services) in the independent India. The new cadre of these officers was, however, not visualised as the successor to the ICS in spirit. They were supposed to be instrumental in promoting national integration and neutralising the divergent regional pulls. It was planned that these IAS officers would move from districts to state capitals, from there to the central secretariat and then back again. It was decided from the beginning that at least half of such officers belonging to a particular state cadre should belong to other states. This was done to avoid parochial approach to the problems and shun favouritism. These plans were quite laudable. They, however, did not take note of the rapid and multi-directional expansion in governmental activities, with the dawn of era of national reconstruction and development. Due to the multiplication of developmental activities, the government was forced to induct into its service the technocrats, the scientists, the engineers, technicians, and doctors etc. These technocrats made a substantial contribution to the country's developmental efforts but they could not attain the coveted top positions in the central secretariat or state hierarchy. Men like Dr. S.S. Bhatnagar and Dr. H.J. Bhabha have been exceptions.

This has led to the controversy as to why not the technocrats be allowed to hold the highest positions in the administrative hierarchy ? Why should the administrative services be given special weightage ? Administration, it is opined, is no longer a simple affair which can be handled by a person equipped with liberal education. The old story of a petty king who got pleased with a barber who could shave him in sleep without disturbing him and appointed him a Tehsildar—a Generalist post is those days—does not fit in the modern days of administrative complexities. Modern complicated administrative processes require a clear cut statement of service rules and conditions and a specialist abreast of these written codes or rules and regulations can do as good as a Generalist, in running modern administration.

Dr. Rajendra Prasad observed, ".....I see no reason why technical personnel and technical services should not be given the same emoluments and advantages as the country's service. I am sure sooner or later, it is bound to happen".[2] Y.B. Chavan, while addressing a meeting of the members of the Institute of Engineers at Patna, stated, "....the present role of the administrator is legacy of the British days. This situation must change now and the scientists, engineers and others with creative power must be given due place".[3] Delivering the convocation address at the Jadavpore University in 1960, Shri Jawaharlal Nehru said, ".....*it is wrong to think that people in the administrative service belong to some upper strata of society where others cannot reach. One can do away with administrators but cannot do without engineers. An engineer can work as an administrator but an administrator cannot work without engineers because he does not know the job at all.*" [4] Similarly,

---

[1]*Sivaraman, B., op. cit. p. 384.*

[2]*Presidential address at the meeting of the Central Board of Irrigation and Power, New Delhi on 27.11.1956, quoted in the Bulletin of the Bihar Engineering Services Association, Vol. II, June 1, 1973.*

[3]*Quoted in the Indian Journal of Political Science, 1962.*

[4]*Ibid : April-June 1975, pp. 161-162.*

Mrs. Indira Gandhi also remarked, "It is odd that the greatest doctors and engineers in the country who would be rated as the leaders of the profession and save lives and add permanent assets to the nation, can rarely hope to receive the pay or status of the secretaries of ministries. *The brightest of our youngmen choose engineering or medicine. If they happen to go into government, they are very soon overtaken by the general administrator. This must change*".[1]

The Estimates Committee of the Third Lok Sabha also argued in favour of assigning administrative responsibilities to the specialists. The Committee hoped that "Government would take practical steps to induct a large number of officers with technical background, training and experience as administrative heads of institutions, departments, ministries dealing with scientific, industrial and technical subjects. The Committee would also like the Secretaries of Ministries / departments to deal with matters of a technical nature in such a way that the technical advisors do not have the apprehension as expressed to the Second Pay Commission that their views do not get properly transmitted to the Minister. The Committee would like to observe that there is a widespread feeling among the services that the officers belonging to the ICS and IAS regard themselves as exclusive group, unnecessarily exacerbating feelings that generate inter-service rivalry. The Committee hopes that the members of the ICS and IAS would avoid such attitudes towards the other services and would, instead by their conduct set a high example of dedicated service which may inspire the other services".[2]

The specialist versus generalist controversy has reached new heights due to competition for senior and top management posts in public sector enterprises. The heavy losses being incurred by the public sector undertakings are attributed *inter alia* to their being headed by the generalists. Further, the Report of the Administrative Reforms Commission has added a new dimension to the controversy. The Commission recommended that a functional field be carved out for the Indian Administrative Service. This should consist of land revenue administration, exercise of magisterial functions and supervisory work in the states in the fields other than those looked after by other functional services. All posts in a functional area, whether in the field or in the secretariat, should be staffed by members of the corresponding functional services.

The demands of the specialists are mainly two : parity with the IAS in the matter of pay-scales and service conditions; and access to administrative positions at the policy-making levels in government. It is due to the prevailing disparity between the pay-scales and service conditions and also the social status of the specialists and generalists that more and more professionals like medical, engineering and management graduates are entering the IAS. According to available data, only four doctors were recruited in 1977, as against 38 a decade later. The number of engineers swelled from 54 in 1977 to 175 in 1987. During 1990 examination, of the 107 who made it to the IAS, 50 were engineers and seven doctors. Twenty of the engineers were IIT graduates. During 1991 examinations of the first 20 in the merit list of the IAS, 12 were engineers, one a doctor and another a veterinarian. This not only creates a drain on the public exchequer which subsidises the professional education, but also results in denial of seats in professional institutions to those who actually desire to become engineers or doctors. There is already a shortage of doctors in per capita terms, especially in the rural areas, so their joining the non-technical services is a setback to the profession as well as to the country. The professionals should be given better pay scales and service conditions in their own fields so that the civil services do not appear to be an attractive alternative proposition.

The administrative positions in the specialist organisations, for example, up to the Directorate level must be filled from amongst the specialist personnel themselves and the practice of appointing members of the IAS as heads of executive organisations must be discontinued. In India the IAS are being appointed as Vice-Chancellors and Registrars of Universities which looks very odd.

We discuss below the arguments advanced by the apologists of both the Generalist and the

[1]*Quoted from R. Rastogi "The IAS and other Services", The Times of India, 11 Nov. 1972.*
[2]*Ninety-third Report of the Estimates Committee, pp. 53-54.*

Specialists before coming to our conclusion.

Arguments for Generalists

(a) A Generalist is known for broad vision and capacity for leadership. He possesses imagination, drive, initiative and enterprise for quick decisions. As such, he alone can advise the Minister—a layman of course—on political aspects of a plan the technical aspects of which already been taken care of at comparatively lower levels. On the other hand, an expert or a technocrat has myopic vision and a stereotyped mentality. Hence his specialised knowledge may prove as a liability rather than an asset. This specialised knowledge may rob him of the proper perspective when envisaging the plan. At the higher level general rather than technical knowledge is essential for getting things done.

(b) A Generalist's approach even if it is portrayed as a layman's approach is an asset to the administration, because it enables him to express proposals and decisions in a way which is easily carried out by the lower administrative machinery.

(c) A Generalist clears the mess created by the ministers, the legislators and the experts and quells the mob fury which may ensue due to such a mess and prove detrimental to the country. Thus far from suffering from inflated ego, they serve the community in the true sense. A politician makes a promise to the people, but after his triumph in the elections he does exactly the opposite. It leads to agitation. The Generalist bears the brunt of the mob fury. Likewise the legislators pass a law which is detested by the people. The Generalist is again faced with predicament. A technocrat builds a factory which fails to function well. The minister is put in the dock on that account at the hands of the parliamentarians. It is the Generalist who comes to the rescue of the ministers by supplying the ministers cogent and palatable answers. Meeting of such situations requires tactfulness, a broader angle of vision and flexibility which the specialists generally lack.

(d) It is contended that a Generalist is comparatively more suited for the Secretariat and departmental posts in the State and at the Centre, as he has to play the role of adviser to the elected government. An adviser must be acquainted with the whole spread of problem before he renders advice to the government on important policy matters. In the words of Sivaraman, "Unless the adviser has the experience and the knowledge of the field at grass-roots and at the same time has a broad grasp of administration as a whole in the State, his advice is valueless.[1] It is emphasised that there are many specialist fields in the State where the adviser knows only his field of specialisation and none others. The Generalist comprehending the interplay and political forces in the various parts of the State, having varied experience in the Generalist field of work in the State, serves as a better adviser than a Specialist in the state.

(e) It is stated by the protagonists of the generalists that an all India cadre approach alone suits our Federal structure. Federation stands for the welfare of the people. The States generally resent that Central policies ignore the local difficulties and problems and not attend to area disparities. Federation in a vast country like India is apt to be a failure if the adviser at the Centre is not aware of the conditions in the field in his portfolio, in any part of the country. A Generalist who is supposed to work in any part of the country possesses a detailed knowledge of the field. Hence he will be able to cater to the needs of the masses more properly. It is, however, admitted that in certain fields the Specialist may prove a better adviser because of his expertise and specialized knowledge. Such fields are generally limited and the Specialists in these fields have already been given due recognition.

(f) The Generalist alone is competent enough to hold management positions in public sector enterprises. He is more committed to the enterprise than a private sector entrant on a term contract. The manager in a public sector, in fact, has to make use of only part of administrative art of which Generalist is the embodiment.

---

[1]*S. Sivaraman, B. (ICS Retd.), op. cit., p. 391.*

(g) The Generalist is apt to prove better than non-technical Specialist as the field of the vision of the latter is narrower than the former. Moreover, in-service training can enable the Generalist to be in tune with the times and cope with the ever-increasing field of operation.

(h) The Generalist suits a democratic setup. He is open to convictions. As such, he will not have the tendency of aggrandisement. He will be more co-operative with the ministers and accept the superiority of the political boss unreluctantly. The Specialist, on the other hand, will be less co-operative and have the tendency to assert. It may affect efficiency of administration as the political bosses may remain at loggerhead with the specialists as the heads of the Departments.

Arguments for Specialists

Administrative Reforms Commission of India and Fulton Committee of U.K. were strongly of the view that in this age of technology and ever-developing science, the departments should be headed by the Specialists rather than the Generalists. The protagonists of technocrats also hold similar views on the grounds stated below :

(a) It is contended that appointing Generalist as the secretary of Government department concerned with the technical subjects to assist the minister who himself is a layman is like the blind leading the blind for instance. It looks anomalous that the Minister for Irrigation and Power himself is advised by a secretary who is a layman — a Generalist—while technologists equipped with specialized knowledge of the subject play a second fiddle. It is apt to affect adversely the working of the Department.

(b) It is wrong to presume that the generalist has a monopoly of good sense and he alone can evaluate and co-ordinate plans and projects and understand their economic and political implications. Further, it is a myth promoted by the Generalist that he alone can make things intelligible to the people. An appraisal of the reports of Union Public Service Commission clearly reveals that the number of first class graduates recruited to IAS has been only about 40 per cent of the total. On the other hand, the number of first class graduates joining the other technical government departments has been twice as high. This reflects that the IAS do not necessarily have higher mental calibre than the technocrats. Rather the latter have been comparatively more intelligent. The technocrats on account of their technical accomplishments and rigorous and intensive training which the Generalist owing to their constant mobility from one department to the other cannot get are, in fact, more capable of handling the plans and projects and dealing with the masses.

(c) It is further asserted that our public sector enterprises headed by the Generalists have become breeding centres of gross mismanagement. It has resulted in heavy losses and consequently a big drain on the national exchequer. On the other hand, a technocrat like Dr. Bhabha proved administrator of great acumen. He was responsible for putting the Atomic Energy Commission on its feet and building up an organisation, we are all proud of.

(d) The critics do not accept the version that the Generalists alone can look financial and political aspects of problems. The political aspect of a problem is not the concern of administrative leadership. It is to fall in the domain of political leadership, *i.e.*, the ministers. The financial aspect can be looked into better by a financial expert rather than a layman—a Generalist — whose only claim to expertise is inflated ego.

(e) It is pointed out that due to emergence of concept of welfare state, the role of administrator has undergone a change. He is no longer concerned simply with the maintenance of law and order and supervising those working under him. He is to perform welfare functions on behalf of the government. As such, he has to manage the economic life of the country as well. This has resulted in inflating his ego and adding to his sense of self-importance. Hence he stands alienated from the people. Thus the gap between the people and the government which is a relic of the alien's rule still persists. The government of independent India is described as a government of the bureaucracy, by the bureaucracy and for the bureaucracy. It has failed to adapt itself to the evolving socialist society of ours. The bureaucrat-politician nexus has destroyed the social fabric and given rise to high mounting corruption. The law and order situation is grave and the country is in the grip of financial bankruptcy. There is hardly any governance in the country worth its name. The generalist administrator has failed on all the fronts. He has become an epitome of self-aggrandisement. Hence, a Generalist must be replaced by a Specialist who alone can keep pace with the challenges of the fast moving technological world.

Fulton Committee in its report held a similar view. They opined that to meet the increasing demands of people in the modern state, the civil services must be far-sighted and must make use of their accumulated knowledge and experience and must be able to take initiative in analysing the needs of the future and meeting them adequately. Criticising the prevalent Generalist concept, the committee said, "*The concept has most damaging consequences. It cannot make for the efficient despatch of public business, when keymen rarely stay in one job longer than two or three years before being moved to some other post, often in a very different area of government activity....The cult (Generalist cult) is obsolete at all levels and in all parts of the service.*[1] *Hence the Committee recommended that "a wide and more important role must be opened up for specialists trained and equipped for it*".[2]

(f) The adherents of 'cult of specialists' contend that the specialist who trains himself to deal with his specialisation in depth and has more interest in the art of analysis and synthesis should not be relegated to the position of comparative inferiority in the policy making hierarchy. He should be assigned a role commensurate with his capability and technical expertise.

(g) The critics are not prepared to accept the theory of Generalist having comprehensive grasp of the entire field of administration. Such administrators are rarely born. They can never be so built up by any known method of administrative development. Hence it is better to bring experts in several sectors together in order to analyse administrative problems and evolve a solution. No worthwhile reforms are possible till the hold of generalist on policy-making is broken.

(h) A specialist as an adviser to a lay politician may prove better, he may not be a suppliant tool and a mere yesman. On account of his expertness and professional training he may succeed in convincing the political chief and thus follow a correct line of action. Such an ideal combination of laymen and experts may result in efficient functioning of democracy. The politicians have vested interests in a generalist administration.

Administrative Reforms Commission's View

As already said, the Administrative Reforms Commission (Govt. of India) appraised the problem of Generalist vs. Specialist in its report on Personnel Administration. It realised the necessity of the change in the role of the Government and keeping in view the great diversification of its functions called for induction of a variety of skills in the higher administration. The ARC made following observations in this direction.

(a) A rational system of filling policy advice positions with men possessing the required qualification and competence needs to be devised. This will mean a fuller use of different services for secretarial work.

(b) Senior management posts may be selected from all the relevant sources—the Generalist and the Specialists. The talent needs to be discovered and developed in all the cadres specially among those who have not hitherto been inducted into the higher administration to any significant degree.

(c) A rational pay structure should be adopted so as to reflect actual responsibilities borne in each job.

[1]*Report, Fulton Committee on Civil Services, 1966-68, London, Chapter 1, p. 11.*
[2]*Ibid, Chapter II, p. 26.*

(d) In order to tone up morale throughout the personnel system, much greater scope than what now exists needs to be created for talent in the lower ranks to move up to higher positions in the civil service on the basis of competence and performance.

(e) The commission broadly classified the higher services into two categories (i) posts in the field, (ii) posts at headquarters. Posts in the field should be occupied by functional services which comprise not only technical services equipped with pre-entry vocational education like Engineering services but also those which specialise after entry in a particular area of administration (such as the Accounts, Income Tax, etc.). The Commission recommended that a functional field pertaining to Land Revenue Administration, exercise of magisterial functions and regulatory work in the states in fields other than those looked after by other functional services recently created and relating to specific functions should be filled by the professionals like engineers, scientists, doctors and economists who possess subject-matter competence.

The Commission rightly concluded, "The Generalist has his place and an important one at that, in the scheme of things, so has the specialist, the scientist and the technologist. In a growing democracy, committed to rapid socio-economic development, the administration has to be good no less than it has to be effective, if a good administration is imperative for the happiness and welfare of the people, an effective administration is a pre-requisite for the strength and prosperity of the country. This twin purpose needs the devoted services of the specialists no less than those of the generalists.....". The Commission went to the extent of suggesting that "preference for the generalist ...should give place to a preference for those who have acquired competence in the concerned field".[1]

Conclusion

The observations made by the Administrative Reforms Commission are worth consideration. The ARC has rightly diagnosed the malady. Too great a reliance on the Generalist is detrimental to the interest of efficiency of administration particularly in the fields of public enterprises and technological development. The bureaucrats having become attuned to red tapism and rule book fail to efficiently manage these fields where a different sort of professional approach is needed. Consequently, the developmental plans suffer and the interests of common man are lost sight of. There is a dire need of inducting the specialists and technical personnel in the top government services. However, they may be assigned only advisory role and not be integrated into the decision-making hierarchy as they may fail to handle men and matters involved in relationship with other departments. We may, therefore, conclude that the administrative services must no longer remain the close preserve of a handful of Generalists—the so-called elite of the country. A maximum utilisation of all available talent necessitates the abolition of artificial discrimination between the Generalists and the Specialists. The agitation for a position of precedence and parity of pay scales is apt to end if the government pays adequate attention to the recommendations of ARC and accords a right place to the Specialists which they richly deserve. Inter-service co-operation is the crying need of the hour. Such a co-operation will prove much more fruitful and productive if it is based on mutual respect and profound regard for each other rather than a sense of superiority or inferiority. Mutual respect and reciprocity is possible if proper status is conferred upon the hitherto neglected technical man, and the latter does not create more irritants by resorting to agitation.[2]

Somehow, in Indian polity the Generalists have been able to hold their ground. The reasons are not far to seek : (*i*) The ministers are apprised of two lines of advice — that of the Generalists and the Specialists — on a particular issue. The Specialist is said to be over-enthusiast. As such he disqualifies himself to this extent from arriving at a final decision. (*ii*) The IAS Generalists

---

[1]*Report on Personnel Administration as incorporated in Administrative Reforms Commission's Report, p. 19.*

[2]*Dr. S.K. Sharma, Paper on Higher Civil Services Policy Formulation, Third Pay Commission view, read in the 17th Annual Conference of the Members, Indian Institute of Public Administration.*

monopolise all realms of higher administration, assisted actively by a caucus of the department of personnel. Since the Cabinet Secretariat and the Prime Minister's office are also IAS monopolies, they succeed in manipulating things to their advantage. The fifth pay commission was faced with the unseemly controversy of Generalist vs. Specialists which has been charged with giving 'step-motherly' treatment to non-IAS officers. It appears that Generalist vs. Specialist controversy is not going to die so long as the role of specialist is not fully appreciated in the context of the developmental administration and technological development being the need of the hour.

However, the Generalists will have to be made more knowledgeable and more efficient in the performance of their assigned tasks. Besides, the Administrative services must acquire specialisation by choosing an area of administration and receiving an indepth specialised training in that area. They should be allowed to stay there for considerable period in order to gain requisite experience. Their transfers too should be limited to linking fields. The future administrator should be a blend of a 'modest measure of technical competence' and a high degree of administrative skill. Efforts may also be made to choose generalist administrators out of Specialists who have exhibited administrative acumen. A staff College on the pattern of the Hyderabad Staff College may be setup to formulate suitable administrative and 'de-specialisation' training courses for such specialist administrators. At present, good Generalists and good Specialists constitute a rare commodity in the administrative services.

(C) VALUES IN PUBLIC SERVICES AND ADMINISTRATIVE CULTURE

Every organization, public or private, has certain rules and regulations governing the conduct or behaviour of its employees. For employees of the government who belong to public services it is of importance that they conscientiously follow the code of conduct and maintain integrity and discipline.

Conduct Rules in India: Conduct rules for public services generally relate to

(a) Maintenance of good behaviour towards superiors and citizens.

(b) Protection of integrity and impartiality of the officials.

(c) Observance of certain code of ethics in the private life of the official.

(d) Regulation of political activities of officials.

Some of the important conduct rules are as follows.

(1) Every member of the service shall maintain integrity and devotion to duty.

(2) No member of the service shall, except with the previous sanction of the Government, permit his son, daughter or dependent to accept employment with firms with which he has official dealings, or with other firms having official dealings with government.

(3) No member of the service shall, except with the previous sanction of the Government, permit his son, daughter or dependent member of the family to accept from any person gift, or ask for or accept contributions to, or otherwise associate himself with the raising of any in pursuance of any object whatsoever.

(4) No member of the service shall, except with the previous sanction of the Government, engage directly or indirectly in any trade or business or undertake any employment. No member of the service shall speculate in any investment. No member of the service shall make or permit his wife to make any investment (lending or borrowing of money) likely to embarrass, or influence him in the discharge of his official duties. No member of the service shall, except with the previous knowledge of the Government, acquire or dispose of any immovable property by lease, mortgage, purchase, sale, gift, or otherwise either in his own name or in the name of any member of the family. A member of the service who enters into any transaction concerning any movable property exceeding one thousand rupees in value, whether by way of purchase, sale or otherwise shall forthwith report

such transaction to the Government. Every member of the service and thereafter at the interval of every twelve months, shall submit a return to the Government of all immovable and movable property held by him.

Neutrality in Politics

Public servants should serve the government and not a particular party. The fortunes of civil services should not be connected with the rise and fall of political parties. Neutrality in politics is necessary for maintaining the integrity and effecting efficiency of administration. Political neutrality is the hallmark of Indian administrative service. A civil service man is debarred from indulging in activities of a political nature or canvassing for political support. He does possess the right to vote but he has to exercise it secretly. His political beliefs are supposed to be his private concern. He is supposed to be loyal to any political party that is victorious at polls. Permanence of tenure and peaceful contented stay at a station necessitates aloofness from politics. However, the concept of neutrality is not to be invoked to shield non performance, poor performance or shoddy performance. Following are some of the rules pertaining to political neutrality:

(1) No member of the service shall be a member of or be otherwise associated with any political party or any organization which takes part in politics nor shall he take part in, subscribe in aid of, or assist in any other manner, any political movement or activity.

(2) No member of the service shall canvass or otheriwse intefere or use his influence in connection with, or take part in, an election to any legislature or local authorioty.

(3) No member of the service shall, in any radio broadcast or in any document published annoymously or in his own name, or in the name of any other person or in any communication to the press, or in any public utterance, make any statement of fact or opinion which has the effect of an adverse criticism of any current or recent policy or action of the Central Government or a State Government or which is capable of embarrassing the relations between the Central Government and the Government of any State or which is capable of embarassing the relations between the Central Government and the Government and the Government of any foreign state.

(4) No Government servant shall, except in accordance with any general or special order of the Government or in performance in good faith of the duties assigned to them, communicate directly or indirectly any official document or information to any Government servant or any other person to whom he is not authorized to communicate such document or information.

In 1964 some more rules were added which are as follows:

(i) Every government servant holding supervisory post shall take all possible steps to ensure the integrity and devotion to duty of all government servants working under him.

(ii) No government employee shall use his position or influence directly or indirectly to secure employment for any member of his family in any private undertaking.

(iii) No government employee shall in the discharge of his official duties deal with any matter or give or sanction any contract to any undertaking or any other person if any member of his family is employed in that undertaking or under that person or any member of his family is interested in such matter or contract in any other manner.

(iv) No Government servant shall engage himself or participate in any demonstration which is prejudiced to the interests of sovereignity and integrity of India, the security of the state, public order, decency or morality or which involves contempt of court, defamation or incitement to an offence.

(v) No government servant shall join or continue to be a member of an association, the object or activities of which are detrimental to the interests of the sovereignty and integrity of India or public order or morality.

An Evaluation

Above we have mentioned the Civil Service Conduct Rules, 1965 and revised thereafter from time to time. Human nature being a blend of vice and virtue need to be tied up under a prescribed code of conduct and discipline. In the case of private individual they are tied down to their religious or social code, whereas the government employees are duty bound to follow the Civil Service Conduct Rules formulated by the Government which in some matter may even be opposed to their religious or social code. A high moral standard of conduct on the part of public services is called for so as to set an example for the people and to run the public administration efficiently and impartially.

It is however a sad fact that public services in India have failed to cultivate high standards of conduct. There are far more lapses on the part of our civil servants. Corruption in civil services is widely rampant. The disproportionate wealth possessed by bureaucrats of the status of chief secretary of a state or chairman of Delhi Milk Scheme., Vice-Chairman of Delhi Development Authority and officers involved in fodder scam case, Jain Hawala case, security scam case and several such other cases speak volumes about the extent of corruption in the Indian Administration. Corruption among public services has become a national problem. There is a deep conspiracy of interests between the politicians and the top civil services who indulge in corrupt practices with a sense of impunity. So far as the lower level employees are concerned the least said the better. One cannot get even one's water connection sanctioned without bribing those authorised to sanction it.

The irony is that India's Civil service is one of the oldest among modern nation-states, set up by its colonial rulers even before Britain got its civil service in 1854 and the United States in 1872. Yet ours is ranked among the top ten corrupt bureaucracies. What we need to free our civil services from the evils of corruption is not only to reform our administrative system and rid it of the evils of red-tapism, procedural delays and vexatious regulations but also to recruit people of competence and integrity, with the spirit of public welfare and give them proper training to meet the challenges of a developing country in different fields. It may also be added that civil servants should self-cultivate professional standards, ethics, attitudes and ideology of public service.

It may also be emphasized that for the achievement of high professional values the responsibility cannot be entirely placed upon the shoulders of the official. The official works in the society in which bribery, political corruption, business criminal nexus, nepotism, favourtism, psychophancy, caste divisions, lawlessness and low public morality exist. A society in which these evils exert cannot have a chaste civil service. The society, therefore, must reform itself. However, the public official can play an effective role in this direction. He is a part of the society but at the same time he is the philosopher and guide suggesting and correcting society. He himself should set high moral standards before the people. In a democracy, all the officials of government are responsible to the people. They must answer to their own consciences, to their own sense of dignity, to the opinion of their fellowmen and to their hopes of esteem for the record they leave behind them. And finally, they should not leave any stone unturned in their honest efforts to work for the total welfare of the people for whom they have been appointed to serve.

Administrative Culture

The word 'culture' is a complex word not to be easily defined as culture differs from group to group. However, it may not be denied that culture is a universal phenomenon which marks every group, nation or society. Thus we use the words Hindu culture, Muslim culture, Indian culture, Western Culture, economic culture, political culture and administrative culture, Administrative culture denotes the attitudes, norms and values, ideals and perceptions and patterns of behaviour of the administrators who constitute a compact group. It is a conglomeration of values, orientations, beliefs, dispositions and its central concern is the perception of the administrative system by the public at large.

India's Administrative Culture

India at the time of independence in 1947 got from the British rulers a system of administration marked by integrity, impartiality, neutrality and efficiency. The bureaucrats of the British rule in India rendered their best advice and never indulged in politiking and criminality. For some years after the Britishers left India the administrators continued to follow the British model of administration. But, thereafter, changes began to take place gradually and slowly with the consequence that Indian administration is now categorised the most corrupt one. The politicians became power hungry and in order to capture power compelled the bureaucracy to change its basic values of honesty, integrity and neutrality. The bureaucracy too became subservient to the political clan and instead of working for the people started serving their interests and of their political masters. There developed a close nexus between the political master and bureaucrat for common interests and benefit. The bureaucrat lost his commitment to the development efforts and adopted the role of committed bureaucracy Expediency values emerged. Loyalty to the nation was displaced by loyalty to political leadership. The bureaucracy got bosses belonging to one or the other political party. Selection of competent senior administrator for the highest post became a thing of the past. Honest and dedicated officers with traditional bureacratic values were relegated to the background. Caste factor also came into play. Caste favouritism, regional considerations, linguistic affiliation came to be openly practised in different spheres of administration. The people came to talk openly and publicly about the politician-bureaucrat-businessman nexus. The political leader needed huge Mass transfer to purchase elected candidates in order to get the requisite majority to form the governments. This money came to him from the business class through bureaucrats. Money of the officers after elections became a usual affair. Those who favoured the party coming to power got lucrative postings while those who did not support it or gave no money for election fund were sent to remote areas or non-lucrative posts.

Subordinates also followed the footsteps of their superiors. There was a price for moving a file or getting any other favour. Running after the file has become a part of our administrative culture. There also developed a barrier of communication between the higher and lower bureaucracy as the subordinate one did not want to take decision himself to avoid responsibility. At the same time, there is a tendency on the part of the senior officer to endorse the note put up the subordinate. The Indian administrative culture is marked by slowness and red tapism. There is also a reluctance on the part of the superior officer to delegate power to his junior. He believes in bureaucratic domination. Bureaucratic arrogance is another trait of administrative culture Visitors keep waiting for long hours to see the officer even during public visiting hours. Further, officers are not available to the visitor as they are busy either with meeting or on tours. The Indian administration lays more emphasis precedents, rules and regulations. Even in emergency they ask for rules before taking any action. They ignore the crisis situation. The administrative procedure is too cumbersome. Another feature is too many reviews and references. A decision is reviewed at too many levels by too many person in too many organs of government in too detailed too repetitive and too negative terms. Fault finding has become a normal trait of administrative procedure. More emphasis is laid on letter of the law caring on its sprit. Any mistake in the type may throw back a file caring little that it is a bonafide rather than mistake and can be corrected by the official. Some of the dysfunctional characteristics of the webrian model still persist with our bureaucracy. It continues to be means oriented than result oriented Administrative culture. To cut short, the Indian administration despite democratic political system is wedded to feudialistic culture.

In the end, Rajiv Gandhi may be quoted on what he had to say about contemporary administrative culture in a speech delivered on December 28, 1985 "...and what of the iron frame of system, the administrative services and the myriad functionaries of the state? but as the proverb says there can be no protection if the fence starts eating the crop. This is what has happened. The fence has started eating the crop. We have government servants who do not serve but oppress the poor and the helpless, who do not uphold the laws but connive with those who cheat the state. They have no work-ethic, no feeling for the public cause, no involvement in the future of the nation. They have only a grasping mercenary outlook, devoid of competence, integrity and commitment".

It may however be emphasised that culture is not something imported or transplanted. It does not grow overnight. It takes several years, even centuries to replace the old cultural values. India after getting independence from British rulers embarked on the way to development and adopted the path of secular and socialistic democracy which require a service oriented, public oriented and integrity oriented administrative culture. That Indian administration should show such orientation need not be emphasized.

TRANSPARENCY AND ACCOUNTABILITY IN INDIAN ADMINISTRATION

The two important values of Public Administration in a democracy are the values of transparency and accountability. By transparency is meant that the government decisions should not be shrouded in secrecy and the facts thereof should be open for public examination. Our bureaucurats, style of functioning has not changed much from the colonial style which was mostly non-transparent. A bureacurat in democratic India should give up his colonial out look a legacy of the colonial rule and have a genuine desire to be transparent and responsible for his actions. A transparent system of administration will be quite helpful to eradicate the evils of red-tapism, delay, corruption and arbitraness. Like wise accountability wild add to efficiency and honesty in administration as the officer will be held responsible for any wrong or injury caused by his acts of omission and commission.

Right to Information Act 2005: An important step taken by the Government of India to make public administration transparent and accountable is the enactment of Right to Information Act in 2005. Right to information is guaranteed implicitly in the Constitution but this Act makes a provision for practical regime for the citizens to secure access to information on all matters of governance. Evidentlly, the Act makes public administration accountable and the decision making process participatroy.

Scope of the Act: The Act extends to all levels of governance and as such has the widest coverage. It applies to the Union, State and local governments– urban and rural and public authorities. It also covers the authorities which happen to be recipient of government grants. There are minimal exemptions first to protect the national interests. However all exempted organisations are also within the purview of right to information by the people if the matter asked for pertains to human rights violation or corruption. Hence it will not be incorrect to hold that the enactment is all comprihensive. Recently on January 6, 2008 the Central Information Commission (CIC) ruled that apex court including the Chief Justice are not exempt from the RTI.

The Act as such is the most progressive of all legislation. The citizens while seeking information are not required to establish their locus standi. The Act overrides all other Acts contrary to it including the Official Secracy Act.

Procedure for seeking information: The procedure for invoking the right to information is very simple. The concerned person has to make a request to the public information officer concerned on a simple paper. The request must indicate the information required and the address on which it is to be communicated. The request is to be made either personally or communicated by post in English or Hindi or in the official language of the area. Through e-mail also the request can be made.

The applicant has to pay RTI fee of Rs. 10 per application either in cash or through bank draft or postal order along with the application.

The applicant can inspect the documents. It also permits the applicants to collect samples of various work.

If the applicant does not receive any intimation within 30 days after receipt of application and within 48 hours if information is concerned with life and liberty or the applicant is dissatisfied with the reply, he can make a first appeal within 30 days to the appellate authority an officer immediately superior to the public information officer. The appellate authority is required to decide the appeal within 30 days of the receipt of the appeal. No fee is payable if the applicant is still not satisfied with the decision of the appellete authority he can appeal second time to the Central Information Commission or the State Information Commission as the case may be within a period of 90 days. The Central Information Commission entertains appeals in case of Public Sector Undertakings or financial institutions under the Central Government and the union territories whereas state Information Commission entertains appeals concerning officers, financial institution, Public Sector Undertaking under the State Government.

Both the Central and State Information Commissions are high powered, independent and impartial commissions. These Commissions are empowered to impose penalties upto Rs. 25000 on the public information officers if they deny information deliberately.

The Government is, however, of the view that the Act has transformed the regime of secrecy into the regime of openness. It's not that information shall be supplied only when a person requests for it. Rather every public authority in order to diseminate maximum possible information is obliged to publish large quantum of information in respect of its organisation "suomotu" so that the public has minimum need to resort to seek information from the public authorities.

Exemption earlier granted

The Central Government has exempted security agencies from seeking information under the RTI' Act except for corruption and human rights violation. The Public Information Office can also reject an application under section 8 and 9 of the Act Section 8 outlines categories of information exempt from the Act *i.e.* data relating to national security. Section 9 refers to disclosure of information if that infringes copy right.

Chief Justice and judges not exempt from RTI January 6, 2008

There has been some doubt as to whether the judges of Apex court or Chief Justice of India can refuse some information. Decision on Jan. 6,2008 makes it crystal clear. As referred earlier the CIC bench headed by Chief information Commissioner Wajahat Habibullah in a decision having far reaching consequences ruled 'the apex court' is not exempt from the Right to Information Act. "The Chief Justice India too will have to provide information under the Act' The CIC remarked" The institution and the head cannot be two distict public authorities. They are one and the same information therefore available with the CJI must be deemed to be available with the Supreme Court also.

Evidently RTI's scope has widened still more after this decision. The Judiciary has been under constant pressure to be more transparent and ready to be open to the public scrutiny.

How land mark ruling emerged?

The landmark ruling is the outcome of an appeal filed by Delhi Resident S.C. Aggarwal who wanted to discover whether the supreme court Judges declared their assets regularly before CIC. The Supreme Court judges declared their assets regularly before Chief Justice of India. The supreme court officials had not provided this information to Aggarwal on the plea that the CJI alone passes this information. In fact, CJI himself also has been holdiing that revealing details of judges wealth is a voluntary practice and not binding on the Judges. "The CIC did not accept this plea and held". The office of the Chief Justice of India is the custodian of the information and cannot be categorised as personal information. "As such the Supreme Court was asked to furnish the required information to the petitioner. Shri Aggarwal-within 10 days".

This version of the Chief commissioner has further widened the scope of the RTI and made our democracy more democratic and transparent.

Evaluation of RTI

Within short span of time the RTI Act is proving to be a catalyst in transforming governance. Across the country 75 lakhs applications were filed in 2008. Possibly the number will further grow in 2009.

In the period of recession all the world over economic wastage puts unpardoable strain on government resources. The RTI provides good opportunity to use it to plug loopholes in our development projects and assist shielding the livelihood of millions of poor and paupers of India. It can also help a wider debate on key policy and development issues and make their evaluation and solution participatory.

Besides RTI is apt to help in checkmating corruption in government departments. In the words of R. H. Tahiliani the perception of corruption has reduced in two years since the RTI law has been enacted.

In the view of social activists like Aruna Roy and Sandeep Pande the RTI has ensured that rural wage earners in Rajasthan and Uttar Pradesh get their due from the National Rural Employment Guarantee Act the only scheme in India that allows social audits on basis of information sought under RTI.

Success stories of RTI are fairly encouraging despite certain bottlenects at the hands of bureaucrats. According to S. K. Sarkar Joint secretary Department of Personnel and Training. "We found that 33 per cent of RTI applicants had to visit the public information offices (P1O) more than once to deposit the application". Over 54 per cent of the applicants found the attitude of PIO towards them as apathetic Kejrival an activist was of the view that the information commissioners should be more proactive in ensuring the people get information fast which is not happening.

However, such teething problems are apt to arise but time is not far off when a rustic villager too uses it to get his or her dues from the local governments. India chief Information officer is optimistic. Hence he remarks, "the shortcomings are just initial hindrances until RTI law users and implementaters mature. Some of the concrete instances as reported in reputed newspapers clearly reflect that RTI has exposed some deficient, evasive and corrupt bureaucrats and their hirling the clerical staff whose corrupt practices have gone to the extreme and are infact a slur on the face of our democracy which aims at attaining a super power status at no distant future. Some instances as quoted in the media are eye openers:

(i) Prateek Pande of Chhatisgarh states "As elsewhere the RTI Act infused some fear among officials. We struggled on various fronts after the Act was implemented owing to hostile reaction from labour "Vote for good governance" in Chattisgarh during the recent elections in Chatisgarh enabled BJP to be triumphant. The real hero of good governance in this tribal impoverished state is the Right to Information Act which prompted the citizens and the activitists to make the government accountable. They expossed irregularities of the States Public Services commission in the conduct of the examination. The disclosure through the Act led to the suspension of the chairman Public Service Commission, its secretary and Controller of examination. The very exam system was overhauled. Likewise the state suppressive order which charged Rs. 10 per page for any query sought through RTI was got scrapped after 8 months struggle through the appellate authority. Thus the invoking of the RRI became afffordable.

(ii) Through RTI, the Income Tax Department revealed the statements of accounts of six political parties. The Advocacy Group camp Association for democratic reforms (ADB) succeeded in knowing that in 2006-2007 political parties received Rs. 309 crores from donation but they disclosed sources of the funds for Rs. 15 crore. Most political parties except (CPM) showed that they spent only 20 per cent of the donations to fund candidates in the election.

(iii) Examination Reforms: The RTI application of a Professor of IIT Kanpur compelled authorities to disclose how the candidates are chosen. It exposed the evaluation system which was changed. 20% cut off marks to pick successful candidates was fixed. In another case a candidate who had failed to pass civil service examination conducted by the UPSC invoked RTI to force the Commission to provide the candidate with the details of cut off marks. The UPSC had to respond.

There are memerous success stories emanating from Orissa, Chattisgarh, Kerala, Madhya Pradesh, Meghalaya, Jammu and Kashmir. The social activists and thousands of citizens have undertaken to make full use of the RTI to expose the corrupt evasive and negligent officials and also political partieis not working in consonance with norms of conduct or ignoring values altogether. Arvind Kejriwal who won Magsasay Award for his campaign on RTI blamed the bureaucrats turned Information Commissioners for failing to protect the rights of information seekers when the PIOs act funny with RTI applicants. Hence he remarked, "The Information Commission should be more proactive in ensuring that people get information fast which is not happening. No doubt the real popularity of the RTI has in the fact that a rustic villager makes use of it and succeeds in getting his dues from the local government and a group of common men begin to demand accountability and answers from the Goverment at all levels. That will usher in era of 'Swaraj' in the real sense when a common man no longer fears the wrath of bureaucrat or of a ruthless policeman or hobnobbing by a politician."

Apex Court to challenge CIC on assets

In 1997 a full resolution was passed by the apex court under the chairmanship of the then CJ-J.S Verma making it mandatory for the Judges to regularly declare their assests and also those of families. However, during arguments before Chief Information Commissioner a 'U-turn was discernable The apex court lawyer partrayed this resolution as 'informal' and any information sought for on the basis of the Resolutaion would amount to breach of confidentiality. As a matter of fact the disclosure of such a 'U turn' emerged when the present CJI- K.G. Balakrishanan hinted that the CIC's, ruling directing the court to provide these details within 10 days might be challenged in the court. He remarked "We do not agree with what the CIC has said. We might appeal it in the court"

Even the Supreme Court Registry had also indicated "it might consider moving the Delhi High court against the ruling made pubilc"?

However former CJI J S verma who had moved and got the resolution passed stated, "How can a resolution adopted in a full court be termed as voluntary and informal. It became obligatory on the Judiciary since the day it was passed in the full court meeting in May 1997 He went to the extent of saying that judiciary should open itself to public scrutiny and not oppose the move". In fact India is the only major democracy in the world where the supreme court and high court judges are not willing to make public the details of their wealth and academic qualifications.

The credit for the exposition of the above controversy goes to 'Right to Information'. It is likely to usher in era of openness and accountability of all the Branches of government and redress the grievances of the common man who is fast becoming a victim of high handedness of government officials at all levels. It will serve as a sword of damoclese on the heads of erring, arrogant and corrupt ones.

D. CORRUPTION IN PUBLIC SERVICES

A Historical Perspective

Corruption is a relic of the past. It has always existed in human society in one form or the other. Kautilya in his famous work — 'Arthasastra'— refers to the various forms of corruption. Evidently corruption prevailed in his times otherwise he could not have given thought to this problem. However, scope of corruption was fairly limited in the past as public administration did not have a sway on all aspects of our lives. A handful of officials, who were required for collection of taxes and enforcing of law and order, did make misuse of their discretionary powers in the absence of written laws or rules.

With the fall of Mughal Empire and the ushering in of a new era—era of British rule in India — corruption assumed alarming proportions. The East India Company — a body of British traders — exploited India, amassed fortunes and brought India on the verge of bankruptcy. The British king appeared in the garb of a benevolent despot seemingly to put an end to the corrupt East India Company's rule and run the administration of India with caution and care. No doubt the British monarchy through its representative, the Governor-General, tried to build up a good administrative machinery in India. Yet some of the Departments, viz., Police, Revenue and Excise which were vested with vast discretionary powers were susceptible to corruption. The lower layer of judiciary also was said to be corrupt to the core. However, till the outbreak of the World War, corruption was confined to the lower strata of administrators. The top officials who were mostly British were not corrupt, firstly because they got highly alluring remuneration, second because they did not remain in touch with the community. Besides, the confinement of the British administrative machinery to a small compass, the depression of economy of British India, the restricted circulation of money were the other reasons responsible for keeping corruption under limits.

The outbreak of war unleashed forces of corruption. The unscrupulous officials got golden opportunity to grab wealth. According to the Bengal Administration Enquiry Committee (1944-45), "The Second World War....breeds conditions which make money making easy....The possession of a licence became a thing of high value and dishonest and unscrupulous persons did not hesitate to offer bribes in order to secure the licence to trade in the commodities effected....War conditions, thus, provided the opportunity, and it cannot be denied that it became all too easy for dishonest men to seize the opportunity of illicit gain by reason of two things, namely, (a) ill-advised administrative action; (b) defects in the Law which make detection of offences difficult and which provide inadequate penalties for convicted offenders".[1]

With the dawn of independence, India embarked upon an era of welfare state. As such the activities of the Government got multiplied. The officials were entrusted new and unfamiliar tasks. This resulted in the emergence of new regulations, controls, licences and permits which provided ample opportunities for corruption. The lust for power and craze for higher status added to the gravity of the malady. Some visionary political leaders like C. Rajagopalachari opposed the licence-quota-permit system, but he was over-ruled by the vested political interests. Some efforts were made to bring the corrupt officials to book, but the methods employed fostered a belief that government was not serious in eradicating corruption. Another notion which gained momentum with the passage of time was that while government stood against corruption, it did not believe in weeding out corrupt officials.

Things became still worse when democratically elected representatives also joined the vicious circle. The so-called custodians of Indian nationalism and sentinels of her territorial integrity themselves became instrumental in wrecking the democratic superstructure. They craved for monopoly in politics, through fair and foul methods. Doling out loaves and fishes to their political adherents and distributing quotas and permits amongst their henchmen resulted in accentuation of suspicion against their integrity. The officials, who danced to the tune of political godfathers also did not lag behind in making hay while the sun shone brightly. Thus the honest and conscientious officials felt frustrated whereas unscrupulous few who obliged their political bosses gained name and fame. The tales of supersession, frequent transfers to god-forsaken places and less prestigious placements for those who could not appease the political high ups, suspension and dismissal, even registration of criminal cases began to be repeated. Thus corruption reached the climax soon after the attainment of independence. Charges of corruption have been levelled in almost all the states of India against the Chief Ministers and other cabinet Ministers, not only by the opposition political parties but also the faction within the party itself. The Das Commission's report against Punjab Chief Minister, P.S. Kairon, is revealing. The Commission unmasked the infirmities of administrative officials in humouring Chief Minister by extending patronage to his sons and giving them maximum possible concessions in the minimum possible time. The Commission remarked, "*The speed with which these officers moved was unusual and remarkable. It is true that there can be no objection to expedition if the thing done is not in itself objectionable.....Such breakneck speed in the disposal of a serious matter for which elaborate rules have been framed to be observed and performed is not at all normal and can be attributable only to some powerful force regulating the speed.*

The disproportionate wealth possessed by bureaucrats of the status of Chief Secretary of a state or Chairman of Delhi Milk Scheme in the sensational revelations by C.B.I—speaks volumes about corruption going into the roots of our administrative structure. The critics go to the extent of saying that corruption has been institutionalised. If we talk of nationalisation of corruption in our country, it will not be an exaggeration. The legislators are playing havoc with their constituents whom they are supposed to serve. The ministers, barring a few exceptions, fleece the needy to fill their coffers with jingling coins. The bureaucrats propitiating their political godfathers at the cost of the distressed masses are more worried about securing their position or place of posting rather than devote attention to developmental activities. The judiciary particularly at the lower level has become a laughing stock on account of its dilatory tactics and inconceivable judgments allegedly due to pecuniary allurements. A Supreme Court Judge, formerly Chief Justice of Haryana & Punjab High

[1]*Hindustan Times, October 29, 1998.*

Court was found guilty of corrupt deeds and financial irregularity by a High-Power-Judicial Committee. The Jain Hawala case (1993), the Security scam, the Bofors scandal (1986), the Animal Husbandry scam, the Sugar import scam, Urea scam, the Telecom scandal, (1996) the Telgi scam JMM Bribery scandal, 1993, Coffin Gate scandal (1999), Tehelka Tape scandal (2001), Cash for Query Scam (2005) MPLADS Scam (2005), Passport scam (2007), Cash for votes scam (2008) and the fraud in several nationalised banks are some notable cases involving political leaders and high level officials. It is contended by the critics that the monopoly of political power in the hands of one political party gives ample opportunities to its members to pull wires from top to bottom. However in a coalition Government the evil is no less serious. The ruling party or alliance is generally hesitant to investigate cases of corruption against its members and henchmen. It has resulted in conspiracy of interests between the politicians and the top civil services who indulge in corrupt practice with a sense of impunity.

Meaning of Corruption

Before we make an appraisal of the causes of corruption among the civil services it is essential to define the term 'corruption'. In general terms corruption is a *"deliberate and intentional exploitation of one's position, status, or resources directly or indirectly for personal aggrandisement whether it be in terms of material gain or enhancement of power, prestige or influence beyond what is legitimate or sanctioned by commonly accepted norms to the detriment of the interests of other persons or the community as a whole"*.[1]

The Indian Penal Code has defined corruption in legal terms : "Whoever being or expecting to be a public servant accepts or obtains or agrees to accept or attempts to obtain from any person for himself or for any other person any gratification whatever other than legal remuneration as a motive or reward for doing or forbearing to do any official act or for showing or to show in the exercise of his official function favour or disfavour to any person or for rendering or attempting to render any service, disservice to any person with the Central or any State Government or Parliament or Legislature of any State or with any public servant as such shall be punished with imprisonment of either description for a term which may extend to three years or with fine or with both".[2]

Extravagant expenditure of public money, provision of employment for kith and kins, friends and supporters, getting of 'speed money' for doing a work, placing governmental machinery at the disposal of candidate for winning the elections, writing of good remarks in confidential reports and personal files after expecting a subordinate to dance attendance at the departmental head, a craving to stay at a station of one's choice by greasing the palm of the concerned boss, entering into transaction with the government by giving some percentage to the officials are some of the modes of corruption which may be kept in mind while discussing the causes of the malady of corruption and efforts to eradicate them.

Causes of Corruption

Ex-President, Dr. Radhakrishnan, in a message to Samyukta Sadachar Samiti correctly remarked, "*Corruption was an evil which has to be fought on all fronts, at all levels*". In all developing democracies corruption has become a malady. Following are the main reasons for the rapid spread of corruption among the employees :

(a) Historical. Corruption in all the developing democracies of Asia is a relic of the colonial past. The erstwhile rulers believed in reserving all the top positions for their own nationals whereas low positions were earmarked for the subject nationals. Naturally the latter developed tendency of exploiting the people to lead a comfortable and more enjoyable life like their bosses, whose way of

[1]*Awasthi, A. & Maheshwari, Public Administration (1974 ed) p. 342.*
[2]*Section 161, Indian Penal Code.*

living made them envious. The scarcities caused due to the World War II resulted in the spread of virus of bribery and corruption among all ranks of civil services. After the attainment of independence, the national governments of these countries undertook to race with the time for effecting economic development. Hence there arose the necessity of controls, permits, and quotas. It opened the gates of blackmarketing. The black money began to be unscrupulously displayed to win over the governmental officials. Thus, a large-scale racket of wholesale corruption became the order of the day.

(b) Economic. Corruption has its economic moorings. The salaries paid to the officers are inadequate. The occasional rise in D.A. hardly helps in neutralizing the ever-rising prices of the commodities. In recent years, the ever-shooting cost of living has brought down the real income of various sections of the community particularly that of the salaried employees. Thus the standard of living has suffered an eclipse. An employee who cannot afford to be a silent spectator to the ever-deteriorating economic standards, takes to accepting of illegal gratification to maintain his standard of living.

In India, rapid growth of population has added to the gravity of the problem. Family planning campaigns have not fully succeeded. The low class employees having no other source of recreation take to multiplication of families. This makes the situation still worse. As fond parents they will not like their children to starve and live in the state of poverty and abject helplessness, hence they are apt to get corrupted. The corrupters — the hoarders of black money — are readily available to pay the 'speed money' to get their work done speedily. The Santhanam Committee rightly stated, "*Possession of larger amounts of unaccounted money by various persons including those belonging to the industrial and commercial classes is a major impediment in the purification of public life*".[1]

(c) Sociological. Corruption is rooted in our acquisitive society where greatness of individuals and nobility of their family is judged by what they possess rather than by what they are. The acquisition of wealth has become *sina qua non* of life. People indulge in acquiring wealth without caring for the means they adopt. Even gods are propitiated by the avaricious people to attain their worldly goals, viz., victory in games, triumph in lottery, acquittal from courts, success in examination, etc. If gods are bribed why should not the civil services—the avaricious mortals—be appeased to gain the motives ? The best way to entice an individual is to grease his palm, thus enabling him to gain status in the acquisitive society.

(d) Procedural Causes. The defective procedural systems and poor anti-corruption law also cause corruption in public services. The Railway Corruption Enquiry Committee revealed lacunae in the rules and regulations which ultimately lead to corruption. The Santhanam Committee also referred to cumbersome and dilatory procedures in government offices. Red-tapism and 'passing the buck' have become the permanent features of Indian offices. The enterprising and shrewd businessmen having lot of black money are thus prepared to pay the 'speed money' to get their work done speedily. The procedural red-tapism has enabled the officers on the verge of retirement to show special favour to the business magnets by speeding up their work and secure jobs in return after their retirement. The economic ministries have become dens of intrigue and iniquity. Touts and lobbyists haunt their corridors and perform 'useful tasks' for the vested interests. In business language they are called "liaison men".

The archaic laws guided by the lofty principle of 'natural justice' have helped the corrupt people in escaping punishment. Our criminal justice system has become the safe refuge of every scoundrel, every corrupt politician and government servant, every businessman who defrauds the bank and refuses to pay tax arrears. Added to this list are the politicians who refuse to pay for the I.A.F. aircrafts used by them, the bureaucrats who refuse to pay their house rent and continue to occupy Government accommodation for years after retirement and the politicians who cease to be

[1]*Interim Report of ARC, Oct. 1966, p. 3.*

M. Ps but do not vacate the spacious house they were once allotted in Delhi. Corruption has poisoned our republic and we use wrong methods to deal with it. Plainly speaking, we have not dealt with corruption effectively; rather we have perpetrated it.

(e) Environmental. The fast urbanization and industrialization have resulted in change of values. Simplicity of primitive and medieval times has given place to ostentatious and luxurious life. Material possessions, administrative status and economic powers are determinant of the status and prestige of a person in a society—may it be a developed or developing. However, in a developing society, the environments are more amenable to corruption. The governments of the developing democracies cannot afford to pay even a bare minimum wage to their employees. On the other hand, enough of black money is available with the industrialists. Naturally the semi-starved employees will be tempted to make use of money which is apt to flow to them on account of the service rendered by them to the industrialists. C. Rajagopalachari rightly pointed out, "The system of permits, licences, allocation of transport routes, quotas and similar attempts to administer the economy of a big and busy nation from the secretariat instead of leaving such things to the consumer and competition in the market is at the root of corruption. The contract between the official and party bosses on the one side and the very clever, far too clever businessman on the other, with a tremendous lot of money expected in the business produces the national malady we call corruption......".

(f) Lack of civic consciousness. Bulk of people in the developing democracies are illiterate. As such, they lack civic consciousness and do not clamour for the redress of their grievances. The civil services being more enlightened take undue advantage of the general apathy, ignorance and indifference of the common men, they indulge in nefarious activities without fearing the public wrath or mass denunciation. The public, in fact, is keen to shield such officers who are pinpricks for the government in developing democracies like India. People feel concerned only when they are individually going to be affected by the action of the officials. Hence, the Railway Corruption Enquiry Committee rightly observed, "......citizens of a free country have the right, nay the duty, to insist that public servants render due service for which they are paid from public coffers......citizens themselves will have to be vigilant and they must insist upon their rights. They should also be prepared to pay, if necessary, the price of such insistence with some temporary loss or inconvenience to themselves. A strong public opinion must therefore be created and a determined effort made to withhold payment of illegal gratification."[1]

(g) Political. Since the ushering in of a democratic era, in a developing democracy like India, corruption has reached the zenith. According to the Election Commission, there are at present seven national parties, 33 state parties and 612 registered but unrecognised parties. The present Lok Sabha has 40 parties. Are we to believe that all these parties are busy working for the people ? Surely not. These are personality-oriented parties to advance the interests of the "leader" and his henchmen. It is not only the ministers at the Central or State levels but also the MPs and MLAs, the Pradhan and the Sarpanches exert pressures on the officials at their respective levels and get the illegal things done. What to talk of the administrative officers, even the judges are not safe from the overwhelming influence of the ruling party and its top bosses. The judges who are committed to the ideology of the ruling party may seek promotion and elevation to higher offices, the others not toeing its line may be bypassed or superseded. The example of supersession of the judges of the Indian Supreme Court particularly when they were opposed to the majority verdict on the 24th and 25th amendments is said to be a glaring example of political corruption of a very high order. Evidently the civil services who dance to the tune of political bosses and act according to their dictates alone can flourish and bask in the sunshine of prosperity bestowed upon them by their political God Father. The electoral system in the country has in its own way contributed to the extent of corruption. The role of money

[1]*Santhanam Committee Report, pp 117-18.*

in elections is so great that it has vitiated the entire democratic process. Those fighting for victory at the hustings by any means fair or foul are not spurred by altruistic motive of service to the common man; they are solely guided by the power that goes with the office and that can be leveraged for personal and sectional ends. The elected members change political sides as one changes his clothes, obviously for money considerations. The JMM bribery case and the Jogi case are notable examples on this score. The efforts of T.N. Seshan, M.S. Gill and J.M. Lyngdoh to cleanse the electoral system of its evils could not bear fruit. The reasons are obvious—the political leaders, apprehension to lose if the electoral system is cleansed and rid of those features which lead to corruption.

(h) ***Special causes.*** (*i*) ***Non-cooperation of Commercial Classes.***

Unscrupulous industrial magnets and commercial classes constitute a major impediment in the purification of public life. It is indispensable to weed out these dishonest agents of corruption so as to end corruption in the public services. The Trade Associations, the Indian Chamber of Commerce can play a vital role in fighting against corruption.

(*ii*) ***Safeguards for public services.*** According to the law of our land, both the giver and receiver of bribes are held guilty. Hence, it is difficult to procure evidence against the guilty. The heads of the departments, though aware of the crime of their subordinates, are not in a position to take action against them for want of adequate proof for their conviction. They are sometimes not even courageous enough to make adverse entries in the confidential reports of their subordinates fearing that they won't be able to substantiate them when challenged by the latter or get adequate support from their administrative bosses if the political bosses are out to support erring subordinates who earned adverse report at their hands.

(*iii*) ***Security of Tenure.*** There is too much security of tenure assured to bureaucracy in India. No civil servant shall be dismissed or removed by an authority subordinate to that by which he was appointed. Moreover, no such person shall be dismissed or removed or reduced in rank until he has been given a reasonable opportunity of showing cause against the action proposed to be taken in regard to him. However, according to the 15th amendment of the Constitution, effected in 1963, instead of two full-fledged opportunities of defence, the accused employee can only make one representation against the penalty proposed to be imposed upon him, on the basis of the evidence already adduced during the inquiry into the charges against him without the necessity of any fresh evidence or other extraneous matters. This has tightened the noose round the erring employee.

All these causes have led to vitiating of atmosphere in India. Honest and scrupulous employees are becoming rarity. A vicious circle has been created by corrupt politicians, dishonest administrators and the so-called custodians of justice. It is claimed by the present rulers that efforts are afoot to rid the nation of this malady of corruption which is deeply rooted in Indian polity, but sadly enough, corruption is on its ascendancy and we have earned dubious distinction of being ranked the ninth most corrupt country in the world. The Vora Committee Report placed before Parliament on August 2, 1995 speaks volumes about the magnitude of corruption and the close nexus between criminal gangsters, politicians and bureaucrats. In the recent past Punjab Vigilance Bureau could register 169 cases against former ministers and bureaucrats. At least 46 tainted PCS officers have been dismissed for bribing their way through Public Service Commission.[1]

Anti-Corruption Measures in India

(a) Central Bureau of Investigation (C.B.I.). As already said, corruption in public services assumed alarming form during the World War. Hence, the government of India set up special Police Establishment (S.P.E.) in 1941, to investigate cases of bribery and corruption in transactions with which the war and supply departments were concerned. At the end of 1942, cases of corruption in the Railway Department were also entrusted to it.

[1]*Hindustan Times January 6, 2003. p.9.*

In April, 1963, the Central Bureau of Investigation was set up and the Special police Establishment was made one of its Divisions. It did not effect any change in the jurisdiction, powers and functions of the Establishment. The **C.B.I.** plays a supplementary role to the States' Police Forces. To avoid duplication of efforts, the administrative arrangement has been arrived at between the Central and the State Governments regarding the type of cases to be earmarked for the SPE. The cases which essentially and substantially involve Central government employees or their officers, or certain state government employees are referred to the **C.B.I.** The **C.B.I.** can also take up cases against the employees of statutory bodies or public undertakings established and financed by the government of India.

(b) Santhanam Committee's recommendations. With the ever rising corruption, Parliament got alarmed. On its insistence, a committee consisting of seven members—5 MPs and 2 senior officials of the Ministry of Home Affairs and with K. Santhanam as Chairman was appointed in June, 1962. It was authorised to review existing instruments for combating corruption and advising on practical steps to make anti corruption measures more vigorous. In a way it was required to examine the working of the vigilance machinery of the government of India and recommend improvements in their working. It was also expected to suggest improvements in the Government Servants' Conduct Rules and see to the speedy trial of cases of bribery, corruption and criminal misconduct.

The Committee produced a very elaborate report comprising 304 pages.

Suggestions of the Committee

(a) Article 311 of the Constitution may be amended in order to make the judicial process in corruption cases easy and speedy.

(b) There should be a Central Vigilance Commission having autonomous powers.

(c) The Government Servants' Conduct Rules may be amended so as to restrict the re-employment of retired government employees by private businessmen.

(d) Some amendments in the Defence of India Bill, 1962, may be made.

In order to implement these recommendations, the government of India strengthened the **C.B.I.** and vested it with additional powers. Further with a view to improve co-ordination and co-operation between the administration and the C.B.I., the Home Ministry issued a directive to all ministries and departments of the government that their vigilance officers and heads should report to the C.B.I. for investigating such cases in which charges of corruption and bribery are made against public servants. It was suggested that all records and documents required by the C.B.I. should be placed at their disposal for inspection and scrutiny within a fortnight of such a request. Likewise if the C.B.I. suggested transfer of an employee during the course of investigation, it should be readily complied with by the department concerned.

Central Vigilance Commission (CVC)

The Central Vigilance Commission was set up in 1964 by the Central Government in exercise of its executive powers. The central vigilance commissioner is the chief executive of the commission. He is appointed by the President of India for a period of six years or until he attains the age of 65 years whichever is earlier. The commission is located in the Ministry of Home Affairs but accorded autonomous status. Its jurisdiction extends to all employees of the central government and the employees in the public undertakings, corporate bodies and other organisations dealing with matters falling within the executive powers of the central government. Even the Delhi metropolitan council and the New Delhi municipal committee fall within the jurisdiction of the commission. However, it cannot probe cases of corruption against ministers and members of parliament.

Its Functions

(a) To undertake an enquiry into any transaction in which a public servant is suspected or alleged to have acted for an improper purpose or in a corrupt manner.

(b) To investigate into any complaint against a public servant who has exercised or refrained from exercising his powers for improper or corrupt purposes.

(c) To ask for reports from agencies so as to enable it to exercise general check and supervision over the vigilance and anti-corruption work in them.

(d) To take over under its direct control complaints for further action which may be either (*i*) to ask the central bureau of investigation (C.B.I.) to register a regular case and investigate it or (*ii*) to enlist it for enquiry to the C.B.I. or the concerned agency.

(e) To initiate review of procedures and practices of administration which concern the maintenance of integrity in the administration. Recently a Delhi University Professor complained to CVC after being superseded.

The commission is required to submit an annual report to the Ministry of Home Affairs about its activities. The Ministry of Home Affairs places this report before each House of Parliament.

The commission receives complaints from individual persons. It also gathers information about corruption and malpractices or misconduct from other sources such as press reports, audit objections, information through parliamentary debates and other forums etc. The complaints about Central Government employees received by the state vigilance commissions are forwarded by them to the Central Vigilance Commissions.

On receipt of a complaint, the CVC has the following alternatives open to it :

1. The CVC may entrust the matter for enquiry by the administrative ministry/department concerned. In such cases, the vigilance officer of the ministry/department makes a preliminary enquiry to verify the defalcations and submits its report to the CVC. The commission, thereafter, advises the ministry / department concerned for further action to be taken.

2. The CVC may ask the C.B.I. to make an inquiry. The C.B.I. will then submit its report to the commission which will advise the ministry/department as to the course of further action to be taken.

3. The CVC may ask the director of the C.B.I. to register a case and investigate it. The director will inform the commission of the result of the investigation if he is of the view that a prosecution should be launched.

(a) The director, C.B.I. will forward the final report of his investigation to the Ministry of Home Affairs through the CVC. if sanction for such prosecution is required under any law to be issued in the name of the President. A copy of the investigation report will also be sent to the concerned Ministry / department for its comments. After considering the report of the C.B.I. and other relevant records and also the comments of the administrative ministry / department, the CVC will advise the ministry of Home Affairs whether or not prosecution should be launched. The necessary orders will be issued by the Home Ministry.

(b) If any authority other than the President is competent to sanction prosecution, the C.B.I. Director will forward the investigation report to such authority to sanction the prosecution. The comments of the authority received will be forwarded by the C.B.I. to the CVC for advice through the administrative ministry / department concerned. Further action will be taken by the authority concerned after considering the advice of the CVC.

The commission has laid down procedures to be taken by the administrative ministries / departments in the case of complaints received by them. These complaints are to be dealt with by the ministries/departments concerned. The CVC may advise the ministries/departments in respect of all matters relating to integrity in administration. It may also call for reports, returns or statements from all ministries / departments so as to enable it to exercise a general check and supervision over vigilance and anti-corruption work in the ministries / departments. It can also take over under its direct control any complaint or case for further action.

The Central Bureau of Investigation investigates the cases of bribery, corruption, misconduct of central government employees, breaches of law concerning import and export control, foreign exchange regulations, customs and central excise, income-tax, etc. and cases of fraud and conspiracy against the country's security as well as other important cases of crime. The important cases under C.B.I. investigation are the Bofors and Fodder Scam case, Babri Masjid Case. Taj Corridor case, Disproportionate case against Shri Mulayam Singh, Nithari Murder Case and Aarushi Murder case which have led the C.B.I's role into controversy. It will be a sad day in the history of administrative integrity if the high level investigation agencies lose their credibility.

Pursuant to the Supreme Court directions of December 18, 1997, the Government has reconstituted the Central Vigilance Commission by enactment of CVC Act, 2003 and the CBI. The CVC has been given statutory status and made a plural body consisting of four members of whom two will be non-bureaucrats. Thus, it would no longer be a purely bureaucratic body. The Secretary, Personnel would not be an ex-officio member of the commission. The Chief Vigilance Commissioner will be selected by a committee comprising the Prime Minister, the Home Minister and the Leader of the Opposition from a panel of outstanding civil servants and others to be furnished by the Cabinet Secretary. The CBI is the creation of Special Police Establishment Act. The Centre can not use the Agency in a state without the latter's permission. The working of the CBI shows that it has been used by the party in power to serve its politifcal ends. In the Mulayam Singh case (2009) the Supreme Court expressed shock over the CBI stand and admonished it using harsh words against its functioning. A legal luminary even observed that the agency has sold its soul.

There has been a long-going controversy that CBI should be an independent body. Presently it is an executive creation and acts as a govt. department and receives instructions from the Law Ministery to investigate a case, file the charge sheet and follow it up. The government uses it to punish or favour an individual, a leader or a political party. It has been an instrument into the hands of the party in power or the Centre which has put question marks on its credibility. In order to insulate the CBI from political pressure it has been suggested that it should be put under the supervision of the Central Vigilance Commission.

Vigilance Organisation in Ministry

The Santhanam Committee made elaborate recommendations for the strengthening of the vigilance organisation in each ministry / department. An officer in each ministry has been designated as chief vigilance officer and vested with vigilance powers. He acts as a special assistant to the secretary or the head of the department in all matters pertaining to vigilance. He provides a link between the central vigilance commission and the ministries. Likewise, a vigilance officer has been attached with subordinate offices and public sector undertakings. Some of the chief vigilance officers / vigilance officers are whole time officers while others are part time.

Each chief vigilance officer is to be appointed in consultation with the Central Vigilance Commission and the vigilance officers in the attached offices in consultations with the chief vigilance officer of the respective ministry. The chief vigilance officer is of the rank of a deputy secretary and vigilance officers of the rank of under secretaries.

The Central Vigilance Commission has been empowered to assess the work of the Chief Vigilance Officer. The assessment is recorded in the character rolls of the officers.

The Chief Vigilance Officers review the existing arrangements in the organisation under their charge in order to take suitable steps for strengthening the existing setup wherever necessary. All proposals for reorganising or strengthening the vigilance organisation are referred to the Central Vigilance Commission for scrutiny.

Vigilance Machinery of States

There is a State Vigilance Commission in each State. Further in each State as at the Centre, there is a special police establishment. The state vigilance commission deals with matters within executive powers of the State concerned. However, it cannot investigate cases of political corruption. The powers of these commissions with the minor variations from State to State are as follows :

(*i*) To undertake enquiry into any transaction in which a public servant is suspected or alleged to have acted for an improper purpose or in a corrupt manner.

(*ii*) It causes an inquiry or investigation into any complaint that a public servant has exercised or refrained from exercising his powers for improper or corrupt purposes. It holds enquiry into any complaint of corruption, misconduct, lack of integrity or other kinds of malpractices or misdemeanour on the part of a public servant. It also takes under its direct control such complaints, informations or cases it deems fit.

(*iii*) It initiates review of procedure and practices of administration which deal with the maintenance of integrity in administration.

(*iv*) It collects statistics and other information needed for exercising general check and supervision over anti-corruption work.

These commissions are headed by State Vigilance Commissioner who enjoys status of a High Court Judge. He holds office for a period of five years and is ineligible for any employment either under the Union or State Government. Besides the Commissioner, there is a Commissioner for departmental inquiries who conducts departmental enquiries into charges of corruption.

The commission submits an annual report to the state government about its activities. This report is to be laid before the state legislature.

Vigilance at Division and District Levels

At the divisional level, a divisional vigilance board has been set up. It comprises the Divisional Commissioner, Deputy Inspector General of Police and a Division Vigilance Officer.

At the district level, a district vigilance officer heads the vigilance organisation. He is appointed by the District Collector / Deputy Commissioner from among his gazetted assistants in consultation with the Divisional Vigilance Board.

To streamline this quest for integrity, the vigilance commissioners of all States hold an annual conference under the chairmanship of the Chief Vigilance Commissioner. This annual conference provides a forum for discussion of mutual problems and exchange of experiences. Moreover, it gives publicity to vigilance efforts of the government at both the central and state levels. Such a step inspires people's confidence in the government's sincerity of purpose.

Concluding, it may be said that the range and dimension of corruption have increased alarmingly during the past three decades or so. In the sixties, one could count on fingers the number of corrupt persons, but today one can count only a few honest persons in the vast ocean of corruption. Corrupt practices have become a part of governance. **The nexus between the corrupt politician, the corrupt bureaucrat and the underworld Dons remains unabated**. There is no political will to root out corruption and there is no accountability at any level of administration. The corrupt move freely and continue to be in power even when serious charges of swindling public money are registered against them. The criminal justice system is so imperfect that none is afraid of law. The public faith in the government's capacity and will to root out corruption has considerably eroded. Thousands of cases against politicians, bureaucrats, police officers and people accused in massive frauds are lingering on for decades which reminds us of our hypocrisy and dishonesty. To root out corruption, it is essential to safe guard the framework of political arena from its evil effects. Thereafter the administrative and criminal justice structure and system is to be revamped with a view to ensure efficiency in administration and speedy disposal of corruption cases. Transparency in administration with right to information is absolutely necessary for ensuring public accountability at all levels of administration. Last but not the least, eternal vigilance is required on the part of people who are the ultimate beneficiary of a corruption free polity and administration. The rulers also should know that people understand what is what and that the nation is still vibrant. They would be inviting their doom sooner or later unless they follow ethical standards and norms of exemplary behaviour and stop defrauding the nation.

(E) REDRESSAL OF CITIZENS' GRIEVANCES

Corruption is not the only malady of public administration in India; harassment by officials, delay in disposal of cases, arbitrary decisions and maladministration also constitute its black spots. Accordingly, any democratic government — a government of the people, by the people and for the people, has to remove those spots and promote among its citizens a sense of content and satisfaction towards administration. The average citizen is interested more in the devices of redress of his grievances than in the sophisticated manual of organisation and methods of disposal of government business. He wants responsive, sympathetic and courteous administration and it is one of the hard problems of public administration as how to make public officials fair, sensitive, responsible, responsive and how to protect the citizen against administrative arbitrariness.

The functions of modern government have increased manifold and the assumption of manifold responsibilities has resulted in the multiplication of processes. Administrative power and discretion are vested at different levels of the executive, all the members of which are not endowed with the same level of understanding and strength of character. Power means authority and authority is likely to be abused, more so when it is to be exercised in the context of scarcity of goods and services, controls, licences or permits, and pressures. In the absence of any effective machinery for redress of grievances, the executive arbitrariness grows all the more.

The redressal of public grievances is not an easy task. The following steps may help in redressal of their grievances to some extent.

1. Judicial Remedies

The Constitution of India has guaranteed certain fundamental rights to the people and in case there is a violation of any of these rights, the aggrieved person can move the High Court or Supreme Court for enforcement of his rights. A citizen can also avail of the judicial remedy against any arbitrary action or violation of law by a public servant. He can also move the court to seek remedy against any wrong done to him by a public servant in the course of discharge of his public duty. The judicial remedies against the administration may include : suits against the government for quashing of its arbitrary, discriminatory and unlawful orders; reinstatement of employees, payment of salary arrears and other damages; prosecution of the offending government servants for illegal acts such as unlawful detention, torture or harassment; writ jurisdiction of the Supreme Court and High Court which has the effect of quashing administrative orders, prohibiting administration from some act or directing it to do a particular act or not to do it.

The judicial remedies do provide an effective check against official excesses or abuse of power, but these remedies have certain limitations. *First,* the judicial process is very slow and cumbersome. An aggrieved person cannot wait indefinitely to avail himself of the judicial remedy. Tired of the delay he loses hope and gets reconciled to his fate. *Second,* judicial remedy is highly expensive and cannot be taken advantage of by many people. Moreover, the inconveniences involved keep them away from seeking judicial remedy. It may also invite the wrath of the powers that be and the complainant may be subjected to harassment in other subtle ways. In view of the obstacles and risks ahead, people prefer to suffer than to invoke court jurisdiction. *Third,* sometimes the remedies offered by the law courts are inadequate and ineffective. The government also deprives the person of the remedy granted to him by amending the law or modifying rules thereof.

To provide speedy and cheap justice to the people against official excesses, administrative tribunals have been setup. Such tribunals operate with a degree of informality. Formal rules of evidence as found in the law courts are not observed and the lawyers are not needed to argue a case. In India, there are a number of such tribunals, such as Income Tax Appellate Tribunal, Railway Rent Tribunals, Labour Tribunals, recently[1] established Rent Tribunals at State level, etc. The Central Administrative Tribunal setup in 1985 hears the cases of the employees belonging to all India services, Central Services and Central Government offices regarding service matters. Although the administrative tribunals have proved useful to provide cheaper, speedy and adequate justice, yet they can be availed of only by certain sections of the people such as assessees, workmen, government employees, tenants and landlords and the like. For the common man, they do not provide any redressal of his grievances against excessive or dilatory administrative acts.

Consumer courts have been set up at the District levels to protect the people against unfair trade practices and inefficient service by the service departments such as telephone, electricity and housing departments. Any consumer who has suffered any loss may approach the consumer court to seek redress of his grievance by making a simple application and without the intervention of any advocate. Provision also exists for an appeal from the lower consumer court to the higher one.

2. **Parliamentary Procedure**

The principle of ministerial responsibility gives Parliament the right to probe into executive actions. The elected representatives, having been persuaded by their constituents ask questions in Parliament, move adjournment motion, censure motion, call-attention motion to draw the attention of the House to a particular matter. There is also a parliamentary committee, the Committee on Petitions—to which the citizen may submit petitions to secure redress against an act of injustice. In the beginning, only those petitions were admitted which related to pending Bills before the legislature but during 1956, the scope of the Committee was enlarged and it was given the power to consider all representations, resolutions, telegrams, etc. which might be addressed either to the speaker or to the secretary of the Lok Sabha. The committee, if it deems fit, may call upon the concerned department to furnish the facts pertaining to the petition and may also hear the individual and the representative of the department. It may refer the complaint to the concerned department for enquiry. The committee after receipt of the enquiry report considers the report and may ask the department to rectify the cause of complaint or clarify its position. The parliament may also appoint special committees to investigate any matter of administrative corruption, collusion or negligence. The joint parliamentary committee to probe the Security Scam is an example thereof.

However, the parliamentary action is circumscribed by the rules of procedure and speaker's rulings. According to the Administrative Reforms Commission, "*Parliamentary procedure is more suited for the consideration of matters of public importance than for obtaining redress of individual grievances arising in the course of day-to-day governmental administration*".[1]

3. **Complaint Forums**

The government has setup numerous complaint forums at different levels to receive people's complaints and take further necessary action. These complaint cells have been created in various government organisations for speedy disposal of public complaints. One may also air one's grievances before a senior officer against the actions of his subordinates. Complaint officers have been appointed in organisations dealing with the public. Complaint boxes and registers are maintained in many organisations. The bus conductor carries a complaint book wherein a passenger may write his / her complaint about the conductor's behaviour or bus service. One can meet ministers, members of the legislature while on tour and convey one's grievances. Public / district grievances committees under the chairmanship of a minister/district collector have been setup to hear grievances against a department in the district. These committees meet once every month on fixed days and hold open meeting. Open darbars are also held by a Minister on tour or a local officer to hear complaints from the people and provide redress on the spot.

---

[1]*Interin Report of ARC, Oct. 1966, p.3.*

This remedy also is not much helpful because the complaint officers are reluctant to hold their own colleagues responsible. They are afraid to investigate grievances against a decision taken by an officer senior to them. Further, there is a tendency among the officers to protect their subordinates against whom complaint is made. It is also difficult to take any action against an employee/officer having political pulls and patronage for his acts of injustice. The Trade Unionism also cautions the investigating officer to tread the path very diligently.

4. **Enquiries**

There is a provision for instituting departmental as well as public enquiries under the provisions of Public Servants (Enquiries) Act, against a public servant for his acts of misbehaviour. Various commissions have been appointed from time to time by the government to investigate the allegations against the civil servants, for instance, the Chagla Commission, Das Commission, Aiyangar Commission, Venkateswara Iyer Commission, Mundholkar Commission, etc. While these commissions have done useful work, the remedy is not effective to provide redress to the common man against his grievances regarding day-to-day matters. Generally serious matters of maladministration and corruption are the subject-matter of public enquiry.

5. **Central Vigilance Commissioner**

As described earlier, a Central Vigilance commission headed by a vigilance commissioner was setup in 1964 consequent to the recommendations of the Santhanam Committee to investigate corruption charges, complaints of misconduct, lack of integrity or other kinds of malpractices on the part of public servants. In 1966, a Commissioner for Public Grievances was also appointed. There is also a Department of Personnel, Public Grievances and Pensions under the Government of India under the charge of Minister of State. The role of Vigilance Commission is limited because it has only advisory role. Further, the procedure of investigation is so vexatious that people do not desire to be involved in long and unpleasant proceedings. The role of the Commissioner for Public Grievances is just one of post office who forwards the complaints to the concerned departments for necessary enquiry and action.

Public Grievances and Administrative Reforms

The Department of Administrative Reforms and Public grievance may be portrayed as the nodal agency of the government planning and for effecting administrative reforms and also for redressing the public grievances concerning the states in general and those related to the Central Government in particular.

Functions: (a) The department disseminates information on vital activities of the Government concerning administrative reforms and looks to redressal of grievances through publications and documentation.

(b) The department undertakes activities in the field of international exchange and cooperation to promote public-service reforms.

(c) The department acts as a facilitation to improve governmental functioning through systematic changes in consultation with ministries and departments of Centre, States and Union Territories.

(d) It sets up commission for the Review of Administrative laws. It actually did so on May 8, 1998 in order to identify proposals for effecting amendments in the existing laws, regulations and procedures. On the submission of Report by this commission on September 30, 1998 out of 1382 central laws recommended by the commission for repeal, 415 Acts including five war time ordinances have been repealed by the govenrment.

The Second Administrative Reforms Commission was set up in 2005, under chairmanship of Verappa Moiley to prepare a blue print for revamping the public administrative system. This commission was required to suggest measures to achieve a proactive, responsive, accountable sustainable and efficient administration for all levels of government in the country. The commission submitted five reports to the government: (a) Right to Information (June 9, 2006) (b) Unlocking Human Capital - Entitlements and Governance (31st July 2006) (c) Crisis Management-From despair to Hope (31st October 2006) (d) Ethics in Governance (12th February, 2007) (e) Public order - (June 25, 2007). Under the chairmanship of Parnab Mukherjee a group of ministers have been deputed to make an appraisal the pace of Implementation of Administrative Reforms recommended by ARC. They are required to provide guidance as well for the implementation of the recommendations.

Institution of PM Award 2005: The Department had instituted in 2005. "Prime Minister award for Excellence in public administration. This was an incentive for excellent and innovative work done by the central and state government officials. The award was constituted of (a) Medal (b) scroll (c) Cash award of Rs. one lakh. In case a group of officers collectively do excellent work they will be entitled to Rs. five lakhs (one lakh for each person to the maximum). On April 21, 2007 such awards were given by the PM in Vigyan Bhavan on Civil Service Day.

Development of a Model

The department has developed a Model (SEVOTTAM) for benchmarking service delivery standards by the departments.

The project aimed at setting standards in consultation with user group and include these standards in the citizens charter. It also had devised a framework to use the performance against the standards and to measure improvement and achievements of these standards.

Thus the Model stands for bringing about excellence in service delivery standards in various government organisations.

Thus the Department of Administrative Reforms and Public Grievances has brought out good governance practices in the country. Its multi pronged strategies include. seminarrs, publications, regional conferences, lectures, Documentary films and a quarterly magazine. It also brings out monthly News letter Civil Service News. All these steps create awareness and also lead to share experiences.

Administrative Tribunals

Article 323-A of the Constitution empowers the Central Government to establish Administrative Tribunals through an Act of the Parliament. In 1983 Administrative Tribunal Act was enacted. It opened a new era in the domain of administering justice to the aggrieved government servants.

These Tribunals stand for adjudicating disputes and complaints regarding recruitment and conditions of service of employees appointed to varied services in the states and the union governments. These tribunals exercise original Jurisdiction in respect of service matters of employees. In a judgement on March 18, 1997 the apex court held that the appeals against the orders of an Administrative tribunal shall lie before the Division Bench of the concerned High Court.

The jurisdiction of Administrative Tribunals has been clearly laid down. It extends to service matters of the litigants enumerated in the Act.

The procedure in these courts is very simple. An aggrieved person can appear before such courts personally. The government can present its case through its departmental officers or legal practitioners.

Justice in these courts is speedy and comparatively inexpensive.

Central Administration Tribunal (CAT)

The Central Administrative Tribunal was set up on November, 1, 1985. Presently it has 17 regular benches which function as the courts. These benches hold circuit sitting at other seats of High courts.

The Tribunal consists of a Chairman, Vice Chairman and other members. The members are drawn both from judicial and administrative wings. That enables the CAT to make use of expertise and calibre of both legal and administrative streams.

Need for Lokpal

The different avenues described above suffer from limitations and have failed to provide effective redress of individual grievances of a citizen against administrative agencies and political leadership. The Administrative Reforms Commission, setup in 1966, was asked, *inter alia*, to examine the problem of redressal of citizen's grievances. Specifically, it was asked to examine :

(*i*) The adequacy of existing arrangements for redress of grievances; and

(*ii*) the need for introduction of any new machinery or special institution for redress of grievances.

The ARC in its interim report on the "Problems of Redress of Citizens' Grievances" observed : "In the circumstances of today, with the expanding activities of government, the exercise of discretion by administrative authorities howsoever large the field may be, cannot be done away with nor can it be rigidly regulated by instructions, orders or resolutions. The need for ensuring the rectitude of the administrative machinery in this vast discretionary field is not only obvious but paramount. Where the citizen can establish the genuineness of his case, it is plainly the duty of the state to set right the wrong done to him...an institution for redress of grievances must be provided within the democratic system of government. It has to be an institution in which the average citizen will have faith and confidence and through which he will be able to secure quick and inexpensive justice".

On the question of setting up of Ombudsman type of institutions, the ARC observed : "After having carefully evaluated the pros and cons...we are of the view that the special circumstances relating to our country can be fully met by providing for two special institutions for the redress of citizens' grievances. There should be one authority for dealing with complaints against the administrative acts of ministers or secretaries to government both at the Centre and in the states. There should be another authority in each state and the Centre for dealing with complaints against the administrative acts of other officials. All these authorities should be independent of the executive as well as the legislature and judiciary". The first authority was to be called the Lokpal and the second one the Lokayukta.[1]

The commission also held the view that "the setting up of these authorities should not, however, be taken to be a complete answer to the problem of redress of citizens' grievances. They only provide the ultimate setup for such redress as has not been available through the normal department or governmental machinery and do not absolve the department from fulfilling its obligations to the citizen for administering its affairs without generating, as far as possible, any legitimate sense of grievance. Thus, the administration itself must play the major role on reducing the area of grievances and provide remedies, wherever necessary and feasible. For this purpose, there should be established in each ministry or department, as the case may be, suitable machinery for the receipt and investigation of complaints and for setting in motion, where necessary, the administrative process for providing remedies. A large number of cases which arise at lower levels of administration should in fact adequately be dealt with by this in-built departmental machinery. When the machinery functions effectively, the number of cases which have to go to an authority outside the ministry or the department, should be comparatively small. In some states and at the Centre, there is now some provision for a governmental authority to hear grievances and attempt to secure remedial action through the administration. The tendency is to setup such authorities independent and outside the departmental machinery. After the setting up of the authorities we have recommended above, there would be no need for those functionaries. We would in the circumstances strongly advocate that the responsibility of the departments to deal adequately with public grievances must be squarely faced by them.....[2]

---

[1]*Lee, Hahn-Been, "Bureaucratic Models and Administrative Reforms" In Arne F. Leamans ed. The Management of Change in Government, p. 114-125.*

[2]*Ibid.*

It may be noted that the proposed institutions of Lokpal and Lokayukta were not to supplant the existing remedies available within the departmental setup or at the levels of judiciary and administrative tribunals. These institutions were to provide remedy only in respect of those matters for which such remedies were not available or where it was not reasonable to expect a citizen to take recourse to legal proceedings. The Lokpal and Lokayukta devote their attention and energies only to those cases in which *prima facie* the need for redressing an act of injustice or maladministration exists.

According to the Commission, both the institutions of Lokpal and Lokayukta should be characterised by the following features :

1. They should be demonstrably independent and impartial.

2. Their investigations and procedures should be conducted in private and should be informal in character.

3. Their appointment should as far as possible, be non-political.

4. Their status should compare with the highest judicial functionaries in the country.

5. They should deal with matters in the discretionary field involving acts of injustice, corruption or favouritism.

6. Their proceedings should not be subject to judicial interference.

7. They should have the maximum latitude and powers in obtaining information relevant to their duties; and

8. They should not look forward to any benefit or pecuniary advantage from the executive government.

The Commission recommended that the Lokpal will have the power to investigate an administrative act done by or with the approval of a Minister or Secretary to the government at the Centre or in the States, if a complaint is made against such an act either by an individual or by a corporation who is affected by it. The Lokpal may also in his discretion inquire into a complaint of maladministration involving not only an act of injustice but also an allegation of favouritism to any person, or of the accrual of personal benefit or gain to the administrative authority responsible for the act. The Lokpal may *suo moto* investigate administrative acts which may come to his notice otherwise through the complaint of an adversely affected person.

The following matters were to be excluded from the purview of the Lokpal :

1. Action taken in a matter affecting the relations or dealings between the government of India and any foreign government or any international organisation or state government.

2. Action taken under the Extradition Act, 1962 or Foreigners Act, 1946.

3. Action taken with respect to protecting the security of state including action taken with respect to passports.

4. Action taken in the exercise of power in relation to determining whether a matter shall go to the court.

5. Action taken in matters which arise out of the terms of contract governing purely commercial relations of the administration except complaints of harassment or delays in the performance of contractual obligations.

6. Action taken in respect of appointments, removals, pay, discipline, superannuation or other personal matters.

7. Grant of honours and awards.

8. A decision taken in the exercise of his discretion by an administrative authority, unless the act shows that no discretion was at all exercised.

9. Any action in respect of which a person aggrieved has or had a right to go before a court or tribunal.

10. An administrative action more than twelve months ago before the date of complaint.

Lokpal Bill

The Government of India accepted the recommendations of the ARC in general terms and a bill styled the Lokpal and Lokayukta Bill, 1968 was introduced in the Lok Sabha in 1968. After the consideration of the Bill by the House, it was referred to a joint committee of the two houses. It was thereafter passed by the Lok Sabha on 20 August, 1969 and sent to the Rajya Sabha for its consideration. The Bill, however, lapsed due to the early dissolution of the Lok Sabha in December, 1970. A fresh Bill on the subject was introduced on 11 August, 1971, but this Bill also lapsed on the dissolution of Fifth Lok Sabha. The Janata Government on coming to power in 1977 introduced the New Lokpal Bill. The two main features of this Bill were : first, the Prime Minister was brought within the ambit of enquiry by the Lokpal; second, the Lokpal was to have his own independent administrative machinery to carry out investigations. The Bill was referred to the joint select committee which submitted its report in July 1978, but when the Bill was under consideration as reported by the Committee, the Lok Sabha was dissolved and the Bill lapsed. The Rajiv Gandhi government revived the proposal and introduced the Lokpal Bill in 1985. The Bill was referred to the Joint Committee whose report was placed in the parliament on December 6, 1988. The Government, meanwhile had introduced a motion for the withdrawal of the Bill and bring forth a comprehensive legislation to deal with redressal of public grievances. The committee considered the notice of the government together with the reasons, and recommended that leave be granted for the Bill's withdrawal. On December 29, 1989, Janata Dal Law Minister introduced the Lokpal Bill. The Bill brought within the purview of the Lokpal the Prime Minister as well. It was not to have any jurisdiction to conduct enquiry into the allegations against the President, Vice-President, the Speaker, the Chief Justice or any Judge of the Supreme Court, the Comptroller and Auditor General, the Chief Election Commissioner, the Chairman or any member of the UPSC. The Lokpal was not to have jurisdiction to enquire into any matter concerning any person if any of its members has any bias in respect to person or matter concerned. The Lokpal was also not to enquire into any matter referred to enquiry under the Commission of Enquiry Act or into any complaint made five years after the date of offence mentioned in the complaint. However, the Bill could not be enacted as Parliament was dissolved. The Narasimha Rao government even failed to introduce the Bill as its policy was "Let sleeping dogs lie". The Bill was introduced for the sixth time by the United Front government led by H.D. Gowda in 1996. The proposed bill was scrutinised by the Parliamentary Standing Committee, but before its recommendations could be incorporated in the Bill, the U.F. government went out of power and fresh elections were held in Feb., 1998. The Vajpayee government introduced the Lokpal bill on August 3, 1998. This was for the seventh time, but since the Vajpayee government also resigned (May 1999) and the Lok Sabha stood dissolved, the Lokpal Bill introduced by it had run ground. The Bill was again introduced by the present govt. on August 14, 2001. The P.M. was brought within its purview but M.P.s excluded. The Lok Pal Bill sets up a watch dog body to check corruption in high places including the office of P.M. The exclusion of MPs from its ambit would, however, defeat its purpose. N. Vittal-C.V.C. felt that the Bill would be tooth less if MPs escape inclusion

There are two fundamental issues involved. *First*, the hidden unwillingness of the ministers including the Prime Minister to submit themselves for enquiry by an independent authority other than the parliament to which they are already responsible under the principles of parliamentary democracy; *second*, the functional jurisdiction of the proposed Lokpal. Should the Lokpal take up the cases of corruption only or should it be also invested with the task of redressing citizens' grievances in respect of injustice caused by maladministration of officials. Infact, the citizen is interested in redressal of his individual grievances as the existing avenues do not provide him easy, speedy and cheap redressal. Hence the existence of an agency independent of government control is indispensable.

The institution of Lokpal on the pattern of Ombudsman is apt to prove an appropriate institution for dealing with the average citizen's complaints about unfair administrative action. It differs from the traditional methods of dealing with grievances and has important advantages over those methods. *First,* the Lokpal is to be an officer of the legislature and not of the executive. *Second,* he is to be independent of political control and will be an impartial investigator. *Third,* his reports to the parliament will serve as an effective weapon of publicity against the excesses of the government. *Last,* he can start investigations *suo moto and* his method of handling cases will be as such direct, informal, speedy and cheap. It is, therefore, hoped that the Ombudsman type institution of Lokpal will be an asset in the Indian political scenario.

Lokayukta

Although no institution of Lokpal has yet been established at the Centre, there are states like Maharashtra, Madhya Pradesh, Karnataka, Bihar, Orissa, Himachal Pradesh, Haryana, Rajasthan, Assam, Gujarat, Andhra Pradesh, Uttar Pradesh, Kerala etc., which have appointed Lokayukta for dealing with public grievances on the lines suggested by the Administrative Reforms Commission. Maharashtra was the first state to enact such legislation in 1971. The other states legislations were based on more or less on the Maharashtra legislation which provides the Lokayukta with exclusive power to look into complaints against state ministers, secretaries and other senior officers. Section 12 of the Himachal Pradesh Lokayukta Act, 1983, provides, "If, after enquiry in respect of a complaint, the Lokayukta is satisfied...that all or any of the allegations made in the complaint have or have been substantiated either wholly or partly, he shall, by report in writing, communicate his findings and recommendations to the competent authority and intimate the complainant and the public servant concerned about his having made the report". The competent authority examines the report and has to communicate to the Lokayukta within a period of three months of the receipt of such report, the action taken thereon. It may be noted that the Lokayukta is only a recommending authority. Its recommendations have no legal sanctity, nor are these binding. The final judgement in respect of the offence lies with the competent government authority. Prof. Donald C. Ravat, an internationally known expert on the Ombudsman institution has highlighted some pertinent defects in the Ombudsman system in the states of India. According to him, "the main defect in the Indian plan has been the attempt to combine the Ombudsman institution with the machinery for fighting corruption, and the consequent treatment of grievance complaints in almost exactly the same way as allegations of misconduct and corruption. This has had two unfortunate results. The fear by senior officials and ministers of allegations against themselves or their colleagues has meant that they have given the plan weak support bordering on actual sabotage of its effective working. Secondly, it has resulted in forbidding formal procedure, designed for allegations, being applied equally to grievance complaints. The extreme example is that of punishment to the complainant unfortunate enough to have made a false complaint. The Ombudsman elsewhere is widely regarded as the little man's friendly helper and defender against the bureaucratic juggernaut of the modern state..."[1]

To sum up, the institutional devices for redressing citizen's grievances in India are many and varied (legislative, administrative, judicial and quasi-judicial). Several institutions at the Central, State and local levels exist for the purpose but still dissatisfaction with the governmental functioning and mis-behaviour of employees is widespread. The administrative machinery is inertia ridden and corrupt. Under such circumstances, the Lokpal is likely to be swamped with overwork but to remedy the situation his jurisdiction is not to be too diminished. Further, as pointed out by ARC, the setting up of Lokpal and Lokayuktas is not the complete answer to the problem of redress of citizens' grievances. In the ultimate analysis, the government should manage its affairs without generating any legitimate sense of grievance. But an efficient and clean system of administration is the by-product of a similar political culture. In the present Indian environment of falling standards of

[1]*Quoted by U.C. Aggarwal in 'A case for a National level ombudrman.' Managements July-Sep. 1986,p.149*

political morality and high level bureaucratic corruption it is feared that institutional devices also will fail to check administrative malpractices, because like the other independent agencies they cannot remain free of the overwhelming bureaucratic apparatus and the overpowering political forces. Whether the Lokpal, would prove an effective functionary and whether the deep rooted corruption and widespread maladministration would be checked or minimised, remains to be seen.

(F) PEOPLE'S PARTICIPATION IN ADMINISTRATION

Shri Jawaharlal Nehru once said, "Public administration, apart from the normal features that it should have, should be intimately concerned with public cooperation. The idea of a public servant sitting in a world apart and doling out impartial justice is completely out of place in a democratic society and much more so in a dynamic democratic society which is moving forward because the very pace of moving forward depends not on the public servant but on the people and if there is no intimate connection between the people and the public servant there may be efficiency but there is no moving forward".

The preamble to the Constitution of India envisages the creation of a new social and economic order through democratic process in which both the civil servant and the people have to play an active part to translate into action the developmental goals. India has embarked upon planning for development and any planning to be successful must ensure people's participation in the implementation of development plans. Although after 1947, the Britishers withdrew, yet the machine of administration remained not only as a manual of office procedures, physical buildings and human bodies but also established habits, prejudices, interests and class barriers. There was hardly any departure from the past, and innovations were few. Bureaucracy nurtured on colonial traditions continues to exhibit the traits of impersonality, compulsive professionalism and procedural rigidity.[1]

Today, in India the people's grievances against civil servants are increasing day-by-day which exhibit themselves through frequent *bundhs* and agitations, even sometimes leading to violence and 'gheraos'. The upsophisticated and illiterate as most of them are, they generally face injustice, harassment and persecution. Hence, the people, in general, have got alienated from the administration. They have little faith in the integrity and impartiality of the administrative officials. Instead of assisting the administration, the people keep themselves aloof and away from it. In a democratic system of government, the citizens and the public servants are not two separate entities. Much of the success of public administration depends on its capacity to enlist public participation in the administrative process. Many of our developmental programmes like family planning, community development and social welfare have failed due to the lack of citizens' participation in them. One of the main reasons for the failure of municipal administration to provide adequate civic amenities to the people is its failure to enlist people's cooperation. The fifth plan, having recognised the need for the people's participation in planning, states, "The involvement of the people and their elected representatives is a pre-requisite for effective planning. A plan which does not take into account the people's aspirations and preferences can have no operational validity, especially since its successful implementation can be ensured only if the majority of citizens, functioning as entrepreneur decision-makers in relation to consumption, savings, investments etc. endorse the envisaged policies and programmes by their whole hearted participation".[2]

Thus, both democratic administration and development administration call forth people's participation in order to successfully achieve the goals of democratic socialism enshrined in the Constitution of India. It may be pointed out that democratic political system does not necessarily ensure democratic administration. After independence, we adopted a democratic system of government by bestowing the right of adult franchise and enabling the citizens to elect the legislators and making the government responsible to the elected representatives of the people. But the

[1]*Jaganadham and H.R. Mukhiya, 'Citizen, Administration and Lokpal, p.27.*

[2]*Planning Commission, see fifth Five year plan.*

administration still retains its colonial authoritarian legacies in character and style of functioning which has generated hostile alienation among the people.

Meaning of People's Participation

Participation, according to a UNESCO document is "collective sustained activity for the purpose of achieving some common objectives, especially a more equitable distribution of the benefits of development.[1] The term 'participation' varies in meaning and content from context to context. Its interpretation may range from taking passive interest in national affairs such as by reading newspapers, listening of radio, viewing TV and discussing matters with others to taking part in national activities like attending meetings, conferences etc. and taking part in demonstrations and processions. It may even include protest actions like strikes, dharnas, etc.

Broadly speaking, the term 'people's participation' refers to the role of members of general public, as distinguished from that of appointed officials, including civil servants, in influencing the activities of government or in providing directly for community needs. It can be at various levels and by different sets of people on different issues in each case drawing different segments of community. It may occur from the village to the country level. It may manifest itself in different forms. It may only be advisory, as in the case of an advisory committee to a minister or district officer; it may involve decision-making as in the case of local self-governing bodies; and it may extend to actual implementation as occurs when villagers / town dwellers decide to carry out a community self-help project. The participation may be direct, as in the community projects and in the work of private welfare organisations, or it may be indirect, through elected representatives or officials.

The Report of the team for the Study of Community Projects and National Extension Service, 1957 states : "People's participation is not merely their providing a certain proportion of the cost of a particular work in cash, kind or manual labour. It is their full realisation that all aspects of the community are their concern and the government's participation is only to assist them where such assistance is necessary. It is the gradual development of their faith in the efficacy of their own cooperative action in solving their local problems.[2]

To sum up, people's participation in administration refers to all those activities which show the people's involvement in the processes of administration that is, participation in policy formulation and programme planning, implementation and evaluation of policies and programmes meant for development of particular target groups. Generally speaking, people's participation is mobilised through institutional structures which is called institutional participation.

Problems of People's Participation

The degree and extent of people's participation in public administration in India is greatly conditioned by the basic nature and operational peculiarities of Indian administration, and the socio-economic ethos of the country. Extensive empirical studies on the nature and degree of citizens' participation in India have revealed that the colonial legacy, social diversity, poverty and illiteracy and the peculiarity of the political process combine to greatly restrict popular participation in the public administration in India.

The reasons for indifferent, disinterested, apathetic and even disgusted public attitude towards administration are the following :

(*i*) *Colonial Legacy.* The public administration in India even after independence retains colonial elements. A new class – administrative elite – has come into existence which has monopolised decision-making on all major issues of public policy. The bureaucracy acts in an autocratic manner,

[1] *UNESCO, Division for the Study of Development, p. 15.*

[2] *Report, Nov. 1957, p.3.*

under-rates the intelligence and capability of the people to offer any suggestions for improvement of administration, gives priority to the maintenance of law and order and does not even extend the normal courtesies to the people. The officers consider themselves embodiment of law and forget that they are public servants. There is no adequate machinery for redress of people's grievances and give them expeditious justice. The people get disenchanted with the administration. A research study in Eldesveld, Jagannadhan and Barnabas has revealed that large proportions (60 per cent urban, 32 per cent rural) hold that their dealings with officials are unsatisfactory, and the majority sense that their probabilities of gaining access to officials and being successful in processing their complaints with them are low. Over 50 per cent feel that officials in certain agencies are not fair, that a citizen can do little by himself, and from 60 per cent to 75 per cent feel that political pull is important in getting administrative action. Consequently, the administrators have failed to solicit extensive public participation.

(*ii*) *Administrative Corruption.* The widespread corruption in public services has caused loss of faith and trust of the people in administration. The common people have to experience a lot of inconvenience, disappointment and frustration when they have to get their ordinary and just matters cleared and are made to run from pillar to post to get their legitimate grievances inquired into and removed by the competent authorities and to realise in the ultimate analysis that they cannot get justice without bribing the officials. They learn to their shock that it is only the few well-to-do, influential and elite sections of society who are favoured with better quality of service. Corruption in public life is rampant and our political masters are so helpless to minimise it, nothing to speak of rooting it out, that people have stopped agitating against it and accepted it as a normal part of administration. Obviously, people have lost faith in the integrity of public services and do not heed their appeals for public cooperation. Any such appeal from corrupt officials and politicians is just considered a hoax.

(*iii*) *Social Structure.* The Indian social structure is characterised by numerous cleavages along religious, ethnic, linguistic and caste lines. The Indian people move within their narrow community groups. They do not intermix socially. There is no loyalty to the nation. The citizens, in general, exhibit an attitude of aloofness, even hostility at times which is a peculiar personality trait reared by the social and communal groups. The minorities, and scheduled castes/tribes have been provided numerous advantages. These classes in order to reap the benefits of the special concessions provided to them do not want to join the mainstream of national life and zealously guard their separate identity.

(*iv*) *Poverty and Illiteracy.* Widespread poverty and illiteracy in the country have facilitated the dominance of powerful socio-economic groups in society who monopolise the fruits of development and progress. The people are not aware and conscious about their rights and obligations and the role they are expected to play in the administration of the country, nor does the government make any serious efforts to create such an awareness among the people. It does not involve the people in decision-making in respect of the plans, projects or schemes. Indian planning is highly centralised and the planning commission has assumed the role of super cabinet. Though District Planning Councils, and State Planning Boards have been set up, they do not play an effective role in the finalisation of the District Plan or State Plan. The Planning Commission is the final authority to determine the size of a state plan and its targets. The people are thus denied the opportunities for participation in the plan proposals which are going to affect their lives.

On account of appalling poverty, people are busy day and night to make the two ends meet. They have neither the time nor the incentive to participate in the task of national reconstruction. Good citizenship and people's participation cannot be expected to emerge from bad living conditions.

(v) Slow pace of Development. The government has no doubt established a wide network of developmental activities in both rural and urban areas, but apparently these have not made deep impact on the life of citizens whose enthusiasm and cooperation are not forthcoming. Citizens would have been more involved in the planning, modernisation and development processes, if they had felt their demands and expectations are in the process of realisation. On the other hand, there is wide gap between the rich and the poor; the rich having easy access to administration and the general tendency of officials to avoid the poor and underplay their needs and interests. There is inordinate delay in getting the wheels of the administrative machinery in motion. The Community development programmes have failed to generate the necessary enthusiasm and rural initiative, and donations in cash and kind were not as forthcoming as were required to make the movement a success. It turned out to be more of a 'government's programme' instead of 'people's programme'. Planning has not eradicated widespread poverty, inequality and unemployment. The fruits of development have not reached the target groups (the rural and urban poor, landless farmers, small artisans and backward classes), these have been cornered by a few feudal nobles and political leaders. In the existing milieu of slow pace of development and failure of rising expectations, it is small wonder that the people were turning increasingly hostile, critical and cynical.

(vi) Failure of Panchayati Raj. The Panchayati Raj institutions were established as institutions of grass root democracy and of democratic development with the objective to operationalise the concept of democratic decentralisation and devolution of real power and responsibility to the local mass for the development of their areas. In the recent past, the system has lost its old moorings, its ethos and objectives. The Panchayati Raj bodies have made the existing caste and caste division in rural society more acute. As told earlier, the Panchayati Raj institutions have become hotbeds of deep political rivalries and another appendage of criminalised politics and political criminalisation. They are in no sense representative institutions of rural self-government. Consequently, they have failed to involve the rural people in the socio-economic development of the country.

(vii) Poor image of Leadership. Citizens become what their leaders make them to be. In the ultimate analysis the quantity and quality of people's involvement in the socio-economic development in India is set by the political and administrative leadership. The present-day crisis in India is the crisis of finding administrative leaders who can give new dimensions to administration in line with our concepts of democracy, secularism, planning and socialism. The administrative leadership is marked by authoritarian attitude and bureaucratic style. The work culture is poor. The concept of participative management is missing. About political leaders the least said the better. The legislators once elected do not bother about the electorates. They seldom visit their constituencies and try to create awareness among their voters about the need of their active participation in administration. People are considered as only vote banks by them. The legislators of today are mediocre – some of them illiterate, semi-educated and devoid of the spirit of dedication and service. Their violent behaviour on the floor of the House is disgusting. The country can hardly expect enlightened leadership from a clan of leaders who do not hesitate to indulge in the worst kind of political manipulation and sordid corruption to keep themselves into power. The common man in India is fed up with the vicious role of political leaders in the administration of the country. A close nexus has developed between the politician, the bureaucrat and the capitalist. Citizen participation demands certain preconditions. Of these, the most important are enlightened political leaders, conscientious civil servants and an informed public; all the three of which are conspicuous by their absence in the Indian scenario.

If the above reasons are analysed, it would become clear as to why the people do not come forward to help the police in investigation, as to why they are apathetic to the civic problems of insanitation and pollution and as to why they do not actively participate in the tasks of social upliftment and economic development. The people dread approaching the administration and prefer to suffer. The administrative system has become so polluted that the average person keeps himself aloof and away from it so long as he can afford. The administration feels demoralised while the citizen feels disgusted.

Measures to promote People's Participation in Administration

Despite the desirability, advisability and rationality for people's participation in administration, not much planned effort is visible either to involve people in development processes, projects and schemes or even to offer them incentives to find their own solutions for their local problems. The system of democratic decentralisation introduced in India did not really devolve power on the masses. Planning has remained more bureaucratic than democratic. The dominance of powerful socio-economic and political groups has alienated the common man from the national mainstream. The colonial legacy of law and order administration by an administrative elite stands in the way of the administrator's soliciting extensive public cooperation. The fifty years of planning has failed to ameliorate the living conditions of the masses to any appreciable extent. Poverty, unemployment and inequality are still widespread. Most of the citizens feel helpless and frustrated before the mighty power of the administration and have learnt to reconcile to the corrupt political system.

Obviously, the causes responsible for lack of people's participation in administration have to be removed and various measures need to be initiated to exploit their potential to the maximum. These may include : constant contact of the legislators with their constituents, change in the attitude of bureaucrats, strengthening of Public Relations agencies to inform the people and serve as a bridge between them and the administration, providing adequate mechanism for redressal of citizens' grievances, competent administrative leadership, constructive role of political parties and revamping of established procedures and restructuring of administration so as to make it more democratic, responsive, transparent and people-friendly.

A word may also be said about the role of voluntary organisations and advisory committees which are useful media to secure people's participation in administration. The planners have very often expressed their keenness not only to secure the willing assent of the people to a democratic plan but also to seek their active participation in the process of planning and implementation. In other words, it is no longer a question of associating the people or their agencies through indirect representation with a plan officially framed and administered but of evolving a joint partnership in the entire process of development. It is, in fact, a step towards translating into reality the concepts of participating democracy. In the long history of social work in India, voluntary organisations have always played a pioneering role. The administrative machinery being impersonal in nature, it cannot lend that "human touch" to administration which a voluntary organisation can provide. The personal approach is more necessary in development administration. The government should strengthen voluntary organisations and streamline their activities. They should be freed from bureaucratic rules and procedures and political interference, which unnecessarily hamper their functioning. There should be a healthy relationship between the government and voluntary agencies which is a relationship of 'partnership' in a common endeavour to play their respective roles in national development.

People also participate through advisory committees / boards constituted to tender advice to the government. Such committees / boards may be appointed at Central, State and local levels. There may be representative advisory bodies consisting of representatives of different groups and other persons besides official nominees. There may also be expert committees, consisting of experts in a particular field to advise the government. The establishment of a rationally organised system of advisory committees would keep "the government appraised of what they (people) expect, what they apprehend, and what they would resist". It provides an opportunity to the Government to test the efficacy of its policies and actions. Through a network of advisory committees, the feeling of alienation among the people gets reduced and their feeling of participation gets strengthened.

In conclusion, people's participation in administration means active cooperation and involvement of the general masses and the targetted public in the various interfaces of decision-making process and implementation and evaluation of development programmes at all levels. It is "a cumulative and continuous process, which has to be nurtured and gradually developed with the help of the people themselves through close rapport, communication, their organisations, decentralised and integrated approach." Public participation in the public administration in India must become a mass movement, for, it is not only a means to national development but is in itself a development goal.

(G) IMPACT OF INFORMATION TECHNOLOGY ON PUBLIC ADMINISTRATION

The most significant development in the field of public administration in the twentieth century has been the emergence of new public management in the form of electronic methods and tools. The classical modes of administration with emphasis on division of work, rule book, written word, defined regulations, lines of authority, written manuals, filing system, record maintenance, huge paper work, communication through post and telegraph, face to face personal exchange of various hand written or typed correspondence and delayed delivery of service have given place to new what is called E-Governance or administration. Public administration is now making more and more use of electronic devices and information technologies.

The advent of computerisation in the 1960s ushered in a new discipline of Information Technology. It is computer based communication system *i.e.* E-mail, tele and video conferencing and Internet. Internet is self-regulated global network of computer net-works. It is a loose amalgam of hundreds of thousands of computer network connecting a widely diverse community of government departments, public undertakings, universities, research institutions, commercial establishments and millions of individuals all over the world.

At the time of independence Indian scientific and technological infrastructure was neither strong nor organised as compared to the developed world. We depended on imported teachnologies for growth in economic, commercial and infrastructural fields. But during the past few decades an infrastructure and technological capability has been created minimising our dependence on other countries. There is, now a reservoir of expertise well aquainted with the most modern advances in basic and applial areas to provide a framework for future national development.

In the field of Public Administration, the use of information technology has brought about the following changes:

(i) Urban Services. Information Technology has facilitated the accounting, delivery, compliance and payment for services like water supply, the telephones and electricity. The bills are now prepared on computer and paid through electronic system. We need not visit personally the public offices for this purpose. It has added to the efficiency and speedy delivery of service. Likewise, citizens in urban areas can now obtain necessary information and forms for applying for any service and submit the form through Email.

(ii) Computation and Payment of Taxes: The tax authorities are now making use of electronic devices for computation of taxes to be paid by user. The citizen can now file his income tax, sales tax, house tax etc. and other duties payment form and make payment electronically. This has eliminated the need for a personal visit to the concerned departmental official. This has also reduced the inconvenience to the tax payer and also speeded the payment of taxes.

(iii) Filing of Complaints: A system of filing complaints has been introduced in some offices like telephone, electricity and water supply etc. electronically which has led to the speedy redressel of grievanus and avoided the harrassment caused by personal visit to a far located complaint centre. In some police stations the system of lodging a FIR online has been introduced.

(iv) Public Recruitment: Online filling up the forms and examination system has been introduced which has avoided huge paper work, saved the time spent on holding such examination, avoided the inconvenience to the candidates caused in visiting the centre situated at far off places and made it possible to declare the results within a short time. Several eminent institutions and centres of excellence have adopted the 'On line' admission system.

(v) Data-maintenance: A large number of Government departments like Land-Revenue, Public Relation, advertisement and publicity, Transport and Communication, Health, Education, Industries, Employment and Social Welfare etc. have pur up the data on internet concerning their departments which can be easily accessed for securing any necessary information.

A special mention in this connexion may be made of the Indian Railway which have introduced online reservation system and tickets can be issued for any train, class and destination on any day. Return journey can also be got reserved 'on line'. This has resulted in a large saving in queuing hours for the passengers and at the same time saved the time of the booking clerk spent by him in routine chores such as elaborate tallying of cases. In the Airlines also similar system has been adopted. It may also be mentined that some offices issue computerized receipts for payment received and acknowledgement of application which has reduced corruption to some extent.

(vi) Departmental websites: Most of the ministries/Departments have developed their own websites wherefrom we can get the desired information immediately. Earlier under colonial administration it was very cumbersome to get any information from a government department but now with the introduction of information technology all the relevant and useful information has been put on the websites.

(vii) Harmonious Headquarter-field Relations: Information Technology has brought the Headquarter field establishments nearer and closer to each other. Through E-mail devices any information can be immediately sought from the field and the field staff can get easily advice or clarification on any. The issue communication distance between the two has been reduced and greater harmony in the working of administratin achieved. The method of Tele-conferencing is being used by the senior officers to address their staff in the field, seek their views, know their problems and invite suggestions for improving the efficiency in administration. Tele-conferencing has led to economy in expenditure in calling departmental conferences and paying TA/DA to the participants and also avoided the inconvenience caused to participants in travelling and attending the conference at outside stations.

(viii) Transparency in Administration: Use of IT in delivery of public services and adequate dissemination of information has made administration more transparent and responsive. It satisfies people's right to information and facilitates their empowerment with the required data easily available on the web site. The citizen can know the how and why of a decision taken by the Government and in case he feels dissatisfied with the decision, he can make a representation on line or seek further information. Information Technology has facilitated administrative decentralization. From the far flung area official information regarding progress of various development projects can be gathered in no time and utilized for devising more affective implementation.

The general changes brought about by I.T. Administration may be listed as below:

(i) Unwieldy paper files have been replaced by computer based files.

(ii) Information kept hidden in file has been put on website to be shared by the people.

(iii) Expenditure oriented administration has been replaced by performance oriented administration.

(iv) Earlier, public administration was inspection or compliance oriented, now it is achievement oriented.

(v) The old public administration suffered from delayed service; now under IT administration the citizen gets instant service.

(vi) The IT administration operates through on 'On Line' processing whereas under the traditional method public Administrator operated through 'Batch' processing.

(vii) In old Public Administration much of the time of the employee was spent in routine work; under IT administration he gets sufficient time for creative work.

(viii) The old Public Administration was marked by ' Status-quo', administration is trying to make continuous improvement by inventing better and highly electronic devices.

(ix) The old Public Administration was heavily staffed administration. The IT administration has down sized the staft, reduced time and increased customer satisfaction. Information-keepers and file pushers have been eliminated. People have been replaced by technology. IT administration seeks to eliminate the age-old and archaic procedures and offer a package of efficiency, time boundedness and cost-effectivity along with transparency.

However the important point may not be missed that information Technology has been used to a very limited extent and only in a few aspects of administration. Its greater use is being made in the business, commercial, financial and investment fields and that too in private sector. In public administration the application of information Technology is in its initial stage PCS have been available to senior rank officials. Websites have been set up for making forms available and enabling their submission and publishing information in the public domain including Acts and Rules and activities carried by the department. The pay roll accounting system has been computerized in most of the ministries and departments. As regards electronic work flows like e-mail, on-line notice board, use of grievance redress software, submission of forms on line and on-line delivery of services about one-third of the Ministries/Departments have made progress. The Government of India has started numerous programmes and projects for e-Governance. The country is producing highly important software technologies through its Indian Institutes of Technology, and other Centres of Excellence Indian Software Engineers are much in demand by the software companies like Infosys, T.C.S, Wipro, Cisco etc. The Government can utilise their expertise and knowledge for bringing IT revolution in Public Administration field. It needs no emphasis to say that Technology provides competitive advantages, financial gains, better delivery of services besides bringing in accountability, transparency and speed to the working of administration. To keep pace with the changing global phenomenon Indian Administration should not lag behind in constantly homing the capabilites of the administrators in IT based technologies.

H. GLOBALISATION – IMPACT ON PUBLIC ADMINISTRATION

After the end of second world war and establishment of the United Nations Organization the idea of 'World Government' was mooted to promote community interests and ideals. But the idea could not bear fruit in view of the concept of supreme national sovereignity. However, the need for international cooperation was constantly felt. In the present era the concept of gloablisation has been put forward encompassing economic, social, political and cultural activities.

Globalisation has been defined as "increased and intensified flows between countries. These flows are of goods, services, capital, ideas, information and people, which produce non-border integration of a number of economic, social and cultural activities". Thus, globalisation has a multi-dimensional characteristic and is today widely used to find solution to common problems of poverty, unemployment, international trade. Both the developed and developing countries feel that without mutual cooperation and efforts they can neither provide all the services for the welfare of their people, nor assure a conflict free society. The main indicators of globalisation are internationalism i.e. cross-border relations, border openness by removing regulatory barriers and protectionist measurs, free enterprises and plural democracy and a constant process of expansion of newer opportunities for increasing capital acumulation at the global level. Globalisation is, thus a search for new society. It believes in global market and integrates the national economics into global economics. Under the impact of globalisation the particular markets of nation states are getting incorporated into a single world wide a market. The development of fast means of transport and communication has facilitated the movement of people and goods at inernational level. The revolutionary advances in information technology have facilitated inter connectivity. Eventually a new global society and a new global culture have emerged.

Impact on Public Administration

Globalisation is increasingly changing the economic and political scenario of India. The interdependence has increased to the extent that economic recession in the United States has caused global recession down slowing the economic growth of all the States. India also has become the victim of global slow-down. Thousands of workmen have been removed and rendered jobless. New avenues of employment have shrunk. People have been hard put to meet their both ends. The budget deficit has increased due to slow growth of industrial production and less revenue receipts from taxes. The financial sector is in bad shape. Due to poor liquidity of money with the banks, credit has squeezed and investment fallen. The economic disturbance caused by global recession has adversely affected the law and order situation. Crime graph has increased and public discontentment against the Government is spreading widely. Under the present disturbed conditions Public Administration in India is faced with the challenge of reshaping its structure, nature and functioning to cope with the challenges of globalisation.

The impact of globalisation on Public Administration may be seen in the following areas:

(i) Re-inventing Government: The traditional Public Administration was marked by rules, regulations and red-tapism. Globalisation has led public administration to reinvent itself through new prescriptions like deregulation, decentralisation, debureaucratisation and market like mechanisms. It is known New Public Management. It has been said by the advocates of NPM that Public Administration should not only adopt the techniques of business administration but also adopt the values of business. The basic principles of reinventing government are: steering rather than raving, empowering rather than servicing, injecting competition into the service delivery, transforming rule-driven organisation, meeting needs of the customers not the bureaucracy, from hierarchy to participation and bringing change through the market. The NPM lays emphasis on performance and efficiency, and not on policy making. Public officers should become service providers, agencies delivering services to the people on user basis. They should adopt marketing techniques and act in a spirit of competition. They should not go by a traditional theory but function as a management expert aiming at cutting cost, reducing public expenditure and increasing performance through maximising enhanced output.

(ii) Enterprenurial Government: Under the impact of globalisation, public administration has adopted enterprenuerial form of Government. Efficiency and productivity are the two pillars of enterprenuerial goverment. Public sector orgnisations are now under global pressure to enhance their productivity by increasing efficiency.

(iii) Changing Role of Bureaucracy: With the extinction of USSR it has been proved that state socialism is not the answer to lead economic growth. Privatisation and liberalisation are the basic formulations to increase productivity and efficiency. The government shoud not undertake business functions. It is a political and not an industrial organisation. Developmental activities can not be managed by civil bureaucrats. They are wedded to rule-book and lay more emphasis on strictly following the prescribed regulations. In the present era of economic globalisation only business management experts can deliver the goods. The bureaucrat has to function as a helper and accelerator and not as a director/manager.

(iv) Good Governance: Good Governance is the first priority towards reforms of public administration. Good Governance is more than discharging allocated functions and following prescribed rules and regulations. It is equivalent to purposive and development oriented administration which is committed to improvement in quality of life of the people. It is citizen friendly, caring and responsive administration. It is the process of building bridges between the state and the society at large through people oriented mechanisms of administration.

(v) E-Governance : E-Governance is the chief feature of good governance. E-Governance is the application of information Technology to the process of government functioning. The present day public admministration is making great and greater use of electronic devices like videos, audio, computer and internet which has made it more responsive, transparent and efficient.

(vi) Empowering citizen: Globalisation has also witnessed the rise of grass-roots, people's participation at the local level in areas such as women empowerment, education for all, human rights, consumer rights, environmental protection and decentralisation. Thus empowerment of citizens has been an important component of reforming public administration.

(vii) State Retreating: Under the impact of globalisation the state is withdrawing itself from numerous sectors wherein it once used to play controlling and ownership roles. Thus some public enterprises have been handed over to private entrepreneurs or government shares have been reduced therein. It is said that economy should operate as per market forces and not as per government policies, preferences, rules and regulations. Private enterprise and non-state sectors such as voluntary agencies, cooperative institutions, self-help groups and community based organisations have entered several areas of development like education, health, human rights and welfare of the poor.

Under the impact of globalisation, public administration is required to play a changed role. Firstly, the older regime of controls, regulations, restrictions, licences, secrecy and delay should be disamantled. Secondly, the bureaucracy should become citizen-oriented, people friendly, responsive, open, transparent and competitive. Thirdly, redundent rules, laws, procedures and practices should be eliminated. Fourthly, corruption, nepotism, favouratism and politicisation of administration should be removed.

Today state interference in the lives of individuals has been reduced. The state has now assumed the new role of regulator and facilitator. The role of public administration is towards good governance than of direct involvement. It is to play enabling, collaborative, cooperative and regulatory roles. Public administration is no more a question of revenue administration or law and order maintenance. It is now required to come to grip with a socio-economic challenges of development and globalisation.

***

ADMINISTRATIVE REFORMS IN INDIA

...... *"What we need in India is revolution in administrative system without which no enduring change can be brought about in any field* **— Late Prime Minister Indira Gandhi**

ADMINISTRATIVE REFORMS IN INDIA

At the time of independence in 1947, India inherited a colonial administration which was primarily designed for the performance of limited functions of an imperial government, and naturally unsuited to serve the needs of a secular, independent, democratic and socialistic Republic of India. Consequently, since Independence the question of reforming the administrative machinery gained importance in order to make it adequately suitable to the new goals of public administration in India. The founding fathers of Indian Independence saw an advantage in not scrapping the old colonial administration altogether but rather refashioning and remoulding it to meet the needs of democracy, development and efficiency.

Meaning of Administrative Reforms. The term 'Administrative Reforms' has been defined by Prof. Gerald E. Caiden as the 'artificial inducement of administrative transformation against resistance'.[1] This definition seems to be too flexible to include those matters which do not qualify the term. John Montgomery defines administrative reform as "political process designed to adjust the relationship between a bureaucracy and other elements in a society or within the bureaucracy itself in order to change the behaviour of the public service.[2] This definition does not clarify the term 'reform'. According to Lee, Administrative Reforms is an "effort to apply new ideas or combinations of ideas to an administrative system with a conscious view to improving the system for positive goals of national development".[3] Deor defines Administrative Reforms in terms of "directed change of main features of an administrative system".[4] Backoff defines administrative reforms as "improving performance by identifying the attributes and rates of bureaucratic adaptability".[5] In simple words, administrative reforms mean changes in the machinery of government to promote cleanness, openness, accountability, decentralisation, public ethics and citizens' satisfaction in public administration. These changes may pertain to its structure, process, personnel and behaviour.

Writing on the "Priorities in Administrative Reforms", M. Sunder Raj observed that, "The administrative organisation is a tool for conducting the economic and political affairs of the society

[1]*Gerald E. Caiden, "Administrative Reform", p. 8.*

[2]*John Montgomery, "Source of Bureaucratic Reform". A Typology of Purpose and Politics, Ralph Braibanti (ed.) Political and Administrative Department, p. 73.*

[3]*Lee, Hahn-Been, "Bureaucratic Models and Administrative Reforms" In Arne F. Leamans ed. The Management of Change in Government", p. 114.*

[4]*Deor, Y. "Strategies for Administrative Reform". Development and Change, pp. 19-35.*

[5]*Backoff, Robert, "Operationalizing Administrative Reform for Improved Governmental Performance". Administration and Society", p.73.*

in a disciplined and orderly manner, and for effectively achieving social and economic progress. Like all tools, it has to be shaped to suit the environment in which it operates, and the nature of the materials which it has to handle. The environment and the material are continuously changing and if administration is to serve its purpose it has to continuously adapt itself to these changes. Moreover, it is not feasible to lay down a blueprint for a perfect administrative system. Nor is such perfection achievable pragmatically but what is practicable, is to improve on the quality of an existing administration by exercising a constant and vigilant watch over the areas of efficiency, and affecting a timely change whenever necessary. There always is a need and scope for reforms in any administration".[1] (Late) Prime Minister Indira Gandhi once observed, "Our patterns of administration were drawn or designed at a time when the government's main business was to keep law and order. They are inadequate for the challenge which we face today. What we need, therefore, is revolution in the administrative system without which no enduring change can be brought about in any field".

The main defects in Indian administration are : faulty structure and organisation, archaic rules and regulations, poor work culture, procedural delays, lack of integrity and efficiency, people's apathy towards administration, lack of accountability and transparency, politicisation of administration, erosion of public faith in the government's capacity to solve people's problems, etc. To remove these failures and defects, administrative reforms are needed. It was stated in the Third Five-Year Plan that "The primary aim must be to ensure standards of integrity, efficiency and speed in implementation. The process of improving administrative efficiency is a continuous once and progressively through work studies and improved systems of office administration, and in other ways, better methods have to be devised. It is recognised, of course, that while changes in organisation and procedures can go some distance to remove causes of delay and to achieve greater speed, they have to be supported by greater attention to the training of personnel, to supervision and to reporting and evaluation. Nevertheless, without a concerted attempt to make the administration much more action-oriented than at present, these measures may not yield enough results".[2]

Reforming Administration

In our country both the Central and State governments have been taking a keen interest since independence in bringing about administrative reforms through various committees as under.

Ayyangar Committee, 1949. The first committee setup to undertake a comprehensive review of the machinery of central government towards the end of 1949 was Gopala Swami Ayyangar Committee, 1949, which dealt with organizational changes, improvement in calibre of personnel and improvement in methods of transaction of governmental business. The committee recommended a distinction between a 'Ministry' and a 'Department'. While the ministry would be identified with the Minister's charge, a Department would be identified with a Secretary's charge. It was also recommended that the Central Secretariat should be divided into 37 primary units of organisation consisting of 28 departments, 8 Central Administrative offices and a Cabinet Secretariat. Twenty-eight departments should be accommodated with twenty ministries. It also recommended the setting up of an "organisation and Methods Division" in the Home Services Department of the Ministry of Home Affairs and the appointment of Standing Committees of the Cabinet like Defence Committee, Economic Committee, Parliamentary and Legal Affairs Committee and the Administrative Organisation Committee.

Gorwala Committee, 1951. In 1950, the government setup the Planning Commission. An important term of reference was to consider whether the present administrative machinery and methods were adequate to the requirements of planned development. The Commission felt that it should obtain an independent and objective assessment of the problems of public administrations and requested Mr. Gorwala, a retired ICS officer to make a study and suggest measures for bringing

[1]*Indian Journal of Public Administration, April-June 1967, p. 204.*
[2]*Third Five-Year Plan – "Administration and Plan Implementation", pp. 271-73.*

about reforms in public administration, especially in relation to the implementation of the development programmes of the Central and State governments. Mr. Gorwala submitted his report to the Deputy Chairman of the Planning Commission on 30th April, 1951, after completing it within a short period of two months. He felt that the administrative machinery was rundown and its efficiency was impaired. There was considerable public dissatisfaction with it due to delay, lack of integrity, undue interference and corruption, as also lack of personal touch which led to lack of confidence in administration.

Gorwala Report

The main recommendations of Gorwala Report were :

(*i*) Parliamentary government with a cabinet system on the British model cannot be effective, unless the standard of morality of those who work it, is high and the general public believe it to be so. Gorwala insists on the maintenance of moral standards among ministers, legislators and administrators and ascribes the fall in standards of public administration to corruption, patronage and influence. It vitiates policy, weakens administration and undermines public confidence.

(*ii*) He suggested proper relationship between Administrative Ministries and the Finance Ministry. Financial control is desirable but financial interference should be avoided.

(*iii*) The Minister should confine himself to matters of policy and leave the initiative to the Secretary.

(*iv*) There should be created an O and M branch in the government and a Board of two members should be setup to provide necessary drive and direction to administration.

(*v*) Parliamentary control over the working of Ministries and more especially over expenditure is most desirable.

(*vi*) More junior officers and less clerks should be appointed.

(*vii*) Discipline in government offices has been first victim of independence. To bolster the discipline, he recommended promotion on the basis of good work.

(*viii*) Whitley Councils on the pattern of U.K. should be established.

(*ix*) Training, besides aiming at precision and clarity in the conduct of business and improvement of staff morale, must also encourage the civil servant to see his work in its widest context and to preserve with his own educational development. It must prepare him for higher work and greater responsibilities and attune his outlook and methods to the needs of changing times.

(*x*) The principal of the IAS Training School should be absolved of other departmental responsibilities.

(*xi*) Director of Training and Organisation and Methods with requisite staff and office should be immediately appointed.

(*xii*) Recruitment to all grades of government service should be conducted in a manner which eliminates scope for patronage and suspicion of patronage. All posts, whether temporary or permanent, should be filled up by the Public Service Commission.

The Government of India accepted Gorwala's recommendation to setup an O and M branch in the government and allowed the rest of the report to lie on the shelf.

Appleby Report, 1953

In the closing months of 1952, C.D. Deshmukh, the Finance Minister at the time, invited Paul H. Appleby, a noted authority on public administration in the U.S.A. to make a survey of public administration in India. He wrote his report mainly for policy-makers and the executive authorities. He was less concerned with details of administrative machinery and more with the basic principles and concepts. Appleby felt that Government of India was making the best effort in the world today to bring development through democracy. He analysed factors making for unity and disunity. Amongst the factors responsible for weakening of administration, he mentioned the absence of any nucleus field structure of the Centre. He suggested a strong Centre for administration of programmes. He also commented on the lack of action-mindedness in Indian administration and lack of capacity to take action in situations.

Appleby submitted his Report in 1953. The main recommendations were the following :

(*i*) An Organisation and Management of Public Administration office directly under a minister of the government should be setup. It should focus attention and study on proposals concerning the improvement of governmental structure and procedures.

(*ii*) An Institute of Public Administration for India should be established. It should serve as a nucleus of a professional journal, expansion of studies and development of literature towards advancement of administrative knowledge.

(*iii*) An academic graduate programme in public administration should be evolved for young persons in association with this institute.

(*iv*) Procedures at different levels of government should be simplified and expedited in all developmental and social action fields.

(*v*) The administrative hierarchy should take a more truly pyramidal form with more executives at most levels. The number of levels should be increased.

(*vi*) More flexibility and discretion should be allowed to administrative agencies in co-operation with the P.S.C. in regard to recruitment of personnel.

(*vii*) Extensive and sustained personnel development programmes to maximise the potentialities of public personnel should be undertaken.

An O & M Division was accordingly setup in the Central Secretariat in 1954 and the Indian Institute of Public Administration was also established in the same year at New Delhi. In 1958 the government of India provided for the delegation of financial powers to administrative departments and attached Financial Advisors to each such department for local guidance and control.

Appleby Report, 1956

The setting up of public enterprises in India after Independence had created additional problems of introducing reforms in India's administrative system. The key to the successful operation of business enterprises lies in the rapid decision-making and rapid action. Prof. Appleby was asked to re-examine India's administrative system with special reference to the Government's industrial and commercial enterprises. He submitted his second report concerned more specifically with public undertakings in 1956.

The main recommendations of this Report were as follows :

(*i*) New levels of co-ordination below the level of cabinet and below the level of Minister should be provided structurally.

(*ii*) Provision should be made for recruitment and training of generalist administrator and technical administrator.

(*iii*) Structural and procedural arrangements should be made for the growing size of administration.

(*iv*) An official called Programme Expediter or Plan Expediter should be appointed in the Central Secretariat who will be responsible for overcoming all hurdles, viz. red-tape, inadequate staff, and for overseeing the fulfilment of the Plan.

(*v*) There should be appointed a Finance officer with the parent ministries to develop financial and budgetary competence.

(*vi*) There should also be appointed an Expenditure Secretary in the Finance Ministry to accelerate decision-making. None of the three officers should be deemed permanent additions to the administrative structure but should be setup as temporary expedients to hasten reviewing and decision-making functions and to provide speed to governmental processes by eliminating reviewing agencies at all stages.

(*vii*) The Reports of the Comtroller and Auditor-General contain too much trivial matters. These ought to be shorter and selective.

(*viii*) The principle of delegation should be applied to the field of administration. The parliament should not go into petty details in the name of parliamentary control and public accountability. It should raise itself to the appropriate high level of direction. Its role should be a positive one where it would stop looking for things to criticise and begin looking for things to praise.

(*ix*) Board of Directors for companies and corporations should work on the principle of delegation. The Board should have two functions, one of evaluation and the other co-ordination.

(*x*) Central Purchase and Central Construction retard operation of large undertakings.

(*xi*) The Comptroller and Auditor-General should be relieved of the responsibility of audit. The auditors should not assume the role of judges of policy, administrative judgements or public interest.

(*xii*) The layout, the hierarchical structure and the location of plant of the public undertaking should be determined with a view to future growth and enlargement.

(*xiii*) The public employees should be paid adequate salaries. "Since future prosperity of the country is dependent on the success of the Indian government, people must be willing to pay what adequate and successful government will cost".

Only a few of Appleby's recommendations have been accepted by the government and action taken thereupon.

Administrative Reforms Commission (1966-70)

The appointment of Administrative Reforms Commission was an important landmark in the history of administrative reforms in India. The Commission was setup on January 5, 1966, under the chairmanship of Morarji Desai, with five other members - K. Hanumanthaiya, H.C. Mathur, G.S. Pathak, H.V. Kamath and V. Shankar (member-secretary). During its life, the commission saw several changes in its membership. The chairman left the commission on becoming the Deputy Prime Minister and Sh. K. Hanumanthaiya took over as Chairman. G.S. Pathak left on being appointed the Governor while H.C. Mathur died in the third year of the commission's functioning. In 1970, the last year of the Commission, its membership consisted of K. Hanumanthaiya (Chairman), H.V. Kamath, K. Mukherjee, V. Shankar, T.N. Singh as members.

The commission was asked to examine and report on a vast array of subjects. As many as ten major areas were included in its terms of reference which were the following :

1. The Machinery of the Government of India and its procedures of work;
2. The machinery for planning at all levels;
3. Centre-State relationships;
4. Financial Administration;
5. Personnel Administration;
6. Economic Administration;
7. Administration at the State level;
8. District Administration;
9. Agricultural Administration; and
10. Problems of redress of citizen's grievances.

Under each topic, a number of items were enumerated.

The Commission was left free to devise its own procedures and appoint committees and advisers to assist it. The Commission worked from January, 1966 to June 1970. It setup 20 study teams, 13 working groups, 4 expert groups and one task force to investigate into specified problems and suggest reforms. The Commission submitted in all 20 reports to the Central Government which contained 578 recommendations. Such a stupendous work was never undertaken before in India.

The Machinery of Government and its Procedures of Work

(*i*) The maximum number of Ministries in the Union Cabinet should be sixteen, including the Prime Minister. Each department/subject be represented in the Cabinet by one or the other Cabinet Minister. The strength of the Council of Ministers should normally be forty; but should in no case exceed forty-five.

(*ii*) A Deputy Prime Minister be appointed for giving institutional support to the Prime Minister. The Deputy Prime Minister should have the charge, in addition to his own portfolio, of such subjects and *ad hoc* assignment as the Prime Minister considers appropriate.

(*iii*) A Department of Personnel should be setup under the Prime Minister and its main functions should be the formulation of personnel policies and review of their implementation, talent-hunting, development of personnel for senior management and processing of appointments to senior posts, manpower planning, training and career development and research in personnel administration.

(*iv*) There should be only two levels of consideration below the Minister, namely : (*i*) Under Secretary / Deputy Secretary, and (*ii*) Joint Secretary / Additional Secretary. Work should be assigned to each of these two levels on the lines of the 'desk officer' system in which the officer concerned will himself dispose of a substantial amount of work with the necessary staff assistance.

(*v*) The role of the Cabinet Secretary should be that of a general coordinator and principal staff adviser to the Prime Minister, the Cabinet and the Cabinet Committees.

(*vi*) Responsibility for overall co-ordination with a Ministry which has more than one Department Secretary, should be specifically assigned to one of the Departments/Secretaries most appropriate for this purpose.

(*vii*) The existing O & M units in different Ministries / Department should be reactivised.

(*viii*) The Department of Administrative reforms should be placed directly under the Deputy Prime Minister.

Centre-States Relationships

(*i*) An Inter-State Council should be constituted consisting of the Prime Minister as Chairman, the Finance Minister, the Home Minister, the Leader of the Opposition in the Lok Sabha and five representatives one each from the five Zonal Councils. Its functions will be as indicated in Article 263 of the Constitution.

(*ii*) Powers should be delegated to the maximum extent to the States with regard to their work on projects in which the Centre is directly interested or which are carried out by them as agents to the Central Government.

(*iii*) The Finance Commission may be asked to make recommendations on the principles which should govern the distribution of Plan grants to the States. The appointment of the Finance Commission may be so timed that when making its recommendations it will have before it an outline of the five year plan as prepared by the Planning Commission.

Personnel Administration

(*i*) The Government servants should have no right to strike and their grievances should be settled through Joint Consultative machinery and Civil Service Tribunals.

(*ii*) There should be unified grading structure for the entire Civil Service, so as to facilitate the movement of officers from one area to another for which they are qualified and in which they may be required.

(*iii*) The present system of confidential reports should be replaced by performance reports in which every government servant will have an opportunity of giving a resume of his performance during the year and getting his merits properly assessed for the purpose of promotion.

(*iv*) Greater opportunities should be provided to government servants of lower ranks to rise rapidly, as high as their competence and performance warrant.

(*v*) There should be an improvement of recruitment policies and procedures, pruning of excessive personnel, simplification and codification of rules, rationalisation of holidays and strict limitation of overtime work and transfers.

(*vi*) The functions of government have become greatly diversified. Wherever the numbers involved in a particular function are viable, the posts should be grouped into regularly constituted services.

(*vii*) A functional field must be carved out for the IAS.

(*viii*) There should be setup a Central Training Division in the Department of Personnel.

(*ix*) A civil servant may be allowed to retire voluntarily after he has completed 15 years of service and given proportionate pension and gratuity.

(*x*) Both the husband and wife should not be employed under government at the same time to relieve the problem of mounting unemployment.

(*xi*) The quantum of pension admissible may be raised to 3/6ths of the average emoluments of the last three years as against the existing 3/8ths.

Finance, Accounts and Audits

(*i*) The departments and organizations which are in direct charge of development programmes should introduce Performance Budgeting, which would inter-relate financial outlays with physical targets and achievements and present estimates and expenditure in terms of functions, programmes, activities and projects.

(*ii*) Audit should aim at a positive and constructive approach directed towards seeking improvements in organizational efficiency and effectiveness of financial rules and procedures.

(*iii*) The present system of internal financial advice should be strengthened, as to develop financial competence within each Ministry or Department.

(*iv*) On the 1st of November should begin the Financial year, so as to facilitate a more realistic assessment of revenue and an even spread of expenditure.

(*v*) The Commission did not consider the question of separation of Audit from Accounts.

Economic Administration

(*i*) A high powered Commission on 'Prices, Cost and Tariff' should be setup to assist the government in evolving rational price policies and in creating a climate of cost consciousness and also to take over the functions of the Tariff Commission.

Public Sector Undertakings

(*i*) The practice of deputing government officers on temporary service in public undertakings should cease.

(*ii*) 'Sector Corporations' one for each major area of enterprise should be setup with the main function of promotion and development in that area including the setting up of new projects.

(*iii*) The Bureau of public Enterprises should be reorganized so as to make it a more effective service agency for the Ministers and the public undertakings.

(*iv*) Four or Five Audit Boards should be constituted, each for a specified section of public enterprises, for conducting efficiency audit and appraisal of performance.

The Planning Commission

(*i*) The Planning Commission should confine itself to the formulation of plans and evaluation of plan performance; it should have no executive function and authority.

(*ii*) The National Development Council which is at present composed of the Prime Minister, Deputy Prime Minister, if any, and of the Chief Ministers of all the States, should have also the Union Ministers of ten important departments.

Redress of Citizens' Grievances

(*i*) Special officers should be appointed for the redress of citizens' grievances. There should be one authority – Lokpal – dealing with complaints against the administrative acts of Ministers or Secretaries to government at the Centre and in the States.

(*ii*) There should be another authority – Lokayukta – in each State and at the Centre for dealing with complaints against the administrative acts of other officials.

State Administration

(*i*) The Council of Ministers in a State should be compact and homogeneous, its size being determined by administrative needs. In big States, the number of Ministers may range between 8 and 12.

(*ii*) The full Cabinet should meet at least twice a month.

(*iii*) Ministers should not intervene in the day-to-day administration except in cases of grave injustice, serious default or maladministration on the part of civil servants.

(*iv*) The Standing Committees of State Legislatures may be setup in selected areas of administrative activity for promoting detailed legislative review.

(*v*) The existing executive departments should be so reorganized that needless multiplicity is removed and diffusion of functions and responsibility is avoided.

(*vi*) In departments dealing with specific subjects, there should be setup two 'staff' cells, namely, (*a*) combined cell on planning and policy; and (*b*) a finance cell.

(*vii*) A Department of Personnel should be setup under the charge of the Chief Secretary and be placed under the Chief Minister.

(*viii*) There should also be setup in each administrative department a Policy Advisory Committee.

(*ix*) The proliferation of personnel under the State Governments must be checked. O and M Division must be activised.

(*x*) A convention should be established where the Public Service Commissions are consulted by State governments before the latter exempts any case or types of cases from the purview of the State PSC.

District Administration

(*i*) The judicial work of the collector should be transferred to the judiciary.

(*ii*) the District Administration should be divided into two sectors — one concerned with 'regulatory' functions and the other with 'development' functions. The District Collector should be the head of the former and the Panchayati Raj Administration should have the responsibility for the latter.

(*iii*) There should be only two administrative units whose heads are invested with power of decision-making in the district administration the one in the tehsil, taluka or a group of tehsils /

talukas or a sub-division and the other at the headquarters of the district.

(*iv*) The district level officers in charge of development departments should be transferred to the jurisdiction and charge of the Zila Parishad.

(*v*) A District tribunal consisting of the Collector and a Subordinate Judge should hold inquiries in cases where removal of members of Panchayati Raj bodies is involved.

Evaluating the work of the Administrative Reforms Commission, P.R. Dubhashi has observed as follows :

"Though the Administrative Reforms Commission was to deal comprehensively with Public Administrative system in the country, the manner in which they dealt with it left much to be desired. Though they produced twenty reports, there was no necessary balance between them. Its most important report was on the machinery of Central Government. But its report on State Administration was inadequate whereas it did not give any independent report on District Administration which was described in the British days as the pivot of the administrative system. Secondly, the ARC did not go into the field level implementation of the various development programmes or the working of the regulatory administration at the grassroot level. Nor did it deal comprehensively with the concept of people's participation in administration....

"The ARC seemed to have no integrated perspective or perception about public administration. It had no philosophy of administration and it made no attempt to articulate it. Indeed, it had no overall core report on public administration as a whole."[1]

As regards implementation of the recommendations, the primary responsibility rests with the respective Ministries. The Department of Administrative reforms also is concerned with securing the speedy consideration on the recommendations and ensuring prompt implementation of the decisions taken on them. However, the final decision rests with the Cabinet.

The major recommendations accepted by the government are:

1. The Government has agreed to create the institution of Lokpal and Lokayukta. In this direction Lokpal Bills were presented in 1968, 1971, 1977, 1985, 1989, 1996 and 1998 which however could not be enacted and each time the Bill lapsed due to dissolution of Lok Sabha. Recently on august 14, 2001 Lok Pal Bill was tabled in Lok Sabha. P.M. is within its purview.

2. The Department of Personnel was setup in 1970 which was raised to a Ministry in 1985 called, the Ministry of Personnel Administrative Reforms, Public Grievances and Pensions.

3. In January 1970 the Government also setup a Bureau of Industrial Costs and Prices in the Department of Industrial Development.

4. The Performance Budgeting System was introduced from the financial year 1968-1969 in respect of four ministries, gradually extended to cover more ministers from 1975-76.

5. Most of the recommendation regarding the composition of the Planning Commission have been accepted. However, the Prime Minister and Finance Minister continue to be its Chairman and member respectively.

6. The Government accepted the recommendation that no officer of a Ministry should be made chairman of a public undertaking, nor should the secretary of a ministry be included in its Board of Management.

7. The Government has accepted the recommendation that combined audit parties comprising the staff of audit boards and the professional auditors should be formed for carrying out their work in an undertaking concurrently and collectively.

8. It has been accepted that the Prime Minister should continue to be associated with key appointments.

[1] *P.R. Dubhashi, "Administrative Reforms", p.42*

The Second Administrative Reforms Commission was set up by the Government of India i. August 2005 under the chairmanship of Shri Verrappa Moily to prepare a detailed blueprint for revamping public administrative system and suggest measures to achieve a proactive, responsive, accountable, sustainable and efficient administration for the country at all levels of the government. The commission had four members besides the chairman and the member secretary.

The following areas were identified for consideration of the ARC:

(i) Organisational structure of the Government of India.

(ii) Ethics in governance.

(iii) Refurbishing of personnel Administration.

(iv) Strengthening of financial management system.

(v) Steps to ensure effective administration at the state level.

(vi) Steps to ensure effective District Administration.

(vii) Local Self Governent/Panchayati Raj Institution

(viii) Social Capital Trust and Participative public service delivery

(ix) Citizen-Centre Adinistration

(x) Promoting e-governance

(xi) Issue of federal Polity

(xii) Crisis Management.

(xiii) Public Order

Among the important recommendations of ARC on Refurbishing of Personnel Administration the following ones need mention.

(i) Minimum and maximum age at the entry point should be between 21 to 25 for general category, 21 to 28 years for OBC and 21 to 29 years for SC/ST.

(ii) Lateral entry may be allowed on earmarked posts to attract qualified and competent people from outside.

(iii) Automatic promotion from State Civil Services into the I.A.S or I.P.S should be weeded out. The Commission says, " let them take an exam". All those who have completed 8 to 10 years of service in grade 'A' posts be made eligible to take the exam. A maximum of two chances may be allowed and the upper age limit be fixed at 40 years for entry.

(iv) For specific specialised posts All India. Service and the Central Civil Service officers who have completed 13 years of service be eligible to apply, preference being, given to one who possesses the knowledge of the domain applied for. Once an officer is selected for a particular domain, he or she will remain posted in that field only.

(v) Non-performing bureaucrats should be booted after 20 years of service. There will be two reviews of the performance of an officer, first after 14 years and seemed after 20 years of service. If one is not considered fit for continuing in service he should be removed from service.

(vi) To cut short the long time taken in the conduct of Civil Services Exam, the Moily Commission is of the view that both the Preliminary Exam, having an objective type paper and the main Exam having convential type paper should be administred at one stage one after another in consecutive days. The multiple choice objective type paper for the preliminary exam may be evaluated first and thereafter evaluation of Main exam paper could be undertaken for only those candidates who have scored a thresh hold level of marks.

(vii) A formal degree course in public policy and management may be introduced in the higher educational curriculum for candidates seeking a career in civil service.

(viii) There should be set up a Civil Services Authority headed by a five-member body and appointed by the President which will virtually administer the services for all practical purposes including promotion. It will interview the candidates applying for specific specialised services requiring a practical domain knowledge.

(ix) An exhaustive code of ethics should be redrawn besides simplification of the procedure for punishing an erring bureacrat or an official.

(x) Suitable measures be put in place for mandatory training of officers periodically at all levels-senior, middle and lower in addition to the induction stage. The quality of training should improve. It should seek to impart the functional knowledge, skill and aptitude necessary for performing their jobs diligently.

(xi) Senior positions in the senior Administrative Grade should be filled through competition by opening these positions to the All india and Central Servics. This will reduce the bitterness presently prevaling among officers of other services against the monopoly of the IAS.

(xii) Aquisition of domain competency is imperative for All India Service officers in the present context of development administration and globalisation. The Civil Service Authority will undertake the responsibility of assigning domain to the officers. For this purpose, it may invite the resumes from all officers in the government who have completed 13 years of service.

(xiii) The ARC has suggested 12 functional domains of civil services. These are, namely, general administration, urban development, security, rural evelopment, financial management, infrastructure, HRD, social empowerment, economic administration, tax administration, agricultural development, natural resources administration and health management.

Administrative Reforms in Five-Year Plans

Besides, the above three major reports concerning administrative reforms in India, the subject of 'Administrative Reforms' has also figured in the Five-Year Plans. The First-Five Year Plan laid stress on securing integrity, efficiency, economy and public cooperation in administration. It suggested strengthening of the Prevention of Corruption Act, 1947, and further suggested changes in modes of work and organization, It was suggested that there should be a clear line of responsibility between the secretariat and the department. As regards modes of work it was proposed to have an Organisation and Methods Division. It recommended delegation of responsibility, supervision and inspection including surprise checks and promotion of human relationships between different grades of employees. It also suggested that systematic evaluation of plan projects should become a normal administrative practice.

The Second Five-Year Plan reiterated the suggestion made in the First Five-Year Plan and emphasized the importance of integrity and efficiency in administration. It recommended continuous assessment of personnel, their methods of work and achievements. The factors which contributed to corruption and malpractices should be minimized. It recommended the appointment of a vigilance officer in every ministry and department. A committee on Plan Projects was constituted to ensure efficiency in implementation of projects. It was also suggested that O and M Divisions should be setup in the States as well.

The Third Five-Year Plan again emphasized high standards of integrity, efficiency and speed in implementation. It laid stress on administrative planning in the shape of specification of tasks, means to be employed, obligations of various agencies and the time sequence. It emphasized simplification of work procedures and recommended that there should be no rapid transfer of officials.

The Fourth Five-Year Plan noted that there had been a significant gap between planning and implementation. It pointed out that planning and administration are interrelated. Administration should be action-oriented and performance budget system should be introduced. Management techniques like work-study should be adopted. Relations between Secretariat, department and executive agencies should be clearly defined. Adequate power should be delegated. Short tenures and frequent transfers

5. To prepare simultaneously the ground for a comprehensive investigation of the entire administrative system in the country.

6. To continue the earlier work of the Organization and Methods (O & M) division.

Later, the work of processing the recommendations of the ARC and to give management advice to various government agencies and to promote management techniques were also added to its functions. The department was also assigned the responsibility of organizing training programmes to spread awareness among public employees of the value of administrative analysis as a tool of improvement and to impart education of modern management techniques and administrative practices.

In 1973, the Department of Administrative Reforms was merged with the Department of Personnel and transferred to the Cabinet Secretariat. This merger formed a new Department know as the Department of Personnel and Administrative reforms. In 1977, it was transferred to the Ministry of Home Affairs. In January 1985, this Department was converted into a Ministry called the Ministry of Personnel, Training, Administrative Reforms, Public Grievances, Pension and Pensioners' Welfare. The work of the Ministry is divided into three Departments : Department of Personnel & Training, headed by a Secretary, Department of Pension and Pensioners' Welfare under an Additional Secretary and Department of Administrative Reforms and Public Grievances under the charge of an Additional Secretary.

From the above analysis, it is clear that there has been a constant attempt to reorganize and improve the administrative machinery since 1947. The Committees and Commissions appointed have highlighted the weaker areas of Indian administration and made useful suggestions for reforms at macro, micro and meso levels. At the macro level these suggestions are related to reforms in the economic, political, electoral and constitutional system. At the micro level suggestions have been made to improve the working and image of public offices where the citizen steps in for his problems. The Macro level suggestions are concerned with the reforms in the administrative system proper. These are mainly related to reforms in organization, procedure and methods of work, management of personnel, administrative planning and monitoring.

Though, the ills affecting public administration in India have been thoroughly examined yet ere mere diagnosis is of little comfort unless and until the remedies suggested are implemented ators seems to be a preoccupation with rituals rather than with performance. Our leaders and adm sheer are never tired of publicly emphasizing the need for reforms in administration. But al is what hypocrisy without any meaningful determination to improve the things. An admir observe the the political rulers want it to be. The British rulers wanted the Indian administr als of public , administration ends of imperialism and so it was shaped and developed. In free India, th vative, objective, administration are democracy and development and in order to realize tandards of integrity has to be participative, accountable, transparent, efficient, effective, fair, just, goal-oriented and people-friendly. It has to be clean and political leaders. In order and honesty. It has to be people-oriented and not procedure the political system of the

Public administration has been ravaged by illegitimate code of political ethics. The to rid the administration of undue political pressure, people and not their political country are needed, there is also a more urgent ne sition and gain political mileage. political leaders must realise that administration well-defined procedures and norms. ends. The ruling party should not make it a to mation Act has been enacted which The administration should be allowed to o about the public authorities-Govts. at It is heartening to note that the much ncy in Administration though to limited provides for freedom to every citiz the Centre and in the States. That h extent. For details see last chapter.

The bureaucracy also is to change. In the words of Wallace S. Sayer, "The bureaucracy has a somewhat ambiguous role in the matter of innovation. Its precepts and training emphasise its role as the guardian of continuity, stability, coordination, prudence and precedents. These are the qualities which, however desirable otherwise, cut across the grain of innovation making the bureaucracy more often a vetoer than a sponsor of innovations".

The Madhya Pradesh Administrative Reforms Commission in its Report submitted in 1972 had observed : "..........during the entire course of consultations and discussions with officials and non-officials, we were painfully made aware of a widespread feeling that our labour is an exercise in futility as the political unwillingness to make radical change and obscurantism at the official level would together ensure that no reforms are in fact made".[1]

The above observation is a sad commentary on the political and bureaucratic attitude towards administrative reforms. The rhetoric of reforms is a more familiar phenomenon than is the fact of implementation. The ills of Indian administration cannot be cured by mere pious declarations and half-hearted or isolated measures. Whatever reforms have been introduced are piecemeal and have proved ineffective as the same were implemented in isolation from the political, economic and social context. The failure of Panchayati Raj institutions and urban local bodies are glaring examples of administrative failure.

Concluding, it may be said that our administrative machinery, as it exists today, is inadequate to meet the new challenges of development administration and globalisation Let us give it a new thrust and a new orientation. At a time when the country is threatened by militancy and terrorism aided by foreign powers and there is deep frustration and resentment among the people, the stakes are too high to afford apathy to administrative reforms. A nation which loses faith in the integrity and honesty of its political leaders and capacity and capability of its administrative machinery is sooner or later doomed to disaster. Let the history not repeat itself.

***

ANNEXURE–I

OFFICE ADMINISTRATION

A. PROCEDURE OF WORK IN GOVERNMENT

Government in popular parlance is an organisation of several Ministries and Departments. It is usually known after the name of the Prime Minister, for example, Nehru Government , Indira Government or Vajpayee Government, although the executive power of the Union constitutionally vests in the President and is excercised in his name. He is empowered under Article 77(3) of the Constitution to issue rules for the convenient transaction of the business of the Government. These rules are :

(*a*) The Government of India (Allocation of Business) Rules and

(*b*) The Government of India (Transaction of Business) Rules.

The allocation of Business Rules allocates the business of the Government among the different Departments which are assigned to the charge of the Ministers by the President on the advice of the Prime Minister.

The transaction of Business Rules seeks to define the authority, responsibility and obligations of each department in the disposal of business allotted to it. These rules also specify:–

(*a*) What matters will be submitted to the President, the Prime Minister, the Cabinet or its committees for their consideration and approval, and

(*b*) The circumstances in which the department concerned with the business under disposal will have to consult other departments concerned and get their approval before taking final decisions.

Department

A department is the main unit of a Government. It holds the responsibility for the formulation of policies of Government within its sphere of work. Besides, it executes and reviews that policy. The following are the secretariat functions of an Administrative Department.

(*i*) To assist the Minister in policy making and its periodical review.

(*ii*) To frame legislation, rules and regulations.

(*iii*) To formulate programme and sectorial planning.

(*iv*) To frame budget of the department and exercise control over its expenditure in respect of its activities.

(*v*) To accord and also secure administrative and financial approval to operational programmes and plans and their subsequent amendments.

(*vi*) To excercise supervision and control over the execution of policies and programmes by the executive departments and semi-autonomous field agencies and evaluate their results.

(*vii*) To coordinate and interpret policies, assist other branches of Government and keep up contact with the State Administration.

(*viii*) To initiate measures for effecting greater personnel and organisational competence in the Ministry and its allied executive agencies.

(*ix*) To render assistance to the minister in the discharge of his parliamentary responsibilities.

Attached (or Subordinate) Offices

If the execution of the policies of the Government requires decentralisation of executive action and/or direction, the department is assisted by executive agencies termed 'Attached' and Subordinate Offices for the purpose.

Their Functions

(*i*) The attached offices provide executive directions necessitatd in the implementation of policies formulated by the Department to which they are attached.

(*ii*) They provide technical information and advice to the Department on technical aspects of questions dealt with by them.

(*iii*) They serve as field establishments or agencies responsible for the detailed execution of the policies of Government. They function under the direction of an attached office. However, where the volume of executives direction involved is not substantial, they work directly under the department. In the latter case, they help the concerned department in dealing with technical matters in their respective domains of specialisation.

Functions of Various grades of Officers

1. Secretary : The administrative head of a Ministry or Department is Secretary to the Government. He acts as prinicipal adviser of the Minister on all matters of policy and administration concerning the Department. His responsibility is indivisible and his responsibility is complete.

2. Additional Secretary /Joint Secretary/Special Secretary : If the work of a Ministry is voluminous and beyond the manageable limits of a single individual one or more wings are created with Additional Secretary/Joint Secretary/Special Secretary as incharge of the wings. He is equipped with the maximum measure of independent functioning and is entrusted with responsibility in respect of the business falling within the purview of the wing. However, overall responsibility of the Secretary for the administration of the wing persists.

3. Director/Deputy Secretary : The Deputy Secretary or the Director acts on behalf of the Secretary. He is made incharge of a Secretarial Division and is responsible for the disposal of Government business conducted within the Division. Ordinarily he disposes of the majority of the cases under his own responsibility. It is his discretion to seek directions or orders of the higher officers on more important cases verbally or in writing.

4. Under Secretary : An Under Secretary holds a Branch in a Ministry which comprises two or more sections. He excercises control over the Branch as regards despatch of business and maintenance of discipline. The sections under him send the work direct to him. He disposes of as many cases as possible on his own responsibility. However, on important cases he gets orders of the Deputy Secretary or other higher officers.

5. Section Officer : He is quite a pivotal officer. His duties are multifarious as given below.

(*a*) General

(*i*) He is concerned with maintenance of discipline in the section.

(*ii*) He is to coordinate the work of the section.

(*iii*) He is responsible for assigning work to the assistants as evenly as possible.

(*iv*) He is to assist, advise and train the staff.

(*v*) He is to maintain list of residential addresses of the staff.

(*b*) To attend to Dak

(*i*) He is to attend to the daily correspondence.

(*ii*) He is to pursue as to which receipts (Dak deliveries) are to be communicated to the Branch Officer and which are to be sent to the higher officers.

(*iii*) He is to see to the prompt movement of Dak and check any hold up.

(*iv*) He scrutinizes the diary of the section once a week and sees to its proper maintenance.

(c) Issue of Drafts

(*i*) He is to see that draft prepared is in perfect order and all corrections are duly effected before submission to higher authorities.

(*ii*) To see whether or not all relevant documents are attached with the draft (shown as enclosures).

(*iii*) To indicate priorities on the draft.

(*iv*) To explain mode of despatch.

(*v*) To suggest number of spare copies required.

(*d*) To see to expeditious disposal of work

(*i*) He is to see that cases are not held up at any stage.

(*ii*) He is to see that arrears of work and other returns are submitted in time.

(*iii*) He is to appraise periodical returns every week and take prompt action on items necessitating attention next week.

(*iv*) To inspect Assistants' tables to ensure that no paper or file have been overlooked.

(*v*) He is to maintain a note of important receipts and keep a regular watch on progress of actions.

(e) Independent functionship

(*i*) He is to take independent steps regarding procuring or supplying of factual information of a non-classified nature.

(*ii*) He is to issue reminders to negligent officials under him.

(*iii*) The government can authorise him to take any independent action.

(*f*) Recording and Indexing

(*i*) To ratify the recording of files and their classification

(*ii*) To supervise periodic weeding of unwanted spare copies

(*iii*) To ensure proper maintenance of registers in the section.

(*iv*) To review the file which is to be destroyed.

(g) Miscellaneous

(*i*) To deal with important and complicated cases personally

(*ii*) To ensure neatness and tidiness in the section

(*iii*) To see to the strict compliance with Departmental security instructions

6. Private Secretary/Personal Assistant

(*i*) He is to keep the officer free from the worries of a routine nature by (*a*) mailing correspondence (*b*) filing papers (c) fixing appointments with his boss (*d*) arranging meeting and collecting information

(*ii*) He takes dictation in short hand and transcripts it.

(*iii*) He is to screen the telephone calls and the visitors tactfully

(*iv*) He is to maintain an accurate list of engagements and meetings and keep his officer duly informed

(*v*) He is to keep a note of the movement of files passed by his officer and other officers if necessary.

(*vi*) He carries out the corrections to the officers reference books.

(*vii*) He is to relieve the boss of much of his routine duties and assist him in a manner directed by him.

7. Assistant :

(*i*) He prepares a draft without unnecessary noting where line of action in a case is clear or where the section officer has given clear instructions.

(*ii*) In other cases, he puts up a note keeping in view as to whether all facts have been correctly stated.

(*iii*) He points out any mistakes or mis-statements of the facts.

(*iv*) He draws attention to precedents or rules on the subject.

(*v*) He places the Guard file if necessary before the boss and supplies relevant facts and figures pertaining to cases before him.

ACTION PLAN AND MONITORING

(A) Formulation of Plan

In order to implement the programmes and projects in a systematic way each department formulates an annual action plan in the month of January. The action plan reveals the manner and time frame of action on certain activities, the extent of target to be achieved month wise during the next financial year.

(B) Accountability

The action plan identifies the levels of accountability-direct and supervisory, for the execution of each action point. Attainment of action plan targets constitute a substantial element of performance appraisal of each employee.

(C) Finalisation

Two copies of action Plan will be communicated to the Cabinet Secretariat and one copy each to the Prime Minister's office, Planning Commission and Ministry of Programme Implementation by the Department by January 31. In the month of February, the Plan will be thoroughly thrashed and finalised at meetings to be held for the purpose.

(D) Review

Each officer is to review weekly the progress shown against action points within his charge and take proper steps for effective implementation of the tasks assigned to him. The Secretary heading the department will appraise the performance of the department as a whole regarding the action plan items in a monthly meeting with the senior officers.

(E) Monitoring

Monthly performance report on the activities of the Action Plan revealing details of the targeted and actual performance with comments on deviation, if any, will be communicated to PMO, Cabinet Secretariat and Ministry of Programme Implementation. Besides a quarterely report on the progress attained in most important Items and the indicators identified by the PMO for special monitoring will be communicated to that office.

B. DRAFTING AND CORRESPONDENCE

Drafting

The entire government business, inspite of other modern means of communication like telephones, radio telephones, PABX, Intercom, E-mail, Internet and cellular phone is conducted by written words which can take the form of letters, circulars, memos, notifications, communiques and endorsements etc. Before any of these mediums is used for communication, the format of written words is to be decided upon, i.e., through which medium the communication is to be sent. After a decision is taken, the necessary draft of the communication is prepared. Thus draft is a rough sketch of an official letter, a memorandum, circular or notification etc. Before assuming its final shape, a draft passes through various channels. It is prepared at the level of Assistant who submits it to the officer for his perusal and approval who may make corrections, modifications, amendments etc. While preparing the draft, the concerned Assistant looks into the previous correspondence, notes, resolutions, rules and other relevant material.

Essentials of a Good Draft

Drafting is an art and it needs not only adequate understanding of office procedure, Government laws and rules but also sound knowled[illegible]ge along with clarity of thought and expression. The following are the essentials of a goo[illegible]

***(i)* Correctness**

A draft should not only be correct in its la[illegible]ut all the statements, numbers, figures, rulings, regulations and references made therein sh[illegible]riably be correct to avoid any further correspondence and inconvenience to the party it conc[illegible]n a wrong date may lead to serious consequences. Therefore, the drafting assistants should be v[illegible]ful in the matters of dates, figures, rules and regulations. An incorrect letter not only shows th[illegible]ssness and inefficiency of the office but also bring a bad name to the officer who has signed it. [illegible]usly, the officer who initials the draft should carefully check the references and figures etc.

***(ii)* Completeness**

The draft should give all the information asked for in reply to a lette[illegible] The Assistant should read the letter very carefully and see that no point is left unanswered. The reply should be such that there may be no need of further elucidation or correspondence. An incomplete draft will not only lead to delay in disposal but also add to the cost and causes avoidable inconvenience.

***(iii)* Conciseness**

Brevity is the soul of wisdom. The draft should be as brief and to the point as possible. Of course, clarity and completeness is not to be sacrificed at the cost of brevity. There are words or phrases which can be used for a long sentence. While draft is not a litrerary piece, superficial words and compound/complex sentences should however, be avoided.

***(iv)* Clearness**

The draft should very clearly communicate the message. It should not be shrouded in obscure language and use of verbose words. An appropriate format is to be preferred. Personal observations are not to be made. The letter should be correclty punctuated, as wrong punctuation may change the meaning of words. The usual technical words adopted in official language should be used.

***(v)* Courtesy**

Courtesy implies no cost, rather it wins friends and turns rivals into well-wishers. An official letter should be courteous in tone and language. Even if a request has to be refused or a proposal not approved, one must use such a language that the other party does not feel offended. Unparliamentary language should be avoided. Instead of writing "your statements are wrong and false", one can write "the facts stated in your letter do not appear to correspond with the facts."

***(vi)* Convincing**

The language and the arguments used in a communication should convince the other officer of the soundness and logic of the proposal and the advisability of the plan, suggestion or proposal made therein. In other words, the proposal must be supported by facts, rules and regulations and it must be consistent with the objectives, policies and programmes of the Government.

***(vii)* Medium**

The medium of communication/draft to be adopted should be in conformity with the nature and purpose of the message to be conveyed and it should be written in accordance with the prescribed format. The different types of medium are official letters, demi-official letters, memorandums, circulars, endorsements, notifications, communiques, memorials, resolutions, despatches and proclamations. Of these, the proper medium should be carefully selected to suit the particular needs. The cost of preparing the draft of such medium may also be taken into account.

Letters

It may be noted that most of the correspondence in Government offices is carried on through letters. A post-card is seldom used. The parts of an official letter are :

(*i*) The number of communication.

(ii) The name of the office or the M ...he Department.

(iii) The place and date of issue. ...er of the letter.

(iv) The name and designation ...whom the letter is addressed.

(v) The designation of the of...

(vi) The subject matter.

(vii) The salutation.

(viii) The body of the le...se.

(xi) The complimenta...

(x) The signature ...nd enclosures.

(xi) Identity mar...

A specimen lett... is as follows :

No INSPColl...es/Fbd/2002-145

From

S.P. Yadav,
Principal,
Govt. College,
Faridabad..

To

The Commissioner of Higher Education
Haryana, Chandigarh

Dated Fbd., 25th September, 2002

Sub : Inspection of Govt. College, Faridabad.

Dear Sir,

With reference to your letter No.............dated...............2002 informing us of the proposed inspection of our college on ....02 by a U.G.C. team for the purpose of accreditation, I have the pleasure to inform you that the team will be provided with all the necessary information and record for their perusal and we shall put up our best show.

Yours faithfully
(S.P. Yaday)
Principal
Govt. College
Faridabad

Demi-Official Letter

The objective of writing a demi-official letter is to invite the personal attention of the addressee. The style of writing D.O. is direct, friendly and personal. Active voice is to be used e.g. " I notice" rather than it is noticed. The issue is to be taken up forthwith in the D.O. letter. A D.O. letter should not be a lengthy one; preferably it should be of one page or less than that. Arguments, if any, can be appended as 'enclosures'. The subject matter should be condensed in few small simple sentences in a manner that grips the attention of the addressee.

A specimen D.O. letter is as follows :

J.P. Tandon
Higher Education Commissioner

Office of the Higher Education Commissioner
Haryana.

D.O. No......... Chandigarh 25th June, 2002

Dear Mr. Garg,

Please refer to the office letter NO...............dated.............about Sh. S.R. Gautam, lecturer in your college. As the question of his promotion to senior scale is under consideration, please let me have your report about his integrity at an early date.

With kind regards.

Yours sincerely

....

To

Mr. R.S. Garg

Principal, Govt. College

Faridabad

As regards other mediums of communication.

Memorandum, generally called 'Memo' is a kind of official communication which is used.

(*i*) between departments and offices of equal standing; or

(*ii*) in reply to petitions or applications; or

(*iii*) when the matter is not very important; or

(*iv*) when the addressee is an ordinary person or is an official of a subordinate rank; or

(*v*) when a reminder is to be sent to a person.

A memorandum is written in a brief form in third person, signed by a junior officer or Superintendent and there is no complimentary close like 'Yours faithfully'.

A speciment is as under

No 33/03

Government of Haryana

Education Department

Dated Chandigarh, 26th January, 2003

With reference to his application dated 13th December, 2002 for employment in this office as a typist, Sh. M.L. Sharma is hereby informed that there is no vacancy in this office.

....

Suprintendent

For Higher Education Commissioner,

Haryana

To Sh. M.L. Sharma

207, Sector 27

Faridabad

Circular form is used when the communication is to be brought to the notice of several offices or individuals. It is written in the first person and issued by the Head of a Department to his subordinate officials. It may be in the form of a letter, a memorandum or an endorsement.

A specimen is as under :

No...............

From

A.S. Upadhyaya,

Registrar,

M.D.U. Rohtak

To

The Heads of Teaching Departments,

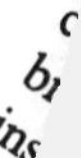

M.D.U.

Rohtak

Dated Rohtak, the 13th Jan, 2003

Dear Sir,

I have to request you to kindly favour me with a list of the foreign students in your Department during the current academic year along with the name of their country and local address. The list is to be incorporated in the Annual Report of the University.

Yours faithfully

( )

Registrar

Endorsements

When a letter received from another office is required to be communicated to a third party for information or to report or to take necessary action etc. on such letter, in such cases the copies (photostat/cyclostyled) copies of the letter are prepared and sent to the concerned party with an endorsement thereupon. It is always dated and numbered, and the name of the office of forwarding the letter is given.

Speciments of endorsement is as under :

No..................

Office of the Chief Commissioner,

Ambala Division

Ambala, 13 Feb., 2001

Forwarded for information and necessary action

....

(Chief Commissioner, Ambala)

A statement showing the designation, address of the person or office and the purpose for which the letter is being forwarded is made at the bottom of the letter itself. e.g.

"Copy forwarded to the Principal, Govt. College, Faridabad for favour of circulation among the members of the staff.

Notifications are written in third person and are published in the official Gazette or leading newspapers. Notifications are not addressed to any particular office or individual but they are meant for information to the officer as well as for the general public interested in the notification.

Communiques are a kind of notification for those who usually do not see notifications published in the offical Gazette. Such communiques are published in the newspapers and not in the official Gazette. The purpose of communiques is to give wide publicity to the subject matter of notification as the people generally read newspapers and do not read the official Gazette The "Employment News" published by the Ministry of I & B, New Delhi publishes notifications important for the people and employment seekers.

B. CORRESPONDENCE

Correspondence is the life-blood of present day public administration because most of the administrative work is done through correspondence, i.e., receiving and sending letters. An office receives communication and sends out communication in the form of letters, circulars, notifications, communique and press notices. Correspondence, therefore, means conveying information in writing from one person to another or between institutions on matters of common interest. Although ommunication can be received and sent through verbal methods like telephone, face-to-face meeting, oadcasts, public meetings etc., however, communication through written word is preferred rather isted upon in public administration.

The following are the advantages of written communication.

(*i*) It provides a written record of what was received and what was sent. The receiver and sender cannot eat their words at a later stage.

(*ii*) It provides time to think and take rational decisions. Both the receiver and sender get time in between the receipt of letter and sending its reply to consult references, take advice from experts and prepare a suitable draft. Thus the time made available minimises the possibility of errors and wrong decisions. Besides accuracy and clarity can be maintained.

(*iii*) Sending letters is less expensive than conveying information through telephones or meetings.

(*iv*) It also helps avoiding unpleasant situations which may take place under face-to-face communication. A negative letter may be written in a non-offending and courteous and in a language to convince the receiver that no injustice has been done to him.

(*v*) Correspondence has become easier and speedy by the introduction of automatic office machines and electronic devices.

(*vi*) Correspondence provides a permanent record for further reference and stands witness if any dispute arises.

Types of Correspondence

Correspondence may be divided into two types :

(*i*) **Internal Correspondence** means the correspondence between one department and another of the same organization or office or between one office of the organisation with another office of a particular department. Correspondence between the Head office and field offices or branches is also considered internal correspondence. Thus the correspondence between the Director Higher Education and Principal of a college, or the correspondence between the Principal and a staff member, fall under internal correspondence.

(*ii*) **External Correspondence** is correspondence between the organisation and the outsiders i.e., the public, any outside agency or organisation like a Teachers Union or voluntary organisation.

It may be noted that the main object of correspondence is achieved through an efficient and economical communication service. Delay and red-tapism are the two great evils of Indian Administration. Wastage of time and stationery are another weakness. Letters received should be speedily replied, cutting red-tape. The cost of correspondence should be kept in view which includes (*a*) the time spent in drafting and typing the reply (*b*) capital cost of the machines like type writers, computer etc. (*c*) Stationery used and wasted, (*d*) overhead expenses (light, rent etc.), (*e*) time spent by messagers and diarists.

Organisation of Correspondence

Proper organisation of correspondence department is a very significant part of efficient administration. If the letters are not speedily replied or not replied even acknowledged, it may create resentment and snowball into an agitation. The aggrieved party writes to the media for failure on the part of an organisation to redress his grievance which highlights the failure and damages the good will of the people. Moreover, if proper record of correspondence is not maintained, it may in future create problems for the administration. Being the life blood of administration a properly organised correspondence system is of utmost importance.

Correspondence can be dealt with in two ways :

(*i*) Centralised correspondence system;

(*ii*) Decentralised or departmental correspondence system.

1. **Centralised Correspondence System** : Under this system all the letters received by an organisation are handled by a specialised department created for the purpose. Correspondence is not passed on to the department concerned. The staff trained in correspondence techniques deal with the letters under a qualified officer. They collect information and relevant references from the clerks of the concerned department and draft suitable reply to the letter received.

Its Merits : The merits of centralised correspondence system are :

(*i*) Effective letters are drafted, since qualified staff are appointed who work centrally.

(*ii*) Uniformity of treatment is ensured because letters of a similar nature are handled by the same member. Under decentralised system, the different departments may interpret the rules differently and take variant decisions.

(*iii*) Since letters are written effectively and all get unifrom replies, resentment is avoided and faith in the rightness of a decision is created.

(*iv*) Correspondence is of a high standard because it is made by trained and qualified staff. It is without error and is flawless.

(*v*) Staff can be trained properly and easily.

(*vi*) It is economical too.

Demerits. The centralised system of correspondence is not without its demerits which are as follows:

(*i*) Though qualified persons are appointed, but since they are not subject experts, i.e., they do not possess knowledge of every subject like agriculture, industry, education, banking, health, defence and external affairs etc., they have to consult the department concerned and seek information or check up the contents of the letter received. This will cause delay in sending reply and also lead to loss of time.

(*ii*) The staff of centralised correspondence department may write out wrong replies based on information received from other departments which may create problems in future. Responsibility gets divided and it becomes difficult to fix responsibility. One may try to pass the buck on the other.

(*iii*) Letters dealing with matters of policy or of important nature are to be drafted by highly knowledgeable persons seated in higher ranks of administration. Such letters cannot be left to be drafted by staff trained only in the techniques of correspondence and working in the centralised correspondence system.

2. Decentralised or Departmental Correspondence System

Unde the decentralised system, correspondence is handled by each department separately. An organisation has several departments among which the work of the organisation is divided, for example the government work is divided among different departments such as education, agriculture, health, industries, transport, social welfare etc. Each of these departments handles its correspondence. These departments are concerned with different subjects and manage the affairs pertaining to the subject entrusted to them, Along with managing the administrative work it receives its own letters called inward mail addressed to it, prepares the reply and sends it to the person concerned. It is called outward mail. The letters received in the receipt section of the department are marked to section superintendent who further distributes them to various clerks who deal with such letters. The dealing clerk goes through the contents of the letter, prepares its reply which he gets approved from the higher authority, sends the draft for typing and after getting the typed letter signed by the signing authority sends it for despatch. In this way, the entire correspondence is handled by the staff of the department concerned.

Its Merits. The decentralised correspondence system is the commonly adopted system under the present day administration. Its merits are :

(*i*) The clerk concerned in the department has got the files, relevant circulars and other information with him. He has not to go to any outside person to collect them. Since the necessary information is already available in the department, replies can be prepared without delay.

(*ii*) The dealing clerk has good knowledge about the subject matter under the scheme of allocations of work. Possessed of such knowledge he can prepare a suitable reply which will be more accurate.

(*iii*) Promptness in handling correspondence can be maintained, since correspondence takes place in the department itself including drafting, typing and despatch. Going to an outside agencies is not required.

(*iv*) Since the dealing assistant has been dealing with a particular subject, say, pension for many years it is easy for him to solve any problem without referring it to the higher offices. Dealing with a subject for years together, he comes to possess perhaps greater knowledge compared to his superiors.

(*v*) In order to boost the reputation of the department for efficient and expeditious disposal of work, the staff works with zeal in discharging its functions because it brings, appreciation for them.

Its Demerits : These are as follows

(*i*) Specially trained persons in the technique and methods of correspondence cannot be appointed in each department because the volume of correspondence work is not so large as to require special staff. It is thus deprived of specialized service.

(*ii*) Along with correspondence, the dealing assistant has also to deal with administrative and routine work. He may have under his charge different types of matters to look after, for example, he may be dealing with leave, retirement and disciplinary cases. Burdened with work, he may not find sufficient time to properly look after correspondence. The departmental heads have often to draft letters.

(*iii*) As the dealing assistant is not a specialist in correspondence matters and has to deal with correspondence of different categories, he might commit mistakes and errors may creep in. An error in the case of any matter of public importance may lead to serious situations and media bashing.

(*iv*) Lastly, under decentralised correspondence system, it is not possible to maintain uniformity in correspondence because different departments may adopt variant form of letters marking a departure from standardised form.

To conclude, it may be said that under the present day administration, the common type of correspondence is decentralised correspondence system. Each department of the government has its own correspondence system.

Inward and Outward Correspondence

Inward correspondence consists of the letters received by a department by post or through messenger/peon or delivered by the sender himself in person. It is also called incoming mail.

Outward correspondence consists of letters written and sent by the departments under the signature of competent authority.

It is very important to see that the incoming letters should be properly taken care of lest any of these letters gets misplaced or lost. For this purpose, the letters received are stamped to show the date of the receipt, entered in the receipt register giving brief particulars of the letters with entry number recorded on the letters, sorted out subject-wise and distributed to the clerks concerned for necessary action. Letters marked as "Private", "Confidential", "Personal" are not opened in the Receipt branch but are sent unopened to the persons concerned.

As regards outgoing letters, it is necessary to see that the letter is complete in every respect with enclosures, appendices (if appended), and signed at the proper place by the competent authority. It is the superintendent or the head clerk who is to ensure the above. The letters are sent to the despatch branch where these are entered in the despatch register with brief particulars there of and despatch number is mentioned on the letter. Thereafter, the outstation letters are properly folded and inserted in Government envelopes. The despatch clerk writes the address on the envelope carefully to ensure correctness of the address. After affixing proper stamps, the envelopes are handed over to the peon to post them.

(C) REPORTS

Every organisation in order to improve its working and produce result needs accurate and up to date information based on facts for policy formulation and action plan. Such information is made available through what are called 'Reports'. A report is a presentation of facts, which have been drawn from investigation, analysis, survey, office records, interview and public opinion etc. It is prepared in a coherent style in clear, correct and unambiguous language.

Meaning of Report

Some of the definitions of report are :

1. "Organisational distance, specialisation and limitations of human comprehension force management to rely heavily upon reports in communicating information both downward and upward. Reports are basically summaries of information." —Littlefield

2. "Report is written statement based on collection of facts, events and opinions which usually expresses a summarised and interpretative value of this information. It may deal with past accomplishments, present conditions or probable future developments." —George R. Terry

3. "A good report is a communication that contains factual information organised and presented in clear, correct and coherent language." —Johnson

On the basis of above definitions it may be concluded that a report is an organised statement of facts relating to a particular subject, prepared by an individual or a committee after an independent investigation and presented to the interested persons with or without recommendations.

Difference between Returns and Reports

1. A report comprises a narrative form with proper headings and sub-headings. Hence there is always a scope for its further elaboration and expression of personal opinion.

Returns are in a tabular form, the format being prescribed by the demanding authority and there is little scope for expressing personal opinion.

Importance of Report

Reports play an important role in the successful working of an organisation. In the present day administration their value has grown on account of the following reasons :

(*i*) The enhancement and growing complexity of activities of organisations and organisational distance between the top and the lower managements.

(*ii*) Ever increasing trend of decentralisation and consequent delegation of authority necessitating provision of means for measuring executive performance.

(*iii*) In consonance with the interests of lower officers sending of reports to higher officials is apt to help the former to seek solution to their problems they are confronted with and have failed to solve.

Reports serve the following functions.

(*i*) They help in the process of planning.

(*ii*) They provide necessary information to those who need and use it. Research scholars make use of them.

(*iii*) They make the people aware of the activities and performance of the government in the particular field dealt with in the report.

(*iv*) The act of coordinating is best performed with the help of reports.

(*v*) They present actual facts to the highups in order to exercise control.

(*vi*) Regular reporting system can check unsatisfactory trends in performance and corrective measures can be taken in time.

(*vii*) They help in measuring the utility of an organisation and its employees on the basis of which such organisation may either be wound up or its working improved.

Types of Reports

Reports are usually of two types (*i*) Routine Ordinary Report and (*ii*) Special Report.

1. Routine Reports

Routine reports are prepared in the department from internal sources and may be daily, weekly, monthly, quarterly and annually dealing with specific topics such as revenue collected, expenditure incurred, targets achieved, quantity produced, loans granted, scholarships awarded to Scheduled

Castes and other backward classes, number of complaints received, link roads constructed, and new industries registered/started Such reports are factual and do not contain comments, suggestions or recommendations.

Routine reports may be categorised as under :

1. *Performance Report* : The source for preparation of this report is internal. It stands for enabling the higher officers to excercise control. It furnishes information regarding achievement of targets, production of goods, collection of revenues, sales, construction of roads etc. These reports are periodical and their frequency is high.

2. *Monitoring Report* : It is analogous to the above report. The difference lies in the fact that it lays emphasis on progress or otherwise in certain important areas viz., industrial relations, public complaints, research and development activities.

3. *Exception Report* : It stands for excercising control. It points out significant deviations from fixed schedules or shortfalls in targets or to report unusual features. There are three objectives of exception reporting :

(*i*) To eliminate irrelevant details; (*ii*) to intimate higher management of deviations or unanticipated trends; (*iii*) to draw attention of higher management to those situations which are not remediable at lower levels.

These reports are submitted occasionally. As such, their frequency is low. The source of information in their case also is internal.

4. *Demand Report* : The demand report is both for planning and control. Such reports are specially demanded either *both motu* or to procure additional information regarding points arisen from the above mentioned reports. Their source of information is internal and frequency variable.

5. *Planning Report* : The Planning Report exists for strategic planning. It assists in forecasting trends, evaluating investment opportunities, planning future activities, appraising political and economic trends, fiscal policies and competitors activities. The informational content in this case is unstructured and invariably decided by the sender. Frequency of such report is low though pre-determined—half yearly or annually. The source of information is internal as well as external. It is a periodical report.

2. Special Reports

As the name itself suggets, special reports are written for a special purpose and are not routine ones. When a circumstance arises and some decisions have to be taken, special reports are prepared. These circumstances may be a farmers agitation, employees strike, railway/air accident, police firing over a community, communal violence, misappropriation of public funds, high level corruption cases like fodder scam, spurious defence deal, sugar scam or any other scandal. For preparing such reports a particular person or a committee is appointed to investigate the matter and submit the report which contains the opinion or recommendations of the reporting person or committee.

Special reports, as said above, are not the usual feature. They are prepared when some occasion arises with a special object in view, for example, to check corruption in administration, to prevent rail/air accident, or to ensure better law and order, to improve police administration etc. Vora Committee Report on corruption, Appleby and Gorwala. Reports on administrative reforms, National Police Commission Report on police reforms, Kelkar Committee Report on taxes are some of the examples of special reports.

Report Writing

A routine report is written first by the clerks or subordinates on the basis of data or records available with them. Thereafter the concerned officer of the organisation drafts and edits it and submits it to the officer concerned e.g., the reports on the revenue collected and expenditure incurred may be submitted to the Accountant General or the report on the scholarships awarded to backward classes may be submitted to the Director, Social Welfare Department. These reports are matter-of-fact reports and based on facts and figures. They are usually short, give only the facts and do not include any comments, opinions or recommendations. They are routine reports prepared daily, weekly, monthly or annually or on demand. However, they should not be considered as a matter of routine and due care should be taken to prepare and send them in time.

The special reports are not of routine type. They are prepared with some special object in view and, therefore, it is necessary that the reporter—individual or committee, must properly understand the terms of reference and their scope. He must clearly know (*i*) why is the report wanted, i.e., the object or the purpose of investigation. (*ii*) who is to take decisions on the report to be submitted, i.e., to whom it is to be submitted and (*iii*) the time by which the report is to be submitted. Timely submission of report is very essential; otherwise it may lose its utility. An interim report may also be submitted.

The reporter is himself to find out the sources from where information is to be collected. The **primary sources** of information are (*i*) direct personal observation, (*ii*) indirect personal interviews through investigators, (*iii*) local reports, and (*iv*) questionnaires.

Under direct personal observation, the reporter personally interviews the people and collects the data; but when the field of enquiry is vast, indirect personal interviews are held through interviewers appointed for the purpose. They visit the informants and collect information personally. The interviewers must be qualified person and should not be biased. Under local reports, information is collected through local agents or correspondents.

Questionnaire is the common and popular method of collecting information. It is a list of questions sent to the persons who may be in possession of facts and figures relating to the enquiry. It is printed or cyclostyled having enough space for writing the answers to the questions listed. It may be sent by post or personally handed over by the interviewers. The correctness and the quality of the data collected through questionniare will depend upon which questions have been selected and how they have been framed. In this connexion the following hints are useful :

(*i*) The questions should be simple and in understandable language.

(*ii*) The questions should be such whose answers do not need writing long paragraphs. One or two sentences or simply 'Yes' or 'No' should complete the answer.

(*iii*) The questions should be clear in content and avoid ambiguity.

(*iv*) The number of questions should not unnecessarily be too many which may bore the informants and take a great deal of their time.

(*v*) The questions should be such that in replying them no calculations are required to be made by the informant.

(*vi*) No personal questions should be asked. These should be related to the subject matter of enquiry .

(*vii*) The questions should be arranged in logical order.

(*viii*) The question should not hurt the pride of the informant.

(*ix*) The questions should not be intermingled. Each question must seek a different information.

(*x*) The informant may be told the purpose of enquiry and his cooperation should be thankfully solicited. He should be told that the information given by him will be kept confidential and that his identity will not be disclosed.

To prepare a good questionnaire requires hard work, thorough understanding of the subject and scope of enquiry and its purpose along with the knowledge of human psychology. The analysis of the replies to the questionnaire also requires good knowledge of statistical methods.

It may also be mentioned that most people do not reply to the questionnaire and that therefore, the questionnaire should be sent to a sufficient number of people so that the information gathered looks representative of different sections of the people and broad enough to draw inferences.

The **Secondary sources** consist of official publications, journals, committee reports, publication by research institutes and universities etc., books by eminent authors and departmental records. Since secondary data is available in ready form, it is easier and cheap to use. However, it may not be forgotten that the secondary data may be biased and it should be, therefore, used with caution.

Essentials of a Good Report

A routine report is prepared in the department from internal sources for departmental perusal of the performance of a unit, its progress, shortfall and deficiencies. As such, it must ensure accuracy. There is a tendency in India to manipulate facts and figures about the achievement of an organisation to show its good performance but such a tendency defeats the purpose of the report. The report should be submitted timely so that necessary action may be taken before it is too late. Of course, it is to be submitted in the prescribed format and style.

A special report is written for a particular purpose after proper investigation of facts and ascertaining public/experts, opinion on the subject of report. The general format is :

(*i*) *Heading* : which indicates the subject matter dealt in the report.

(*ii*) *Preface or Introduction* : It contains the purpose of the report and the terms of reference.

(*iii*) *Table of Contents* : As in the case of a textbook, a report mentions its contents chapter-wise along with their page numbers.

(*iv*) *Body of the Report* : This forms the main part of the report. It states how many meetings of the committee were held along with their dates, the number of witnesses examined and their views or opinions, whether these views were accepted or rejected and why, difficulties, if any, experienced by the committee or its members.

(*v*) *Findings or Recommendations* : This part of the report contains the findings which are based on facts and data collected e.g., whether there was police firing, how many people were killed, whether timely medical aid was provided etc.

The committee also makes its suggestions and recommendations to improve the matters in future.

(*vi*) *Summary* : In case of a lengthy report, a brief summary is also given.

(*vii*) *Appendices* : These may be statistical tables, graphs, lists of witnesses, questionnaire issued etc.

It may be noted that the recommendations/findings of the committee need not be unanimous. If some disagree with the views and recommendations of the majority of the members, they may give their dissenting opinion which fact may be stated in the body of the report and such opinion be given in the Appendix.

The report is to be signed by all the members. The minority report is signed by the disaggreeing members only.

The essentials of a good report are :

(*i*) It should be in the format as described above.

(*ii*) Its recommendations should be based on factual data supported by facts and figures, if possible.

(*iii*) Its language should be simple and unambiguous.

(*iv*) The rules of grammer should be strictly followed so as to avoid confusion of meaning.

(*v*) The report must be readable and understandable by those for whom it is meant.

(*vi*) The report should deal with the matter as concisely as possible.

(*vii*) If it is a lengthy report, each paragraph should be numbered.

(*viii*) Technical terms must be avoided in the report. Clarity is more important.

(*ix*) The recommendations and suggestions may be in capital letters so as to draw the attention of the readers.

(*x*) The report should be submitted in a presentable form i.e., in a bound book form or file and its outer appearance should be pleasing.

It may be remembered that the main purpose of a report is to help the authorities to know the facts relating to the subject under report and take necessary suitable action. A report which is based on hearsay and unverified information and is more journalistic than realistic, serves no useful purpose, nor does it justify the labour and cost incurred in its preparation. To sum up, a good report should contain all the relevant facts sought through proper investigation and study, marshal the facts without any bias, analyse them in logical order, arrive at natural conclusion and make workable recommendations.

(D) FORMS

The forms play a vital role for the effective management of an agency. They furnish information for formulating policy, controlling and improving informations and evaluating performance. They serve as guides to movement of materials, the performance of services, the authorization for expenditures and payment of money. They constitute a basis of clerical and executive actions.

Forms have been defined as "printed or typed documents with blank spaces for the insertion of information". According to Prof. J.C. Denyer, a form signifies "*a piece of paper or card on which entries are to be made bearing pointed or otherwise marked headings, captions or descriptive matter intended to define entries.*" According to Wylie and Brech, "*Office forms are the vehicles by which various statistics are brought together either by accumulation from many points or by individual recording at a single point for the purpose of analysis, establishment of records or uniformity of procedure.*" Broadly speaking, forms comprise all pieces of paper designed to facilitate the work of an organisation. They are used to procure, convey or record information necessary to its operation. In short, forms are standardised medium of collecting, analysing, transmitting and recording information. They make clear what information should be collected and in what manner. They facilitate the furnishing of information. Examples of forms are the admission forms, leave application form, Income Tax Retrun form, Sales Tax Assessment form, Purchase Order form, Passport Application form, Visa form, Money order form, cheque deposit form. money withdrawal form, birth registration form, license form, Annual Confidential Report form, requisition forms, purchase bills, tender form, house allotment application form etc.

Objects of Office Forms

Forms are described as the basic tools of office. Frank Knox said, "Nothing happens in an office except by means of pieces of paper." Form are the medium to maintain the records of the enterprise and serve as the basis of records management. The following are the objects of the office forms :

(*i*) No piece of information which is of some importance is to be held back intentionally or unintentionally.

(*ii*) Only the relevant information is to be supplied and irrelevant information is to be held back.

(*iii*) The concerned party in receipt of the filled form is to be made fully alert of the fact that no information has been suppressed.

(*iv*) Lot of time of the typist or clerk concerned is saved by simply filling up the gaps through a few words.

(*v*) Information conveyed through office forms is easily collected and thoroughly analysed.

(*vi*) The forms help enhancing the clerical efficiency and the output of the work.

Advantages of Office Forms

(*i*) Only relevant information is intimated as the heading of the columns are self revealing.

(*ii*) Big economy is effected in overhead expenses of the office as lot of time and labour is saved.

(*iii*) Only standard information is presented.

(*iv*) It becomes easier to analyse the data.

(*v*) Uniformity in presenting information is possible through forms only.

(*vi*) Multiple copies can be preferred.

Disadvantages of Office forms

A few disadvantages of office forms are also there as follows :

(*i*) Lot of time is wasted in their designing and then their printing.

(*ii*) A badly designed form creates confusion and results in wastage of time, labour and money.

(*iii*) The clerks consider the filling up of forms as monotonous.

In order to make the forms more effective, they should be properly designed and drawn up.

Types of Forms

The forms may be categorized as under :

(*i*) On the basis of use :

(*a*) *Internal Office Form*

These forms are used by employees of the business viz., accounting form, requisition form, memorandum form.

(*b*) *Enternal Contact Form*

These forms are sent to customers, creditors namely purchase order forms, order forms etc.

(*ii*) On the basis of operation (function)

Forms are classified on the basis of functions they perform, purchase form, application form, material requisition form fall in this category.

(*iii*) On the basis of copy

There are two types of forms in this category

(*a*) Single Copy Forms : which are complete in themselves and usually assume the shape of source document.

(*b*) Multiple Copies Forms : They are made in duplicate or more than two copies. They are used to transmit information or serve the function of supplying additional records.

Form Designing

As said above, forms are basic tools of office system. They are the chief medium of collecting information in a systematic way. It is therefore necessary that they should be well designed and complete in all respects. As ill designed form can cause delay, invite errors, make processing costly and difficult. Besides a badly framed form can have adverse sociological reaction and convey a poor image of organisation. In Muthaswamy's words "Forms are the ambassadors of an organisation outside and a good workman inside".

Design of Form

Some significant steps are to be taken before designing a form :

(*i*) A careful examination explaining the purpose of the form—Whether designed for collecting and analysing certain information or for standardization of the method or procedure of handling a specified work.

(*ii*) To examine the nature of work requirng collection of information or the procedure which is to be standardized. Such an examination is fruitful as it obviates the necessity of devising a new form as the same can be used with slight modification. As regards standardization a check list already in use for examination of a particular personnel matter can also be used for examination of another similar case e.g., sanction of advances from Provident Fund and a case of withdrawal from the same fund.

(*iii*) The source of the collected information. It will reveal the periodicity and frequency, use of the language in which it is to be couched and also the shape of the form.

(*iv*) Methods and equipments to be used for processing, recording and perserving the informations gathered through the form e.g., manual processing and automatic or electronic data processing methods will be necessitating different types of forms.

A minute examination of the above will be useful in determining the content of the form i.e., the different entries to be effected in it, the manner in which the entry is to be made, the language to be used, the material to be made use of e.g., paper or card, thin or thick paper coloured or white paper and size and shape of the form e.g., whether single or multiple copy form.

(*v*) **Cost** : Lastly, it is necessary to keep in view the cost factor while designing the form namely cost of production, processing, distribution and storage.

Guidelines for Form design

The basic quality of a perfect form design lies in its pleasing appearance. Besides, it should be easy to fill up, interpret and process. The following guidelines, if followed, can give the form a proper shape.

(*i*) The form should have a proper title which should be clearly indicative of its purpose and also the number to facilitate identification.

(*ii*) The language should be appropriate to its purpose and as simple and pleasant as possible. It should be in consonance with the official requirements. Loose wording should be avoided as it may not convey the correct information.

(*iii*) Departmental high sounding jargons may not be opted for as the people will fail to comprehand them.

(*iv*) The size, quality and colour of paper may be standardized to minimise cost of production and avoid avoidable confusion.

(*v*) The layout of the form should be good. A logical sequence; a continuous flow of writing; provision of box design for providing ample scope for variable answers to a particular question and facilitating compilation of variable data; the layout of the form suiting the particular requirements of the machine if used for compilation, provision of enough space for making entries by writing or typing, laying down of adequate instructions for completion of the form; specimen entries to be indicated for guidance; to be foldable and useable as envelope, to enable it to seek information from the public; provision of a predetermined space for mentioning of mailing address are the requisites of a good layout of the form.

To sum up, the designing of forms is an important matter for office administration. It is, therefore, essential that this function should be handled by a trained and competent officer who has the knowledge not only of the nature and needs of the office work and procedure but also of printing technology and paper quality. Anybody and every person can not efficiently look after this job. A properly designed form will facilitate the information, processing the information and assist in achieving the office purpose.

Form control

Littlefield defines form control as a "means of excercising management control over the costs of producing and processing forms". J.C. Denyer holds "*Forms are important in any organisation therefore, there should be proper management control of them to ensure that they are efficient and economical in design as well as in use.*" In the modern era forms constitute the basic tools of office work. Efficiency in office work is attributed to them. They save time of the office as need of writing for processing information is eliminated.

The control on forms should be centralised under one agency like the O and M unit or a form Control Committee comprising various user Departments. The Unit or Committee performs the following functions :

(*i*) To maintain folders of forms function wise/number (*ii*) design new forms, classify and codify them for easy identification, storage and distribution (*iii*) To eliminate obsolete forms and redesign the existing forms after a review, examine the possibility of introducing multi purpose forms in place of multiple forms. (*iv*) To effect economy in the production, distribution and use of forms.

Infact, no new form should be introduced till the Unit or Committee, whatever the case may be, is consulted.

So far as possible the tendency to have multiple forms should be checked. Such tendency minimises their relative importance and their striking advantages are lost sight of. Hence it is imperative to exercise proper control over the forms in order to enhance their effectiveness.

The centralized committee or the department unit should be equipped with the authority of design, printing, issue etc. The unit should keep a Form Book or Form Register. The Form Book should contain a copy of each form. Whenever any modification in the form is effected the same may be notified in the Form Book as well. On the receipt of the revised form it may be placed on the old form or tagged with it.

Steps in Form Control

Forms control comprises of proper designing, printing, economical use and supply of forms for the efficient and effective performance of office work. The following steps are essential for proper forms control.

I. Need of Centralized Authority

In large organisations there is a dire necessity of forms control department under the charge of a forms control supervisor. In the alternate a committee of experts in Forms may be constituted. Such a Forms Control Department or Committee will perform following functions.

(*a*) Introduction of new forms.
(*b*) Modification of existing forms
(*c*) Elimination of irrelevant forms
(*d*) Blend of two or more forms.
(*e*) Fixing contents of forms.
(*f*) Designing of forms.
(*g*) Production of forms.
(*h*) Storing and issue of forms.

II. Necessity of a Forms Register

The centralised forms control authority may collect at least two copies of each office form being used in the office and place them in the Forms Register or Forms Book. An index of all forms in the Forms Book may also be made.

III. Listing of office routine

A list of the office procedures which require the use of forms may be prepared. The relevant forms may be classified, marked and then numbered in accordance with the procedure of the department making use of them.

IV. An analytical Appraisal of the Forms

All forms may be periodically analytically appraised so as to eliminate those not required and to effect an improvement if needed. The departments may at this stage be asked to give concrete suggestions for the redesigning of the existing forms and also furnish requisition for the new forms. Thereafter, the Forms Control supervisor may determine the elimination of the irrelevant forms and the consolidation and the modifications of existing forms and the introduction of the new forms.

V. Proper designing and production

In order to effect efficiency and economy of operations the forms are to be properly designed. After designing the decision is to be taken regarding the production of the number of copies of each form. The Forms control supervisor is to determine the method of reproduction of forms with the assistance of a duplicator and also get them printed from suitable outside agency.

VI. Obsolete Forms to be Disposed of

The Head of department using a particular form is required to give in writing that the form is obsolete. Then the form is submitted to the office manager who is to accord the recommendation under his signature that it be disposed of. Therafter, the form not required is disposed off. The approval of the officer is pasted on the form and the same is placed in the Form Book marked as 'dead' and date also is mentioned if possible.

To sum up there is always a scope for improvement of form design with the changing needs and new developments and experiences. In the course of working, the office staff may face difficulties caused by the use of forms or the people may feel inconvenience in filling up forms. Today, at every step forms are required to be filled up. Too many forms are used than necessary. It is therefore, necessary that form control programme should be a continuous affair and all forms should be analysed periodically.

Inventory and Storage

Most of the forms used in public office have become obsolete and outlived their utility so that there is need for their redesigning. As such it is imperative that an inventory of the existing forms used in an office be made as a part of forms control programme. The inventory may be in the form of 'Master Form Control Schedule' which may be in the following format with modification as required by the office needs.

Master Form Control Schedule

(Deptt. of Education)

S. No.	Title Name of form	Purpose of the form	No. got printed	How prepared	Wherefrom printed paper	Cost of printing including	Year of printing	Total copies printed
1	2	3	4	5	6	7	8	9

Last Balance in stock	Total in stock	Old Forms if any in stock
10	11	12

To justify the continuance of a form, the following facts may be kept in consideration and debated :

(*i*) The purpose of the form and the type of information it is expected to convey. Is its title correct? For example, the form evaluating the performance of an employee should be called Annual Confidential Report or Self Assessment Form.

(*ii*) Does it comprise irrelevant columns?

(*iii*) Does it include all the relevant columns?

(*iv*) Does any column affect the sensitivity of the sender?

(*v*) Is the format convenient and comprehensible?

(*iv*) Is the information supplied interpretable, quantifiable or encodable for computerisation purpose?

(*vii*) Is it in use?

It is evident that through a well planned system of forms inventory, the forms can be used more usefully and economically and wastage can be avoided. It is seen that there is much wastage of forms in offices. Sometimes, these are used for non-relevant purposes, issued mindlessly and taken away by the junior employees for their children to be used for rough work. It may not be forgotten that each form costs money, howsoever little, and therefore, economical and proper use of forms is called for in the interest of economy.

Storage

The forms used in public offices under the present day administration are got printed in several thousands and, therefore, the problem of storing such vast number of forms is quite difficult to solve. The forms may get spoiled, torn or misplaced in case they are not properly stored. If the different types of forms get mixed up, the problem of their being issued promptly may crop up. The space problem is another hindering factor in proper storing.

Presently, the forms are stocked in gunny or polythene bags which are thrown in the available vacant space either in some room or corridors. The dealing clerk who issues them to the individuals who need such forms keeps them in a bundle placed either on the top of his *almirah* or the vacant space near his table. Both the methods are not satisfactory. The two essential requirements of storage, i.e., safety and accessibility are lost sight of under the above arrangement.

Essentials of Good Storage System

(*i*) *Proper Classification* : The forms used in an office are of different kinds and further there are a number of offices or departments where office work is carried. So, the quantity of forms is very large. Under such conditions, they should be properly classified, tagged title-wise, placed in different bundles/bags. The title of the form should be written on the cover of the bundle/bag.

(*ii*) *Accessible Location* : The forms should be stored in an easily accessible location to facilitate the issue. A different building or a far off corner may create inconvenience and delay in issue.

(*iii*) *Safety* : Forms should be bundled carefully so that they do not get damaged. The cover used for storing should be stout and properly tied. It should also be ensured that they are not damaged by rats, insects, rain, fire, etc., and proper safety steps may be taken in this direction.

(*iv*) *Less space* : Economy of space is of great importance in all organisations. So it is necessary to see that storing requires minimum floor space but not at the cost of easy accessibility. Forms which are much in demand and use may be placed in a front line and easily approachable space while the less frequently used forms may be stored in a farther corner.

(*v*) *Equipments* : Various types of storage equipments should be procured to store the form. A sufficient number of almirahs, racks, boxes and fixed wooden shelfs etc. should be made available. Efforts should be made to see that the packings of forms are not thrown haphazardly without any systematic arrangement on the floor. Insecticides may be sprinkled from time to time to protect the forms from being damaged by rats, insects, dampness etc. Fire proof equipments should also be installed.

(*vi*) *Training* : Trained staff should be posted to handle the storage. It should not be left to be looked after by a peon or any other class IV employee.

(*vii*) *Decentralised System* : Storage of forms is generally the departmental responsibility. The different departments look after it independently. Each department has its own forms which may differ according to its requirements and nature of its functions. This system is more simple, easy and suitable than the centralised system. The forms are easily and quickly available.

(*viii*) *Deal Forms* : Forms which have lost their purpose and utility and are no longer usable or have become shabby in appearance or have been damaged may be declared non-usable and condemnable. Such forms should be disposed of to make space available.

To sum up, the most important points in storage are that the forms should be safely stored, properly protected and be easily and quickly available.

(E) MANUALS

Administration today is not a matter of personal whims and prejudices. It is required to follow a definite policy, a definite set of rules and a specific working procedure. When the policy, rules and procedure are reduced in writing in a book form, it is called a 'manual'. As such, manual is a compendium of information and knowledge regarding the rules and procedures operative in an organisation—business or a Government one. It contains general information, general office rules and regulations, safety instructions, organisational policies, job description, office facilities, standard practices and general instructions etc.

The manual clearly lays down :

(*i*) What has to be done? (*ii*) When it has to be done? (*iii*) Where it has to be done? and (*iv*) By whom it has to be done?

In the government such manuals constitute a normal features : Income Tax Manual, Service Manual, Finance Manual, Police Manual, Jail Manual are examples of some of the important manuals.

Purposes and advantages of Manuals

The important purposes of manuals are :

(*i*) To make instructions definite and clear;

(*ii*) To find answers as regards office procedures;

(*iii*) To effect improvement in administrative control;

(*iv*) To ensure stability and uniformity in office work.

The Advantages of Manual are

(*i*) It makes easier for the management to supervise as the staff gets acquainted with the procedures. In case of doubt the staff can cast a glance as the office manual.

(*ii*) The manaul serves as an authority on the procedures.

(*iii*) Amendments are possible in view of the experience gained after practical work in the procedure

(*iv*) The training of the personnel also becomes easier. Manual can serve as a source of training.

(*v*) The employee understands the job well because the method of doing the job, i.e. how the job is to be done, is written in the manual.

(*vi*) The employee can get necessary information easily. He need not run to other employees or offices for the purpose.

(*vii*) Responsibility can be fixed on the individuals who do not follow the manual in the discharge of their functions and cause delay, loss or irregularity.

(*viii*) The people can easily know the procedure to be followed in getting their job done and the information required for the purpose. An individual can easily find out from the Income Tax manual, the procedure for submitting the Return and the information to be given by him. He has not to go to an officer. The manual is there to guide him. It is thus a convenient method in public dealings.

(*ix*) Chances of error are minimised and efficiency increases.

(*x*) A well written manual leads to efficiency in office work and makes it convenient for the people to contact the office. A liaison is thereby developed between the public and office.

In Public administration, manual plays more vital role than in any other large scale organisation as it is responsible to the people. For all their activities, public personnel are accountable to some superior and ultimately to the legislature and public. As such, all office activities have to be recorded and performed in accordance with the laws, rules and regulations. Manual is the first requirement of an organisation.

Disadvantages of Manual

Some disadvantages also have been pointed out in Manual system. They are :

(*i*) It is expensive and time consuming to prepare a manual. Sometimes, it takes years to gather full information of the relevant rules and regulations to prepare the Manual. It is not an easy task to prepare a manual.

(*ii*) A manual may become out of date due to the changing circumstances and growing complexities of administration. It is difficult to keep a manual up to date and revise it from time to time.

(*iv*) A manual may be misinterpreted if it is not written clearly and is ambiguous.

(*v*) It may lead to red tapism and other concomitant evils as the rules mentioned therein are to be followed strictly irrespective of the exigency of the case.

What is good Manual ?

The disadvantages of manual pointed out above can be minimised or removed if there is a good manual. Good manual is that which is well adapted to achieve the desired ends. But what are the 'desired ends' and whether the procedure is well adapted to achieving them, pose big problems. The ends sought by administration are complex and intangible. Hence, it is difficult to determine which of them is to be served by a procedure and in what proportions? A change in government may bring a change in the ends and procedure of administration. From a democratic administration it may change to autocratic with the change in the complexion of the government. However, generally speaking, manual should be simple ensuring prompt action. It should not be too rigid as to leave no discretion in exceptional cases. Its language should be unambiguous and clear which is easily understandable by a common citizen. It should try to cut short the channels so far as possible. It should help rather than hinder the progress of the work. It may never be forgotten that manual is a means to facilitate the work, not an end in itself. Too much insistence on the letter of the rules leads to red tapism and corruption—the two main evils of present Indian Administration.

Types of Manual

Manuals may be classified as

(*i*) Institutional Manuals and

(*ii*) Working Manuals.

(*i*) Institutional Manuals

Institutional Manuals pertain to staff, housekeeping service or auxiliary function. They cover mail and communication, meetings and conferences, travel, internal reporting, preparation, issuance and distribution of documents, space, files, records, clerical services, procurement, clearance and review, budgetary and fiscal administration and all aspects of personnel administration. Service manuals, Records maintenance, files, journey/TA rules, Reports, Pay and allowances manual, financial Returns, Audit Manual, Inter-departmental correspondence manual, Purchase and disposal manual are some examples of institutional manuals. The laws, rules and regulations contained in such manuals are prescribed by statute or delegated legislation. They apply uniformly in all the departments of the Government with some exceptions in view of the nature and functions of an agency like C.B.I., Intelligence, Judiciary, Defence and External Affairs etc.

(*ii*) Working Manual

Working manuals are meant for accomplishing an agency's particular objectives. These are of two types, viz. those publicly issued and those not publicly issued. Publicly issued manuals contain rules for the agency and any individual affected by the statute. They specify the agency's sense of the procedural requirements of law and also its conception of what is customary, fair and expedient. They tell all persons affected "What, where, when and how" of things. For example, how to lodge a report with the police, get a telephone connection, make an appeal against tax-assessment, apply for a post under the government, submit a tender for a contract, apply for a licence or loan, and so forth.

Manuals not publicly issued are meant for the internal working and administration of an office e.g., the functions of superintendent, allocation of business, noting on papers, file maintenance, receipt and despatch etc.

It may be noted that manuals are enforceable. The office staff and people are to abide by the rules mentioned therein. If any action is ultra-vires of the manual, it can be challenged or disciplinary action can be taken against the erring employee.

Organisational Policy Procedure Manual

A manual is not only a compendium of the rules of office procedure defining the responsibilities and duties of different office employees and officers, it may also contain the organisational policy procedure. The main purpose of any organisation is to successfully implement the policy of the government and its departments. Therefore, those working in the organisation should get well acquainted with the organisational policy so that rules of working procedure may be faithfully followed. If it is the policy of the Government to assist the weaker sections of society in their unliftment, it is desirable that they should be given special benefits and concessions. As such the education manual should contain necessary rules for adequate facilities to them which the employees should faithfully execute.

Policy, it may be noted, is prior to every action. It provides the framework within which all actions for the accomplishment of objective are to be activated. It sets the tasks for administration and guides the adminstrators. Policy is not same thing as 'rule' because policy is dynamic and flexible, whereas rule is specific and rigid. It is also neither the same thing as 'rule of procedure' because the latter exists to effectuate the former.

Policy-making is a legislative function although administration can not be completely divorced from policy-making. Public officials are associated with policy-making in three ways. *First,* it is they who supply facts, data and material for policy making; *second* in many cases the initiative for policy-making emanates from the administration because it is the administration which is in constant touch with the general public and better knows their problems and difficulties; *third* , the legislature passes acts in skeleton form and leaves the framing of rules, regulations and bye-laws to the administration.

Policy Formulation. Policy means a decision as to what shall be done and how, when and where. It is guide to administrative action. It deals with basic issues, basic to the working of the whole administrative machinery. These issus may be simple and limited in nature or they may be complex and numerous.

There are two sources of policy formation body legislative or administrative. Under parliamentary system cabinet is the main body to decide upon a policy which is presented to the legislature for approval. The important polices like Industrial policy, agricultural policy, import-export policy, monetary policy are approved by the legislature. However, it is the administrative policy which falls under the subject of public administrative. Administrative policy is largely concerned with

(*i*) the determination and establishment of appropriate machinery and procedure for the implementation of legislative polices

(*ii*) selling the timetable or work programme of activities

(*iii*) guidance of its staff through rules, regulations or orders in the performance of their duties, and

(*iv*) taking precedent making decisions on specific new issues which may arise in the course of day-to-day administration.

Policy whether legislative or administrative must be based on factual data and actual information. To the legislature, it is the administration which supplies the meesary information. The administration, however, collects its information through (*i*) internal sources, (*ii*) external sources, (*iii*) special investigations, and (*iv*) research and study.

To sum up, the precess of policy formulation consists of the following steps :

(*i*) Understanding and analysing the present environment, both external and internal;

(*ii*) Identification of policy alternatives to achieve the goals in the anticipated environment;

(*iii*) Examination of the alternatives;

(*iv*) Elaboration of the consequences of various alternatives;

(*v*) Effect of alternatives and consequences on preferred values and norms;

(*vi*) Selection of policies.

It may be noted that under the impact of information technology, mass media is playing an important role in building pressure on policy making.

Procedural Manuals

Procedural manuals are working manuals. In general terminology they are called 'Office Manuals' which specify the rules of procedure to be followed in the conduct of office work. Generally, these are prepared and issued departmentally. The rules are formulated by the Head of the department in the context of organisational objectives. (See also above 'Working Manuals').

A word may be said about office procedure. The office machinery starts functioning when some letter or application from outside reaches the department. That letter or application is received by a clerk known as Receipt Clerk. The clerk registers that in the Receipt Register and the Receipt number is put on it. The Receipt Clerk sends it to appropriate operating section. At this stage it enters the file and now the file moves. It goes to the Section Assistant who forwards it to the Section Officer with his noting. The section officers puts his note upon it and sends it up to the Branch Office; Superintendent who further forwards it to the Deputy Secretary. The Deputy Secretary passes it on to the Secretary or Joint Secretary. Finally it reaches the Minister, Prime Minister and lastly to the President. During this journey of the letter, rules are consulted, precedents discovered, old records looked into, information from various sources gathered and consultation if required with high up held. By this time the file becomes a file of correspondence, notes, minutes and memoranda. At long last there begins the downward journey of the file. Ultimately, the file reaches the Assistant through downward channels who despatches the final draft approved to the typist. The typist types it, sends in to the examiner who passes it on to the section officer for signature. After his signatures are obtained the draft goes to the Registry office for despatch and thereafter the file goes to the record office for record.

Preparation of Manuals

As told above, office procedures reduced in writing in a book form constitute a manual. It is the duty of the Heald of the Department to lay down the procedure of work in his department and frame appropriate rules for the conduct of business. While framing these rules the following principles are to be kept in mind :

(*i*) There should be no bottleneckes in order to have good flow of work.

(*ii*) Duplication of work and records should be avoided.

(*iii*) The movement of the staff should be curtailed to the minimum during the course of working

(*iv*) Unnecessary forms and information should be avoided i.e., paper work should not supersede the objective or in other words-adequate safeguards may be taken against red-tapism.

(*v*) Effort be made to use the modern electronic devices provided the output is more and time consumed is less.

(*vi*) Complicated procedures should be avoided to minimise irritants and simplified procedures be opted.

(*vii*) The exisiting rules of procedure should be studied thoroughly before making any amendments therein or replacing them from the view point of acheiving the objective of the organisation and improving efficiency of work in the department.

(*viii*) The rules should be welcome to the staff and encourage their interest and participation wholeheartedly in the office work.

(*ix*) Due recognition should be given to the field staff and efforts be made to secure full cooperation and co-ordination between the Headqaurters and field offices.

(*x*) There should be proper delegation of duties and authority to the junior officers and field staff.

(*xi*) Allocation of business among the employees should be fair and workable, seniority of an employee should not be ignored.

To sum up, Manuals should be so prepared as to ensure that the organisation works smoothly, that no part of it repeats what the other part does, that employees are well-conversant with their duties, that there is no unnecessary paper work, that rules are simple and understandable, that no employee works at cross purposes and the objectives of the organisation are successfully achieved.

Sources of Material for Manuals

Rules of procedure contained in a Manuel for the working of an organisation though in some cases may be inlcuded in a statute enacted by the legislature, are generally framed by the administration. Broadly speaking, administration collects material for rule-making from the following sources :

(*i*) *Internal Sources* : Every organisation is a centre to which flow periodic reports, returns, statements, accounts and varied material or information from field establishments. These reports and other material reveal certain facts and problems which become the basis for framing the rules. The employees may also bring facts and problems to the notice of the administration which they come across during their working.

(*ii*) *External Sources* : To supplement the internal data which may not be sufficient, the administration takes help from external sources. It establishes contact with private bodies, unions, associations, chambers etc., in order to know their problems and suggestions, for example, Director of Education may call the leaders of Students Union and Teachers Associations to know their views about the procedure and rules regarding admission rules, teaching schedule, evaluation methods and students facilities. Likewise, the representatives of Chambers of Commerce may be invited to seek their reactions to the Tax assessment and collection procedure. Further, the media also through its editorials and news may inform the administration of the public opinion about its functioning. The information received through these sources is duly considered and used for rule making or amendments in the rules contained in the manual.

(*iii*) *Special Investigations* : Whenever some incident like Ayodhya or Godhara takes place or agitations/protests are held against some matter, committes of enquiry for finding facts and making recommendations are appointed. It may be one man committee or include more than one person. These committees have specific terms of reference; they examine witnesses, both official and non-official and obtain facts and views and submit their report which may serve as the basis for manual-making and effecting reforms in the procedure of work. Such committees may be appointed by the government on its own also to study a particular matter and make recommendations concerning it. The Administrative Reforms Commission, Radhakrishnan Commission, Vora Committee, Kelkar Committee, National Police Commistion are some of the examples.

(*iv*) *Research and Study* : Research and study may be organised by the government and non-official agencies to find out certain facts and views. The O and M units in the departments are such organisations whose job is to study the organisation of public offices and their work procedures in order to effect efficiency and improvement in both. Efficiency signifies elimination of duplication, waste and delay by reshaping the organisation and by simplification and acceleration of procedures. Similarly non-official agencies like Indian Institute of Public Administration, Institute for Manpower and Research, Business Schools, Management Institutes, and various Research Institutes also conduct research and supply vast information and material which are taken cognizance of by the manual framers.

Technique of Designing Manual

As told above the Head of the Department is to lay down the rules of office procedure and compile them in the form of manual. It is necessary that before undertaking this task he should have a vivid picture of the office in his mind. He must be aware of the objectives of the offce; the amount of work to be done in the office; a list of office workers; the responsibilities to be earmarked to each one of them; the methods to be pursued for the performance of each operation, the snag in the procedures, if any, and to see how best work is to be done.

After getting aware of the office routine he should examine the justification of a particular operation and conclude whether efficiency can be attained without without such an operation. He has to discover the bottlenecks which impede flow of work thus causing reduction in the total output. Hence he has to strive to remove such bottlenecks.

He has also to visualise whether there is any duplication of work anywhere. He is to make efforts to avoid such duplication. Avoidable filling up of forms or operations of procedures should be eliminated. Time and motion study is of immense value while framing office procedures and designing manual.

Maintenance and Preservation of Manuals

In order to ensure efficiency of work and achieve the objectives of an organisation, it is essential that the office manual should be kept up-to-date. It may be noted that the nature of work is fast changing with the growing complexities of administration and vastness of problems. Under such conditions, Government organisation can hardly remain static for a long true. It must adjust itself with the changing times for the sake of its own survival. Such adjustments are often piecemeal. They are responsible for unplanned development both of the organisation and the methods of work. Duplication of rules takes place and consequently efficiency suffers.

Maintenance of manuals requires that rules should be updated in the light of experiences gained and the growth of problems. An obsolete manual serves no purpose because it is outdated and is not in consonance with the changing circumstances and improvements in technology. The Jail Manual and Police Manual contain several rules which make a mockery. Although the role of police has changed in free India from that of ruler-friendly to that of people-friendly, the manual of British days still continue to govern the police functioning. Likewise, the Jail Manual drafted during British rule remains still operative despite the rehabilitative approach of today's jail administration.

Office manual is a basic document; hence its proper preservation is of utmost importance. It should be stoutly bound lest its pages get loosened. At the same time, it should be easy to open and read it. It should be kept at a place wherefrom it can be made readily available because speed and accuracy of office functioning depends upon the easy availability of the manual.

A manual is a part of office record. It is to be safely preserved for future reference. Past manuals, may be needed for further study and at the time of formulation of a new manual. They are helpful in locating the errors and identifying the wastes occuring in the organisation. Information about the history of the organisation, its past functions and working procedures is useful for improving upon its earlier rules and making them up to date so that they may properly serve the needs of the changed conditions and be in consonance with the technology and policy of the current era. Further the need for referring to manuals, past and present, may also arise for legal purposes, for example, settlement of cases between the department and employee or between the department and the citizen. Manual is a good piece of evidence. The importance of proper preservation of a manual can not be exaggerated in the modern days when there are pulls and counterpulls over the administration, and pressures to bend it in one direction to serve vested interests.

ANNEXURE–II

SALIENT FEATURES OF THE INDIAN CONSTITUTION

Immediately after the attainment of Independence the Indian leaders of the times started contemplating about the framework of the Constitution of free India. A Drafting Committee under the chairmanship of Dr. B.R. Ambedekar was constituted to draft the Constitution. The Committee took 141 days to frame the draft. Eight months period was approximately spent on its hair splitting. After its presentation to the Constituent Assembly, out of 165 days, 114 days were spent on the consideration of the Draft of the Constitution. 7635 amendments to the Draft Constitution were tabled, out of which 2473 amendments were actually moved. It took Assembly 2 years, 11 months and 20 days to complete the finishing touches to the Constitution. Nehru and Patel were the soul behind the Constitution. They are therefore called the founding fathers of the Constitution. Dr. K.V. Rao[1] called Dr. Ambedekar as the '*Mother of the Constitution*'. *In his words "...Dr. Ambedekar had to bear in fact other ideas and nurture them and bring them out as his own and he did remarkably well.*"

In fact, the Constitution of India which was drafted after going through many constitutions of the world is a blend of good features of prominent Constitutions of USA, UK, Ireland, Canada, Soviet Union (now extinct). Some critics, however, go to the extent of calling it a bag of 'borrowing' and a 'hotch potch' Constitution.

It is an exaggerated view. The framers were governed by the rich experience of top democracies and even a socialist state like erstwhile USSR. They adapted their good features to their circumstances and brought out a voluminous constitution for their country. The basic postulates of our constitution are federalism, secularism, democratic socialism, parliamentary democracy and independent judiciary. The following are the salient features of our Constitution in brief :

1. Written and Lengthy

In the initial stage, the Indian Constitution comprised of 395 Articles and 12 Schedules. Presently it is the lengthiest document comprising 443 Articles. The bulk of the Constitution is attributable to the following reasons.

(*a*) It makes provision for administrative machinery not only at the centre but also of the states and union territories.

(*b*) The Federal Scheme adds to its volume. Enough space has been devoted to the Union and State relations.

(*c*) The details of the Fundamental Rights and later inclusion of Fundamental Duties by 42nd amendment add to its length.

(*d*) Provision of chapter on Directive Principles of State Policy.

(*e*) Special provision of the constitutional safeguards for the minorities.

(*f*) Inclusion of Articles on three types of Emergencies.

(*g*) Provisions concerning citizenship, national language and regional languages, Elections, the services, trade, contracts etc.

(*h*) Subsequent addition of certain amendments.

---

1. *K.V. Rao : Parliamentary Democracy in India : A critical commentary (Ed.) pp. 1-2.*

Some of the details are said to be irrelevant and could have been avoided. The more of these details the less is the room for adaptability.

2. Sovereign Democratic Republic :

Sovereignty is reflected through internal independence and avoidance of any external control. Our membership of Commonwealth of Nations accepting British Monarchy as the presiding genius of the Commonwealth and membership of United Nations do not detract a bit from our sovereign status.

India no longer owes allegiance to the Crown. It only accepted the monarch as the symbol of Commonwealth unity only till implementation of our constitution. India nor can sever its connections with Commonwealth at its own will.

Fair, free and impartial periodical General Elections both for Parliament, State Legislatures and the Local Bodies; provision for Civil Liberties; the existence of Pressure and Interest Groups and their decisive influence on the rulers of the country without fear indicate the democratic character of the Constitution.

Unlike that of UK, which has hereditary king as the head of the state, India has opted for an elected functionary as head of the state. President heads the state though he is a mere constitutional ruler unlike that of the USA, where President is both a head of the state as well as that of the government. As such the latter is the real elected ruler of the country. In case of India, real powers are vested with the Prime Minister who heads the Government and President is only a signing machine.

3. Centralised Federation (Quasi Federal)

The Constitution has opted for federalism though word 'Federal' has not been used. Instead India is called 'Union of Indian States'. This accords it a unique status. Dr. Wheare holds "*The Indian Constitution establishes a system of government which is at the most quasi-federal.....a unitary state with subsidiary federal features rather that federal state with unitary features.*" Dr. B.R. Ambedekar also confesses, "*The constitution has not been set in a tight mould of federation*".

Its federal characteristics are :

(*i*) A written constitution;

(*ii*) Rigid constitution;

(*iii*) Dual Polity;

(*iv*) Division of powers between the Union and the State Governments.

(*v*) Provision of Supreme Court as the final interpreter of the Constitution.

(*vi*) Existence of a second chamber to accord equal representation to the units of the federation. The last point exists only in name. Unlike the American Federation equal representation has not been given to the units of Indian federation :

The Indian Constitution is partially flexible partially rigid.

Its centralised features are :

(*i*) Over riding powers of the Central Government.

(*ii*) Single citizenship (unlike USA and Switzerland which have opted for double citizenship).

(*iii*) Emergency powers of the President which enable him to convert the country into a unitary state. The Union Parliament during emergency legislates for the country.

(*iv*) Parliament can alter the name, the size, and the boundaries of a state.

(*v*) A single unified judiciary. The Indian High Courts are branches of the Apex Court unlike USA, where the double set of Judiciary exists.

(*vi*) Appointment of Governors, the Attorney General Accountant and Auditor general by the Centre.

(*vii*) Election Commission is a central body though it conducts elections of the states as well.

(*viii*) On concurrent matters, the will of the centre prevails ultimately.

(*ix*) In certain circumstances the Central Legislature can make laws on the subjects in the State List if resolution is passed to that effect by the Rajya Sabha.

Keeping in view the centralised features D.D. Basu remarks *"Constitution of India is neither purely federal nor unitary but is a combination of both"*.

4. Parliamentary Form of Government

India opted for parliamentary form of government like that of British democracy. The Prime Minister—the real head of the Government alongwith Council of Ministers is collectively responsible to the Lok Sabha—the lower directly elected House. The President like British monarch is the Head of the State equipped with only constitutional authority. *Secondly*, the ultimate control over legislation and financial matters lies with the Lower House. *Thirdly,* healthy and effective opposition is the pre-requisite of parliamentary democracy. The leader of the opposition is duly recognised. He enjoys cabinet status. In India opposition parties do exist but due to lack of dual party system opposition has failed to play healthy and effective role. However, the leader of the opposition enjoys the cabinet rank and opposition is as such legally recognised.

A Chapter on Fundamental Rights and Fundamental Duties

Part III of the Constitution incorporates chapter on Fundamental Rights. In the initial stages seven rights were embodied in the Constitution viz., right to equality; right to freedom; right against exploitation; right to freedom of religion; cultural and educational right; right to property; right to constitutional remedies. At a later stage the 44th amendment Act 1978 deleted right to property from the list of fundamental rights. Thus there are six Fundamental Rights now. However, these rights are subject to certain restrictions. In the interest of public order, decency or morality, reasonable restrictions can be imposed on these rights. Any of these rights can be suspended during emergency. They can be abrogated through Constitutional Amendment.

The provision of Fundamental Duties did not exist prior to the passage of 42nd Amendment Act in 1976. These Duties though called fundamental are not enforceable. Some of the important duties are:

(*i*) To uphold sovereignity and protect the unity and integrity of India.

(*ii*) To promote harmony and the spirit of common brotherhood amongst all the people of India.

(*iii*) To abide by the Constitution and respect its ideals and institutions. To defend the country and render national service when called upon to do so.

(*iv*) To protect and improve the national environment including forests, lakes, rivers and wildlife.

(*vi*) To safeguard public property and abjure violence.

(*vii*) To develop the scientific temper, humanism and spirit of enquiry and reform.

6. Directive Principles of State Policy

The Directive Principles of State Policy constitute part IV of the Constitution. They are non-justiciable but they are considered fundamental in the governance of the country. The states are to strive to keep these principles in mind while legislating. These principles constitute the national objectives and the national conscience and the party victorious at the hustings cannot offered to ignore them if they are keen to secure their future electoral prospects. These principles are Gandhian, socialistic, liberal intellectualistic and a few of general category.

Some of the socialistic principles comprise—(*a*) Avoidance of concentration of wealth. (*b*) Ensuring adequate means of livelihood to the citizens. (*c*) Assistance in cases of unemployment, old age, sickness and avoidance of concentration of means of production to the common detriment etc. (*d*) Right to work.

Gandhian Principles include (*a*) Prohibition of intoxicating drinks; (*b*) Establishment of Panchayati Raj.

The Liberal Intellectualistic principles comprise (*a*) preservation of ancient monuments and articles of historic interest; (*b*) separation of Judiciary from the executive; (*c*) promotion of international peace and security; (*d*) promotion of cottage industries.

Articles 36 and 37 constitute general categary

These principle are not enforceable by a court of law and they are fundamental in the governance of the country. The state is duty bound to keep them in view while framing laws. The 42nd amendment (1976) enjoins upon Government to protect environment and wildlife.

These principles have been described as moral precepts, pious wishes, noble aspirations and economic maxims which ultimately degenerate into sublime nonsense. However, this is an exaggerated statement.

Some of the decisions of the Supreme Court have given precedence to the Directive Principles over the Fundamental Rights in the recent past. They have proved insurance against extremes. M.C. Setalvad (ex Attorney General of India) remarks "...*These fundamental axioms of state policy though of no legal effect have served as a useful beacon light to the courts..*"

Rigid cum Flexible Constitution

The Constitution of India is a blend of rigidity and flexibility.

How rigid? (*i*) Article 368 explains its rigidity. Some of the matters viz. Fundamental Rights and Directive Principles and all other provisions except few specified relating to judiciary or the Rights and Powers of the units require support of majority of the total membership of Parliament and 2/3 of the members present and voting. **(*ii*) Special Majority and ratification by States :** Some of the provisions as enumerated below necessitate the ratification of each House of Parliament by majority of total members of both the houses and 2/3 majority of the members present and voting. Besides, such amending bills are to be ratified by the legislatures of not less than one half of the states. Following are the matters falling in this category :

(*i*) The extent of executive powers of the union and the states (*ii*) Manner of election of President of India (*iii*) High Courts of Union Territories (*iv*) Legislative relations between Union and the States (*v*) Articles dealing with representation of states in Parliament (*vi*) Provisions dealing with amendment of the Constitution (Article 368) etc.

How Flexible? About 2 dozen articles can be amended by Parliament by a simple majority. These articles pertain to (*i*) qualifications of citizenship (*ii*) creation of new states, changing of their names and boundaries (*iii*) creation and abolition of upper chambers in the states (*iv*) salaries of judges of Supreme Court and High Courts.

Keeping in view these two methods of amendment one can conclude that ours' is a rigid cum flexible Constitution. Till Dec, 2003 ninety-seven constitutional amendments had been effected—the last one dealing with Defection, replacing the Anti-Defection Act of 1985.

8. A Secular State

Right to Religion and Preamble of the Indian Constitution clearly reflect that Secularism is the cardinal principle of the Indian Constitution. A secular state does not have state religion. It allows freedom of faith, conscience and worship to all without any discrimination. A secular polity believes in complete religious neutrality and does not accept man-made barriers on the basis of religion. It stands for fellowship, tolerance and equality. In the words of H.V. Kamath "..A secular state is neither a Godless state nor an irreligious nor an anti religious state..". Dr. B.R. Ambedekar also opined. "..All that a secular state means is that this parliament shall not be competent to impose any particular religion upon the rest of the people."

9. Bicameral Legislature

The framers of the Constitution opted for a bicameral legislature. The Lok Sabha—the lower House is a directly elected chamber. The adults who are 18 years of age (previously 21) or more are the eligible voters. The country is divided into single membered constituencies to elect the M.Ps of the lower House. Presently 545 are the total members of the lower House. They are inclusive of 2 Anglo Indians who are nominated members of the lower House. Rajya Sabha is the upper House presently consisting of 245 members to the maximum. Its members are indirectly elected. The members of the State Assemblies (M.L.As) cast votes for the members of the Rajya Sabha. According to the Constitution twelve members of Rajya Sabha are nominated by President. They are to be nominated out of the eminent artists, scholars and those who have rendered social service. Prithvi Raj Kapoor, Nargis Dutt, Dalip Kumar, Vijayanti Mala, Raj Babbar, Shabana Azmi are some of the prominent artists who got this privilege.

The Lower House is more powerful than the upper like its prototype in UK. It controls the purse. It can oust the Council of ministers by vote of non-confidence. It initiates important legislation. The Rajya Sabha can detain a non-money bill maximum for a period of one year. Both the Houses have co-equal powers regarding election of the President and Vice President, and also their removal. Both participate in the amending procedure of the Constitution. The emergency proclamations are subject to approval by both the Houses.

Through a resolution of Rajya Sabha, a subject provided in the state list can be transferred to the unit list, if it is deemed of national importance. Evidently, ours being a parliamentary democracy the Lok Sabha enjoys ascendency over the Rajya Sabha.

10. Impartial and Independent Judiciary

Judiciary has been accorded supremacy so far as the interpretation of Constitution or safeguarding of Fundamental Rights is concerned. Vesting of judicial review authority with the Supreme Court necessitated the existence of impartial and independent Judiciary in the country.

The method of appointment of Supreme Court and High Court judges, their high qualifications, security of tenure, their handsome emoluments chargeable on Consolidated Fund of India and the debarring of Court judges from practising after retirement reflect that sincere efforts have been made to make Indian Judiciary impartial and independent. Indian Judiciary at the Apex is said to be envy of democratic world. The judges have set the precedent of being impartial and above board in all times and climes. Their power of judicial review has sometimes raised the eyebrows of the critics. They have been at times protraying it as 'judicial despotism' and at times "judicial high handedness". Like that of American Supreme court our apex Court has also been categorised as a 'third chamber' and its power of judicial review has been commented upon as 'judicial veto'. However, these are exaggerated remarks. The Supreme Court in particular has proved to be a 'saviour of Constitution' and palladium of peoples liberties though at times judicial activism has been a great irritant for the government-both the Parliament and the Executive.

11. Single Citizenship

Generally, a federal form of polity opts for double citizenship—citizenship of Federation as a whole and citizenship of each component unit (state). The constitutions of USA and Switzerland cater to double citizenship. In case of India an Indian residing in any part of the country is known as Indian citizen. He cannot claim separate citizenship of the state where he lives. This is unlike that of other federations as stated above. This has been done to inculcate the spirit of true nationalism amongst people who witnessed partition of the country and drama of barbarism and carnage on the vivisected soil of this subcontinent. Dr. B.R. Ambedekar remarked "There is only one citizenship for the whole of India. It is Indian citizenship. There is no state citizenship. Every Indian has the same right to citizenship no matter in what state he resides."

12. Sovereignty resides in the people

The Premable of the Indian Constitution states 'India is a land of people of India. The people are the authors of constitutional law. The union government can not claim sovereignty because its authority is derived out of the Constitution which can through its amending process deprive it of its powers. The same is the case with the individual states. The Supreme Court can challenge the act of both—the Legislative and Executive organs of the Government. But the Supreme Court also like other organs of Government is eventually controlled by the Constitution. The Constitution itself is not sovereign, as its provisions can be amended by the constitutional process of amendments. In fact, sovereignty resides in the people of India. The authority emanates from the people. They have beastowed powers upon the organs of the Government. They have enacted the Consitution. They can unmake it. The Preamble highlights the source of Constitution as'The people of India' The Constitution of India was framed and adopted by the people of India in their Constituent Assembly. Organised in the Parliament and state legislatures they are empowered to amend the Constitution. The supreme political power vests with constitutionally qualified electorates but the legal authority to amend the Constitution has been entrusted to the electorates as organised through their representatives in the determinate form in Parliament and State Legislatures. In fact our Constitution is a peoples' Constitution and a Constitution which gives free and ample scope to the people of India to make experiments in socialism or any other 'Ism' which they feel will take their country ahead and make it least in the sunshine of prosperity.

13. Establishment of a Welfare State

The ideals as contained in the Preamble of the Constitution constitute the cornerstone of a welfare state. The Constitution prohibits artificial barriers and manmade inequalities. Discriminations have been ended; however interests of the backward classes have not been ignored. Article 46 specifies that the state shall promote with special care the educational and economic interests of the weaker sections of society. Article 15 authorises the state to make special provisions for the advancement of socially and educationally backward class of citizens, the Scheduled Castes and Scheduled tribes. The President of India and Governor nominates the representatives of Anglo-Indian community to the Lok Sabha and State-Legislative assemblies respectively, if they are not otherwise adequately represented. Articles 29 and 30 allow the minorities to preserve their language and culture and administer institutions of their choice. Article 29 was amended to authorise the state to reserve seats in the state colleges for socially and educationally backward class of citizens or for Scheduled Castes and Scheduled Tribes. Reservation in appointments for backward classes has also been provided. Likewise, the interests of women have been safeguarded. Equal pay for equal work for men and women has been provided. K.M. Munshi aptly remarked "*The Constitution was an instrument not only of ensuring material betterment and maintaining a democratic set up but that it recognized that the personality of every individual is sacred*". A state looking after the interests of each and every section of people can be categorised as a welfare state.

Conclusion

An appraisal of the salient features of the Indian Constitution reflects that Indian Constitution is neither a 'bag of borrowings' nor a 'hotch potch' Constitution. It is not to be categorised as mere glorified edition of 1935 Act. It is in fact a conglomeration (blend) of good points of constitutions of the world, duly adapted to our circumstances, congenial to Indian environment and in consonance with national heritage. No doubt it is not an original document but it is certainly a workable and a well conceived document. In the words of Basu *"The Constitution of India is remarkable for many outstanding features which will distinguish it from other constitutions though it has been prepared after ransacking all the known constitutions of the world"*.

***

Appendix I

"Introduction of Aptitude Test – A Substitute of Prelims from 2011"

On March 10, 2010 the Minister of Personnel informed the Lok Sabha on the floor of the House that the Prime Minister has accorded his approval to the proposal for introduction of CSAT (Civil Services Aptitude Test) in place of the existing CS Preliminary Examination. In a written reply he said "CSAT is expected to come into effect from Civil Services Examination 2011".

According to the changes so contempleted "candidates will appear for two objective papers having emphasis on aptitude and ethical and moral dimensions of decision making. Both the papers will have equal weightage. Change will be effective only for the first stage of the CSE from 2011".

Evidently, 'aptitude' rather than 'knowledge of the subject' will henceforth be given due importance. In other words, specialization in a particular subject may no longer be considered necessary for selecting a good civil servant. An official said, 'The new system will also provide a level playing' field and equity since all candidates will have to attempt common papers unlike the current format which provides for only one common paper. [1]

In fact, a scaling system is in vogue in the preliminary examination which ensures that no candidate opting for any particular optional paper gets undue advantage because of its inherent scorability or varying degree of difficulty of other papers. Still complaints persisted. Hence, the change was thought indispensible.

[1] *The Times of India March 11, 2010, p.11*

APPENDIX II

"Recommendations of II Administrative Reforms Commission (Decmeber 12, 2008)" headed by M. Veerappa Moily

1. *Lowering of the upper age limit*. The upper age limit for writing the Civil Service Exams will be 21-25 for General Candidates ; 21 to 28 for the Other Backward Classes (OBC) and 21 to 29 for Scheduled Castes and Scheduled Tribes and also for physically challenged candidates.

2. It suggested that the number of permissible attempts in Civil Services Examination should be 3, 5 and 6 for the General Candidates OBC and SC/ST and physically challenged aspirants respectively.

3. The present system of evaluation of performance based on annual confidential report he must be done away with. Instead there should be a concept of annual performance agreements to be signed between the Minister concerned and the secretary or Head of the Department providing physical and verification details of the work to be done during a financial year. The actual performance should be assessed by the third party.

4. The Report suggests discouragement of coaching centres. A Post-School Grooming System for civil services aspirants should be substituted for the coaching centres and suggested a formal degree course in public policy.

5. A Central Civil Authority should be set up for the above purpose. It should be a 5 membered body with the chairperson appointed by the President on the recommendations of Prime Minister and Leader of the Opposition .

6. The Government officials should not be allowed to go on deputation to private commercial organisations.

7. To increase accountability there should be a periodic review of the performance -one on completion of 14 years of service and the other on completion of 20 years. The first review will serve the purpose of initimating an individual about his/her performance and the second is mainly to assess the fitness of the officer for his/her future continuance in the service.

8. It suggests the scrapping of 23 optional papers. It has recommended to test the candidates knowledge knowedge in only one or two general studies papers. It also suggests that the subjects for Preliminary and Main Exams should be on constitution legal system economy, polity, history and culture. Evidently, technical degree holders stand ruled out.

domain. The applicants will have to undergo interview which will be conducted by a panel of the Civil services authority. Once selected for a particular domain the officer will remain confined to that only. Likewise for all senior posts in civil and Police knowledge will be given top priority.

10. The first review of the public servants will be done at 14 years of service completed. It will primarily more than aware of their strengths and drawbacks. The second reviews will be at 20 years of service completed. It will determine the fitness of the officer for continuation in service. In case of unfitness the service will be discontinued.

11. An attempt has been made toward out the automatic entry from the state civil services into the Indian administration services. It has suggested such an entry only through an examination. All these who have completed 8 to 10 years of service in Grade A parts will be eligible. Maximum two attempts will be allowed and the upper age limit will be 40 years for entry in IAS. This was done to motivate state civil services for better projects.

The commission under the headship of Veerapa Moily released the Reports on "refinishing of personnel administration – scaling new heights" on December 12, 2008. Is what extent these recommendations are accepted is yet to be seen. Much depends on the political leaders at the helm of affairs.

NEW ELECTION COMMMISSIONER TO TAKE OVER

As per Government's Notification dated 27 July, 2010 S.Y. Quraishi will be the new Chief Election Commissioner of India and will take over the charge from the present incumbent — Navin B. Chawla on July 30.

[1]*Hindustan Times dated July 28, 2010, p.1*